International Relations of the Middle East

FOURTH EDITION

Edited by

Louise Fawcett

OXFORD

UNIVERSITY PRESS

OXFORD
UNIVERSITY PRESS

Great Clarendon Street, Oxford, OX2 6DP,
United Kingdom

Oxford University Press is a department of the University of Oxford.
It furthers the University's objective of excellence in research, scholarship,
and education by publishing worldwide. Oxford is a registered trade mark of
Oxford University Press in the UK and in certain other countries

First edition 2005
Second edition 2009
Third edition 2013

Impression: 1

Published in the United States of America by Oxford University Press
198 Madison Avenue, New York, NY 10016, United States of America

British Library Cataloguing in Publication Data
Data available

Library of Congress Control Number: 2015955920

ISBN 978-0-19-870874-2

Printed in Italy by L.E.G.O. S.p.A.

Preface to the fourth edition

In the few years that have passed since the third edition was published, the Middle East has continued to experience momentous changes. Most notable of these, are the consequences of the 'Arab Spring' uprisings, which started late in 2010, but continue to have enormous impact across the region and the wider world. In revising their chapters for this edition, the different authors have fully taken on board the possible impact of these, as well as other, recent developments on the international relations of the region. In addition, there is one new chapter which looks specifically at the impact of the Arab Spring on the International Relations of the region. The online resources that accompany the book have been revised and brought up to date to offer students continuing additional support.

As with the previous editions, a number of people have been involved in assisting the smooth progress of this manuscript. As in the past I have benefited from the expert assistance of the OUP editorial and production teams and I would like to thank them for their efficiency and support. I am particularly grateful to Francesca Mitchell for her careful editing and many suggestions for improvement. And, as before, I am enormously grateful to all of the authors who have been generous and forthcoming with ideas and suggestions for this revised volume.

Finally, I would like to acknowledge the support of the Middle East Centre, St Antony's College, Oxford.

Louise Fawcett
Oxford
April 2016

Guided tour of the Online Resource Centre

www.oxfordtextbooks.co.uk/orc/fawcett4e/

The Online Resource Centre that accompanies this book provides students and registered instructors with additional teaching and learning resources.

For students:

Interactive map

An interactive map of the Middle East provides key information about each state, helping you to expand your knowledge of the region.

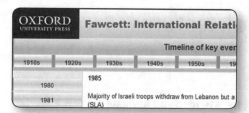

Timeline

An interactive timeline outlines the key events in the Middle East using the chronologies in the book.

Web links

Web links direct you to useful sources of interest and information, enabling you to take your learning further.

Chapter exercises

Web-based questions that are directly related to each chapter of the book help you to extend your knowledge and test your understanding.

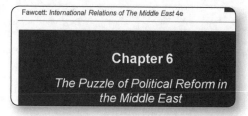

Links to news sites

Links to news sites direct you to sources of up-to-date information on current events in the Middle East.

For registered instructors:

PowerPoint® slides

These fully adaptable slides complement each chapter of the book and are a useful resource for preparing lecture presentations or class handouts.

Guided tour of textbook features

This text is enriched with a range of learning tools to help you navigate the text material and reinforce your knowledge of international relations of the Middle East. This guided tour shows you how to get the most out of your textbook.

Overview

Overview

International relations theory takes many forms and poses a wide range of that can be addressed using Middle Eastern cases. Structural realist theory do the field, complemented by neoliberal institutionalism, the English School, h sociology, and constructivism. Statistical studies of world politics offer useful that demand further exploration, as do power transition theory and pow theory. Conceptual contributions from regional specialists also merit elabora

The Overview outlines themes and issues within the chapter and indicates the scope of its coverage.

Boxes

Box 1.1 What is the 'Middle East'?

How to delineate the Middle Eastern international system in conceptual, geographical, terms is a long-standing problem. Leonard Binder (1958) pr consists of the former territories of the Ottoman Empire, along with neigh religious opposition movements have challenged Western-style nationalis 'the Middle East proper stretches from Libya to Iran, with fringe areas incl and the Maghrib, and a core area including the Arab states and Israel' (Bin that relations among these states cannot be explained in terms of the dyn

Interspersed throughout the chapters, boxes provide further insights into specific topics and issues.

End-of-chapter questions

Questions

1. What aspects of the security dilemma have the greatest imp relations in the Middle East?
2. Constructivism appears to be a useful way to explain trends Eastern international relations, but how can constructivists of regional culture that reinforce long-standing stereotypes?
3. Under what circumstances did Westphalian sovereignty tak

Questions are provided at the end of each chapter to help you check your understanding and critically reflect on your learning.

Key events

Key events

1839	Gülhane Reform Decree initiates the period of Ott Tanzimat
1856	Reform Decree confers equality on non-Muslir reform of the Tanzimat
1876	Promulgation of the Ottoman Constitution

Chronological lists draw out key Middle Eastern events to strengthen your understanding of regional history.

Further reading

Further reading

Brown, L. C. (1984) *International Politics and the Middle Eas* (Princeton, NJ: Princeton University Press)
An excellent study that traces the evolution of the nineteenth-rab state system of the twentieth century.
Fromkin, D. (2000) *A Peace to End All Peace: Creating the M*

Reading lists are provided to help you find out more about the topics covered in the chapter by directing you to the key academic literature in the field.

Contents

International Relations of the Middle East

Giacomo Luciani teaches at the Paris School of International Affairs (SciencesPo) and at the Graduate Institute of International and Development Studies in Geneva. His latest book is *Political Economy of Energy Reform: The Clean-Energy–Fossil Fuel Balance in the Gulf* (Gerlach Press, 2014).

Peter Mandaville is Professor of International Affairs in the School of Policy, Government & International Affairs at George Mason University. He is the author of *Islam and Politics* (London: Routledge, 2014).

Augustus Richard Norton is Professor of Anthropology and International Relations, Pardee School of Global Studies, Boston University, and Sultan of Brunei Fellow, Oxford Centre for Islamic Studies. His most recent book is *Hezbollah: A Short History*, 3rd edition (Princeton, NJ: Princeton University Press, 2014).

Eugene L. Rogan is Professor of Modern Middle Eastern History at the University of Oxford and a Fellow of St Antony's College. His most recent book is *The Fall of the Ottomans: The Great War in the Middle East, 1914–1920* (New York: Basic Books/London: Allen Lane, 2015).

Larbi Sadiki teaches international affairs at Qatar University. He is editor of the *Routledge Handbook of the Arab Spring* (Abingdon: Routledge, 2015).

Avi Shlaim is Emeritus Fellow of St Antony's College and Emeritus Professor of International Relations at the University of Oxford. His books include *The Iron Wall: Israel and the Arabs* (expanded and updated edition, 2014).

Peter Sluglett is Director of the Middle East Institute, National University of Singapore. He is co-author (with Marion Farouk-Sluglett) of *Iraq since 1958: From Revolution to Dictatorship*, 3rd edition (London: I. B. Tauris, 2001).

Charles Smith is Professor Emeritus of Middle East History, School of Middle East and North African Studies, University of Arizona. He is the author of *Palestine and the Arab–Israel Conflict*, 8th edition (Boston, MA: Bedford/St Martin's Press, 2012; 9th edition forthcoming in 2016).

New to this edition

- A new chapter on the Arab Spring and its impact.
- Fully updated to include coverage of the so-called Islamic State or ISIS group.
- End-of-chapter questions designed to encourage critical reflection.
- An increased number of case studies to link theory to real-life situations.

Introduction:
The Middle East and
International Relations

LOUISE FAWCETT

The book and the title

This book aims to provide the reader with a comprehensive, up-to-date, and accessible guide to understanding the international relations of the modern Middle East. Few parts of the world have been quite so buffeted by conflict and war; few parts of the world have been so much written about and debated in recent times, while remaining subject to misunderstanding and stereotype. As one scholar, reflecting on the legacy of fifty years of academic study of the region, claimed: 'Middle Eastern political processes defy observation, discourage generalization and resist explanation' (Bill 1996: 503). This observation has been borne out by the unpredictable series of events since the start of this century, including 9/11 and subsequent terrorist attacks; the Iraq War of 2003; the 2011 Arab uprisings and their consequences, including the rise of so-called Islamic State (IS)[1] and a refugee crisis of enormous proportions. These have deeply unsettled the region, bringing about the fall of long-established regimes and causing a 'deep structural transformation' (Lynch 2012).

The two major disciplines of international relations (IR) and Middle East studies with which this book is mainly concerned are highly interdependent, as any cursory survey of major works shows. No book on the contemporary politics of the Middle East can possibly ignore the way in which external forces have shaped and continue to shape the development of the region's politics, economics, and societies. If the former colonial powers were involved in the very creation of states, post-colonial powers have maintained extraordinarily high levels of interest and involvement in their politics, economics, and security, for reasons relating to resources, geographical location, and culture (Milton Edwards 2011). Similarly, no international relations text can ignore the rich cases that the Middle East has supplied, and how they illuminate different theories and concepts of the discipline (Binder 1958), whether in respect of patterns of war and peace or international political economy. Many works have been published on either side of the Middle East studies–international relations divide, but until recently there were rather fewer titles that took on the challenge of integrating the two disciplines. There has been a rather standoffish attitude between political scientists and area studies scholars, which has held back joint enterprises. Area studies specialists criticize IR and social science methods for ignorance or selective use of facts to suit their theoretical purposes. IR specialists criticize area studies scholars for being unscientific, too descriptive and empirical, and 'methods light'. This state of affairs contributed to what scholars have called a 'crisis' in Middle East studies, in part the product of such disciplinary divides, but also because academic research on the Middle East has mostly failed to provide a good template for policymakers (Kramer 2001; Gause 2011a; Lynch 2014).

Notwithstanding such criticisms, this situation has changed in recent years, with a growth in efforts to integrate political science and Middle East studies. This is evident in the area of comparative government (for example, Anderson 1987; Tessler et al. 1999; Bellin 2004; Posusney and Angrist 2005). As regards the international relations of the region, there have been, since the 1980s, some significant works including L. C. Brown, *International Politics and the Middle East* (1984), T. Y. Ismael, *International Relations of the Contemporary Middle East* (1986), F. Halliday, *The Middle East in International Relations* (2005), and R. Hinnebusch, *The International Politics of the Middle East* (2015b). Together, these books have made important contributions to the subject, offering different approaches and perspectives informed by contemporary international relations debates. Yet it is probably fair to say that, despite such advances, there is still something of a gap in the literature, which suggests that work remains to be done in bringing the subject areas together, to close an imaginary fault line that has for a long time held them apart (Valbjorn 2004b). Further, and to state the obvious, there is enormous contemporary interest in a subject and a region that poses some of the central security challenges of the first half of the twenty-first century. These include the destabilizing regional and international effects of the Iraq War (Fawcett 2013), the Arab Spring (Gerges 2014), Iran's foreign policy orientation and nuclear programme, and the still unresolved Palestine–Israel conflict. This volume is therefore a direct response to this interest and to continuing demand for further scholarly engagement between the two disciplines, in order to help us better understand the international politics of the region.

In moving beyond the international relations–area studies divide, it seeks also to challenge arguments of 'exceptionalism' that have been applied to the Middle East. Such arguments, which are addressed in Edward Said's classic text *Orientalism* (1978), find in it unique qualities—such as its Arab and Islamic character—that make it different, explaining, for example, the stubbornness of authoritarian rule—even beyond the Arab Spring (Kedourie 1992; Springborg 2011). Rejecting such approaches, it seeks to offer a nuanced and integrated approach in which key ideas and concepts in international relation, and key themes and developments in Middle East Studies, are brought together and discussed in a systematic way. In this new edition it responds to a call from those who engage in 'Global International Relations',[2] which incorporates more critical and expansive approaches to international society. Global IR demands that we consider the contributions of the entire globe in the making and remaking or IR (as opposed to focusing on the advanced industrialized countries or the West). Such a view is becoming more and more relevant, not only because the West is no longer the only or even the most important centre of power, but also because voices from the 'non-West' have proved to be equally important in illuminating the pathways of modern international politics.

Studying the international relations of the Middle East

With this in mind, it is useful further to explore some of the particular problems that arise in studying the international relations of the Middle East and how this volume tackles them. Two issues are relevant here: the first relates to the nature of the subject matter itself; the second, to the scholarly approaches on offer.

One difficulty in discussing the international relations of the Middle East lies in the very definition of the region itself. This is not a problem unique to the Middle East: common to many world regions is the question of identifying the territorial space that any region occupies and classifying its 'regional' characteristics. For example, despite obvious commonalities, scholars have long debated whether or not Latin America constitutes a distinct region or is better understood as a set of subregions; there is currently debate about whether or not East Asia can be classified in this way, one that has produced conflicting views about the nature and quality of 'regionness'.

The term itself, the 'Middle East', slipped into common use after the Second World War, replacing the more limited definition of the 'Near East', but interpretations over its extension have varied over time. Both terms, it should be noted, derive from the West's perspective of the region for the 'East' was, obviously, conceived of in relation to its geographical position to Western Europe. Today, it is commonly understood to include the Arab states of West Asia and North Africa (members of the Arab League), and the non-Arab states of Iran, Israel, and Turkey (see **Figure 0.1**). Some have argued in favour of narrowing the region to exclude the African Arab states west of Egypt, which have strong Mediterranean links. Others suggest further expansion to include the Muslim republics of Central Asia whose links to the region are closer since the end of the Cold War and break up of the USSR of which they formed a part. Both these regions are linked, through the Arab language, Islam, or both to the 'Middle' East so there is an obvious logic to inclusion; however the Central Asian republics are not generally included. With so much geographical, historical, and cultural variety, one might well ask whether it is meaningful to speak of the Middle East as a coherent region. Can we make general claims about the international relations of such a diverse group of states?

Although there are a number of problems with this definition, it may be argued that the region, as currently defined, does indeed possess some common properties and unifying characteristics, whether political (low levels of liberalization/high levels of authoritarianism), economic (rentier economies/low levels of economic liberalization), or cultural (predominantly Arab/Islamic), such that we may consider it a distinguishable unit, or a 'subsystem' within the bigger international system (Gause 1999). It also shares a common security dilemma making it therefore a regional security 'complex' (Buzan 1991: 210). If we consider the effects of the Arab Spring which included countries from North Africa (Tunisia, Egypt, and Libya), the East Mediterranean (Syria and Iraq), and the Gulf (Bahrain), but also have resonated in the non-Arab states of Iran and Turkey, this notion of an inter-related system is again demonstrated. This does not, however, imply that the region behaves in a uniform or static way, as the different contributions to this volume demonstrate. Some would argue that elements of regional cohesion visible in the Cold War period have been weakened, with the Gulf states, mostly immune from the Arab uprisings, for example, forming a distinct regional subsystem characterized by strong economies based upon

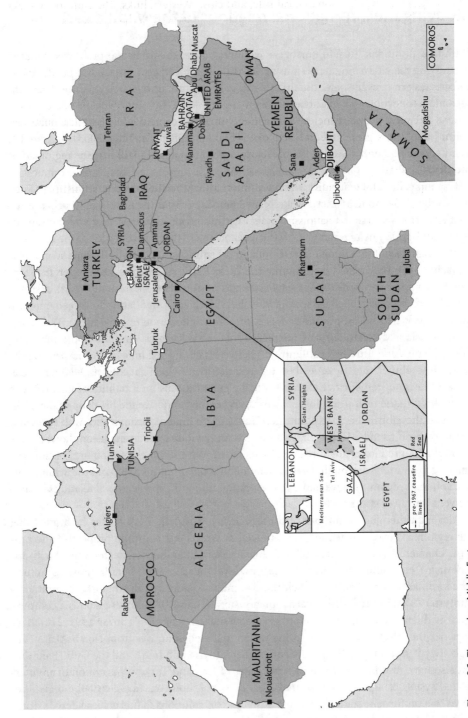

Figure 0.1 The modern Middle East

oil income, conservative monarchical rule, and close Western links. The Gulf today seeks to operate as a kind of fulcrum, or power balancer, in respect of the region's international relations.

If defining the Middle East presents challenges, international relations, for its part, is an evolving and often imprecise term to describe an evolving and imprecise social science. Once limited to the analysis of interstate relations, recent international relations scholarship moved beyond this traditional state base encompassing a broader range of interactions between peoples, societies, and governments, to include webs of transnational politics and trans-governmental networks (Frankel 1988; Slaughter 2003). Global IR, as noted above, contributes to this development by expanding still further the range of enquiry.

This expansive and expanding notion of international relations is useful for this book in many ways. Much of the volume is concerned, of course, with the mechanisms and institutions of formal interstate relations, but also with less formal interactions and patterns of behaviour operating above and below the level of states. The consequences of the Arab uprisings are particularly relevant here as states have been weakened by civil war and external intervention and the region has seen the rise of new non-state actors which operate across state boundaries and challenge the foundations of the system. These seem especially pertinent: for many regional scholars, the non-state domain has often been the default position from which to approach the Middle East.

To illustrate this point, much of the territory of the modern Middle East was formerly part of the Ottoman Empire. Few recognizable states existed. For sizeable parts of the twentieth century, even after the emergence of a states system, the two linked ideologies comprising Arabism and Islam constituted important elements in the international relations of the region. Tribal and religious identities both preceded and transcended state boundaries in shaping regional behaviour (Khoury and Kostiner 1990). In the early twenty-first century, although some states looked stronger than before, such ideologies, particularly that of Islam, have remained salient. As two leading scholars argue, 'No student of Middle East international politics can begin to understand the region without taking into account the ebb and flow of identity politics' (Telhami and Barnett 2002: 2). This point was forcefully brought home by the rise and increased significance of transnational Islamic movements (see **Chapter 8**), particularly evident after the turn of this century and again after the Arab uprisings. Such groups and their actions, facilitated by sophisticated communications networks, both challenge and erode the fragile legitimacy of many states, while making them subjects for external intervention. The charge, for example, that Afghanistan and Iraq had encouraged such networks contributed to the US-led interventions in 2002 and 2003, respectively, and the subsequent dismantling of incumbent regimes. In the twenty-first century, in contrast (alongside continuing radicalism), more moderate voices of Islam have been heard, as witnessed in Turkey, for example, and through the success of Islamic parties in post-Arab Spring elections.

However, it is a finding of this volume, as well as of other scholarly works on the Middle East, that the transnational or subnational case, while important, should not be overstated (Brown 2001; Owen 2004). Despite its contested and at times fluid properties, the state system in the Middle East has proved remarkable for its survival and durability, and it is the contention of some that the older features of regional identity—notwithstanding their recent and sometimes violent manifestations—have increasingly surrendered to, or at least been conditioned by, more powerful considerations of *raison d'état*. Pan-Arabism has slowly declined as a dominant ideology (Dawisha 2005) and the Arab Spring, despite resonating among Arab publics gave rise to further fragmentation visible in inter-Arab sectarian divides. While political Islam has captured spaces once occupied by Arabism, it has also emerged as a fragmented force, one that must coexist with, not replace, the existing state system. There are different versions of political Islam on offer, from the statist and more moderate Turkish example, or the stricter Saudi and Iranian interpretations to those, like that of so-called Islamic State (IS, a group also known as ISIS, ISIL, and Daesh), that envision the end of the state system itself. Still, it remains clear that a wholly state-centric approach is inadequate, or at least needs balancing with a thorough consideration of other actors and movements that compete with states for authority and popular support. This argument applies to any region, but the Middle East can arguably be singled out for the interconnected relationships that its peoples and societies have enjoyed, and their often poor fit with a still relatively new system of states, an argument frequently heard in the post-Arab uprising environment.

Strong criss-crossing currents of regional homogeneity thus persist in a variety of forms, and are reflected in repeated patterns of cooperation within the region and in its interactions with the outside world. From people power in the Arab Spring (see **Chapter 15**), to continuing Arab solidarity in the face of external challenges (see **Chapter 9**). However the theme of conflict is also prevalent and this juxtaposition of conflict and cooperation is a prominent thread that runs through the different chapters of the book.

Indeed for IR scholars the term 'conflict' appears unproblematic, even natural when applied to the Middle East and its international relations. Conflict is seen as the default state of affairs in international relations; cooperation is a realm entered only with caution, and where certain observable criteria and conditions are in place, offering material benefits for all. The widespread and persistent perception of the region, and one that has pervaded academic as well as popular circles, is that of a zone of conflict and war. It provides, for some, an illustration of an (international) state of nature described by Thomas Hobbes: a world that, in the absence of a powerful Leviathan, sees the prevalence of anarchy and power struggles. It is characterized by both 'old' and 'new' wars (Kaldor 1999). The Middle East is still an 'unfinished' region, like other parts of the developing world, with weak states and regional institutions, where territory and borders are contested, and interstate conflict persists. The kinds of cooperation of rational actors seeking maximum payoffs in terms of security and power, identified and parsimoniously explained by international relations scholars, are rarely seen. Yet against this vision of disorder there is a contrasting and equally compelling vision of order, one long familiar to regional scholars: of peoples cohabiting a relatively seamless space, of tolerance and diversity—cultural, linguistic, and religious (Hourani 2002). Although this vision has often been obscured by events in the last century, it was recaptured in the spirit of the Arab Spring when Arab peoples joined in expressing their disapproval of governing regimes.

These observations lead directly into identifying the second problem in undertaking a study of the international relations of the Middle East. This relates to the appropriateness of the scholarly approaches on offer: their shortcomings help to explain the longstanding reluctance of area studies specialists to engage with international relations scholarship. As noted, international relations theories are often too crude, regionally insensitive, and ill-informed to be of real service, a problem arguably exaggerated by trends in quantitative analysis which lose sight of real-world relevance. Indeed, those scholars brave enough to span the divide—and this includes a number of contributors to this volume—have found themselves obliged to wear 'two hats', as Avi Shlaim once eloquently expressed it. Middle Eastern hats are exchanged with international relations hats to suit different fora and publics.

A particular difficulty that has arisen in observing the international relations of the Middle East—one that the region shares with other parts of the developing world—is that, traditionally, most of the observers have come from, or were trained, outside the region, and their observations are based on rather different understandings of the traditions and practices of states (Neumann 1998; Tickner 2003): international relations theory was made *for* the Middle East, but not *by* the Middle East. Although the very creation of the modern states system in the Middle East—part of the territorial settlements that took place after the First World War—closely coincided with the development of international relations as an independent discipline, the two have hardly grown up together; rather, they have long resisted constructive engagement. Until quite recently, international relations was mostly the preserve of scholars from English-speaking countries. Indeed, it was not that long ago that Stanley Hoffmann (1977) described international relations as an 'American Social Science'.

The early language and vocabulary of international relations were designed to fit and to explain the experience of the United States and its allies, or those who had closely followed the US and European paths. When applied to the Middle East and other parts of the developing world, it had a certain resonance, of course, not least because it was the language used by dominant states and other states felt obliged to use it also. Western IR is widely taught in universities across the developing world. Few would disagree that there are certain features that all states share. But, in its attempt to describe state behaviour, to devise universal theories to fit all state types, early international relations theory has failed to capture difference. It ignored the importance of local circumstances and actors whose influences lent a distinctive flavour to a region's interactions with the outside world (Acharya and Buzan 2010).

The original realist and liberal paradigms—the mainstays of international relations theory—were both guilty of observing the world in this way, leading to the kind of generalization critiqued in the foregoing paragraphs. Generations of international relations scholars were content to view the Middle East, and indeed the rest of the world, through the realist lens of anarchy and balance-of-power politics. Liberal views of cooperation, order, and institution-building appeared of little relevance, except as thinly disguised attempts by strong powers to bring order and to discipline the weak. States were the main focus of attention and were catalogued precisely according to their relative strength and weakness, highlighting the importance of the distribution of power in the international system. There was little interest in exploring the particular conditions under which states developed, or what made weak states weak. A classic work on international conflicts by a leading scholar, Joseph Nye (1997: 163–73), describes how the pattern of conflict in the Middle East is 'consonant with the realist model'. Another work by Stephen Walt (1987), using the Middle East as its case study, argues for a modified balance-of-power approach in which the behaviour of states is based on threat assessment.

As noted, some of the elements of realism were always useful and remain so. The Middle East must make its way in the world, as other regions do, in an international system in which power and security remain an important currency. Middle Eastern wars have borne similar attributes to the wars of other regions; the Arab–Israel wars, or the Iran–Iraq war, for example, both set in the context of the bigger Cold War, obeyed many of the rules of balance-of-power politics. So too, arguably, have the Western powers' more recent wars with Iraq. However, as Middle East scholars themselves have frequently noted, much international relations theory often seems strangely irrelevant or peripheral to their concerns. While international relations scholars have retained a tight focus on the unitary state as the primary object of analysis, Middle East scholars have told and retold a different story, one that places material interests alongside identity and domestic concerns at the centre of their analysis.

Their impatience is understandable. As Arnold Toynbee wrote in his critique of Western historians:

> [They] have gone wrong because they are egocentric, in diverse ways: because they deal only with Western history, or because they consider other histories only in so far as they are relevant to Western history, or because they look at other histories through categories applicable only to Western history, or because they think of themselves as somehow standing outside history and so able to judge it.
>
> (Quoted in Hourani 1961: 3)

Toynbee's views were controversial (and he was a Western historian!), but his statement remains pertinent to many contemporary interpretations of the modern Middle East, with obvious consequences for policymakers.

From a somewhat different perspective, Edward Said, in his essay 'Travelling Theory', notes how explanations that have developed in a particular context evolve and change as they move through space and time, and may lose their original meaning and purpose:

> A theory arrives as a result of specific historical circumstances . . . What happens to it when, in different circumstances and for new reasons, it is used again and . . . again? What can this tell us about theory itself—its limits, its possibilities and inherent problems?
>
> (Said 2000: 199)

Again, the uncritical export of dominant international relations theory to different parts of the world, including the Middle East, has been often problematic.

Despite such limitations, the positions of the two camps have not remained static and much has changed in recent years. Notably, both sides have responded positively to the demands of scholars and policymakers alike to address the shortcomings of their respective approaches. On the one hand, Middle East studies has reacted to increasing criticism for isolating itself from mainstream social science; on the other hand, international relations scholarship has increasingly freed itself from its Western origins (Bilgin 2008): it has slowly become 'globalized', with more and more critical voices getting heard, and thus can no longer be described as an exclusively 'American' social science. It has also expanded into new areas of enquiry, making possible in particular a more region-sensitive approach. The much-talked-of crisis in Middle East studies is not over, at least from a policymaking viewpoint, but new templates have been devised for breaching the interdisciplinary divides.

The explosion in international relations theory that followed the end of the Cold War has facilitated this bridge-building in the sense that it has provided scholars with a bigger array of theories upon which to draw. Constructivism, in particular, has helped to open up the possibility of a more nuanced approach to the roles that culture or identity may play in international politics. International anarchy and the self-help behaviour that characterizes it, as one of the early constructivist works reminds us, is not a given; rather, it is socially constructed, that is the product of different societies' histories, beliefs, and interactions (Wendt 1992). Leading the way in making the connection between the roles that identity may play in defining the behaviour of Middle Eastern states, Michael Barnett (1998: 5) has offered 'a narrative of politics that is theoretically distinctive and historically instinctive' (see also **Chapter 1**).

While most scholars welcome the opening up of the field that constructivist accounts have offered, for some constructivism is too modest in its goals—only a facilitator for realist accounts that continue to reify the state and its actions. Critical theorists would thus resist the notion that the Westphalian state model, with all its familiar attributes, should be enthusiastically accepted as the central unit of analysis (Seth 2013). Others remain cautious of embracing wholeheartedly constructivist claims. As Ray Hinnebusch (2003) reminds us, the debate about *how much* identity really matters remains unresolved; elsewhere, he has advocated a form of 'modified realism'. There is no such thing as an 'Arab' or an 'Islamic' foreign policy, for example, and neither the major Arab institution, the Arab League, nor the Organization of the Islamic Conference have so far aspired to promoting one. Hence identity clearly does matter, but as a means of influencing perceptions and thus state behaviour, rather than displacing states and state power.

Other scholars of the region remain cautious of the new paradigm shifts, as work by the late Fred Halliday (2005) reveals. Critical of what he calls the post-realist 'fetish' for culture, he forcefully reminds us that, when it comes to the Middle East, 'the cultural perspective was always there'. He advocates, as in his previous works, a firm grounding in historical sociology as an essential starting point for any analysis of the region. Many contributors to this volume would agree.

In sum, it would be wrong not to recognize recent advances in the attempt to bridge the divides between international relations and area studies; the theoretical and analytical gaps have narrowed. This book continues and develops this trend by demonstrating above all that the international relations of the Middle East are incomprehensible without appreciating first the regional and domestic, as well as the international, frame within which states operate, and second the juxtaposition of the features of cooperation alongside persistent conflict. Understanding these relationships provides in turn important clues to interpreting patterns of both war and peace, as well as the continuing story of state-building in the region.

Organization of the volume

Given the subject matter and the diverse array of approaches on offer, the organization of a volume such as this presents a number of challenges. As the existing literature demonstrates, there are a variety of alternative routes to approaching the international relations of the Middle East. Hence different entrées to the subject have been provided, for example, through a history of its societies and peoples (Hourani 2002; Rogan 2009), its political economy (Cammett, Diwan, Richards, and Waterbury 2015), or its foreign policy or diplomatic practices (Brown 2004; Korany and Dessouki 2008; Hinnebusch and Ehteshami 2014). There are many fine case studies of individual states and crises, and of 'great power' relations (Gerges 1994; Sela 1998). Finally, there is the growing trend towards bringing core international relations approaches and themes to the Middle East in discussions of the roles of identity, security, globalization, regionalism, resources, and power (Telhami 1990; Yergin 1991; Korany et al. 1993; Barnett 1998; Hudson 1999; Henry and Springborg 2001; Lawson 2006; Buzan and Gonzalez-Pelanez 2009).

While all such approaches are helpful in illuminating different aspects of the international relations of the region, this book aims to bring them together in a single, all-encompassing volume. It is deliberately designed to reach a wide student public drawn from different disciplines. It is also designed to draw on the strengths of individual authors, all well-known scholars in their respective areas of study. The objective therefore has been to include a range of perspectives, rather than to favour any single approach, or indeed to try to apply a set of uniform questions across the different chapters of the volume.

With the above in mind, the book is divided into three parts, as follows.

1. **Part 1** offers a broad theoretical, historical, and thematic overview of the international relations of the Middle East. The first theoretical chapter is designed to provide the reader with a solid and accessible background to diverse international relations theories and their application to the region. The historical chapters that follow also provide vital and enduring points of entry into understanding the international politics of the region: 'All history is contemporary history', as one historian of the early twentieth century observed (Croce 1941: 19). The historian's eye for detail and analysis can tell us much of what we need to know about the present by engaging us, in the words of E. H. Carr (1961: 30), with 'an unending dialogue' with the past. The importance of such a dialogue today is of particular relevance in understanding the course of events leading to the Arab uprisings. The call for a revision of the post-First World War boundaries is embodied in the demands of radical groups, particularly those demanding a return to the Islamic caliphate of the Ottoman period.

2. **Part 2** of the book covers important contemporary themes in Middle East international relations. These include topics such as political economy, the role of ideas and identities (particularly Arabism and Islam), democratization and political reform, the management of regional relations, and patterns of war and security. In considering these themes, the different authors utilize a variety of international relations theories and approaches, and assess their relative usefulness in understanding the region and its interactions with the rest of the world.

3. **Part 3** looks at key regional case studies incorporating historical, contemporary, and theoretical perspectives. It covers both region-specific conflicts and events, and the role of different internal and external actors in shaping the international relations of the region. Included here are the foreign policy practices of different states, the Arab–Israel conflict and attempts at its resolution, the international relations of the Gulf, the Arab Spring and its consequences, and finally the policies of both US and European powers in shaping the region's political and economic development.

Although not exhaustive in their coverage and highly interdependent, the three parts provide a set of discrete, yet interconnected, insights. In offering this wide menu for choice, the volume aims to reach a broad readership among graduate and undergraduate students of

Middle East politics and international relations. For the former the chapters will provide useful introductory material; for the latter a set of core readings and entry points to understand the IR of the region. The different chapters are intended to stand alone for those who wish to focus on a particular historical period, event, or theme, but can be read together, and thus provide the opportunity of acquiring a solid, well-rounded perspective on any given question.

Within the three parts of the book, the selection of individual chapters was necessarily a difficult and subjective one, and there are some obvious pitfalls of overlap, repetition, and exclusion. Following current fashions in political science and international relations might suggest a different choice. In a world in which the state, for some, has become an outmoded concept, or in which security may be viewed through a different lens—for example, that of environmental security, or of 'human security', as suggested by former United Nations Secretary General Kofi Annan and in the 2008 *Arab Human Development Report* (UNDP 2012)—the subject might be approached in a different way. Here, rather than current trends, the relative weight or salience of topics over time has been a guide. A central question asked in the organization of the volume is: which are the topics and issues that students of international relations and Middle East studies most commonly seek to address? In contemplating the contemporary region in broad terms, we find that traditional, alongside newer, security concerns—notably, issues of war and peace, relations with external powers, the processes of economic and political liberalization, and the politics of identity and alliance formation—all feature prominently. This book tackles such questions while acknowledging that the questions themselves may change, or may already be changing. A book on the international relations of the Middle East written in 2050 might read rather differently.

Chapter outlines

Part 1: Theoretical and Historical Overview

In **Chapter 1**, Fred Lawson offers an overview of the different theories and approaches that characterize the study of international relations, and then considers their application to the region. Wide-ranging in theoretical terms and extensively referenced, the chapter constitutes both an essential starting point and a useful set of tools for students wishing to understand the region's international relations.

In **Chapter 2**, Eugene Rogan traces the origins and the entry of Middle East states into the international system after the First World War. His analysis is influenced by the ideas of the 'English School' of international relations, for whom international relations is understood in terms of an 'international society', one in which shared norms, values, and practices develop that states find in it their interests to nurture and preserve (Bull 1977). The emergence of the Middle East saw states entering and participating in this society. Against this backdrop, however, there were elements of resistance and revolt, where the state system failed to meet the needs of different peoples and became synonymous with oppression and inequality, the consequences of which still reverberate today.

Chapter 3 continues with the story of the Cold War in the region. Here, the evidence of which factors drove regional developments has been contested by international relations and regional scholars alike. In the historiography of the Cold War, traditional interpretations attribute importance to external agency and are linked to the dominant realist paradigms in international relations. US policy is seen as a reaction to the Soviet threat—and vice versa—and moulded accordingly in balance-of-power and containment terms (Gaddis 2005). Later accounts, informed by the release of post-Cold-War archives, add nuance and detail, placing much more importance on the role of domestic actors or regional agency in shaping events. Peter Sluglett's account emphasizes the persuasive power of realism and the dominance of material interests. Although mindful of the regional framework, he argues that the Middle East in the Cold War was very susceptible to superpower influence, and he demonstrates this in a case study of Iraq.

Chapter 4 deals with the post-Cold-War era. Rather than providing a chronological record of historical events and developments, the chapter introduces some the key themes that have come to dominate the contemporary international relations of the Middle East: oil; new and old conflicts; the impacts of globalization; and religio-politics. It therefore provides a bridge between the first and second parts of the book. In sorting what he calls our post-Cold-War 'conceptual lenses', Bahgat Korany advocates the use of the term 'intermestic' to highlight the multiple linkages between domestic and international politics—linkages vindicated by the events of the Arab Spring.

Part 2: Themes in International Relations and International Political Economy

The chapters in the second part of the volume explore some of the topics introduced by Korany in more detail. In **Chapter 5**, Giacomo Luciani tackles the omnipresent question of oil. If oil is at the centre of debates about the domestic politics of the region, it is also at the heart of its international relations. Luciani demonstrates the compelling links between oil and the consolidation and evolution of the modern state system. Yet he also finds that, while outside powers have invariably used oil in their calculations of Middle East policy, it has figured less prominently in the foreign policies of Arab states, whose concerns remain of a more parochial kind: the oil weapon has been little used. As regards domestic politics, the rentier model developed by Luciani shows how oil has conditioned economic *and* political outcomes in oil-rich and oil-poor states, slowing down the prospects for reform. However, if the Arab Spring gives way to democratic consolidation, even the wealthy Gulf states will feel the winds of change.

In **Chapter 6**, Augustus Richard Norton tackles the critical issue of political reform in the light of these winds of change. He avoids the term 'exceptionalism', but acknowledges that the Arab world has been slow to respond to the global processes of democratization, and here highlights the political economy of states, the persistence of conflict, regime type, and the ambiguity over the relationship between democracy and Islam. This relationship is not necessarily a contradictory one. Norton points out how much Islamic discourse—past and present—is marked by participation and diversity rather than by rigidity and intolerance. Further, as the Arab Spring has illustrated, civil society is vibrant and growing in many states across the region. Responses from the West to political reform have been lukewarm, with stability privileged over democracy, although this is also changing. The evidence from the region, even before the Arab uprisings, is that peoples want better, and more representative government, even if they remain unclear as to what type of government that should be.

Chapter 7 by Raymond Hinnebusch and **Chapter 8** by Peter Mandaville offer critical reviews of the explanatory power of identity and culture in understanding the region's international relations. In **Chapter 7**, Hinnebusch focuses on Arabism and other regional ethnicities as sources of political identity. The importance of these identities within the region has been accentuated because of the poor fit between identity and states and regimes—a colonial legacy, but one that remains pertinent today, as revealed in the Arab uprisings. Indeed, he argues that the persistence of conflict in the Middle East must be understood through this 'incongruence of identity and material structures'. Focusing on pan-Arabism, as well as the irredentist and separatist movements that have characterized the history and political development of the region, such as the Kurds in Turkey or Iraq, Hinnebusch shows how the interaction of identity with state formation and development has contributed to numerous wars, and most recently to the evolution of regional developments following the Arab Spring.

In **Chapter 8**, Peter Mandaville takes up the story of identity from an Islamic perspective. In a historically informed account, he shows how Islam, in a variety of forms, has interacted with the domestic, regional, and international politics of the region. Its influence, however, has ebbed and flowed alongside different currents in regional and international relations. In this regard, globalization has been a facilitator of transnational Islam, but by no means a force for union. Notwithstanding its evident importance, there has been little substantive presence of religion in the foreign policies of Middle Eastern states, even in those more overtly Islamic ones such as Saudi Arabia and Iran. However, the popular uprisings in the Arab world have created new opportunities and challenges for the Islamic movement, which could affect states' foreign policies.

Identity also features in **Chapter 9** by Louise Fawcett, which offers an overview of the changing dynamics of regionalism and alliance-making in the region, processes that are closely related to and reflect states' foreign and domestic policy choices. The idea and practice of regionalism, broadly interpreted, are examined alongside international relations approaches that focus on the role of ideas, interests, and domestic and external agency in explaining efforts to build consensus and cooperation around core issues. In considering the history of such efforts in comparative perspective, the chapter demonstrates the loose fit between traditional, international-relations-type concerns and regional realities: the EU, for example, cannot be considered an obvious model for a region like the Middle East. Domestic-, regional-, and international-level factors combine to explain the region's slow record in terms of successful institution-building, although some recent precedents suggest some alternative regional scenarios.

Chapter 10, by Marina Calculli and Matteo Legrenzi, offers a contemporary analysis of the region's security dilemmas. Its perspective is informed by a critical reconsideration of the balance of power and threats in the light of the Arab uprisings, which have fundamentally altered prevailing security dynamics. In this balance, external actors are still important, as is regime security. However, an important feature of the current scene is the 'securitization of identities' whereby rival regimes mobilize different identities to preserve and consolidate their positions against the destabilizing effects of change. Their more activist foreign policy and pro-Western orientation of the Gulf states reflects their new roles as conservative managers of the status quo.

Part 3: Key Issues and Actors

This final part comprises a number of more focused and issue-based case studies that are designed to inform and illuminate further aspects of the region's international relations. **Chapter 11**, by Ray Hinnebusch and Anoushiravan Ehteshami, offers an analysis of foreign policymaking by regional states based on a 'complex realist' approach. This acknowledges the weight of realist (or power based) arguments, but highlights other factors such as the level of dependency on the US, processes of democratization, and the role of leadership in informing states' foreign policy choices. To illustrate this approach, it examines decision-making by four leading states—Saudi Arabia, Iran, Turkey, and Egypt—in relation to the key events and crises of the last decade.

The following two chapters deal directly with what has been—at least until the present decade—the most central and contentious security issue in the international relations of the modern Middle East: the Arab–Israel conflict, and attempts at its pacification and resolution. There are many lessons here for international relations scholars concerned with questions of war and peace. In **Chapter 12**, Charles Smith explores the different aspects of the Arab–Israel conflict over time—military, political, and economic. In line with other chapters and themes already set out, he demonstrates how both realism and the contours of identity politics inform the position of different states. Even the high point of the conflict, the 1967 War, was as much about Arab identity and leadership as it was about the struggle with Israel. Tracing the conflict from its origins in 1948 to the present, Smith shows how the Palestinian question remains today at the heart of debates about the normalization of regional relations.

Following this analysis, we turn to **Chapter 13**, in which Avi Shlaim covers the landmark series of negotiations between Arabs and Israelis in the early 1990s, culminating in the Oslo accords (1993), which marked the first sustained effort at peaceful resolution of the Arab–Israel conflict. These events, which dominated the regional panorama and captured the international imagination, assist our understanding not only of the nature and direction of Middle East politics, but also their positioning within the emerging international order as outlined by then US President George H. W. Bush. At first, it seemed that the accords, in reconciling the two major parties to the conflict—the Israelis and the Palestinians—were a demonstration of an emerging and more liberal international system. Yet the fragility of this system, in the Middle East as elsewhere, was soon exposed. Domestic, regional, and international politics conspired against peace in the Middle East; the opportunity was lost and has yet to be regained.

The Gulf states have faced different challenges in addressing their own pressing security dilemmas, as M. Legrenzi and F. Gregory Gause III demonstrate in **Chapter 14**. Considering the shifting security dynamics in this crucial region, they closely examine the policies of two major players, Iraq and Saudi Arabia, as well as the growth of US involvement. Iran's roles, its nuclear programme and relations with the Arab Gulf states are also examined. In line with other chapters, Legrenzi and Gause argue that the classical realist tool, the balance of power, only partly explains the positioning of states. The domestic framework and its (positive and negative) interactions with transnational influences and external actors are crucial to understanding the environment within which local states operate—whether revolutionary Iran, Saddam Hussein's Iraq, or the Gulf monarchies. Given that regime security drives states in their foreign policies, the need to cope with both internal and external threats is compelling. Outside actors are important in as much as they supply or help to combat such threats. The withdrawal of US forces from Iraq and the relative immunity of the Gulf monarchies from the effects of the Arab Spring have afforded these states greater regional influence and autonomy.

In **Chapter 15**, a new chapter, the Arab uprisings and their outcomes are given detailed attention. They are conceived of as popular uprisings against aged and mostly despotic governments, which have long silenced popular dissent. Larbi Sadiki argues that the Arab uprisings demonstrate the weakness of traditional IR with its focus on states and power by showing how much the people matter. Even if the Arab uprisings have not yet delivered on popular expectations, and the Arab world continues to be subject to external interference, they are part of a process of global protest and change, facilitated by new media and technology, which challenges the dominant IR theories.

In **Chapter 16**, Michael Hudson offers an in-depth study of the evolution of US policy towards the region. Starting with a review of its origins and development over the past century, he ends with critical assessments of the Bush Jr and Obama administrations. Interwoven into his analysis—and an implicit critique of realist approaches—is the crucial and interdependent relationship between different domestic constituencies in the US, and the conduct of US foreign policy: a relationship that, in the early twenty-first century, brought about the so-called 'neo-conservative revolution'. That revolution damaged the reputation of the United States in the Middle East as credible ally and peacemaker. President Obama's attempt to reset relations with the region has, so far, produced mixed results with a possible Iran agreement in sight, but continuing regional turmoil following the Arab uprisings and the rise of IS, and still no real progress on the Israel–Palestine question.

Chapter 17, by Rosemary Hollis and the last of the volume, explores the evolution and development of European approaches to the Middle East. A central question relates to the relevance and significance of Europe as an actor in influencing patterns of politics and development in the Middle East. Why is it that Europe, despite its economic and soft power resources, remains a political pygmy in a region of such profound historical and contemporary interest? Realism would point to the relative irrelevance of institutions such as the European Union and the limits to cooperation. Yet medium powers, if Europe can be understood thus, can influence outcomes in international relations and there are Middle Eastern states that have looked to Europe to supply this balancing effect, in both normative and policy terms. This potential has been demonstrated in the development of the Euro-Mediterranean Partnership Programme (1995) and subsequent initiatives, which may yet provide a cornerstone for further development. Yet Europe has been slow and often clumsy in responding to the events of the Arab Spring, caught between conflicting loyalties and interests (Peters 2012). A common security policy with respect to the region is yet to emerge and the 2015 refugee crisis has exposed new divisions.

Within this framework, the different chapters in the three parts of the book offer a balance between Middle Eastern studies and international relations perspectives. The authors do this in different ways, reflecting their own interests and preferences. There has been no attempt to turn area specialists into international relations scholars, or vice versa—an exercise that would run the risk of being artificial and superficial. Rather, in locating their chapters within the broad remit of the international relations of the Middle East and considering different axes of conflict and cooperation, continuity, and change—themes that run throughout all of the chapters of the volume—there is an invitation to each author to play to his or her respective strengths, but with an eye to developing a theme or idea that is intelligible to both disciplines. The result is a blend that aims to bring them a little closer together. Each chapter, in its own way, thus contributes to a broader understanding of the patterns of relations between Middle Eastern states and societies and other states and societies, at different moments and in different settings.

The international relations of the Middle East and the future

In place of a concluding note, it may be helpful briefly to highlight a few general points that emerge from the volume that could inform thinking about the future direction of studies on the international relations of the Middle East. All of these points are reinforced by a consideration of the momentous changes taking place in the region that scholars and policymakers failed to predict, and which they are still struggling to understand (Lynch 2012).

- History provides an enduring and essential entry point to understanding the contemporary region, its politics, and society.
- The region's international relations cannot be understood without close and constant reference to domestic actors, regimes, and an array of local factors that make each region unique in its own way.
- Models derived from the experience of Western states do not necessarily provide a good fit with local conditions and practices.
- Western policymakers (whether US or European) have as yet failed to devise successful and acceptable strategies to promote economic and political development and security.
- A regionally sensitive and regionally informed approach is an essential starting point for scholars and policymakers. Such an approach has often proved elusive at the cost of regional stability and development.

Describing the region's experience with modernization in the nineteenth century, the historian Albert Hourani wrote:

> It would be better ... to see the history of the period as that of a complex interaction: of the will of ancient and stable societies to reconstitute themselves, preserving what they have of their own while making the necessary changes in order to survive in a modern world.
>
> (Hourani 1993: 4)

And writing of the region at the end of the twentieth century, another historian, Avi Shlaim, notes how the Middle East has yet to overcome its 'post-Ottoman syndrome' in reference to the settlement that was imposed on the region by the European powers after the First World War (1995: 132).

At the start of the twenty-first century, these reflections have lost none of their relevance, and continue to inform the region's politics and international relations. They are all the more appropriate from the perspective of 2016 as the region continues to wrestle with the implications of its colonial past, its fractured modern history and multiple encounters with globalization.

Further reading

Gerges, F. (2014) *The New Middle East. Protest and Revolution in the Arab World* (Cambridge: Cambridge University Press)
A valuable recent addition to the post-Arab Spring literature.

Halliday, F. (2005) *The Middle East in International Relations: Power Politics and Ideology* (Cambridge: Cambridge University Press)
A survey of the region's history and politics informed by different international relations approaches.

Hinnebusch, R. (2015) *The International Politics of the Middle East*, rev. edn (Manchester: Manchester University Press)
An interpretation of the international politics of the region, offering a 'modified realist' approach.

Lynch, M. (2012) *The Arab Uprisings. The Unfinished Revolutions of the New Middle East* (New York: Public Affairs)
Historically informed analysis of the uprisings that have swept the Arab world.

Milton Edwards, B. (2011) *Contemporary Politics in the Middle East*, rev. edn (Cambridge: Polity Press)
A comprehensive introduction to contemporary regional politics.

Owen, R. (2004) *State Power and Politics in the Making of the Modern Middle East*, rev. edn (London: Routledge)
An authoritative text offering an excellent introduction to the history and politics of the region.

Notes

1. Otherwise known as ISIS, ISIL, or Daesh. In this volume all these terms are used.
2. 'Global IR: Regional Worlds' was the title given to the International Studies Association conference in 2015. It refers both to the development of the discipline beyond its Western origins and to the exploration of different global forces, actors, and movements in the development of IR theory and practice.

Part 1

Theoretical and Historical Overview

International Relations Theory and the Middle East

FRED H. LAWSON

Overview

International relations theory takes many forms and poses a wide range of puzzles that can be addressed using Middle Eastern cases. Structural realist theory dominates the field, complemented by neoliberal institutionalism, the English School, historical sociology, and constructivism. Statistical studies of world politics offer useful insights that demand further exploration, as do power transition theory and power cycle theory. Conceptual contributions from regional specialists also merit elaboration.

Introduction

International relations is a broad field of academic inquiry that has generated a variety of theoretical approaches. Mainstream theories focus on the ways that states interact with one another under circumstances in which there is no overarching authority that governs their behaviour—in other words, under conditions of anarchy. For structural realists, also known as neorealists, the anarchic character of the international arena compels states to look out for their own interests, and to distrust the motives and actions of others. Neoliberal institutionalists, by contrast, recognize the importance of self-interest and suspicion in world affairs, but expect states as rational actors to create institutional arrangements that can reduce tension and facilitate cooperation. Such institutions clarify the objectives and intentions of the states involved, and thereby reduce the incentives to engage in self-aggrandizing behaviour at the expense of others. Similarly, scholarship on relational contracting suggests that, even though the world looks as though it is anarchic, there are mutually agreed relationships that lay the foundation for international hierarchies. These may be hierarchies of power, wealth, or prestige, which generate ties of patronage and dependence between great powers and subordinate states.

An important alternative perspective—the English School—argues that, even under anarchic conditions, there is a high degree of orderliness in world affairs. English School theorists posit that, at any given time, there exists a society of states that operates according to accepted norms of behaviour and shared conventions, most notably ones governing diplomacy and warfare. This tradition of scholarship sets out to explain why one cluster of norms and conventions—rather than any other cluster—regulates international relations at a particular moment, as well as why different kinds of international societies, or states-systems, emerge, flourish, and deteriorate.

Less conventional approaches criticize structural realists, neoliberal institutionalists, and the English School alike for assuming that states constitute the elemental and fixed actors in world affairs. Constructivist theories assert that states take shape in specific historical and political-economic contexts, and that the conditions under which states coalesce and become socialized to one another play a crucial role in determining not only how they interact, but also how they conceive of themselves and formulate their basic interests. Moreover, constructivists claim that there can be many different sorts of international anarchy: sometimes, the absence of an overarching authority structure accompanies pervasive rivalry and mistrust among states, but under other, equally anarchic, circumstances, states get socialized to interact in a more benign and collaborative fashion.

Constructivist theories are sometimes associated with the philosophical position that all knowledge is bound up with concepts that dictate what is considered to be factual and what is not. In other words, radical constructivists reject the positivist claim that theories can (and indeed must) be tested against empirical data; they assert instead that knowledge derives from concepts that interpret what goes on in such a way as to promote justice, equality, or peace. A growing body of scholarship that declares itself to be post-structuralist, or even post-modernist, insists that interpretive theories offer the only meaningful insights into world politics. For scholars in this research programme, the quest to build a scientific discipline of international relations is at best wrong-headed and at worst masks—and advances—the interests and agendas of statespeople.

At the other end of the spectrum from these radical approaches stands an assortment of quantitative studies that offers an impressive body of empirical findings about international relations, accumulated through the meticulous collection of events data and the employment of sophisticated statistical techniques. Quantitative research at first focused almost exclusively on the association between alliances and war, but has gone on to address more complex dimensions of international conflict. Among these are the dynamics that characterize militarized interstate disputes, territorial conflicts, and enduring rivalries. Equally empiricist in nature is a handful of quantitative and qualitative—that is, case study—explorations into questions raised by power transition theory and power cycle theory.

There thus exist a great many alternative theories of international relations that can be investigated, debated, tested, elaborated, and refined by examining events and trends in the Middle East. Some broad theoretical controversies have already trickled into scholarship on Middle Eastern affairs. Raymond Hinnebusch (2003), for instance, incorporates constructivist notions of identity and structuration into his survey of regional developments; Fred

---

Box 1.1 What is the 'Middle East'?

How to delineate the Middle Eastern international system in conceptual, rather than purely geographical, terms is a long-standing problem. Leonard Binder (1958) proposes that the region consists of the former territories of the Ottoman Empire, along with neighbouring countries in which religious opposition movements have challenged Western-style nationalism. 'On this basis,' he argues, 'the Middle East proper stretches from Libya to Iran, with fringe areas including Afghanistan, Pakistan, and the Maghrib, and a core area including the Arab states and Israel' (Binder 1958: 416). Binder asserts that relations among these states cannot be explained in terms of the dynamics of the global order, but instead require close attention to local history and internal politics. 'If power were to be likened to rays of light,' he observes, 'we might say that extra-area power is 'refracted' when projected into the Middle Eastern element' (Binder 1958: 415).

Paul Noble (1991), by contrast, focuses on relations among the Arab states, excluding Iran, Turkey, and Israel on the grounds that they do not share the weak state institutions, common values, and ideologies—in particular an affinity for pan-Arabism—or permeability of political boundaries that one sees in the Arab world. Gregory Gause (2004) counters that the Middle Eastern system is made up of states that are held together by bonds of asymmetrical interdependence. Alternatively, it has been proposed that the Middle East forms a regional security complex: a set of states in which policies carried out by one state generate externalities that ignite, escalate, or mitigate conflicts in other states (Lake 1997). In these terms, the Middle Eastern regional system delineated by Binder has expanded in recent years to incorporate the Caucasus, Central Eurasia, and South Asia (Lawson 2007b; al-Hariri 2011).

Halliday (2005) wrestles with the reciprocal impact of state institutions and transnational processes, as well as with influential theories of nationalism; Barry Buzan and Ana Gonzalez-Pelanez (2009) have even made a preliminary attempt to apply English School concepts to this part of the world. But for the most part, international relations and Middle East studies remain strictly segregated from each other. One of the major tasks for future scholarship is to combine state-of-the-art theorizing with up-to-date analysis undertaken by specialists in this particular region (**see Box 1.1**).

Structural realism, neoliberal institutionalism, and relational contracting

Under anarchic circumstances, states look out first and foremost for their own security interests. For structural realists, this means that states give top priority to maximizing their individual well-being, and do their best to guard against being attacked, conquered, or otherwise exploited by others (Waltz 1979). In pursuit of this objective, states can be expected to act rationally, primarily because the most pressing dangers they confront are so glaringly obvious that leaders can easily figure out the broad outlines, and secondarily because states set up dense networks of government agencies to gather information and interpret what is happening around them.

Unfortunately (and structural realists call this the 'underlying tragedy of world politics'), the steps that states take to maximize their own security jeopardize the interests of other states. In other words, the policies that any one government implements to build up its armed forces, mobilize its population, or boost its economic productivity put other states at a strategic disadvantage. The others immediately take steps to catch up, and their responses undermine whatever benefit might have been gained by the first state. Consequently, all states end up no better off than they were at the outset or—as a result of the expense of armaments programmes and the animosity created by the cycle of hostile action and reaction— actually worse off. This dynamic is known as the 'security dilemma', and structural realists argue that it drives interactions among states under anarchy (Jervis 1978; Glaser 1997; Booth and Wheeler 2008).

Analysts of international relations in the Middle East frequently employ the term 'security dilemma', but almost always do so in a loose or simplistic fashion. Instead of examining crucial features of the irresolvable paradoxes that states face when they deal with one another in an anarchic environment, Middle East scholars generally use 'security dilemma' as a synonym for 'security problem' or 'security challenge'. Only a handful of studies has employed the concept in a rigorous way (Yaniv 1986; Stein 1993; Lawson 2011).

Even though the security dilemma tends to spark arms races and aggravates mistrust and antagonism among states, it does not necessarily lead to war. A major puzzle that structural realists continue to investigate concerns the precise circumstances under which interstate wars break out in an anarchic environment. The literature on this topic is enormous, and much of it deals with comparisons of relative power. Geoffrey Blainey (1973), for example, argues that war is more likely to occur when statespeople disagree about how power is distributed among states, while the chances for peace improve markedly whenever leaders find themselves in agreement about the distribution of power. Other neorealist scholarship explains the outbreak of war in terms of the 'offense–defence balance'—that is, whether weapons and strategies that improve states' ability to mount an attack are more effective than weapons and strategies that can protect against attacks or limit the damage if an attack comes (Van Evera 1999). Major studies in this research programme have tried to determine just what factors make offensive forces and strategies dominant over the defence, and how the rise of attack-oriented armaments shapes decision-making in a crisis (Lynn-Jones 1995).

Still other structural realists connect the likelihood of conflict and instability to specific distributions of power. There is a long-standing debate between scholars who claim that severe conflict is more likely to erupt if there are three or more states competing with one another (a multipolar world) (Waltz 1964) and those who assert that there is a higher potential for system-changing warfare if two states confront one another head-on (a bipolar world) (Deutsch and Singer 1964). The debate originally dealt with the international system as a whole, but it has been extended to the regional level (Weede 1976). Some scholars who have undertaken statistical research on this question define multipolar worlds as ones in which power is less concentrated and bipolar worlds as ones in which power is highly concentrated (Siverson and Sullivan 1983; Wayman 1984); others define multipolar worlds as ones that have three or more groups of states and bipolar worlds as ones with a pair of grand coalitions (Singer et al. 1972). Such reformulations of the concepts of multipolarity and bipolarity have made most quantitative studies tangential, if not actually irrelevant, to the original debate (Moul 1993). It would therefore be useful to explore the question of whether the Middle East tends to be more peaceful and stable at those times when there are two predominant actors in regional affairs, or when there are more than two major rivals.

Structural realists generally claim that states try to block or undercut any state that pursues an overtly aggressive foreign policy or sets out to change the underlying structure of the international arena. This implies that countries almost always engage in balancing behaviour when they confront actual or potential aggressors, and that balancing among states plays a key role in preserving the stability of the system as a whole (Waltz 1979). A minority view argues that, under some conditions, weaker states choose instead to align themselves with the aggressor, in the hope that they will either be rewarded for their support or spared the harmful consequences of resisting—a policy known as 'bandwagoning' (Labs 1992; Schweller 1994). Large-scale, quantitative studies indicate that balancing predominates in the modern era (Fritz and Sweeney 2004; Levy and Thompson 2005), despite a bit of quibbling over definitions (Schroeder 1994). Systematic analyses of historical cases reach the same conclusion (Wohlforth et al. 2007), although methodological shortcomings cast doubt on the results of large-scale qualitative research (Eilstrup-Sangiovanni 2009).

Scholars of international relations in the Middle East have contributed a good deal to our understanding of balancing and bandwagoning. Stephen Walt (1987) demonstrates that states in the Arab world most often take steps to block any one country from gaining a dominant position in regional affairs, despite persistent calls for Arab unity, concerted efforts by one government or another to exert leadership in inter-Arab affairs, and the presence of the State of Israel as a common adversary. Walt goes on to argue that concrete measures of power have less impact than more fluid notions of threat in determining how Middle Eastern states interact. Alan Taylor (1982) describes in detail the kinds of balancing behaviour that have characterized regional affairs, as do the pioneering studies of Patrick Seale (1965) and Malcolm Kerr (1971). Elie Podeh (1993 and 2003) surveys the shifting alignments that permeated inter-Arab relations during the era of Egypt's greatest influence. James Lebovic (2004), by contrast, asserts that Walt defines terms in such a way as to overstate the frequency and centrality of inter-Arab balancing. Laurie Brand (1994) adds that fiscal considerations play a pivotal role in determining how Middle Eastern governments ally with one another, while Richard Harknett and Jeffrey VanDenBerg (1997) account for Jordan's puzzling 1990–91 alignment with Iraq in terms of a convergence of foreign and domestic threats.

Gregory Gause (2003) advances the argument that Arab states give higher priority to some kinds of threats than they do to others when it comes to deciding how to respond to adversaries. Threats that put a country's domestic stability in jeopardy are more salient and consequential than those that involve foreign affairs alone. Consequently, 'Middle Eastern leaders balance against the state that manifests the most hostility toward their [respective] regimes, regardless of that state's aggregate power and geographic proximity' (Gause 2003: 283; see also Ryan 2009). Similar reasoning has been used to account for the emergence of the Gulf Cooperation Council (Priess 1996), although the formation of the GCC can also be explained in terms of overlapping external and internal threats (Cooper 2003–4).

Structural realists expect states to form alliances only if such partnerships improve their capacity to protect themselves, or in some other way augment their security. Alliances that coalesce on the basis of shared ideology will tend to be rare and fragile, since strategic alignments entail substantial costs and impose significant restraints on the freedom of action exercised by member states (Snyder 1997). Moreover, it is hard for states to manage relations with allies and adversaries at the same time. Policies that strengthen the alliance may enable a state's partners to drag it into conflicts in which it has no intrinsic interest, while attempts to improve relations with the adversary are likely to prompt a state's allies to abandon it. Whether entrapment and abandonment occur equally often is open to question (Kim 2011).

The dilemmas associated with alliance management have only begun to be explored using Middle Eastern cases (Lawson 2007a).

Evidence from the Middle East lay at the heart of an earlier, but now largely forgotten, literature on alliances that emphasizes states' incentives to maintain regional stability by creating delicately counterpoised coalitions. Brian Healy and Arthur Stein (1973) assert that states form alignments that exhibit structural balance—in other words, that produce ally–adversary configurations that consist of even numbers of antagonistic linkages. Frank Harary (1961) shows that a marked tendency toward structural balance propelled alliance-making among Egypt, Israel, Britain, France, the United States, and the Soviet Union in the months leading up to the 1956 Suez War; David Lai (2001) delineates analogous alliance patterns among the Arab states, Israel, the US, and the Soviet Union. Vestiges of this research programme can be discerned in studies that highlight the strategic triangles that characterize successive periods of Middle Eastern diplomacy (Mojtahed-Zadeh 1994; Fuertig 2007).

Another major debate among structural realists concerns whether states are primarily concerned with maximizing their overall security, wealth, and prestige, or instead worry most about their position compared to others. Proponents of the former line of argument assert that states pursue absolute gains, and that this predisposition helps to reduce the severity of the security dilemma (Snidal 1991). Those who claim that states are more keenly interested in relative gains conclude that it is almost impossible to escape the security dilemma, so any action that states take will heighten mistrust and conflict (Grieco 1988). This debate lost some of its intensity after Robert Powell (1991) put forward the sensible proposition that states worry about relative gains whenever war looks imminent and give greater consideration to absolute gains if the prospects for war seem slight. Nevertheless, the controversy regarding absolute versus relative gains leaves open the question: under what conditions will leaders emphasize the overall well-being of their respective countries and what factors induce states instead to put greater weight on their position vis-à-vis others?

Neoliberal institutionalists make almost all of the same theoretical assumptions that structural realists do, but shift attention away from interstate conflict and highlight the factors that facilitate cooperation (Keohane and Martin 1995). For these scholars, states are much less likely to act belligerently and exploit one another under some circumstances than they are in others. In particular, if the worst possible outcome facing two states happens when one state acts cooperatively and the other takes advantage of it, then—under anarchic circumstances—each state has no incentive to cooperate. This situation is usually called the 'prisoner's dilemma' (Oye 1985). If, however, circumstances make it much more costly for the two states to exploit one another, and the best possible outcome is either mutual cooperation or mutual non-cooperation, then each one will make an effort to coordinate its actions with those of the adversary. Situations like these are known as 'assurance games' (Martin 1992).

For neoliberal institutionalists, the key analytical task is to examine the context in which states interact, in order to determine what sort of incentive structure they face. Because states are assumed to act rationally, conditions that decrease the level of mistrust coalesce into formal or informal institutions (Martin and Simmons 1998). When institutions emerge, interstate cooperation becomes more prevalent and stable. Institutions that promote cooperation can take many different forms: states gravitate toward a small number of major currencies; the United Nations consists of both a tiny Security Council and a much larger General Assembly; airline pilots around the world speak English; the Arab League takes decisions on the basis of consensus among member states, whereas the short-lived Arab Cooperation Council was constructed on the principle of majority rule (Lawson 2008). How and why various institutional arrangements come into existence and evolve over time constitutes the heart of the neoliberal institutionalist research programme.

One offshoot of neoliberal institutionalism analyses the emergence and consolidation of regional organizations (Mansfield and Solingen 2010). Studies of Middle Eastern regionalism remain almost entirely descriptive, rather than explanatory (Aghrout and Sutton 1990; Tripp 1995; Zorob 2008; see also **Chapter 9**). Moreover, the existing literature tends to lump together regionalist projects that differ profoundly from one another in structure and mode of operation. Thus Paul Aarts (1999) presents the Arab Maghreb Union (AMU), Arab Cooperation Council (ACC), and Gulf Cooperation Council (GCC) as equivalent types of regional formation; Michael Hudson (1999) puts the United Arab Republic, Federation of Arab Republics, AMU, ACC, and the Joint Arab Economic Action Initiative in the omnibus category of 'subregional groupings'. More firmly grounded in the international relations literature on regionalism stands Melani Cammett's (1999) focused comparison of the AMU and the GCC, which argues that these two formations more closely resemble instances of what Andrew Hurrell (1995) calls bottom-up 'regionalization' than they do the state-sponsored initiatives that one finds in other parts of the world.

International governance structures have been analysed somewhat differently by scholars who apply the concept of relational contracting, drawn from neo-classical economics. David Lake (2009) asserts that states constantly engage in bargaining with one another and the relations that take shape among countries over time represent mutually agreed outcomes of these ongoing negotiations. As they bargain with each other, states do their best to keep transaction costs and governance costs to a minimum. This implies that as soon as it becomes too expensive to administer a specific territory, whichever state controls that territory will accord it a degree of autonomy. Empires emerge whenever governance costs happen to be particularly low; protectorates appear as governance costs increase; spheres of influence come into being as governance costs rise even higher. These costs will change depending on the frequency of interactions among the political entities involved (Kim and Wolford 2014). Relational contracting can be used to explore conceptual and empirical issues related to the emergence, adjustment, and collapse of regional institutions throughout the Middle East, from the Ottoman Empire to the European protectorates of the early twentieth century to today's Greater Arab Free Trade Area. The trick is to come up with ways to define and measure transaction, governance, and enforcement costs that are not inherently circular.

International society, political culture, and historical sociology

Hedley Bull (1977) famously postulates that even though individual human beings find existence under anarchic circumstances to be intolerable, because any single person can be killed at one blow by any other individual, states have a greater capacity to survive in anarchy, because they are much harder to destroy. As a result, Bull argues, the anarchic international arena gives rise to some form of society among states, albeit one that is fundamentally different from societies made up of human individuals. Societies of states are characterized by significant levels of rivalry and mistrust, but the degree of conflict they exhibit can be, and most often is, limited and managed by means of astute statecraft.

Later scholars in this theoretical tradition, who refer to themselves as the English School, advance the stronger claim that societies of states, or states-systems, exhibit rules and conventions that constrain governments from engaging in what Thomas Hobbes calls a 'war of all against all' (Watson 1992; Little 2000; Linklater 2009). The most important of these rules and conventions are bound up with the concept of sovereignty—the notion that states, as a matter of principle, respect each other and refrain from interfering in one another's internal affairs. States-systems in which sovereignty operates exhibit much less friction and belligerence than those in which sovereignty is absent. Sovereignty in this sense, which Stephen Krasner (1999) labels 'Westphalian sovereignty', arose in Western Europe at some point after 1648—precisely when remains in dispute (Osiander 2001)—and spread to other parts of the world over the next three centuries. Along with the global diffusion of Westphalian sovereignty came the emergence of other commonly accepted practices, most notably legitimate intervention in countries that stand outside the international society of the era (Keene 2013).

Investigating the ways in which regions outside Europe became incorporated into the global, sovereignty-based states-system constitutes a major area of investigation for the English School. Early writing on this topic emphasized the transformations in diplomatic practice, political discourse, and alliance-making that accompanied the integration of non-European areas, including the Ottoman Empire (Naff 1984), into the Europe-centred states-system. Newer work examines the local political-economic trends that set the stage for the emergence and consolidation of Westphalian sovereignty throughout the former Ottoman domain (Kashani-Sabet 1999; Lawson 2006).

Precisely how sovereignty operates in the contemporary Middle East is a controversial topic. Students of regional politics usually take at face value the pronouncements that have been made by generations of local statespeople and argue that an aspiration for unity permeates relations among Arab states. In other words, most observers consider pan-Arabism to be a cardinal principle of Middle Eastern diplomacy (Valbjorn 2009; Valbjorn and Bank 2012), and claim that the drive toward Arab unity contradicts the conventions of Westphalian sovereignty (Barnett 1998). A subtler reading of the statements made by Arab governments demonstrates that calls for unity almost always point toward some sort of loose federation that retains a substantial degree of state autonomy, especially with regard to internal affairs, but also concerning matters of war and peace. The most prominent experiment in Arab unification, the United Arab Republic that resulted from the merger of Egypt and Syria in 1958, collapsed after only three years of existence, largely due to the fact that Egyptian leaders carried out policies that infringed on the autonomy of their Syrian counterparts (Podeh 1999).

A parallel debate rages over the role of political culture, and more specifically religion, in shaping international relations in the Middle East. The conventional view asserts that Islam stands in stark opposition to the tenets of Westphalian sovereignty, and that the basic incompatibility between these two clusters of principles injects a high degree of conflict into regional affairs (Hashmi 2009; Mendelsohn 2012). It seems more accurate to observe that Islam has, from the very beginning, accommodated a wide variety of diplomatic and strategic practices, including ones that closely resemble Westphalian sovereignty (Piscatori 1986). For the English School, religious doctrines and institutions make up a crucial, but frequently overlooked, component of international society—whether in medieval Europe, nineteenth-century East

Asia, or the contemporary Middle East (Thomas 2000). The extent to which the rise of radical movements like the so-called Islamic State in Iraq and the Levant (ISIS) has altered such
fundamental conventions as respect for territorial boundaries represents an aspect of Middle
Eastern affairs that English School scholarship might fruitfully address (Dessouki 2015).

Alongside the English School's analysis of international society runs a parallel research
programme rooted in historical sociology. This theoretical approach plays down the centrality of the state and highlights the political, economic, and social dynamics that shape
the expansion and contraction of governmental capacity (Jarvis 1989). Two variants of this
research programme can be discerned: one inspired by Max Weber (Hobson 2000), the
other by Karl Marx (Gills 2002). Recent work in historical sociology explores the impact of
multiple and competing modernities in shaping relations between imperialist Europe and
parts of the world that fell under European domination. John Hobson (2009) makes the pro-
vocatively counter-intuitive claim that Westphalian sovereignty came to Europe from East
Asia, by way of the trade routes that straddled the Middle East. Studies of Middle Eastern
international relations that illustrate the usefulness of historical sociology are just starting to
appear (Cummings and Hinnebusch 2014).

Constructivism, post-structuralism, and post-modernism

Perhaps the most energetic research programme in the field of international relations over
the past decade involves constructivist theory. Initially, constructivists claimed that all actors learn how to think about themselves and what they value most highly through their interactions with one another. In other words, states develop both identities and interests by
means of a learning process that can lead in dramatically different directions. The world of rivalry and mistrust that is envisaged by structural realists is only one possible outcome, which
takes shape in a specific context and should not be generalized (Wendt 1992). More importantly, constructivists argue that structural realists, neoliberal institutionalists, and English
School theorists alike overemphasize the importance of the international structures that are
presumed to determine how states interact with each other. They insist to the contrary that
states-as-actors and structural features of the international arena arise simultaneously and in-
separably—in other words, that these phenomena are 'mutually constituted' (Hopf 1998: 172).

Constructivists go on to highlight the role of meaning in world affairs. States are not simply, to use a famous analogy, billiard balls that bounce against one another and come to rest
in kaleidoscopic patterns; they are instead conscious actors that develop common understandings that influence how they deal with one another (Ashley 1988). Such understandings provide the basis for shared expectations, which spell out what kinds of interaction are
appropriate under the circumstances ('norms')—and norms change as time goes by. In order
to explain what happens in the world, scholars must pay careful attention to meanings and
other forms of 'intersubjective understanding' (Mitzen 2005). As Ted Hopf remarks:

> Determining the outcome will require knowing more about the situation than about the distri-
> bution of material power or the structure of authority. One will need to know about the culture,
> norms, institutions, procedures, rules, and social practices that constitute the actors and the
> structure alike.
>
> (Hopf 1998: 173)

Key to constructivist theory is the concept of 'discourse'. Discourse refers not only to the language, rhetoric, and symbols that states use to express their identities and interests, but also to the practices that they undertake in order to carry out their strategic objectives (Bigo 2011). Whereas neorealists and neoliberal institutionalists conceive of power in terms of concrete resources, such as battleships and steel mills, constructivists claim that material power must be combined with 'discursive power' in order to understand why some countries prevail while others do not. In R. B. J. Walker's (1984: 3) words, 'it is important to recognize that ideas, consciousness, culture, and ideology are bound up with more immediately visible kinds of political, military, and economic power'. Discursive power often arises as part of a social process, in which the interpretations and responses of others play a part in conferring greater capabilities on one state or another. Egypt, for example, wielded considerable influence in Middle Eastern affairs during the late 1950s not only because it was the most populous and best-armed Arab state, but also, and more crucially, as a result of its dominant position in regional culture and the admiration that leaders and citizenries throughout the region accorded President Gamal Abd al-Nasser (Barnett 1996; Teti 2004).

Discourse lies at the heart of power, but also stands at the core of the manifestation and recognition of threats. Constructivists argue that changes in the distribution of power among states do not, by themselves, precipitate arms races, alliance formation, or economic mobilization; it is only when power dynamics get constituted as threats to a state's security that governments gear up for military action. Hopf (1998: 187) refers to this pivotal process as 'threat perception', but much more than perceptions are involved. Threats take shape in the context of conflicts of interest, cultural disharmonies, ideological incompatibilities, hostile rhetoric, belligerent activities, and a whole host of other circumstances that transcend mere perceptions. The question of how threats emerge has sparked the growth of securitization theory, a branch of constructivism that deals with the puzzle of why aspects of everyday life sometimes get transformed into matters of national security (Balzacq 2011). Dynamics associated with securitization have caught the attention of several scholars of Middle Eastern international relations (Aras and Polat 2008).

Many components of constructivist theory fit comfortably into structural realism and neoliberal institutionalism, and look perfectly compatible with the English School as well. Yet there exists profound disagreement among constructivists over just how much of the world is socially—or, more accurately, 'intersubjectively'—constructed (Guzzini and Leander 2006). Does a country's gross national product or the size of its nuclear arsenal play any part in determining its power and interests? Or is the primary determinant the interpretations that a country's own leaders and the leaderships of surrounding states entertain and share among themselves? Radical constructivists reject the assumption that state identities and security interests have any solid basis in the world (Zehfuss 2002). The purpose of scholarly inquiry for radical constructivists is not so much to explain what happens as it is to expose and critique the meanings that statespeople and scholars have attributed to particular events.

For the most part, constructivist writing on the international relations of the Middle East retains an empiricist, philosophical realist bent, and stands firmly anchored in what Emanuel Adler (1997) calls 'the middle ground' of the conceptual spectrum. Bruce Jentleson and Dalia Kaye, for example, argue that greater regional security cooperation took shape in the wake of the 1990–91 Gulf War as a result of the Egyptian leadership's worries that:

Egypt's status interests . . . were being threatened by another Arab state, Jordan, delineating and seeking to legitimize an alternative Arab position. This became an additional impetus for Egypt to link all of the [Arms Control and Regional Security] agenda to the [Israeli] nuclear issue, as the very multilateral nature of the ACRS process was providing other Arab states a venue for asserting independent positions; that is, for genuinely multilateralizing the process in a manner that threatened the position and status of Egypt as [Arab] bloc leader and monopolistic interlocutor.

(Jentelson and Kaye 1998: 232)

Michael Barnett (1996) connects the burst of regional cooperation that appeared in 1991–2 to a shift in norms that involved not only states' conception of their respective interests, but also emerging notions of 'the desired regional order'. Arshin Adib-Moghaddam (2006) likewise situates current trends in the Gulf in the context of long-standing cultural attributes that have engendered competing norms and rival discourses between actors based on the Persianate northern coast and others located on the Arabian southern shore.

Radical constructivism bears a close resemblance to conceptual approaches to international relations that reject conventional notions of theory altogether. Attempts to find causal explanations for events and trends in world affairs may well turn out to be illusory. States—or, more precisely, the human beings who hold influential positions in government agencies—have little in common with the minerals, gases, and biological organisms that inspire the physical sciences. In addition, international relations deals with matters that affect people who are systematically excluded from the policymaking process every bit as much as they do the wealthy and powerful.

Post-structuralists thus pay close attention to the way in which certain topics get routinely overlooked or set aside by mainstream theories. These writers usually begin by noting that Western science coalesced in the context of philosophical and political developments that privileged a peculiar analytical viewpoint, one that values 'technical control over nature and administrative control over humans' (Campbell 2010: 218). Post-structuralist scholarship explicitly opposes theories that go hand in hand with any and all forms of domination, and does its best to illuminate and encourage ideas and movements that expand the range of human freedom (Weber 1999). Rather than tacitly accept analytical distinctions such as citizen/immigrant, security/insecurity, or Israeli/Palestinian, this research programme sets out to analyse 'the cultural practices through which the inclusions and exclusions that give meaning to binary pairs are established' (Campbell 2010: 225). Deconstructing the discourse of academics who write about world politics is every bit as vital as deconstructing the discourse of statespeople, since the theories that have been developed by scholars usually set the terms of reference and frames of action for diplomats and military commanders.

At its core, David Campbell declares:

Poststructuralism is different from most other approaches to international politics because it does not see itself as a theory, school, or paradigm which produces a single account of its subject matter. Instead, poststructuralism is an approach, attitude, or ethos that pursues critique in particular ways.

(Campbell 2012: 234–5)

It is especially concerned with exposing the ways in which power operates at and across various levels of world politics. In the intellectual tradition of Michel Foucault, post-structuralists assert that there is an intimate connection between power and knowledge, and focus their energies on the task of unravelling the linkages that permit oppression and exploitation to persist and flourish (Edkins 1999). They also emphasize the importance of investigating various forms and dimensions of agency in world affairs, and reject the assumption that actors are fundamentally constrained by fixed (structural) arrangements (Knafo 2010).

Post-structuralists remind observers of international relations that, just as scholarly ideas shape the actions of statespeople, so their own thinking reflects developments in the world. It is therefore vital for scholars and students to recognize the reflexive interaction that exists between theories of world politics and ongoing political trends. Explicit recognition of reflexivity can be autobiographical in form or it may focus on the institutions that nurture intellectual life (Hamati-Ataya 2013). Among students of Middle Eastern international relations, Morten Valbjorn (2004a), Andrea Teti (2007), and Pinar Bilgin (2011) exemplify broadly post-structuralist approaches.

Most post-structuralists bridle at the suggestion that their conceptual perspective is equivalent to post-modernism. The latter perspective abandons theory entirely, and celebrates ideas and practices that express the entire spectrum of human creativity (Bleiker 2001). Like post-structuralism, post-modernism abhors domination and exploitation, but, unlike the post-structuralists, post-modernists devote their primary attention to issues of meta-theory and ontology rather than matters of epistemology or methodology (Brown 2012). Analogies or parables that elucidate some previously ignored or fundamentally misconstrued aspect of world affairs are, for post-modernist writers, perfectly acceptable contributions to academic literature and debate (Constantinou 1994).

Key findings from quantitative research

Arguably the most significant finding that has come out of the quantitative scholarship in international relations is the proposition that liberal democratic countries do not go to war with other liberal democracies. This statistical finding has been tested in all sorts of ways, and has been validated time and again (Ray 1995; Oneal and Russett 1999; but note, on the other hand, Spiro 1994). Early work claiming that liberal democracies are less war-prone in general than other types of states has been effectively rebutted, and the Gulf Wars of 1990–91 and 2003 demonstrate that even well-established democracies such as the United States and United Kingdom harbour few, if any, inhibitions about engaging in warfare against non-democratic countries. The robustness of the finding that liberal democracies do not engage in war with one another raises the question of whether interstate conflict in the Middle East might diminish in frequency or severity if this form of government were to gain a firm foothold in the region. Etel Solingen (2003) argues that it would; Michael Hudson (1992) intimates that it would not.

Optimism that the establishment of liberal democracy would bring peace to the Middle East might well be tempered by quantitative studies that investigate the likelihood of war during the initial stages of democratization. Edward Mansfield and Jack Snyder (1995) show that, even though mature democracies seem to have no chance of going to war with one another, states that are just starting to democratize face intense pressure to act belligerently. This finding has been brought into question (Narang and Nelson 2009), and deserves further investigation. It would probably be useful to integrate the research programme on belligerence in new democracies with statistical studies that explicate the association between revolutions and outbreaks of war (Walt 1996; Colgan 2013). And if things were not murky enough, the quantitative literature also demonstrates that dicatorships are just as likely to keep the peace among themselves as are democratic regimes (Peceny and Beer 2002). Elucidating the factors that promote peacefulness among authoritarian states seems like a particularly promising area of research for Middle East specialists.

Statistical studies require a large number of cases in order to reach reliable conclusions. Since the number of wars that one finds, even in comparatively bellicose parts of the world like the Middle East, remains too small to support sound quantitative research, scholars have turned their attention to the dynamics of militarized interstate disputes (MIDs). MIDs consist of instances of belligerent action that involve the threat or possibility of war, but do not eventuate in armed combat (Gochman and Maoz 1984). Bombastic public speeches, military exercises along the border, economic embargoes, and 'accidental' artillery discharges represent examples of MIDs of varying degrees of intensity. Most germane to the Middle East is the finding that states whose regimes consist of a single political party engage in fewer MIDs with other single-party regimes than they do with countries that do not have that type of government (Peceny and Beer 2003). On the other hand, countries ruled by personalist dictatorships or military juntas turn out to be more likely than others to become involved in MIDs, and much more likely to initiate warlike interactions (Peceny and Butler 2004; Weeks 2012; Colgan and Weeks 2015). Formulating plausible explanations for these findings would be an important contribution that students of international relations of the Middle East could make to the field as a whole.

Whether or not oil-producing states are more prone to involvement in MIDs has been the subject of recent research. It seems clear that governments that derive a substantial proportion of their total income from non-tax revenues engage in a greater number of MIDs (McDonald 2007). Georg Struever and Tim Wegenast (2011) demonstrate that oil-producing countries turn out to be more likely to initiate MIDs than non-oil-producing countries, whether or not the oil states are liberal democracies. Such states possess the financial resources to purchase and deploy large quantities of high-quality weapons, and may be accorded greater leeway to brandish these armaments against actual and potential adversaries by the international community, most of whose members' economies rely on oil imports. Oil-producing states that experience a revolutionary upheaval are especially prone to aggressive behaviour (Colgan 2010).

Territorial disputes exhibit a particularly strong association with the outbreak of both wars and MIDs (Hensel 1996). For the years between 1945 and 1987, states that share a border with one another and that harbour some kind of boundary dispute are forty times more likely than other countries to be involved in war (Kocs 1995). Disagreements over territory are especially likely to be associated with the escalation of MIDs to warfare (Huth 2000: 90). And the incidence of armed conflict over territory is just as high for the period after 1945 as it is for the era stretching from 1816 to 1945, despite all of the improvements in transportation and communication that took place after the Second World War (Hensel 2000: 66). Moreover, conflicts arising from territorial disputes turn out to be both more severe and substantially harder to resolve than other types of interstate conflict (Hensel 2000: 73).

Studies of territorial disputes in the Middle East remain few in number and largely descriptive in nature. Gwenn Okruhlik and Patrick Conge (1999) survey long-standing border conflicts around the Arabian peninsula, as do John Wilkinson (1991) and John Peterson (2011). A detailed analysis of the dispute between Abu Dhabi and Saudi Arabia over the oasis of al-Ain/Buraimi is undertaken by Richard Schofield (2011), while the boundary conflict between Saudi Arabia and Yemen is explored by Ahmad al-Ghamdi (1996). Asher Kaufman (2001, 2006, 2009) details the simmering conflict among Lebanon, Syria, and Israel over a collection of contested villages in the Golan. One step beyond simple narrative can be found in Shahram Chubin and Charles Tripp's (1993) explication of the link between the consolidation of 'state-based nationalism' and territory-based conflicts among the Arab Gulf states.

Large-scale statistical studies have discovered that only a handful of countries accounts for most of the wars and MIDs that have occurred since 1815. In other words, participation in major international conflicts is not randomly distributed among states. There is a limited number of pairs of states (dyads) that fight each other over and over again, which can be labelled 'enduring rivalries'. Various operational definitions of enduring rivalries have been proposed; the most widely accepted version holds that an enduring rivalry exists whenever two states use, or threaten to use, force against one another at least six times over a period of at least twenty years. The finding that wars and MIDs cluster among a small number of states raises the question of why some episodes of armed confrontation get transformed into recurrent military contests (Mor 2003; Vasquez 2009), as well as why enduring rivalries eventually draw to a close. Surprisingly, and despite all of the quantitative work that has been devoted to the dynamics of enduring rivalries, these two crucial questions remain unanswered. Janice Gross Stein (1996), Zeev Maoz and Ben Mor (2002), and Karen Rasler, William Thompson, and Sumit Ganguly (2013) have extended the study of enduring rivalries to the Middle East.

Paul Huth (1996) finds that disputes over territory are particularly likely to set the stage for the emergence of enduring rivalries. Huth argues that territorial disputes are apt to generate recurrent conflict if:

a)   the land in question has 'strategic value' rather than merely economic value;

b)   there are linguistic or ancestral groups that spill across the contested border that have ties to the state that is challenging the territorial status quo;

c)   the two states are roughly equal in military power; and

d)   internal instability gives the state that is challenging the status quo an incentive to mobilize its populace for war.

Paul Diehl and Gary Goertz (2000) further assert that some kind of 'political shock' tends to accompany the initiation of an enduring rivalry, although they frame the notion so broadly that almost any substantial disruption in political, economic, or diplomatic affairs might count as such a shock. Two cases demonstrate the importance of territorial disputes for the origin and entrenchment of enduring rivalries in the Middle East. Recurrent warfare between Baath Party-dominated Iraq and the Islamic Republic of Iran can be traced, despite obvious ideological incompatibilities between the two states, to profound disagreement over control of the Shatt al-Arab waterway (Swearingen 1988; Karsh 1990). Similarly, the enduring rivalry between Iraq and Kuwait grows out of deep-seated grievances connected to the demarcation of permanent borders and other territorial matters (Rahman 1997).

Power transitions and the power cycle

Straddling the line between quantitative and case study research stands a growing body of scholarship that elaborates power transition theory. This conceptual approach, which was initially formulated by A. F. K. Organski and Jacek Kugler (1980), assumes that the international arena is organized in a hierarchical fashion, with no more than a handful of states situated at the pinnacle of power and prestige. Power transition theory hypothesizes that whenever the differential in power separating the dominant great power from its primary challenger starts to diminish—that is, whenever the challenger begins to overtake the dominant state—the chances of major conflict increase dramatically. If the challenger is deeply dissatisfied with the existing international order or has interests that diverge sharply from those of the dominant state, then war becomes even more likely. By contrast, the possibility is virtually nil that major conflict will occur if the dominant state occupies a much stronger position than the primary challenger, or if the challenger is on the whole satisfied with the institutional arrangements that have been put in place by the dominant state.

Power transition theory suffers from significant conceptual shortcomings (DiCicco and Levy 1999; Lebow and Valentino 2009), but has nevertheless inspired empirical investigations into the circumstances under which war breaks out in various parts of the world (Lemke 1996). Statistical studies indicate that armed conflicts seldom erupt if the dominant state in a particular region enjoys a substantial surplus of power over its primary rival, and that war does not take place whenever the challenger is satisfied with the existing regional order. Detailed case studies, for the most part, confirm the utility of power transition theory as an explanation for the occurrence of large-scale warfare (Copeland 2000).

Although power transition theory has not yet been used to explain episodes of war in the Middle East, power cycle theory has been applied to Middle Eastern conflicts. Power cycle theory posits that all countries experience upswings and downturns in their relative economic and military capabilities over time (Doran 1991). At each stage in the cycle of power, some actions are appropriate for a state to undertake and others are not. Whenever a state adopts policies that are inappropriate to its location on the power cycle, conflict with other states is apt to occur (Spiezio 1993; Hebron et al. 2007). In particular, countries that reach the pinnacle of power relative to others and begin to decline, but do not scale back their strategic ambitions, are likely to provoke diplomatic and military confrontations that they cannot afford. By the same token, states whose relative position takes a turn for the better, but whose leaders neglect to take advantage of their improved circumstances, will most likely find themselves exploited by rivals before the proper adjustments can be made.

This analytical perspective can explain crucial aspects of Iraq's relations with its neighbours after 1975. Andrew Parasiliti (2003) shows that Baghdad's invasion of Iran in September 1980 took place in the context of sharply rising Iraqi power, plunging Iranian power, and a marked levelling off of Saudi Arabia's power. In the run-up to the 1990 invasion of Kuwait, by contrast, Iraq's power relative to that of its neighbours had notably diminished, Iran's was rapidly growing, and Saudi Arabia's had started to recover after a sustained slump. In both situations, the Iraqi leadership confronted a strategic crisis, which accompanied a persistent 'ambition for a greater role in both Gulf and Arab political affairs' (Parasiliti 2003: 160). The conjunction of power trends and role conceptions led Iraq, in each case, to launch a risky military venture (see also Gause 2002b). Trita Parsi (2005) extends power cycle theory to explain the unexpected jump in Israeli hostility toward Iran at the end of the 1980s. He shows that this shift occurred in the context of falling Israeli power and rising Iranian power, which:

> prompted a rivalry with Iran, which in turn necessitated improved [Iranian] relations with Israel's Arab neighbors, particularly since Iran sought increased role [sic] by playing the Arab street card against governments of the pro-Western Arab states through its harsh rhetoric and anti-Israel ideology.
>
> (Parsi 2005: 261)

Charles Doran, the inventor of power cycle theory, has toyed with a complementary analytical perspective, which he labels the 'conflict cycle'. This conceptual framework takes various kinds of hostile action and categorizes them according to degree of bellicosity and severity; it then charts the incidence of these events in order to generate a cluster of 'leading and lagging indicators' that is associated with the outbreak of war (Doran 1980: 28). In the case of the Arab–Israeli war of June 1967, troop mobilizations and informal warnings were the primary leading indicators. More importantly, Doran (1980: 34) shows that the eight leading indicators of that war rose, crested, and trailed off in a sequential pattern, with 'each subsequent breakpoint in the conflict cycle occur[ring] at a higher level of tensions'. Consequently, there was no single turning point in the crisis, after which war became inevitable. An earlier collection of statistical studies of conflict interactions among Middle Eastern states explores other dimensions of the conflict cycle that culminated in the 1967 war (Burrowes and Muzzio 1972; Wilkenfeld et al. 1972).

Contributions from regional specialists

With the notable exception of Stephen Walt's work on alliance formation, writing about the Middle East has had no discernible impact on the broader field of international relations. Scholarship that deals with the region occasionally tests or revises concepts that have been developed to understand things that occur elsewhere, but innovative theories formulated to explain Middle Eastern cases tend to get relegated to the area studies ghetto. Nevertheless, there are at least two research programmes coming out of the Middle East that merit wider recognition.

Benjamin Miller (2006) accounts for the exceptionally high incidence and severity of conflicts in the Middle East in terms of the lack of congruence that exists between states and nations in this part of the world. Middle Eastern states tend to be poorly institutionalized and suffer from a basic incapacity to mobilize and manage resources. At the same time, state boundaries rarely coincide with 'the national aspirations and identities of the people in the region' (Miller 2006: 665–6). State leaders consequently have a strong incentive to redraw existing borders, and ethno-sectarian minorities have an equally strong incentive to secede. Pervasive irredentism and secessionism end up 'exacerbat[ing] other causes of war such as the security dilemma, power rivalries, and diversionary motives', while increasing the advantages of striking first in a crisis (Miller 2006: 670–1). Miller applies this argument to the Middle East as a whole, rather than demonstrating that state–nation imbalances in one part of the region or at some particular moment push countries toward war. Moreover, the analysis makes sweeping assertions about the effects of pan-Arabism, even though spelling out congruences and incongruences between states and local nationalisms would be more apposite. Still, this looks like a promising explanation for variations in regional conflict, in the Middle East and beyond.

Philip Robins (2014) proposes a distinction between states that operate inside an established regional order ('milieu states') and 'cusp states' that stand at the edge of adjacent regions. Cusp states display unusually complex patterns of antagonism and alignment, which reflect the powerful cross-currents they have to navigate. Relations between a cusp state and its neighbours can be expected to be tenuous and fragile, and subject to unexpected twists and turns, since the cusp state finds itself forced to respond to changing circumstances in two (or more) regional arenas at the same time. Moreover, cusp states occasionally get pulled into one of the regions it abuts, only to be dragged back to another, resulting in major reconfigurations in both regions. So far, the concept has been used to explain the foreign policies of a handful of individual states (Herzog and Robins 2014). Exploring the dynamics of interaction between cusp states and milieu states in a systematic fashion will uncover new ways to comprehend regional, and inter-regional, politics in the contemporary world.

Conclusion

Scholars of the Middle East have so far addressed only a small fraction of the many theoretical debates and controversies that propel the field of international relations. Most studies that explicitly engage with broader conceptual questions have been framed in terms of structural realism, although a growing literature draws inspiration from one branch or another of the constructivist research programme. Quantitative scholarship at one time paid close attention to events and trends in the Middle East, and one influential statistical database was created from events that transpired in this part of the world (Azar 1972). Yet widespread and persistent unfamiliarity with the facts of Middle Eastern cases—past and present—severely restricts the audience for scholarship that is firmly grounded in regional expertise.

Moreover, it may not be possible to conceive of the Middle East as a regional order, or states-system, that is autonomous enough to operate according to its own dynamics. To the extent that the United States, Russia, the People's Republic of China, Europe, and other external actors intervene in Middle Eastern affairs in a routine and sustained fashion, many of the analytical questions that exercise scholars of international relations will turn out to be mis-specified or irrelevant. For the moment, however, abandoning the quest to integrate international relations and Middle East studies seems premature, and both intellectual enterprises can be enriched by sustained and deliberate cross-fertilization.

Further reading

Burchill, S., Linklater, A., Devetak, R., Donnelly, J., Nardin, T., Paterson, M., Reus-Smit, C., and True, J. (2010) *Theories of International Relations*, 4th edn (London: Palgrave Macmillan)
   Cogent, accessible overviews of the most influential theoretical approaches to world politics.

Carlsnaes, W., Risse, T., and Simmons, B. A. (eds) (2013) *Handbook of International Relations*, 2nd edn (London: Sage)
Short, authoritative summaries of key analytical arguments and conceptual controversies.

Dunne, T., Kurki, M., and Smith, S. (eds) (2010) *International Relations Theories: Discipline and Diversity*, 2nd edn (Oxford: Oxford University Press)
Comprehensive survey of the field by major scholars.

Linklater, A. and Suganami, H. (2006) *The English School of International Relations: A Contemporary Assessment* (Cambridge: Cambridge University Press)
Lucid appreciation and critique of English School scholarship.

Senese, P. D. and Vasquez, J. A. (2008) *The Steps to War* (Princeton, NJ: Princeton University Press)
Compelling synthesis of a wide range of quantitative findings.

Smith, S., Booth, K., and Zalewski, M. (eds) (1996) *International Theory: Positivism and Beyond* (Cambridge: Cambridge University Press)
Seminal contributions by theorists outside the mainstream.

Questions

1. What aspects of the security dilemma have the greatest impact on international relations in the Middle East?

2. Constructivism appears to be a useful way to explain trends and patterns in Middle Eastern international relations, but how can constructivists avoid highlighting features of regional culture that reinforce long-standing stereotypes?

3. Under what circumstances did Westphalian sovereignty take root in the Middle East?

4. Why did the conflict between Egypt and Israel become an enduring rivalry?

5. On the basis of evidence drawn from the Middle East, can we conclude that major wars are most likely to occur whenever a dominant state starts to be overtaken by a rising, dissatisfied state?

2

The Emergence of the Middle East into the Modern State System

EUGENE L. ROGAN

Overview

The modern states of the Arab Middle East emerged from the collapse of the Ottoman Empire and the post-First World War settlement. The fall of the Ottoman Empire left the Turks and Arabs ready for statehood, although unprepared for dealing with the international system. The experience of Ottoman reforms had left an important legacy of statecraft in the Arab world. While the Arab people were thus prepared for statehood in 1919, they had little prior experience of diplomacy. In Ottoman times, relations with the European powers had been mediated through Istanbul. Moreover, the Arab lands constituted provinces of a common state, rather than distinct states with their own national boundaries, and thus had no experience of dealing with other Arab communities as foreign states. The Arabs had no say in the post-war partition of their lands under League of Nations auspices, distributed among the victorious powers as a new form of colonial state known as 'mandates'. Nationalist movements emerged within the confines of these new states in opposition to colonial rule. This legacy would leave the Arab world struggling between a widely held ideal of Arab unity and a reality of nation-state nationalism reinforced by nationalist struggles for independence. The Arab states post-independence were divided by factionalism and infighting. These divisions were apparent in the first issue to test the independent Arab state system: the Palestine crisis (1947–49). The new states of the Middle East have proven remarkably stable, although in their genesis lay the foundations for many of the conflicts that have subsequently troubled the region.

Introduction: the Arab entry to international relations

The Arab world made its entry into international relations at the Versailles Peace Conference following the First World War. Prior to the war, the Arab lands of North Africa had
been colonized by France, Italy, and Britain, while the majority of the Asian Arab lands had
been under Ottoman rule. The Arab delegations, newly independent of the defeated Ottoman Empire, came to Versailles to seek those essential attributes of independent statehood:
juridical equality with other states, and absolute sovereignty (Bull and Watson 1984: 23).
They faced two major impediments. To start, there was no consensus among the Arabs on
the post-war state structure that was to be sought. While some delegations came to present demands for discrete national states like Egypt or Lebanon, others pursued a broader
vision of Arab statehood. The Arab delegations were thus working at cross-purposes. The
Europeans posed the second impediment to Arab ambitions. As Hedley Bull asserted, 'non-
European states entered an originally European club of states as and when they measured up
to the criteria of admission laid down by the founder members' (Bull and Watson 1984: 123).
The Arabs faced real disparities of structural power in negotiating with the Europeans, who
harboured imperial interests in the Eastern Mediterranean and whose soldiers still occupied
Egypt, Palestine, Syria, and Iraq.

The dilemma that the Arab delegations to Versailles faced was common to all newcomers
to the international order: admission to international society was conditional on recognition of sovereignty and 'states do not have sovereignty apart from recognition of it by others'
(Bull 1984: 122). The entry of many Asian and African states to international society would
face the same constraints (Bull and Watson 1984; Clapham 1996). The very institutions governing the workings of international society in 1919 were little changed from the previous
century. The governance of the system was in the hands of the great powers, which played
a decisive role in codifying the norms of the system in a set of regulatory rules of war and
peace known as 'international law'. The powers met and applied international law to resolve conflicts through congresses such as Versailles. Outside periods of conflict, relations
between states were maintained through diplomatic missions (Watson 1984: 24–5, 27).

Almost without exception, the new states of Asia, Africa, and the Middle East were alien
to the institutions of the European system of international relations. Those North African
states already under European colonial rule before the outbreak of the First World War had
surrendered control of their foreign relations to their colonial masters. Those Arab territories that had formerly been part of the Ottoman Empire had never known formal relations
with outside powers, because the Empire's foreign relations had been conducted through the
imperial capital, Istanbul. Indeed, the Ottomans themselves were relatively recent entrants
to the European system of diplomacy.

Ottoman diplomacy

The Ottoman Empire was a nineteenth-century newcomer to the European state system. Up
to the reign of Sultan Selim III (1789–1807), Ottoman relations with Europe were based on
a unilateral system whereby European ambassadors were received by the Porte (the central

government), but no Ottoman permanent missions were sent to European capitals. Ottoman ambassadors were dispatched infrequently, for specific missions, and returned to Istanbul, often with extraordinary stories of the alien culture that they had encountered (Itzkowitz and Mote 1970; Göcek 1987). European states conducted their relations with the Ottomans through trade companies such as the English Levant Company (established 1581). European merchants resident in Ottoman domains enjoyed extraterritorial rights to be judged by their own nation's laws, as set out in a series of bilateral treaties known as the 'Capitulations'. The first Treaty of Capitulation was drafted in 1352 with Genoa, followed by similar treaties with Venice and Florence. In 1535, a commercial treaty was negotiated between France and the Porte, and a formal negotiated Capitulation concluded in 1569, followed by similar instruments with England (1580) (Hurewitz 1975: 1–10). The Capitulations were drafted when the Ottomans were the dominant Mediterranean power and saw little need for more formal relations with Christian Europe. Selim III's first experiment of reciprocal diplomacy, establishing embassies in London, Vienna, Berlin, and Paris in the 1790s, was most remarkable for its bad timing: the French Revolution and the Napoleonic Wars were low points in the European state system.

It was only when Europe began to intervene in Ottoman affairs to prevent the fall of the Sultan's government that the Ottomans were assimilated into the European state system. The two Egyptian crises (1831–32 and 1839–40) led the European powers to enter Ottoman domains to contain the ambitions of Egyptian governor Mehmet Ali Pasha—and each other. The London Convention of 1840, resolving the Second Egyptian Crisis, marked the Ottoman entry to continental European politics. It was the first European convention signed by Ottoman diplomats on behalf of the Sultan. What is more, British Prime Minister Lord Palmerston drafted a secret 'self-denying protocol' adopted by Britain, Austria, Prussia, and Russia, pledging that no power would seek territorial or commercial gains in Ottoman domains to the exclusion of any other power (Hurewitz 1975: 271–5).

The Ottomans formally joined the Concert of Europe in 1856 when they signed the Treaty of Paris marking the end of the Crimean War, along with Britain, France, Austria, Prussia, Russia, and Sardinia. The Ottomans were entering a system whose rules they had no say in drafting and of whose terms they had at best an incomplete knowledge. The Ottoman foreign ministry had been established only in 1836. In the course of the nineteenth century, permanent embassies were opened in European capitals and Istanbul received ambassadors from the great powers, which residences still grace the European quarters of Istanbul. Diplomacy in Ottoman domains was thus almost exclusively confined to the imperial capital. While European consuls were posted to key provincial cities such as Jerusalem, Beirut, Damascus, and Aleppo, their interaction was with Ottoman governors, mediated through Istanbul. Local Arab Muslims had little or no contact with these foreign dignitaries and no experience of the international system.

By 1878, Palmerston's 1840 'self-denying protocol' had lapsed. The Ottoman Empire had declared bankruptcy to its European creditors (1875). Battles with Bulgarian nationalists seeking independence from Ottoman rule had been reported in the European press in terms of atrocity and led to a disastrous war with Russia in 1877–78. Utterly defeated, the Ottomans were forced to accept enormous territorial losses: Britain claimed Cyprus as a colony; Britain and Germany gave France the nod to occupy Tunisia; and, in the Treaty of Berlin, the Ottomans were forced to cede some two-fifths of their territory, mostly in the Balkans. In 1882, Britain occupied Egypt, still officially Ottoman territory. The European powers had embarked on the dismemberment of the Ottoman Empire that would reach its climax in the secret agreements concluded in the course of the First World War.

Yet, in the last quarter of the nineteenth century, the collapse of the Ottoman Empire was far from inevitable. Despite Ottoman territorial losses to European states and Balkan nationalist movements, reforms proceeded apace in the institutions of statecraft. The influence of these reforms would prove an enduring legacy in Arab lands.

An Ottoman legacy of statehood

It was the common wisdom of the peacemakers at Versailles that the Arabs had no experience of statecraft when, following the collapse of the Ottoman military in the First World War, they first emerged among the community of nations. The exceptions were those North African countries that had developed instruments of statehood, all of which were under direct colonial rule in 1919: Morocco, the oldest formal Arab state, became a French protectorate in 1912; Tunisia had been under French rule and Egypt under British rule since the 1880s. Algeria, the first Arab territory to come under European colonial rule (1830), was assimilated to metropolitan France and never had the chance to develop autonomous instruments of rule to the same extent as the other North African states.

When speaking of 'the Arabs', the victors at Versailles were referring to the Arab provinces of the Ottoman Empire. The Arab lands formally under Ottoman rule in 1914 were Yemen, the Red Sea province of the Hijaz, Greater Syria (comprising the modern states of Syria, Lebanon, Jordan, and Israel/Palestine), and Iraq. Tenuous Ottoman claims to the Najd region of central Arabia, and the Persian Gulf sheikhdoms stretching to Qatar, had lapsed by 1913 (Anscombe 1997). Britain and France, intent on adding these territories to their colonial possessions as spoils of war, claimed that the newly liberated Arab lands were not ready for independence, but would first require a period of tutelage in statecraft.

While none of these lands comprised a state in its own right, each had enjoyed extensive exposure to Ottoman instruments of state, particularly since the period of reforms in the second half of the nineteenth century. The Ottoman reforms, known as the 'Tanzimat' (1839–76), were in small part designed to preclude European pretexts to intervene in Ottoman affairs. Arguably, the chief aim of the reforms was to make for a more viable Ottoman state and to consolidate Istanbul's hold over its Asian provinces as nationalist movements led to the progressive secession of the Balkan provinces.

Much of the literature on the Tanzimat has focused on issues of minority rights, and the equality the reforms established between Muslims and non-Muslims. This was a measure taken by the Ottomans to prevent the European powers from exploiting minority issues to intervene in Ottoman domestic affairs. However, as a reform process the Tanzimat was far more significant in the realm of domestic governance and financial regularity. Seen in this light, the milestones of the Tanzimat were not the major policy pronouncements made by the Sultan (the Reform Decrees of 1839 and 1856, and the Constitution of 1876) so much as the 1858 Land Law, the 1864 Provincial Governance Law, and the promulgation of the civil law code known as the 'Mecelle' (1870–76). These were the measures that introduced rational bureaucracy, fiscal regularity, a consistent rule of law, and growing contact between Ottoman subjects and their government. What is more, the era of reforms did not end in

1876, but continued across the reign of Sultan Abdülhamid II (1876–1909), dubbed by one author as 'the culmination of the Tanzimat'. As Stanford Shaw argued, 'Every aspect of the Ottoman system was included [in Abdülhamid II's reform agenda]—the military, the central administration, the provinces, the law courts, finance, the economy, public works, education, fine arts, and the administration' (Shaw and Shaw 1978: 221). The reforms in this sense extended from 1839 through to the first decade of the twentieth century.

Arguably, the Arab provinces of the Ottoman Empire were initiated in statecraft in the last quarter of the nineteenth and the first two decades of the twentieth centuries. This education involved direct knowledge of and contact with the government bureaucracy, and a subordination to the 'rule of books' through the census, land registration, the tax office, and military conscription. Arab Ottomans came to know the complexity of government, at both the provincial and the imperial levels. The Arabs also had their first experiences of elected office at this time, both at the provincial level, to town and regional councils, and to the Imperial Parliament, in 1876 and again after 1908. A consistent rule of law was applied and enforced by police and gendarmes in the countryside and by courts in the towns.

What is more, residents of the Arab provinces came to associate certain benefits with the exercise of statecraft. The extension of the rule of law brought a new degree of security, particularly in the countryside. The rapid expansion of the primary and secondary school system in the provinces broadened literacy and witnessed a growing number of locals entering the civil service—in the Arab provinces as well as in Turkish Anatolia (Findley 1989; Somel 2001). A clear sense of 'citizenship', with attendant rights and responsibilities, appears in correspondence written by Ottoman subjects to Ottoman officialdom. Arabs in the provinces found a political voice assertive of individual rights, property rights, constitutional law, justice, and humanitarianism in their telegraph communications with Ottoman officialdom (Rogan 1998: 123–6).

It is striking how the victorious European powers shaped the Arab state system in the image of Ottoman provincial government. After the 1864 Provincial Reform Law, Ottoman provincial capitals were the focus of extensive investment and construction. Government buildings (administrative offices, courthouses, barracks), communications infrastructure (post, telegraph, roads, trams, and railways), and commercial and residential quarters underwent rapid development in the later nineteenth century. Provincial capitals such as Jerusalem, Beirut, Damascus, and Baghdad were easily adapted to make national capitals in the mandates of Palestine, Lebanon, Syria, and Iraq.

Taken together, these aspects of late Ottoman rule constitute a legacy of 'stateness' that had prepared the Arab people for some degree of self-rule by 1919 (Rogan 1999). To some extent, this was acknowledged in the Covenant of the League of Nations:

> Certain communities formerly belonging to the Turkish Empire have reached a stage of development where their existence as independent nations can be provisionally recognized subject to the rendering of administrative advice and assistance by a Mandatory until such time as they are able to stand alone. The wishes of these communities must be a principal consideration in the selection of the Mandatory.
>
> (Article 22)

Given their more advanced state of development than the other mandated territories, in Central and South-Western Africa, as well as in the Pacific Islands, the Arab lands were designated 'type A' mandates—that is, proto-states in need of interim tutelage in preparation for independent statehood. However, this was not to be. For the whole of the inter-war years, all Arab states bar Iraq remained under de facto British or French colonial rule. The origins of this colonial division date back to the time of the First World War.

Wartime plans for the partition of the Middle East

In the course of the First World War, Russia initiated the wartime diplomacy for the partition of Ottoman territory. In March 1915, as Allied warships assembled outside the Dardanelles, the Tsarist government staked claims to the Ottoman capital Istanbul and the strategic waterways linking the Black Sea to the Mediterranean—the straits of the Bosporus, the Sea of Marmara, and the straits of the Dardanelles. France responded by declaring its interest in securing Syria and the Cilician coastline for its empire. Britain at that stage had no clear territorial interests in Ottoman domains but went along with its allies' demands, reserving the right to make its own territorial claims at a later date. The Constantinople Agreement, concluded between Russia, France, and Britain in March 1915, was the first of four wartime agreements that would determine the shape of the modern Middle East (Hurewitz 1979: 16–21).

Britain struck the second wartime agreement to conclude an alliance with the Arab movement against the Ottomans. Between July 1915 and March 1916, British High Commissioner for Egypt Sir Henry McMahon and the Sharif of Mecca, Hussein ibn Ali of the Hashemite family, negotiated the terms for an Arab revolt against Ottoman rule. In exchange for opening this internal front against the Ottomans, Sharif Hussein sought British support for an enormous Arab kingdom stretching from Mersin and Adana (in modern Turkey) to Persia in the north, to the Persian Gulf, the Indian Ocean, the Red Sea, and the Mediterranean, excluding the British colony of Aden. McMahon responded, in his famous letter of 24 October 1915, with British acceptance of these boundaries, with the sole exclusion of the 'two districts of Mersina and Alexandretta and portions of Syria lying to the west of the districts of Damascus, Homs, Hama and Aleppo' and those areas in Mesopotamia of strategic interest to Great Britain (Hurewitz 1979: 50). With these assurances, Sharif Hussein initiated in July 1916 the Arab Revolt made famous by T. E. Lawrence.

While Britain's representatives in Cairo were negotiating with Sharif Hussein, the British Foreign Office initiated negotiations with the French Ministry of Foreign Affairs to reconcile the pledges to the French made under the Constantinople Agreement with McMahon's promises to the Arabs. This third agreement, known by the names of its British and French authors, Sir Mark Sykes and Charles François Georges-Picot, was approved on 4 February 1916 and gained Russian support in March 1916 in exchange for Anglo-French agreement to Russian territorial demands in Eastern Anatolia. According to this agreement, France would establish an administration in those areas that Sir Henry McMahon had excluded from the Arab kingdom—the 'two districts of Mersina and Alexandretta and portions of Syria lying to the west of the districts of Damascus, Homs, Hama and Aleppo'—while Britain would establish an administration in Mesopotamia. The inland territories between these areas were to be divided into British and French spheres of influence, with Palestine internationalized to prevent disagreement between British, French, and Russian claims to the Holy Lands (Hurewitz 1979: 60–4).

Finally, on 2 November 1917, the British government gave formal support to the aspirations of the World Zionist Organization to establish a Jewish national home in Palestine. The Balfour Declaration, transmitted in a letter from Foreign Minister Arthur James Balfour to Lord Rothschild, confirmed Britain's support for 'the establishment in Palestine of a national home for the Jewish people' (Hurewitz 1979: 106). The Balfour Declaration contradicted both the pledge to Sharif Hussein and the Sykes–Picot Agreement, and further complicated the post-war settlement at Versailles (see **Box 2.1**).

Upon the fall of Damascus and the subsequent Ottoman retreat from the Arab lands in September 1918, Britain found itself in sole possession of the Arab Middle East. Now faced with a post-Ottoman reality, Britain had to square conflicting interests with wartime pledges to its Entente allies. This difficult task was left to the negotiations at Versailles.

Box 2.1 Zionism and anti-Zionism, 1919

The World Zionist Organization, bolstered by the British government's 1917 commitment to create a Jewish National Home in Palestine, submitted a memorandum to the Supreme Council at the Paris Peace Conference in February 1919. The boundaries that it claimed ran from the town of Sidon in the north (in modern Lebanon), east to the Hijaz Railway (in modern Jordan), and south to the Egyptian frontier in the Sinai. The Zionists asserted a historic claim to Palestine: 'The land is the historic home of the Jews', the memo claimed. 'By violence they were driven from Palestine, and through the ages they have never ceased to cherish the longing and hope of a return.' They also made a humanitarian argument:

> In some parts of the world, and particularly in Eastern Europe, the conditions of life of millions of Jews are deplorable . . . the need of fresh outlets is urgent, both for their own sake and in the interest of the population of other races, among whom they dwell.

Finally, they argued, 'the land itself needs redemption. Much of it is left desolate. Its present condition is a standing reproach' (Hurewitz 1979: 137–42).

These claims were rejected by the General Syrian Congress in July 1919, which submitted its resolutions to the King–Crane Commission for transmission to the Paris Peace Conference:

> We oppose the pretensions of the Zionists to create a Jewish commonwealth in the southern part of Syria, known as Palestine, and oppose Zionist migration to any part of our country; for we do not acknowledge their title but consider them a grave peril to our people from the national, economical, and political points of view. Our Jewish compatriots shall enjoy our common rights and assume the common responsibilities.
>
> (Hurewitz 1979: 180–2)

Because the King–Crane Report was never presented to the Supreme Council, there is no reason to believe that the views of the Syrian Congress were ever communicated to the peacemakers at Paris.

The post-war settlement, 1919–22

Two features of the post-war settlement are apparent: the weak bargaining position of the Arab delegates to Versailles; and the duplicity of the great powers. For Britain and France, the colonies and territories of the vanquished German, Austrian, and Ottoman empires were seen as spoils of war (Ulrichsen 2014: 173–201; Rogan 2015: 385–406). The United States, somewhat naively, espoused a much more liberal view of a new world order, set out by President Woodrow Wilson in his well-known 'Fourteen Points' address to a joint session of Congress on 8 January 1918. Wilson spoke to the aspirations of Arab political elites in his twelfth point:

> The Turkish portion of the present Ottoman Empire should be assured a secure sovereignty, but the other nationalities which are now under Turkish rule should be assured an undoubted security of life and an absolutely unmolested opportunity of autonomous development.

The Arab delegates to Versailles were early proponents of President Wilson's vision. However, they would prove no more successful than President Wilson himself in imposing a new order on old world diplomacy, a complex science of which they had little understanding and less experience.

The Arabs in Versailles

A number of delegations from former Ottoman domains sought the opportunity to press their claims before the victorious Entente powers for recognition. The Greeks pressed for territory in Anatolia. Armenians presented their case for statehood. The Hashemites, in de facto control of geographic Syria (roughly corresponding to modern Syria, Lebanon, and Jordan) and the Hijaz, sought to secure the Arab kingdom promised them by the Hussein–McMahon correspondence. The Zionist movement was active to uphold the Balfour promise of a Jewish national home in Palestine. And in Egypt, the British refusal to permit a delegation to go to Paris to present Egyptian claims for independence prompted a nationwide uprising in 1919 that led to a reversal of policy and the dispatch of an Egyptian delegation to Paris. In some regards, the Paris Peace Conference marked the entry of the Middle East as a region into the prevailing system of international relations. The experiences of the Arab delegations revealed the disadvantages of having their relations with the European state system mediated through Istanbul for the length of Ottoman rule.

Egypt and the *wafd*

The nationalist movement in Egypt had been gaining momentum in the early years of the twentieth century. Under British occupation since 1882, Egypt had already developed the institutions of independent statehood. The monarchy could trace its origins back a century to the appointment of Mehmet Ali Pasha as governor of the Ottoman province of Egypt in 1805. The Pasha was to rule Egypt for forty-three years and set the province on a path to autonomy. His descendants had ruled the country ever since. The 'khedives', as the rulers of Egypt came to be designated, governed in consultation with a cabinet of ministers whose portfolios conformed to formal government divisions (for example, foreign affairs, finance, education, health). There was even a proto-parliament, known as the 'Chamber of Delegates', which met regularly between November 1866 and March 1882 (Schölch 1981). Occupation came as a result of financial and political crises, starting with the Egyptian bankruptcy in 1876 and ending with a military-led revolt against European control and Khedive Tawfiq, believed by many in Egypt to be himself under excessive European control (Owen 1981).

By the end of the nineteenth century, nationalist parties were formed and their views aired in a range of newspapers. Their main agenda was to end the British occupation. Such nationalist activity was contained during the long years of the First World War. Egypt was formally separated from the Ottoman Empire in November 1914, following the Ottoman entry into the war on Germany's side, and declared a British protectorate. The Khedive was now designated a Sultan, raising expectations of independence in the aftermath of war. When the victorious Entente powers began to plan for a peace conference in 1918, Egyptian nationalists again mobilized. There is some dispute over who first proposed to send a delegation (in Arabic, *wafd*) to represent Egypt's claims, although the men who called on British High Commissioner Sir Reginald Wingate were associated with the Ummah Party. Headed by Sa'd Zaghlul, a former judge and minister of education, the delegation was rebuffed. The Egyptian public responded with petitions and growing anger. When the British authorities arrested and exiled Zaghlul and his supporters to Malta, a mass uprising followed. The 'Revolution of 1919' rendered Egypt ungovernable, and the British were forced to recall Zaghlul from exile and arrange for him to address the delegates at the Versailles Peace Conference.

Egyptian nationalists were to return from Versailles empty-handed. On the day on which Zaghlul and his party arrived in Paris, the American delegation issued a statement recognizing Britain's protectorate over Egypt. Egyptian hopes pinned on Woodrow Wilson's support, raised by his Fourteen Points, were dashed. Zaghlul and his colleagues, no strangers to European politics, had learned that colonized people could change imperial politics only through domestic disorder. The Egyptian delegation returned to alternate periods of political disorder and negotiations with the British, leading up to the 1922 Treaty that ended the protectorate while preserving British influence over Egypt.

The Hashemite Arab kingdom

Following the Ottoman retreat from Damascus in 1918, Amir Faisal (crowned King of Syria in March 1920) found himself de facto ruler of Syria, which, at that time, had no recognized boundaries or formal government. Faisal sought to consolidate his position in Syria at the Versailles Peace Conference. The greatest threat to his position came from Britain's other wartime promises. Faisal came to terms with the Balfour Declaration and signed an agreement with Zionist leader Chaim Weizmann in January 1919, conceding Palestine to the Zionist movement on condition that his demands for an Arab kingdom be otherwise accepted by the powers (Laqueur and Rubin 1985: 19–20). Faisal first learned of the Sykes–Picot Agreement when the Bolsheviks published the secret treaties of the Tsarist government in 1918, at the height of the Arab Revolt. While Faisal saw no alternative to continuing with the Revolt, the threat of French rule hung over his new state and he held few cards to improve his position at Versailles.

Faisal presented the Supreme Council of the Paris Peace Conference with a memorandum setting out Arab aspirations in January 1919. Faisal appeared before the Supreme Council, accompanied by T. E. Lawrence, the following month (6 February). In his memo, Faisal wrote that 'the aim of the Arab nationalist movements ... is to unite the Arabs eventually into one nation'. He based his claim on Arab ethnic and linguistic unity, on the alleged aspirations of pre-war Arab nationalist parties in Syria and Mesopotamia, and on Arab service to the Allies' war effort. He acknowledged that the various Arab lands were 'very different economically and socially', and that it would be impossible to integrate them into a single state immediately. He sought immediate and full independence for Greater Syria (including Lebanon, Syria, and Transjordan) and the western Arabian province of Hijaz; he accepted foreign intervention in Palestine to mediate between Jewish and Arab demands, and in Mesopotamia, where Britain had declared its interest in oil fields; and he declared the Yemen and the central Arabian province of Najd outside the scope of the Arab kingdom. Yet he maintained a commitment to 'an eventual union of these areas under one sovereign government'. He concluded:

> In our opinion, if our independence be conceded and our local competence established, the natural influences of race, language, and interest will soon draw us into one people ... To achieve this [the great powers] must lay aside the thought of individual profits, and of their old jealousies. In a word, we ask you not to force your whole civilization upon us, but to help us to pick out what serves us from your experience. In return we can offer you little but gratitude.
>
> (Hurewitz 1979: 130–2)

As subsequent events would prove, it was not realistic to expect Britain and France to act in so disinterested a fashion.

A second set of claims was made in the name of the Syrian people by the chairman of the Central Syrian Committee, Shukri Ghanim. Ghanim's recommendations were diametrically opposed to those of Amir Faisal. Stressing Syria's lack of preparation for self-rule and need for foreign assistance, Ghanim asked the Council of Ten to place Syria under the tutelage of France for reasons of alleged historic attachment, demonstrating a capacity to reconcile Muslims and Christians and, perhaps most improbably, its lack of imperialist interest in the region. It would later be revealed that Shukri Ghanim was a French citizen who had been away from Syria for thirty-five years (Helmreich 1974: 54–5). Indeed, France sought by all means to undermine Hashemite claims to Syria and to keep to the spirit of the Sykes–Picot disposition of Arab territory.

Faced with divergent claims on behalf of the Syrian people, with disagreement between Britain and France over the future of the Arab lands and American disapproval of the secret wartime agreements as a whole, the United States proposed to dispatch a commission of inquiry to establish the wishes of the Syrian people, and gained British and French agreement to do so. Faisal was delighted, writing to President Wilson in March 1919 to express his gratitude for granting the Arabs the opportunity to express 'their own purposes and ideals for their national future' (Howard 1963: 35).

The King–Crane Commission

President Wilson named Oberlin College President Henry Churchill King and Chicago businessman Charles R. Crane as commissioners. Wilson 'felt these two men were particularly qualified to go to Syria because they knew nothing about it' (Howard 1963: 37). Knowledge here was conflated with interest and Wilson sought men of integrity with no prior interests in the region. In fact, both men had extensive knowledge of the Middle East, King as a scholar of biblical history and Crane through his travels in Ottoman lands, dating back to 1878. When the British and French withdrew from the Commission, the Americans set out for Syria in May 1919 with instructions to meet local representatives and to report back on the aspirations of the Arab peoples in Syria, Iraq, and Palestine. The Commission arrived in Jaffa on 10 June, and spent six weeks touring Syria and Palestine. It held meetings in more than forty towns and rural centres, and collected more than 1,800 petitions. As James Gelvin (1998: 35) has argued, 'while the entente powers had charged the commission with a simple fact-finding mission, its presence in Syria catalysed a mobilization of the Syrian population that was unprecedented in scope'. The local Arab government distributed sermons to be read in Friday prayers in Syrian mosques, political and cultural associations were enlisted to prepare petitions for the Commission, and the headmen of villages and town quarters were mobilized to encourage an enthusiastic response to the Commission.

In August 1919, the Commission withdrew to Istanbul, where King and Crane drafted their report, which was delivered to the American delegation in Paris at the end of the month. The report went no further. There is no evidence that it was ever consulted by the British or French, and it was made public only in 1922, well after the post-war settlements had been signed. Yet the King–Crane Report serves as a yardstick against which to measure the gulf that separated Arab claims of self-determination made to the commissioners from the mandate system that they received.

King and Crane summarized their findings after five weeks of collecting testimony. While noting explicit Syrian preference for full independence, they recommended a fixed-term mandate under American or, as second choice, British authority (but explicitly ruling out French administration), leading to full independence. Syria, including Palestine, should be established as a single monarchy under Faisal's rule, with Lebanon given extensive autonomy within the Syrian state. King and Crane called for major restrictions in Zionist settlement in Palestine, noting that 'more than 72 per cent—1,350 in all—of all the petitions in the whole of Syria were directed against the Zionist program' (Hurewitz 1979: 196). In Iraq, they called for another unified monarchy under British mandate. In essence, the recommendations of the King–Crane Commission overturned the Balfour Declaration and Sykes–Picot Agreement. It is no wonder that the British and French chose to ignore the document and proceed with a modified partition plan.

San Remo and the mandate system

By the time that Britain and France reached the peace conference, the Sykes–Picot Agreement had been overtaken by events. Most importantly, the Bolshevik Revolution had led to the withdrawal of Russia's claims on Ottoman territory. The Soviets, preoccupied with securing their state against outside menace and internal challenge, would not play a major role in Arab affairs through the inter-war period.

The British position had changed in many ways since 1916 as well. For one, its armies had occupied Syria and Iraq, which gave it a better sense of its strategic imperatives and an improved bargaining position to assure them. Two areas in particular were to come under revision: the northern Iraqi region of Mosul, allotted to the French sphere of influence; and Palestine, which was to come under international control. These were important points of difference and they needed formal agreement.

The premiers and foreign ministers of Britain, France, and Italy, and two delegates from Japan, met in San Remo in April 1920 to agree the partition of the Arab lands. They were not alone. As Lord Curzon complained: 'Syrians, Zionists, Armenians … They take rooms in the same hotel as we are in and they dog our footsteps wherever we go' (Nevakivi 1969: 242). The lobbyists did not manage to influence events, because the decisions on the Arab lands had largely been negotiated and agreed between Britain and France months beforehand. France was to obtain mandates over Lebanon and Syria, spelling the end of Faisal's Arab kingdom in Damascus. In return, France conceded its claims to northern Iraq (although Mosul would not be formally conceded to the Iraq mandate until 1925) and acknowledged Britain's rule over Palestine, including the lands east of the River Jordan stretching to Iraq that would later be made into a separate mandate of Transjordan. The British and French established a boundaries commission to agree the frontiers between their respective territories. On 24 July 1922, when the League of Nations sanctioned the decisions taken at San Remo, the boundaries of the mandates had already been agreed between Britain and France.

Britain had, with some modification, met its commitments to both the Sykes–Picot Agreement and the Balfour Declaration; only the promises to the Hashemites had been disregarded. At the end of 1920, Britain called Faisal, the deposed King of Syria, to London to gain Hashemite acceptance of the San Remo division of the Middle East. In return, Britain would place its new mandates under the sons of Sharif Hussein. This plan came to be known as the 'Sharifian solution', both a way in which partially to redeem Britain's promises to its wartime allies and 'an interlocking political grid whereby pressure on one state could win obedience in another' (Wilson 1987: 49; Paris 2003). The Sharifian solution was made policy by Colonial Secretary Winston Churchill in the Cairo Conference in March 1921.

Churchill and the Hashemites

The two territories conceded to Britain at San Remo were Iraq and Palestine. Given that these were mandates rather than traditional colonies, Britain needed to devise governments for the new states. Iraq was the first item on the agenda at the Cairo Conference and it was quickly agreed that Faisal would be placed on the throne in Baghdad. A mechanism was yet to be found to gain Iraqi public acceptance of Britain's choice, although this was left to Britain's colonial agents on the ground. A referendum was held and Faisal was confirmed as King of Iraq in August 1921.

The next item on the agenda was Palestine—or rather those lands to the east of the River Jordan stretching to the Iraqi frontier that had been claimed by Britain as part of Palestine. Faisal's brother, the Hashemite Amir Abdullah, had ridden with a group of supporters from the Hijaz to the Transjordanian town of Ma'an in a bid to reclaim Damascus from the French. While no one had any illusions that Amir Abdullah might succeed in this aim, they saw his presence in Amman as threatening to destabilize the new borders between the French and British mandates. Churchill and a delegation from the Cairo Conference proceeded to Jerusalem and met Abdullah. They struck an agreement with Amir Abdullah, who agreed to serve as provisional ruler over Transjordan for a six-month probationary period. He was given a stipend of £5,000 and assigned to contain both anti-French and anti-Zionist activity. Churchill held out the prospect of a throne in Damascus if Abdullah proved his merits to the French—a prospect that must have looked as improbable at the time as it does in hindsight.

Yet with Iraq, Transjordan, and the Hijaz under Hashemite rulers, Churchill could claim to have gone as far as he could to redeem Britain's pledges to Sharif Hussein and his sons (Paris 2003). (Sharif Hussein assumed the kingship of the 'Arab Countries' in 1916, although he was recognized by Britain only as King of the Hijaz. He abdicated in favour of his son Ali in 1924; Ali ruled until the Saudi conquest of Hijaz in 1925.)

As for Palestine itself, Britain chose to rule the mandate directly under a High Commissioner, and to develop the structures of statehood in cooperation with the Arab and Jewish communities. Neither the cooperation nor the structures were forthcoming, because Palestine came to be the arena of two rival nationalist movements, Zionist and Palestinian.

The colonial framework

In the four years following the Ottoman retreat from Arab lands, the map of the modern Middle East was drawn. The failure of the Arab parties to attain their national aims at Versailles revealed the weakness of their bargaining position when challenging European imperial interests. Given this somewhat compromised genesis, it is all the more remarkable just how enduring the borders of the Middle East have proven.

The Middle East that emerged from the post-war negotiations was almost exclusively an Anglo-French preserve (see **Figure 2.1**). Algeria was a full French colony; Morocco and Tunisia protectorates; Syria and Lebanon were held as League of Nations mandates.

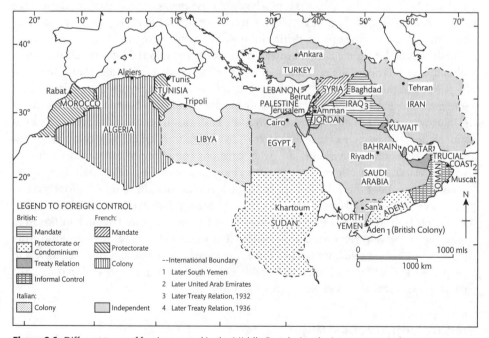

Figure 2.1 Different types of foreign control in the Middle East during the inter-war period

Source: State, Power and Politics in the Making of the Modern Middle East, Roger Owen. Copyright 2004, Routledge. Reproduced by permission of Taylor & Francis Books UK.

Egypt gained nominal independence in 1922, but continued to be under British influence through a restrictive treaty. Sudan was held as a 'condominium', ruled jointly by Britain and Egypt. Aden, or South Yemen, was a British colony; Palestine, Transjordan, and Iraq were held as mandates; Britain's interests in the Persian Gulf were upheld through treaty arrangements with the ruling families in Kuwait, Bahrain, Qatar, and the sheikhdoms known as the 'Trucial States' because of the anti-piracy treaties, or 'truces', signed between them and Britain. Muscat and Oman were similarly under informal British control. Libya, an Italian colony since 1911, was an exception to this Anglo-French division of the region.

Three states in what is now called the Middle East escaped some form of colonial rule. Turkish nationalists rallied around General Mustafa Kemal (later known as 'Atatürk') in opposing the draconian terms of the Paris Peace Conference, culminating in the Treaty of Sèvres (August 1920) that reduced the Ottoman Empire to a rump state combining parts of northern and western Anatolia with Istanbul as its capital. The Turkish War of Independence (1921–22) resulted in the Republic of Turkey, the sovereignty and independence of which were recognized in the Treaty of Lausanne (24 July 1923). In the aftermath of the First World War, Iran was occupied by both British and Soviet forces. British attempts to establish a protectorate by treaty (1919) were stoutly resisted by a proto-nationalist movement. In 1921, the commander of the Iranian Cossack Brigade, Reza Khan, led a coup that brought down the Qajar dynasty and gave rise to the Pahlavi state that would rule Iran until the Islamic Revolution in 1979. And in Arabia, the forces of Abdul Aziz Al Saud (known in the West as 'ibn Saud') succeeded in uniting the Arabian Peninsula from the Persian Gulf to the Hijaz Province on the Red Sea by 1924. Britain recognized Abdul Aziz as King of the Hejaz and Nejd in 1927, and in 1932 the kingdom was renamed 'Saudi Arabia'. These three nation states pursued their own development independent of European political domination, although, in the case of Iran, British influence remained profound.

For the rest of the Middle East, the inter-war years were a period of national self-definition within the boundaries of the new states and a battle for self-determination against the colonial powers. In this, the Middle East shares a common experience with those parts of Asia and Africa that emerged into the community of nations through European imperialism in the inter-war years. The difference in the Middle East was the enduring appeal of a supranational identity based on a range of greater Arab nations transcending the colonial boundaries. The Hashemites envisioned an Arab kingdom combining the Arabian Peninsula, Greater Syria, and Iraq; others saw Egypt as an integral part of the greater Arab state; others yet saw the whole of the Middle East and North Africa, stretching right to Morocco, as part of a common Arab Islamic nation. The enduring legitimacy enjoyed by the vision of the greater Arab nation was to prove to the detriment of interstate relations in the Arab world. Those who put their own narrow nation-state interests before those of the ideal 'Arab Nation' were deemed collaborators in a European agenda of 'divide and rule'. Yet, as was to be expected, the nationalist leaderships and the confrontations that they endured with the colonial powers gave rise to vested interests within states.

'French' North Africa and Libya

The French colonial possessions in North Africa experienced limited nationalist agitation in the inter-war years, gaining their independence only in the 1950s and 1960s. This had the effect of limiting the involvement of North African states in the international relations of the Middle East more generally. Algeria, the first Arab state to be occupied by a European colonial power (1830), was the last to gain independence, after a violent war spanning the period 1954–62 that claimed more than a million lives. Morocco and Tunisia were protectorates rather than formal colonies, and were ruled by France through their own monarchies. Given their own institutions of state and a much smaller French colonial settler community, both Tunisia and Morocco achieved their independence earlier, with far less confrontation. Morocco's King Muhammad V wrote demanding independence of France in 1952. His exile gave rise to an armed resistance movement that forced a French reversal and recognition of Moroccan independence on 2 March 1956 (Pennell 2000). Tunisia initiated autonomy talks with France in 1955, achieved independence as a monarchy in 1956, and declared a republic in 1957. As for Libya, following the execution of Omar al-Mukhtar in 1932, Italian rule went unchallenged until the British occupation in 1942–43. The United Nations oversaw Libya's independence as a monarchy in 1951 (Anderson 1986).

Morocco, Algeria, and Tunisia, and to a lesser extent Libya, were bound by similar colonial histories and the timing of their independence. This has marked North Africa as a distinct subunit of the broader Arab world known as the 'Mahgreb'. Although members of the Arab League, the Mahgreb states, along with Egypt, are active in the Organization of African Unity, these four states are also marked by a special relationship with the European Mediterranean—especially Spain, France, and Italy. While tensions between Mahgreb states have been pronounced—between Morocco and Algeria in particular—there have been numerous attempts to create a union of Mahgreb states, given their common interests and geographic proximity. Yet these very differences have set the Mahgreb apart from the rest of the Arab world, hinged to some extent by the keystone Arab state, Egypt.

Egypt and the Sudan

Following the nationwide disturbances of 1919, the British sought to normalize relations with Egypt in such a way as to preserve their strategic interests while giving the semblance of independence. The result was a treaty replacing the protectorate with a nominally independent monarchy bound to Britain. The 1922 Treaty recognized Egypt's independence while preserving four areas under British control: the security of imperial communications in Egypt (primarily the Suez Canal); the defence of Egypt against outside aggression (assuring Britain base rights for its military); the protection of foreign interests and minorities (as enshrined in the extraterritorial rights of the Capitulations); and the Sudan. These limits on Egyptian independence were sufficiently intrusive as to prevent Egypt's admission to the League of Nations and were an enduring source of nationalist grievance.

The inter-war years have been termed Egypt's 'liberal age' (Hourani 1962; Botman 1998), an era of party politics and parliamentary elections. Britain continued to dominate Egyptian politics by playing the monarchy and the parliament against each other. The most popular party by far was the Wafd, founded by Sa'd Zaghlul. In every free election, the Wafd won by landslide majorities. By the late 1930s, the death of King Fuad and accession of his son Faruq, combined with the return of the Wafd to power under the premiership of Mustafa al-Nahhas, set in motion renewed negotiations with the British authorities. On 26 August 1936, a new Anglo-Egyptian treaty was signed. The twenty-year treaty was essentially a defence pact that recognized Egypt's sovereignty as an independent state and paved the way for Egyptian admission to the League, in 1937. Egypt could now establish embassies and consulates for the first time. In return, the Egyptians permitted Britain to station a maximum of 10,000 troops in the Suez Canal zone during peacetime and guaranteed Britain base rights to protect its imperial lines of communications in emergency. The treaty also preserved the status quo in the Sudan, which would remain under Anglo-Egyptian rule until 1953 and gained independence only in 1956.

The mandates

Unlike the other colonial arrangements, Britain and France were held accountable by the League of Nations for their rule in the mandates. They were required to submit annual reports to the League secretariat outlining their progress in establishing the institutions of statehood deemed prerequisite for national independence. In theory at least, the mandates were meant to be tutorial exercises in self-rule rather than out-and-out colonial rule. The experience varied widely from country to country, although in each case the combination of colonial state formation and nationalist agitation for independence set in motion the evolution of nation states from the former provinces of the Ottoman Empire.

Iraq and Transjordan

In every regard, Iraq was deemed the role-model mandate. Through an admittedly rigged referendum, King Faisal I was installed at the head of a government composed of many Arab nationalists who had fought in the Arab Revolt in the First World War. In close alliance with Britain, the institutions of statehood were established, including a constitution, a cabinet government, and an elected parliament. Oil and agricultural resources combined to endow Iraq with a viable economy. Yet the majority of Iraqis resented the British presence deeply. A nationwide revolt broke out in 1920 similar to anti-British riots in Egypt in 1919. Popular opposition to the British presence continued through the 1920s and encouraged the British to reconsider their position in Iraq. The initial treaty of alliance of October 1922 imposed the sort of limits on Iraq's sovereignty that precluded admission to the League, as had been the case in Egypt. Persistent nationalist agitation, and domestic British opposition to paying for unproductive colonies, led to the drafting of a treaty of alliance in 1930 that allowed for the termination of the mandate. Britain supported Iraq's application to the League of Nations and, in 1932, Iraq's sovereignty was recognized with membership of the League. As in the Egyptian treaty of 1936, Britain retained base rights in Iraq, transit facilities for its military, and preferential relations in diplomatic and military spheres. These restrictions notwithstanding, Iraq's emergence into the community of independent states was the envy of the Arab world (Tripp 2000).

The only other Arab state to negotiate the end of its mandate was Transjordan, although its mandate outlived the League itself. The long duration of the mandate reflects the low level of opposition to what was in fact a very light British presence. Amir Abdullah secured his rule over the Transjordan and was maintained on a modest British subsidy. The main objective of Abdullah's politics was the aggrandisement of his modest state. His first target was Damascus and he enjoyed close ties with some Syrian nationalists, such as Dr Abd al-Rahman Shahbandar, as well as with Druze leaders in southern Syria. Both the French mandate authorities and the majority of Syrian nationalists opposed Abdullah's 'Greater Syria' plans. Abdullah also looked to Palestine for access to the Mediterranean. His quick acceptance of partition plans for Palestine when first pronounced in 1937 led to widespread Arab criticism of Abdullah (Wilson 1987). Abdullah, whose introduction to international diplomacy came through representing his father Sharif Hussein in his wartime negotiations with Sir Henry McMahon, developed extensive experience of international relations through his long rule (1921–51) and close ties to Britain. He was one of the most active leaders in inter-Arab relations and had the most exchanges with the Jewish Executive in Palestine (Shlaim 1988). However, his first attempt at negotiating the end of the mandate in 1946 led to so partial an independence that the United States refused to recognize the state and blocked Transjordan's entry to the new United Nations (Dann 1984). It was not until 1948, when Britain and Transjordan signed a treaty less restrictive of its sovereignty that Transjordan gained American recognition—and not until 1955 that the country was admitted to the United Nations.

Palestine

If Iraq was the most successful British mandate and Transjordan the easiest, Palestine was to prove the most unsuccessful and difficult of British colonial possessions in the Middle East. The origins of the problem may be traced to the contradictions inherent in the Balfour Declaration. Arguably, there was no mechanism for Britain to establish a Jewish national home without disadvantage to the rights of the indigenous Palestinian Arabs. The mandate structure and the Jewish nationalist ideology of Zionism gave rise to an active Palestinian nationalist movement demanding full sovereignty over all Palestine, an end to Jewish immigration, and an end to the British mandate that provided the framework for the Jewish national home. Palestinian resistance to the mandate and refusal to participate in its institutions prevented the building of any enduring state structure. On the other hand, the Yishuv, as the Jewish community in Palestine was called, cooperated fully with the British and initiated a process of state-building, establishing a trade union movement, a modified cabinet government, and even its own military. With their close links to the World Zionist Organization, the Jewish Executive enjoyed a degree of experience in negotiations with European powers that the Palestinians would never match. In essence, the Palestinians could force changes in British policy only through confrontation. Riots, economic boycott, and an all-out armed revolt lasting nearly three years (1936–39) produced commissions of inquiry, a raft of White Papers, and finally in 1939 a programme of reduced Jewish immigration and the promise of independence in a decade. The terms of the 1939 White Paper were rejected by the Zionists and, between 1945 and 1947, radical Jewish groups engaged in a terror campaign against the British authorities in Palestine. Britain conceded defeat in 1947 and referred the Palestine problem to the United Nations for resolution. The UN voted for the partition of Palestine into Jewish and Arab areas, setting off a war that raged within Palestine through the spring of 1948 and, following the British withdrawal on 14 May, exploded into the first Arab–Israeli War (Segev 2000).

Syria and Lebanon

The French created very different mandates in Syria and Lebanon. In Lebanon, they merged the highlands of Mount Lebanon with the coastal plain from Tyre to Tripoli and the Biqa Valley, stretching between the Lebanon and Anti-Lebanon Mountain chains, to create the state of 'Grand Liban', or Greater Lebanon. The aim was to create the largest territorial expanse, while preserving a Christian majority. While this plan was opposed by Sunni Muslims and Druzes, the colonial power enjoyed the ardent support of their Maronite allies and the tacit agreement of other Christian communities. Greater Lebanon was established by decree of General Henri Gouraud, commander-in-chief of French forces in the Levant and High Commissioner, and declared an anomalous 'independent State under French Mandate' (Salibi 1977: 164). After six years under French military governors, the Lebanese Republic was founded in 1926, with an elected chamber of deputies, an appointed senate, a constitution, and a president selected by the two chambers. There were, of course, nationalists who opposed the great influence the French mandate authority exercised over the nominally independent Lebanon, symbolized by the original national flag, which imposed a Lebanese cedar on the French *Tricolore*. While the Lebanese enjoyed autonomy in domestic affairs, France assumed full responsibility for Lebanon's foreign relations and defence. During the 1920s and 1930s, the institutions of the Lebanese state came increasingly into conflict with the mandatory power and sought fuller independence. A range of nationalist movements pulled Lebanon in different directions: some called for Lebanon to be reattached to Syria; others sought the end of the mandate and full independence.

The French enjoyed virtually no indigenous support in their Syrian mandate. They sent a military force to drive out King Faisal and his supporters, and to occupy Damascus. The French engaged a small force of irregulars at Khan Maysalun on 24 July 1920, entered Damascus the following day, and asked Faisal to leave on 27 July. This blatant disregard of Syrian self-determination for colonial ends blighted Franco–Syrian relations from the start. Subsequent French efforts to break Syria into four smaller units based around Damascus, Aleppo, and two minority statelets for the Alawites and Druzes provoked fierce opposition for the clear attempt at divide and rule. In July 1925, the Druze launched a proto-nationalist revolt against French administrative measures that spread to Damascus and the rest of Syria, and which raged for two years. Peace was restored only when the territorial integrity of Syria was respected. These events consolidated nationalist forces fragmented by the years of fighting the French into what came to be known as the 'National Bloc', which sought to attain Syrian independence through negotiations (Khoury 1987).

The end of the mandates in Syria and Lebanon followed similar trajectories. France sought to curtail nationalist dissent with treaties granting independence to both states in 1936. Modelled on the Anglo-Iraqi Treaty of 1930, the Syrian treaty was widely accepted, while the treaty in Lebanon proved very controversial, provoking clashes between its advocates and its detractors. Neither instrument was ratified by the French Chamber by the outbreak of war in 1939. The mandates looked slated for termination in 1941, with the Allied occupation and the Free French declaration of the independence of Syria and Lebanon. In practice, though, the French sought to preserve their authority. The Lebanese were the first to achieve independence. General elections were held in Lebanon in the summer of 1943. The new chamber elected Bishara Khuri president and purged all French prerogatives of the mandate from the constitution. French efforts to arrest Khuri and his government, and to reassert their prerogatives, provoked nationwide resistance and a reversal of policy that led to full Lebanese independence. In Syria, too, independence was initiated through constitutional reform, and by 1944 both Syria and Lebanon gained international recognition. By declaring war on Germany in 1945, both Syria and Lebanon were invited to the conference founding the United Nations. However, France retained forces in both Syria and Lebanon, and sought preferential treaties before withdrawing. It was only after Syria and Lebanon had brought UN pressure to bear that France withdrew its troops from Syria (April 1946) and Lebanon (December 1946), and both countries could claim full independence.

The colonial experience: an assessment

These brief historical overviews demonstrate that, while each Middle Eastern state had a distinct inter-war encounter with imperialism, the colonial experience left certain common legacies. The post-war settlement created a number of new states. Within their new, European-drawn boundaries, a process of state formation was initiated under strict imperial control. The new states were insulated from foreign affairs by their colonial masters. Politics were overwhelmingly domestic, and domestic politics were dominated by the search for national independence. The struggle for independence created vested interests in the individual nation states that conflicted with popular notions of a greater Arab nation. By the time independence was achieved, in nearly all cases in the aftermath of the Second World War, the newly emergent states of the Middle East were hardly better integrated to the prevailing system of international diplomacy than they had been at the end of the First World War. Relations between Arab states were fraught with rivalries and factionalism that undermined regional organizations such as the Arab League, and the Arabs were ineffectual in such international arenas as the United Nations and in great power diplomacy. These weaknesses were apparent in the Arab handling of the Palestine crisis of 1947–49.

The Arab states and the Palestine crisis

Following the Second World War, Britain found its position in Palestine increasingly untenable. Armed conflict with Jewish groups and demoralizing terror attacks placed a burden on British armed forces when the shattered post-war economy could least bear it. In the end, Foreign Secretary Ernest Bevin referred the Palestine question to the United Nations for resolution.

The UN resolved in November 1947 to partition Palestine into two states. The six Arab members of the United Nations (Egypt, Lebanon, Saudi Arabia, and Syria were founding members; Iraq joined in December 1945 and Yemen in 1947) all opposed partition, but had no impact on the debate within the General Assembly. They failed to build a coalition of nations to support Arab claims to Palestine and were outmanoeuvred by the Jewish Agency. The final vote in the General Assembly was thirty-three to thirteen, giving the necessary two-thirds majority to ensure the passing of the Partition Resolution (Hurewitz 1976: 301).

While one might make allowances for the difficulties that the Arab states encountered in going against policies advocated by such great powers as Britain and America, they were hardly more accomplished in inter-Arab diplomacy, as witnessed by the ineffectual actions of the Arab League. The Arab states were deeply divided and distrustful of one another. King Faruq of Egypt and King Abdul Aziz ibn Saud of Saudi Arabia sought to contain the Hashemite kings of Iraq and Transjordan. King Abdullah of Transjordan and Hajj Amin al-Husseini, the leader of the Arab Higher Committee of Palestine, loathed each other. The President of Syria, Shukri al-Quwwatly, feared King Abdullah's ambitions in Syria (Rogan and Shlaim 2007). The Arab League engaged in a series of fruitless summits to address the growing crisis in Palestine across 1947 and 1948.

The incongruous territories allotted to the Jewish and Arab states were not acceptable to either party (although the Yishuv formally accepted the terms of the UN Resolution), and the Partition Resolution gave rise to a civil conflict in Palestine in which Jewish forces occupied several Palestinian cities in the autumn of 1947 and spring of 1948 (most notably Tiberias, Safad, Haifa, and Jaffa). Even when war was inevitable, the Arab League decided only two days before the end of the mandate in May 1948 to dispatch the armies of Egypt, Iraq, Syria, and Lebanon into Palestine, along with Transjordan's Arab Legion. This last-minute invasion involved a fraction of the national armies involved: only 10,000 Egyptian soldiers, 3,000 Syrians, 3,000 Iraqis, and 1,000 Lebanese, in addition to the 4,500 Transjordanians—well below the forces necessary to achieve a strategic advantage over Jewish forces. King Abdullah was named commander-in-chief of the Arab forces, but each nation's army operated under its own commanders without any overall coordination.

Immediately following the termination of the mandate and the withdrawal of British troops from Palestine on 14 May 1948, Israel declared its statehood. The armies of Syria, Lebanon, Iraq, Transjordan, and Egypt invaded Palestine to engage the Jewish forces. Between 15 May 1948 and the end of hostilities on 7 January 1949, the State of Israel contained or defeated all of the Arab armies and expanded its boundaries to embrace 78 per cent of the Palestine mandate. The military defeat in Palestine reflected both a failure by the newly emergent Arab states in international diplomacy and the legacies of the colonial experience. In effect, the nationalist leaders who oversaw the transition to independence within the boundaries of the colonial states fell at their first hurdle when they failed to live up to their rhetoric and save Arab Palestine from the Zionist threat (Rogan and Shlaim 2007). The Arab defeat in Palestine was to continue to plague the international relations of the region into the early twenty-first century.

Conclusion

The Palestine crisis brought to light Arab weaknesses in the international arena and in regional affairs that were a legacy of the way in which the colonial powers shaped the emergence of the modern Middle East. It was also a harbinger of the problems that would plague the region for decades to come.

Coming out of the Ottoman experience, the Arabs aspired to national independence. Promises of a new order of international relations, set out by US President Wilson in his Fourteen Points, generated expectations of national self-determination; instead, the Arabs found themselves denied any say in the disposition of their lands and under British or French colonial rule. Within the parameters of these new states, again shaped without the consent of those governed, Arab politics were primarily focused on gaining independence from colonial rule. The new Arab states had little or no exposure to the international order so long as their colonial masters oversaw their foreign affairs. This extended to inter-Arab affairs, often divided between those states under British and those under French rule. Thus divided, domestic interests prevailed over broader Arab interests in a way that allowed the colonial powers, and later even the young State of Israel, to play the Arab states against each other.

The manner in which the Middle East was shaped in the inter-war years produced a number of stable states that have, with time, established themselves in the community of nations.

It also gave rise to enduring problems that have troubled the region and the international order. The most obvious example was in Palestine, where the rival national claims have made the Arab–Israeli conflict an enduring feature of the international relations of the Middle East. French efforts to create the largest possible state for their Maronite clients in Lebanon, and the sectarian system that they helped to shape to govern the many religious communities that fell within its boundaries, laid the foundations for one of the most violent civil wars in the Arab world (1975–91). Yet it is Iraq that has proved the most unsettling to the international system. The decision to create a state of the three Ottoman provinces of Mosul, Baghdad, and Basra laid to rest promises of a state that would have served as a homeland to the Kurdish people. Instead, the Kurds distributed between Turkey, Iran, Iraq, and Syria have known periods of intense nationalist agitation and civil war. Noteworthy examples were the Kurdistan Workers' Party (PKK) insurgency in Eastern Turkey of the 1980s and 1990s, and the numerous Kurdish uprisings in Iraq, repressed with increasing brutality by the Baathist regime, including the use of gas against the villagers of Halabja. Yet it was Iraq's claims to territories formerly associated with the Ottoman province of Basra in the modern state of Kuwait (1937, 1961, and 1990) that have provoked the greatest wars to rock the region (see **Box 2.2**). Saddam Hussein's invasion of Kuwait on 2 August 1990 divided the Arab world and led to war in 1991, twelve years of sanctions, and a second war in 2003. The emergence of the state system in the Middle East is thus a history both of the creation of stable states and of destabilizing conflicts.

Box 2.2 Iraqi claims to Kuwait

In the late nineteenth century, the Ottoman Empire sought to extend its sovereignty over a number of Arab territories in the Persian Gulf, including Kuwait, Qatar, and the Hasa region, now the Eastern Province of Saudi Arabia. It conferred titles on local rulers and claimed their territories as integral parts of Ottoman provinces. Members of the ruling Sabah family of Kuwait were recognized as district governors and their territories nominally attached to the Ottoman province of Basra. Britain, which had long sought to preserve the Persian Gulf under its exclusive influence, sought to counter Ottoman efforts at every turn. In 1899, the British government concluded an exclusive agreement with the ruling sheikh of Kuwait, Mubarak al-Sabah (1896–1915), by which:

> the said Sheikh Mubarak-bin-Sheikh Subah [sic] of his own free will and desire does hereby pledge and bind himself, his heirs and successors not to receive the Agent or Representative of any Power or Government at Koweit [sic], or at any other place within the limits of his territory, without the previous sanction of the British Government.

(Hurewitz 1975: 475–7)

The Ottomans were never reconciled to Britain's protectorate over Kuwait. With the creation of the modern state of Iraq after the break-up of the Ottoman Empire, the independence of Kuwait was to be challenged on three separate occasions.

- In 1937, Iraqi King Ghazi asserted Iraq's sovereignty over Kuwait as part of a general criticism of Britain's position in Iraq and the Gulf. Two years later, Ghazi died in a car crash and nothing came of his claims.

- The issue was revived in 1961, when Kuwait was given its independence by Britain. Iraqi President Abd al-Karim Qasim tried to revert to Ottoman practice, declaring the sheikh of Kuwait a district governor subordinate to the governor of the Iraqi Province of Basra. Britain responded by dispatching troops to Kuwait and referred the matter to the United Nations, before Iraq withdrew its claim.

- Saddam Hussein's invasion of Kuwait in the summer of 1990 was thus the third and most forceful Iraqi claim to its oil-rich Gulf neighbour, justified, as in the past, on anti-imperial and pan-Arab grounds, undoing the divisions imposed on the Arab world by the British Empire.

Key events

1839	Gülhane Reform Decree initiates the period of Ottoman reforms known as the Tanzimat
1856	Reform Decree confers equality on non-Muslims, the most controversial reform of the Tanzimat
1876	Promulgation of the Ottoman Constitution
1882	British occupation of Egypt
1914	Ottoman Empire enters the First World War in alliance with Germany
1917	British government declares official support for Zionism (Balfour Declaration)
1918	Surrender of Ottoman forces and occupation of Ottoman territory by Entente powers
1919	Paris Peace Conference
1920	Anglo-French partition of former Arab territories of the Ottoman Empire agreed at San Remo
1922	Partial independence for Egypt and election of Wafd government headed by Sa'd Zaghlul
1929	Anti-Zionist riots in Palestine
1932	Anglo-Iraq treaty terminates the mandate in Iraq, which is admitted to the League of Nations
1936	Anglo-Egyptian treaty confers nominal independence on Egypt, which is admitted to the League of Nations
	Independence treaty concluded between France and its two Levantine mandates, Syria and Lebanon; French parliament fails to ratify the treaties
1936–39	Arab Revolt in Palestine
1941	Free French declaration of Syrian and Lebanese independence
1946	Full independence in Syria and Lebanon, with the withdrawal of all French troops
1947	United Nations passes Resolution to partition Palestine to create Arab and Jewish states
1948	End of the British mandate in Palestine, declaration of Israeli statehood, and the first Arab–Israeli War
1949	Colonel Husni al-Za'im overthrows Syrian government in a military coup
1951	Assassination of King Abdullah of Jordan
1952	Free Officers' Revolution overthrows the Egyptian monarchy and brings Gamal Abd al-Nasser to power

Further reading

Brown, L. C. (1984) *International Politics and the Middle East: Old Rules, Dangerous Game*
(Princeton, NJ: Princeton University Press)
An excellent study that traces the evolution of the nineteenth-century 'Eastern Question' into the troubled
rab state system of the twentieth century.

Fromkin, D. (2000) *A Peace to End All Peace: Creating the Modern Middle East, 1914–1922*
(Harmondsworth: Penguin)
This book discusses the formative period of the First World War and the Versailles Treaty in shaping the
Arab state system.

Hourani, A. (2002) *A History of the Arab Peoples* (London: Faber & Faber)
A magisterial study, among the best general histories of the Middle East in the twentieth century.
See especially Parts IV and V.

Hurewitz, J. C. (1975) *The Middle East and North Africa in World Politics: A Documentary Record,*
vol. 1 European Expansion, 1535–1914; (1979) *The Middle East and North Africa in World Politics:*
A Documentary Record, vol. 2, British–French Supremacy, 1914–1945, 2nd edn (New Haven, CT:
Yale University Press)
A two-volume compilation that comprises the best collection of documents on the diplomacy of the
Middle East.

Rogan, E. (2009) *The Arabs: A History* (Harmondsworth: Penguin)
An interpretation of the history of the Middle East and North Africa, from the Ottoman conquests to the
present day, which expands upon the treatment of the modern period in Hourani (2002).

Rogan, E. and Shlaim, A. (eds) (2007) *The War for Palestine: Rewriting the History of 1948*, 2nd edn
(Cambridge: Cambridge University Press).
An edited volume that traces the inter-Arab divisions underlying Israeli victory in the first Arab-Israeli War.

Yapp, M. E. (1987) *The Making of the Modern Near East, 1792–1923*; (1991) *The Near East since the*
First World War (London and New York: Longman)
A highly recommended two-volume history.

Questions

1. What was the Ottoman legacy of statecraft in the modern Middle East?

2. Why did the Arabs lose out on wartime plans to restructure the region?

3. Which states fared best/worst in the post-war settlement?

4. Which were the strengths and weaknesses of the mandate system?

5. Why did the Palestine question prove so hard to resolve?

3

The Cold War in the Middle East

PETER SLUGLETT

Overview

This chapter attempts to examine the effects of the Cold War upon the states of the Middle East. Although the region was not so profoundly affected as other parts of the world in terms of loss of life or major revolutionary upheaval, it is clear that the lack of democracy and many decades of distorted political development in the Middle East are in great part a legacy of the region's involvement at the interstices of Soviet and American foreign policy. After a brief discussion of early manifestations of USSR–US rivalry in Greece, Turkey, and Iran at the beginning of the Cold War, Iraq is used as a case study of the changing nature of the relations between a Middle Eastern state and both superpowers from the 1940s until the collapse of the Soviet Union. Considerable attention is devoted to the ways in which various Iraqi regimes were able to manipulate the two superpowers throughout the period. A final section attempts to assess the overall effects of the Cold War on the region as a whole.

Introduction

It seems something of a truism, but apparently a truism not universally accepted, that the Cold War had deep, lasting, and traumatic effects upon the Middle East. Thus Fred Halliday considers:

> For all its participation in a global process, and the inflaming of inter-state conflict, the Cold War itself had a limited impact on the Middle East; in many ways, and despite its proximity to the USSR, the Middle East was less affected than other parts of the Third World.
>
> (Halliday 1997: 16)

Specifically, there were no significant pro-Soviet revolutionary movements and the overall casualties arising from the Arab–Israeli conflict between 1947 and 1989 (about 150,000 Arabs and 11,800 Israelis) were very much lower than those in wars elsewhere; compare the casualties in Korea (4 million) or Vietnam (2–3 million). However, in addition to prolonging the region's de facto colonial status, it seems clear that the constant struggle for influence waged by the United States and the Soviet Union effectively polarized and/or anaesthetized political life in most Middle Eastern countries, encouraged the rise of military or military-backed regimes, and generally served to stunt or distort the growth of indigenous political institutions. Recent scholarship also emphasizes the importance of seeing the period as part of the broader context of decolonization rather simply in the straightforward binaries US/Middle East versus USSR/Middle East (*International Journal of Middle East Studies* 2011: 317, 320; Laron, 2013). In addition, the regional clients of the superpowers made generous contributions to the destabilization of the region by attempting to involve their patrons in the various local conflicts in which they were engaged.

Of course, much the same might be said for many other regions of the non-Western world, and it is undeniable that a number of 'intrinsic' or specific factors—including the presence and development of oil in much of the Middle East, and the perceived need by the rest of the world for unfettered access to it, as well as complex local issues such as the Palestine conflict and the invention and growth of political Islam—all would have had, and of course did have, their separate and cumulative effects on the political and socio-economic development of the region, Cold War or no Cold War. Thus, although it helped to facilitate the once hopeful but by now largely defunct Oslo peace process (see **Chapter 13**), the end of the Cold War ultimately had little major impact on the Arab–Israeli conflict, at least not in the direction of bringing about a settlement, which, it was sometimes alleged, was being prevented by superpower rivalry. In much the same way, well before the end of the Cold War, the Iranian Revolution (although it included leftist forces) 'broke with the pattern that revolutionary insurgencies against the established order came mainly from the Marxist-inspired left' (Westad 2005: 288).

It is also important not to exaggerate the extent to which each superpower—especially the United States, whose influence was usually stronger, since it could offer more, and generally better quality, inducements—was able to control the actions, or force the obedience, of its local clients (Gaddis 2005: 128). Thus both the US and the Soviet Union were unable to prevent Israel and Egypt going to war in 1967 (Tibi 1998: 65); in 1980, Iraq did not inform the Soviet Union of its intention to invade Iran until the invasion had taken place (which resulted in Soviet exasperation, expressed in the form of a temporary stoppage of arms deliveries). As already suggested, the amount of manipulation exercised by individuals such as Gamal Abd al-Nasser, Hafiz al-Asad, Saddam Hussein, and others should not be underestimated; the phenomenon of the 'tail wagging the dog' was very much in evidence over these decades. It now seems obvious (as historians can say with hindsight—although presumably it was not so clear at the time) that local actors could and frequently did take advantage of superpower rivalry to play the US and the USSR off against each other for their own or their country's benefit. Particularly given this latter consideration, it is important not to subscribe, as many in the region do, to a culture of 'victimhood': the notion that peoples and governments are merely the playthings of immeasurably stronger international forces—a notion that, if accepted, denies any agency to local peoples, governments, and states.[1]

The immediate origins of the Cold War

It is not difficult to see why, almost immediately after the Second World War, the struggle for control or influence over the Middle East became sharply contested between the United States and the Soviet Union. (While the example, and occasionally the influence, of China was certainly important in the Middle East, China's regional role at the time was more significant in terms of the Sino–Soviet conflict than of the wider struggle between 'East' and 'West' being conducted by the Soviet Union and the United States.) Among many important areas of concern were, first, the desires of the superpowers to gain strategic advantage in the region given the departure, or imminent departure, of Britain and France, second, the fact that the region contained some two-thirds of the world's oil reserves in a context in which oil was becoming increasingly vital to the economy of the Western world, and, third, the fact that, in a novel way that made it quite distinct from previous power struggles, the Cold War represented an ideological conflict between two very different political, social, and economic systems. As Stalin observed to Tito and Djilas: 'This war [the Second World War] is not as in the past; whoever occupies a territory also imposes on it his own social system . . .' (Kuniholm 1980: 117).

In terms of what might be called 'traditional' strategic considerations, the former Soviet Union shared a common frontier with two Middle Eastern states, Turkey and Iran (or three, if Afghanistan is included in the Middle East), and, in the case of Iran, a particularly long one. Given that more-or-less overt hostility between the two powers surfaced soon after, even sometimes before, the end of the Second World War, it did not take long for the Soviet Union to see itself facing actual or potential threats from its southern neighbours, while its southern neighbours were equally quick to see actual or potential threats from the north. At the risk of stating the obvious, an important difference in the situations of the two superpowers before the development of long-range or intercontinental ballistic missiles in the 1960s was that while an invasion of the Soviet Union could be launched, or threatened, from Iran or Turkey, the Soviet Union had no comparable access to the United States from the territory of any of the latter's neighbours. At the same time, while the United States would have to send troops halfway across the world to assist its friends and allies in Iran or Turkey, it was rather easier for the Soviet Union, for example, to train and supply Greek guerrillas from Bulgaria and Yugoslavia (see the map in Kuniholm 1980: 403), or to support or encourage potentially friendly autonomist/separatist movements in Iranian Azerbaijan and Kurdistan (Sluglett 1986; Fawcett 1992).

The conflicts in Iran and Greece were among the earliest manifestations of Cold War activity in the Middle East, and were the result of the coincidence of a number of different factors. In Greece, for example, to simplify a complex reality, the communists had gained a fair-sized following by the mid-1940s as a result of their leadership of the resistance to the German occupation after the Allied evacuation in April 1941. However, they were fiercely opposed to the American plan of supporting the return of the exiled king, to which, to complicate matters further, the British were almost equally strongly opposed. By the end of 1944, the Soviet Union was also becoming keenly interested in the situation in the Balkans; Bulgaria and Romania were occupied by Soviet troops in September and October, at more or less the same moment that the Soviet Union was pressing Tehran for oil concessions in north-western Iran. Between the end of the war in Europe in May 1945 and early 1947, the Greek communists, like the Iranian 'autonomists' a little earlier, sought to capitalize on a combination of their own gathering strength, the Soviet connection, and Britain's declared intention to withdraw its occupation forces (Kalyvas 2006).

Faced with this situation, of an armed leftist movement with powerful external support, coupled with the imminent prospect of British withdrawal—reflecting Britain's economic prostration after the war rather than a 'positive' political choice (Louis 1984: 11–15)—and with parallel (if not quite so alarming) developments in Turkey, the United States announced the Truman Doctrine, which promised American assistance specifically to both Greece and Turkey, in February–March 1947. Truman's speech has an oddly familiar ring today (see **Box 3.1**).

The situation in northern Iran, which flared up at much the same time, was at least equally, if not more, complicated. Briefly, many Azeris and Kurds sought either autonomy for their area(s), or, more modestly, a genuine reform of the machinery of central government in Tehran, which would eventually trickle down to the provinces.[2] Such aspirations had been encouraged by the course of the Bolshevik Revolution, by the Jangali movement in neighbouring Gilan, on the south-western shore of the Caspian, between 1915 and 1921, by the short-lived Soviet Socialist Republic of Iran (Kuniholm 1980: 132; Chaqueiri 1995), and also, especially among the Iranian Kurds, by the more repressive aspects of some of Reza Shah's centralizing policies in the 1920s and 1930s.

Box 3.1 The Truman Doctrine

One of the primary objectives of the foreign policy of the United States is the creation of conditions in which we and other nations will be able to work out a way of life free from coercion. This was a fundamental issue in the war with Germany and Japan. Our victory was won over countries which sought to impose their will, and their way of life, upon other nations.

... We shall not realize our objectives, however, unless we are willing to help free peoples to maintain their free institutions and their national integrity against aggressive movements that seek to impose upon them totalitarian regimes. This is no more than a frank recognition that totalitarian regimes imposed on free peoples, by direct or indirect aggression, undermine the foundations of international peace and hence the security of the United States.

...

At the present moment in world history nearly every nation must choose between alternative ways of life. The choice is too often not a free one.

One way of life is based upon the will of the majority, and is distinguished by free institutions, representative government, free elections, guarantees of individual liberty, freedom of speech and religion, and freedom from political oppression.

The second way of life is based upon the will of a minority forcibly imposed upon the majority. It relies upon terror and oppression, a controlled press and radio, fixed elections, and the suppression of personal freedoms.

I believe that it must be the policy of the United States to support free peoples who are resisting attempted subjugation by armed minorities or by outside pressures.

I believe that we must assist free peoples to work out their own destinies in their own way.

(Full text in Kuniholm 1980: 434–9; also available online at http://avalon.law.yale.edu/20th_century/trudoc.asp retrieved: July 2015)

In August 1941, as a result of the change in the international constellation of forces after the German invasion of Russia and because of Reza Shah's evidently pro-German leanings, British and Soviet forces entered and occupied Iran. The British remained south of an imaginary line connecting Hamadan, Tehran, and Mashhad (roughly 35° North), while Soviet forces occupied northern Iran, eventually controlling about a sixth of the total land area, but, in Azerbaijan alone, about a quarter of the population of Iran. At least initially, neither of these incursions was rapturously received by the local populations. The two new allies were no strangers to the area, having interfered in Iran's internal affairs continuously and generally quite blatantly since the early nineteenth century (Sluglett 2014). However, on this occasion, perhaps not entirely to Britain's liking, a new political situation had come into being.

The nature of the wartime occupation of Iran and the forced abdication of Reza Shah ushered in a sudden flowering of political freedom, which not only benefited organized political groups, especially the communist Tudeh Party, but also paved the way for the appearance of a relatively free press and the formation of labour unions and professional associations. However, Britain controlled the government in Tehran (Kuniholm 1980: 155); in addition, most of the government officials, as well as many of the wealthier elements among the population, quickly left the north for the British zone in the south when the Russians came (Fawcett 1992: 201–21). Initially, things changed little when the United States entered the war after Pearl Harbor, but, in time, British (and Iranian) apprehensions of what might turn out to be the 'true nature' of Stalin's future policies were communicated to the Americans. The result of this, in December 1943, was the joint Allied Declaration regarding Iran (signed by Churchill, Roosevelt, and Stalin), which guaranteed, inter alia, Iran's future sovereignty and territorial integrity (Kuniholm 1980: 167).

However, some two years later, a few months after the war had ended, events in the north seemed to be proceeding somewhat at variance with the Declaration. While most Azeris and Kurds probably had not initially regarded the Soviet occupation as a possible means of freeing themselves from the control of Tehran, it seems that, after four years—that is, by the time of the provincial elections in November and December 1945—a number of politicians in both regions had decided that autonomy within Iran, with Soviet support, was both practicable and desirable. Accordingly, a Kurdish autonomous republic and an Azeri autonomous government were declared soon after the provincial elections, which looked, or were represented as looking, somewhat threatening from London, Washington, and Tehran.

However, in spite of these developments, it soon became clear that there were great limitations on the Soviet Union's freedom of manoeuvre. In addition—and here is a theme that recurs again and again throughout the Cold War—there were clear limits to the risks that the Soviet Union would take in any confrontation with the United States. In spite of threats and cajolery, it ultimately proved impossible for the Russians to wrest the oil concession that they wanted out of the Iranian majlis. After a relatively brief bluster (they were supposed to have left by March 1946), Soviet troops were withdrawn by the middle of May 1946 (Louis 1984: 62). After this, the Soviet Union had virtually no leverage in Azerbaijan and Kurdistan, or indeed in the rest of the country. The three Tudeh cabinet ministers (for health, education, and trade and industry) who had been appointed to the government of Ahmad Qavam in August 1946 were dismissed by November. In December 1946, Iranian troops marched into Tabriz and Mahabad, and the two autonomous entities came to an abrupt end (Alvandi 2014; Fawcett 2014a).

It remains unclear what the Soviet Union's objectives were in Iran, although the opening of both Soviet and Azerbaijani archives have helped to expose both the nature and extent of Stalin's ambitions (Hasanli 2006). The USSR certainly sought an oil concession in the areas around the Caspian and a friendly local government on the other side of the border. No significant oil deposits have ever been found in northern Iran, although it is possible that the Soviet Union was angling for a share of the Anglo-Iranian Oil Company concession further south. It seems far-fetched to imagine that the Soviet Union actually wanted, or thought that it would be permitted, to annex north-western Iran permanently (Rubin 1981: 31). Given the political constellation in the region at the time, the Soviet Union's support for minorities in Iran probably raised warning flags for other governments with sizeable minority communities, such as Iraq and Turkey, although both states were already so firmly anti-Soviet in outlook at the time that this must have served only to confirm already deeply held suspicions (Carrère d'Encausse 1975: 12). In many ways, these two sets of incidents—in Greece and Turkey, and in Iran—were emblematic of later developments in the Cold War in the Middle East, in the sense that, on the one hand, the Soviet Union wanted to take whatever fairly limited measures it could to assure the safety of its frontiers, while on the other the United States found itself equally obliged to defend 'free peoples' wherever it judged that their freedom was being threatened. We will return to the matter of these 'perceptions' later on.

Oil in the Middle East

One obvious lesson of the Second World War was that the future oil needs of the West were going to be met increasingly from the oil production, and from the huge oil reserves, of the Arab world and Iran. In chronological order, Iran had been exporting oil since 1913, Iraq since 1928, Bahrain since 1932, Saudi Arabia since 1938, and Kuwait since 1946, although all on a fairly limited scale. Demand had risen enormously in the course of the war and oil rapidly became a major strategic factor in the region.[3] By the mid-to-late 1940s, US oil companies controlled at least 42 per cent of Middle Eastern oil, as well, of course, as having majority interests in companies nearer home (in Mexico and Venezuela, and in the US itself). Between the 1950s and 1970s, the Middle East gradually became the principal source of oil for Western Europe and Japan, aided in time by new discoveries and exports from Algeria, Libya, Qatar, and the Trucial States.[4]

The Soviet Union hardly participated here, importing only insignificant quantities of Middle Eastern crude—although, in a different context, Soviet technical assistance and sales guarantees were crucial preconditions for the nationalization of Iraqi oil in 1972 (Farouk-Sluglett and Sluglett 2001: 123–6, 145–8). While much was made, and is still made occasionally, of the potential damage to the world economy that could be effected by a potential hostile group of 'revolutionaries'—or more recently (and almost equally implausibly) 'terrorists'—gaining control of one or more Middle Eastern oilfields, the history of the post-Cold War Middle East has shown such fears as largely groundless. It cannot easily be assumed that the deterrent effect of strong links with the US has played a significant role. Thus even the most eccentric or 'extreme' regimes that came to power in the region (in Libya in 1969 and Iran in 1979) did not take long to direct their oil exports towards exactly the same markets as those favoured by their 'reactionary' or 'amoral' predecessors. Similarly, although it certainly caused a major price hike, the oil embargo that began in October 1973 had almost ceased to function by the spring of 1974 (Stork 1975: 210–56). Thus, to play the counter-factual card, if a group opposed to the Āl Saud had come to power in the 1970s or 1980s and seized the oilfields, it is difficult, given the monocultural nature of the Saudi economy, not to imagine that they would sooner or later have begun to sell their country's oil to its former customers.

Hence it is difficult to pinpoint the true role played by oil during the Cold War. Like many other features of this period, it was something of a chimera, to be evoked in passionate discussions of American and European 'vital interests', or as an excuse for supporting this or that more-or-less undemocratic regime, but given that the Soviet Union had immense resources of its own, oil never really functioned as a contentious issue between East and West. Even oil nationalization, a heady rallying cry for countries eager to control their own economies, soon degenerated into a damp squib, given the despotic nature of most Middle Eastern governments. In the first place, the economic independence of individual states was a thing of the past by the 1970s and, in the second, much of the money so gained went not into the pockets of the toiling masses of the country concerned, but into those of the unscrupulous cliques in charge, whether in Iran, Iraq, Libya, or Saudi Arabia. Only the first of these moves, the nationalization of Iranian oil in May 1951, was carried out by a more-or-less democratically elected government, and it was, of course, frustrated by Britain's resolute refusal to countenance it.[5]

A clash of ideologies

The role played by the Soviet Union after its entry into the war on the Allied side in June 1941 was vital—probably decisive—in the Allies winning the struggle against the Axis. One consequence was that it quickly became necessary for Britain and its Allies to present their new partner in a favourable light, partly to show their appreciation, and partly to rally support from the broad left and the labour movement throughout the world. In consequence, Middle Eastern communist and leftist parties enjoyed a few years of relative freedom before being pushed firmly back into the closet (or the prison cells) in the late 1940s and 1950s. We have already mentioned some of the consequences of this in Greece and Iran in the 1940s, but this period of respite also put the Iraqi Communist Party in a better position to lead the clandestine opposition to the *ancien régime* in the late 1940s and early 1950s, and permitted communists to rise to the leadership of almost all of the principal labour unions (Farouk-Sluglett and Sluglett 1983).

There can be no doubt that ideology played an important role in defining the nature of the competition between the two powers for the hearts and minds of Middle Eastern regimes and, although in different ways, of Middle Eastern peoples. In 1945, with the exception of Afghanistan, Iran, Saudi Arabia, Turkey, and North Yemen, the whole of the Middle East and North Africa either had been, or was still, under various forms of British, French, or Italian colonial control, at least since the end of the First World War. Even the excepted territories had been subjected to economic or other kinds of pressure by the European powers. Thus Iran, although never actually colonized, had been fought over by Britain and Russia for economic and strategic reasons well into the twentieth century. Initially, of course, with the process of decolonization under way after 1945, both the United States and the Soviet Union (which was at pains to dissociate itself from its Tsarist past) could point to their clean hands, their lack of colonial/imperial involvement in the region.

In the context of the process of decolonization in particular, there was a certain degree of ambiguity in the attitude of the United States, which took several episodes to resolve. Thus the United States was very publicly opposed to Britain over Palestine and over Iranian oil nationalization (during the Truman administration), did little to discourage the Egyptian Revolution in 1952, and, in spite of having less-than-cordial relations with Abd al-Nasser after his decision to buy arms from the Soviet Union in 1955, showed itself both firm and single-minded in its opposition to the tripartite invasion of Egypt by Britain, France, and Israel in November 1956 (Laron 2013). Of course, things gradually became less confusing as Britain's withdrawal from the region increased in momentum. Indeed, by January 1968, Dean Rusk described himself as 'profoundly dismayed' at the prospect of Britain's military withdrawal from South-East Asia and the Middle East, which he considered 'a catastrophic loss to human society [sic]'.[6]

In broad terms, the United States offered its own vision of modernity: initially that of a disinterested senior partner that could offer assistance, in terms of both goods and 'advice' to young nations struggling to become members of the 'free world' that was emerging after the devastation of the Second World War. 'Communism'—and this was long before the extent of the excesses of Stalinism was fully known—was represented as the incarnation of evil totalitarian forces, bent on world conquest, and in particular as inimical to the spirit of free enterprise, an activity considered on the western side of the Atlantic as one of the most vital expressions of the human spirit. However, for many people in the region, the Soviet Union, parts of which were at least as underdeveloped as much of the Middle East in the 1940s and 1950s, offered an alternative vision: of an egalitarian society in which class divisions had been, or were being, abolished and in which a benevolent state would look after the interests of its citizens from the cradle to the grave. Both visions of the world, and of the future, had their partisans and adherents in the Middle East (Ismael 2008). At this stage, of course, few people from the region had had the chance to study either system at first hand.

As has been noted in the context of Iran and Greece, it became apparent soon after the end of the Second World War that the depleted financial and military resources of Britain and France would not permit them to resume the paramountcy that they had enjoyed in the region in the inter-war years. As Westad (2005: 86) comments, 'there is little doubt that it was the second war in Europe that destroyed both the will and the ability of European elites to keep their colonial possessions'. In addition, something of a power vacuum was going to be created by their departure, and indeed by any major reduction in their regional role. France's departure from Lebanon and Syria in 1945 and 1946 was both more or less final and fairly abrupt, although the decolonization of North Africa, particularly Algeria, would take longer and would be extremely painful and costly. As far as Palestine was concerned, the Labour cabinet first wanted to cling on, and then, seeing that it would get no support from the United States for the creation of a binational state, decided at the end of 1946 that it would make better sense to refer the matter to the United Nations (Louis 1986). Similarly, the increasingly anachronistic nature of Britain's position in Egypt (and a few years later, but in much the same way, in Iraq), the narrowness and isolation of the clique that supported the continuation of the British connection, and the relentless forward march of nationalist or anti-colonial movements meant that the question became 'when', rather than 'if', Britain would depart. Into the vacuum thus created stepped, in different ways and at different times, the United States and the Soviet Union.

Naturally, the role of ideology, and the relative appeal of the Soviet Union and the West, changed quite dramatically as the Cold War unfolded. In the first place, the two powers took some time to define their respective roles. For one thing, after the events in Greece and Iran just described, the Soviet Union went into a period of relative isolation (not only, of course, in the Middle East), from which it began to emerge only after the death of Stalin in 1953. The only major exception to this was the Soviet Union's hasty recognition of Israel as an independent Jewish state in May 1948, on the well-known, but still rather extraordinary, grounds that Israel, founded on what the Soviet Union believed to be 'socialist principles', provided a 'last chance to destabilise the Middle East from within' (Carrère d'Encausse 1975: 14–15).

Throughout the Cold War, this action on the part of the Soviet Union vis-à-vis Israel always remained one of the choicest of the many big sticks that their local rivals were to use time and again to beat the Middle Eastern communist parties. Apart from this, and the episodes already discussed, Stalin's main concern, both before and after the Second World War, was the internal reconstruction of the Soviet state (the doctrine of 'socialism in one country'), and Soviet foreign policy was directed to that end. Given the situation in 1945, the subjugation of the states of Eastern Europe can be understood in terms of the pursuit of that goal. A further important factor, which became a serious challenge to much of the received thinking in the Soviet Union, was that, even in the early 1950s, and even to the most diehard partisans of political correctness in Moscow, it was becoming uncomfortably clear that the imminence of the 'crisis of capitalism', on which a great deal of Soviet thinking had been predicated, was largely a product of wishful thinking in the Kremlin and had very little foundation in fact.

In the late 1940s, the East–West conflict was symbolized particularly by the Berlin blockade and the Korean War: after the early incidents already noted, it was some time before the Middle East developed into an arena of conflict. In fact, Soviet interest in the developing world in general remained fairly subdued until after the death of Stalin in March 1953 and its main concern outside its own borders was assuring the 'stability' of the states of Eastern Europe. For its part, the United States was fairly active in organizing the defence of the 'Free World', with the creation of the North Atlantic Treaty Organization (of which Turkey became a member in 1952). In 1955, the United States created (although it did not join) the Baghdad Pact, which brought Britain and the states of the so-called 'Northern Tier'—Iran, Iraq, Pakistan, and Turkey—into an anti-Soviet alliance. The Soviet Union was somewhat slower to take action in the region, and in fact the formal embrace of the Warsaw Pact (May 1955) never extended beyond the Soviet Union's allies in Eastern Europe.

The relationships of the two great powers with the states of the Middle East were quite complex and nuanced in nature, and cannot simply be written off as imperialist or neo-imperialist. They also changed markedly over time, especially as the limitations on the freedom of manoeuvre of the Soviet Union and the East European countries became increasingly apparent in the late 1970s and 1980s. To some extent, they can be described as 'patron–client' relations (Osterhammel 1997: 115–17), with the peculiarity that some of the clients (in the Middle East and elsewhere in the developing world) were able to switch patrons, and often to have more than one patron at once, in the case of both poor and rich countries—Egypt and Iraq, for example.

One of the most remarkable aspects of the Cold War in the Middle East was the agility with which the various Middle Eastern states acquired the ability to play one superpower off against another. This meant that relations were often competitive, especially in terms of the provision of goods and services. An obvious example here was the willingness of the Soviet Union to finance the Aswan Dam when the United States would no longer support the project, because Egypt had bought or ordered arms from the Soviet Union. Bargaining over arms supplies was a major point of leverage, since the United States would not supply the kinds of arms to the Arab states that might enable them to defeat Israel. But it took quite some time for it to become clear that the Soviet Union would not do so either, and those years of uncertainty marked the heyday of 'Arab–Soviet friendship'.

Elements of a case study: Iraq, the Soviet Union, and the United States, 1945–90

Iraq's changing and complex relations with the superpowers offer an interesting example of the extent to which the Middle Eastern tail was so often able to wag the superpower dog. As has already been mentioned, the decision of the Soviet Union to join the Allied side in 1941 ushered in a brief, but important, period of political freedom for the left in both Iran and Iraq. However, since Iraq had defied Britain in the 'Thirty Days War' of April–May 1941, the liberalizing effects of the Soviet membership of the alliance did not become apparent until after Nuri al-Said's resignation from the premiership in June 1944. One of the major, if indirect, beneficiaries of this relaxation in the political climate was the Iraqi Communist Party, which had been founded in 1934. Although its numbers were small, it was able to wield considerable influence, especially among workers in the modern industrial sector (Basra port, the Iraq Petroleum Company, the Iraqi railways) and among 'intellectuals'. Between late 1944 and the spring of 1946, sixteen labour unions, twelve of which were controlled by the Communist Party, were given licences, as were a number of political parties. However, the enforced resignation of Tawfiq al-Suwaydi's ministry (as a result of pressure from the Regent and Nuri al-Said) at the end of May 1946 brought this brief period of political freedom to an end.

A number of British officials and some British ministers in London had come to realize that 'with the old gang in power this country cannot help to progress very far' (quoted in Louis 1984: 309). Nevertheless, there were limits to the amount of pressure that Britain, and behind it the United States, was prepared to bring to bear on Iraqi governments immediately after the war. Given Nuri al-Said's very close ties with Britain, the debacle in Palestine was evidently a serious embarrassment for him, especially since it came close on the heels of the hostile atmosphere created by the Iraqi government's botched attempt to renegotiate the Anglo-Iraqi Treaty at Portsmouth in January 1948. Yet, with a combination of ruthlessness and repression, and the rapid rise in oil revenues in the late 1940s and early 1950s (from 2.3 million Iraqi dinar, or ID, in 1946, to ID13.3 million in 1951, to ID84.4 million in 1955), the *ancien régime* was able to put off what seemed to many observers to be the inevitable for another ten years.

The Baghdad Pact was effectively an eastward extension of NATO, representing an attempt on the part of the United States to create an anti-Soviet alliance of states bordering, or close to, the Soviet Union. At this stage, the Soviet Union was slowly emerging out of the post-war isolation that Stalin had imposed upon it and was beginning to make its first cautious forays into the politics of the Middle East. Early in 1955, in the wake of an audacious Israeli raid on Gaza, Egypt had asked the United States for arms and had been rebuffed. In April–May 1955, Nasser, Sukarno, and Tito formulated the doctrine of 'positive neutralism' (neither East nor West) at the Bandung Conference. In September, evidently acting on behalf of the Soviet Union, Czechoslovakia announced that it would sell arms to Egypt (and later to Syria). This greatly enhanced the Soviet Union's image and popularity in both countries, as well as in Iraq, although under the conditions then prevailing in Iraq, listeners to East European radio stations faced the prospect of hefty fines or prison sentences if caught.

At this stage, the main objective of the Iraqi opposition (which was composed of a wide gamut of largely incompatible elements) was to make Iraq truly independent of Britain and to set up a national government. Although there was no mistaking the US hand behind the Baghdad Pact, anti-American feeling in Iraq was probably secondary to anti-British feeling, since the long-standing British presence, British bases, and the regime's obvious dependence on Britain were daily realities. Hostility to Britain increased with the tripartite invasion of Egypt in November 1956, an episode that transformed Nasser from an Egyptian to an Arab political figure with almost irresistible appeal. It is not clear how far Iraqis understood the extent to which US intervention had been crucial in bringing the Suez crisis so swiftly to an end.[7] Thus, while it became increasingly obvious over the ensuing months that the United States was alarmed by the possible consequences for the rest of the region of Nasser's 'victory', the US had not managed to damage its reputation irrevocably in the eyes of all anti-British Iraqis by the time of the Iraqi Revolution of July 1958.

The Eisenhower administration's responses to Suez, the attempt to build up King Saud of Saudi Arabia as a counterweight to Nasser, and the pledge to come to the aid of nations threatened by 'international communism' (the Eisenhower Doctrine) had little immediate impact on Iraq (Kunz 2002). The Iraqi public's imagination had been much more excited by the announcement of the setting up of the United Arab Republic (UAR) of Egypt and Syria in February 1958 (Sluglett 2002). However, the declaration would set alarm bells ringing in Washington: the Iraq Petroleum Company's pipelines to the Mediterranean crossed Syria and, by the spring of 1958, the UAR was threatening Lebanon—or so the United States' friends in the Lebanese government were alleging (Kunz 2002: 88).

As has been shown elsewhere (Sluglett 2002), it is most unlikely that there was any direct involvement of either Egypt or the Soviet Union in the Iraqi Revolution of 1958. Of course, both countries welcomed the change of regime in Baghdad, especially early indications that the country would tilt in the direction of 'Arabism', or 'positive neutralism', or both. But, for all of his talk of Arab unity, Nasser was actually quite wary of extending his remit further across the Middle East. The UAR had been the Syrian Baath's idea rather than Nasser's, and the pressure for post-revolutionary Iraq to join the UAR came, again, from Arab nationalist groupings in Iraq, not from Cairo.

As for the Soviet Union, the notion gradually developed in the Kremlin and its think tanks in the late 1950s and early 1960s that national liberation movements that pursued the 'non-capitalist road' when they came to power could be considered worthy allies and partners. However desirable it might be that they should immediately choose the 'socialist road', few newly independent states either did so or showed any particular desire to do so—Cuba being the exception. This explains the complex and uncertain relations between the Soviet Union and, say, Egypt, or Iraq, or Syria, throughout the Cold War. The military regimes that seized power in the Middle East in the 1950s and 1960s were nationalist and anti-imperialist, and sought, and generally achieved, independence for their countries, but they were not, however Western analysts might choose to portray them, socialist or communist. Indeed, for the most part they were highly suspicious of and hostile to socialism and communism, and of those who espoused such ideas locally (Ismael 2008; Sassoon 2014). At the same time, while the Soviet Union was keen to intervene in, and exert influence upon, regional conflicts, it would not do so to the extent of seriously endangering or threatening its generally status-quo-upholding relationship with the West. Soviet military planners also knew that, in the event of a military confrontation, they would not be equipped to challenge American superiority.

These limitations on Soviet power, and greater or lesser degrees of local understanding of them, explain much of the 'now hot, now cold' relationship between the Soviet Union and the Arab states. The West would not give the Arab states weapons that might result in them gaining military superiority; the Soviet Union would not either, but it did supply, generally on rather easy terms, the kind of bread-and-butter military hardware that the Arab states could roll out for their publics on Army Day or National Independence Day.[8] In brief, Iraq and the Soviet Union went through something of a honeymoon period for much of the first twenty years of the republic (until the late 1970s), especially after the (fairly early) souring of the Soviet–Egyptian relationship. Throughout the period, Iraqi public rhetoric was almost entirely anti-American (anti-imperialist) and anti-Zionist, while being full of praise for 'our Soviet and socialist friends'. Of course, the Soviet Union was obliged to swallow some fairly bitter pills along the way, including the massacre of much of the communist left in 1963, the Baath's crude national socialist demagoguery, and the abandonment of any pretence that it was following a 'non-capitalist road' after the late 1970s (Ismael 2008; Franzén 2011). There were some little triumphs, perhaps most notably the nationalization of Iraqi oil in 1972, which had been undertaken with generous (and widely acknowledged) technical assistance from the Soviet Union. Although oil nationalization was wildly popular in Iraq and added greatly to the cachet of the Baath government, lack of accountability meant that a large proportion of the proceeds of the nationalized oil went into the pockets of Saddam Hussein and his cronies, and was indeed a major factor in enabling them to stay in power for so long.

For the United States, obsessed by its crusade against communism, the overthrow of Qasim in February 1963 and the massacre of the left that followed were regarded as positive developments, akin to the overthrow of Musaddiq ten years earlier and the overthrow of Allende ten years later. While the Shah was alive, it was reckoned that he would be able to contain the Iraqi regime and act as the US policeman in the Gulf. Until the 1970s, Iraq could be written off as hopelessly 'socialist' and 'pro-Soviet', and as such was an object of fashionable concern and approval in some more short-sighted and forgetful European leftist circles (Farouk-Sluglett 1982). After the oil price rise that followed the Arab–Israeli War of 1973, Iraq's income from oil tripled within two years, and went up almost tenfold between 1973 and 1982. With the disappearance of Iran from the scene in 1979–80, Iraq became the second largest market in the Middle East, after Saudi Arabia, for European, American, and Japanese goods.

Finally, with the fall of the Shah and the rise of the Islamic Republic, the United States became very anxious to find another policeman to take the Shah's place. Thus, while initially cautious, it eventually threw its weight behind Iraq's invasion of Iran in 1980, probably thinking, along with Saddam Hussein, that the chaos within Iran would mean that the new regime would fall with comparative ease. When it became clear that this was not going to happen, the United States supplied Iraq—either directly or through third countries—with the latest military technology and advanced weaponry, and either gave Iraq, or otherwise allowed it to receive, the means to manufacture chemical (and most probably biological) weapons (Farouk-Sluglett and Sluglett 2001: 266–8), often in contravention of its own laws. Soviet–Iraqi relations had been under intense strain since 1978 (and GDR–Iraqi relations even more so: see Sassoon 2014), when the Baath had turned against the communists again, and Iraq was moving steadily closer to the United States. However, after Khomeini banned the Tudeh Party and cancelled a number of agreements with the Soviet Union, and especially after Iran began to gain footholds within Iraq in 1982–83, the Soviet Union shifted its support back to Iraq, although only for the duration of the war (Golan 1992: 47–53). Thus the Cold War came to an end with the Soviet Union having spent its final few years on the same side as the United States in the war between Iran and Iraq.

Conclusion

To return to a theme mentioned at the beginning of this chapter, let us discuss briefly some of the distortions that the Cold War created in the internal politics of the states of the Middle East. Although counterfactual history is thought to be a rather risqué activity for historians, it clearly has its uses in international relations and political science (Nye 1997: 42–5). Thus it is reasonable (if the speculation remains within the parameters of common sense) to speculate on how Middle Eastern history and politics might have developed if such-and-such had or had not happened, or if such-and-such an action had or had not been taken. This speculation, however, will form the subtext, rather than the main body, of what follows.

It is often alleged that democracy has no 'natural' roots in the Middle East, or more generally in the Islamic world, and hence that the growth of democratic institutions in such stony soil cannot and should not be expected. It is worth pointing out to such doubters, first, that Egypt, Tunisia, the Ottoman Empire, and Iran all had constitutions of a kind before 1914; second, that Western/Westminster democracy has no roots in Japan; and third, that such roots as there may have been in Weimar Germany or Italy were extirpated almost entirely by the excesses of the 1930s and 1940s. However shakily, all three countries (as well as Turkey and India in their own ways, while not exactly the obvious heirs) have maintained a fair semblance of democracy for some six decades. Whether this is natural or unnatural is rather beside the point.

In the geographical space between Western Morocco and Eastern Iran, only two countries, Turkey and Israel, have more-or-less recognizable parliamentary democracies in which the opposition can and has become the government on several occasions. Even here the record is less than spotless, given the number of military interventions in Turkish politics and the fact that at least a third of those whom Israel rules have virtually no say in most of the basic aspects of their governance.

It was not always so. In the inter-war and immediately post-war period, there were lively and contested parliamentary elections in Iran, Iraq, and Syria, and perhaps also in Egypt. Part of—perhaps most of—what killed this off in the 1950s was the pressure of the Cold War. Mostly founded in the 1930s, the Middle Eastern communist parties had fairly limited connections with Moscow, which, as we have seen, did not have particularly strong ties with the region. Unfortunately, the nature of the East–West conflict meant that, for example, when the monarchy was restored in Iran after the overthrow of Musaddiq, or the United Arab Republic of Egypt and Syria was set up, or Qasim's regime was overthrown in Iraq, such events were followed by the round-up and imprisonment, torture, and (especially in Iraq in 1963) the execution of thousands of local communists and leftists and their suspected sympathizers.

If one looks at what the communists were actually advocating or at what they did achieve in the limited arenas in which they were able to take some brief charge, it was quite modest and restrained: the creation of trade unions; the fundamentals of compensated land reform; the nationalization of leading industries; free health and welfare programmes; and so on. In fact, with the exception of land reform, which was not on the agenda in Western Europe, these goals were prominent on the platforms of almost all Western European social democratic parties. In Britain, for example, mostly during the post-war Labour government between 1945 and 1951, the railways and the mines were nationalized, a national health service was put in place, there was a free educational system from elementary school to university, and so on.

In the Middle East, the communists and the left were increasingly persecuted and driven underground in the 1950s and 1960s. This group included, it is reasonably safe to say, most of the leading intellectuals of their day, those who could not be bought and/or co-opted by the regimes that came to power. Their influence on the cultural life of the region was paramount and lasting. For the most part, potentially leftist or left-leaning regimes were replaced by more or less vicious forms of national socialist dictatorship, or, in the case of Iran under the Shah, by an autocracy that became increasingly less benevolent as the years passed.[9] The US and British intelligence agencies were behind the coup that overthrew Mussadiq and restored the Shah in 1953; perhaps less well known is the fact that the CIA was involved in the coup that overthrew Qasim in Iraq in February 1963 and that it had also been in touch with members of the Baath party, most probably including Saddam Hussein, since the late 1950s, on the grounds that the party was both the 'force of the future' and virulently anti-communist (Farouk-Sluglett and Sluglett 2001: 327, n. 3). Obviously, being a leftist in Egypt was somewhat less dangerous than being a leftist in Syria or Iran, and being a leftist in Syria or Iran was still less dangerous than being a leftist in Iraq. In any case, survival—or at least not being persecuted—was largely a matter of chance and connections.

Perhaps the most unfortunate general consequence of this pathological fear, or hatred, of local communists and leftists that the Cold War encouraged, even if it did not actually engender it, was that secular opposition was driven underground almost everywhere in the Middle East. In such circumstances, 'politics' either became extraordinarily dangerous or degenerated into sycophancy. Opposition to, or criticism of, the regime, or of the leader's policies, became tantamount to treason and could be punished as such (Makiya 1998; Sassoon 2012). As a consequence, what opposition there was drifted into the hands of religious organizations of various kinds, since, in Islamic countries, governments cannot ultimately close down the mosques.

This, then, seems to have been one of the more tragic consequences of the Cold War. The obsession with persecuting and reducing the influence of the left had two results: first, the maintenance in power of a series of unattractive, unrepresentative, and generally dictatorial regimes of whatever political hue; and second, the rise of the religious right. In the case of the latter, we are now faced with uncontrollable forces that believe, or purport to believe, in place of more rational political programmes, that 'Islam is the only solution'. The Soviet Union has collapsed and the Cold War has come to end—but the scars that this conflict has left on the Middle East will not quickly go away.

Key events

1945–46	Autonomist movements in Iranian Azerbaijan and Kurdistan
1948	Israel recognized by the United States and the Soviet Union; 750,000 Palestinian refugees created
1952	Egyptian Revolution
1951–53	Iranian oil nationalization crisis
1954–55	Egypt and Syria purchase arms from the USSR via Czechoslovakia
1956	Suez Canal Crisis
1958	Iraqi Revolution
1963	Overthrow of Qasim regime in Iraq, masterminded by US Central Intelligence Agency
1967	Six-Day Arab–Israeli War: Israel gains control of Gaza, Golan Heights, West Bank, Sinai Peninsula
1968	Baath Party (nominally pro-Soviet) takes power in Iraq
1973	October (Ramadan) War between Israel, Egypt, and Syria
1974	Palestine Liberation Organization (nominally supported by Soviet Union) recognized as sole legitimate representative of the Palestinians
1975	Lebanese civil war
1978	Camp David accords: treaty between Egypt and Israel
1979	Fall of the Shah; installation of the Iranian Revolution
1980–88	War between Iran and Iraq
1981	Assassination of Sadat; smooth succession by Mubarak
1990	Iraq invades Kuwait

Further reading

Abrahamian, E. (1982) *Iran between Two Revolutions* (Princeton, NJ: Princeton University Press)
In-depth study of the formation and activities of the Tudeh (Communist) Party of Iran.

Batatu, H. (1978) *The Old Social Classes and the Revolutionary Movements of Iraq: A Study of Iraq's Old Landed and Commercial Classes and of its Communists, Ba'thists and Free Officers* (Princeton, NJ: Princeton University Press)

A study of the Iraqi Communist Party that charts the chequered and tragic progression of this organization for much of the Cold War.

Carrère d'Encausse, H. (1975) *La Politique Soviètique au Moyen Orient, 1955–1975* (Paris: Presses de la Fondation Nationale des Sciences Politiques)
The clearest account of the beginnings of Soviet involvement in the Middle East after the death of Stalin.

Farouk-Sluglett, M. and Sluglett, P. (1983) 'Labor and National Liberation: The Trade Union Movement in Iraq, 1920–1958', *Arab Studies Quarterly*, 5(2): 139–54
This article traces the linkages between the struggle for national independence and the activities of the Iraqi Communist Party.

Fawcett, L. (1992) *Iran and the Cold War: The Azerbaijan Crisis of 1946* (Cambridge: Cambridge University Press)
A comprehensive account of attempts to form an independent Azeri government in northern Iran with Soviet assistance.

Franzén, J. (2011) *Red Star over Iraq: Iraqi Communism before Saddam* (London: Hurst)
Discusses the widespread influence of the Iraqi Communist Party in the second half of the twentieth century.

Ismael, T. (2008) *The Rise and Fall of the Communist Party of Iraq* (Cambridge: Cambridge University Press)
A thorough account of the influence of the Soviet Union, and particularly of the Communist Party of the Soviet Union (CPSU), on the leadership of the Iraqi Communist Party.

Kuniholm, B. (1980) *The Origins of the Cold War in the Near East: Great Power Conflict and Diplomacy in Iran, Turkey and Greece* (Princeton, NJ: Princeton University Press)
See in particular the sections on Greece and Turkey.

Laron, G (2013) *Origins of the Suez Crisis: Postwar Development Diplomacy and the Struggle over Third World Industrialization, 1945–1956* (Washington, DC: Woodrow Wilson Center Press)
A more Egypt-focused account of the crisis.

Louis, W. R. (1984) *The British Empire in the Middle East 1945–1951: Arab Nationalism, the United States and Postwar Imperialism* (Oxford: Oxford University Press)
The most authoritative account of the gradual replacement of Britain by the United States as the dominant power in the Middle East.

Louis, W. R. and Owen, R. (eds) (2002) *A Revolutionary Year: The Middle East in 1958* (London: I. B. Tauris/Washington, DC: Woodrow Wilson Center Press)
The volume contains a number of useful essays on the various crises of 1958.

Nye, J. (1997) *Understanding International Conflicts* (New York: Longman)
Immensely helpful in trying to understand the wider ramifications of the Cold War.

Sayigh, Y. and Shlaim, A. (eds) (1997) *The Cold War and the Middle East* (Oxford: Oxford University Press)
The most comprehensive work on this period.

Questions

1. How was the Middle East drawn into the early Cold War?
2. Did the Cold War impede the process of democratization in the Middle East?
3. Which superpower best achieved its goals in the Middle East?

4. Were regional states superpower pawns or did they demonstrate independent agency? Give examples.

5. Why were communist parties relatively unsuccessful in the Middle East?

Notes

1. 'Only when we begin to allocate full agency to Arab governments can we allocate full agency to the populations; a deterministic worldview of a hegemonic United States or West has a disempowering effect, since it locates the source of all ills exclusively in the West' (Farouk-Sluglett 1994: 105). On 'victimhood', see Makiya (1993: 253–60).

2. It probably also reflected local disappointment at the fact that much of the promise of the Constitutional Revolution had not been fulfilled (Fawcett 1992: 12). See also Sluglett (2014).

3. 'It has been taken for granted … that American interests must have actual physical control of, or at least assured access to, adequate and properly located sources of [oil] supply' (Herbert Feis, wartime economic adviser to the State Department, quoted in Stork 1975: 29).

4. In 1970, 6.8 per cent of OPEC crude oil went to North America, 55.8 per cent to Western Europe, and 21.3 per cent to the Far East. In 1990, 22.7 per cent went to North America, 34.9 per cent to Western Europe, and 30.7 per cent to the Far East. Relatively small amounts of OPEC crude, mostly from Iran and Iraq, went to the USSR and Eastern Europe: 0.2 per cent in 1970 and 2.3 per cent in 1990. Although Soviet oil production doubled between 1970 and 1990, it represented only about 0.6 per cent of world production in 1970 and 1.3 per cent in 1990 (OPEC 1991: Tables 25, 26; this source does not separate the Middle Eastern/North African members of OPEC from the non-Middle Eastern/North African members—Ecuador, Gabon, Indonesia, Nigeria, and Venezuela). In 1970 and 1990, oil exports from these countries accounted for 20.8 per cent and 23.3 per cent of the OPEC total, respectively (OPEC 1991: Table 23).

5. The incident caused a major, if temporary, rift in Anglo–American relations, since the United States had already accepted the principle of fifty–fifty profit-sharing between ARAMCO and the government of Saudi Arabia, and could not understand why Britain did not see that it would eventually have to bow to the inevitable and follow suit (see Louis 1988). In *The British Empire in the Middle East 1945–1951*, Louis (1984: 655) quotes George McGhee, the Assistant Secretary of State for the region, himself an independently wealthy oil man, as having 'left the British in no doubt whatever that he believed "Anglo-Persian" to be niggardly and short-sighted'.

6. Admittedly, this lament was uttered in the context of very considerable European hostility to US policy in Vietnam. Echoing the Blair government's support of the United States in 2002–03, the British government was one of the US's few unwavering supporters in the late 1960s (Louis and Owen 2002: 1–25).

7. In the sense of this comment by the associate dean of the Faculty of International Affairs at Columbia University at a conference in December 1968: '[The West] accepts the idea of full national self-determination in the Middle East, as elsewhere. The last doubt on that score was dissipated by the clear United States stand in the Suez crisis of 1956' (Mosely 1969: 227).

8. Thus Iraq spent US$12 billion on materiel between 1985 and 1989, of which US$7 billion worth was purchased from the Soviet Union. Iraq's second largest supplier was France, which received US$2 billion.

9. ' … for every Iranian, including me, the great, paramount fact about the US government was that it had overthrown Mossadegh, helped to create a terrifying secret police, and, as we saw it, used its immense power to control our monarch for its own purposes, just as the British always had' (Farman Farmaian and Munker 1992: 349).

4

The Middle East since the Cold War: the Multi-Layered (In)security Dilemma

BAHGAT KORANY

Overview

This chapter analyses some key features of the evolving regional security situation since the Cold War's ending. It argues that continuity, as well as change, character-izes regional security. While longstanding issues like the Arab-Israeli conflict and the nuclearization of Iran still characterize the regional security context, the biggest game changer has been a series of domestic events dubbed the 'Arab Spring' (see **Chapter 15**). This Arab Spring refers to the continuing tsunami of mass protests since 2011 that reflect the fight for political space between authoritarian regimes 'from above' and people 'from below' (Korany and El-Mahdi 2012). In considering old and new security challenges—economic, political, and social—this chapter emphasizes throughout the role of 'intermestics', that is, the close connection between the inter-national and domestic politics of the region.

Introduction

In the spring of 2015, the 26th Arab Summit—focused on 'Arab national security'—was concluding its deliberations. The first summit was summoned by Nasser in 1964 to contain the Arab Cold War between the 'revolutionary/socialist' camp headed by Egypt and the 'conservative/reactionary' one headed by Saudi Arabia. The objective was still 'Arab national security', but threats were defined differently: that is, to contain Arab fragmentation in order to mobilize Arab forces against their 'main enemy: Israel'. Cursory content-analysis of these two summits—separated by fifty-one years—gives a glimpse of the magnitude of regional change.

In this 26th summit, the Arab–Israeli conflict still figures—we are officially told—as central. In reality, however, attention is focused on an 'Iranian threat' undermining Arab regimes and pushing, after its rising influence in Iraq and Syria, for a Shia crescent, even encircling Saudi Arabia by deciding the fate of Yemen's civil war in Iran's favour. Saudi Arabia, along with most of the members of the Gulf Cooperation Council (GCC, established in 1981), now also joined by countries such as Jordan, Egypt, and possibly Morocco, wanted to use the 26th Summit for an Arab consensus to contain Iran, and prepare military intervention in Yemen. They were overtaken by events. Yemen's president had to flee the capital, Sanaa, after being detained by Houthi tribal forces and then again flee Aden in the south after failing to stop the Houthi advance. The Saudi Air Force launched a massive bombing campaign, with US and European military coordination in terms of logistics and intelligence. The 26th summit, for its part, was increasingly mobilized to 'Arabize/Islamize' Saudi action after, rather than before, the fact. Events are moving so fast in the region, that some influential talk shows with established 'news analysts' recorded only 2–3 days earlier have had to be substantially 're-edited' or simply replaced.

What general patterns do the Arab Summits' changing agenda, the Yemeni episode, and Saudi-led GCC military intervention reveal?

1. Although the emerging mobilization is against Iran, regional conflict patterns and dynamics are no longer 'Arab versus non-Arab', as Pakistan is joining the Saudi–GCC coalition, and Israel and Turkey are in support. Whatever delimitation existed of an 'Arab regional system' distinct from a Middle East one is now increasingly blurred.

2. Although on the face of it, the traditional (in)security dilemma of interstate conflicts and high politics are still supreme, Iran is not perceived as only another state but rather the incarnation of both revolutionary and Shia Islam. Although the ongoing conflict between Iran and a number of Arab states looks like a conventional interstate one, for the main protagonists and some of their people, the conflict is an inter-group and trans-state one. This is where dominant International Relations theories—especially realism, old and new—are partial in the dual sense of the word: incomplete and biased. In being obsessed with the state while black-boxing it, these schools limit themselves to the tip of the iceberg and overlook the basic infrastructure of international interactions 'coming from below'.[1]

3. The dominant conflict patterns are increasingly related to domestic polarization, socio-economic as well as political; state-authority decline and incapacity to cope with governance challenges; and regime fragmentation, with or without the multiplier of foreign intervention (Korany 2014). The present (in)security dilemma evokes the Algerian analyst, Malek Bennabi's concept of 'colonializability' of the early 1950s, another substantiation of 'intermestics'. According to the Fragile/Failed State Index, Yemen, Iraq, and Somalia have been among the first dozen fragile/failed states for the last decade with Syria also joining the top 25 since 2013 (http://fsi.fundforpeace.org). Since the beginning of the conflict in 2011, Syria's bloody civil war has seen over 220,000 people killed, hundreds of thousands more maimed, almost 4 million international refugees, and millions more internally-displaced persons. In terms of development, the country has regressed to 40 years earlier as measured by its 2010-Human Development Index. The Middle East and North Africa (MENA) region is reflecting the characteristic recent world conflict patterns: the decline of traditional inter-state wars and the rise instead of intra-state ones.[2]

4. This pattern is becoming more complex and chaotic with the increasing influence of non-state actors such as ISIS, Al-Qaeda, and various tribal militias, aided or not by external actors.

Although features of the MENA situation such as the Arab–Israeli conflict, and the nuclearization of Iran still characterize the regional context, the biggest change in recent years is a domestic event: dubbed the 'Arab Spring' (see **Chapter 15**). This Arab Spring refers to the tsunami of mass protests of 2011 that reflects the fight for political space between authoritarian regimes 'from above' and people 'from below' (Korany and El-Mahdi, 2012).

Continuity and change

Notwithstanding the primacy of such changes (Korany 2010), we should not go to the other extreme and overlook elements of continuity. In this constantly-evolving situation, the best methodological approach is to look for the dialectics between forces of continuity and forces of change. This chapter places emphasis on some basic factors that show this continuity/change dialectic and how it continues to determine interactions.

The chapter is analytical rather than chronological. It emphasizes some milestones in the region's evolution in the last quarter century to tease out dominant patterns and characteristics. US military unipolarity in the region notwithstanding, the chapter analyses three factors synonymous in the public mind with this region: oil, the primacy of conflicts/'new' threats, and religio-politics. It also continues to emphasize the imposing crisis of governance, a reflection principally of the gap between vertiginous social change and fossilization of political authority, national and regional. This gap is reflected in the primacy of youthful population (not only numerically but as a social phenomenon with all that youthfulness entails) and the persistence of ageing/ailing political leadership of both government and opposition. ICT is also playing its role. An alternative media—blogs and the empire of Facebook—is increasingly impacting the region. In Syria, as in Gaddafi's Libya before, they are the only sites available to air political opposition, and survive despite governments' efforts to block them.

Both during and after the Cold War, the MENA region occupied centre stage, despite initial concern that the end of the Cold War would devalue the region's worth and deprive its members of their capacity to manoeuvre in a unipolar system. Fear of the region's strategic devaluation was perhaps greatest in Turkey, a NATO member, a listening post on the Soviet Union, and guardian of the Dardanelles Straits.

But the end of the Cold War coincided with the 'Second Gulf War' of 1990–91. The building up of an American-led international coalition to expel Iraqi invading forces from Kuwait dissipated doubts that the region might become marginalized. The attacks of 11 September 2001 ('9/11') against New York and Washington; Al-Qaeda's jihadism; President Bush's crusade against 'the axis of evil'; the 2003 Anglo-American invasion of Iraq; the Israel-Hezbollah war in Lebanon in 2006; and the Gaza (Israel-Hamas) Wars of 2008–09 and 2014; the Iran nuclear problem; and the fallouts of the Arab Spring all confirmed the region's centrality and its dubious distinction as an epitome of conflicts, both old and increasingly 'new'. As a result, factors shaping MENA and its interaction with the global system have not changed post-Arab Spring—at least on the surface. But their ranking and varied combinations give the region a different texture and chemistry. For despite differences between opponents of globalization (a majority in the region) and its proponents (a minority), all agree that this reality liberates us from the blinder of state-centredness and shows internal/external connectedness in social dynamics. In-deed, MENA after the Cold War might help clarify and confirm intermestics, rather than extreme state-centrism and the perception of a state as a well-delimited closed entity. Whereas the all-familiar state-centred geopolitics are still asserted, the new socio-politics of globalization and the growing crisis of governance are increasingly impacting behaviour, domestic and international.

Thus the story of MENA in the post-Cold War world is one of increasing globalization, and of increasing mobility of ideas and people, including migrants or post-Arab Spring 'boat people' across the Mediterranean.[3] It is also the world of contradictory tendencies: increasing integration in global interactions has been accompanied by a rise in particularistic ethnic and religious identification. Topping these contradictions is the yawning gap between rich and poor, not only between oil-producing states and the rest of the region, but within individual countries. Arab satellites—from Al-Jazeera to Al-Arabiyya—make people aware of these contradictory tendencies; for instance the rising oil power, combined with global marginalization and denigration of their religion (as in the Danish anti-Islamic cartoons in 2009, and in France's Charlie Hebdo in 2014).

In January 1996, at the time of the first election in Palestine following the 1993 Oslo Agreement (see **Chapter 13**), some members of the group of international observers under the leadership of Jimmy Carter pondered on whether Palestine and the region would evolve more like a Singapore or a Somalia. The 2007 Hamas/Fatah fights, the repeated Israeli military actions, and the vagaries of the Arab Spring point at present—a Dubai pattern notwithstanding—to the Somalia pattern. Although not exactly in the same condition of civil war as Somalia, socio-political fragmentation is demonstrated in Iraq, Sudan, Syria, Libya, and Yemen. A different pattern of socio-political fragmentation exists in Lebanon. This country existed for seven months in 2007–08 without a President, despite eighteen attempts to elect one, and its 2014 elections also failed to achieve a quorum. Further elections have been postponed until 2017.

The influence of tiny Qatar highlights the other pattern in Middle Eastern politics and economics: the Dubai global outpost model with its high-rise towers mushrooming in the desert among oil-wells. Until 2012, oil exports from Arab oil-producing countries continued to increase, with record prices of $150 a barrel in 2008. (Indeed, between 2003 and 2006, six such states saw their oil exports increase by almost 260 per cent, and the surplus in their balance of payments by 300 per cent.) Despite a decrease in exports from 2013 and decreases and fluctuations in prices throughout 2014 and 2015, Qatar's per capita income is almost fifty times that of another Gulf country: Yemen. Amidst these extreme variations and contradictory patterns of politics and economy, the region continues to be in flux. To the continuing interstate conflicts, new and intense societal ones have been added. Intermestics, described in the following section, attempts to make this MENA complexity and its contradictions intelligible.

The chapter's other four sections deal with what are considered in the public mind to be synonyms of the region. The first deals with oil, its assets, but also a hidden 'resource curse'. The second deals with traditional insecurity concerns or conventional geopolitical conflicts: the ongoing Arab–Israeli conflict, some Arab–Arab conflicts, and their global repercussions (e.g. Gulf Wars). The third section draws attention to socio-political threats and conflicts including newer socio-economic deficits and the highly conflictual domestic environment. It also deals with religio-politics: its mobilization effect and electoral behaviour as well as its non-state actors and their international spillover. Although attention is drawn to the importance of religion in the region generally, the emphasis is on Islamic institutional protest. A fourth section considers the much debated claim of Arab 'exceptionalism'.

Decoding the Middle East: intermestics

A limited survey of the regional satellite channels and influential yearbooks shows that dominant conceptual lenses to explain the post-Cold War world do not decode MENA. Instead of the popular lens provided by Fukuyama's (1992) 'End of History', MENA geopolitics and conflicts show the continuation of history or even its return. Meanwhile, the 1980–88 Iran–Iraq war and Iraq's factional in-fighting; Iraq's 1990-invasion of Kuwait; and rising Sunni–Shia rifts show Huntington's (1996) influential 'Clash of Civilizations' thesis to be a self-fulfilling prophecy if not a misleading conceptual lens.

The alternative conceptual lens suggested here is intermestics.[4] This neologism (the International Relations equivalent of the economists' now well-established 'stagflation') denotes the organic interconnectedness and overlapping between INTERnational and doMESTIC dimensions of socio-political processes and interactions. Intermestics as a conceptual lens is thus a reflection of the creeping globalization, characterized by the retreat and/or fragility of the state and its traditional sovereignty, and the intensity instead of trans-state societal interconnectedness and speedy circulation of ideas and people. Major MENA characteristics, from oil wealth and its impact to religio-politics and its international spillover, demonstrate the dominance of intermestics. For instance, in the region, threats multiply and insecurity deepens, due not only to traditional state-centred, military threats but increasingly to people-centred human (in)security ones (UNDP 2009; Korany 2014).

Thus repeated pro-subsidy or food riots (e.g. Egypt's or Morocco's 'martyrs for bread') show the pitfalls of globalization and its translation for the majority of the region's people in extreme external dependency (in basics). They also show a crisis of governance. While issues of traditional security in Iraq or Palestine have not declined, they are compounded by new 'low politics' ones: cultural invasion, identity politics, and urges for democratization. These basic and divisive debates take place amongst islands of both severe poverty and extreme wealth—especially oil wealth.

Consequently, intermestics, as globalization's rising characteristic, finds the region highly prone to conflict because of an increasing resource-gap. A resource-gap should be understood here not only in the limited material sense, but also in the wider one of deficits. Deficits could be in capital, both financial and social, in management capacity, both of human resources and of conflicts, and in the availability of goods necessary for nourishing body and mind. As a result, among the myriad factors helping to decode MENA's present international relations, the three factors of oil, the primacy of conflicts (especially so-called 'low politics' conflicts), and religio-politics are particularly emphasized.[5]

Oil: a mixed blessing?

Although **Chapter 5** is devoted to oil, some aspects must be noted here. Oil is still a highly strategic energy supply, and MENA—despite US shale extractions—occupies a central position in providing it. OPEC countries command 81 per cent of world oil reserves and Middle East countries account for 66 per cent of these (OPEC 2015). Since, contrary to previous optimistic estimates, Caspian Sea oil reserves are equivalent only to those of the North Sea, MENA retains its prime place as *the* oil-provider par excellence. Indeed, although the US has reduced its dependency on MENA oil, Western Europe continues to be quasi-totally dependent on it for its oil supplies. Moreover, growing energy needs in 'emerging powers' in Asia increase pressure on Middle Eastern oil.

For the peoples of the region, oil has proved to be a mixed blessing. The Middle East accounts for 66 per cent of OPEC's total reserves. Oil has intensified world interest and involvement in their fate since the 1930s and the industry reveals at present the perilousness of counting on an extremely extraverted and one-product economy. On average, Gulf economies rely on oil for over 80 per cent of their national income. This leaves them victims to the vagaries of the world economy. For example, between 1981 and 1986, Algeria's oil revenues dropped from $26.3 billion to $6.2 billion and Libya's from $46 billion to $7.1 billion. This story is representative of all oil-producing countries. Thus Saudi Arabia's revenues soared from less than $3 billion in 1972 to $113 billion in 1981, before plummeting to less than $23 billion in 1987. In 2014 and 2015, oil prices have been in a constant decline, from $115 per barrel in 2014 to less than $60 per barrel in March 2015. The IMF estimated that in 2015, Gulf state economies were likely to lose $300 billion in oil revenues due to lower oil prices, amounting to about 21 per cent of their GDP (http://www.inss.org.il/index.aspx?id=4538&articleid=8990).

Indeed, most oil states' budgets have serious structural deficits and open or concealed internal debt: the budget deficit for the period 1996–2000 was on average 10 per cent. Moreover, population growth could offset any increase in oil revenues. Saudi Arabia, for the period

1980–2000, saw its population grow from 9.9 million to 22 million, a rise of over 120 per cent (the figure for 2011 was 2.28 per cent; Cammett et al. 2015). Meanwhile, its per capita income decreased from $21,425 to $3,000, or a seventh of what it had been two decades earlier (Cammett, Diwan, Richards, and Waterbury 2015). Yet, accustomed to the easy money of the rentier state that derives substantial revenue from foreign sources in the form of rent (as opposed to really 'sweating for it'), the population does not easily accept hardships. It is not only the state and its economy that are rentier, but it is as if the contagion trickles down into the society'sstructure and organization and even to individual mind-sets. In such a socio-economic context, reward does not depend on work or productive efficiency but provides an incentive for effortless spending. The serious problem in governance starts when this 'easy money' suddenly declines, as we will see in the sections on the yawning resource gap and religio-politics.

Hardship or not, the fluctuation of financial flows are not allowed—by conviction or by persuasion—to affect 'national security'. Consequently, many of these countries 'recycle' a substantial sum of their petro-dollars in arms purchases from Western countries, especially the United States. Despite the two Gulf Wars proving that none of the six GCC members could adequately defend itself—individually or collectively—against either Iran or Iraq, these states nevertheless invested more than $85 billion of their oil wealth in the purchase of weapons systems between the end of the Cold War and 2000. Between Iraq's invasion of Kuwait in 1990 and 2000, the Saudi government signed contracts for US weapons systems worth $36 billion, or 32 per cent of US global arms exports. From 1996 to 2006, Saudi Arabia increased its military expenditure by about 80 per cent, Libya by about 75 per cent, and Algeria by a hefty 230 per cent (SIPRI: Arms Transfers data, April 2008: 2–3, 5). Subsequently, between 2006 and 2014, Saudi Arabia increased its military expenditure from $29,581 million to $80,762 million. In the same period, in Libya, this expenditure jumped from $614 million to $3,340 million; and in Algeria from $2094 million to $11,862 million (SIPRI: Arms Transfers data, 2014). This militarization of the MENA region will be further explored in the section on traditional insecurity and the geopolitical context.

Oil not only provides substantial revenues, but also political influence. This is why we used the term 'petro-politics', which is increasingly substantiated at present. Thus, either to prevent the winds of (Arab Spring) change from engulfing the Gulf or to direct the inevitable change in a certain direction, GCC countries seem to be in the driver's seat, including in the League of Arab States (LAS). For instance, under GCC influence, the LAS has committed a volte-face of its conventional anti-foreign intervention policies and supported the NATO intervention in Libya which finally overthrew the Gaddafi regime. The GCC has also directed the efforts, first in the League, then in collaboration with the UN, to dislodge Asad's regime in Syria. Moreover, the GCC directed the change from Yemen's President Saleh to his vice-President Mansour, supporting the latter militarily. Earlier, the GCC prevented any seismic domestic change in Bahrain, associating any domestic restructuring in favour of the Shia majority with the rise of Iran.

Petro-politics—in a different way—has also been associated with the crisis of governance and social tensions, before and after the Arab Spring. Although oil and its revenues initiate in the GCC aspects of the welfare state, it is becoming a problem in some other countries, like Egypt and Algeria. These two countries have been paying huge subsidies to keep domestic energy prices low, reaching, in the Egyptian case, 20 per cent of its budget. With the population increase, domestic consumption has been eating at exports and hence revenues, at a time when such revenues are sorely needed to prevent rising social demands and protests. Despite Egypt's decision in 2014 and Iran's in 2015 to reduce oil subsidies, in such a tense social situation, no government will risk reducing such sub- sidies all at once. It is a catch-22 situation for many oil-producing countries, including some in the GCC who, given their demographic growth, must deal with such issues in the future.

Traditional (in)security: the geopolitical context

The Arab-Israeli conflict

In an examination of traditional (in)security in the Middle East, the ongoing Arab–Israeli conflict (see **Chapter 12**) remains crucial, at least in rhetoric—as seen in the 26th Arab sum- mit in March 2015. It is a protracted social conflict, in which religious, political, cultural, economic, and psychological elements pile up and feed on each other to create a seemingly indissoluble impasse. Consequently, it is so central to MENA's regional dynamics that these are mostly analyzed through its prism. Eight regional wars as well as two Intifadas have shaped both interstate and inter-society phenomena: state-formation, regime patterns, re- gional alignments and realignments, and collective psychology as well as the region's overall process of negotiations and governance. Historically, this conflict even shaped the balance between the two superpowers in the Cold War. In the 1950s, it brought in the USSR to foil the Western arms monopoly, and ended by promoting non-alignment. In the 1970s, its peace process marginalized Soviet regional impact, as in the negotiations at Camp David that initiated the first peace treaty between Israel and an Arab country, Egypt. The Arab– Israeli conflict is even supposed—through lobby politics—to influence elections to top political positions in the United States.

At the regional level, the Arab–Israeli conflict—directly or indirectly—continues to influ- ence the rise of the so-called *national security state*, and make MENA one of the most mili- tarized regions in the world. For instance, three coups d'état took place in Syria in the first year following the Arab defeat in the 1948 Arab–Israeli war, and the Nasserist coup in Egypt (1952) was primarily motivated by the debacle in Palestine. Average military spending as a percentage of government expenditure for some individual states is very high. Between 2000 and 2012 the figures were 12 per cent for Israel; 30 per cent for Saudi Arabia; 13 per cent for Turkey; 8 per cent for Iran and 9 per cent for the United Arab Emirates (Cammett et al. 2015: 359). Despite a relative decline over the previous decade, this is still far above the world average, and this will likely continue to be the case, especially in the tense Gulf sub-region.

According to 2015 statistics, Saudi Arabia's defence budget of $30.3 billion corresponds to $25,401 per capita; spending by Oman, at $3.7 billion, equates to $21,688 per capita; and the UAE's 13.9 billion in 2013 equates to $44,552 per capita. The ratio is even higher for Kuwait—an equivalent of $44,850 per head for its $4.84 billion defence budget in 2014. Finally, the budget for Qatar in 2013 was $4.35 billion with a per capita figure of $98,986 (IISS 2015).

In 2013, Iran was listed among the top twenty countries in the world when it comes to military expenditure in PPP dollar terms (purchasing power parity). It spent $14.8 billion, which includes figures for national defence but does not fully include spending on the Revolutionary Guards, which constitutes a considerable part of Iran's total military expenditure (IISS 2015). The amount is equivalent to $4,769 per head of the country's population.

Even if this military expenditure is no longer directly motivated by the Arab–Israeli conflict, it has often been presented as such. The most extreme example was Iraq's Saddam Hussein's justification for invading Kuwait in 1990, allegedly to liberate Jerusalem. The main point, however, is that the dominance of such geopolitical conflicts as that between the Arabs and Israelis lead to arms races, and both phenomena feed on each other to make the Middle East a highly-militarized region.

However, the end of the Cold War presaged an initiative towards a collective peace process with the convening of the Madrid Conference in October 1991. Typically, this conference got bogged down in procedural polemics and ended without even fixing another meeting. Because of this failure, negotiations moved to the bilateral level that Israel always preferred: for example Syrian–Israeli negotiations in Washington. But it was *second track or informal diplomacy* that proved the most capable of making things move. The secret Israeli–Palestinian negotiations in Oslo in 1993 (see **Chapter 13**) were the result. Oslo was indeed a qualitative shift for at least three reasons: (a) the two main protagonists announced mutual formal recognition; (b) there was agreement on a specific programme of action and timetable for Israeli withdrawal from Gaza and most of the West Bank, and the emergence of an internationally recognized formal Palestinian authority (e.g. internationally-supervised Palestinian elections took place in January 1996); and (c) it allowed other protagonists to join—officially—the peace process (e.g. the signing of the Jordanian–Israeli peace treaty in 1994). Optimism was so widespread that talk of the 'New Middle East' joined the rhetoric of the new world order. The idea was best expressed in 1993 by Shimon Peres, Israel's former head of the Labour Party, Prime Minister and President:

> Peace between Israel and its Arab neighbours will create the environment for a basic reorganization of Middle Eastern institutions. … Our ultimate goal is the creation of a regional community of nations, with a common market and elected centralized bodies, modelled on the European Community.
>
> (Peres and Noar 1993: 62)

At present, the situation is quite the opposite. The reason for this regression is that lobbying for peace lost its main constituency, especially in Israel. Israeli Prime Minister Yitzhak Rabin was assassinated in 1995, and Israel is currently run by a right-wing government now in its fourth term, led by Likud head Benjamin Netanyahu. Moreover, the expected peace dividends did not materialize: the ill-fated regional economic conferences offer an eloquent indicator. Four of these took place between 1994 and 1997, in Casablanca, Amman, Cairo, and Doha respectively. All of them ultimately failed.

Border disputes

Related to traditional geopolitical interstate conflicts are the myriad *border disputes* in the Middle East. Almost every MENA country has a border-demarcation problem with its neighbour(s). This applies even to the GCC countries which intend now to transform their Gulf Cooperation 'Council' into a 'Union', but whose borders' 'lines in the sand' become lines of dispute with oil exploration and discovery.

An Arab–Arab conflict between Algeria and Morocco in 1963 (just one year after Algerian independence) was about the tracing of their borders. This conflict continues to poison their relations—for example in the Western Sahara conflict. Despite the presence of a Union project (UMA or *Union du Maghreb Arabe*), during the fifty years of Algeria's independence, the border with Morocco was closed, on and off, for more than thirty years. In addition to this, the eight-year war between Iran and Iraq (or the First Gulf War—the largest and most costly war in the post-Cold War era) was ostensibly about the tracing of borders on the Shatt El-Arab waterway. Rough estimates suggest that there were more than one and a half million war and war-related casualties and millions were made refugees. Iran acknowledged that nearly 300,000 people died in the war, while Iraq suffered an estimated 375,000 casualties. The final cost is estimated at a minimum of $200 billion (http://www.globalsecurity.org/military/world/war/iran-iraq.htm).

The Second Gulf War (1990–91), beginning with Kuwait's invasion, was also about (colonial) border-demarcation. Globalization and technological advance left their impact. Although much shorter, the war's cost was staggering: according to US estimates, more than 100,000 Iraqi soldiers died, and 300,000 were wounded. Many human rights groups claimed a much higher number of Iraqi casualties. In purely monetary terms, estimates of this war's cost range from $61 to $71 billion (CNN- http://edition.cnn.com/2013/09/15/world/meast/gulf-war-fast-facts/). The Third Gulf War, the 2003 US-led invasion of Iraq, substantiates a multiplier effect. Other than the high cost for the US itself, the reconstruction of Iraq will require at least $20 billion a year. The indirect impact of the war cannot be neglected. In Europe, though the euro appreciated against the US dollar during the war, the European Commission lowered its forecast for economic growth from 1.8 per cent to 1 per cent. The aviation and tourism industries were two of the worst hit sectors with many countries cancelling their flights to the region. The war also brought unpredicted risks to the shipping industry. Insurance companies increased the so-called special war premium for shipping stationed around the Gulf to as high as 1 per cent per week. The fee is much higher if the ship is owned by the US, as it is more likely to be a target for attack. The result of this primacy of conflicts is that MENA has, as mentioned, become a highly-militarized region, even when compared to other turbulent zones in the developing world. Compared to nuclearized South Asia for the 1997–2006 period, the BICC's Global Militarization Index (GMI) 2013 reveals that

> Israel, Syria, Jordan and Kuwait ... are among the top 10 countries on the GMI, with the rest of the Middle East region ranking in the top forty militarized states in the world. This high level of militarization is demonstrated, among other things, by the ratio between military expenditure and Gross Domestic Product, which is well over seven percent in some states and thus far in excess of the world average of approximately 2.5 percent.

On the surface, the Gulf Wars have brought to the fore the looming danger of weapons of mass destruction, from chemical and biological weapons to nuclear proliferation. Among the countries of the region, pressure is building to carry out the economists' 'demonstration effect', the 'keeping up with the Jones', a 'contagion effect' to accelerate proliferation both of nuclear and chemical-biological weapons. If there is a crisis of this type at the global level, it will manifest itself very vividly and dangerously in the MENA region. For instance, Israel is perceived by its Arab neighbours as being increasingly nuclearized, with 'no less than 264 nuclear bombs … in addition to tactical neutron bombs … all supported by a sophisticated delivery system' (*El-mustaqbal Al Arabi*, January 2000, 175–82). As a result, Iran's prestige because of its nuclear intentions is soaring. There is a huge pressure from vocal sectors of Arab civil society on their governments to go nuclear to attain the level of nuclear deterrence of their Israeli adversary. A conference at the Center for the Study of the Future (Assiut University, Egypt, November 1999) suggested that Arab governments abstain—in the case of the failure to establish MENA as a nuclear-free zone—from signing the NPT and work seriously to establish an active nuclear programme, individually or collectively. In 2015, amid renewed calls for a nuclear free Middle East, it remains to be seen how the P5+1 agreement on Iran's nuclear programme will play out at the regional level.

Meanwhile, new and old regimes are facing the continuing fall-out of the Arab Spring, reflecting 'low politics', threats, and demonstrating intermestics.

Socio-political threats and conflicts: the new high politics

Long before the Arab Spring, on average all *comparative socio-economic indicators* for the twenty-year period 1980–2000 were negative, arguably showing this development shortfall as the new threat to stability and security in the MENA area. GNP growth rates were less than half those achieved in South Asia, and comparison with East Asia-Pacific rates makes the Middle East situation look particularly poor (World Bank 2000: 23). In this context, the Arab Spring was to be expected.

The development gap in real terms is much worse when demographic trends are taken into account. With globalization and increased standards in health and health education, the populations of MENA countries have increased on average by more than three times in the last fifty years—in Algeria four times, and Saudi Arabia seven times. Analysts agree that true development normally requires an annual economic growth rate that is 2 per cent higher than population growth, so if the MENA population growth hovers around 2–3 per cent on average, an economic growth rate of a minimum of 5 per cent is needed to avoid negative growth. For the period 1991–95, the comparative figures of real per capita GDP growth were unfavourable to MENA at –0.2 per cent, compared to 2.2 per cent for South Asia and 8 per cent for East Asia (Cordesman 2001: 48). Although the overall region's GDP grew by an average of 6.2 per cent in 2005, there was a huge gap between the oil-rich countries and the resource-poor countries, as the latter's GDP dropped from 4.8 per cent in 2004 to 4.0 per cent in 2005. Because the region's economic growth is highly-affected by oil prices (even in non-oil-producing countries through labour remittances), the 2008–09 global crisis, which caused a decrease in the price of a barrel of oil, resulted in a decrease in the average growth rate of the region from 6.4 per cent in 2008 to 2.4 per cent in 2009. Some recovery was witnessed in 2010 in the entire region, whereby Egypt for example was growing at 5.5 per cent and other non-oil rich countries growing between 4.5 per cent and 6 per cent, while oil-rich states were growing at an average of 6.3 per cent. However, the political turmoil in the region since 2011 has slashed those numbers and increased the gap between oil-rich and oil-poor countries. In 2011 for example, Egypt's growth rate decreased to 1.2 per cent, while Syria's dropped from 5.5 per cent to 1.5 per cent (http://www.oecd.org/mena/investment/49171115.pdf). That said, more recently, the performance of these economies has been mixed, with high-income countries growing at 4.9 per cent in 2014 (indeed, GCC countries are expected to lead regional recovery), compared to only 0.7 per cent growth in poorer states. This weak performance is attributed to the region's political transitions and their consequences.

Rather than an exception or surprise, the Arab Spring was a ticking time-bomb in terms of potential social upheavals and their possible spill-overs into external conflicts. Indeed, the relationship between demographics, social upheaval, and external conflict is no longer guess-work. Based on an analysis of forty-five conflicts in developing countries in the period 1945–71, one of the findings is that the higher the rate of population growth, the more salient a factor population increase appears to be in the development of conflict and violence (Choucri and North 1975).

The demographics/resource gap in MENA has another aspect: the region's 'youthening' dilemma where 40 per cent or more of the population is aged 14 or younger. This age bracket is certainly a potential asset, but at present it is taxing the system in terms of educational needs and job opportunities. Often unemployed, these young people are easily recruited to protest ideologies and militant pseudo-religious organizations. Yet resources to drastically increase employment opportunities are unavailable. Since 2000, budget deficits in the region have been seriously increasing: from 0.9 per cent of GDP in 2001 to 5.5 per cent in 2010, and 8.5 per cent in 2012. Moreover, activities in the private sector tend to emphasize imports and related services rather than real economic development (http://www.dailynewsegypt.com/2013/02/05/cutting-deficits-without-damaging-growth/).

The region failed to compensate for its resource gap by attracting foreign resources through trade or FDI (foreign direct investment). For the period 1980–2000, the FDI gap between MENA and the rest of the world was a large one, although this improved over the following decade. Whereas MENA's exports rose by 5 per cent, the rate for the Latin America-Caribbean (LAC) area was about 350 per cent, for South Asia-Pacific more than 400 per cent, and for East Asia 550 per cent. Even for sub-Saharan Africa, the growth rate was almost five times that of MENA, at 24 per cent (Cordesman 2001). In general, in 2006, MENA's growth relative to the developing world on a per capita basis was found to lag; only LAC and sub-Saharan Africa performed worse that year (Nabli 2007). Between 2006 and 2008, FDIs increased from US$28 billion to $30.2 billion (World Bank 2008). However, after the onset of the global crisis in 2008/09, OECD 2013 data show that countries of the MENA region only received 6 per cent of FDI (http://www.oecd.org/mena/governance/Marie%20Rey.pdf) (Cammett et al. 2015: 496–500).

Moreover, the region failed to make up for this shortfall in FDI (and the haemorrhage of increasing external debt) by raising its *productivity*. In fact, whereas East Asian-Pacific productivity rose by 54 per cent, MENA productivity dropped by about 6 per cent in the period 1960–90 (Cordesman 2001: 79). While GDP in MENA registered an annual increase of 5.5 per cent in 1993–2003—the second highest in the world—productivity, which measures how efficiently resources are used, increased by only about 0.1 per cent annually during the same period (for a total of 0.9 per cent over the ten-year period). The only region to fare worse was sub-Saharan Africa, which registered negative productivity (Raphaeli 2006).

Even oil-producing countries were not immune to the negative societal effects of this deteriorating resource gap. For instance, most oil states' budgets have serious structural deficits and open or concealed internal debt. As a group, oil economies have actually under-performed compared to the rest of MENA. The result is that population growth will more than offset a probable increase in oil revenues. For instance, for the period 1980–2013, Saudi Arabia saw its population rise from 9.9 million to 29.1 million—a rise of over 193 per cent, which is bound to affect per capita income if oil prices do not increase or even stay the same. There has been an increase in per capita income in Saudi Arabia, reaching $25,961 in 2013, and a budget surplus of 6.4 per cent, in 2014 (http://www.tradingeconomics.com/saudi-arabia/government-budget). This occasional or cyclical rise in oil prices remedies the situa-tion momentarily. But it also reflects the vagaries of extreme dependence on one commodity and its world market. In non-oil exporting countries, the widening resource gap continues to have a negative effect.

This worsening economic situation—with all its facets—increases *societal stress* and leads to a situation of overall insecurity for both society and state. Between 2005 and 2007, Egypt—where official strikes are not allowed—experienced twenty-one labour strikes and 124 sit-ins; a precursor of the 2011 political explosion in Tahrir. This overall insecurity, to-gether with the state's legitimacy deficit, feeds discontent and protest.

These new threats, euphemistically dubbed 'low politics', continue to influence domestic politics and regional–international interactions, as the wars in both Yemen and Syria amply show. As we shall see, social tensions often take a religious form in a highly religious region. It is in this sense that an intermestics lens is the most appropriate. Religio-politics further magnifies this intermestics lens.

Religio-politics: mobilization, electoral performance, and international spill-over

It is well known that the Middle East region witnessed the birth of three major world re-ligions: Judaism, Christianity, and Islam. Although the dominant Western media tend to talk mainly about Islamic fundamentalism, the whole MENA region is characterized by the politicization of religion. Lebanon suffered from two protracted civil wars in the 1950s, 1960s, and 1970s because of the distribution of political posts between different Muslim and Christian communities and their sects. Israel's identity and very existence are based on its Jewishness. At the spring 2003 US–Israeli–Jordanian–Palestinian summit in Aqaba, Jordan, President Bush had to accept that Israel's national security rested on it keeping its Jewish character. Many of the present Israeli laws, from the law of return to the recent ban on marriage between Israeli Arabs and Palestinians, cannot be understood without remem-bering this link between Israel's Jewishness and its national security. Moreover, the nagging settlements problem is associated with orthodox Jews, causing deep divisions within Israeli society itself. But because more than 95 per cent of the population of the Middle East are Muslims, the phenomenon of the Islamization of politics and protest should be emphasized in the space available here.

In Algeria, Egypt, or even the Islamic Republic of Iran, Islamic movements have tried to topple the ruling regimes. As a recent illustration, in Egypt, about 1,200 people were killed following terrorist action or police repression between 1990 and 2002, and such losses rose after the military deposed the elected Muslim Brotherhood president and replaced him with one of their own in 2014. Press reports indicated 1,641 'terrorist' acts in the first quarter of

2015, equal to one incident every 1.5 minutes (*El-Sherouk* newspaper, 17 March). On the World Peace Index, Egypt ranked 52nd in 2010, but 113th in 2013 (Baseera, Egyptian public Opinion Poll No. 283, December 2013). Despite the purely domestic character of such movements, there seems to be an overall contagion effect.

Religio-politics is also leading Turkey, an officially secular country, to an acute crisis of governance, manifestly concerning the status of hijab. This is exemplified by the fact that the wife of current President Erdogan of the Islamist AKP—Justice and Development Party wears a hijab. Since wearing hijab is barred from many official functions and institutions, Erdogan's wife could be excluded from attending many official functions. Hijab, therefore, has become a symbol of both identity and political crisis. Amid massive demonstrations for and against legalizing wearing hijab in universities after the AKP was re-elected in 2007, there was even a demand to ban the governing AK party itself as contravening Turkey's secular orientation. If globalization is associated with mobility and secularist ideas, religion is becoming a symbol of the defence of threatened identity.

The West exploited the importance of religious identity during the Cold War to defeat Marxism and the Soviet presence worldwide. In 1982, between 20,000 and 30,000 Muslims from all over the globe joined the war in Soviet-occupied Afghanistan, and indeed managed to make Soviet troops bleed and finally withdraw. This in reality marks the international origin of the Al-Qaeda organization and its 'Afghan Arabs' which immensely benefited from Saudi-Gulf funding and US training. But Al-Qaeda is not the only transnational group: the *Encyclopaedia of World Terrorism* lists no less than sixteen Islamic organizations and groups that have international objectives.

Before the events of 9/11, scholars usually focused on the domestic dimension of Islamic protest (Karawan 1997: 68). It is true that Islamized opposition movements can prosper in countries that are extremely different in per capita income, domestic political organization, and international orientation: as in Algeria, a paradigm of erstwhile Third World revolutionism; and in Saudi Arabia, an Islamic orthodox state. Socio-economic ills are certainly an important factor in the rise of Islamic opposition, but so are the threats to identity in an intrusive globalization context—hence the contradictory phenomenon of an Islamic opposition in an Islamic orthodox state.

But such underlying societal insecurity cannot be camouflaged forever and eventually has to come out in the political arena. In this situation, political conflict comes to the forefront and the legitimacy deficit increases, even in Saudi Arabia. Moreover, this opposition can spill beyond state borders. This is the case with the Afghan Arabs and Osama Bin Laden (deprived of his Saudi citizenship in 1994) who constituted an extreme and bloody example of uncivil society contesting global governance.

Consequently, at present many more scholars are in search of systematic evidence to emphasize the transnational dimension of Islamic cells as network actors. 'Network actors' refers to non-formal illegal and clandestine groups not necessarily tied to a state, and usually supported by a sophisticated financial network—*Hawalah* or financial transfer. Whether terrorist or not, they are increasingly part of the global civil society and since their funding and logistical networks cross borders, they are neither dependent on formal state interaction nor disrupted by economic sanctions. They have capitalized on available technologies to communicate quickly and securely. The root factor of the mushrooming of political Islam as a mobilization force lies in the legitimacy deficit of many regimes in this area and the increasing threats to identity by uncontrolled forces of globalization.

So-called domestic religio-politics, then, has international spill-over: for example, fifteen of the nineteen 9/11 hijackers were Saudi citizens. Attacks on tourists (e.g. Luxor, Egypt, 1997; Tunisia, 2015) are meant to embarrass governing regimes, threaten their economic base, and guarantee international visibility. While the West generally is identified as the distant enemy (as in the 2015 Charlie Hebdo attacks in Paris), the US and its citizens are usually the prime target. There is a wide range of examples, including the 1995 truck bombing of the National Guard headquarters in Riyadh which killed at least five US servicemen; the 1996 bombing of the Khobar Towers which killed nineteen US servicemen; the 1998 attacks on the US embassies in Kenya and Tanzania which left 257 dead and almost 6,000 injured; and of course, the 9/11 Al-Qaeda attacks against the World Trade Center and the Pentagon which killed almost 3,000 people. Al-Qaeda under the financial leadership of Bin Laden took the US as a major target because it incarnates the largest power in the region, because it has close ties with Israel, and because attacks on the US produce the most worldwide publicity, and act as a proxy for less popular attacks on Middle Eastern regimes.

In addition, we have witnessed the expansion of the activities of Al-Qaeda to reach countries such as Morocco and Algeria. For example, on 12 April 2007, a suicide bomber blew himself up beside the office of the Prime Minister in Algeria, killing twenty-three people and injuring 160. Previously, on 13 February 2007, at least six people were killed and thirteen injured in a series of bomb blasts targeting security forces in north-eastern Algeria. Bin-Laden's assassination notwithstanding, such attacks in Al-Maghreb or in the Arab Peninsula have been linked to Al-Qaeda, which has often claimed responsibility for them.

Al-Qaeda has offshoots in other parts of the MENA region, but Al-Qaeda seems to be eclipsed now by more home-grown Islamist organizations focusing on the 'near enemy': governing regimes. The most notable example is the so-called Islamic State, Daesh, or ISIS group. The group was formed by Abu Musab al-Zarqawi in 2000, pledging allegiance to Al-Qaeda and becoming a subset of it. This was until ISIS was disowned by Al-Qaeda in 2013, leaving the group Jabhat al-Nusra (JN) as the official Al-Qaeda affiliate in Syria. ISIS, which has now taken over parts of Iraq and Syria, ruling as an 'Islamic State', has also admitted to the 2015 Charlie Hebdo and November 13th attacks in Paris. It is clear that offshoots of Al-Qaeda are taking control of their own organizations and overriding the power of Al-Qaeda in their own regimes.

The primacy of change over Arab exceptionalism

In relation to this religio-politics, the most important result of the 'Arab Spring' is the opportunity it gave to Islamists to rule through elections. The 2012 Egyptian parliament had an Islamist two-thirds majority. Similarly in Tunisia, the Islamist El-Nahda party reached political power, and in Libya, Islamist political forces are in the making. Even the reform initiated by the royal palace in Morocco has led to a post-election Islamist-dominated government. In some respects then, the 'Arab Spring' thus became an Islamist Spring. But in international relations terms, such changes have not led to the rise of an Iranian-type foreign policy in any of these countries.

The region is, however, reflecting world patterns of change and transformation and defeating the stereotype of 'Arab exceptionalism'. Arab exceptionalism asserts that while the world is changing, this region—especially its authoritarian pattern—is not, but instead remains stagnant. This view is now denting, if not ending (Korany 2010). Whereas some constants will continue, both domestic governance and its regional environment are changing. As noted earlier, the LAS itself is reflecting some major aspects of this change. Its pro-active policy toward both Libya and Syria post-Arab Spring reflects a change in both initial conception and general behaviour across its seventy years of existence.

The LAS was established before the UN, but there was a certain ambiguity in its objectives. On the surface, it responded to the 'Pan-Arab' dream of 'one nation with one language' and it even seemed to embody this aspiration. In reality, however, the LAS is based on strict respect of the territorial Arab State and its traditional concept of state sovereignty. The content analysis of speeches and official statements at the time of its establishment show the primacy of protecting 'state sovereignty'. The forty-eight articles of its charter repeated this concern for state sovereignty no less than twenty-two times. Rhetoric aside, rules of voting and actual behaviour confirmed the primacy of the 'state' over the 'nation'.

In 2011, however, the LAS went out of its fossilized way and allied itself with the internationalization of domestic protests against some Arab regimes. Thus in the case of Libya, the LAS supported UN Security Council Resolution 1973 on the 'no-fly zone' and accepted NATO military action to enforce it. In Syria, the LAS's newly-elected Secretary General, El-Araby, met with the Syrian Transitional Council, sent Arab observers to Syria to supervise regime action against its people, and kept its seat empty rather than being occupied by the Asad regime. It finally supported international action to send former UN Secretary General, Kofi Annan, to Syria as a representative of the international community to censor regime actions. Thus in both Libya and Syria, the LAS sided with the internationalization of domestic revolts against their regimes—a noticeable game-changer compared to traditional LAS behaviour.

However, it is still too early to conclude that this behavioural change represents a transformation in LAS orientation and structure. What is certain is that this behavioural change reflects another case of power restructuring at the regional level—call it a Gulf moment. Indeed, since its establishment in 1945, the LAS mirrored—rather than triggered—the regional power structure and its different phases. Thus at its initiation, Cairo was chosen as its headquarters, which reflected Egypt's relative socio-political weight and especially the role of its monarchy as a balancer in the dynastic rivalry between Al-Saud and the Hashemites that ruled in Iraq and Jordan. The arrival of post-1952 Nasserism maintained this Egyptian hegemony but with a revolutionary flavour. The 1967 defeat in front of Israel indicated the decline of Egypt's hegemony—representing the revolutionary pole—and the rise instead of the 'conservative' political petrolism around Saudi Arabia. In fact, the Khartoum Arab Summit in November 1967 codified this transformation when Egypt and Syria had to accept petro-dollar subsidies in order to survive the loss of their territories by occupation and the closure of the Suez Canal and to consolidate resistance against Israel. The fourth Arab–Israeli war and the oil-embargo in 1973, leading to successive huge rise in oil prices and accumulation of petro-dollars, confirmed this power transformation at the regional level (for details, see Korany 2010, 2012). This power transformation, with an increasing emphasis on GCC regional hegemony, is making itself felt in the LAS and its actions toward Libya and Syria.

The Gulf's IR moment

In the countries that underwent regime change during the Arab Spring—Tunisia, Egypt, and Libya—the structural patterns of their international relations still continue. This continuity is less related to the change in domestic regimes than to the pattern of post-Cold War international politics. As this post-Cold War global system is much less polarized on ideological lines, major alternatives of alignment–realignment for new domestic regimes do not really exist. Some bilateral adjustments might take place, as in Tunisia which is more open to the US after the fall of Ben Ali's regime which had close French links. Or Egypt, bothered by US criticism of Cairo's human rights record, might strengthen relations with Moscow or Beijing. These are, however, tactical moves rather than strategic restructuring. A regime change in Syria, however, could lead to a different pattern. Such change could lead to a corresponding change in alliance patterns with present Iran and Lebanon's Hezbollah. Regional restructuring could follow.

A similar restructuring was initially deemed possible with the arrival of the Muslim Brotherhood in Egypt and its impact on what we can call the Camp David regional order. At the basis of Egyptian foreign policy and indeed the 'new Middle East' is the trilateral pattern of relations between Egypt, Israel, and the US, inspired by the 1978 Camp David Accords. These accords initiated a different 'international regime' in the region. The 1979 Peace Treaty between Egypt and Israel had profound effects on the Arab–Israeli conflict processes and opened the way for similar 'peace' arrangements, not least the 1982 Arab Peace Plan. Subsequently, in 1993, Israel and the PLO 'recognized' each other in the Oslo agreements, and in 1994, Jordan and Israel signed their own peace treaty. The years 1999–2000 witnessed, through Turkish mediation, peace negotiations between Israel and Syria. The Camp David accords were thus much more than pure bilateral relations between Israel and Egypt: they were a plan for a reorganization of the region.

With the establishment of the new regime in Egypt following the 2011 uprising, there was talk of amending the Egyptian-Israeli peace treaty, building on public opinion in favour of revision during the Mubarak regime. In fact, the Mubarak regime was taken to the supreme constitutional court by some Egyptian activists. They accused the government of exporting oil and/or gas to Israel far below world prices and asked for either fair prices or stoppage of these exports. They won their case, but despite this (and the significant pressure of public opinion), the exports continued. This governmental resistance and its lack of transparency increased mistrust about the hidden part of the Egyptian-Israeli 'partnership'. As a mirror of this public mistrust, gas pipe-lines to Israel (and Jordan) were blown up thirteen times in the year following the regime's overthrow. Consequently, demands for revision of the 1979 Egyptian/Israeli Treaty were bound to increase, with a potential impact on the Camp David order involving US policy in the region. The Muslim Brotherhood, however, stayed in power for just one year, and did not show a clear tendency to re-open the Camp David order chapter during this period.

In fact, the impact of the global system—especially global financial institutions—will continue and even intensify in the wake of the Arab Spring. Many of the countries that saw regime changes are economically bruised. For instance, more than 10 per cent of the economies of both Tunisia and Egypt were dependent on tourism, but tourism has declined by more than 60 per cent. The same applies to foreign direct investments. Even in a country that did not go through protracted mass protests or civil war, such as Bahrain, the economy has suffered: Bahrain's stock exchange declined by 20.15 per cent by the end of 2011, while the level of investments declined by 28.8 per cent that year (*Khaleej News*, 20 March 2012). As a result, the need for financial support from Arab and/or Western sources will be sorely felt. Voices have been raised for the elaboration of a 'Marshall Plan' to help democratic transition reach its destination. This financial need explains the rise of the GCC led by Saudi Arabia. The GCC seems intent on buying a certain political order. Press reports estimated that Saudi and UAE financial contributions to support the post-Muslim Brotherhood government in Egypt amounted to $20–25 billion over the 2012–14 period. At the time of writing, Saudi Arabia, under a new king, is going beyond a reactive foreign policy towards a pro-active one. After leading GCC military forces in Bahrain in 2012, it has championed operation 'Decisive Storm' in Yemen.

The fluid post-Arab Spring context is affecting Arab/non-Arab interactions. This chapter has alluded repeatedly to the case of Iran, whether in relation to Bahrain, Syria, or Yemen. Turkey is also increasingly involved in regional affairs, from the Arab–Israeli issue to inter-Arab affairs, to having a major say in the evolution of the Iraqi and Syrian systems. Turkey is filling a regional power vacuum driven by Arab fragmentation and turbulence. Moreover, it is increasingly looked at in the post-Arab Spring context as a potential model of a successful combination of Islamic identity and democratic rule. In addition, it is referred to as an example of how to manage civil–military relations, an element of heightened tension in post-Muslim Brotherhood Egypt where the military are in the driver's seat.

Conclusion: which direction the Middle East?

Given the one-dimensional nature of the Gulf moment, this question is still valid and indeed is all the more applicable after so many seismic changes in the region. The Arab Spring has witnessed the rise and demise of new political actors, the proliferation of non-state actors, GCC regional assertion amidst problems of generational succession, and on-and-off discussion of Iran's denuclearization. The Middle East political space is over-crowded with actors and factors in an extremely fluid environment of shifting alliances where elements of change and continuity are closely-entangled and constantly evolving.

In addition to the conventional impact of external factors and traditional insecurity issues, newer security questions maintain their primacy on the region's international relations. These include socio-economic factors, such as the demographic bomb and its impact on such social sectors as education or unemployment; religio-politics and its multiple regional and international consequences; and the yawning gap between ageing-ailing leaderships and the increasingly young population. Another factor of note is the important role of IT and its impact on social mobilization, as discussed in **Chapter 15**.

If these triggers of change are not managed, we might see an increase in the number of 'soft' or even 'failed' states, especially during the post-protest transition period and before a new system replaces the *ancien regime*. During this fluid period and until rules of democratic process are internalized, rising political forces face each other in an almost Hobbesian environment. A period of political instability and social tension is bound to persist.

Contrary to a conventional view of international relations focused primarily on traditional 'high politics' or military–diplomatic interactions, this chapter has consistently emphasized issues of so-called 'low politics' and socio-economic threats, which are conceived here as the basic infrastructure of International Relations. In retrospect, these proved to be at the root of the seismic changes that took place in 2011, becoming indeed the new 'high politics'. Despite the discipline's inherent bias to emphasize 'high politics' and inter-state diplomatic interactions, the chapter's emphasis has been a plea for an emphasis on socio-political dynamics, international relations from below, or 'low politics' becoming the new high politics. These socio-political dynamics shape what we see 'above' in interstate diplomatic interactions, whether routine and peaceful or crisis-laden and violent.

Further proof of this can be found in the example of the water resource gap in a barren region and potential 'water wars'. They heighten tension at present between Egypt and Ethiopia, due to the latter's building of the El-Nahda dam and its potential impact on Egypt's Nile water quota. In fact, the decline of water per capita in MENA is far greater than the world average. Whereas between 1960 and 1990, world decline was 43 per cent and by 2025 the decline is estimated to be 64 per cent, the respective figures for MENA are more serious. They are: for Jordan 58 per cent and 83 per cent; for Yemen 54 per cent and 75 per cent; for Iran 63 per cent and 82 per cent; for Iraq 64 per cent and 86 per cent; for Oman 67 per cent and 90 per cent; for Libya 71 per cent and 90 per cent, for Saudi Arabia 71 per cent and 91 per cent, and for the UAE 94 per cent and 96 per cent. Ominous as they are, these figures may be rather conservative since real population increase could be more than has been factored in. Indeed World Bank/OECD statistics for 2010 show population growth in the Middle East to be among the highest in the world (IEA 2010).

Moreover, a major part of MENA lives divided in time due to the invasion of IT, satellite TV, and especially the Internet. In 2014, the number of Internet users in the Arab world reached 135,610,819 (roughly one-third of the total population) with a penetration percentage of 35.8 per cent. This is compared to a world average of 39 per cent. Additionally, Facebook usage in 2012 was 45,805,180 (Internet World Statistics 2014). With increasing efforts to introduce computers in schools, these figures are perhaps too modest.

Issues like those of water and the impact of IT cannot be settled by routine conflict management. They raise the issue of socio-economic change given the region's double problem of ageing leadership but youthful population. In 2011, Egypt's Mubarak had been in power for thirty years, and the revolutionary Gadhafi for forty-one years. Syria, Morocco, and Jordan had their succession in place when their leaders died: Asad senior after thirty-one years, Hassan II after forty years, and Hussein after forty-seven years. It was a process of pure political inheritance with sons replacing fathers. But no major socio-political restructuring has taken place in these systems until now and the future remains uncertain. Although democratically confirmed in 1996, Palestine's Arafat also remained in power for forty years before he died in 2003. Before his death, he faced increasing marginalization under pressure from the Israelis and the Americans.

Religio-politics will also impact on the type and direction of change in the region. The present debate is about which pattern of religio-politics will shape the future direction of the region and its place in the world. Will it be the orthodox Saudi/Salafi-type increasingly under fire both internally and externally? Will it be the Iranian revolutionary type, increasingly factionalized between reformers and radicals, a factionalization that goes against any monolithic view of 'political Islam'? Will it be the Turkish type, attempting to combine Islam and Western democracy? Or will it resemble the restrictive pluralism of regimes in Jordan, Kuwait, or Morocco which continue to experiment with finding the appropriate formula to satisfy internal pressures and external aid donors?

Although it was domestically-focused and driven, the 'Arab Spring' has been a real game-changer, with consequences both regionally and globally, separating the 'before' and 'after'. It is yet another demonstration of *intermestics*, this organic linkage between the international and domestic elements. However, the domestic/regional situation continues to be fluid, making teasing out patterns as difficult as shooting at a moving target. The prevalence of seismic change and intermestics are adding to regional complexity. However, some patterns are already discernible:

1. The notion of 'Arab exceptionalism' is increasingly challenged if not ending altogether, even if forces of transformation suffer setbacks and elements of continuity persist (for example the Arab–Israeli conflict, and Iran's self-assertion).

2. The MENA state, although still authoritarian and even fierce, is increasingly fragile. In addition to traditional shifting alliances, new political actors—tribal, religious, or generational (e.g. youth with their new media tools) are crowding the public political space.

3. Whereas the Middle East environment continues to be conflictual, some long-term conflicts, such as the Arab–Israeli conflict are being momentarily outranked.

4. Regional rather than global powers are contesting for regional leadership and their interactions tend to shape the MENA environment. In addition to traditional aspirers such as Egypt, Iran, Israel, or Turkey, the GCC and specifically Saudi Arabia are becoming self-assertive, even militarily.

5. Change—often uncontrolled—is the order of the day. Even a fossilized regional organization such as the LAS—as shown—is feeling the winds of change and is adopting new international postures in Libya and Syria.

'Intermestics' has thus continued to characterize the Middle East since the end of the Cold War. In this organic internal/external interconnectedness, the region could be a learning laboratory for the different social sciences. For instance, dominant international relations theory should moderate its focus on states and regimes, on diplomatic history and obsession with top chancelleries, to analyse the impact of action 'from below', and decode its influence on patterns of state rise and demise. Through the literature, I have drawn up an inventory of various factors of instability, including new or socio-political threats: for example the youth bulge; unemployment; religio-politics; identity; non-state actors; and potential 'water wars'. These conflicts will intensify given the yawning resource gap. These infrastructural aspects of international relations, notably an accumulation of deficits—economic, political, and social—will make the distinction between internal and external crises or cooperation even harder to discern.[6]

Key events

| 1987 | Palestinian intifada begins |
| 1988 | Iran–Iraq War ends |

1990	Cold War ends
	Iraq invades Kuwait
1991	Gulf War
	Madrid Conference initiates Arab–Israel peace process
1994–97	Regional economic conferences in Casablanca, Amman, Cairo, and Doha
1995	Assassination of Israeli Prime Minister Yitzhak Rabin
1999	Death of King Hussein of Jordan (succeeded by Abdullah II)
2000	Death of Syrian President Hafiz al-Asad (succeeded by Bashar al-Asad)
	Camp David summit, the failure of which marks end of the peace process
2001	9/11 terrorist bombings of US targets in New York and Washington
	US initiates attacks on Afghanistan
2002	US President Bush delivers 'axis of evil' speech
2003	US invasion of Iraq begins
	'Road map' launched for an Israel–Palestine settlement
2004	Death of Yasser Arafat
2005	Assassination of Lebanese Prime Minister Rafiq Hariri
2006	Hamas wins in Palestinian elections
	Israel–Hezbollah War in Lebanon
2007	Annapolis Conference, Maryland
2008–09	Gaza War (Israel–Hamas)
2010	Start of 'Arab Spring'
2011	Regime change in Tunisia, Egypt, Libya, and Yemen
2014	Gaza conflict (Israel–Hamas)
2015	Charlie Hebdo and subsequent attacks in Paris
	P5+1 Agreement on Iran's nuclear programme

Further reading

An important characteristic of recent MENA literature are contributions by scholars publishing in their own 'native' languages and the rise of *Gulf-based think-tanks*. For Arab readers, *The Arab Strategic Yearbook* (Al-Ahram Centre of Political and Strategic Studies, Cairo) is both solid and balanced in its analyses as is CAUS: State of the Arab Nation. *El-Siasa El-Dawliyya* (*International Politics Quarterly*, Cairo), *El-Democratiyya* (Cairo) and *El-Mustaqbal El-Arabi* (*Arab Future*, Beirut, monthly) provide a wealth of information. From Tel-Aviv, *Middle East Survey* though no longer publishing, has good chronological analysis. Among newspapers, *Al-Hayat* (daily, London) and *Al-Ahram Weekly* offer good coverage and reliable analysis.

Brynen, R. C. et al. (2013) *Beyond the Arab Spring* (Boulder, CO: Lynne Rienner)

A lucid build-up on the original liberalization/democratization analyses of the 1990s confronted with the transitions of the 2011 context.

El-Suwaidy, G. and El-Safty, A. (eds) (2014) *Islamic Political Movements and Authority in the Arab World* (Abu Dhabi: ECSSR)
Solid comparative analyses by well-established experts in the region.

Gerges, F. (ed.) (2014) *The New Middle East* (Cambridge: Cambridge University Press)
Seasoned analysts move between International Relations and Comparative Politics to dissect the Arab Spring as a milestone.

Heydemann, S. (ed.) (2000) *War, Institutions and Social Change in the Middle East* (Berkley & London: University of California Press)
One of the few analyses on the region that goes beyond analysing war as an interstate phenomenon and integrates it with wider national and regional dynamics.

Kamrava, M. (ed.) (2014) *Beyond the Arab Spring* (Oxford: Oxford University Press)
A well-conceived collection, coherently-designed around the concept of political bargaining. Based on fieldwork by most of the authors.

Kadhim, A. (ed.) (2014) *Governance in MENA* (London and New York: Routledge)
The most recent book on an aspect that is still under-researched.

Korany, B. (ed.) (2010) *The Changing ME* (Cairo & New York: American University in Cairo Press)
Almost foretelling the Arab Spring, emphasizing limitations of status-quo approaches and issuing a wake-up call about forces of change.

Korany, B. (ed.) (2014) *Arab Human Development in the 21st Century* (Cairo and New York: American University in Cairo Press)
Designed and written as the tenth anniversary volume of the well-established Arab Human Development series by UNDP. It analyses new issues such as inter-Arab conflicts and the role of religious education.

Sifry, M., and Cerf, C. (eds) (2003) *The Iraq War Reader* (New York and London: Simon and Schuster)
An excellent collection of historical documents and political analyses with appendices.

Tessler, M., Nachtwa, J., and Banda, A. (eds) (1999) *Area Studies and Social Science: Strategies for Understanding Middle East Politics* (Bloomington and Indianapolis: Indiana University Press)
A credible effort to combine general concepts and specific cases in decoding the region's different facets.

Questions

1. Why did the end of the Cold War not see the beginning of 'long peace' in the Middle East?

2. Rather than being separate, so-called 'high' and 'low' politics in the ME are dialectical and interactive. Explain using examples.

3. Has the 'Arab Spring' failed? Debate its balance sheet and challenges. Is it really 'good to be a monarchy' in the region?

4. Briefly trace 'Arab/non-Arab' relations and explain the changing pattern of regional conflicts.

5. The Middle East could be described today as history moving fast forward. Identify some of the principal features explaining this change.

Endnotes

1. Though Darby talks about International Relations (IR) as a 'Disabling Discipline?' (with a question mark) and D. Blaney and N. Inayatullah favour 'IR from Below', they do not go far enough. See Reus-Smit and Duncan Snidel (eds), *The Oxford Handbook of IR* (Oxford: Oxford University Press, 2008), pp. 994–105 and 663–74, respectively. Established IR is deficient in what Sadiki calls in his chapter the 'peoplehood approach'. For my analysis of the impact of 'IR from below' on Pan-Arabism, see B. Korany, 'The Arab Spring, the New Pan-Arabism and the Challenges of Transition'; and for a much more critical approach of 'ME studies from above', see B. Korany and Rabab El-Mahdi, 'The Protesting ME', both in B. Korany and R. El-Mahdi (eds) *Arab Spring in Egypt: Revolution and Beyond* (Cairo and New York: American University in Cairo Press 2012), pp. 271–94 and 7–16, respectively.

2. The critique of militarized 'strategic studies' and the development of an alternative 'human security' approach is now becoming widespread. For an early critical assessment, B. Korany 'Strategic Studies and the Third World', *International SocialScience Journal* 38 (1986): 547–62. An application of human security is in the UNDP 5th Arab Human Development Report (AHDR): *Challenges to Human Security in the Arab Countries* (New York: UNDP, 2009). An important aspect about the relative decline of interstate wars in relation to other forms of violence are the research findings on terrorism. According to the Global Terrorism Index (GTI 2015), since 2000 there has been more than a five-fold increase in the number of people killed by terrorism.

3. According to *Foreign Policy Magazine* (19 May 2015) at least 51,000 people reached Europe while more than 1,800 drowned in the Mediterranean.

4. As far as I am aware the neologism 'intermestics' was first used in the 1990s by a colleague from Singapore in discussing trade relations, but without any conceptual content or general application. Relatedly, the debate on the relative weight of 'domestic' vs 'international' or external determinants in both MENA and Third World Studies generally has been long since it started in the 1960s/1970s on 'Modernization' vs 'Dependancy' theories. The controversy has been over-played by each side, using almost zero-sum terms rather than mutual interaction between a crisis-laden governance realm and an exploiting or 'multiplier' effect by outside forces. See B. Korany (ed.), *Arab Human Development in the 21st Century* (Cairo and New York: American University in Cairo Press, 2014), especially pp. 3–19 (the Arabic edition is published by the Center for Unity Studies, Beirut).

5. For a detailed analysis of the four high-level economic conferences to substantiate 'peace dividends', to integrate Israel and promote regional interdependence, please refer to this chapter in the 1st and 2nd editions for details.

6. For my assessment of IR as a discipline and its neglect of 'infrastructural' aspects, see my acceptance speech of the Global South Scholar Award of the International Studies Association, ISA 56 Annual Convention, New Orleans, 20 February 2015, http://gscis.blogspot.com/2015/05/remarks-of-distinguished-scholar.html

Part 2

Themes in International Relations and International Political Economy

Oil and Political Economy in the International Relations of the Middle East

GIACOMO LUCIANI

Overview

Oil and oil-related interests have had, and continue to have, a profound influence on the political economy of the Middle East—domestically, as well as from the point of view of international relations. Indeed, it is often difficult to resist the temptation to conclude that practically everything is related, conditioned, and justified by oil; hence the widespread, yet simplistic and essentially erroneous, 'conspiracy theory', according to which the 'black gold' is the only value that matters. The aim of this chapter is to offer a synthetic, yet balanced, view of the impact of oil—presenting the multiple ways in which oil has shaped the recent history of the Middle East, but also making it clear that oil is not the only relevant explanatory variable.

Introduction

Oil is commonly considered a political commodity. Because of its pivotal importance as a primary source of energy, governments are concerned with its continued availability and seek to minimize import dependence.

In fact, whether oil deserves to be considered a political commodity is debatable. For the past century or longer, oil has been in abundant supply, and the leading industrial players—the major international oil companies in the past; the Organization of the Petroleum Exporting Countries (OPEC) producers today—have been primarily concerned with avoiding excess supply and a consequent collapse in prices. Tightness in global oil supplies became the dominant narrative around the turn of the century, but the exponential increase in US shale oil production eventually reversed global perceptions in this respect, leading to a collapse of oil prices in the second half of 2014.

Indeed, estimates of global proved oil reserves have systematically increased over the past two decades, passing from 1.04 to 1.69 trillion barrels between 1993 and 2013. The definition of proved reserves requires that oil should be commercially recoverable from such reserves, meaning that they are also a function of oil prices: evidently the increase also reflects the fact that reserves which were not deemed to be commercially viable in 1993 became viable due to the increase in oil prices. The geographical distribution of proved reserves has also changed: the share of the Middle East has declined from 64 to 48 per cent of the total, while the share of Latin America has increased from 8 to 20 per cent, that of North America from 12 to 19 per cent, and that of Africa from 6 to 8 per cent. Today the country claiming the largest proved reserves is Venezuela. Saudi Arabia, which used to be in first position, is now second and it is followed by Canada. Iran, Iraq, Kuwait, and the UAE, which used to immediately follow Saudi Arabia, have correspondingly fallen back in the list.

For about three decades, from the 1930s to the 1960s, control of large oil reserves—notably in the Middle East—allowed a small group of international oil companies to reap extraordinary profits. Governments at the time may have been justified in making sure that such profits were preserved or bypassed, depending on whether the international oil companies were national or foreign. Since 1973, it has been the governments of the OPEC countries—and of those non-OPEC producers that benefit from the fact that OPEC keeps prices high—that have reaped extraordinary rents from oil. Prices, however, have not been steadily high, but followed three long cycles: a high-price period from 1973 to 1985; a lower price phase between 1985 and 2003 (with a short-lived price rally in 1990, due to Iraq's invasion of Kuwait); and a second high-price episode between 2004 and 2014.

Apart from rents generated because Middle East oil is generally cheap to produce, control of oil reserves or logistics has not entailed special political or military benefits, and conversely the lack of such control has not exposed individual countries to special costs. Oil is essentially allocated through the market, not through power and appropriation; and the logistics of international oil flows have repeatedly proven to be flexible and highly reliable.

Nevertheless, the Middle East plays a special role in the international oil industry (see **Table 5.1**). Five Gulf producers possess 46 per cent of the world's proven oil reserves. Their oil is by far the cheapest to produce, and if oil were a competitive industry, they would probably be the almost-exclusive source of world oil. However, because oil is not a competitive industry, the Middle Eastern producers' share of global production has been kept low—well below their share in global reserves. Over the years, this has been especially true of Iraq, this being both a cause and a consequence of Iraq's difficult relations with the rest of the world.

Figure 5.1 illustrates the evolution of production from the major Gulf countries. Iran was the first country in the Gulf to become an oil exporter and retained pride of place until 1950. That year, the controversy between the company controlling all Iranian production—the

Table 5.1 Proven oil reserves, Middle East and North Africa, end 2014

Country	Barrels (1,000 m)	Share of world total (%)
Middle East		
Iran	157.0	9.3
Iraq	150.0	8.9
Kuwait	101.5	6.0
Oman	5.5	0.3
Qatar	25.1	1.5
Saudi Arabia	265.9	15.8
Syria	2.5	0.1
United Arab Emirates	97.8	5.8
Yemen	3.0	0.2
Other Middle East	0.3	–
Total	*808.5*	*47.9*
North Africa		
Algeria	12.2	0.7
Egypt	3.9	0.2
Libya	48.5	2.9
Tunisia	0.4	–
Total	*65.0*	*3.8*

Source: BP (2015)

Anglo-Iranian Oil Company—and the nationalist government of Iranian Prime Minister Muhammad Mussadiq erupted. Following the nationalization of Anglo-Iranian, all international oil companies boycotted Iranian oil; production collapsed to almost nothing in 1952 and 1953, and recovered only after the coup that overthrew Mussadiq and the formation of the Iranian Consortium, in which Anglo-Iranian's share was reduced to 40 per cent.

Production in Iraq started in 1928, but remained low because of a long-lasting controversy between the Iraq Petroleum Company (IPC) and the Iraqi government. Saudi Arabia began producing in 1938, but its production was constrained during the war and took off only after 1945. Kuwaiti production began only in 1946, but grew very rapidly; by 1953, it had already overtaken Saudi production. The production of all three countries—Iraq, Saudi Arabia, and Kuwait—increased rapidly to compensate for the collapse of Iranian production in 1951–54, but while Saudi and Kuwaiti productions remained high, Iraq's declined.

- Kuwaiti production reached a maximum of 3 million barrels per day in 1973 and then declined. It was reduced to almost zero by the Iraqi invasion in 1991, but has since recovered.

- Iranian production peaked in 1974 and declined precipitously after the revolution in 1979. It continued to decline after the onset of the Iran–Iraq War in 1980, but recovered after the war ended in 1988. More recently, it has been affected by sanctions due to Iran's nuclear fuel enrichment policy.

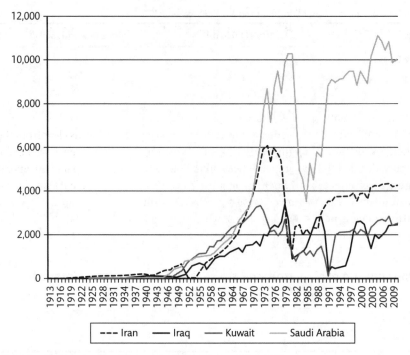

Figure 5.1 Historical production of four main Gulf producers, 1913–2010

Source: 1913–64: OPEC Annual Statistical Bulletin 2005; 1965–2010: BP Statistical Review of World Energy 2011

- Iraqi production peaked in 1979, before the war with Iran. It recovered in the final stages of the war, but collapsed again when Kuwait was invaded in 1990. It recovered once more under the United Nations Oil-for-Food Programme, only to collapse again in 2003, when the Coalition invaded and occupied the country. Since then, it has recovered slowly.

- Saudi Arabia's production peaked in 1980, when it had to compensate for the loss of Iranian and Iraqi oil. It then declined precipitously until 1985, when the kingdom was playing the role of the world's swing producer. Having abandoned that posture, production recovered gradually and averaged around 9 million barrels per day throughout the 1990s. In the last decade, it increased further as Riyadh attempted to resist the excessive increase in prices and compensate for shortfalls from other regional producers due to political upheaval.

In discussing the Middle East, oil is inescapable. It has influenced the region's relations with the rest of the world—notably, the great powers. It has influenced relations within the region, because it is not uniformly distributed; on the contrary, it is highly concentrated, creating a very distinctive polarization between 'oil haves' and 'oil have-nots'. It has also influenced the domestic politics of the Arab countries, allowing the consolidation of regimes that, in the absence of the oil rent, would probably not have survived to the twenty-first century.

Oil and the consolidation of the Middle Eastern state system

The presence of oil in the Middle East has had a crucial influence on the consolidation of the regional state system. Interest in Middle Eastern oil focused initially on Kirkuk—then part of the Ottoman vilayet of Mosul—and southern Persia, and was already active at the turn of the twentieth century. Oil was discovered in Persia in 1908 (Stocking 1970: 8–14; Yergin 1991: 135–49), and the involvement of the UK imperial government was clear from the start (Stocking 1970: 14–22; Yergin 1991: 150–64). Winston Churchill, then First Lord of the Admiralty, decided that the imperial fleet should be converted from coal to oil, and argued for direct government involvement by acquiring a controlling interest in Anglo-Persian—as Anglo-Iranian was then named—as a way in which to guarantee cheaper supplies to the fleet. The strategic interest in oil, at a time when none of today's Gulf states (other than Persia) could be said to exist, was already quite obvious.

Oil, the collapse of the Ottoman Empire, and British imperial interests

Oil interests fundamentally shaped British policy in the Gulf, first emphasizing freedom of navigation and later guaranteeing the independent existence of the 'trucial states', as they were called at the time, against the momentum of Saudi expansionism.

Oil was also a major factor in the shaping of states that emerged from the collapse of the Ottoman Empire. However, interest in the political control of oil reserves was not uniformly shared: it continued to be a quintessentially British objective to which other powers did not give the same importance. After the First World War, the San Remo Conference attributed to the United Kingdom the mandate of a newly formed country called 'Iraq', composed of the three Ottoman vilayets of Mosul, Baghdad, and Basra. Previously, the Sykes–Picot Agreement had attributed Mosul to France, but the latter surrendered that choice morsel and was content with a minority participation in the IPC, the producing consortium that acquired a concession to Kirkuk oil.

The political rationale behind the composition of the IPC shareholding group is obvious, especially when we take into account the evolution from its early version—the Turkish Petroleum Company, which Calouste Gulbenkian sponsored before the war, and which included German and Italian interests—to its final shape (47.5 per cent to British companies; another 47.5 per cent equally divided between American and French companies; the remaining 5 per cent to Gulbenkian) (Stocking 1970: 41–6; Yergin 1991: 184–206).

Not all UK policies in the Middle East were a function of its oil interests. The Balfour Declaration, which was to have such a momentous impact on the future of the region, was certainly not conceived in connection with oil; nor was British support to the Hashemite revolt, later contradicted by the Sykes–Picot Agreement; nor was its acquiescence to the expansionary policies of Abdul Aziz ibn Saud, which led to the disappearance of the Hashemite Kingdom of Hijaz and the formation of contemporary Saudi Arabia. Contemporary British oil interests simply completely overlooked the possibility that Saudi Arabia might have significant oil deposits and were not interested in seeking a concession there, thus opening the door to a total parvenu on the scene, Standard Oil of California. The United States quickly filled in any space that the UK had left unoccupied and thus contributed to the consolidation of some of the region's states, Saudi Arabia first and foremost (Stocking 1970: 66–107; Yergin 1991: 280–92).

Oil production in the Gulf before 1972 was controlled by producing companies, or consortia within which the major international oil companies cooperated in a web of interlocking interests (see **Table 5.2**). Producing consortia held huge concessions and frequently were the only producers in the country, thus commanding enormous bargaining power vis-à-vis the national government. The company with the largest reserves in the Gulf by far was Anglo-Iranian. It changed its name to 'British Petroleum' following Mussadiq's nationalization and is today's BP. The cornerstone of the system, however, was IPC. Five of the eight major international companies were present in IPC, equity in which was carefully divided between British interests (represented equally by Anglo-Iranian and Royal Dutch-Shell), American interests (represented equally by Standard Oil New Jersey—one of the companies issued from the break-up of John D. Rockefeller's Standard Oil in 1911, later known as Esso Oil Company, and today as ExxonMobil, after its merger with the latter—and Mobil—previously known as Standard Oil Company of New York, or SOCONY, another offspring of Standard Oil), and French interests (represented by the *Compagnie Française des Pétroles*; today's Total). The internal rules of IPC were designed to discourage competition between the IPC partners in the downstream markets as well as upstream elsewhere in the region. The partners were bound by the Red Line Agreement not to enter into any other producing venture in the former Ottoman Empire except in the same combination as in IPC. Hence many other producing consortia—notably Abu Dhabi onshore—exactly mimic the composition of IPC. Kuwait, however, which was not considered to have been part of the Ottoman Empire, allowed Anglo-Iranian to take 50 per cent of the concession, sharing it with Gulf Oil (an American company later taken over by Chevron). Saudi Arabia, on the other hand, *was* part of the Ottoman Empire, and the IPC partners showed no interest in acquiring a concession there; consequently, it went to Standard Oil of California (or SoCal, another Standard Oil offshoot; today, Chevron), which discovered oil alone, but was taken aback by

Table 5.2 Composition of major producing consortia in the Middle East before 1972 (%)

Consortium	Kuwait Oil Company (KOC)	Iraq Oil Company (IPC)	Arabian American Oil Company (ARAMCO)	Abu Dhabi Marine Areas (ADMA)	Iranian Consortium
British Petroleum	50	23.750		66.6	40
Royal Dutch Shell		23.750			14
Standard Oil New Jersey		11.875	30		7
Standard Oil California			30		7
Texaco			30		7
Mobil		11.875	10		7
Gulf	50				7
CFP		23.750		33.3	6
Others		5.000			5

Source: Adapted from Penrose (1967)

the magnitude of its discovery and started looking for partners, with the active participation of the US State Department—which at some point even considered taking a direct interest (Anderson 1981), much as the British government had a direct interest in Anglo-Iranian. SoCal brought in first its regional partner Texaco, in a joint venture called Caltex (today, Chevron and Texaco are merged in a single company); later, it also brought in Standard Oil New Jersey and Mobil.

The Iranian Consortium was formed after the 1953 coup that overthrew the Mussadiq government and paved the way for the return of the Shah (the US Central Intelligence Agency had been instrumental in orchestrating the coup). Anglo-Iranian, the original sole concession holder, maintained a 40 per cent interest, but had to surrender the rest to Royal Dutch Shell (14 per cent, so that British interests still controlled a majority) and various American companies. (It is at this point that Anglo-Iranian changed its name to British Petroleum.) The system collapsed after 1972, when most producing companies were nationalized.

Although the Truman administration finally decided against acquiring an equity stake in SoCal's Saudi concession, the keen interest of the US in Middle Eastern oil affairs is demonstrated by its insistence in obtaining an American participation in IPC and in the Iranian consortium. But the predominant US interest has always been towards Saudi Arabia, ever since the almost mythical meeting between President Roosevelt and King Abdulaziz on 14 February 1945, on board a US ship anchored in the Bitter Lakes, along the Suez Canal (Bronson 2006).

The US–Saudi alliance is, at the same time, an immutable pillar of regional international relations, second only to the relationship between the US and Israel, and a source of recurrent frustrations for both sides. Ever since the 1970s, successive US administrations have proclaimed the objective of making the US independent of Middle East oil—just as US oil import dependence has been increasing. Most notably, US oil imports from Saudi Arabia have been decreasing over the years (see **Figure 5.2**), and the boom in non-conventional oil

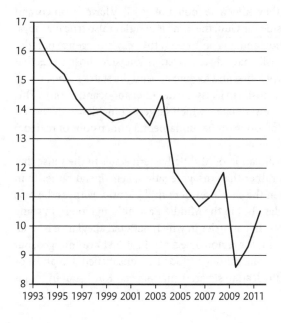

Figure 5.2 US imports from Saudi Arabia as a percentage of the total

Source: US Energy Information Administration (2011)

production in Canada and the US since the mid-2000s has led to the suggestion that North America might be independent of net oil imports by 2035 (IEA 2011; BP 2012). This leaves Israeli security the only compelling motivation for continuing active US involvement in Middle East affairs.

Oil and Middle Eastern boundaries

As we look at today's political map of the region, we find that oil has had little influence in determining boundaries and state structures within the former French mandate (that is, Syria and Lebanon) or in the Mediterranean portion of the British mandate (that is, Jordan and the Palestinian–Israeli conundrum). It has, however, had a fundamental influence in shaping the boundaries and independent existence of all other states in the Middle East.

The British action that stopped Saudi expansionism to the north (towards Iraq) and to the east (towards the trucial states) was clearly dictated by the wish to see the region subdivided into several, competing states, avoiding excessive concentration of powers and resources in the hands of a single state (the old Roman strategy, divide and rule). This can be understood only in the light of oil interests, and the need to maintain control of oil resources through diversity and competition. We can speculate what the political map of the Gulf might have looked like in the absence of oil, but most historians would agree that the United Arab Emirates (UAE), Qatar, Bahrain, and possibly even Kuwait would not have survived as independent entities without their oil.

It is possible that even Saudi Arabia would not have survived. The third Saudi state, established by King Abdul Aziz, would have had a hard time consolidating itself purely on the basis of revenue from the pilgrimage (hajj) and domestic taxation of an extremely poor population. It is oil that allowed the consolidation of the Saudi state, providing sufficient financial resources to pay for a modern state bureaucracy and eliminating the urge to conquer in order to replenish empty coffers. Similarly, it is oil money that has allowed the Gulf emirates to develop modern state structures, of which they otherwise could not possibly have dreamed, and to establish themselves on the map. Outside the Gulf, the same is certainly also true for Libya.

In short, oil has led to the consolidation and, in some cases, the very emergence of independent states—that otherwise might easily have disappeared—alongside those states that have deeper roots in history, such as Egypt—first and foremost—and the states in the French sphere of influence (Morocco, Algeria, Tunisia, to a lesser extent Lebanon, and Syria).[1] This dichotomy between the older and the newer states, which largely coincides with the 'oil haves' and the 'oil have-nots', has come to be one of the fundamental dimensions of regional and international relations of the Middle East.

Oil was also instrumental in the consolidation of Middle Eastern states in the sense that it predominantly favoured aggregation rather than disaggregation, centripetal rather than centrifugal forces. The same has not been the case elsewhere in the world: witness the case of Biafra[2] and, more recently, South Sudan. But in the Middle East, although oil is, in some cases, the prerogative of one region only—in countries in which national allegiance is weak and regional allegiance is strong—demands for regional decentralization have emerged, but no truly separatist temptations. Although one cannot exclude that unsatisfied demands for greater regional autonomy may eventually lead to separatism, not even Kurdistan in Iraq is currently interested in secession.

Finally, oil has been instrumental in encouraging the definition of boundaries and accepting international arbitration in contested cases. The definition of boundaries has frequently been a successive stage to mutual acceptance and recognition. The potential for finding oil has been an incentive to adopt a tougher negotiating stance, but at the same time also to seek a speedy resolution. This has been the case in the Gulf (between Bahrain and Qatar; Qatar, the UAE, and Saudi Arabia; Saudi Arabia and Yemen; and so on), as well as elsewhere (for example, between Libya and Tunisia). The problem of oil fields straddling across boundaries (for example, between Qatar and Iran, Iraq and Kuwait, and Libya and Algeria) was not eliminated and, in most cases, such trans-boundary fields continue to be independently exploited on the two sides of the frontier, because the solution based on unitization and condominiums has not taken root. The original 'neutral zones' between Kuwait and Saudi Arabia, and between Iraq and Saudi Arabia, have been divided up, further demonstrating a preference for clear division over joint exploitation. Although Iraq mentioned Kuwait's pumping of oil, which Iraqis claimed to be theirs, as a reason for invading Kuwait, it would be difficult to argue that this was an important, even less a determinant, reason. So far, potential conflict over the sharing of common resources has not erupted, leading at most to competition in developing each country's side of the field more rapidly. In contrast, several non-oil-related boundary conflicts have not been resolved, one suspects primarily because neither side has a strong interest in resolving them. In this sense, and possibly counter-intuitively, oil has contributed to the peaceful solution of boundary conflicts rather than to their exacerbation.

This conclusion runs contrary to the main thrust of a large body of literature that has argued that an abundance of oil (or other valuable resources) is frequently associated with conflicts (Collier and Hoeffler 2004; Solingen 2007; Ross 2012). Certainly, the Middle East has witnessed, and continues to witness, multiple conflicts, both inter- and intra-state, and large-scale bloodshed. However, the connection with oil has rarely been proven: oil-related interests may, at best, be a supporting cause to the onset of violence. Oil, however, certainly plays a role in the duration of conflict, because it gives one or both belligerents the means for extending the fight in time and it discourages compromise.

Oil and the international relations of the Middle East

Oil is a very important factor in the international relations of the Middle Eastern states, both with respect to regional, or inter-Arab, relations and with respect to international relations at large—that is, relations with industrial and other developing countries.

The West and Arab oil

It is quite evident, and amply documented in the historical literature, that preoccupation with oil has been paramount in shaping the attitude of the UK, and later the US, towards the region. We have noted this already in relation to the formation of the state system in the region, but almost all policies of the key outside players towards the region were evaluated mainly in terms of their implications for oil. Consider, for example, the key episode of Iraq's independence, the final granting of which was subordinated to the interests of the IPC—or the overthrow of the Mussadiq government in Iran, which was tied primarily, although not exclusively, to the nationalization of Anglo-Iranian Oil Company. Similarly, the US, as already noted, entered into very close alliances with Saudi Arabia and Iran, the latter having developed following the inclusion of American companies in the Iranian consortium that became possible after Mussadiq's demise and the return of Muhammad Reza Shah.

The diplomacy of other countries was also shaped by oil, albeit at a lower level of intensity, simply because they had far fewer assets and were rather more interested in a reshuffling of the cards than in the continuation of the existing order. Thus France attempted to hold on to Algeria and did what was necessary to protect the interests of CFP (today's Total) in the UAE, but otherwise tried to distinguish itself from 'the Anglo-Saxons' by taking a line emphasizing 'cooperation' with the oil-producing countries. Other examples of this are France's immediate acceptance of the Iraqi nationalization in 1972, its refusal to become a member of the International Energy Agency when it was established in Paris in 1974, its promotion of diplomatic initiatives for a 'new international economic order' and later for the International Energy Forum, and finally its active undermining of US sanctions against Iran until the end of the Chirac presidency and its flirting with Saddam Hussein's regime for oil concessions in the 1990s—a love story that was never consummated because of UN sanctions.

Italy too supported the creation of a national oil company, ENI, which became the prime mover of Italian diplomacy towards the Arab countries, leading to active support of the Algerian war of liberation (raising the suspicion that the bomb that downed Enrico Mattei's plane in 1962 might have been planted by the French secret services), as well as support for Muhammad Reza Shah when he fled Iran in conflict with Mussadiq, and finally to the close relationship with Libya.[3] In actual fact, however, none of these attempts were ever terribly successful: ENI got its best results from purchasing oil from the Soviet Union (a move that made the US furious) and finding oil in the Sinai, in Egypt.

Oil has influenced diplomacy towards the region, but in most cases diplomacy has failed to yield the results that were expected of it, at least as far as oil is concerned. In more recent years, oil has more frequently been used as a tool, rather than as an objective: witness the American sanctions against Iran, which continue to this day, then Libya (1982–2004), and the UN-imposed sanctions against Iraq (1990–2003). In all cases, the major industrial powers have made their own access to oil more difficult in order to pursue a political priority. Or is it the case that oil needs not only to be abundant and cheap, but also politically correct, in the sense of coming from a country with a 'friendly' government? Many seem to believe that this is indeed a priority, or even a requirement, and rank suppliers in accordance with political proximity, although there is no empirical support for the belief that oil produced from a friend is either cheaper or more reliable than oil produced elsewhere.

Middle Eastern oil exporters and their international relations

The oil-producing countries have naturally taken notice of the importance attributed to oil by the major powers and have attempted to take advantage of it, acquiring guarantees for their security against external and internal challenges, as well as access to sophisticated weapons systems. The guarantee against internal challenges was 'lifted' from Iran by US President Jimmy Carter, who wanted to uphold basic human rights and democracy, and thus allowed the Pahlavi regime to collapse—with consequences that most observers would, to this date, consider disastrous. Following the 11 September 2001 terrorist attacks ('9/11'), a current of thought in the US depicted Saudi Arabia as part of the problem, rather than the solution,[4] and argued in favour of regime change in the kingdom as well as in Iraq. But the meeting between President Bush and then Crown Prince Abdullah in Crawford, Texas, in April 2005 reiterated the close alliance between the two countries (Bronson 2006). With the onset of the Arab Spring, the US has followed a course very close to that advocated by the countries of the Gulf Cooperation Council (GCC),[5] except for being critical of the repression in Bahrain. The GCC has been unhappy with the US refusal to intervene in Syria, and of continuing negotiations with Iran aimed at reaching an accommodation on the nuclear fuel enrichment issue. Nevertheless the US has consistently reiterated the security guarantee against external challenges—notably the threat of a nuclear Iran—and has approved massive weapons sales. Finally, the turnaround in US oil production, substantially decreased reliance on imports and, in perspective, even a potential return to a net exporting position for North America, has not led to the feared disengagement of the US from the Middle East, confirming that oil is not the only nor possibly the most important American interest in the region.

The less obvious point is that, in fact, oil does not appear to be a prominent preoccupation in shaping the foreign policy of the oil-producing countries. International oil policy is entrusted with a minister of petroleum or energy, who is generally regarded as a technician; it is discussed in OPEC or other similar forums, which have a narrow, technical mandate. The only case in which there was an attempt to use oil as a weapon—in 1973—was a short-lived affair and oil never truly became physically scarce (see **Figure 5.3**).

At the outbreak of war between Israel and its Arab neighbours in October 1973, the Organization of Arab Oil Exporting Countries (OAPEC) declared an embargo against the US and the Netherlands (Yergin 1991: 588–612). Prices increased rapidly on oil markets, precipitating the first 'energy crisis'. **Figure 5.3** shows that the embargo was fictional: Middle

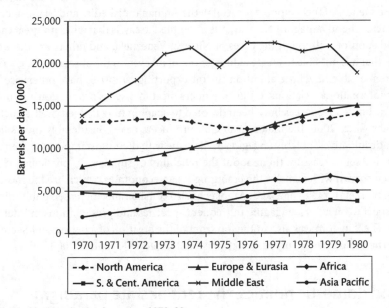

Figure 5.3 World oil production by region, 1970–80

Source: BP (2007)

Eastern oil production increased steadily and rapidly until 1974; it declined the following year because of the recession and decrease in oil demand triggered by the increase in prices. In fact, oil was never used as a weapon. Nevertheless, commentators still refer to OAPEC's decision as a dangerous precedent and proof of the unreliability of Gulf oil supplies.

That episode was a success, since it provoked an increase in prices, but politically it was a disastrous failure, which the Gulf oil producers still regret today. In fact, the perception that Gulf oil supplies are insecure and unreliable is still based essentially on only that one decision, and persists notwithstanding the fact that, since that time, Gulf producers have demonstrated more than once that they are able to deliver all of the oil that is required even when there is conflict in the region.

More recently, OPEC's decision, prompted by Saudi Arabia with the support of Kuwait and the UAE, not to lower production quotas in November 2014 has been interpreted in some capitals as being politically motivated, and possibly suggested or endorsed by the United States, in order to punish or weaken other oil exports such as notably Russia, Iran, or even Venezuela. However, such conspiracy theories do not hold water in the face of the intractable excess of supply and unwillingness of some OPEC producers (Iran, Iraq) and all non-OPEC producers to consider reducing their respective exports.

Mostly, the diplomacy of the oil-producing countries has been busy pursuing objectives that are either irrelevant or dysfunctional to their position as major exporters of oil—be it the promotion of Islam or the fight against Israel, pan-Arabism, or some milder form of pan-Africanism, or sheer military expansionism. Indeed, many oil-producing countries should blame their ill-advised foreign policy initiatives for most of the problems in which they find themselves mired. Even the Gulf countries, which have a record of less pernicious adventurism than Iraq, Libya (culminating in the Lockerbie bombing), or even Algeria (still mired in conflict with Morocco on southern Sahara, a late heritage of its 'Third World-ism'), still bear the consequences of their support for Arafat, the Afghan mujahedin, and Islamist tendencies everywhere. The advantage of Norway, one is tempted to say, is that it has no 'great cause' that it should sponsor—although the cases of Nigeria, Venezuela, and others are there to demonstrate that it is possible to create a disaster out of oil even in the absence of such a cause.

It is remarkable how little attention the oil-exporting countries have otherwise devoted to oil in international relations. OPEC members meet to discuss production and prices, but otherwise limited resources have been devoted to shaping fully fledged, well-structured oil diplomacy. Since 2000, the major Arab Gulf producers have considerably diversified their diplomatic initiatives, notably engaging in dialogue with their most important clients in East and South Asia to reassure them about the reliability of supplies. In particular, closer ties have been shaped with some of the emerging Asian economies, which are the most rapidly growing markets for Gulf oil. Saudi Arabia has also considerably increased public diplomacy with respect to oil affairs, engaging in frequent speeches and presentations in international forums. The kingdom was also in the forefront of the creation of a permanent Secretariat to the International Energy Forum, which was established in Riyadh in 2003.[6]

Oil and domestic politics: the rentier state paradigm

The availability of oil resources profoundly affects the domestic political order and contributes to explaining the Middle Eastern particularity. Several authors have dealt with the interplay between oil and domestic politics, and a lively discussion has developed in the literature. Without attempting a complete survey, this chapter will introduce the 'rentier state paradigm', which was proposed originally by Hossein Mahdavy (1970), and systematized by Beblawi (1987) and Luciani (1987); it has become a common tool in the interpretation of the political dynamics of oil-producing countries.

The rentier state paradigm

The essence of the 'rentier state' concept is this: in 'normal' countries, the state is supported by society and must, in order to pay for itself, establish a system to extract from society part of the surplus that it generates; in oil-exporting countries, the state is paid by the oil rent, which accrues to it directly from the rest of the world, and supports society through the distribution or allocation of this rent, through various mechanisms of rent circulation. Hence the distinction between 'production' states, in which society is the source of value added and the state pays for itself by imposing taxes, and 'allocation', or 'distributive' (or rentier) states, in which the state is independent of society and directly or indirectly supports a large part of society through the process of spending domestically the rent that it receives from the rest of the world.

The emphasis in this approach is on the fiscal function of the state. The (production) state is viewed essentially as a tool with which to subtract resources from the actors originally possessing them and reallocate them in a way that is different from that which the original owners would have chosen. Politics in (production) states consist in justifying the predatory function and influencing the destination of the 'booty' in the name of an asserted common interest. In order to justify this process, states need the acquiescence or acceptance of their people, and seek legitimacy, including through democratic institutions. In contrast, rentier states do not need to tax, or may tax more lightly, and their primary function is the distribution of resources accruing from abroad. These resources enter the domestic circulation and have an impact on the domestic economy only to the extent that they are domestically spent by the state. Spending is therefore the essential function of the rentier state, and generosity (as opposed to accountability), the essential virtue of its ruler.

Not all Arab states are rentier. The details of the definition of rentier state are essential, and generalizations that blur our understanding of reality rather than improve it should be resisted. In particular, the following points must be made.

1. It is essential that the source of the rent be the *rest of the world*. States that use the control of a specific domestic source of rent to extract surplus from society are not rentier states, because they are supported by society rather than vice versa.

2. It is also essential that the rent should accrue *directly* to the state. Some authors consider the inflow of remittances from workers having migrated to the oil-exporting countries (believed to incorporate a share of the oil rent) to be a potential base for a rentier state in the receiving country. There is, however, a double fallacy here: first, because expatriate earnings, if they contained an element of rent in the past, certainly do not do so any longer, beyond the normal differences in remuneration levels in different labour markets; and second, because, in any case, remittances are private income flows and the state must resort to taxation in order to appropriate them.

The rentier nature of the state is empirically connected primarily to the case of oil exporters, but there may exist other sources of rent, which might have essentially the very same impact.

These may be tied to control of: strategic assets, generating payments from other governments; important logistical assets, such as the Suez Canal; other minerals, such as diamonds in Africa; or drug production or trade, such as in Afghanistan, among others. However, these activities are not always controlled by the state, in which case the political impact is quite different: for example, the production of qat is not controlled by the Yemeni state, the production of opium in Afghanistan supports the Taliban resistance, and the drugs cartel in Colombia is in conflict with the state; for many years, diamonds allowed the National Union for the Total Independence of Angola (Unita) to continue in civil war against the Angolan government.

In historical experience, the oil rent suddenly increased for approximately a decade, from 1973 to 1983, and 'flooded' the entire region, engulfing everybody in the process of rent circulation. But this was a limited experience: oil-exporting states were rentier, in the sense of being essentially independent of domestic taxation, before 1973 and continue to be so in the twenty-first century. To the rest of the region, the encounter with large-scale oil rent was short-lived.

The rentier state, taxation, and democracy

The most important feature of the rentier state is that—being financially independent of society and indeed having, in a sense, society on its payroll—it is autonomous (that is, it can initiate policies with a degree of independence, although it cannot eventually ignore public opinion entirely) and does not need to seek legitimacy through democratic representation. It is a historical fact that demands for democratic representation and government accountability arose out of the attempt of the ruler to impose new taxes. The rentier state paradigm has become most popular through the reversal of the well-known saying 'no taxation without representation' into its mirror image: 'no representation without taxation'. In fact, neither of the two is, strictly speaking, correct, yet both capture a simple casual link, which remains fundamentally true.

Rentier states inherit a political order from history; they do not create their own political order. A few were democracies when they acquired access to external rent and remained democracies, although perhaps with a slightly different modus operandi. A majority were authoritarian, and the advent of the rent allowed them to reinforce and consolidate authoritarian rule. Patrimonial states ruling segmented (tribal) societies are a specific subset among the authoritarian rentier states: it has been argued that this specific form of government is particularly adapted to the rentier state, because the state is viewed as the property of the ruler and the distributive function, which is played in order to maintain a desired balance in the segmented society, is understood as the essential function of government.

The link between oil and authoritarian rule has been belaboured in the literature in numerous studies based on statistical analysis of panel data (Ross 2001b, 2012; Herb 2005), which suffer from many predictable problems, including a limited number of observations, the arbitrary quantification of essentially qualitative variables, a low dispersion of values, the arbitrary specification of equations to explain variables that clearly are determined by complex, multifaceted societal processes, among other things. At the same time, this approach has a tendency to propose simplistic explanations of the nexus between oil and authoritarianism (because complex explanations cannot be tested statistically). For example, saying that oil money allows the ruler to 'buy off' the opposition and acquire consensus through government expenditure is pointing to a power strategy that is common in all polities, including democracies, and not exclusive to oil producers. Similarly, pointing to the fact that oil money allows the state to pay for a strong repressive apparatus points to another feature that is surely not exclusive to oil-exporting states; indeed, relatively speaking, oil-exporting states are probably less repressive than their non-oil neighbours. In both cases, the strategies in question can be pursued on the basis of income from domestic taxes quite effectively. The difference in oil states is that power holders do not need to take money from their citizens—and this changes the nature of their relationship very substantially.

It is to be expected that rentier states will not be subjected to important pressure from below to allow for proper democratic rule. The reason is not that citizens are indifferent to outcomes (clearly, they are not), nor that they do not have opinions or have no wish to express them, but that they are likely to be sceptical about the effectiveness of elections as a tool with which to select the best rulers. If we focus on the Arab countries, it is clear that issues such as the political irrelevance of the educated and potentially liberal elite, the role of religion and the potential manipulations that it may allow, and the overwhelming importance of expatriates in the resident population all militate against betting on elections.

The point is that 'democratic transitions' in rentier states are very likely to produce authoritarian governments. Everybody understands that a democratically elected ruler will be seriously tempted to turn authoritarian as soon as he acquires control of the oil rent and the great power that this gives him over society. The possibility of alternation is essential to democracy: no opposition will remain loyal to democratic institutions if it does not stand a chance of ever winning elections; and no political force will accept a transition to democracy if the first elections are also likely to be the last.

The difficulty of establishing representative democracy in a rentier state is an objective fact. It has been clearly demonstrated in Iran, where a clerical elite has progressively established a stranglehold on power, and where elections are controlled and increasingly fabricated. It has been demonstrated also by the difficulty of establishing democratic institutions in Iraq. Early on in the debate about the democratization of Iraq, it was clear that the distribution of the oil rent would be a crucial determinant of the resulting power equilibrium: if the rent is left entirely in the hands of the central government, whoever wins the first elections has a huge opportunity to consolidate power. Hence it was proposed by some that oil revenue should be distributed directly to individual citizens in equal instalments (a negation of politics and of the state) and hence the 2005 Constitution allocates priority control over oil affairs to provinces rather than to the central government—a stipulation that many find incompatible with national unity and sovereignty. The lack of a national consensus on control of the oil rent amounts to disagreeing on political institutions and the constitution—and both remain unresolved more than ten years after the collapse of the Saddam Hussein regime. The divisive policies of Prime Minister al Maliki, who appeared only interested in consolidating his personal power (Dodge 2012) led eventually to his demise. It remains to be seen whether his successor, Haider al-Abadi, will succeed in reversing the trend and avoid the complete collapse of the Iraqi state.

Another crucial test case is Libya. The collapse of the regime of Muammar Gaddafi was precipitated by the tide of the Arab Spring and made possible by Gaddafi's style of government (inimical to institution building; incapable of delivering any economic diversification or even decent infrastructure; exclusivist, violently repressive). Still, international intervention was necessary to allow the internal opposition to dislodge the autocrat. However, once that task was accomplished, Libya was left on its own and progressively descended into civil war and state failure. At the time of writing, the country is a battleground of different factions, and a UN effort at shaping a minimum national consensus is not achieving the hoped-for improvement in the situation. Oil production has collapsed because of insecurity, and declining volumes compound with much lower prices to create very difficult economic conditions, on top of political and security concerns.

While democratic transitions are difficult in rentier states, this does not mean that there is no political participation (Khalaf and Luciani 2006). The Gulf countries exhibit, to variable degrees, a style of authoritarian rule coupled with consultation (shura) which is meant to integrate and involve as much as possible all components of society. Shura is not democracy, because the ruler remains absolute, is not elected, and has the final say on all decisions. But he listens to his people through formal or informal channels—from the establishment of appointed or elected (increasingly) parliaments, to selective access to the ruler for people in positions of influence (including those who have influence on expatriate communities), to police control of social media and communications. Through the practice of consultation, the ruler impresses upon his people the idea that it may be better to have a chance to be listened to, even if your advice is not always followed, than to be a marginalized minority under inflexible majority rule. Indeed, the key difference between the Gulf monarchies and the rentier republics (Iraq, Libya, Yemen) has been the inclusivist practice of consultation as opposed to an exclusivist reliance on a restricted circle of praetorian supporters. As a result of the sectarian divide, Bahrain has not been able to sufficiently integrate its Shia majority and will never recover political stability until integration is accomplished. The remaining Gulf countries (in descending order, from Kuwait to Oman, to Saudi Arabia, to Qatar and the UAE) all appeared to be more advanced on the road of political participation than most other Arab countries—until the advent of the Arab Spring. However, since the outbreak of the Arab Spring the space for public debate and consultation has considerably narrowed. Turmoil in Syria, Yemen, and Iraq and the rise of ISIS constitute a direct threat to the GCC regimes and have led to a further emphasis on security.

The question of democracy in non-rentier states and root causes of the Arab Spring

Conversely, it may be expected that non-rentier states, because they need to rely on taxation, will experience pressure from below to allow for democratic representation. However, when faced with pressure to democratize, non-rentier states can, first and foremost, resort to repression—a task facilitated by constant refinement of control methods and technology; second, they can make the most of whatever small sources of external rent might be available; and finally, they can develop forms of taxation that are less politically demanding—from taxes on international trade, to money creation and inflation. The region offers examples of various combinations of all of these, and they succeeded quite well in delaying the transition to democracy that would otherwise have taken place about twenty years earlier (the Algerian transition started in 1988 and collapsed in 1991; Mohammed Bouazizi set himself on fire on 17 December 2010).

The ability of authoritarian governments to resist economic, fiscal, and political reform is indeed considerable. The common assumption, whereby economic stagnation will breed dissatisfaction and fuel demand for participation, has frequently been disproved in reality: having a hard time simply to survive leads to passivity and fatalism, rather than to the revolt of those 'having nothing else to lose than their chains'.

Yet, faced with decreasing legitimacy, the non-rentier states have been unable to muster sufficient resources to promote development and maintain at least a stable supply of public goods to a growing population. The state has been forced to cede ground, reluctantly and gradually, to the private sector, but has conducted the process more with an eye to rewarding selected supporters (Heydemann 2004) than to maximizing the potential benefit in terms of economic growth (Luciani 2013). In the absence of substantial rent, the state has increasingly relied on circulation of the spoils. The state thus lost capacity in all domains, including repression, and remained an empty building behind a crumbling facade.

The survival strategy of the state has, in other words, consisted in its progressive withering away in order to avoid establishing legitimacy on new, democratic foundations, as would have been necessary to open the door to a new development strategy. The Washington Consensus provided a convenient narrative to justify the withering away of the state, but did not produce much development.

That said, recent research aiming at understanding the root—specifically economic—causes of the Arab Spring has found that the countries where the revolt erupted were not doing badly at all in the years immediately preceding (Luciani 2015). The Arab countries experienced a decade (or more) of rapid growth before 2010. Income disparities seemingly did not increase, and income distribution remained more egalitarian than that of other key emerging countries, when measured at the national level. Research has also found increasing corruption and cronyism, both traits capable of increasing the alienation of the population from the state. However, overall these phenomena hardly explain the sudden, spontaneous wave of revolts which very rapidly engulfed the entire region: a common, regional underlying cause must have existed to generate the Arab Spring.

A possible hypothesis is that the common underlying cause be in fact the rapid increase in oil prices, which exacerbated economic distances between oil and non-oil Arab economies, and created conditions in which tactical positioning and political connectedness became much more important than productive investment. The regionalization of media brought images of Gulf consumerism and irresistible progress to the homes of the poor and marginalized in Egypt, Tunisia, Yemen, or Syria, exacerbating the feeling of exclusion and hopelessness, which combined with the desire for political freedom, and was expressed as a request for dignity.

In this interpretation, high oil prices are a corrosive factor for regional relations and domestic stability in each of the region's states, because of the difficulty of managing rent circulation in the region in such a way that it may become a trigger of development. Beginning from the fact that the oil exporting countries of the Gulf prefer to rely on immigrant labour from South and South-East Asia rather than from neighbouring Arab countries; and considering that private investors are more attracted by financial or real estate placements and projects in the industrial countries or in distant emerging economies rather than in fellow Arab countries, it is clear that key potential mechanisms of rent redistribution are not functioning in favour of greater regional integration.

With the exception of Tunisia, the Arab Spring has yielded neo-authoritarian regimes or civil wars and failed states. Such regional developments now represent a direct threat to the stability of the GCC regimes, prompting them to greater regional activism. Saudi Arabia and the UAE have thus supported the coup that toppled the Muslim Brotherhood government in Egypt and have since extended massive economic aid to the government of General Sisi. Whether this may succeed in stabilizing the latter in the long run, or whether progress can be made in national reconciliation in Yemen, Iraq, Libya, or Syria is the challenge lying ahead for the rentier states of the Gulf.

Oil and inter-Arab relations

Oil has had a fundamental influence on inter-Arab relations, primarily because of the dialectic between oil-poor and oil-rich states. Interestingly, the oil-rich states, as stressed earlier in the chapter, are also relatively 'new' in history, while the oil-poor states have deeper historical roots. Finally, the oil-rich states are rentier, while the oil-poor states became rentier only for a short period, as recipients of unilateral transfers from the oil-rich states.

The dichotomy between oil-rich and oil-poor states is certainly not the only factor in the extraordinary divisiveness of Arab regional relations, but it has been significant.

The call of pan-Arabism

Pan-Arabism has been the dominant discourse in regional relations in the Middle East. Pan-Arabism is not, in itself, directly related to oil—although it is a reaction to the Balkanization of the Arab region, which, in turn, is certainly also related to oil—but quickly became entangled with it, hardening the conflict between the historically longer established, progressive, more developed, but oil-poor Arab states and the newly formed, traditional, conservative, oil-rich states in the Gulf and North Africa.

Nasser's ideology was not primarily conceived of as a tool with which to destroy the oil monarchies and assert control over their oil riches, but it was soon perceived by these monarchs as aiming precisely at this outcome. Nasser was defeated not only by his inability to deliver progress with respect to the Palestine–Israel issue, but also, and perhaps even more so, by his inability to come to terms with the oil monarchies—or, to be precise, with all oil-exporting countries in the region—even when they shed their monarchies and followed the 'revolutionary' path. He lost his battle when he could not prevail in the civil war in Yemen; nor was he able to overcome persistent rivalry with Iraq (even before 1967). The advent of a regime with strong Nasserite and pan-Arab temptations in Libya received little more than an opportunistic and profiteering response from Egypt. Simply put, the 'historical' Arab states have been unable to accept that the basis of power in the contemporary world has changed: not only are oil barrels more important than guns, but also money is more important than population size.

The constant temptation of Arab oil exporters to become embroiled in issues that transcend their national boundaries and are not functional to their national interest is indeed a feature of rentier states. The authoritarian rentier state has not needed to refer to a 'national myth', because it is supported by a rent accruing from the rest of the world and does not impose taxes on the domestic economy. A national myth is necessary to justify the redistributive function of the state, which needs to be based on a concept of collective good and legitimacy. Rentier states simply distribute without the need for taxes and tend to deny that 'the people' should have a say in the way in which the rent is distributed, presenting 'the state' as invested with some superior or wider mission. The authoritarian rentier state thus has tended rather to assert its legitimacy by reference to a constituency that is larger than its own population— Islamic in Saudi Arabia or the Islamic Republic of Iran; Arab in Iraq or Libya; technocratic in Dubai. Inevitably, these assertions of legitimacy tend to compete and conflict with each other, creating a difficult regional climate. Partly in reaction to the unwanted consequences of pursuing values transcending national boundaries, rentier states have, in the past decade, devoted greater attention to asserting their respective national consciousness and identities; the strength of shared identities (Arab, Islamic, Shia, Sunni, and more) remains very strong, however, and has been furthered by the emergence and success of regional media (satellite television, first and foremost).

For their part, the oil-poor states have articulated a claim to a share of the oil rent that the oil-rich states never truly accepted as legitimate. The primary recipients initially accepted mechanisms to circulate the rent regionally—direct budget subsidies to their neighbours, as well as labour migration and remittances—but expected a political return, which was denied to them. This has little to do with the nature of the regime, because it has been true of the Gulf monarchies as well as of Libya and Iraq. The claim to sharing in the rent combined with a statist ('étatist') ideology, which attributed the primary role in promoting economic development to the state, leading to a vision of regional integration based on politicized government-to-government relations. This approach proved totally sterile.

It is interesting to note how both oil-poor and oil-rich states sometimes embraced the same ideological discourse, but with quite opposite intentions. Hence pan-Arabism in Egypt and Baathism in Syria were meant to lay a claim to a share of the oil rent of neighbouring countries, while the same pan-Arabism in Libya or Baathism in Iraq were used to justify the rentier state's bid for hegemony.

Egypt turned its back on pan-Arabism and Nasser's legacy when it signed its separate peace with Israel. It also turned its back on the oil money of its neighbours, embracing, in theory, the credo of openness to international trade and market-based development. But implementation of the new strategy was painfully slow. It is only since 2000 that Egypt has been moving more aggressively towards economic reform, and the shift came about essentially because it became clear that this was the way in which to attract private investment from the Gulf—that is, again tapping the oil rent, albeit in a different form. The Gulf oil producers have always combined a leading role of the state in promoting development—an essential facet of circulating the oil rent—with openness to international trade. In so doing, they have nurtured a domestic private sector that has grown more competitive within and been better integrated into the global economy. Attracting private Gulf investment became the corner-stone of economic development strategy in all Arab countries, including Syria; in this way, the Gulf countries hegemonized development throughout the region.

The ascendance of the Gulf rentier states

In the 1970s, the increase of the oil rent was so sudden, and its concentration so extreme, that the rentier states felt it was prudent to be generous outside, as well as inside, their boundaries.

They therefore created institutions to redistribute a share of the rent internationally and engaged in granting direct subsidies to neighbouring governments. Jordan, Syria, the Palestine Liberation Organization, and, until it made peace with Israel, Egypt were major beneficiaries of these direct grants. Later, Iraq became a recipient during its protracted war with Iran.

However, the effectiveness of such generosity in purchasing lasting goodwill was dubious, to say the least. Iraq's decision to invade Kuwait, and the attitude that Jordan, Yemen, or the Palestinians took on that occasion, proves that generosity sometimes breeds resentment. More recently, the fact that Al-Qaeda turned against the Saudi regime is again a demonstration of a client turning against its patron.

So, after a short period of time in which the tide of the rent rose so high that it covered the entire region and almost every government became rentier (in the sense of being primarily occupied with capturing oil or strategic rents under the form of direct grants), we have returned to a condition that was common before 1973—that is, of a region dominated by the dynamics between rentier and non-rentier, or oil-rich and oil-poor, states, and the seemingly impossible integration between them.

In the meantime, the private sector in the rentier states has become much stronger: rentier states can therefore propose a much more conventional model of regional cooperation, based on free trade and private investment, be it direct or financial. They can rely on international organizations such as the International Monetary Fund, the World Bank, or the World Trade Organization to promote this model, playing down the Arab nationalist discourse and dimension. However, the shared Arab regional identity refuses to die and, as argued above, may be responsible for the regional dimension of the Arab Spring and subsequent political turmoil.

Slowly, but surely, the balance of power (of opportunities and capabilities) has shifted in the region, away from the older established, but oil-poor, states and in favour of the newly consolidated, oil-rich ones. Furthermore, within the latter group some have wasted their opportunities, engaging in regional adventurism and ill-advised state-led investment policies. The GCC states, certainly the most fragile at the beginning of the process, have bred a wealthy, sophisticated private sector, which is reasonably well integrated in the currents of globalization; they therefore have a much better chance of succeeding than the rest of the region.

The regional balance in the Arab region has been moving relentlessly away from the historically better established states towards the oil-rich 'parvenus'. As military power loses importance—in a world in which only one superpower counts—and traditional industry and agriculture are less important than services and the e-economy, the traditional centres of Arab politics are in decline, while the oil exporters enjoy all of the opportunities.

The regional and international environments and the political order in the Middle East

In the early years of the twenty-first century, a major attempt was made by Western powers to change the region's political landscape radically through outside intervention. Motivated by, or using as a pretext, the terrorist attacks of 9/11, the United States and a number of other countries decided to intervene militarily in Iraq to eliminate the Baath regime of Saddam Hussein. This was perceived as the first move in a broader plan aiming at establishing democratic regimes throughout the region, as well as changing the rules under which the region's oil resources are exploited and commercialized internationally.

Whether the Iraqi adventure was motivated primarily by oil interests or by political objectives is a discussion that is likely to continue for some time. The fact that Iraq is potentially a much more important exporter than it has been historically certainly played a role in the decision-making process—at least in giving credence to the idea that the war and reconstruction could, and would, be paid for by Iraq itself. Nevertheless, it is clear with hindsight that if the purpose had been to make more oil available to the international market and to allow international oil companies to return to the country under favourable contracts, it would have been more fruitful to accept the deals that the Saddam regime was offering in the 1990s, which the companies, keen as they were to accept those terms, were prevented from signing by international sanctions. The war and its difficult aftermath delayed investment in Iraqi resources by a minimum of ten years, and the companies (those that ventured into the country—and not all did) have been forced to accept service contracts and considerably tougher terms rather than the production sharing agreements that were on offer in the previous decade.

The intervention in Iraq was also motivated by the desire to establish a 'model' democratic regime that would trigger a wave of democratization throughout the region—beginning with the regime in Saudi Arabia. But the infant Iraqi democracy has proved to be inferior as a model, and it is not clear that it had much of a role in triggering the Arab Spring and the wave of authoritarian regime collapses that ensued.

The revolutionary movement that started in December 2010 has rapidly engulfed several states in the region, including one major oil producer (Libya) and some minor (Egypt, Syria, Yemen). It has had less of an impact—at least for the time being—on the Gulf states (except Bahrain) or Algeria. Thus it appears that while being an oil exporter is not an absolute guarantee against revolutionary contagion, it helps. In the case of Libya, outside intervention was needed to help the rebel forces to defeat the regime and again the question was: was intervention motivated by the oil? It is possible that considerations related to oil—especially the danger, and the potential consequences, of a long, drawn-out civil war—might have played a role in precipitating the decision. However, Libyan oil was always accessible (except for sanctions, imposed by other countries on Libya); oil companies were busy investing in the country and, after 2004, had received the active support of their respective governments, which had been generous in bestowing accolades on the intractable Gaddafi.

The end of the oil price cycle (2004–14) and the unresolved dilemmas of regional relations

There is a close connection between regime change in Iraq and the onset of the oil price cycle that began in 2004 and came to a dramatic end in the latter part of 2014. At the turn of the century, oil prices were recovering from the abysmally low levels reached in 1998–99, and the dominant narrative was that of peak oil. Following the terrorist attacks of 9/11, some tension emerged on the markets due to fear for oil supplies—Saudi Arabia at that time being portrayed as part of the problem rather than part of the solution. However, in the run-up to the allied intervention in Iraq, the expectation was that the demise of the Saddam regime would bring about an end to the Iraqi sanctions, the opening of the country to international oil companies' investment, and rapid increase in oil production. As it became apparent that the outcome of the Iraqi adventure was very much different from what had been expected, oil prices started increasing gradually. The upward trend found little immediate resistance: demand for oil showed no sign of decreasing—indeed China's appetite for imported oil exploded; the industrial countries were not plunged into recession; and alternative sources of oil were not immediately forthcoming. The market became convinced that prices could grow much higher, and eventually created a bubble. The financial crisis subsequent to the collapse of Lehmann Brothers suddenly drained liquidity from the oil futures market, leading to a collapse in prices in the latter part of 2008—but this proved temporary. Prices recovered quite rapidly and kept climbing until 2011. The outbreak of the Arab Spring contributed to again creating a fear that oil supplies from the Middle East might be seriously disrupted, although this was in fact not the case.

In the meantime, supply from alternative sources, which had not been forthcoming in the previous decade, started growing exponentially. The fastest growing, but not unique, component of additional supply was from shale oil in the US, which revolutionized the global oil market outlook. The shale oil revolution was also viewed as liberating the US from their dependence on Middle East oil, thus potentially undermining the close relationship between Washington and the GCC oil exporters.

Between 2011 and 2014, the market became progressively oversupplied, and in the summer of 2014 price softness became apparent. Nevertheless, many expected that OPEC, and specifically Saudi Arabia, would cut production in order to shore up prices. Such expectation proved unfounded: in November 2014 OPEC decided to keep quotas unchanged, opening the door to a major price collapse. This downturn is unlikely to be reversed soon, because all signs point to abundant supplies until at least 2020.

We can therefore identify a clear oil price cycle, which began approximately in 2004 and came to an abrupt end in 2014. This price cycle had momentous consequences in the Middle East region: it further emphasized the distance between the oil exporters of the Gulf and the rest of the region, and, as we argued, created the underlying conditions for the regional upheaval of the Arab Spring.

It is clear that the period of very high prices led to greater regional instability rather than the opposite. Not only did it enhance the distance between the major oil exporters and the rest of the region, fuelling the resentment of the latter; it also provided ample resources to regional spoilers (facilitating Russia and Iran in their support to the Asad regime, or the Houthi rebellion in Yemen; and private donors' money to flow to Islamic extremists). But the collapse of oil prices cannot be expected to have a symmetrical outcome, that is, to lead to a resolution of conflicts.

The Arab Spring posed a major challenge for the major Gulf oil producers and they frequently appeared to be divided in their response. Saudi Arabia offered refuge to Zine al-Abidine Ben Ali and supported Mubarak until the last moment (and beyond); Qatar was in support of the revolutions in both countries, and maintained its support of the Muslim Brotherhood government even beyond its demise; Saudi Arabia and the UAE, in contrast, welcomed the coup staged by Field Marshal Abdel Fattah al-Sisi, and strongly supported his new regime with finance and investment. The GCC as a group reacted to the outbreak of the Arab Spring by offering membership to Jordan and Morocco, two non-oil monarchies: but there was no practical follow-up to this opening. The group was unanimous in helping the Bahraini monarchy crush the Shia rebellion; yet in Yemen the organization was very active in seeking a way of easing Ali Abdullah Salih out of power. The Gulf countries also very actively supported the rebellions in Libya and Syria. In December 2011, King Abdullah of Saudi Arabia called for the transformation of the Gulf Cooperation Council into a Gulf Union, to better face the worsening regional challenges. This proposal met with the hostility of Oman and Qatar, both jealous of their sovereignty in the conduct of regional policy. Divergences between Qatar on the one hand and Saudi Arabia, the UAE, and Bahrain on the other led to the withdrawal of the latter countries' ambassadors from Doha between March and December 2014. The lack of cohesion of the GCC will inevitably weaken the organization's ability to pursue the return to peaceful conditions in the region.

Conclusion

This chapter has attempted to map the multiple ways in which oil has influenced international relations and domestic politics in the Middle East. Historically, interest in oil—especially in the UK and the US—strongly influenced attitudes towards the Middle East and the formation of the state system in the region, following the collapse of the Ottoman Empire. However, not everything can be explained by oil.

The chapter has stressed the dynamic between states that have deeper roots in history, but generally little oil, and states that were formed only much more recently and consolidated primarily thanks to their oil resources and the rent that these generated. The polarization in the region between oil-rich and oil-poor states is an essential tool of analysis. The parallel distinction between rentier and non-rentier states helps to explain how oil affects the domestic political development of the oil-rich states, and influences their regional relations.

Rentier states feel little pressure to become democratic, while this pressure exists in the non-rentier states. Yet, faced with the need to engage in economic reform, non-rentier states are in a much more difficult position—because of the weakness of their private sectors—than rentier states—notably the Arab Gulf states, whose governments always supported private business. This is one reason why there has been little progress towards democracy and economic reform in the non-rentier states; quite the contrary, the state progressively barricaded itself behind an increasingly intrusive repressive apparatus. In contrast, rentier states in the Gulf moved towards economic reform as well as wider political participation; the latter, however, is falling well short of democracy, as normally recognized. The game suddenly changed in December 2010, with the onset of the Arab Spring.

Such domestic dynamics are important because they underlie regional relations. The progressive ascendance of the oil-rich, rentier states has been made possible by their much greater adaptability to the dictates of globalization. The oil-poor states are facing a political turning point, which may or may not open the door to economic revival.

International organizations, the United States, and the European Union all pursued, albeit at times in competition with each other, an agenda aiming at economic and political reform in the region. However, faced with the new political landscape, external actors found that their tools are limited and intervention frequently counterproductive.

Oil is important because it affects the power balance within the region, as well as outside attitudes. As the price of oil increased significantly between 2004 and 2014, the impulse towards reform in the rentier states has moderated. The priority attributed to the strengthening of the role of the private sector remained essentially unchanged. Concern for the employment of nationals, with the closely correlated emphasis on education reform and even more acute alarm for excessive dependence on expatriate labour (which is the other side of the same coin), remained high on the political agenda.

At the regional level, the high oil price cycle had important destabilizing effects, and opened wounds that will not be mended easily. The prospect of two important oil exporters, such as Iraq and Libya, slowly turning into failed states inevitably has important international repercussions and invites outside interference from various sides. But outside intervention has already been attempted and has not yielded appreciable results.

By the same token, GCC financial support for the new Egyptian al-Sisi regime also smacks of *déjà vu*. Maybe what was tried before and failed will succeed when tried a second time, but scepticism is justified. Continuing political unrest and civil war in several of the countries of the region and failure to create a positive development dynamic in Egypt would force the Gulf countries to further isolate themselves from the rest of the region, and clamp down on domestic dissension. At the same time, a successfully stabilized and economically prosperous Egypt would not wait long before reasserting its regional hegemony, confining the GCC countries to paymasters of its regional ambitions. In other words, there is no escape from the inevitable tension between oil-rich and oil-poor countries in the region, nor from the call of the Arab regional identity.

Further reading

Aarts, P. and Nonnemann, G. (eds) (2005) *Saudi Arabia in the Balance: Politics, Economics and International Relations between 9/11, the Iraq Crisis and the Future* (London: Hurst)
   The best collective effort at understanding Saudi Arabia currently available.

Bronson, R. (2006) *Thicker Than Oil: America's Uneasy Partnership with Saudi Arabia* (Oxford: Oxford University Press)
   The most exhaustive discussion of US-Saudi relations and the role that oil has played—or not played.

Kerr, M. H. and ElSayed, Y. (eds) (1982) *Rich and Poor Nations in the Middle East: Egypt and the New Arab Order* (Boulder, CO: Westview Press)
   A classic for understanding the regional dynamics between oil-rich and oil-poor countries in the Middle East.

Khalaf, A. and Luciani, G. (eds) (2006) *Constitutional Reform and Political Participation in the Gulf* (Dubai: Gulf Research Center)
   An exploration of the different dimensions and limits of political liberalization in the GCC.

Legrenzi, M. and Momani, B. (eds) (2011) *Shifting Geo-Economic Power of the Gulf: Oil, Finance and Institutions* (Aldershot: Ashgate)
   Contains essays discussing several aspects of the growing economic power of the Gulf countries.

Luciani, G. (ed.) (1990) *The Arab State* (Berkeley, CA: University of California Press)
   Includes the essential reference work on the rentier state paradigm.

Ross, M. (2012) *The Oil Curse: How Petroleum Wealth Shapes the Development of Nations* (Princeton, NJ: Princeton University Press)

The most recent argumentation of the theory according to which oil is a curse; has relatively little on the Middle East specifically, but is a very useful reference for the oil/resource curse theory.

Salamé, G. (ed.) (1994) *Democracy without Democrats: The Renewal of Politics in the Muslim World* (London: I. B. Tauris)
The best study of the question of democracy in the Middle East.

Schlumberger, O. (ed.) (2007) *Debating Arab Authoritarianism: Dynamics and Durability in Non-Democratic Regimes* (Stanford, CA: Stanford University Press)
The most recent comprehensive debate on economic and other roots of authoritarianism in the Arab countries.

Stocking, G. W. (1970) *Middle East Oil* (Knoxville, TN: Vanderbilt University Press)
An account of the history of the development of Middle Eastern oil that presents all of the important details very effectively.

Yergin, D. (1991) *The Prize: The Epic Quest for Oil, Money and Power* (New York: Simon & Schuster)
A history of the oil industry that is the best introductory reading to get the basic facts and references. It differs from Stocking (1970) in as much as it covers more than just the Middle East and has a lot of entertaining details, which, however, are not always truly important.

Useful websites

http://gulf2000.columbia.edu The Gulf 2000 Project, established at Columbia University, provides very extensive documentation on the Gulf.

http://www.eia.doe.gov The US Energy Information Agency (US EIA) offers the largest freely available source of information on energy affairs on the Internet.

http://www.grc.net The Gulf Research Center is a privately sponsored research and documentation centre on the Arab Gulf.

Questions

1. It is commonly maintained that access to oil is the main interest justifying the activism of European countries and the United States in Middle Eastern affairs. Does historical evidence support this view?

2. Access to oil revenue has, at different times and under different circumstances, had a stabilizing or destabilizing effect on Arab regimes and states. Give examples of such divergent effects and discuss their causes.

3. The Arab world is sharply divided into oil-rich and oil-poor countries. How does this affect regional relations?

4. Throughout the history of oil in the Middle East, Iraq has played a controversial role, which has prevented it from reaching the level of production that might be warranted by its vast resources. Discuss the specific trajectory of Iraq as an example of how history bears on contemporary developments.

5. To what extent would you say that the foreign policy of Iran or Saudi Arabia is functional to their respective oil interests?

Notes

1. Ilya Harik (1990) has argued that, contrary to the frequently held view according to which all contemporary Arab states are a creation of the colonial powers, most of them have substantial roots in history. This is certainly the case not only for Egypt, but also for the Maghreb—although in the case of Libya, the three constituting provinces of Tripolitania, Cyrenaica, and Fezzan have greater historical legitimacy than the unitary state that has emerged. The situation is different in the Mashreq, where the division between Syria, Iraq, and Jordan (the latter a state invented totally *ex novo*) was shaped by the colonial powers; Mount Lebanon had a clearly recognizable separate identity in history, but today's Lebanon was deliberately defined by the French with considerably wider borders than the historical precedent. In relation to Israel/Palestine, the impact of the British mandate is only too obvious. In the peninsula, a Saudi state has existed in the Nejd (central Arabia) almost without interruption since the eighteenth century, but today's kingdom includes the historical Hijaz and the emirate of Hail, which have disappeared. Kuwait has roots in history, but all other Gulf emirates were such small and unimportant places that to discuss their 'independent' existence in history is moot.

2. Biafra is the province in Nigeria where oil is concentrated. Biafra tried to secede from the Nigerian federation, but lost the ensuing bloody civil war (1966–70).

3. Enrico Mattei was the charismatic founder of the Italian state oil company ENI, which brought together two pre-existing companies, Agip and Snam. He died in the crash of the company's plane in very bad weather while returning to Milan from Sicily; the causes of the crash were never satisfactorily clarified (Yergin 1991: 530–1). Mattei battled the major international oil companies (he coined the term 'the Seven Sisters') and sought to find independent reserves for his company in Iran and Libya, but was especially successful in Egypt.

4. For a recent re-statement of a virulent anti-Saudi position, see Stern (2011).

5. The Gulf Cooperation Council—or, more accurately, the Cooperation Council of the Arab States of the Gulf—is the regional group reuniting Bahrain, Kuwait, Oman, Qatar, Saudi Arabia, and the United Arab Emirates. It was established in 1981 as an association of the rulers of the six patrimonial monarchies, with collective security and a mutual security guarantee as primary objectives. It has since evolved into a regional economic integration project, pursuing the creation of a common market, a common currency, and freedom of movement for nationals and capital. In response to the Arab Spring, in December 2011 King Abdullah of Saudi Arabia issued a call 'to move from a phase of cooperation to a phase of union within a single entity', but the proposal was resisted in particular by Oman and Qatar.

   The GCC member countries are all major oil exporters, with the exception of Bahrain, whose oil production is now down to a trickle.

6. The International Energy Forum is a conference of the major industrial, developing, and oil-producing countries, which was convened for the first time in 1991. The eighth International Energy Forum was convened in September 2002 in Osaka, where the decision to establish a permanent Secretariat based in Riyadh was made. A Secretary General was appointed in June 2003.

The Puzzle of Political Reform in the Middle East

AUGUSTUS RICHARD NORTON

Overview

With only a handful of exceptions, Middle East governments have failed to govern either fairly or competently, and ruling elites have generally been more intent on keeping power in their hands than on improving the lot of their citizens. Although reform initiatives have been announced periodically, business as usual has been the normal outcome. Individual or organized complaints about corruption or abuses of power have often been punished and thwarted, and many of the region's judiciaries have served as instruments of state power. The persistence of autocratic rule in the region stems from several factors, including the dominant role of the state in the economy, a 'ruling bargain' whereby citizens were promised prosperity in return for restrictions on freedom, and the preference of external great powers for stability over democracy. In the resource poor states, the ruling bargain became increasingly untenable vis-à-vis fast growing, better informed populations and state efforts to restructure economies (often under international pressure) produced widening unemployment and spread economic pain. After 11 September 2001 ('9/11'), the United States and several European powers declared their intention to foster reform and to spread democracy in the Middle East, but little was accomplished. Even so, dissatisfaction with government remains pervasive. In the extraordinary political upheaval that began in 2011, the accumulated rage against autocratic governments erupted into a quest for dignity (karāmah) and widespread demands for better governance and freedom. These demands remain largely unfulfilled, and solutions to the puzzle of reform remain elusive.

Introduction

The wellsprings of anti-government enmity fed by false promises and thwarted hopes became apparent in 2011 when protests erupted in many Arab world locales. As the year began, protests were accelerating in Tunisia and, on 14 January, President Zine al-Abidine Ben Ali fled into exile in Saudi Arabia. In neighbouring Egypt, the Tunisians' accomplishment lent momentum to widespread demonstrations, especially after 25 January 2011, designated (following Tunisia's example) as the 'Day of Rage' (*yaum al-ghadib*). Eighteen days later, after more than 800 demonstrators were killed by security forces and government-linked thugs, President Hosni Mubarak, who had ruled Egypt for three decades, resigned from office under pressure from the military. Across the Arab world, emulative protests spread in nearly every country, with varying success and sometimes with horrendous bloodshed. In Libya, a strongman met his demise; in Yemen, a dictator retreated from the presidency; in Bahrain, protesters demanding reform and equitable treatment were suppressed within weeks by a Saudi-led force that was intended to stymie demands for reform; and in Syria, chants of *Irhal! Irhal!* ('Go! Scram!') were met by brutal government violence and a descent into a civil war that by mid-2015 had claimed at least 230,000 lives and uprooted about half of Syria's population of 23 million people. (See '**The Arab uprisings of 2011**' later in the chapter for case studies illustrating the widely variant and sometimes catastrophic outcomes of popular demands for reform in Tunisia, Egypt, Bahrain, Libya, Syria, and Yemen.)

In Arab discourse, 2011 has been described by many people as *al-sahwah* ('the awakening'), or *al-nahdah al-thaniyah* ('the second Arab renaissance'), or even *al-thawrat al-'arabia* ('the Arab revolutions'). Challand (2011) succinctly refers to a new sense of collective autonomy, *tasayir dhati*, in Arab societies. In Western circles, the burgeoning protests, which typically included the trademark demand *al-sha'ab yurid usqat al-nizam* ('the people want the fall of the regime'), were styled an 'Arab Spring' (*al-rabi'a al-'arabi*), but the seasonal metaphor implies a transformational episode whereas mass protests need to be understood as part of a long process of political change.

Although largely unnoticed outside of the region, the first decade of the twenty-first century witnessed numerous demonstrations by organized labour, and other economic segments affected by economic reforms and high levels of under-employment and unemployment. The governments' stifling of political dissent by secular groups lent further momentum to culturally entrenched Islamists. As disillusionment with government spread, a variety of Islamist groups that offered religious answers to complex political and economic questions benefited and significant segments of the population lent them support.

Arguably the core demand of the protests was a clamour for respect and dignity. All too often, it is argued, Arab governments have treated their subjects and citizens with disdain, sloughing off their legitimate demands. Whether in terms of monarchy or Arab republic, authoritarianism in the Arab world has been characterized by the depoliticization of public space. Other than political humour, politics in many corners of the Arab world have been consigned to a private sphere, and even then broached only cautiously with trusted intimates. The depoliticization of public space is illustrated in places such as Saudi Arabia, where a hint of dissent provokes an iron fist response (as well as prophylactic cascades of money—after 2011, US$36 billion in new funding and subsidies to address domestic concerns was announced).

The authoritarian state model

In order to appreciate the immense challenges that face proponents of political reform in the Middle East, it is important to consider the legacies of state formation that shape the contemporary political systems, as well as the changing economic and social parameters of societies in today's Middle East. The following sections discuss the formation of modern states, many of which emerged only after the Second World War, as well as the institutional and political impediments to political reform, and particularly to democratization.

Most Middle Eastern states won their independence from European domination only in the latter half of the twentieth century. The new governments that emerged faced formidable challenges, particularly in promoting prosperity and sustaining growth in late developing economies that were ill-equipped to compete in the world economic system. The chosen path centred on a large statist economy that, in time, swelled government employment and disadvantaged private enterprise.

Another challenge was to foster a collective sense of civic identity, the essence of citizenship. In general, personal freedom was sacrificed in the interest of state security, often with reference to the Arab–Israeli conflict, which has continued since 1948. If political space was dominated by the state and controlled by ubiquitous police apparatuses, this reflected a tacit compact between government and citizen that was wearing thin. In short, in return for loyalty to the state, the citizen would be offered a healthier, more prosperous life. Unfortunately, clientelism and its handmaiden, corruption, often came to define the relationship between ruled and ruler.

Democracy was not much discussed. 'Democracy' refers most basically to the ability of citizens to hold their governments accountable and to change their political leaders at regular intervals. Instead, accountability to the public has been generally weak in the region, and particularly in the Arab world rulers were more likely to change as a result of actuarial realities than a withdrawal of public confidence. In 1979, a revolutionary regime came to power in Iran, and promised to offer a distinct model of political development to the Middle East and the Muslim world, but the promise has not matched the reality. In the nearly four decades since the revolution toppled the monarchy and established the Islamic Republic in Iran, some institutions of democracy, such as competitive elections for parliament, gained popular legitimacy, but the levers of power remain in the hands of conservative clerics who evince little enthusiasm for loosening their grip on power. When President Mahmoud Ahmadinejad won re-election in the 2009 elections, many Iranians suspected that the balloting was rigged in order to deny victory to Mir-Hussein Mousavi, a former prime minister who espoused a modest reform agenda. The green movement, which had been inspired by Mousavi's campaign, launched massive protests, but the protesters were confronted with an iron fist and leading opposition figures were either arrested or kept isolated under long-term house arrest, or simply intimidated into silence. The Iranian case illustrates that, even in the face of broad disenchantment, militarized regimes retain an impressive capacity to forestall change through coercion and repression but the underlying popular appetite for reform continues. In 2013, Hassan Rouhani, a reformist cleric who was hardly favoured by the entrenched political elites, enjoyed overwhelming support and was elected President of Iran.

The exceptions to the rule of a non-democratic Middle East include Israel and Turkey. With more than half a century of democratic experience, democracy is still strikingly incomplete in Israel and Turkey, where ethnic minorities (some non-European Jews and especially Arab citizens in Israel, and Kurds in Turkey) often find their freedoms curtailed and quite incomplete.

Human development and democracy

Given that the exceptional cases of Israel and Turkey entail predominantly non-Arab societies, it is clear that the democracy deficit applies significantly to the Arab world. An appropriate first task is to weigh what is known about the correlates of democracy and to determine what patterns emerge in Arab states. In a ground-breaking study published by a United Nations agency, a group of respected Arab scholars examined political, social, and economic conditions in the Arab world (UNDP 2003). This incisive and rich report attracted wide attention in government circles and in the press.

The authors identified thirty-one indicators reflecting the level of democracy and freedom. These indicators are summarized in three major clusters: government process; government capacity to implement and shape sound policy; and the level of respect displayed by both citizen and state for social and economic institutions. When these clusters of indicators are correlated with measures of human development and then compared to those of the rest of the world, the findings show clearly that even wealthy Arab states provided fewer outlets for political expression, fair government, and responsive government than states with comparable incomes and quality of life outside the region. Using a carefully designed composite measure, fewer than 9 per cent of Arab citizens rank in the middle level of material well-being and freedom, and none are found in the highest level. Only sub-Saharan Africa has a poorer record of fairly applying the rule of law.

Across the region, utter poverty (living on less than US$1 per day) is relatively uncommon and afflicts fewer than 2 per cent of all Arabs. Yet, in the poorer Arab countries the United Nations reports that 25 per cent of the population is malnourished. It has often been argued that as income and other measures of well-being increase, the chances for democracy grow. In the aggregate, per capita income in the Middle East is considerably higher than either East Asia, or Africa, yet both regions have shown much more democratization than the Middle East. The Arab middle class varies widely in size, but in many countries, such as Egypt, Saudi Arabia, and Algeria, it is quite large. However, since the government sector is often massive and employs a large percentage of the middle class, government employees are reluctant to slap the hand that feeds them. For example, despite programmes in recent decades to shrink the public sector, the government employs one person for every two-and-a-half people in the private sector. The corollary is that the large state sector stifles the development of market economies that might produce more challenges to the autocratic state.

Explaining the democracy deficit

The weak progress of democracy in the Middle East has fascinated many scholars. Some offer a 'one size fits all' cultural explanation of the absence of democracy. The late Elie Kedourie asserted that 'the idea of democracy is quite alien to the mind-set of Islam' (Kedourie 1992: 1).

This implies that only by changing the mindset of the adherents of Islam is democracy likely to be embraced—and Kedourie held that to be improbable. Yet it is apparent that Muslims do practise democracy in a variety of settings, including India, Indonesia, Holland, Lebanon, the United Kingdom, and the United States. To discover whether Muslims embrace democracy, one may learn less by examining non-democratic settings than by considering democratic contexts. The notion that Muslims are unwilling to embrace democracy for deeply seated cultural reasons simply does not stand up. Given the opportunity to play by democratic rules, Muslims have been quite adept at forming political parties and interest groups, and building effective coalitions.

Prior to the awakening of 2011, a variety of scholars and policy experts eschewed cultural explanations for their cynicism about the prospects of democratic reform, the activism of a vibrant civil society in the Arab world, or the relevance of oppositional voices. Instead, they focused on adaptive authoritarian tactics. The prevailing perspective on the dim prospects for Arab democracy was captured in Steven Heydemann's widely cited monograph on 'authoritarian upgrading', which was published by the Brookings Institution, one of Washington's leading think tanks (Heydemann 2007). He argued that the Arab regimes had adopted sophisticated techniques with which to dampen domestic demands for reform. These techniques included a sophisticated combination of limited political reforms, middle class co-optation, patronage, surveillance, and coercion.

Eva Bellin offered a conceptually rigorous account showing how the educated middle class has been co-opted by autocratic regimes. She emphasized the coercive apparatus of regimes and the prevalence of patrimonial leadership that is common in the Middle East. She did not see much prospect for major political demonstrations. Writing in 2004, she said that the region was characterized by a 'low level of popular mobilization for political reform' (Bellin 2004: 150).

Once the momentous events of 2011 were under way, there were *mea culpas* from some scholars—notably Gregory Gause, who admitted his own blindness to the emerging social forces in the region. He also noted that many academic experts had got it wrong by succumbing to 'groupthink' about the durability of authoritarian regimes (Gause 2011a). To be fair, some experts understood how vulnerable the Arab regimes were and how deeply rage penetrated Arab societies. In a much-discussed book, Nazih Ayubi emphasized the 'hollowness' of the 'fierce' regimes (Ayubi 1995). Some of the more prescient scholars tended to be on the margins of the policy world, which may have insulated them from the dangers of groupthink. Asef Bayat, for example, anticipated the potency of popular demonstrations by 'ordinary people' in a number of his writings, including *Life as Politics* (Bayat 2010). In relation to Egypt, Joel Beinin and others (2010) were alert to the widespread and spreading labour unrest and strikes that the Egyptian government proved helpless to stop.

Public opinion

Viewed from the West, political attitudes in the Middle East are often hidden not only by barriers of language and distance, but also by metaphors that betray stereotypes rather than reveal reality. An example is the use of 'the street' to refer to opinion in Muslim countries, especially in Arab countries. Arab journalists and others use the term, often in a sense that corresponds with a Lebanese proverb, *ra'i al-baqir ahsan min siyasa al-bashar* ('the opinion of a cow is better than the politics of the people'). Certainly, in Western usage, the term 'the street' implies a formless mass of people swayed by the sentiments of the moment and ma-nipulated by autocrats—a modern parallel to 'the mob' in revolutionary France. 'The street' implies that there are few nuances of opinion and no need to stratify points of view to dis-cern class, gender, age, regional, or occupational distinctions. 'The street thinks ... ' intone sage-sounding commentators, as though talking about tidal movements (Norton 2003).

The evidence does suggest that many people wish they were governed better than they in fact are. A number of leading polling firms, such as the Pew Research Center, Gallup and Zogby Associates, have turned their attention to the region and the broader Muslim world.[1] In addition, a cadre of regionally based public opinion specialists has produced high-quality scientific surveys of opinion (for example, Khalil Shikaki, the Palestinian scholar).

The picture that emerges from these opinion studies are highly differentiated views that confound easy generalizations. For example, when questioned about US policy in Iraq or in the Arab–Israeli conflict, views are overwhelmingly negative, with approval ratings of less than 5 per cent. In contrast, US democracy, education, and technology evoke robust approval ratings. Of course, the opinions vary by age and education, with younger people (those aged 18–35) more likely than older respondents to offer a favourable view (Zogby 2002).

The role of outside powers

While Western diplomats and political leaders paid lip service during the 1990s to encourag-ing democracy in the Middle East, there was little real pressure on the region's governments to permit people an expanded voice in politics. Major powers, not least the US, the UK, and France, preferred stability over the uncertainty of democratization. Those who wielded power in Cairo, Tunis, and Riyadh, and other Arab capitals, grew accustomed to empty Western rhetoric about democratization. In the US, President Bill Clinton spoke melodi-ously in the 1990s about the promotion of democracy around the globe, while his adminis-tration's leading Middle East diplomat, Martin Indyk, simultaneously disparaged the notion of democracy for Arab states as destabilizing and threatening to the 'peace process' and to Israel. Western governments were perfectly happy to cling to autocratic rulers, rather than to gamble on the uncertainties of more open political systems (Indyk 2002).

For many years, regional governments were able to fragment or suppress those groups that were calling most strenuously for reform, with few criticisms from Western capitals. The Islamist political movements of various stripes, the best organized opposition forces, posed a direct challenge to the monopoly on power held by the ruling elites. Where parlia-mentary elections were held, the Islamists' participation was carefully circumscribed (as in Egypt), if not outlawed completely (as in Tunisia). When Islamists were allowed to partici-pate fully in elections in Algeria, they proved to be a popular alternative to the discredited secular ruling party.

Thus the contemplation of democracy in the Arab world prompted major outside powers and local dictators to see eye to eye in terms of the virtue of continuing the status quo and sustaining stability, which has been the obsessive focus of Western and, in particular, US officials.

The Al-Qaeda terrorist attacks of 11 September 2001 ('9/11') changed Western, and particularly US, perspectives on political reform dramatically. Officials now argued that stagnant political systems and stifled hopes were a formula for further disasters. Former US Secretary of State Madeleine K. Albright noted, in a revealing 2003 comment, that she regretted not pushing harder for reform and she admitted that Middle East democracy was not a priority during the eight years of the Clinton presidency:

> We did nudge at times, supporting Kuwaiti leaders in their initiative to give women the vote and encouraging the creation of representative bodies in Bahrain and Jordan. But we did not make it a priority. Arab public opinion, after all, can be rather scary.
>
> (Albright 2003)

In November 2003, President Bush declared a sea change in policy that would see America exchange its obsession with stability for the promotion of democracy, arguing that:

> Sixty years of Western nations excusing and accommodating the lack of freedom in the Middle East did nothing to make us safe—because in the long run, stability cannot be purchased at the expense of liberty. As long as the Middle East remains a place where freedom does not flourish, it will remain a place of stagnation, resentment, and violence ready for export.
>
> (Bush 2003)

Given the broad disdain for US policies in the Middle East—especially Bush's fulsome support for Israel, even when it acts in morally obnoxious ways against Palestinian civilians under occupation—such pronouncements evoked incredulity.

Powerful external powers, especially the US, now embraced secular democracy as a panacea for the region's ills. Top officials referred frequently to the 'freedom deficit' in the Middle East, and concluded that economic failure and political oppression fed despair, and conditioned people to succumb to ideologies of hatred and violence. President George W. Bush declared in February 2003 that: 'The world has a clear interest in the spread of democratic values, because stable and free nations do not breed ideologies of murder.'

In fact, evidence suggests that democratizing states are actually more prone to instability than authoritarian systems (Mansfield and Synder 1995). Thus while there are other good reasons to wish for more freedom for Middle Easterners, the project of democratization may not produce the democratic peace presumed by some officials and observers, at least not in the foreseeable future.

Iraq as a model?

When the US and Britain invaded Iraq in 2003, officials and war proponents asserted that, by toppling Saddam Hussein from power, Iraq would be transformed from a republic of fear into a republic of freedom. Iraq would lead the way as a beacon of democracy for the region. Speaking before the US Congress in July 2003, Prime Minister Tony Blair declared: 'We promised Iraq democratic government. We will deliver it.'

Like Blair, Bush promoted Iraq as a poster child for democracy, especially after the predicted massive stockpiles of weapons of mass destruction that were supposed to be uncovered by the March 2003 invasion proved evanescent. Ironically, one of the most influential Iraqi advocates of this transformation from fear to freedom was dissident Iraqi intellectual Kanaan Makiya, who argued persuasively in 1989 that the regime of Saddam Hussein had obliterated civil society, the middle space between citizen and state, leaving Iraqis exposed to the naked power of the state and able to find security only in the basic institutions of family and tribe—and sometimes not even there (Makiya, writing as Samir al-Khalil, 1989). If a democracy is to be durable, then an essential ingredient is a vibrant civil society, which certainly requires much more time than the few months anticipated initially by the US architects of the invasion.

The US and Britain's opportunistic embrace of democracy initially prompted some ruling autocrats to clean up their acts a bit, but the effect did not last. Neither the US nor Britain anticipated the difficulties that they would face in consolidating their occupation of Iraq following the toppling of Saddam Hussein's regime. Some ill-considered decisions, such as the much-regretted edict to dismantle the Iraqi army shortly after the capture of Baghdad, only exacerbated the problems. The deadly resistance to the Allied occupation, the anger of many Iraqis at an often club-footed US response to violence, and an onslaught of bombings and assassinations against international and Iraqi institutions made a mockery of the project of democratizing Iraq.

While the advocacy of democracy by the US initially provoked considerable heated debate in the Arab world, the chaos unleashed by the war in Iraq discredited the idea. By 2005, even sympathetic Arab thinkers were looking at Iraqi 'democracy' as an exemplar of *fitnah* (that is, disorder or chaos). Autocrats who had felt compelled to respond to Bush's democracy initiative when it was announced, such as Mubarak in Egypt, began using Iraq as an argument against expanding freedom.

In any case, given the political economy of most of the region's regimes, reform, not to mention democratization, needs to be understood as a long-term process of change rather than as a 'two aspirins at bedtime' prescription.

The political economy of the state

In Iraq, as elsewhere in the Middle East, the public sector is massive and any thoughtful effort to promote political reform must address the state's overarching economic role.[2] The Middle Eastern state extends well beyond the seraglios of the rulers. Outside of agriculture, the state is the leading employer. Thus many citizens have a stake in the state and their interests do not lie in destroying it, but in improving its performance. Government dominates the formal economy, in some instances through a phalanx of public sector companies; in others, through the flow of oil earnings and other 'rents' directly into the state coffers. As a result, government expenditures in the Middle East often make up a larger share of the gross national product than in other countries of comparable income level outside of the region. In some cases, government spending amounts to nearly half of GNP (for example, Egypt), compared to less than 25 per cent in middle-income countries generally (al-Sayyid 1991).

While the state's grip on the economy is important, considerable economic activity and resources lie outside of the state's control. A significant amount of largely undocumented economic activity occurs in the realm of the informal sector, which encompasses an array of craftspeople, doctors, lawyers, petty traders in legal and illicit goods, workshop operators, pieceworkers, and many others whose income is undocumented by the state. The informal economy has long been an important site for undermining and quietly contesting the state's authority (Singerman 1995).

Rentierism

Yet the prevalence of rentier states in the Middle East means that governments are highly resistant to change. Unlike states that depend on taxation extracted directly from citizens, rentier states distribute rents rather than extract taxes. Rents are direct payments to government that may derive from natural resources, especially oil, as well as other significant transfers such as foreign aid. (For example, Egypt receives over US$1.5 billion in annual military and development assistance from the US, which reduces the state's dependence on conventional taxation.) In 2014, the European Union provided €650 million in development aid, not including bilateral support by individual European states. Some of the smaller states in the region, such as Qatar or the United Arab Emirates, receive almost all of their income from oil or natural gas sales, rendering the government much more removed from public pressure than governments that depend upon taxation.

The prevalence of the rentier state in the Middle East has had a detrimental effect on both economic development and political liberalization. The state has, in effect, attempted to satisfy the population at large through provision of a host of services and economic activities paid through rent income. As long as rents from the outside world are available, the state will respond only to those concerns of the population that it finds necessary to maintaining its power and position. Moreover, the rentier state's often extensive economic programmes tend to co-opt the bourgeoisie and reward it economically in projects conceived and funded by the state. Hence the bourgeoisie's fortunes come to centre on the state and its defined economic goals.

The rentier state tends to become increasingly autonomous from society. The state can use the income from rent to enlist compliance and to pursue goals not necessarily in the best interests of society. Since most of the state's revenues are not extracted from the population, the corollary sense of obligation and responsiveness to society does not necessarily develop. So long as the rent continues to flow, rentier states have no incentive to liberalize their political systems. As Luciani has indicated in **Chapter 5** and elsewhere, the oil rent becomes 'a factor perpetuating authoritarian government' (Luciani 1994: 131).

A state facing fiscal crisis and forced to resort to increased taxation will generate demands from within the society for accountability. Programmes of political reform in Jordan and Morocco bear out this argument, in that each state sought, through political reform, to salve the pains of extensive economic belt-tightening and tax increases. However, the idea promoted by major international financial institutions, such as the World Bank and the International Monetary Fund, that the path to democracy begins with economic liberalization has proven arguable. This may be true over the long term, but the short-term consequences of economic liberalization are often reduced freedoms. The case of Syria illustrates that economic crisis followed by a relatively steady economic liberalization does not lead to political reform. Similarly to some other authoritarian states, Syria controlled the bargaining process in its economic liberalization programme by confining it to a privileged few (Heydemann 1993).

Divergent paths in rentier states: Iran and Turkey

The examples of Iran and Turkey also shed some light on how rentierism influences the prospects for political reform. In Iran, rentierism came to define the state in the 1970s. Its systematic growth was conclusively evident after the oil boom that followed the 1973 Arab–Israeli War. Supremely confident of its economic and political positions in domestic, regional, and international arenas, the state's economic policies resulted in two simultaneous developments. It created a heavily dependent commercial and industrial modern bourgeoisie that benefited enormously from the state policies, but remained subservient to it. The private sector's influence 'was limited to implementation. Being totally dependent on the state, Iran's rentiér bourgeoisie had neither the incentive nor the means to "capture the state"' (Shambayati 1994: 320–1).

The growth of rentierism also made the state essentially oblivious to the concerns and priorities of civil society. The pre-revolutionary Iranian state decided what was good for society and acted accordingly. When the state was eventually challenged during the revolutionary years, it was the traditional bourgeoisie from the bazaar, which had preserved some of its autonomy from the state, that took the lead and in reality bankrolled the revolution. Using the well-established bazaar–mosque alliance networks, the opposition legitimized its attack on the Pahlavi state by utilizing powerful Islamic ideology. The sharp lines of cleavage were defined in cultural and moral terms, much more so than economic ones, in order to mobilize support and attack the state where it was most obviously vulnerable (Ashraf 1988, 1990; Shambayati 1994).

The Turkish case offers a sharply different model. Although certain features of rentierism—remittances from workers abroad—are also present in Turkey, the state's income is based primarily on domestic sources, not external rent; hence rentierism has not dominated the Turkish economy. To increase revenues in the 1970s, the state had to increase taxation and domestic production. A number of policies, including import substitution and industrialization, were adopted to increase domestic production and to reduce external dependence. Although these attempts did not help Turkey's negative trade balance and foreign exchange crisis, they did prompt the state to engage in serious bargaining with the business community through chambers of commerce and industry. The ensuing cleavages within the private sector led to the creation of several organizations devoted to the management of commerce and industry. It is instructive that an early Islamist group, the National Salvation Party, was established to protect the interests of petite bourgeoisie against some of the more prominent organizations that were tied to the interests of larger industrial and commercial capitalists. Economic issues, rather than religious ones, defined much of the political agenda of this Islamist party, as well as the industrialists, in their interactions with the Turkish state. Structured as a set of autonomous organizations, the private sector was a serious force in the society at large and in its relationship with the state (Shambayati 1994).

In the absence of fully developed rentierism, increasing domestic taxation and extraction, foreign exchange crisis, and the willingness to engage opposition from within the society in an inclusionary way combined to increase prospects for democracy in Turkey. This pattern stands in sharp contrast to the Iranian case in the pre-revolutionary decade, during which rentierism and exclusionary politics were dominant.

The pressure mounts

While literacy rates in the Middle East may be unimpressive by Western standards, the simple fact is that access to education has proliferated, including at the university level, so that many people's expectations have become more complex. In an era of straitened resources, government's capacity to sustain the loyalty of citizens through patronage and subsidies is strained, and often overwhelmed, in the less wealthy states.

Especially in the 1980s and 1990s, the manifest failures of state-dominated models of economic development became undeniable. Repression lightened as a means of accommodating dissent and reducing government's culpability for failure. The population pressures are immense, as reflected in the aggregate figures on youths aged 14 or younger, who account for about 30 per cent of the Middle Eastern population according to 2011 data, and over 40 per cent in some cases, such as Syria and Palestine (Dhillon and Yousef 2009). Equally relevant is that 50 per cent of the total population of the Middle East and North Africa were aged 24 or younger in 2011. It is easy to visualize the serious challenges that this 'youth bulge' poses for government, not least in terms of schooling and job creation. While per capita measures of gross domestic product increased by an average of over 3 per cent in the first decade of the twenty-first century, in recent years growth rates have sometimes been negative and have not risen above 1.8 per cent annually (World Bank Group 2015, 141–8).

In the swelling working-class neighbourhoods of the region's largest cities, rural-to-urban migration has fuelled massive urban sprawl. To begin to grasp the sheer magnitude of the phenomenon, consider that some cities, such as Riyadh in Saudi Arabia, grew so quickly that populations doubled in as little as seven years, while already-massive cities, such as venerable Cairo, become home to millions of new residents each decade.

Where political space opened, individuals began to organize, giving new breath to long-suppressed associational life. The result was a rapid expansion of civil society, the melange of associations, clubs, syndicates, guilds, and other groups that enjoy a measure of autonomy from the state's control, and which ideally serve as a buffer between the citizen and the raw power of the state (Norton 1995). As early as the 1980s, more than 70,000 such groups were counted in the Arab world (Ibrahim 1995). While the components of civil society that attracted the most international attention were oriented to the protection of rights, such as the Egyptian Organization of Human Rights, or the Palestinian al-Haqq, the vast majority was not overtly political, and focused instead on aiding the indigent and the ill, or providing religious or educational resources. In cities such as Cairo, Istanbul, and Algiers, intricate networks defined by kinship, locality, and reciprocity intersect with other elements in civil society, the informal economy, opposition political movements, and government functionaries to define a complex setting for politics (Singerman 1995; White 2014).

Equally, if not more importantly, large informal and undocumented sectors of the economy grew. Across the region, vast numbers of labour migrants were attracted to the employment opportunities in the oil economies of the Gulf. These workers, as they returned home to Syria, Egypt, Lebanon, Jordan, and Yemen, among other countries, brought hoards of hard currency that would be used not only to improve their families' standards of living and to start businesses, but also to fund opposition groups—especially Islamist movements.

Muslims and the question of political reform

There are now over 1.6 billion Muslims in the world, including 525 million in the Middle East, and more than 370 million in the Arab world alone according to 2013 World Bank data. While it might be thought convenient if a preponderance of Muslims were to embrace

Western secular ideals, not to mention Western-style democracy, the picture is more complex. A relative handful of Arab liberals *do* share and espouse Western ideals, but they do not have a broad constituency. The dominant oppositional forces in the broader Muslim world, not least in the Arab world, have typically been hostile to secularism—particularly when 'secularism' is understood to mean that Islamic values have no place in politics—but they also embrace representative democracy. In a region in which religion is an important source of personal identity, any opening of the political system brings with it a debate about the proper role of religion in society and the relationship of religion to the state, but Middle Eastern governments have generally not been willing to experiment in political reform and allow that debate to occur.

In Middle Eastern societies the embrace of piety (*taqwa*) is common, but the content of that piety is actively contested and reimagined, especially among the youth. Islam has become increasingly personalized under conditions of growing urbanization, globalization, and the commercialization of identity, not to mention a new horizon for political imagination (White 2014). Political groups cannot help but be influenced by what Asef Bayat (2010) calls the 'quiet encroachment of the ordinary', whereby subtle individual actions resocialize religious movements and governments, and thereby create new identities and opportunities for change, including democratic change.

There are many variants of democracy, but a core component is the conduct of reasonably fair competitive elections. In many of the countries of the region, where credible political 'secular' parties have been repressed, Islamist groups are poised to seize the opportunity of open elections. Justifiably or not, this prospect generated unease in Western circles. At best, major external powers, such as the US, promoted a 'go slow' approach, but more typically sought to undermine elections that brought Islamists to power. The cases of Algeria and Palestine are instructive.

Algeria

In the face of horrible unemployment, discontent, and economic failure, Algeria attempted democratization in the late 1980s and early 1990s. The ruling National Liberation Front (FLN) had monopolized power for three decades, ever since Algeria won its hard-fought independence from France in 1962. The FLN was soundly trounced by the Islamic Salvation Front (FIS) in Algeria's first free elections, including municipal and then parliamentary elections. The Algerian army intervened in January 1992 to prevent the FIS from realizing its victory and civil war ensued. It is impossible to know whether the FIS might have ruled competently or incompetently, and whether it would have been able to impose its religious values on a divided society split between secularism and religious conservatism.

More than 100,000 people died in the internal war and Algeria became a cautionary tale invoked routinely by Middle East dictators, secularly inclined intellectuals, and Western officials alike. The failure of the Algerian reform experiment certainly illustrated the likely fate of ruling parties when exposed to reasonably free elections.

Algerian secularists who enthusiastically supported the coup in 1992 now often concede that it would have been far better to permit the FIS experiment to go forward, especially since the option of intervention would have continued to be an option for the Algerian generals who continue to wield enormous power.

Hamas and the 2006 elections

When Palestinian legislative elections were conducted in January 2006, at US insistence, the unexpected, but clear-cut, winner was the Islamist group Hamas (Lesch 2007). Palestinian voters were expressing their anger at Israel's occupation and the burgeoning of illegal settlements on occupied Palestinian territory, as well as the notorious corruption of the Palestinian Authority and Fatah. Contrary to a sanguine acceptance of the wholly unexpected result, the US led a campaign to isolate the new Gaza-based Hamas government and to starve it of funds, which also entailed starving large numbers of aid-dependent Palestinians. European diplomats and some US officials urged a path of incremental inclusion instead, but the US rejected any attempt to co-opt Hamas as long as it refused to forswear terrorism or to accept Israel's legitimacy.

The policy was not successful and it has left Gaza impoverished, in large measure as a result of a blockade imposed by Israel and supported in recent years by Egypt. Hamas seized complete control of Gaza in 2007 and a rival Fatah-oriented government resides in the still Israeli-occupied West Bank. Despite a series of Israeli raids and bombardments that have killed many civilians—including military campaigns in December 2008 and January 2009, and in July and August 2014—Hamas continues to dominate Gaza and enjoys significant support in the occupied West Bank. Arguably, the path of incremental inclusion (as respected international diplomats urged) rather than exclusion would have been a wiser response to the Hamas electoral triumph. Hamas is indisputably an entrenched player in Palestinian politics.

The Arab uprisings of 2011

Given the, at best, tepid external support for substantial political reform, particularly entailing the inclusion of Islamist opposition groups, and considering the hostility of Arab governments to meaningful political reform, the puzzle is: under what circumstances would the ruling structures be compelled to succumb to popular demands for change? For years, public space in Arab countries has been depoliticized, so that even ephemeral attempts to organize or mobilize opposition were met with repression and intimidation. Short of an unlikely epiphany within the political class, only sustained popular demonstrations and resistance that dwarf the capacity of the repressive apparatus might convince those who work the levers of power of the imperative for embracing reform (the sincerity of the embrace would be another matter). When are people willing to go to the street, to act collectively and put their lives at risk for change? A solution to the puzzle arrived in Tunisia, when fruit seller Mohammed Bouazizi set himself alight in the city of Sidi Bouzid, on 17 December 2010, in a desperate quest for dignity and massive protests followed.

Not to diminish the profound sacrifice of Bouazizi, the more important fact was that within weeks an enduring Tunisian dictator was forced from office and fled into exile as millions watched the events unfold on satellite television and celebrated the event in text messages, and on social media, particularly Facebook, Twitter, and YouTube (few of the region's governments then anticipated the importance of such platforms). These were exhilarating moments of enthusiasm when the people imagined they could topple a regime.

Popular despair gave way to anger in 2011. For the multitudes of men and women across the Middle East with limited access to government services, who struggle daily to make ends meet, live in fear of abusive police and witness government corruption regularly, a credible opportunity for better lives elicited tremendous excitement. Young people in their teens, twenties, and beyond, hoping for a good job, accumulating the resources necessary to marry or simply finding a decent place to live, were galvanized by a chance to level the playing field. Unlike in Europe, Japan, or North America, in many Middle Eastern societies there is an inverse relationship between higher education and employment, which is to say that better educated people are more likely to be unemployed than less well-educated people. While the duration of protests varied, in the early months of 2011 large-scale, sometimes huge demonstrations occurred in nineteen Arab countries, most momentously in Tunisia, Egypt, Libya, Syria, Bahrain, and Yemen.

In reality, as events unfolded it would be all too clear that displacing a few men at the top of a regime hardly constituted a revolution. Often left intact was the 'deep state'—the webs of bureaucratic power centres, including military and security agencies through which power is exercised, not least in Egypt. The one exception is Tunisia, where consequential and perhaps enduring changes have occurred.

Tunisia: the Jasmine Revolution

Of all of the North African countries, Tunisia would seem to enjoy the best chance for a democratic transformation. The population of 11 million is generally well educated, and there is a sizeable middle class and an impressive civil society. Tunisia has also been a pioneer in its commitment to women's rights, which are arguably more respected in Tunisia than in any of the other North African countries. The small Tunisian military, which includes fewer than 40,000 people under arms, is led by a professional official corps that has neither been the power behind the curtains nor infiltrated the civilian economy in the same way as the behemoth Egyptian military has done.

North Africa, the Maghreb ('the West') is a region of remarkable cultural and political diversity. While the population is predominantly Arab, there are also ethnic minorities, especially the Berbers, who comprise important and often restive minorities in Algeria and Morocco (with sizeable numbers as well as in Tunisia and Libya). While this may change, within Tunisia, the Arab–Berber divide has been far less important than it is in either Morocco or Algeria, where the Berbers have insisted on education in the Berber language, as well as cultural autonomy.

Tunisia's Islamists are led by Rachid Ghannouchi, who is often celebrated as a moderate figure. He returned from exile only in February 2011, after years of living in London, where he played an important role as a voice for Muslim accommodation in Europe. The Renaissance Party (al-Nahdah), which Ghannouchi founded, managed to survive years of state suppression by maintaining a covert presence in society and cultivating a youthful leadership. Tunisia is also known for its strong labour union movement—one that is without parallel in North Africa, or the Arab world for that matter. At moments of political impasse, the Tunisian General Labour Union (UGTT), which boasts a membership of more than 500,000 and is one of the most powerful institutions in the country, played a decisive role by brokering compromises between al-Nahdah and its secular opponents.

Transparent and well-designed elections for seats in the proportionately distributed 217-member National Constituent Assembly were held on 23 October 2011. The Assembly is charged with writing a new constitution. Thirty parties participated, but six won three-quarters of all seats. While al-Nahdah won the largest share, with ninety seats, a variety of ideological and regional groups won representation, and nineteen seats were allocated to Tunisians living abroad.

Time and again since December 2010, Tunisians rallied to preserve the momentum of the Jasmine Revolution. In contrast with other Arab states, the Tunisians have revealed a penchant for reform. Thus, while the Secretary-General of al-Nahdah, Hamadi Jebali, became Prime Minister in December 2011, the Constituent Assembly named Moncef Marzouki, a highly respected human rights activist and physician, Acting-President (a weaker position than the premiership).

Over time, al-Nahdah lost support, particularly for failing to address Tunisia's deep economic problems, including the unemployment crisis. In parliamentary elections in October 2014, al-Nahdah came in second to Nada' Tunis (Call of Tunis), a party bringing together figures from the former regime, liberal opposition figures and elements from the UGTT. To its credit, the Islamist party gracefully conceded defeat and turned over power to the victors. In December 2014, Mohamed Beji Caid Essebi, the octogenarian founder of Nada' Tunis, was elected Tunisia's first freely elected President.

In his seminal article, Dankwart Rustow (1970) conceptualized the process of democratization as a process of habituation whereby the players learn and grow used to the democratic rules of the game. This is an important insight when considering Tunisia because it is unrealistic to presume that democratic systems begin with all parties fully imbued with democratic principles; indeed, even mature democracies are still evolving, still democratizing.

As in Egypt and across the Arab world, conservative and sometimes violent Salafists have asserted themselves in Tunisia, often targeting secular institutions such as universities for failing to adhere to strict moral standards, including permitting men and women to study together, or for not permitting veiled women to enter campus. While the Salafists are politically weak in Tunisia, neighbouring Libya provides a ready sanctuary and training site. So jihadist-oriented Salafists constitute a security threat to Tunisia and its economy, particularly in light of several attacks on key tourist destinations.

Elsewhere in the Arab world, Tunisia may prove to be the exception that proves the rule, namely that the legacy of decades of authoritarian rule is a weak foundation for the political reform. Arabs may be watching political developments in Tunisia with envy, but the short-term possibility of any Arab political system following the Tunisian example is slim indeed.

Egypt: the 25 January Revolution and its aftermath

Egyptians chafed under the Mubarak dictatorship for years. While opposition activities were often stymied by repression and dampened by fear, labour strikes were increasingly commonplace and political activists continued to highlight regime abuses. Within opposition Islamist circles, there was much debate and discussion about themes of civil society, democracy, and tolerance (el-Sherif 2011).

Using word of mouth, text messaging, and social networking tools (especially Facebook, which had become a locus of opposition communication by the previous autumn),

25 January was declared a 'Day of Rage'. A variety of groups was involved, but for many the memory of Khalid Said, a young computer activist who was savagely beaten to death by police the previous summer in Alexandria, was vivid.[3] Tens of thousands turned out, especially in Cairo's Tahrir (meaning 'Liberation') Square, a central site adjacent to Egypt's famous archaeological museum, where chants of *Irhal! Irhal! Irhal!* ('Scram! Get out! Leave!') became commonplace. Although the momentum was tenuous, especially when armed thugs were unleashed by the government to foster a climate of lawlessness, the 'revolution' succeeded in a mere eighteen days in toppling Hosni Mubarak, who had ruled Egypt since 1981, when he had notoriously pledged to serve only one six-year term.

The old order was shaken, but no revolution occurred in Egypt. The massive Egyptian military holds the reins of power. It was the senior generals who told Mubarak that his time was up and pledged to superintend a transition to elections. The military has a big stake in the present distribution of resources and privileges, and it begs credulity to imagine that the uniformed brass will accept any political arrangement that challenges their vested interests. This is a gargantuan constraint on reform.

In March 2011, the Egyptians went to the polls and overwhelmingly approved (more than 77 per cent voted 'yes') a series of constitutional amendments intended to permit parliamentary and presidential elections. Despite promises by the ruling Supreme Council of the Armed Forces (SCAF) that the new constitution would be drafted in an open process, the military unilaterally amended fifty-five articles of the existing constitution after the referendum. The full dimensions of the generals' agenda became clear on 1 November 2011, when SCAF distributed its 'Guidelines' for the drafting of a new constitution. These guidelines include provisions that there will be no scrutiny of the military budget by civilian authorities and that the military will retain veto power over any proffered drafts of a new constitution. (Two subsequent constitutions have greatly broadened the protections and prerogatives of the military.)

Although there were about twenty legal parties in Mubarak's time, few enjoyed anything approaching national organization. Ad hoc groups that played leading roles in the Tahrir Square demonstrations that toppled Mubarak, would have to start from the ground up to create a political party. The only opposition group that could boast national organization was the Muslim Brotherhood, which founded the Freedom and Justice Party. A variety of other Islamist parties have emerged, including the Hizb al-Wasat, the reformist Islamist 'Centre Party' that was finally granted legal status in 2011, after sixteen years of struggle.

The growing vitality of Salafist parties is noteworthy. The Salafists are generally contemptuous of profane politics, but they proved to be quite pragmatic in exploiting political opportunity in order to advance their goal of instilling a conservative Islamic order in Egypt. Salafi groups have long been especially active in Alexandria, but they also enjoy a national following.

Parliamentary elections were concluded in December 2011, and the Muslim Brotherhood's Freedom and Justice Party and allied parties won nearly half of the 508 seats, with the Salafists coming in second with a quarter of the seats. The secularly oriented groups that played such a formative role in launching and sustaining the Tahrir Square demonstrations came in a distant third, with votes scattered among an admixture of small parties.

Presidential elections followed in June 2012. Non-Islamist candidates for the presidency included former Air Force General and Prime Minister Ahmad Shafik, a long-term Mubarak ally, and leftist Hamdeen Sabahi. Non-Islamist voters split their votes between Sabahi and Moussa, so law-and-order man Shafik came in second and then entered a run-off against Muhammed Mursi, the Brotherhood's candidate. After days of suspense (and rampant suspicions that the results were being 'cooked'), Mursi was declared the winner, with about 52 per cent of the vote. What seemed to be a watershed moment in Egypt's political history became a catastrophe. Mursi proved to be an inept leader with a penchant for harangue rather than consensus. He and his colleagues in the Brotherhood were unprepared for the immense challenges confronting Egypt, and they were regularly undermined by components of the deep state that remained well-entrenched in power.

By early 2013, a massive anti-Mursi movement gained force—with generous support from rich opponents of the president, as well as massive funds provided secretly by the army by Saudi Arabia, Kuwait and the United Arab Emirates.[4] The army led by Field Marshal Abdel Fattah al-Sisi, deposed Mursi in July 2013, and pro-Mursi demonstrators were brutally suppressed. In August, police and soldiers slaughtered almost 1,000 protesters. The toppled president and thousands of Brotherhood members have been jailed and face long prison terms (and death sentences, as in the case of Mursi), often under ludicrous charges in a court system that has inspired international derision. The Brotherhood was subsequently declared to be a terrorist organization. Public assembly has been severely restricted, and some of the leading secular figures in the so-called 25 January Revolution have been imprisoned for mounting peaceful protests. Meanwhile, jihadist groups unrelated to the Brotherhood (and now aligned with the so-called Islamic State, or ISIS) have mounted numerous attacks, particularly on security personnel, such as in October 2014 when five dozen soldiers were killed in Egypt's Sinai.

The deep state, led by the army, has clawed back power. In March 2014, Field Marshal al-Sisi won the presidency with 97 per cent of the vote, a result that is reminiscent of the Mubarak era. The economic problems that helped provoke the 2011 demonstrations remain largely unresolved, Egyptian society is now deeply divided along ideological lines and there is certainly less freedom today than during the authoritarian rule of Mubarak.

Libya: the 'Mukhtar Revolution'

Muammar Gaddafi's strategy of ruling was premised on weak state institutions and alliances with favoured tribes.[5] His self-styled *jamahiriya* ('people's republic') was intended to preclude challenges to his power by diffusing power throughout society. Hence the Libyan Army was weak and fragmented; particularly in the case of the eastern units, it centred on the city of Benghazi. The judiciary was fragmented and the police forces lacked a central authority. As for civil society, any initiative that suggested establishing anything resembling autonomous local actors was suppressed or crushed by the state. This meant that any group seizing the state immediately confronted the task of building national institutions, as well offering impetus to civil society.

In Libya, swelling protests began in mid-February. On 17 February 2011, a proclaimed 'Day of Rage' inspired by the models of Tunisia and Egypt prompted a deadly response, especially against demonstrators in Tripoli's Green Square. A vindictive Gaddafi promised to tolerate no dissent, declaring that his opponents were drug-addled terrorists led by Al-Qaeda and calling on Libyans to fight the 'greasy rats'.

As the groundswell of opposition to Gaddafi's rule expanded in February and March, an inchoate civil society could be observed—but Libya lacks either an established political opposition or established legal institutions other than tribal-based traditions of customary law. The Muslim Brotherhood does enjoy considerable support, especially in the eastern cities including Benghazi, and Salafist groups have been picking up pace in recent years. The venerable Sufi or mystical orders, especially the Sanusiyya, played an important role in Libyan history, including leading the anti-colonial campaign against the Italians. Having been ruthlessly repressed by Gaddafi, the Sanusiyya are resurging.

In an extraordinary meeting on 12 March, the League of Arab States (LAS) voted to support international action to protect Libyan civilians, which was followed five days later by United Nations Security Council Resolution 1973. The Resolution enabled the US-European intervention to create 'no-drive' and 'no-fly' zones to stop attacks on Libyan civilians. The NATO effort evolved into a transparent campaign to destroy the military apparatus of the Gaddafi regime in support of opposition forces that were engaged in dangerous on-the-job training.

Gaddafi's capture on 20 October 2011, and his bloody, ignominious end, came amidst reports not only of government atrocities and mass executions, but also of scores of summary executions of regime loyalists by opposition militias. The legacy of disregard for legal processes and disrespect for fundamental human rights by both sides suggested that rocky days lay ahead in liberated Libya, where militias remain heavily armed.

Credible elections for the General National Congress or parliament were held in 2012 with over 60 per cent of eligible voters participating, but by 2014 less than 20 per cent of voters turned out to elect representatives to parliament. An admixture of Islamist groups performed poorly in the latter election, and the weak Supreme Court has challenged the legality of the election. A coalition of groups, notably the Muslim Brotherhood, supported by Qatar and Turkey claims to be the legitimate government and is based in Tripoli. The elected government resides in eastern Libya in Tobruk, near the border of Egypt; from which is it receives significant support as well as from the United Arab Emirates and Saudi Arabia. Neither authority effectively controls it own territory and power is widely fragmented and alliances shift often, as might be expected in a state in which durable national institutions are largely absent. The prospect for a consolidated authority emerging by 2020 is not good.

'The Syria Revolution'

Following the death in 2000 of Hafiz al-Asad, who had ruled Syria for twenty-seven years, there was hope that his son and successor, Dr Bashar al-Asad, would shepherd Syria toward more freedom. Whatever Bashar's intentions, he promptly revealed his dependence on the authoritarian structure of power that his wily father had mastered. After a flush of excitement in 2000, opposition voices were soon stifled by the state.

The chant that became famous in Tunisia, Egypt, and Libya was *al-sha'ab yurid usqat al-nizam* ('the people want the fall of the regime'), but in Damascus the regime was smugly confident that Syria would not be affected by the upheaval. Not only were the many agencies of the security apparatus vigilant to control dissent, but President Bashar al-Asad also presented himself as a reformer. In 2011, he gave a long interview to the *Wall Street Journal* (2011), in which he argued that Syria was stable:

> We always say that we need reform but what kind of reform? This is first. Second, if you want to make a comparison between what is happening in Egypt and Syria, you have to look from a different point: why is Syria stable, although we have more difficult conditions? Egypt has been supported financially by the United States, while we are under embargo by most countries of the world. We have growth although we do not have many of the basic needs for the people. Despite all that, the people do not go into an uprising. So it is not only about the needs and not only about the reform. It is about the ideology, the beliefs and the cause that you have. There is a difference between having a cause and having a vacuum. So, as I said, we have many things in common but at the same time we have some different things.

February passed with only a few small demonstrations, but by March it became clear that Syria was by no means immune: a surge of demonstrations began in the southern Houran district of Syria, particularly in the Sunni town of Deraa. The demonstrations were provoked by the arrest and heinous mistreatment of teenagers, who had been arrested by the police for posting anti-regime graffiti. The initial protests evoked a bloody response from the regime, but the demonstrations spread throughout the southern region, despite widespread arrests and indiscriminate killings by the army and police. As in Egypt, government thugs, known locally as *shabiha*, were commonly employed as well. No serious efforts have been made by the government to accommodate any of the demonstrators' demands, either in 2011 or since.

The initial waves of protests were peaceful, but within months an armed insurrection was underway, including significant number of soldiers who deserted to join the opposition. By mid-2015, credible estimates put the total deaths in what has become the Syrian civil war at nearly 250,000 people. In addition, nearly half of the country's population of 23 million have fled their homes. Over four million people have sought safety in neighbouring countries (primarily Iraq, Jordan, Lebanon, and Turkey) or in Europe, while millions more have been impelled to seek safe haven wherever they may find it in Syria.

The dominant forces opposing the regime have often been hostile to non-Sunni minorities, especially so in the case of Daesh (or Da'ish, the Arabic acronym for the so-called Islamic State of Iraq and Syria; ISIS, which calls itself the Islamic State). Especially in Damascus and Aleppo, as well as in areas dominated by minorities such as Christian sects, Alawis, Kurds, or Druze, the regime has retained significant support. A majority of Syrians (about 65 per cent) are Arab Sunni Muslims, who dominate the opposition (yet many urban-based Sunni merchants have stuck with the regime).

Key elements within the military remain loyal to the regime, but casualties have taken a massive toll on what had been a standing force of 400,000. Tens of thousands of desertions and defections among non-Alawi soldiers and officers have eroded the military's strength, although these losses have typically been from less important units. For more than forty years, the Syrian regime has been dominated by the minority Alawi community, which accounts for about 11 per cent of Syria's population of 21 million, and the Alawis control all senior positions in the army. The Alawi sect is an offshoot of Shia Islam, but the sect is quite unique in its practices and structure. For generations, the Alawis were poor and disadvantaged, but their path to influence and power was the military. Unlike either Tunisia or Egypt, where professional army officers broke with the president, this is unlikely to happen in Syria. The two most important army divisions are controlled by relatives of Bashar al-Asad—particularly his brother Maher, who has taken the lead in attempting to crush the growing insurrection brutally.

International efforts to foster a negotiated solution to the conflict have failed. The regime and its adversaries reject the principle that facilitated a negotiated end to the fifteen-year civil war in neighbouring Lebanon in 1990, namely 'no victor, no vanquished'. The major combatants have rejected compromise out of hand. Yet, neither side has the power to vanquish the other and to dominate Syria. This suggests that Syria will be a country-in-fragments for many years to come. Even if the level of violence recedes over time, the rebuilding of Syria's infrastructure will be a gargantuan if not impossible challenge, not to mention meeting the basic needs of millions of impoverished people struggling to live day-by-day.

Renewed dissent in Saudi Arabia and problems next door

Significant demonstrations took place in Saudi Arabia and in Bahrain. In Saudi Arabia, the minority Shi'i Muslim community of the Eastern Province, who may account for 10 per cent of the country's population, mounted a 'Day of Rage' on 11 March—also styled the 'Hanin Revolution of 11 March', in reference to a document drafted by Shi'i intellectuals in 2010, which was presented to King Abdullah. The document calls for respect for the civil rights of the Shia, including the end of long-term imprisonment without trial (citing the case of some prisoners who have been held for fourteen years without trial). The police responded to the protests by about 800 people by arresting several dozen protesters, some of whom were alleged to have been involved in the 1996 bombing of the al-Khobar Tower barracks. The knee-jerk response of the Saudi authorities has been to describe Shi'i protesters as serving Iranian purposes, often with fallacious or weak evidence. Whether in the Eastern Province, in Bahrain, or elsewhere in the Gulf or in Yemen, the Saudi narrative grants little or no credibility to either local grievances or the distinctive qualities of various Shi'i communities. Instead, it is claimed that Iran's agenda is the key factor.

The government in Riyadh was also concerned that restive Sunni citizens would be inspired to protest. By March, several obliging senior clerics in the holy city of Mecca issued a religious opinion declaring that it was forbidden to protest because this undermines security and stability. Simultaneously, King Abdullah announced a large stimulus package to be spent on creating jobs, housing, and medical facilities. The expanded expenditures eventually totalled nearly $130 billion. Subjects were also threatened with punishment if they mounted illegal demonstrations (and there is no possibility of 'legal' demonstrations).

Under King Abdullah some modest reforms were announced, including a September 2011 promise that women would be permitted to vote and stand for local elections beginning in 2015. With Abdullah's demise in 2015, and the installation of King Salman, even tepid reforms initiated under his predecessor are in doubt. Prior to ascending the throne, Salman served as the Governor of Riyadh for 48 years and he earned a reputation as the royal family's stern disciplinarian, probably not an obvious credential for a reformer.

Meanwhile, neighbouring Yemen, the Arab world's poorest country, was collapsing into civil war by 2014. Long-term dictator Ali Abdullah Salih was nudged from power with Saudi help in late 2011 after months of demonstrations and violence. The conflict in resource-poor Yemen is extraordinary complex, and involves competing regional, ideological, and especially tribal interests. Major combatant forces include a formidable local branch of Al-Qaeda, elements of the military that remain loyal to Salih, military units that remain loyal to the legitimate government, pro-Saudi tribes and Houthis (Shi'i tribesmen who follow a different sect of Shi'ism than Iranians). The Saudi response to the unfolding civil war was to fall back on its narrative blaming Iran for inciting and arming insurgents, although Iran's role has been far more limited, as western diplomats are quick to note. Thus, rather than focusing on the need to accommodate competing Yemeni interests, Saudi Arabia decided to intervene militarily through a campaign of aerial bombardment beginning in March 2015 (with some support from other GCC states). While considerable physical damage has been caused by the bombing, as well as the deaths of hundreds of civilians, the internal balance of power in Yemen has not been meaningfully changed. Short of an enormously difficult ground invasion of Yemen, which was attempted with disastrous consequences by Egypt in 1962, the Saudi's capacity to impose a political solution on Yemen appears dim.

The tragedy of Bahrain

In the small Gulf state of Bahrain, many of the complaints coincide with sectarian differences and disparities in privilege that are extraordinary because they are so readily noticed. Although Shi'i Muslims account for nearly 70 per cent of the small population (excluding expatriate workers, the Bahraini citizens number about 600,000), they have typically been on the short end of the stick in terms of access to government employment and favours. On a journey from the cosmopolitan capital of Manama to the predominantly Shi'i and very distressed Shi'i city of Sitrah, the differences are abrupt and stunning. Sitrah, along with many of the Shi'i villages in Bahrain, is a dreadful place to live. Unemployment and per capita income data speak volumes about the inequity that defines Bahraini society.

On 14 February 2011, protests were mounted by predominantly Shi'i demonstrators, although some reform-minded Sunni Muslims also joined them. Many of the demonstrators gathered around the Pearl Roundabout, a downtown Manama landmark where a white concrete pedestal held aloft a pearl, recalling earlier days when Bahrain was a world centre for their harvesting. The demonstrators were overwhelmingly peaceful and police efforts to dislodge them were largely unsuccessful, despite police violence that killed five protesters on 18 February. The government—urged on by the United States—sought a negotiated end to the protests. Crown Prince Salman took the lead in negotiations to initiate a serious dialogue about reform, particularly with Shaikh 'Ali Salman, the softly spoken and moderate head of al-Wefaq (meaning 'the Compact'), which held all of the elected opposition seats in parliament. Hardliners on both sides were sceptical of the proposed dialogue and it was stymied.

On the opposition side, the rival al-Haq movement declared that its goal was to overthrow the monarchy, while within the regime Prime Minister Khalifa bin Salman, the uncle of King Hamad bin Isa and who had served in his post for four decades from the very beginning of Bahraini independence, was hostile to the prospect of reform. The reputedly corrupt prime minister, who enjoys close ties to Saudi Arabia, has long frustrated reformist efforts, not least those pursued by his grand nephew the Crown Prince. US efforts to encourage the reform dialogue seemed to be bearing fruit in early March, but any talk of dialogue ended on 14 March when troops from Saudi Arabia and the United Arab Emirates troops crossed the causeway linking the main island to the mainland to lead a crackdown on the demonstrators. The Saudi-led incursion was clearly a riposte to the US, which King Abdullah felt was much too quick to jump on the bandwagon of reform and far too reticent to support old friends (including President Mubarak of Egypt). Within days, the very symbol of the protests, the Pearl monument, was demolished.

All talk of reform came to a crashing halt. Shi'i employees were dismissed from state jobs as punishment for having demonstrated and hundreds were arrested. Health professionals, who treated injured demonstrators and those accused of trying to overthrow the regime, were tried by military courts and sentenced to long terms in prisons. Under international pressure, some of the most egregious military trials have been overturned and referred to civilian courts, but little has been done to address the underlying disparities that gave rise to the protests, which continue periodically. The risk is that the majority Shi'i population, which has long been surprisingly moderate, especially given the discrimination that they face routinely, will be radicalized and that charges of foreign meddling by Iran will prove to be self-fulfilling.

Conclusion

Never in the modern history of the Middle East have so many millions demanded the dismantling of their autocratic regimes with such unanimity, perseverance, and—it must be emphasized—courage as they did in 2011. Unfortunately, in all but one instance where rulers were toppled, the results have been horrendous. Embedded political elites have clawed back power, oppression and bloodshed have increased, and many people are living lives more miserable than they were before the protests. The authoritarian states have proven neither 'nimble nor effective' in their efforts to retain power.[6] Three countries are in the grips of civil war (Libya, Syria, and Yemen); Egypt is kept afloat by boatloads of cash from the rich Gulf states while a spreading jihadist insurgency replaces jailed moderates of the Muslim Brotherhood; and Bahrain imposes a police state on the majority of its population.

However, the memories of collective protests cannot be easily erased, as well as the lesson that public space can be reclaimed and repoliticized. The path of reform will indeed be long, far longer than so many people imagined in the uplifting days of 2011, but there is space for new political imaginaries. We need to ensure that our assessments allow room for surprise, including radically changing terms of reference for politics. Demands for accountability and a responsive political system may have subsided, but they have not disappeared.

Further reading

Bayat, A. (2010, 2013) *Life as Politics: How Ordinary People Change the Middle East* (Stanford, CA: Stanford University Press)
  A prescient, nuanced, and richly informed study of youth politics, Islamist politics, activism, and the prospects for mundane politics to foster reform.

Cammett, M., Diwan, I., Richards, A., and Waterbury, J. (2015) *A Political Economy of the Middle East*, 4th edn (Boulder, CO: Westview Press)

Extensively updated edition of the seminal reference on the interplay of politics and economics. The book combines lucid analysis with rich detail and well-reasoned insights.

Hilsum, L. (2012) *Sandstorm: Libya in the Time of Revolution* (New York: Penguin Press)
Exceptional reportage by a veteran journalist who witnessed the Libyan Revolution first-hand. Her account is noteworthy for its lucidity and its insights.

Ismail, S. (2013) 'Urban Subalterns in the Arab Revolutions: Cairo and Damascus in Comparative Perspective', *Comparative Studies in Society and History* 55 (4): 865–94.
For the urban underclass their primary interface with government is with the police, who are much dreaded and feared. For many protesters, as Ismail reveals, the police became the primary target for their rage.

Norton, A. R. (ed.) (1995, 1996) *Civil Society in the Middle East*, 2 vols (Leiden: E. J. Brill)
The most comprehensive collection of studies on state-society relations in the Middle East, covering almost every country in the region.

Owen, R. (2012) *The Rise and Fall of Arab Presidents for Life* (Cambridge, MA: Harvard University Press)
A very timely political history of the Arab world that explains how colonialism, the drive for sovereignty, and political economy gave shape to Arab political systems.

Salamé, G. (ed.) (1994) *Democracy without Democrats: Renewal of Politics in the Muslim World* (New York: St Martin's)
A ground breaking volume that explores the prospects for democracy in a region where leading opposition forces may initially spurn the concept.

United Nations Development Programme (UNDP) (2002, 2004, 2005, 2008, 2009, 2012) *Arab Human Development Reports* (New York: United Nations Publications), available online at http://www.arab-hdr.org/reports/regionalarab.aspx
These candid and penetrating studies by scholars from the Arab world examine the factors that impede freedom in the region, including corruption, the repression of political life, the status of women, and the role of external powers.

White, J. B. (2014) *Muslim Nationalismand the New Turks* (Princeton, NJ: Princeton University Press)
The author's extensive fieldwork in Turkey is the basis for her engaging study of 'Muslimhood'—a model for incorporating pious individuals and principles into the public sphere without excluding non-Muslims.

Questions

1. What is the 'ruling bargain' that defined the relationship between many people in the Middle East and their governments? What factors have undermined the ruling bargain?

2. Many Middle Eastern states depend heavily on 'rents' as opposed to taxes to finance the government and provide service. Why might rentier states be more autonomous from society than states dependent upon taxes?

3. Islamist groups have attracted significant support in most, if not all Middle Eastern states. Given the opportunity to participate in the political systems, how have Islamist groups fared?

4. What factors motivated multitudes of people to take to the streets in mass demonstrations in 2011?

5. Ruling figures were toppled in Tunisia, Egypt, Libya, and Yemen as a result of the 2011 protests, and in Bahrain and Syria profound challenges were posed to the sitting rulers. In a number of these cases, the results have been dismal. What factors explain the poor outcomes?

Notes

1. The Pew Charitable Trust also offers extensive polling reports. See the widely discussed Pew Global Attitudes Project, which includes a lot of material on the Middle East, online at http://www.pewglobal.org/

2. This section draws upon work originally completed jointly with Professor Farhad Kazemi.

3. See http://www.elshaheeed.co.uk/

4. See S. Heydemann and R. Leenders (2014) 'Authoritarian Learning and Counterrevolution' in M. Lynch (ed.) *Authoritarian Learning and Counterrevolution. The Arab Uprisings Explained: New Contentious Politics in the Middle East* (New York: Columbia University Press), pp. 75–92.

5. Omar Mukhtar was a revered leader of the anti-colonial struggle against the Italians and was hanged in 1937.

6. Leaked transcripts reveal that by 2014 the cash infusions from the Gulf totalled $39.5 billion, and perhaps as much as $50 billion by 2015. See http://www.middleeasteye.net/columns/does-sisi-retain-support-his-top-generals-1452666191

7 The Politics of Identity in Middle East International Relations

RAYMOND HINNEBUSCH

Overview

The incongruence of identity and material structures has produced a conflict-prone Middle East. Imperial boundary-drawing, in frustrating identity, left behind states facing competition for the loyalties of their populations from both sub- and supra-state identities. Irredentism was built into the fabric of the states system, generating conflict. Identity has played a role in the foreign policies of regional states. Finally, identity has motivated, but material power structures have frustrated, efforts to create a regional security community.

Introduction

If there is anything special about the international politics of the Middle East, it is the power of identity. Identity is two-sided. Within the group, it facilitates cooperation and mobilizes agents for change, overcoming the collective action problem; where identity converges with shared territory and economic interdependence, resulting in a nation state or regional security community, the result is legitimacy and stability. Conversely, where, as in the Middle East, identity is often incongruent with state boundaries, it becomes a source of revisionism, contributing to high levels of regional conflict. Moreover, because identity presupposes an 'other' against which the self-defines itself and because its construction 'excludes' others, when identity differences correspond to struggles over scarce material resources, notably land, the result is protracted conflict, as between Israel and the Palestinians.

This chapter will explore these issues in five contexts: the problem of nation-building where identity and territory are incongruent; how irredentism from such incongruities generates regional conflict; the identity consequences of the Arab uprising of 2011; identity's role in state foreign policies; and the relationship between identity and material factors in shaping regional order.

The challenge of nation-building: from empire to states system

In an age of nationalism, argues Anthony Smith (1981), identity communities that believe they are nations seek statehood, while state leaders seek to forge a shared national identity among their populations; claiming to represent the nation is the key to contemporary legitimacy, and the nation state, able to mobilize its people to fight and pay taxes, is so successful in international power struggles that pre-national states cannot compete. Modern nationalism was exported to the Middle East from the West, where its ideal, 'one nation, one state', has been widely embraced. Yet here, more than elsewhere, nation-building is complicated by incongruence between the state (territory and state apparatus) and the still-powerful sub- and supra-state identities of the populace.

The idea of the nation state in MENA had little historical tradition on which to build. In an arid region of trading cities and nomadic tribes, the strongest identifications attached to sub-state units—cities, tribe, religious sects—or the larger Islamic *umma*. The region's crossroads position generated an exceptionally diverse ethno-linguistic and sectarian 'mosaic': not only was Islam divided between Sunni and Shia, but the latter also produced several offshoots—notably the Druze, Ismailis, and Alawis in Syria and Lebanon, and the Zaydis in Yemen, and a multitude of surviving Christian minorities were divided by the languages of their liturgies or allegiances to Eastern Orthodoxy vs Rome. According to Weulersse (1946: 79–83), loyalties to territorial states were tepid because these were typically established in the expansion of ephemeral, nomadic, religio-tribal movements that disintegrated after a few generations, with states' boundaries being redrawn by the next state-building movement (although this was less so in areas where the state rested on substantial peasantries attached to the land, as in Iran and Egypt). In parallel, identification with the larger Islamic *umma* was congruent with the region-wide trade interdependence fostered by Islamic empires. The most successful and durable of Middle East states, the Ottoman Empire, run by a multi-communal elite, legitimized in Islamic terms, and embracing a multitude of partly autonomous communal groups, was the antithesis of the nation-state.

However, the single most important factor obstructing nation-building in the region was the imposition under Western imperialism of a deeply flawed version of the Western states system. Begun through the great powers' separation of parts of the Ottoman Empire, it was completed by their division among themselves of the remaining Arab provinces of the empire after the First World War. The boundaries that great powers imposed arbitrarily fragmented the region into a multitude of weak, competing, and often 'artificial' states on the basis of the great powers' interests, not indigenous wishes (Ayoob 1995: 33). These frequently cut across sub-state identities and violated the pre-existing or emergent supra-state identities, Islam and Arabism, which continued to retain popular loyalties more effectively than most states.

Despite this, the ingredients of nation-building are not lacking in the region: 84 per cent of Middle East states have a dominant ethno-linguistic majority (Fearon 2003). Turkey, Israel, and Iran most closely approximate the nation-state model, partly because indigenous state-builders were better able to ensure a rough correspondence between territory and the dominant ethno-linguistic group (Turkey and Israel), or built on pre-existing histories as imperial centres (Iran and Turkey). Nevertheless, technically speaking, even these are multi-national states and face the unfinished task of integrating minorities. Turkey and Israel have been at odds with sub-state identity groups—Kurds and Palestinians. Iran is the premier multi-ethnic society, its Persian core flanked by Azerbaijanis, Kurds, Turkomans, Arabs, and Baluchis. While their relative congruence of identity and territory has made it easier to assimilate or exclude these minority identities, they have still had to work at continually reproducing their national identities, in part against the neighbouring Arab 'other'.

The ethnically homogeneous Arabs certainly constitute a 'proto-nation', but, by contrast to the non-Arab peoples, the imposition of the regional state system shattered their potential territorial unity. In consequence, the Arab states are territorial states rather than 'nation states' as traditionally understood since mutually exclusive identities do not separate them from each other (Kienle 1990: 31). On the contrary, their shared Arabic culture, language, and historical memories of unified Arab empires—critical ingredients of nationhood—are reflected in the very durable belief of many Arabs that they all constitute a single nation, the fragmentation of which ('one nation, many states') violates the nationalist norm of 'one nation, one state'.

For the leading theorist of Arab nationalism, Sati al-Husri, Arab identity is the product of both the Arabs' collective historical accomplishments and the standardization of modern Arabic (Choueiri 2000: 119–20), a view congruent with Karl Deutsch's (1953) analysis of the ingredients of nationalism. Arabism was not, however, inevitably the dominant political identity in the individual Arab states, for identities are constructed and fluid, and usually multiple, with rival identities tested through debates among elites, intellectuals, and publics (Lynch 2006). Hence the rise of Arabism was the work of a generation of Arab historians and publicists, and of political entrepreneurs invoking shared threats, interests, and grievances against the 'other'—the non-Arab states and imperialism—and it was always contested by alternative identities corresponding to different interests (Gelvin 1997). Arab identity within the Ottoman Empire first emerged in reaction to Turkification policies, with Arabs demanding that Arabic be given parity with Turkish. But the identity vacuum left by the collapse of the empire and the reaction against the Western imperialists' occupation and dismemberment of Arab lands, frustrating hopes for a unified Arab state in the Mashreq and disrupting many regional economic links, fuelled the rise of Arab nationalism. Even then it was initially the ideology of the modern educated elite, challenged by traditional notables championing more local identities or Islam. Pan-Arab identity (*qaumi*) developed parallel with more state-centric (*watani*) nationalism, stimulated by the parallel independence struggles in each state (Muslih 1991), although they largely converged on demands for the self-determination of a community of Arab states linked by some form of confederation. The construction of Arab nationalism in multi-religious states as *secular* and linguistically based, resulting partly from the involvement of religious minorities in movements such as the Baath, allowed inclusion in the putative Arab nation of the significant Arabic-speaking Christian and Islamic heterodox minorities, but not non-Arabic speakers such as the Kurds. In more religiously homogeneous Sunni Egypt and North Africa, nationalism had a strong Islamic content. Arab nationalism and Islamism were rivals, yet overlapped and were stimulated by the same shared causes, anti-imperialism and the struggle over Palestine, which, from the 1930s undermined inward-looking alternatives, such as the Wafd's Egypt-centric identity. Indeed, it was several all-Arab conferences provoked by the struggle in Palestine that crystallized the increasingly widely embraced idea of a common Arab nation.

From the 1950s through the mid-1970s, pan-Arab nationalism was the hegemonic ideology in most of the Arab states, eclipsing, but not eliminating, its Islamic and state-centric rivals. In this doctrine, all Arabic speakers formed a nation; reflective of this, thirteen of fifteen Arab state constitutions defined the nation as the 'Arab' nation (Ayubi 1995: 146). In its most ambitious form (as in Baathism and the Arab Nationalist Movement), Arab nationalism sought a solution to the 'one nation, many states' dilemma in Arab unionist projects, such as the 1958–61 United Arab Republic (UAR) of Egypt and Syria, seen as steps toward the unification of the entire nation in a pan-Arab confederated state. A less ambitious version of Arabism, promoted by Nasser, was the belief that a pan-Arab *national interest* ought to concert the foreign policies of the individual Arab states.

Stronger versions of Arabism resulted from the rise of Nasser as pan-Arab hero in Egypt in parallel with the political mobilization of the new middle class across the region, in response to the West's attempt to maintain the region as a sphere of influence, and amidst the chronic shared conflict with Israel. Arabism was facilitated by Egyptian teachers employed throughout the Arab world (to help socialize the emerging middle classes), and the spread of the transistor radio (which enabled Radio Cairo's *Sawt al-Arab* to reach the Arab 'street') (Hudson 1977; Jankowski and Gershoni 1997). A widespread feeling of belonging to a distinct Arab world (*al-'alam al-arabi*) emerged. Surveyed majorities in the Arab states into the 1980s agreed that the Arabs constituted a *nation* artificially divided (Reiser 1984; Korany 1987: 54–5). This feeling corresponded to the persistence, even deepening, of transstate social communication and interactions. Niblock (1990) argues that the interests of the separate states were intertwined by labour supply, investment funds, security, water, and communications routes. Extended family ties frequently crossed borders and cross-border immigration, from Palestinian refugees to labour migration to the Gulf oil-producing states, was continual. Standard newspaper and radio Arabic made the language more homogeneous, stunting the evolution of national dialects into the linguistic basis of separate nations. From the 1990s, Arab satellite television sharply reinforced cross-border participation in a new 'Arab public sphere' (Telhami 1999; Lynch 2006). The Arab world, in the words of Noble (1991: 56), is a 'vast sound chamber' in which ideas and information circulate widely, giving rise to an 'imagined community'.

Just as important in sustaining Arab identity is the ongoing struggle with the 'other', which continues to be experienced collectively in spite of state boundaries. The loss of Palestine, the 1967 defeat by Israel, and the 2003 conquest of Iraq were all seen as shared Arab humiliations; the 1973 Arab–Israeli War and oil embargo, Israel's evacuation of southern Lebanon under Hezbollah pressure in June 2000, and Hezbollah's ability to withstand the full force of the Israeli military machine during the 2006 war in Lebanon were experienced as shared victories. Long after the supposed death of Arabism, Israel's longstanding battle with the Palestinians continued to arouse the 'Arab street'. Arabism was continually reinforced by historical memories of greatness under unity and more recent experience that the Arabs are successful when they act together, and are readily dominated when divided.

The death of Arabism has been announced and debated a number of times: with the failure of the UAR and other unionist initiatives; after the defeat of the main Arab nationalist states by Israel in 1967 made Arab collective security appear unrealistic; by the vacuum left after the 1970 death of the pan-Arab hero and the failure of would-be successors such as Muammar Gaddafi or Saddam Hussein to fill Nasser's shoes; by Arabism's inability to constrain states' sacrifice of all-Arab to state interests (notably, Sadat's separate peace with Israel); and by inter-Arab wars, such as the Iraqi invasion of Kuwait and the conflicts between the Yemens (Ajami 1977–78; Faksh 1993). The alternative view is that Arabism persists, albeit diluted and adapted to state sovereignty, mixed with Islamism and a still-powerful force at the societal level (Abu Khalil 1992; Sirriyeh 2000).

What has evidently changed since the height of pan-Arabism is that identifications with the state and with Islam started to exceed Arab identity. In surveys in the decade before the Arab uprising (Telhami 2006, 2007b, 2011), the distribution of identifications averaged 24 per cent as citizen of the state, 28.5 per cent as an Arab, and 32 per cent as Muslim. At the level of foreign policy, Arab and Islamic identities appear partly to have merged, in that they were associated with very similar foreign policy preferences, as symbolized by posters across the region depicting 'Nasser 1956' alongside 'Nasrallah 2006' during the Lebanon war, when Hezbollah leader Hassan Nasrallah was the most popular leader in the region (Telhami 2006; Valjborn and Bank 2007). The proportion of survey respondents who thought that elites should act in the Arab or Muslim interest rather than that of their individual state fluctuated between a half and a third (Telhami 2006, 2011). Arab publics still evaluated foreign states on the basis of their attitudes toward all-Arab issues such as Palestine and Iraq, not those states' behaviour toward their own state (Furia and Lucas 2006). Regardless of their regimes' alliances with the US, large Arab majorities (72 per cent) saw America as a threat—exactly because of Palestine and Iraq while only 11 per cent feared Islamic Iran, even in the Gulf. While Arabism was increasingly excluded from the calculations of state policymakers in the 2000s, it had survived in the Arab 'street', where it was fused with Islamism. In the post-Arab uprising period, however, this tendency has reversed, with secular Arabism increasingly squeezed between Islamism, sectarianism, and state-centric identities.

What is remarkable, given the persistence of powerful supra-state identities having no parallels elsewhere, and recurrent revisionist challenges, from Pan Arab unionist projects of the 1950-60s, to the Islamist project of a caliphate, is the durability of the regional states system. The borders imposed at its birth outlasted the pan-Arab movements that sought to overthrow them. From the outset, ruling elites and state apparatuses acquired vested interests in the post-Ottoman fragmentation, with state-builders tenaciously defending their sovereignty against a redrawing of boundaries. The state system was partly frozen in place by external power: the fragmentation into weak states balancing against each other and periodic external interventions to defend the sanctity of borders against would-be regional hegemons (Lustick 1997) obstructed Bismarkian solutions, such as Saddam Hussein's attempt to annex Kuwait. Without this, the elimination of the most 'artificial' entities—for example, 'city states', such as Kuwait, and 'buffer states', such as Jordan—would certainly have taken place and historic Syria possibly reconstructed. The decline of Arabism as a popular organized trans-state movement, owing to its repeated failures, proceeded in parallel with the accumulation of interests attached to the states themselves, making them more immune to Arabism, aided by states' use of oil funded patronage to co-opt the main constituencies of Arabism, the middle classes. The weakening, indeed, seeming state failure, in some Arab countries from combinations of external invasion or intervention (Iraq) and internal insurgency (Libya, Yemen, Syria), may yet de facto (if not de jure) alter particular state boundaries, but is very unlikely to undo the regional states system, per se.

It is, however, one thing to consolidate the state materially, but another to legitimize it by constructing an identity around it. State elites, commanding the instruments of socialization—mass media, mass education—as well as job opportunities in state-dominated economies, have sought with some success to construct state-centric identities drawing on the historical and geographical peculiarities of their particular state, and exploiting chronic conflict with other Arab states. The very durability of boundaries means that new generations would increasingly tend to view their state as the normal framework of political life. On the other hand, these state-centric projects have always been contested by counter-elites using sub- or supra-state identities to mobilize support; unable to marginalize these rival identities, state leaders eschewed the one strategy that would legitimate the territorial state—namely, democratization—and pursued instead authoritarian strategies in which ruling cores were often constituted through manipulation of *sub-state* loyalties (kin, tribe, sect), while *supra-state* identities (Arabism and Islam) were often deployed as official legitimating ideologies, thus keeping non-state identities alive—such as when Baathist Syria claimed to be the special champion of Arabism, or Saudi Arabia of Islam. Others vacillated between, or sought to exploit *both*, state and supra-state identities, as in Egypt. The problem that rulers faced is that, to benefit from supra-state identities, their foreign policies had to be seen to promote the interests of the larger community, but external material constraints (Israeli power, dependence on the US) increasingly prevented this.

These general tendencies aside, state and supra-state levels of identity interact in distinct ways in each of the individual Arab states, reflecting differences in geography and historical experience. Never static, these variations range from cases in which identification with the separate states overshadows without wholly displacing Arabism, to those in which state identities remain subordinate to the sense of being an Arab (or a Muslim). At the first end of the continuum are the oil city-states of the Gulf, such as Kuwait and the United Arab Emirates, where polls show state identification to be highest (Farah and al-Salem 1980: 141–2; Telhami 2006), congruent with their material interest in protecting their oil wealth from the claims of a wider Arab nation and with the emergence of a distinct 'Gulfi' identity. In North Africa, where boundary-drawing by Western imperial powers recognized Ottoman provincial boundaries and Mamluk elites achieved autonomy as Ottoman power declined (Tunisia, Algeria), or where an independent dynasty pre-dated imperialism (Morocco), statehood enjoys historical memories and legitimacy. But neither Arab nor Islamic identities have been effaced, as shown by the strong opposition in the Maghreb to the 1991 Western attack on Iraq; remarkably, in 2006 more Moroccans identified themselves as Muslim or Arab than as Moroccan (Telhami 2006). Harik (1987: 19–46) argued that a potential basis for separate nations existed in geographical entities where minority sects had established autonomous regimes, such as Oman (erected around the Kharajite Ibadies), Yemen (around the Zaydi imamate), and Lebanon (around the Maronite emirate), and where tribal-religious movements founded regimes, as in Saudi Arabia and Libya. Still, Arab identity persists in the minority regimes and Arab-Islamic identity is dominant in the latter states. Thus, despite enjoying a pre-Islamic statehood, Yemenis feel themselves to be part of the wider Arab-Islamic world, with many Yemeni political parties the offshoots of Arab or Islamic movements (for example, Aden's ruling National Liberation Front originated in the Beirut-founded Arab Nationalist Movement).

Egypt has a strong sense of territorial identity based on the Nile valley and a history of statehood pre-dating the Arabs. Yet Egyptian identity is Arab-Islamic in content, and attempts to construct non-Arab definitions of Egyptianness—'Pharaonic' or 'Mediterranean'—have failed. Even in the late 1970s, when Sadat was promoting an 'Egypt first' identity, 71.1 per cent of respondents who identified with 'Egypt first' still said that Egypt was the natural leader of the Arab world (Hinnebusch 1982); in 2006, three-quarters of Egyptians put Muslim or Arab identity ahead of identification with the state (Telhami 2006). As a result, decisions taken on grounds of state interest—Egypt's separate peace with Israel and membership in the anti-Iraq Gulf war coalition, which would be perfectly natural were Egypt a consolidated nation state—were damaging to regime legitimacy.

At the other end of the spectrum is the Mashreq, where externally imposed borders corresponded to no history of independent statehood, much less nationhood, with the result that populations initially saw their states as 'artificial'. It is no accident that the main pan-Arab nationalist movement, Baathism, was born in Syria, and was most successful there and in Iraq and Jordan. If *bilad ash-sham* (historic and geographical Syria) might have supported a viable nationhood, its fragmentation into four mini-states (Syria, Jordan, Lebanon, and Palestine/Israel) prevented the truncated Damascus-centred rump from becoming a strong uncontested focus of identity. The attempt to generate a *non-Arab* Syrian national identity by the Syrian Social Nationalist Party came to nothing, although when pan-Syrian identity is defined as 'Arab' in content, it carries resonance (the current view of the SSNP). In Iraq, the opposite case of an artificial state constructed by throwing rival communal groups together, Arabism was embraced as a solution to bridging the Sunni–Shia gap, but rejected by the Kurds. For the stateless Palestinians, having no historical memories of a Palestinian entity, a distinct Palestinian identity was a function of the forced separation of Palestine from Syria and the struggle with Zionism. Yet, many Palestinians also identified with Arabism until its 1967 failure and Islamism increasingly thereafter. These identities were not, however, mutually exclusive: Palestinian Islamists assimilated nationalism, and nationalist resistance to Britain and Israel used Islamic discourse; and Palestinians never ceased to see themselves as Arabs (Budeiri 1997; Khalidi 1997).

Irredentism and interstate conflict

The way in which externally imposed Middle East state boundaries cut across communities, or even excluded them from statehood, built irredentism into the fabric of the regional states system. As irredentist movements have contested borders, they have often dragged states into conflict with each other (Gause 1992). Several enduring centres of protracted conflict and two war-prone states have resulted. Where nations were left stateless, conflict has been particularly intense and enduring. The Kurds, with their own identity, have displayed separatist tendencies in Turkey and Iraq, and have been used by rival states against their enemies (Binder 1999b). Iran's support under the Shah for Iraqi Kurdish separatism engendered bitterness between the two states; while Iran ended its support for the Kurdish insurgency in return for Iraqi concessions on the Shatt al-Arab waterway that they shared, reversing that concession was part of the motivation for Saddam Hussein's 1980 invasion of Iran. Kurdish rebellions during the Iran–Iraq War led to Saddam's murderous razing and gassing of Kurdish villages. The US destruction of the Baathist central government in the 2003 invasion of Iraq empowered Kurdish autonomy, alarming Turkey, which has been embroiled in chronic conflict with a Kurdistan Workers' Party (PKK) insurgency in the country's southeast. Syria supported the PKK as a bargaining chip to extract a share of the Euphrates river water that Turkish dams controlled, leading the two states to the brink of war in 1998 before Syria bowed to Turkish military threats. Since then, Turkey has been embroiled in similar cross-border conflict with PKK sanctuaries in northern Iraq. Ethnicity, land, and water all interacted to fuel conflict.

Lebanon, an artificial multi-sectarian state, resulted from France's forced addition of Muslim parts of western Syria to Maronite Mount Lebanon. Its constituent sects being overarched by only the thinnest of Lebanese identity, the stability of the resultant state was contingent on a 'national pact' between the pro-Western Maronites and pro-Arab Muslims to divide up power and office, and to keep Lebanon out of Western–Arab conflicts. The breaking of the pact periodically unleashed civil war in which rival sects called on outside forces in their power struggles, which, together with the weakness of the state and its army, made the country an arena for proxy battles between external forces over the wider Middle East. Thus the post-1970 relocation of the armed Palestinian diaspora to Lebanon, making it the most active front in the Arab–Israel conflict, unleashed the 1975 civil war, and turned Lebanon into a battleground between Syria and Israel for nearly two decades, until a Pax Syriana was briefly imposed. Syria's Western-forced withdrawal in 2005 made Lebanon a new battleground in the region-wide struggle of the US and its allies, notably Saudi Arabia, against a Syrian–Iranian axis, each via their Lebanese allies.

Britain's construction of the states system in the Arab Gulf left Shia communities straddling the border with Iran, and Shia majorities discriminated against by minority Sunni rulers in Bahrain and Iraq. Revolutionary Iran tried to use the Shia to spread the Islamic revolution to the Arab side of the Gulf (Herb 1999), while Iraq made its resulting war with Iran into a nation-building project, expelling Shia of Iranian descent to Iran and integrating Arabic-speaking Shia into an Arab army fighting Tehran. Washington's 2003 destruction of the secular Iraqi state allowed expelled Shi'i politicians to return from Iran and take power, provoking a Sunni–Shia civil war and alarming US-aligned Sunni regimes in Egypt, Jordan, and Saudi Arabia with the prospect of a 'Shia crescent' linking Iran, Iraq, and the Hezhollah-mobilized Lebanese Shia. Iraq's Shia were caught in the US–Iran struggle for dominance in the Gulf.

The way in which identity interacts with state formation can embed war-proneness into the very fabric of the state, as illustrated by the cases of Iraq and Israel, two states that have been involved in more wars than any other in the region and the only ones that have seized their neighbour's territory.

Iraq was born an artificial state, with communal groups having a history of animosity thrown together in one state, similar to Lebanon, but with the difference that Iraq had the material potential—land and oil—to be an actor rather than a victim. With no shared Iraqi identity, Arab identity was used by the ruling Sunni elite to integrate the Shia, but thereby alienated the Kurds (Dawisha 1999). After decades of unstable regimes, the Baath found a state-building formula combining hard authoritarianism, co-optation through oil-funded modernization and bureaucratization, and legitimacy based on Arab nationalism. Arab nationalism required foreign policy victories and oil-funded militarization gave the means, making Iraq a 'war state' in the view of Mufti (1996). Saddam used war with Iran (1980–88) to pose as defender of Arabism; when this was not an unequivocal victory, he sought pan-Arab leadership by advocating renewed use of the oil weapon against the US in the struggle with Israel. Among the motives for his 1990 invasion of Kuwait was to impose Iraq's pan-Arab hegemony and to realize its long-standing irredentist claim to Kuwait, seen as arbitrarily detached by Britain from Ottoman Iraq. Iraq's wars are intimately linked to its artificial character, arbitrary borders, and intractable nation-building imperatives (Tripp 2002).

Israel, conceived around the idea of a chosen people entitled to a homogeneously Jewish biblical land of Israel and established at the expense of the indigenous Palestinians (Masalha 2000), was inevitably 'born fighting'. The imperative to 'in-gather' world Jewry generated land and water hunger that put Israelis in competition with their Arab neighbours for scarce resources. A shared identity among the disparate ethnic groups that settled in Israel was constructed against the common Arab enemy. The insecurity of a small state encircled by a much larger hostile Arab world (Brecher 1972) was addressed by a pre-emptive strike doctrine and seizure of 'buffer zones', such as the Syrian Golan Heights. Israel's 1967 expansion ignited irredentist dissatisfaction with the incongruence of Israel's territory with ancient Eretz Yisrael, resulting in a drive to incorporate and settle conquered territories (Judea/Samaria—that is, the West Bank). But if Israel's Jewish identity was not to be compromised, the dense Arab populations of the territories could not be given citizenship and could be controlled only by apartheid-like strategies or expelled (as from the Golan). Against the hostility of the Arab world, Israel could achieve its identity imperatives only through exceptional extraterritorial support from the Jewish diaspora, a transnational identity movement that secured the indispensible backing of the US superpower.

Identity and foreign policy

Does identity shape perceptions of interest in foreign policymaking (as constructivists believe) or is it an instrument in the pursuit of such interests (as realists argue)? The answer must be both. Supra-state identity has powerfully driven regional politics, as manifest in pan-Arab leadership rivalries, the power of the Palestine cause, the prevalence of revolutionary movements, and Arab-unity projects, albeit in a dialectic with material forces that may reinforce or dilute its mobilizing power. Identity is a normative 'soft power', both instrumentally used by elites in their power contests and a constraint on their options. Whether identity is satisfied or frustrated at state formation sets states on quite enduring status quo or revisionist foreign policy tangents. Yet if identity shapes what states *want* to do or tries to do in the short term, material capabilities and constraints, largely outside their own control, determine what, in the longer term, they actually *can* accomplish.

The power of Arab identity amidst material constraints

The embedding of the Arab states system in a Pan-Arab imagined community makes inter-Arab politics distinctive. One manifestation of this is the competition among Arab states for pan-Arab leadership. Only the presumption that the Arab world constitutes an overarching political arena explains this competition (Kienle 1990: 1–30). Only the states' high permeability to trans-state ideological appeals, enabling intervention in the domestic affairs of other states that would be ineffective (and a violation of sovereignty) in a conventional states system, makes such leadership appear realistic to ambitious leaders (Noble 1991). That this contest is chiefly a symbolic struggle over legitimacy and norms—over appropriate behaviour for an Arab state—and that it is waged through discourse suggests that the Arab world constitutes a single political arena or public space with features of domestic politics; very different is the resort to military conflict over territory on the Arab–Israeli and Arab–Persian identity fault lines (Barnett 1998).

Pan-Arab identity also has the power to constrain states. That Arab state leaders feel caught between the conventional material state interests prioritized by 'normal' nation states and a supra-state *'raison de la nation'* (Korany 1987), on which their legitimacy is contingent, indicates that, for their publics, there is an 'imagined community' with its own interests and claims on them. Identity powerfully shapes Arab states' perception of enemies and potential allies; thus while *raison d'état* would have driven weaker Arab states threatened by stronger ones, such as Jordan in the 1950s and 1960s, to align with Israel, this could not be done openly without unacceptable legitimacy costs.

Another manifestation of the power of identity is the revisionism and conflict that it often provokes. The frustration of Arab (or Islamic) identity explains in good part the revolutionary movements and revisionist states that periodically challenge 'imperialism' or the 'artificial' states system. Egypt's export of Arab nationalism and Iran's of revolutionary Islam presupposed a belief that they were the vanguards of a wider supra-state imagined community, and it was the receptivity of publics beyond their borders to this message that empowered their reach for regional hegemony (Nahas 1985).

That Arab identity makes inter-Arab politics different is also manifest in the pursuit of Arab unionist projects. The very idea of giving up state sovereignty is a striking anomaly from a 'realist' point of view, carrying high risks for regimes and driven by perceived legitimacy gains. But the material factor stressed by realism—relative power—determined whether a particular state pursued unionism or was threatened by it: weaker states that had no chance of leading the Arab world and which were likely to be victims of unionist annexation tended to embrace sovereignty as a defence. Also, Mufti (1996) distinguished the use of defensive unionism by weaker states (Syria) to mobilize domestic support and enlist the patronage of a stronger Arab state from the 'offensive unionism' deployed by materially stronger states (Iraq, Egypt) to annex or bring a weaker partner into a sphere of influence. Kienle (1995) argues that states turn to pan-Arabism to the extent that they feel vulnerable to external (Western, Israeli) power, with Syria feeling very insecure compared with Egypt.

While this suggests that identity is often regarded instrumentally by elites, without pan-Arabism's powerful appeal, unionism would not even have been on state agendas.

In spite of the pervasiveness of supra-state identity, sovereignty did, however, constitute an almost insuperable obstacle to unionist projects. Even in the one case in which a state sacrificed its sovereignty—Syria's 1958 merger with Egypt in the UAR—clashing interests destroyed the union. Syrian elites were swept into the union by popular demands provoked by their own outbidding and Nasser accepted it despite his own better judgement, to preserve his stature as hero of pan-Arabism. But the rupture of Syria's commercial links with conservative states and the influx of Egyptian products alienated the Syrian bourgeoisie, while Nasser, unwilling to share power, weakened the union by transferring unionist officers to Egypt (Al-Sayyid 1999). When a Syrian coup terminated the union, Egypt had too little at stake materially to defend it by force, although Nasser's enduring mass appeal made it impossible for Syria's hated 'separatist' (*infisal*) regime to legitimize itself.

The 1963 attempt to construct a new pan-Arab union beginning with Egypt, Iraq, and Syria foundered, despite the shared pan-Arab ideologies of the three states, on elites' unwillingness to risk their power in the absence of a power-sharing formula (Kerr 1971), although the project had such a powerful popular appeal that Israel had to threaten intervention should Jordan be swept into it (Podeh 2003). In the 1970s, when rival branches of the unionist Baath party were again in power in Syria and Iraq, they used unionist discourse to threaten the legitimacy of the other, which rested on being seen to be faithful to Arab nationalism (Kienle 1990). The 1978 shock of Egypt's defection from the Arab–Israeli power balance and the prospect that a Syrian–Iraqi merger would restore the balance put union again on the agenda, but the threat posed by union to the security of the two regimes blocked it.

The enduring impact of Arab identity is perhaps most manifest in the place of the Palestine cause in Arab politics. Palestinians' loss of their land to Israel is the root of the Palestine conflict, but it only became an Arab–Israeli one because the identification of Arab populations with the suffering of their Palestinian 'cousins' forced the fragile Arab states to contest Zionism, often at risk to their material interests. Once identity is constructed around enmity, it assumes an autonomous power that gives conflict extra durability. The Palestinian diaspora radicalized Arab politics and gave rise to the Palestine Liberation Organization, whose challenges to Israel, with the support of some Arab states, were a major factor in a chain of Arab–Israel wars. The immediate driver of the 1967 war on the Arab side was identity—namely, the competitive struggle among the Arab states for pan-Arab legitimacy—contingent on being seen to champion the Palestine cause. The Syrian Baath regime's quest for legitimacy at home by supporting Palestinian fedayeen and the brinkmanship by which Nasser sought to appease his pan-Arab constituency on the eve of the war were largely symbolic challenges to Israel made in defiance of the actual material power balance in its favour. When identity mobilizes mass opinion, it can force leaders into risky decisions that they would otherwise not take, such as King Hussein's joining of the anti-Israeli coalition in 1967 and King Faisal's 1973 oil embargo against his US patron (quickly dropped once passions cooled). That Arab opposition to Israel has remained so enduring despite its high costs is hard to explain without the identity factor.

Yet the long-term outcome of identity-driven policies depends on their congruence with the material balance of power. Nasser outplayed his rivals in the game of symbolic

inter-Arab politics in part because he led the largest and most stable state against their fragile oligarchies. Ultimately, both the Egyptian and Iranian efforts to export revolutionary
identity foundered on the military power of states (Israel, Iraq) that they challenged. Indeed,
material constraints may force alterations in identity. After the 1967 defeat, Sadat had to
downplay Egypt's Arab identity in order to exit from a conflict that had overstrained its material resources, while Asad tempered Syria's promotion of the Palestine cause; these states
were 'socialized' by their experience of the costs of promoting identity in defiance of a power
imbalance.

In summary, in the period of pan-Arabism, revolutionary nationalist regimes—especially
those that had the power to seek all-Arab leadership—were occasionally driven by their
Arab identity, especially as this legitimized them within, into conflicts or unionist projects
at risk to material state interests. More frequently, however, when Arabism threatened state
interests, states—especially weaker ones—resisted it, in so far as they were gradually consolidated enough to defy or co-opt their publics. Up against powerful material constraints,
Arabism's high costs and meagre achievements ultimately disillusioned and demobilized its
constituents.

Identity and foreign policy differences

If identify accounts for some distinctive common features in the foreign policies of the Arab
states, how far do identity *variations*, compared to material interests and factors, account
for foreign policy *differences* in the Middle East? It is, in fact, their *interaction* that gives the
most explanatory power.

On the one hand, identity emerges from a contest within states among social forces promoting perhaps rival identities that correspond to their interests. Whether Arab states embraced the status quo norm of sovereignty or revisionist pan-Arab identity depended on
internal class struggles. Sovereignty was the ideology of satisfied social forces—normally,
traditional oligarchies enriched on economic relations with the West that were threatened
by the anti-Westernism of radical Arab nationalism. Smaller merchants or industrialists operating on the regional market tended to favour an Islamic identity or conservative Arabism
(compatible with the market). Radical socialist-oriented versions of Arabism were the ideological weapons of more plebeian strata challenging the oligarchy in the 1950s. The varying
social composition of ruling coalitions in Middle East states partly explains variations in
state identities; hence radical or conservative foreign policies.

On the other hand, the autonomous power of identity can be seen in the fact that whether
it is frustrated or satisfied, expressed or constrained, it helps to shape this internal struggle
and to set states on distinctive foreign policy tangents. States whose identities (or at least
those of the dominant social forces) are satisfied in state formation (Turkey, Saudi Arabia)
or which are formed around pre-nationalist tribal elites sponsored by imperialism (Jordan,
Kuwait) were likely to assume a sovereignty-centred identity compatible with status quo
policies. In states where identity was frustrated, revolutions against the imperial-established
oligarchy were more likely, issuing in Arab nationalist regimes locked into a revisionist tangent. Admittedly, the revolutionary republics diluted their Arabism and moved toward status quo policies once their elites were embourgeoised and acquired a stake in their regimes,
but this development was retarded in states where identity was particularly frustrated by

state formation (such as Syria) as opposed to states that had an identity substitute for Arabism (such as Egypt).

Turkey illustrates how states enjoying a sufficient correspondence between identity and territory to approximate a nation state tend to be both legitimate and to have little incentive to follow a revisionist foreign policy. Thus the exceptional nationalist legitimacy that Ataturk earned in fighting off imperialism's attempt to dismember the Turkish heartland was invested in the construction of a Turkish nation state, fixed on Anatolia, which eschewed any revisionist ambition to reconstruct the Ottoman Empire or to pursue a pan-Turkish project. Because the idea of a Turkish nation state sufficiently satisfied identity (at least that of a dominant coalition), Turkey avoided conflict with Russia or quagmires in the Arab world, and was spared the anti-imperialist conflicts in which the Arab world, unable to fend off imperial dismemberment, was embroiled. Even after the collapse of communism opened up new opportunities in Central Asia and the Balkans, enabling Prime Minister Turgut Ozal to flirt with Turkism and Ottomanism, in the end irredentism was readily restrained by the material interests invested in a status quo that relatively satisfied identity (Robins 2002).

Egypt demonstrates how elites in Arab states with fairly secure alternative identities can choose among, and then manipulate, them to suit their foreign policy objectives—even as those identities, as they are constructed, make certain foreign policies appropriate and others not. Alternation between more Arab- and Egypt-centric identities has been associated with shifts in different conceptions of Egypt's interests, and hence in its foreign policies. As against the Egypt-centric identity of the Wafd, Nasser promoted the idea of Egypt as Arab— indeed, as leader of the Arab world—in part because politically active Egyptians had been made aware of a shared fate with other Arabs (from events such as the Palestine and Suez wars) and partly for material reasons: it was as Arab leader, rather than standing alone, that Egypt could secure its independence by rolling back Western imperialism in the region, not to mention acquire resources from both East and West. Arabism could even legitimize the claim of the oil-poor states such as Egypt to a share of the Arab oil patrimony, which, owing to imperial boundary drawing, was concentrated in the mini-states of the Gulf.

However, once Arabism obstructed President Anwar al-Sadat's interest in winning economic and diplomatic help from the US, he fostered a rival Egypt-centric identity in its place. While the attentive public still perceived Egypt's interest as inseparable from the Arab-Islamic world (Coldwell 2003), Egypt-centrism helped Sadat to reverse Nasser's Arabist foreign policy. For Egypt's ruling elites, identity seemed to shift, not necessarily from short-term opportunism, but in line with long-term material costs and benefits, which in turn were a function of objective systemic constraint, such as the unfavourable power balance with Israel and deepening economic dependency on the US (Karawan 2002).

On the other hand, the dismemberment of historic Syria after the First World War frustrated identity and generated a permanent irredentism in the truncated Damascus-centred rump state, with pan-Arabism expressing the impulse to merge this artificial creation of imperialism in a wider Arab nation. The initially weak Syrian state was vulnerable to pan-Arab appeals from Egypt and Iraq; the strongest political forces were Arab nationalist and Syria gave birth to the most radical pan-Arab party, the Baath, which eventually captured the state and pursued a revisionist foreign policy over Palestine. Even after the 1967 defeat, Arab identity persisted, albeit in a more Syria-centric form than before, institutionalized in the national security state that Hafiz al-Asad constructed to confront Israel.

But if the frustration of identity alone determines revisionism, Jordan should be equally revisionist: Syria and Jordan were, until severed by imperialism, initially parts of the same country, *bilad ash-sham*. Yet they soon embarked on quite *opposing* foreign policy tangents: status quo in Jordan; revisionist in Syria. Damascus felt itself the *victim* of the dismembering of historic Syria, while Jordan's Hashemite regime was the *beneficiary*. The Hashemites—dependent on British arms and financing to consolidate authority over an artificial newly created state, with their strongest support in the pre-national tribal Bedouin and sharply opposed by Arab nationalist forces among the urban middle class and Palestinians—chose, after Britain rebuffed King Abdullah's unionist ambitions, to accept Jordan's role as a buffer state between Palestine (where Israel was created) and the wider Arab world (Salibi 1998). But as a buffer state, the regime could never attain Arab nationalist legitimacy and hence never escape dependence on Western (or Israeli) protection; a status quo sovereignty-centric identity was thus natural. That the contrary identities of its people certainly mattered was evident from the association of Jordan's brief democratization episodes with breaks in its traditional pro-Western policy—and precisely for that reason, they were all aborted. The Hashemite regime's survival depended on containing, not expressing, popular identity (Hinnebusch and Quilliam 2006).

In summary, variations in the foreign policies of individual states result from a complex interaction between identity and material factors. Status quo foreign policies are most likely when identity is satisfied, while frustrated identity is most likely to be expressed—in revisionist policies—by revolutionary states. Where regimes' material interests or external constraints nevertheless dictate status quo foreign policies, they must seek to construct a compatible identity.

Inter-Arab politics amidst supra-state identity: the rise, decline, and evolution of pan-Arabism

A major debate between realists and constructivists is over the relative importance of identity and material factors in shaping the region. In fact, both are important and it is their *interaction* that must be analysed. Whether state responses to the anarchy of a regional states system can move beyond insecurity, self-help, and a Hobbesian struggle for power depends on an effective regional *regime* or security community. Arab identity has always been seen as a potential base of regional cooperation in the Arab world. But constructing a governance system that corresponds to the supra-state *umma* can succeed only if there is sufficient material congruence between identity and material society, sufficient interests shared by states, and a hegemonic state, or coalition of states, to lead the process.

A liberal institutional solution to anarchy, the League of Arab States (LAS), founded parallel with the Arab state system, attempted to reconcile 'Westphalian' sovereignty, which its Charter acknowledged, with the belief that common Arab interests should be collectively defended. However, the League failed its first test: coordination of the Arab states for the defence of Palestine. Ever since, there has always been a major disjuncture between the all-Arab norms agreed by the League and the actual conduct of states. While the LAS Council periodically assembles state leaders to discuss all-Arab issues, its resolutions, having to be passed unanimously, represent the lowest common denominator. As an intergovernmental organization, the League had no means of collective action or enforcement; hence imple-mentation of its resolutions depended upon leadership by the more powerful states—itself contingent on congruence between their individual interests and Arab identity. When these conditions existed, a relatively autonomous regional order based on shared Arab identity was discernible (see also **Chapter 9**).

For about a decade (1956–67), Egypt's Nasser deployed pan-Arabism to roll back Western dominance in the region and to construct an informal 'pan-Arab regime'. Under it, state foreign policies were expected to be governed by a common Arab interest, as promoted by Cairo, including independence from imperialism and its alliance systems, and support of the Palestine cause. Without Nasser's agency, there would have been no pan-Arab regime. His stature after the 1956 Suez War as a popular Arab hero, enabling Egypt to mobilize the Arab 'street' to pressure recalcitrant governments from below, made overt alignment with the West an enormous legitimacy liability, at least where the middle class was politically mo-bilizing. Nasser-inspired Arab nationalist movements overthrew oligarchies in a number of states, with the 1958 fall of the pro-Western Iraqi regime establishing a powerful pan-Arab norm against foreign treaties and bases. Even if Arabism was manipulated to serve state in-terests, because this took the form of pan-Arab leadership competition, in which ambitious leaders trumpeted their own Arab credentials and impugned those of rivals, the effect was to establish pan-Arab norms of behaviour that constrained all states. Even Nasser, the main architect of the pan-Arab order, found that he too was bound by it, for as long as he wished to retain his pan-Arab leadership (Barnett 1998).

Nasser empowered pan-Arabism as a hegemonic institution in the Arab world—yet favourable material conditions also empowered Nasser. First, it was the emergent bipolar world order, wherein countervailing Soviet power sheltered the Arab world to some extent from direct Western intervention or its full consequences, which allowed Nasser to survive the Suez War—by sharp contrast with the easy British repression of similar challenges in the inter-war years. Further, Nasser was able to impose hegemony on the other Arab states be-cause Egypt, the largest of the Arab powers (not only in terms of population, but also in gross national product and military capability), also possessed the most stable and legitimate re-gime facing weak oligarchies and unstable military regimes (Walt 1987). The coincidence of (bipolar) disunity in the global core and an Arab hegemon imposing (relative) unity in the regional periphery briefly neutralized the normally debilitating effect of the core–periphery structure (core unity, periphery disunity) of world power on the region.

Nevertheless, the pan-Arab regime was inherently precarious. Pan-Arabism was suffi-ciently strong that Egypt could use it to threaten other state elites, thereby exacerbating inter-Arab conflict, but not strong enough to force a durable uniformity of policy. Western-aligned regimes propagated sovereignty-centric versions of Arabism against Cairo. When, in 1958, the anti-Nasser Jordan and Lebanon, appeared to be in danger, Western military intervention in their defence was decisive in checking the pan-Arab high tide. Egypt's one attempt to deploy military power to defend its pan-Arab hegemony, in Yemen, ended in stalemate. As their state formation caught up with Egypt's—the monarchies as their oil rev-enues grew, the new republican leaders as they learned to control their bases in the army—Nasser's rivals became more effective in defending their sovereignty. Even the other Arab nationalist states—Syria and Iraq—threatened by Nasser's dominance, balanced against Cairo by outbidding his commitment to Palestine, setting the stage for the 1967 war with

Israel. Egypt had never enjoyed sufficient economic superiority for hegemony, but after 1967 it became dependent on its main rival, Saudi Arabia, for the financial resources with which to rebuild its shattered army. Egypt's hegemony depended on the trans-state public esteem that Nasser enjoyed; when the 1967 defeat destroyed this, the pan-Arab regime lost its enforcer. It proved too dependent on normative discourse and temporary material conditions that were liable to shift.

If 1967 destroyed the Egypt-centred order, the preparation for and aftermath of the 1973 Arab–Israeli War shaped a new polycentric version of pan-Arabism. After Nasser, Egyptian hegemony was replaced by an axis of the largest (Egypt), richest (Saudi Arabia), and most pan-Arab (Syria) states, facilitated by the greater equality—hence trust—between the main leaders, Sadat, Faisal, and Asad. In the absence of an enforcer, cohesion resulted from the dire need to coordinate against a militarily superior power occupying Arab lands. In the 1973 war, Egypt and Syria coordinated their strategies, while Saudi Arabia financed the military preparations and used the oil weapon. Prestige from the relative war success allowed them to constitute a leading centre for the Arab system. Under the new order, pan-Arab norms now had to be defined by an inter-elite consensus—a return to the half-way house between pan-Arabism and 'Westphalia' established by the LAS, but now with a concert of leading states to operationalize it. Arab summits forged an Arab consensus on a comprehensive peace with Israel, provided that it returned the conquered territories, thus engineering a mutual deflation of the standards of Arabism and marginalizing radical regimes (Iraq, Libya) that still sought to use nationalist outbidding against the peace process (Sela 1998).

Parallel to the move toward political concert was one toward economic integration. The absence of a pan-Arab economy had been widely seen as an underlying reason for the failure of Nasser's pan-Arab order. The imperialist fragmentation of the regional market into state-bounded economies had meant that pan-Arab norms had corresponded to no economic interdependencies; on the contrary, the export of primary products to the 'core' pulled the economic interests of dominant classes (such as westward-exporting landlords) out of correspondence with Arabism. Now, however, trans-state economic ties proliferated from the post-1973 explosion in Arab oil wealth, including a massive flow of labour from the oil-poor to the oil-rich states, and of capital and workers' remittances from the latter to the former. Joint investment ventures proliferated, such as the Egyptian–Saudi Arab Military Industrial Organization and LAS functional specialized agencies. This started the economic integration without which political integration cannot advance (Kerr and el-Sayed 1982).

This order too was aborted by a shift in material factors. First, the US used material incentives to co-opt two of the leading Arab states, trumping their Arab identity. It lured Egypt into a separate peace by brokering the return of the Sinai and with massive economic aid. Sadat's parallel promotion of sovereignty over Arabism released many of the constraints on state-centric behaviour that Nasser had put in place. Saudi Arabia, lacking a minimum self-defence capability, especially in the face of revolutionary Iran, sought security in a massive upgrading of its alliance with the US, requiring the recycling of the bulk of its petro-dollars to the West and ending any prospect of again using the oil weapon on behalf of the Arab cause. Then, in the 1980s, two wars—the 1982 Israel invasion of Lebanon and the Iran–Iraq war—split the Arab states and fuelled military insecurity, turning them increasingly to self-help through military build-ups (Syria, Iraq) or security dependence on the US (Saudi

Arabia and the Gulf). Leading Arab states were 'deconstructing' the Arab system and the consequent popular disillusionment precipitated a decline in mass Arabism that further released constraints on pursuit of *raison d'état*.

In parallel, the new Arab economic order faltered: inter-Arab trade stalled at less than 10 per cent of total Arab trade; most Arab capital surpluses and 98 per cent of private Arab foreign investment were recycled to the West; inter-Arab capital transfers declined after the oil price bubble burst around 1986. Arab migrant workers acquired no rights and had to leave their host countries when oil-driven demand collapsed. Even as interdependence stalled, oil accentuated the income gap between oil-producing and non-oil-producing countries, sharply differentiating their interests and setting the stage for Saddam Hussein's 1990 invasion of Kuwait.

The US co-optation of Saudi Arabia and Egypt, and its defeat of Iraq in the Gulf War, destroyed the remnants of Arab cohesion and opened the door to a restoration of imperial domination over the region. The interests of regional states sharply diverged between the majority dependent on the US (which again welcomed the treaties and bases that are anathema to Arab nationalism) and those threatened by it, which hung on to the banner of Arab nationalism or radical Islam (Syria and Iran). If a thin Arabism survived, it was chiefly around the central identity issue, Palestine–Israel, which periodically precipitated LAS summits and attempts to generate a binding consensus on the terms of peace. The Arab states system, reverting to the minimalist Arabism dominant at its founding, reached an equilibrium point: states' interests were too divergent to sustain any deepening of Arabism, but the legitimacy of state leaders remained too contingent on Arab identity for them to jettison it wholly (Sirriyeh 2000: 60–5).

In summary, the embedding of the Arab states system in a supra-state community has built into it an enduring tension, trapping foreign policymakers between the logic of sovereignty, in which each regime, insecure both at home and amidst the anarchy of the states system, pursues its own interests and security, often against its Arab neighbours, and the counter norm held by their publics, which conditioned the legitimacy of the individual states on their acting together in defence of the shared identity (Barnett 1998: 10–11, 25–7). Arab identity has been a constant, but changing *material* conditions have forced adaptations in its norms. The 'thicker' form of pan-Arabism was possible only in the periods during which bipolarity at the global level coincided with Egyptian hegemony at the regional level, or when the common Israeli threat and oil-driven economic interdependence increased cohesion. Thin versions of Arabism, prioritizing sovereignty, corresponded to periods of regional multi-polar struggle, particularly when militarized, coincident with the enhanced intervention and co-optative power of a global hegemon.

The instrumentalization of identity in the post-Arab uprising regional power struggle

The Pan-Arab era ended as oil revenues allowed the increased material consolidation of the Arab states after the 1970s. Subsequently, however, identification with the individual states faltered, partly owing to legitimacy deficits, partly owing to the declining proportion of oil revenues to population available to governments for the purposes of cooptation.

The weakening of the state in most of the Arab republics, beginning in the 1990s made them more permeable to trans-state discourses and movements, that, in the 'new Arab Cold War' (2000–10), seemed to return the regional system to the identity wars typical of the Pan-Arab period. Rival regimes exploited different identities in this struggle, but only exceptionally could they substantially alter identity at the mass level. Thus, the conflict between the 'Resistance Axis' of Iran–Syria–Hezbollah and Hamas and the so-called 'moderate' Sunni bloc of Saudi Arabia, Egypt, and Jordan exposed the continuing durability of mass Arabism: the attempt of the latter to depict the former as a 'Shia axis' had little effect on mass Sunni publics for whom Hezbollah leader Nasrallah and even Iran's Ahmadinejad were much more popular than their Sunni counterparts because of their perceived resistance to Israel during the Lebanon and Gaza wars and the complicity of the former with Israel (Valbjorn and Bank 2007; Sedgwick 2010).

Yet, with the Arab uprising, and the weakening or collapse of many Arab regimes, key states proved as vulnerable to trans-state identity wars as during the Pan-Arab period (Phillips 2011), with the main differences that, first, the monarchies were on the offensive and the republics the defensive and, second, divisive sectarian discourse displaced more inclusive Arab and Islamic identities and rapidly seeped down to the mass level. Syria was the incubator of this new robust sectarianism. As the Asad regime framed the opposition—that initially had been overtly secular, peaceful, and inclusive—as jihadists and terrorists in order to solidify its support among minorities, especially the Alawis, and also inflicted violence on unarmed protestors, the opposition increasingly adopted anti-Alawi and Islamist discourse. As the opposition was militarized, Islamist ideologies became its most effective recruitment tools. At the grassroots level, as order broke down, the 'security dilemma' kicked in: people fell back on trusted in-groups and legitimized violence on identity (us vs them) grounds. At the same time, in non-government controlled areas of Syria, a war economy grew up wherein those with resources attracted people otherwise deprived of their livelihoods by the civil war; those with the most resources, both arms and money, were the more radical Islamists, who were enabled to spread their jihadist sectarian discourse. They were empowered by financing from the GCC states, which sought Asad's overthrow as a way of weakening Iran and the resistance axis; and Turkey which, in the name of exporting democratization, provided a safe haven from which anti-Asad fighters operated; yet, finding the jihadists the most effective anti-Asad fighters, Ankara switched its support to them from the secular opposition and with it, promoted an increasingly Sunni Islamist discourse. In parallel, Iran and Hezbollah, as well as the Shia-dominated government in Iraq became the main supporters of Asad and Shia militias joined the battle on the ground against Sunni counterparts (Lynch 2012). Secularists and moderates promoting a civic identity were squeezed between the warring camps and many exited Syria.

While one might have expected Sunni forces to prevail given their immense demographic and financial advantages, that they did not was down, in part, to the fragmentation of the Sunni world. On the one hand, Qatar and Turkey backed the modernist Muslim Brotherhood, which, for a while, appeared to rise across the region, winning elections in Tunisia, Morocco, and Egypt (Rahim 2011); but for Saudi Arabia and the UAE, the Brotherhood's democratic-compatible Islam was a threat and they funnelled their support to salafists and even backed the secular Egyptian army's overthrow of President Mursi and its repression and demonization of the Brotherhood as 'non-Egyptian'. Thereafter, Egypt,

Saudi Arabia, and the UAE were in the forefront of a Thermidor seeking to roll back the Arab uprising.

The result was a three-cornered struggle for power between the Turkey–Qatar bloc, backing the Muslim Brotherhood, on the defensive after Mursi's fall; the Tehran–Baghdad–Damascus–Hezbollah Shia-dominant bloc, and the Saudi–Egyptian-led Sunni counter-revolution. Identity wars, driven by this power struggle, were reflected on the ground as the security dilemma deepened where the state had collapsed or lost control of territory, as in Syria, Iraq, Libya, and Yemen, leaving vacuums wherein armed rival movements promoted contrary identities, fragmenting publics among rival identities. In Yemen, the power struggle between the Zaidi Houthis and their Sunni opponents was partly a proxy war between Saudi Arabia and Iran and imparted a sectarian tinge hitherto largely alien to Yemen politics. As elsewhere, the 'Sunni' side was handicapped by the Saudis' conflict with their former Yemen allies, the Muslim Brotherhood-linked Islah party and the ex-president Salih, now aligned with the Houthis. In parallel, the alienation of Sunnis by the Iraqi regime prepared the way for their embrace of the so-called Islamic State in Iraq and Syria (ISIS). ISIS's seizure of Iraqi towns, including Mosul, with the backing of Sunni tribes and ex-Saddam soldiers, its takeover of much of the non-government controlled parts of eastern Syria, at the expense of secular and more moderate Islamist opponents of Asad, and the proclamation of a Sunni Caliphate bridging western Iraq and eastern Syria, polarized the struggle in these two states along ostensibly sectarian lines. While its considerable material resources and brutal intimidation led to considerable bandwagoning with it by Syrian Islamists, its ideological appeal to the virtual global *umma*, from whom youth flocked to join its fight against the Alawi regime in Damascus, was a key asset. In the meantime, despite the similarity between ISIS jihadism and Wahhabbism, Saudi Arabia, feeling threatened, condemned ISIS as Kharijites—another resurrection from the Muslim past of sectarian branding. Ironically, only in sectarian Lebanon was further sectarianism resisted as Hezbollah, the divided Christian camp, and Saudi-backed Hariri movement combined to resist the penetration of Al-Qaeda/ISIS jihadis.

Thus, the regional power struggle had by mid-2015 made a powerful impact on regional identity. The reverses suffered by the Brotherhood in Egypt and the rise of salafists and jihadists, notably in failed states such as Libya, Syria, Iraq, and Yemen, seemed to empower fundamentalist and violent forms of Islamic identity at the expense of modernist Islam and secular Arabism alike, while sub-state solidarities—sectarian or ethnic (Kurdish)—were also strengthened where civil conflicts enhanced the security dilemma and weakened central governments. This had implications for the inherited state system. State weakening and failure amidst the revival of both sub-state (sectarian, ethnic) and rival supra-state (Pan-Islamic, Sunni, and Shia) identities, seemed to leave many regional states less able than ever to command the loyalty of their populations. Despite this, the latest contestation of borders by the border-straddling ISIS movement is unlikely to succeed in its attempt to overthrow the post-First World War 'settlement' in the face of widespread opposition by regional states and global powers. The project for an independent Kurdistan does look more credible amidst dramatic state weakening in Iraq and Syria; but even if this leads to a relative congruence of state and identity—a proper 'nation state' incorporating Kurdish parts of Iraq and Syria—the exclusion from it of Kurds in Turkey and Iran would likely only re-inflame Kurdish irredentism. As such, incongruity between identity and territory seems set to continue destabilizing the region.

Conclusion

Identity is ultimately rooted in shared history, faith, and language, facilitated by 'social com-munication' and aroused by conflict with the 'other' over land or resources. At the level of agency, it is the most powerful force for mobilizing grievances in challenges to domi-nant structures—via trans-state movements and, where they seize power, revisionist states (Nasser's Egypt; Khomeini's Iran). States' conceptions of their interests are powerfully shaped by identity, particularly whether it is relatively satisfied or frustrated. The outcome of foreign policies, however, depends on whether material factors reinforce or dilute identity's agential power, with states' identities in the latter case normally having to adapt to system-level material constraints.

At the level of structure, identity, if satisfied—notably, if congruent with territory—is the most powerful means of legitimizing a material order and, when the two are incongruent, of destabilizing it. The special legitimacy and unmatched power of the nation state, best seen in Turkey and Israel, attests to the former; the widespread legitimacy deficits of the Arab states, to the latter. The pervasive incongruence of identity and territory in the Middle East explains the revisionism and irredentism that has precipitated frequent wars, two war-prone states (Iraq, Israel), and multiple enduring sites of civil war, either originating in artificial states (Lebanon, Sudan) or frustrated nations (Kurdistan, Palestine). Likewise, security communities depend on a congruence of supra-state identity, material interdependence, and leadership by a hegemon or concert. The Arab world has only briefly enjoyed a precari-ous congruence among them in the two-decade (1956–76) pan-Arab interval sandwiched between periods of dominance from without. The consequent insecurity of the regional states system is another basic root of the region's enduring instability.

Further reading

Barnett, M. N. (1998) *Dialogues in Arab Politics: Negotiations in Regional Order* (New York: Columbia University Press)
   The classic constructivist account of pan-Arabism.

Binder, L. (1999) *Ethnic Conflict and International Politics in the Middle East* (Gainesville, FL: University of Florida Press)
   A useful collection of case studies.

Jankowski, J. and Gershoni, I. (eds) (1997) *Rethinking Nationalism in the Arab Middle East* (New York: Columbia University Press)
   A state-of-the-art work on the construction of national identities in the Arab world.

Khalidi, R., Anderson, L., Muslih, M., and Simon, R. S. (eds) (1991) *The Origins of Arab Nationalism* (New York: Columbia University Press)
   A collection of contemporary debates.

Kienle, E. (1990) *Ba'th vs Ba'th: The Conflict between Syria and Iraq* (London: I. B. Taurus)
   An examination of how state rivalry defeats pan-Arab identity.

Lynch, M. (2012) *The Arab Uprising: the Unfinished Revolutions of the New Middle East* (New York: Public Affairs 2012)
   A good account of the early Arab uprising that pays particular attention to identity.

Mufti, M. (1996) *Sovereign Creations: Pan-Arabism and Political Order in Syria and Iraq* (Ithaca, NY: Cornell University Press)
Exposes the varieties, roots, and decline of unionism.

Questions

1. Are Arab states and popular identities becoming more or less congruent?
2. Does ISIS demonstrate the failure of 'artificial' Arab states?
3. Why do some Arab states see supra-state identities as an asset to their foreign policies while others feel threatened by them?
4. Is Arabism dead?
5. What keeps the Arab states system from collapsing?

8

Islam and International Relations in the Middle East: From *Umma* to Nation State

PETER MANDAVILLE

Overview

Key international relations concepts have been present in the Islamic tradition for many centuries and Islam has generally been comfortable with the division of the world into sovereign polities. Modern efforts to defeat European imperialism by mobilizing Muslims around the banner of religion proved less effectual than the alternative model found in national self-determination. The leaders of newly established national-secular states in the Middle East have still found it useful from time to time to explain and justify their foreign policies in terms of religion, and on a more limited scale several countries in the region have sought to set up distinctly 'Islamic' states. Islam was viewed by the West as a useful ally in the Cold War fight against communism, although with unforeseen consequences later. The geopolitical significance of energy has also permitted certain oil-producing states in the region to project Islam in their external relations. In more recent years, the dynamics of globalization has seen the political significance of Islam expand to include a wide variety of transnational networks and media spaces. Recent popular revolutions in the Arab world have created opportunities for Islamic movements to enter the political sphere which, in turn, has created a new regional politics around Islamism.

Introduction

As the dominant religion in most societies of the Middle East and a major socio-cultural force in its own right, Islam has had a significant bearing on how states and other actors in the region both think about and conduct international relations. While often dated to the 'Islamic revival' of the 1970s and, more specifically, the Iranian Revolution of 1979, Islam's relevance to international relations in the Middle East can be said to pre-date both the rise of the modern international system and the formation of nation states in the region. Islam played a role in debates about the post-colonial political order in the Middle East, and—at the level of theory—strongly informed much of the thinking and debate on the nation state in the early twentieth century. Coexisting in distinct tension with a prevailing trend to-wards Arab nationalism after the Second World War, however, political Islam, or 'Islamism', emerged as an ideological critique of the secular nation state in the Middle East. Claiming the identity of an 'Islamic state', other key players in the region, such as Saudi Arabia, sought to use their geopolitical clout and dominant position in global energy markets to claim a pre-eminent role among Muslim nations. Other states in the Middle East, including some of the more secular regimes, have at times sought recourse to the language and symbols of Islam to explain and justify aspects of their foreign policy. Here, Islam has often served to complement, or as a surrogate for, nationalist discourse. The substantive presence of Islam in the foreign policies of Middle Eastern nations—even in the case of those that consider themselves to be Islamic states—is, however, often difficult to discern. While the Organiza-tion of Islamic Cooperation (OIC) has sought to represent Muslim nations in the realm of multilateral diplomacy, the national interests of its individual members have generally pre-vailed over any common Islamic voice or vision. In the wake of the 1979 Islamic Revolution, an event with important repercussions beyond the Middle East, Iran emerged as a competi-tor to Saudi Arabia, criticizing the latter's close relationship with the United States. During the latter part of the Cold War, Islam came to be regarded by the US and some of its regional allies as an effective tool with which to combat communism, particularly in the wake of the Soviet Union's invasion of Afghanistan. Meanwhile, Iran sought to develop transnational ties with Shi'i groups in other parts of the Middle East, thus having an important impact on, for example, the civil war in Lebanon. In the wake of the Cold War, many of the networks and movements associated with this period have endured, leveraging the trappings of glo-balization (the Internet, satellite television, diaspora communities) to find new audiences and to redefine their political goals. Similarly, new actors and voices have also emerged, seeking to articulate the relationship between Islam, globalization, and international rela-tions for a new generation. More recently, popular revolutions in the Arab world generated a temporary rise in the political fortunes of Islamist parties in some countries but renewed conflict—often along lines of sectarian and religious identity—in others.

Islam and international relations: history and key concepts

We made you into nations and tribes so that you may know each other ...

(Qur'ān 49: 13)

The idea of interaction between political communities has been present in the Islamic tradition since it was founded in the seventh century. Not only do the core textual sources of Islam, such as the Qur'ān and Sunna (the traditions of the Prophet Muhammad), make mention of key concepts from the world of international relations such as nations, power, political authority, and even treaty making (Qur'ān 8: 72), but we also see in the first centuries of Islamic history plenty of evidence that Muslim political leaders were actively engaged in diplomacy, trade negotiations, and warfare with neighbouring polities. Indeed, by about the eleventh century, centralized political authority within the Muslim world had more or less disappeared, replaced by various regional empires and sultanates. Although the office of the Caliph, as successor to the Prophet Muhammad and nominal political leader of all Muslims, endured in one form or another until after the First World War, the occupant of this office often served as little more than a symbolic figurehead after the decline of the Abbasid Empire in the thirteenth century. There is also a rich history of cultural and intellectual engagement between Muslims and non-Muslims during this period, with Arab philosophers digesting—and augmenting—Greek philosophy and classical learning. Although it is common to think of countries in the Muslim world as being on the 'periphery' of world power relations, quite a different perspective emerges if we look at the configuration of global trade flows in the thirteenth century. At this time, the Indian Ocean emerges as a teeming basin of commercial and diplomatic activity, connecting eastern Africa to the southern coast of Arabia in the Middle East across to Persia, India, and further east of the Malay archipelago. If anything, Europe—still in its medieval slumber—constituted a periphery to the 'centre' of this proto-globalized world system (Abu-Lughod 1989). Nizam al-Mulk's eleventh-century kingship manual, the *Siyasatnama* ('Book of Government'), for example, anticipates by several centuries some of the key themes relating to power, diplomacy, and warfare later found in Niccolò Machiavelli's classic *The Prince* (1532). Europe rapidly re-emerged onto the geopolitical stage from the late fifteenth century, however, and by the early seventeenth century the Ottoman Empire was acceding to trade and military capitulations demanded by the French, marking a geopolitical shift towards Europe.

Several concepts are of particular importance when discussing Islam and politics, perhaps none more so than the oft-cited claim that, unlike Christianity, Islam recognizes no distinction between religion and politics—an idea embodied in the commonly invoked phrase *al-islam din wa dawla* ('Islam is both religion and state'). Despite some evidence that this maxim was introduced to Islamic religio-political discourse only relatively recently (Piscatori 1986), it has been frequently cited in evidence of the argument that secularism and Islam are inherently incompatible. While Islam does not, in theological terms, draw a sharp categorical distinction between worldly power (for example, 'render under Caesar what is Caesar's ...') and divine authority ('and unto God that which is God's'), representing itself instead as a faith system (*din*), the moral guidelines of which apply to all areas of life, one can find throughout Islamic history no shortage of evidence that Muslim political leaders have operated with a sense of religious authority and political power as differentiated spheres of activity (Brown 2000). The concept of sovereignty (*hukm*) in the Islamic tradition is similarly debated. Certain conservative schools of thought in Islam, on the one hand, will argue that the idea of sovereignty as something that belongs to God alone (*al-hukm l'il-allah*) renders illegitimate the sovereign claims of governments and worldly political forces. On the more progressive end of the spectrum, by contrast, the Islamic green (pro-ecology) movement has used the same logic to argue that humankind—as the custodian of divine creation—has a responsibility to protect the environment. Once again, a survey of the historical record reveals that the theory and practice of territorial sovereignty has had a rich tradition in the Muslim world. This latter point also brings into question the dichotomous world view that some observers ascribe to Islam. It is often said that, according to Islam, the world is divided into two realms, *dar al-Islam* (the domain of Islam) and *dar al-harb* (the domain of war). The former is taken to refer to those lands under the control of a Muslim ruler (and in which, in theory, Islamic law prevails); the latter, to all lands outside Muslim rule and with which Muslims are potentially in conflict. Such a selective and de-contextualized reading leaves one with the impression that Islam considers itself to be at war with any non-Muslim country, and ignores the existence of a wide range of additional categories—such as *dar al-ahd* or *dar al-sulh* (the domain of treaty)—that Muslim political theorists have used at various times to characterize the relationship between Muslim and non-Muslim sovereign lands. Of overwhelming importance, as James Piscatori (1986: 145) has argued, 'is the consensus that has evolved over the centuries that Islam tolerates, even endorses, territorial pluralism'.

Given the centrality of war and armed conflict to international relations, it is also important here to consider briefly the notion and role of jihad in Islam. This polysemic concept has been a source of considerable confusion in recent years, with some writers arguing that the term's primary meaning is martial in nature, while others focus on its spiritual dimensions. One thing that can be said for certain is that the translation of *jihad* as 'holy war' is misleading in its characterization. The Arabic root of the term refers generically to the idea of 'struggle', and early Islamic sources draw a distinction between greater and lesser jihad. The former is regarded as an individual's inner struggle to live in accordance with the precepts of Islam, while the latter refers to the outward exertion of efforts to bring the surrounding society into compliance with Islam. This can take a range of forms from teaching activities, to political struggle, to armed conflict. In this sense, advocates of the spiritualist approach are not incorrect to stress their understanding of jihad as more fundamental to Islam. However, the term 'jihad', in Islamic political and historical writings, has generally carried the connotation of armed struggle—so, from the point of view of conventional usage, the other camp is also not incorrect. Over the centuries and under the custodianship of Islamic legal scholars (*ulema*), a body of jurisprudence relating to armed conflict was developed. This corpus, the *fiqh al-jihad*, shares much in common as regards both *jus ad bellum* and *jus in bello* with Christian and eventually secular just war theory (Kelsay 1993). Jihad, for example, is traditionally regarded as defensive in nature—that is, force is to be used only when Muslim countries come under external threat. This body of thought also makes an important distinction between combatants and non-combatants, and teaches against the disproportionate use of force. In the contemporary period, several revisionist interpretations of this concept have had the effecting of unmooring jihad from its traditional formulations. During the second half of the twentieth century, figures such as Sayyid Qutb, Muhammad Faraj, and Abdullah Azzam systematically dismantled or radically reinterpreted the classical doctrine of jihad—including, for example, the provision stating that a legitimate war can be declared only by the proper political authorities. Arguing that, in the contemporary world, even nominally Muslim rulers had abandoned the true path of Islam, their collective efforts sought to refigure jihad as an individual duty incumbent on every Muslim. While only marginally influential in the Muslim mainstream, such thinking strongly informed the global jihadist movement, and groups such as Osama bin Laden's Al-Qaeda and later ISIS. This call to jihad found particular resonance in the context of various geopolitical events, such as the failure of Arab national armies in the 1967 war with Israel, Anwar Sadat's 1979 peace treaty with Tel Aviv, and the aftermath of the Afghan mujahedin's victory against the Soviet Union.

Finally, the concept of the *umma*, or community of believers (potentially global in scope), has been part of the Islamic political lexicon since the time of the Prophet. As we will see in this chapter, modern political actors have sought to mobilize Muslims around the notion of the *umma* in response to circumstances ranging from European imperialism in the late nineteenth century to US foreign policy in the contemporary period. In practice, being part of the Muslim *umma* has not generally excluded or been viewed as incompatible with membership in other orders or modes of social affiliation, such as tribe or nation. In this sense, the *umma* should not be seen as part of a rigid hierarchy of identities so much as a general sense of belonging to a geographically broad and culturally diverse faith tradition. In recent years, some observers have speculated that the prevalence of information and communication technologies, and the heightened transnational networking associated with globalization, could give Muslims a renewed sense of *umma* consciousness (Mandaville 2001).

Pan-Islam, colonialism, and the modern state

The Ottoman Empire (1300–1922), pre-eminent among modern Muslim polities, was well integrated into the international system, participating in a complex system of alliances with European powers. By the late nineteenth century, Islam had emerged as a focal point of anti-colonial agitation in the Middle East and elsewhere. The pan-Islam movement of Jamal al-Din al-Afghani (1838–97) identified European imperialism as an experience common to Muslims, from Africa across to South-East Asia, seeking to mobilize anti-colonial sentiment around a renewed sense of *umma* consciousness (Landau 1990). As an itinerant political activist who made frequent use of new transnational media—in his case, mass-circulation newspapers and pamphlets printed in France for distribution in the Middle East—Afghani's work prefigures the transnational advocacy networks of today (Keck and Sikkink 1998). Although he built a following of influential figures in locales as diverse as Afghanistan, India, Egypt, Iran, and Turkey, Afghani's pan-Islam project never evolved into a mass political movement. Its appeal was limited in part by the difficulty that Muslims faced in 'imagining' themselves as part of a community so abstract and diffuse as the *umma* (Anderson 1991a). Nationalism, by contrast, with its concrete moorings in local territory, language, history, and experience, proved a far more effective discourse in which to house projects of anti-colonial resistance. By the time of Woodrow Wilson's articulation of the doctrine of national self-determination in the aftermath of the First World War, nationalism had become a leading aspiration for most Muslims. The break-up of the Ottoman Empire, which had entered the war on the side of Germany and the central powers, led to the eventual creation of several new nation states in the Middle East, among them Iraq, Syria, Lebanon, and Jordan.

That is not to say that Islam immediately disappeared from the scene with the fall of the Ottoman Empire. With the founding of the modern Turkish Republic, Mustafa Kemal (later known as Atatürk), a leading modernist reformer, formally dissolved the institution of the

Caliphate in 1924. For some leading religious scholars of the time, this act prompted a crisis of Islamic political theory. Some, such as the Egyptian Ali Abd al-Raziq (1888–1966), saw Islam and the modern nation state as perfectly compatible, arguing that, in relation to questions of governance, Islam did not prescribe any particular institutional arrangements (Abd al-Raziq 1925). Even those who regarded the Caliphate as a necessity, such as Rashid Rida (1865–1935), eventually recognized that, with the recent shift in world order, a revival of the Caliphate was not a realistic prospect—arguing instead that Muslims should focus on realizing the moral system of Islam within the confines of the nation state (Rida 1923). In this last regard, his thinking informed in important ways the intellectuals and activists who founded the modern Islamist movement. These theoretical deliberations also had a more practical manifestation in various abortive attempts to institutionalize a system of international Islamic congresses in Egypt during the inter-war years (Kramer 1986). Since this time, the idea of political mobilization in the name of the *umma* has generally been found only in the programme of certain radical Islamist movements such as the Caliphate-oriented Hizb ut-Tahrir, or the self-declared Islamic State (ISIS) movement that announced the re-establishment of the Caliphate in 2014 in territories it had seized in Syria and Iraq. While the majority of Muslims around the world today give little credence to the idea of a renewed Caliphate, the *umma* as an ideal has continued to serve an important symbolic function as an expression of the aspiration to greater global unity among Muslims.

The period following the World Wars saw an unprecedented expansion of the international system as dozens of former European colonies in Africa and Asia emerged as independent nation states. This process also dramatically transformed the political geography of the Middle East. Numerous countries, such as Turkey, Iraq, Syria, Lebanon, and Syria, emerged out of the rubble of the Ottoman Empire, with several others in North Africa, such as Egypt, Morocco, and Algeria—the latter only after a bitter war with France—gaining their independence from former European colonial powers. Saudi Arabia was a newcomer, while others, notably Iran, had avoided ever becoming formally part of the European imperial system. Egypt and Saudi Arabia represent two particularly useful cases for exploring the relationship between Islam and the establishment of modern nation states in the Middle East.

Egypt, whose independence from Britain was consolidated in the wake of the 1952 Free Officer's Revolution that brought Gamal Abd al-Nasser to power, represents the prototypical national-secular republic in the Arab world. Nasser emerged over the course of the 1950s as the leading exponent of Arab nationalism, developing a devoted following across the Middle East and eventually even a global role as a leading figure within the Non-Aligned Movement during the Cold War. As an ideology, Arab nationalism—or 'pan-Arabism' as it is sometimes known—emphasized the historical and cultural affinity of all Arabic-speaking peoples. As a political project, it reached its apogee with the short-lived union of Egypt and Syria as the United Arabic Republic (1958–61). As the leading symbol of Arab nationalism, Egypt often found itself in conflict with other emerging regional powers, such as Saudi Arabia—a country that sought, by contrast, to emphasize its Islamic identity. Egypt was also the setting for the founding in 1928 of the Muslim Brotherhood, the prototype for virtually all modern Islamist movements. The Brotherhood has evolved considerably over the course of its lifetime, experiencing periods of both political quietism and radical militancy—the latter associated, in particular, with the intellectual leadership of Sayyid Qutb in the 1960s. Consistently present in the Muslim Brotherhood political discourse, however, has been a critique of national-secularism. Convinced that the newly independent Egypt, particularly under the Nasserists, was under threat of losing its Islamic identity through excessive Westernization, the Brotherhood proposed an alternative ideology in which Islam systematically pervades all aspects of life, including public administration and affairs of state. The movement's concrete goals included the creation of an Islamic state and—rejecting the legitimacy of human legislation outside the remit of religion—a legal system based exclusively on Islamic law (sharia). Also implied here is the priority, in global terms, of Islamic causes over the interests and policies of nation-state governments. Hence, in 1948, against the wishes of the Egyptian state, the Muslim Brotherhood sent volunteer fighters to Palestine. While most commonly associated with its original incarnation in Egypt, at the core of the Muslim Brotherhood movement is a broad ideology that went on to inspire the founding not only of Brotherhood branches throughout the Arab world, but also related movements in countries such as Pakistan, Turkey, Malaysia, and Indonesia (Mandaville 2007). This same ideology has undergone important shifts over the years, adapting itself to the differing political environments of specific national settings. For example, Hamas was originally founded out of the Palestinian branch of the Muslim Brotherhood, but has evolved into what is today primarily an Islamic-based movement for Palestinian national liberation. Elsewhere, the ideas of Muslim Brotherhood founder Hassan al-Banna had a strong influence on Abul Ala Maudidi, chief ideologue of the Jamaat-i-Islami, Pakistan's leading Islamist party. Prior to the establishment of Pakistan at the time of Indian Partition in 1947, Maududi was strongly opposed to nationalism, seeing in it a doctrine that contradicted the universalism of Islam.

Saudi Arabia represents another important context in which to explore the interface of Islam, politics, and international relations. Emerging as a sovereign nation in 1932, the political system of Saudi Arabia was predicated on an alliance between a leading tribal family, the al-Saud, and a group of Islamic scholars who lent religious legitimacy to the former's efforts at unifying diverse tribal regions into a single polity. At the kingdom's founding, it was declared to be an Islamic state, with the sharia as its highest law. The enormous oil reserves found within its territory soon vaulted Saudi Arabia onto the world stage, with the US cultivating a particularly close relationship with the kingdom after the Second World War. Over the next several decades, Saudi Arabia would seek to assert itself as a leader of the Muslim world, not only because of its geopolitical clout, but also because of the presence on its borders of Islam's two holiest cities, Mecca and Medina, the setting for the annual hajj pilgrimage that constitutes one of the core tenets of the Muslim faith. The kingdom has, at times, also sought to represent and exert Islamic values in international and intergovernmental forums (see **Box 8.1**). During the Cold War, Saudi Arabia's ambitions in this regard, not to mention its close relationship with the US, would bring it into conflict with Egypt under Nasser (particularly during the height of the latter's dalliance with the Soviet Union) and with Iran in the wake of that country's Islamic Revolution in 1979. Windfall revenues accruing from heightened oil prices in the 1970s allowed the kingdom to propagate its particular interpretation of Islam, known as Wahhabism, through a wide range of surrogate organizations and charitable organizations. This 'petro-Islam', as it came to be known, subsequently had an important impact on political and conflict dynamics in a wide range of global settings.

Box 8.1 Saudi Arabia and the Universal Declaration of Human Rights

Brought before the General Assembly of the United Nations in late 1948, the Universal Declaration of Human Rights (UDHR) was passed by a vote of forty-eight countries in favour, zero opposed, and eight abstentions. Among the latter was the Kingdom of Saudi Arabia, whose delegation felt that several provisions of the UDHR were not in keeping with sharia law and with the kingdom's identity as an Islamic state. Among these were Article 16, guaranteeing equal marriage rights for men and women, and, more particularly, Article 18, which endorses an individual's right to change his or her religion. The austere form of Islam practised in Saudi Arabia views apostasy from the faith as a crime. These views and religious interpretations, however, were not in keeping with majority opinion among Muslim nations, most of which—including other Islamic states such as Pakistan—have adopted the UDHR.

Saudi Arabia, we should note, is not alone in styling itself as an Islamic state. While several other countries in the contemporary world make similar claims—notably Sudan, Afghanistan under the Taliban, and, more recently, the self-styled Islamic State in Syria and Iraq—two, Pakistan and Iran, are of particular importance and make for interesting points of contrast with Saudi Arabia.

Pakistan was founded as a homeland for Muslims of the Indian subcontinent, and while its constitution declares it to be an 'Islamic republic', the exact relationship between Islam and the state in Pakistan has been a matter of considerable political debate over the course of that country's history. Some, such as Pakistan's founder, Muhammad Ali Jinnah, saw Muslims as constituting a nation and sought accordingly to establish a largely secular framework in which they could achieve political independence. Islamists led by Maududi and the Jamaat-i-Islami, by contrast, emphasized the idea that Islam should constitute the ideology of the Pakistani state, arguing for a constitution that would privilege sharia law.

The Islamic Republic of Iran, by contrast, represented the first time that an Islamic state had been created through a popular revolution. Riding a wave of widespread discontent with the ruling Pahlavi aristocracy, the Iranian clergy, led by the charismatic Ayatollah Khomeini, seized power in 1979 through an alliance with disparate political factions, including liberals and communists, and then proceeded to consolidate power by oppressing anyone who opposed their conservative brand of Islamic rule.

The Iranian model is distinctive in a number of regards, not least of all because it represents the only Islamic state in which religious scholars are in direct control of all major government functions. This model is derived from Khomeini's doctrine of *vilayat-i faqih* ('guardianship of the jurisconsultant'), which states that political power should rest in the hands of those possessing the most superior understanding of Islamic law. In the Iranian system, the preponderance of power resides with the figure of the Supreme Leader, who controls the judiciary, the military and police, and the media. While there is no requirement that the president of the Republic be a religious scholar, the functional power of this position is limited. In the realm of international relations, the president is invested with the capacity to negotiate and conclude treaties with other countries, but all matters of security—as well as the 'delineation of the general policies of the Islamic Republic'—ultimately fall to the Supreme Leader. Partly stemming from its rivalry with Saudi Arabia for leadership of the Muslim world, Iran—one of only very few countries whose population is predominantly (in this case, 90 per cent) Shia as opposed to Sunni Muslim—has at times sought to emphasize that, as an Islamic Republic, it operates differently from nation states founded on the Western model. In terms of its conduct in world politics, however, Iran has tended to participate in all of the standard practices and to express many of the norms associated with modern international relations, including membership in major international organizations, treaties, and global legal regimes.

The political economy of Islamic revival

Contemporary 'Islamic Revival' in the Middle East is commonly dated to the period following the 1967 Six-Day War, in which the dismal performance of Arab militaries and Israel's success in capturing Jerusalem revealed the failure of the national-secular model. While the symbolic power of such moments should never be underestimated, a more thorough understanding of Islam's renewed political significance can be achieved by situating the political mobilization of Islamic language and symbols within the political economies of Middle Eastern states, and, from the early 1970s, against the backdrop of rapidly accelerating globalization processes. Indeed, the very notion of an Islamic 'revival' obscures the fact that the cultural resonance and everyday language of religion had always been present in the political discourse of the region.

While our primary focus here is on the growth of Islamist social and political movements, it is important to recognize that such groups have not been the only significant Islamic actors; Middle Eastern states themselves have sought to intervene in the religious field, shaping societal understandings of Islam and deploying religious institutions in pursuit of their own goals. In Turkey, for example, the Kemalist ideology of the ruling elite has sought to circumscribe the practice of religion within very narrow, officially approved boundaries. The government's directorate of religious affairs—or Diyanet, as it is known—controls all mosques in the country and oversees the provision of religious services. In Egypt, the Nasserists brought the institutions of Al-Azhar University, for centuries the pre-eminent world centre of Islamic knowledge production in the Sunni tradition, into the remit of governmental bureaucracy—ensuring that the religious scholars (*ulema*) and their mosques would not function as spaces of public critique. Furthermore, they sought to promote an understanding of Islam that was in keeping with the government's own priorities for Egyptian national development (Starrett 1998).

When it comes to Islamism, it is important to note that the ideology of Hassan al-Banna and the Muslim Brotherhood has always been primarily a middle-class phenomenon. As a distinctly modern and 'systematized' reform project, it was designed specifically to appeal to the sensibilities and aspirations of the Middle East's newly educated middle classes. Islamists found early success by figuring themselves as the cultural buffer to rapid modernization, ensuring that Islam remained central to Arab identity and society. As it became clear, particularly from the 1960s, that modernization under the stewardship of national-secular elites would not translate into continued upward social mobility, urban Arab middle classes—now untethered from community safety nets and traditional patronage structures—began to look for alternative answers. Mobilizing behind the slogan *al-islam huwa al-hal* ('Islam is the solution'), the Muslim Brotherhood seized the opportunity presented by this increasingly prevalent sense of relative deprivation to leverage their programme into a mass social movement. Perceiving the Islamists as a growing threat, the Egyptian government cracked down on the Muslim Brotherhood from the 1950s, banning the group and jailing a number of its leaders. This period of oppression coincides with the Brotherhood's most militant phase. Its chief ideologue, Sayyid Qutb, had become convinced that direct armed confrontation with the state was the only way in which to address what he saw as Arab society's descent—at the hands of pro-Western authoritarian regimes—into a state of *jahiliyyah* (pre-Islamic ignorance). In this regard, his famous treatise *Milestones*, authored while in prison (Qutb was executed by the regime in 1966), can be read as a critique of post-colonial development. As some analysts have noted, however, it would be wrong simply to reduce the phenomenon of political Islam to the class interests of a particular actor (Bayat 2007). Islam as a discourse of transformative social change in the face of modernity goes back to the late eighteenth century and cannot be regarded exclusively as a superstructural effect of contemporary economic development.

The impact of globalization on states in the Middle East is also important to consider in relation to the growing efficacy of political Islam from the 1970s. During this period, Nasser's successor in Egypt, Anwar Sadat, shifted his country's geopolitical orientation towards the West. Egypt's 'open door' (*infitah*) policy was designed to encourage foreign direct investment in the country and to integrate Egypt into the emerging structures of a globalized economy. Sadat, who sought in distinct contrast to Nasser to figure himself as the 'believer president', rehabilitated the Muslim Brotherhood as a social and religious organization (but kept in place the ban on its political activities), in the hope that the Islamists could serve to counterbalance the political left. Those within the Brotherhood still beholden to the ideas of Sayyid Qutb saw the decision by the movement's mainstream leadership to renounce violence and operate within parameters prescribed by the government as a form of co-option. The 1970s saw several militant groups splinter off from the main Brotherhood organization, some of whom would later become part of the global jihad movement and join forces with Al-Qaeda. For these groups, Sadat's ultimate betrayal came in 1979, when he signed a peace agreement with Israel, leading a faction of the Islamic jihad to assassinate him 1981.

Sadat's successor, Hosni Mubarak, pushed Egypt's integration with the West and global capitalism to new heights. With hindsight, it can be said that Egypt's decision to open itself up to external economic forces and increased liberalization ended up creating a political environment highly conducive to the growth of Islamism. Mubarak took Egypt into an International Monetary Fund (IMF)-mandated structural adjustment programme that subjected the country's economy to a number of sudden shocks. The scaling back of the government sector, for example, led to a major reduction in employment opportunities and less provision of social services. The Muslim Brotherhood flooded into the vacuum created by the 'retreat' of the Egyptian state. Through the creation of a vast network of charities and social organizations—in effect, an alternative infrastructure for the delivery of basic services—the Islamists showed themselves capable of outperforming the state. The Brotherhood increasingly colonized civil society spaces in Egypt, capturing control, for example, of all major professional syndicates. While generally banned from participating as a political party, the Islamists nevertheless wielded significant clout through the many influential social nodes that lay within their sphere of influence. At the height of the Islamists' social influence, it was even possible to speak of a separate 'Islamic economy' run through a number of Islamic investment companies—most of which were insoluble and later collapsed. Meanwhile, the

Egyptian government continued, through the 1980s and 1990s, to contend with the violent tactics of the radical Islamist splinter groups.

Egypt's experience with Islamism was by no means unique. In Algeria, for example, a similar socio-economic situation—which here also mapped onto a pre-existing cleavage between the Western-oriented Francophone urban elite and an emerging middle class that tended to be more Arab in terms of its cultural and linguistic identity, and also more religiously observant—led to the rapid emergence in the early 1990s of the *Front Islamique du Salut*. The FIS was poised to win national elections and to take power in 1991 when the Algerian military stepped in to annul the vote, precipitating what amounted to a civil war that would run throughout much of the decade.

Islam and geopolitics

Running in parallel with these global–domestic dynamics was an increasingly prominent role for Islam in Cold War geopolitics. Fuelled by windfall revenues after the oil shock of the early 1970s, Saudi Arabia sought to consolidate its leadership of the Muslim world by significantly scaling up support for activities such as mosque-building and religious education around the globe. This 'petro-Islam' subsequently came to be synonymous with the worldwide propagation of the kingdom's austere Wahhabi brand of Islam, which often cross-fertilized with similarly conservative currents in countries such as Pakistan. In general terms, this initiative was welcomed by the US, which viewed Saudi Arabia's religious outreach as a potential check on the growth of (atheist) communism. The Saudi royal family possessed sufficient political and economic capital to paper over the initial signs of a significant undercurrent of Islamist dissent within the heart of the kingdom itself. This manifested itself in the dramatic siege on Mecca's Grand Mosque in 1979, an event that severely embarrassed Saudi Arabia's own security forces when they were forced to prevail upon foreign forces to quell the uprising. The same event also foreshadowed the emergence of concerted religious opposition in Saudi Arabia in the aftermath of the 1991 Gulf War.

The year 1979 also saw another watershed event in the form of Iran's Islamic Revolution. Mobilizing popular discontent with the regime of Shah Reza Pahlavi, a close ally of the US, long-time political dissident Grand Ayatollah Ruhollah Khomeini united a broad cross-spectrum of ideological forces to topple the royal family and to create the Islamic Republic of Iran. The Iranian elite, as Khomeini put it, was suffering from a 'Westoxification' (*gharbzadegi*) that could be eliminated only by replacing the country's political system with one based on Islamic values. One particularly remarkable aspect of this revolution represented an early example of the political utility of globalized popular media. In the months leading up to the revolution, Khomeini primed his audience by smuggling sermons on audio cassettes from his headquarters outside Paris to Iran, where they were duplicated, widely distributed, and eagerly consumed by shopkeepers, taxi drivers, and in private homes (Sreberny-Mohammadi and Mohammadi 1994). Once the revolution had taken place, however, it soon became clear that what Khomeini had in mind was something different from the open and accountable democracy for which most Iranians had been hoping. Instead, Khomeini put his theoretical model of *vilayat-i faqih*—elaborated earlier in a serious of essays on Islamic governance—into practice through the implementation of direct clerical rule. Any political opposition (even from within the ranks of the clergy) was severely repressed, as Khomeini pushed through a new constitution that enshrined him as the country's Supreme Leader—an office that afforded him direct control of the country's security forces, judiciary, and media.

Iran's Islamic Revolution also had important international repercussions. In so far as it symbolized the successful removal of a secular regime by Islamic forces, Khomeini became a hero to Islamists everywhere—even those of a Sunni persuasion. At a time when the leaders of Saudi Arabia were vulnerable to accusations of collusion with the West, the Islamic Revolution allowed Iran to vault itself into direct competition with the Saudis—and, to some extent, with Zia ul-Haq's Pakistan—for the mantle of Muslim leadership. Over the next decades, Riyadh and Tehran would frequently find themselves engaged in a game of 'holier than thou', with each trying to outdo the other in support of global Islamic causes such as Palestine. Khomeini's fatwa against the British author Salman Rushdie in 1988 can be partly understood in this light. Tehran also began to cultivate its own clients and proxy groups overseas, including significant financial and material support for the Lebanese Shia movement Hezbollah. It is also interesting to note that Iran's revolution had a significant impact even beyond the Muslim world. Khomeini's project had broader 'Third World-ist' appeal, and was viewed in parts of Africa and Asia as a triumph for the developing world that transcended the religion dimension. By appearing to carve a geopolitical pathway autonomous of both the US and the Soviet Union, Iran also seemed to embody the aspirations of the Non-Aligned Movement (Esposito 1990). This aspect of the revolution has even resurfaced in the first decade of the twenty-first century, with Iran reaching out to partners in Latin America and Africa in an effort to form a coalition of emerging powers critical of US hegemony. Closer to home, the aftermath of the Iranian Revolution seemed less inspiring. Khomeini soon sought to distract discontent with his revolution on the home front by focusing on a new national cause in the form of the 1980–88 war with neighbouring Iraq—a situation rendered even more complicated by the fact that, like Iran, the majority of Iraq's population was Shi'i Muslim.

Roughly coterminous with the Islamic Revolution and the outbreak of the Iran–Iraq War, the Soviet Union's invasion of Afghanistan provided yet another opportunity for Islam to become implicated in Cold War international relations. Although it occurred beyond the geographic scope of the Middle East, the struggle of the Afghan mujahedin against the Soviets was intimately tied to political dynamics in the region. Afghan fighters received important financial and material support from the US and Saudi Arabia, often using Pakistan's security services as intermediary. More important to the long term, however, was the flow of volunteer fighters (generally estimated to have numbered in the tens of thousands) from the Arab world—'Arab Afghans' as they came to be known—who flocked to Afghanistan and Pakistan in response to calls for jihad from radical Islamic leaders such as the Palestinian Abdullah Azzam. Azzam, who would prove highly influential in shaping the world view of a young Osama bin Laden, was instrumental in building the religious justification for Muslims to leave their countries of citizenship and to fight abroad in the name of Islamic causes (Gerges 2005). Despite their overwhelming numbers and technological superiority, the Soviets did not manage to defeat the mujahedin and their withdrawal in 1988 after eight years was widely perceived as a victory for the Afghan resistance. For those jihadists harbouring global aspirations, Afghanistan was seen as evidence that it was indeed possible to subdue a world superpower under the banner of Islam. Many went on to join Islamic causes elsewhere, such as in Kashmir or Bosnia, while others returned to the Middle East to continue their battle with local regimes in countries such as Algeria and Egypt. It was in this crucible that Osama bin Laden, a young Saudi from a prominent commercial family who had found his calling in the Afghan jihad, decided to establish an organizational infrastructure to support the conduct of global jihad. Thus, out of a nucleus of Arab-Afghans whose efforts had been at least indirectly supported by (and were strategically in line with) the United States, Al-Qaeda was established in 1988. Over the next decade, bin Laden's group built a shadowy network of operatives and finances that spanned much of the Middle East and beyond, culminating in a series of attacks in New York City and Washington on 11 September 2001 ('9/11') that would have major repercussions not only on international relations in the Middle East, but on th global order more generally. The increased human mobility and communications infrastructure associated with globalization (see **'Islam, globalization, and the Arab Spring'** later in this chapter) were central to the mobilization capacity found in these and other Islamist groups.

Thinking about Islam and foreign policy

Thus far we have explored topics such as Islamic thinking on the nation state, and the impact of Islamist groups and the governments of 'Islamic states' on various domestic and geopolitical dynamics. But how should we understand the relationship between Islam and the behaviour of various international relations actors? How is it possible to know when Islam plays a role in the decision calculus of foreign policymakers? Likewise, by what criteria might we decide that the content of a particular policy choice is 'Islamic'? In approaching these questions, one obviously wants to find a middle way between those approaches—often described as 'orientalist'—that explain all Muslim behaviour (social, cultural, economic, political) by reference to Islam and, on the other extreme of the spectrum, purely instrumentalist approaches that view Islam as representing nothing more than a form of rhetoric used to justify policies the real motivation of which lies elsewhere.

It is, of course, impossible for us ever to claim that we can discern the true intention, motivation, or meaning behind a particular social or political action. This does not mean, however, that, when it comes to so pervasive and deeply inscribed a source of social meaning as Islam, we cannot attempt to account for the role of Islamic norms and symbols in a given political situation. Thus we must broadly concur with Adeed Dawisha when he writes:

> It is simply taken for granted that, notwithstanding the variety of interpretations, there still exists an ideological force called Islam that has a symbolic value, ranging from nebulous to significant among people who call themselves Muslims. If this is true, then one should expect that in the actual making of foreign policy, decision-makers of countries, a substantial part of whose population is Muslim, must take Islam into consideration when formulating their policies. At this level of analysis, therefore, one can legitimately assume that Islam must constitute a part (how significant a part is another matter) of the images and perceptions, even attitudes and value-systems, of decision-makers. However, this does not explain how relevant Islam is to particular policies, for to identify factors is not to trace their influence. To uncover processes that affect external behaviour is not to explain how and why they are operative under certain circumstances and not under others.

(Dawisha 1983: 5)

Theories of international relations have traditionally struggled to take culture and identity into account. Privileging the (objectively defined) national interests of a given state, conceptual traditions such as realism, for example, have tended to find little relevance for religion in their explanatory schemas. More recently, theories such as constructivism have sought to appreciate the inter-subjectively defined meanings through which international political actors define and make sense of the situations in which they find themselves (Wendt 1992). Such approaches, however, can often lead to culture or identity functioning as little more than an 'independent variable'—a methodological position that still posits that somehow the 'Islamic factor' in a given situation can be discerned, defined, and isolated relevant to other factors:

> The effort to isolate Islam from other values and to determine its precise (or at least probable) functional role is usually undertaken by reference to the articulated images of the decision-makers. But this immediately raises a further problem … with a little interpretation nearly anything can be justified through reference to Islam, and as such its power to explain and unravel ambiguities can be questioned.

> (Dawisha 1983: 6)

When it comes to Islam and international relations, therefore, our task cannot be one of trying to identify definitive causal relationships between religious faith or normativity, and particular political behaviours. Rather, embracing the 'Muslim politics' approach outlined by Eickelman and Piscatori (1996), we should seek to understand how language, symbols, and values associated with Islam come to be implicated in the representation and deliberation of world political issues, not only by state policymakers, but also, and especially today, by an increasingly diverse range of social actors.

This does not mean that we cannot essay some judgement as to when, for example, the invocation of Islam by political elites leans towards something that looks like the instrumentalization of religion. It has not been uncommon for political leaders associated with strongly national-secular, and even leftist, ideologies to garb themselves in religion during times of crisis, or when their reputations are suffering. Iraq's Saddam Hussein, for example, sought to rally his nation during the long war with Iran (1980–88) by figuring it as, in part, a struggle against the heterodoxy of Shi'ism. Likewise, in the run-up to the Gulf War of 1991, Iraq's conflict with the US was described through the concept of jihad. In television interviews around this time, Saddam would make a point of breaking off the conversation in order to pray. Such public performances of piety by struggling leaders are not uncommon, with the state media often mobilized to provide comprehensive coverage of, for example, a Middle Eastern leader's journey to Mecca and Medina to perform hajj. For Nasser, Islam was not always an obstacle to the realization of Arab nationalism, but rather could often be woven into the broader narrative of Arab identity. Indeed, Islam has often functioned not in opposition to, but as a form of, national cohesion. Also relevant here is the use of religious scholars (*ulema*) by the state to provide religious justification for particular courses of action (Alianak 2007). Thus we saw Saudi Arabia seeking a warrant from its religious establishment for the controversial stationing on the kingdom's soil of hundreds of thousands of non-Muslim soldiers in the run-up to the Gulf War of 1991. Similarly, the Egyptian state's control of Al-Azhar University (the Grand Sheikh of which is technically a high-ranking civil servant) has meant that the institution can be counted on to buttress the positions of Hosni Mubarak's government. More recently, in the case of the Danish cartoon affair of 2006, we saw certain governments in the region taking seemingly counter-intuitive positions. Syria, for example, whose secular Baathist government rarely rallies around religion, saw fit to allow protests against the cartoons to be held in major cities—seemingly to turn to the attention of Syrians away from a variety of domestic ills.

Islam also has an institutional identity in international relations beyond the policies and actions of individual states and leaders. Of primary importance here is the Organization of Islamic Cooperation (OIC), an intergovernmental forum composed of Muslim-majority countries (and several with significant Muslim minorities) founded in 1969 to represent and advocate for Islamic issues before the international community. With international relations dominated by the pursuit of national interests, it is not surprising to find that, over the course of its history, the OIC has often struggled to reconcile the interests of its more powerful individual members (notably, Saudi Arabia, Pakistan, Iran, and Turkey) with the pursuit of a common Islamic position on world issues. As Murden (2002: 198) notes, the OIC has tended to be most unified—and effective—when serving to aggregate Muslim opinion on broadly agreed-upon issues that do not threaten the direct interests of a particular member state—such as expressions of generic support for Palestine, the Danish cartoon crisis (for which the OIC cleared the agenda of its 2005 summit), or the war in Bosnia, in which few OIC members had a real stake. Within the broader OIC 'family' is a range of organizations that mirror certain functional organs of the United Nations. The Islamic Educational, Scientific, and Cultural Organization (ISESCO), for example, is roughly analogous to UNESCO. The Islamic Red Crescent Society is now an important partner within the worldwide Red Cross movement, and the Islamic Development Bank works alongside other multilateral donor institutions and regional development banks. Working more specifically in the realm of religion, non-governmental entities such as the Muslim World League and the World Assembly of Muslim Youth have served as important conduits for Saudi petro-Islam and transnational Islamist networking (Schulze 1990). In the humanitarian field, a number of Islamic charities and relief organizations, such as Muslim Aid and Islamic Relief, have played a prominent role in recent disasters and complex human emergencies. The influence of religion can also be seen in non-Islamic multilateral forums. For example, during the United Nations Conference on Population and Development in 2002, Saudi Arabia and the Vatican formed a coalition to oppose family planning.

Islam, globalization, and the 'Arab Spring'

Of particular importance in recent years has been a substantive increase in the extent and range of Muslim transnationalism in the Middle East—especially the growing prominence of non-governmental actors. While the region may, in some regards, appear relatively untouched by or unintegrated into many processes of economic globalization (Henry and Springborg 2001), one cannot deny that the phenomenal rise of information and communications technologies commonly associated with globalization have produced a teeming 'media-scape' in the Middle East (Appadurai 1996). Islam is very much part of this new media terrain, with some analysts linking its growth to a significant expansion and pluralization of the 'Muslim public sphere' (Eickelman and Anderson 2003). A number of important new Islamic voices have emerged in recent years through satellite television. Sheikh Yusuf al-Qaradawi, an octogenarian religious scholar from Egypt based in the Gulf sheikhdom of Qatar, became a household name through his show on Al-Jazeera television. For our purposes, Qaradawi's significance lies not so much in the mere fact of his project-ing religious authority via new media, but rather in his ability, through satellite television, to bypass government-censored national media and thereby challenge the boundaries of 'official' Islam (Skovgaard-Petersen 2004). Where the scholars of Al-Azhar, for example, re-frain from addressing matters of foreign policy, Qaradawi does not hesitate to hold forth on the Israel–Palestine conflict or the US war in Iraq. Qaradawi was also instrumental in advocating a Middle Eastern boycott on Danish goods in response to the 2006 cartoons fea-turing the Prophet Muhammad. New kinds of popular religious figure without any formal Islamic training are also leveraging new media to get into the game. Hence we see account-ant-turned-television-preacher Amr Khaled calling for inter-civilizational dialogue in the wake of the Danish cartoons. The fact that the Egyptian government pressured him to leave the country in 2002 shows that states are themselves aware that they are operating in an ex-tremely volatile environment in which individuals and groups can cultivate mass followings and accumulate social capital very quickly.

Conventional Islamist groups have also seen globalization as an opportunity to expand their international political influence. The new generation of Islamists, represented by the ruling Justice and Development Party (AKP) in Turkey, is pro-business, globally savvy, and able to build a broad electoral base through its focus on curbing corruption (here, the reli-gious credentials are crucial) and bringing Turkey into the European Union. We see a similar approach in its namesake in Morocco, the *Partie de la justice et du développement* (PJD) and also in the Egyptian Hizb al-Wasat (Centrist Party). These new 'pragmatic' Islamists are committed to the democratic process and are generally seen to be more interested in achieving results than in towing a rigid ideological line (Nasr 2005). While the political plat-forms, agendas, and priorities of these parties reflect their respective national settings, there is also a sense in which they can be viewed as part of a broader, generational trend in which the Islamist project seeks to accommodate itself—often more effectively than state govern-ments—to the phenomenon of globalization. The leaders of these parties, some of whom studied together in universities in the West, are informally networked and regularly in con-tact. But we should not think that Islamism is uniformly adopting the normative agenda of neoliberal globalization. For some within the Muslim Brotherhood movement, for example, globalization is primarily associated with increased socio-economic inequality around the world. These Islamists have sought to build tactical alliances with the political left in the Middle East (Schwedler and Clark 2007). Among those living in the West, this 'anti-hegem-onic Islamism' has taken the form of opposition to the 2003 Iraq War, or even outreach to environmental groups and the broader global justice or anti-globalization (*altermondialisa-tion*) movements. Iran's recent efforts to link up with partners—particularly leftists such as Venezuela's Hugo Chavez—in Latin America and elsewhere in the name of countering US hegemony are also relevant here.

The landscape of Islamic politics in the Middle East was transformed dramatically in 2011, with popular revolutions that brought down the regimes of long-standing autocrats such as Tunisia's Ben Ali, Egypt's Mubarak, and Gaddafi in Libya. Yemen, Bahrain, and Syria also experienced transitions, protests, and civil war, respectively. Some of the region's mon-archies—notably Jordan and Morocco—undertook pre-emptive reform measures to stave off pressures stemming from deeply entrenched socio-economic malaise and popular frus-tration at the lack of accountable and effective government. In all countries experiencing either transition or new political openings, Islamic political parties—both classic Islamists and newly enfranchised, ultra-conservative Salafis—initially achieved stunning success at the ballot box. For a short time, the Egyptian Muslim Brotherhood and Tunisia's En-Nahda became the dominant political forces in their respective countries after years of oppres-sion at the hands of autocratic regimes. Both parties immediately faced the challenge of transforming themselves from opposition movements into governing parties, all the while struggling to navigate the practical challenges of improving dire economic conditions, and managing the increased scrutiny and scepticism levelled at them by displaced secular forces and external actors. Both generally refrained from talking about religion or pursuing explic-itly Islamist agendas in either their domestic or foreign policies.

Their political success was short-lived, however. The Muslim Brotherhood's failure to tangibly address Egypt's problems coupled with a monopolistic approach to politics led to growing unpopularity, culminating in Brotherhood president Mohamed Mursi being re-moved in a military coup in the summer of 2013. In the months that followed, Egypt's new military-backed government banned the Muslim Brotherhood, detained almost all of its key leaders, and employed deadly violence against supporters of the group—with the result that, only a few years after reaching historical heights of success, the Muslim Brotherhood has been all but removed from formal politics in Egypt for the foreseeable future. En-Nahda in Tunisia fared somewhat better, although it too suffered political setbacks. The party's first year in power was characterized by ongoing tensions with secular groups and a growing po-litical impasse. En-Nahda voluntarily stepped down from power but in subsequent elections failed to regain control of the government. Unlike Egypt's Muslim Brotherhood, however, En-Nahda has been able to keep its seat at the political table and has sought to normalize the presence and participation of Islamists in Tunisia's politics.

Beyond the political fortunes of Islamist parties in individual countries, Islamism turned into a regional 'wedge' issue following the 2013 coup against the Egyptian Muslim Brother-hood. Fearing the rising influence of Islamists, several countries—notably Saudi Arabia, Egypt, and the United Arab Emirates—joined forces in an effort to check the political influ-ence of the Muslim Brotherhood across the region. They sought to brand the Muslim Broth-erhood as a form of terrorism and to liken the group to Hamas, Al-Qaeda, and ISIS. On the other side of this divide was an axis formed by two countries, Turkey and Qatar, who had continued to support Islamists across the region. Tensions between the two camps severely frayed relations within the Gulf Cooperation Council (GCC), a forum generally character-ized by consensus and unaccustomed to open disputes between its members.

The 2003 Iraq War and Arab Spring of 2011 have both also had a significant effect on Muslim transnationalism in the region. Some authors, such as Vali Nasr (2006), have spoken of a 'Shia Revival' marked by an upsurge in sectarian political mobilization following the Iraq War. The war undoubtedly provided Iran with new opportunities to wield geopolitical influence in the region and beyond. The popular uprising across the Arab world in 2011 threw these same issues into even starker relief, with countries ruled by minority sectarian groups—particularly Syria and Bahrain—experiencing high levels of tension and violence, and Iran using the opportunity to exert pressure in key countries. The Houthi Rebellion in Yemen, for example, saw Shi'i rebels backed by Tehran emerge as a major political and military force in Yemen. The global jihadist movement, increasingly fragmented post-9/11, was able to some limited extent to use the widespread unpopularity of the Iraq War to re-constitute its ranks and regional networks. The peaceful, cross-ideological Arab uprisings of 2011, however, severely discredited their claim that political change in the region could come about only through the combination of Islam and violence. With the death of Osama bin Laden at the hands of the US military that same year, the global jihadist movement also suffered an important symbolic blow. The volatility of the region in recent years has, however, allowed those Islamists operating in situations of conflict or weak and failed states, such as Hamas and Hezbollah, to become more assertive. Both have enjoyed considerable electoral success and renewed popular legitimacy as symbols of resistance against external influence, even as they continue to be regarded with considerable scepticism by the West.

The most dramatic manifestation of Islamist militancy to emerge from these develop-ments is the movement known as the Islamic State in Iraq and Al-Sham (ISIS), or simply the Islamic State (IS). ISIS is a successor to Al-Qaeda in Iraq, which was mostly eradicated by combined US and Iraqi military efforts in 2007. The movement re-emerged out of the turmoil of Syria's civil war after 2011, taking and holding significant amounts of territory. In 2014, it swept across the border of Iraq and, taking advantage of festering sectarian griev-ances in that country, dramatically seized the city of Mosul and established itself as a major political and military force in the northern and central regions. Shortly thereafter, ISIS de-clared that it had re-established the Caliphate and would be known as the Islamic State (see **Box 8.2**). ISIS became notorious for committing extreme acts of violence against those it

---

Box 8.2 Is the 'Islamic State' a state?

When Abu Bakr al-Baghdadi, the emir of the so-called Islamic State (IS), claimed the mantle of the Caliphate in 2014, he sought to create a sense of legitimacy for his quasi-state by linking it to a centuries old institution in Islamic political history. To what extent, however, can the Islamic State be considered a sovereign entity according to the conventional norms of international relations? In the early months of its existence, the Islamic State managed to accrue certain trappings of *internal sovereignty*—namely, it exercised a near monopoly of violence, rule of law, and governance over populations in the territories it held. It also managed to generate sufficient financial revenue to sustain these activities for a time. However, many who reside in areas controlled by IS do not regard it as a legitimate political force and cooperate with the movement mainly out of fear, or because they perceive some longer term political benefit after IS collapses or is defeated. Moreover, within half a year of establishing its new Caliphate, the capacity of IS to effectively govern its territories had begun to deteriorate. The Islamic State is especially weak when it comes to *external sovereignty*, that dimension of sovereignty that derives from one's standing within the broader international society of nation states. No other member of the international community has recognized the Islamic State's claim of sovereignty, rendering it impossible for the group to participate in conventional international relations. In declaring a new Caliphate, IS was appealing first and foremost to Muslims around the world. However, with only a few exceptions among certain fringe radical figures, no significant Muslim religious or political leaders have recognized IS and most Muslims around the world have expressed little interest in a new Caliphate. In late 2014, a group of more than one hundred of the Muslim world's most important religious scholars wrote an open letter to the Islamic State explaining that it and its activities have no legitimate basis in Islamic law.

defined as its enemies, including Shia, Sunnis who opposed their vision of Islam, and various non-Muslim religious communities in Iraq. Stunned by the scale and gratuitous nature of this violence, a regional and international coalition, led by the United States, was formed in 2014 to attempt to counter and destroy ISIS. In 2015, IS-inspired attacks in Paris and the downing of a Russian passenger jet over Egypt by suspected Islamic militants led to an increased international commitment to undermine the group's activities including Russian air strikes.

Conclusion

As we have seen in this chapter, Islam has figured in the foreign policies and positions of states in the Middle East in a variety of ways. In concluding, however, we should also note Islam's increased salience within broader international relations. In the aftermath of 9/11 and the declaration by the US of a 'global war on terror', Islam has come to inform the perception and positions of states and other actors outside the Middle East. Terms such as 'jihad' and topics such as the Sunni–Shia divide or ISIS and how to combat it are now the stuff of household conversation across Europe, Russia, and North America. In the field of international security, Islamism has in many regards come to play much the same function as communism during the Cold War, with various policymakers and commentators figuring it as the West's chief ideological 'other'. In a geopolitical environment in which efforts to deter militant Islam carry an increasing premium in the eyes of Western powers, numerous countries have sought to use their stated commitment to fighting terrorism as a bargaining chip in their own efforts to secure increased levels of development assistance or lucrative memberships in international organizations. More recently, a string of popular revolutions across the Arab world—and the instability and conflict that have followed in their wake—have brought renewed salience to debates about Islamism, sectarianism, and the role of religion in politics. Given the continued resonance of religious language and symbols in public life, the pervasiveness of media, and the increasingly broad range of actors—including states, political parties, non-governmental organizations, and transnational networks—Islam will remain an important feature of international relations in the Middle East and beyond.

Further reading

Abu Sulayman, A. (1993) *Towards an Islamic Theory of International Relations: New Directions for Methodology and Thought* (Herndon, VA: International Institute of Islamic Thought)
    An exploration of the possibilities and boundaries of a modern Islamic theory of international relations.

Dawisha, A. (ed.) (1983) *Islam in Foreign Policy* (Cambridge: Cambridge University Press)
    A collection of case studies analysing the role of Islam in the foreign policies of various key states in the late twentieth century.

Hashmi, S. (ed.) (2002) *Islamic Political Ethics: Civil Society, Pluralism, and Conflict* (Princeton, NJ: Princeton University Press)
    A superb collection of essays providing an overview of Islam, international society, territorial boundaries, and just war.

Khadduri, M. (1955) *War and Peace in the Law of Islam* (Baltimore, MD: Johns Hopkins Press)
    A classic account of Islamic legal thought on war and armed conflict between states.

Mandaville, P. (2014) *Islam and Politics* (London: Routledge)
  A broad overview of Islam, politics, and the impact of global factors, with significant coverage of the Middle East.

Murden, S. (2002) *Islam, the Middle East, and the New Global Hegemony* (Boulder, CO: Lynne Rienner)
  An analysis of Middle Eastern political responses to globalization and the role of Islam.

Piscatori, J. (1986) *Islam in a World of Nation-States* (Cambridge: Cambridge University Press)
  Justifiably the standard reference point on Islam and international relations; an excellent overview of Islamic thought and practice regarding the world system of states.

Questions

1. Have IR scholars succeeded in accommodating 'Islam' into their theoretical approaches?

2. What is meant by the 'Islamic revival'?

3. To what extent has Islam influenced the foreign policies of Middle Eastern states?

4. Examine the effects of the Arab Spring on the role of Islam in the international relations of the Middle East.

5. Has Islam been a source of unity or fragmentation in Middle East politics and International Relations?

9 Alliances and Regionalism in the Middle East

LOUISE FAWCETT

Overview

This chapter considers the theory and practice of regional cooperation and the Middle East and how the Middle East experience fits into comparative studies of regionalism. International relations approaches to alliance making and other forms of regional cooperation in the Middle East have been influenced by the politics of power, or, in IR language, realist approaches. Interstate cooperation has been frail and transient; alliance-making, reflective of internal and external power balances; and regionalism, the policies of regional institutions, underdeveloped, particularly in contrast with other areas. In reviewing the experience of the Middle East in light of the international relations literature, this chapter suggests that it is more complex and diverse, both analytically and empirically, than commonly assumed. The Middle East is not a region without regionalism. There have been many forces making for cooperation, particularly in the Arab world, based upon common identity, interests and beliefs; multiple alliances that intersect the Arab and non-Arab world, and the potential for cooperation in both broader and narrower regional settings like the Gulf. However, regime insecurity, local rivalry, instability, and external influence inhibit attempts to create regional community. Global as well as regional trends and influences push the Middle East into new arenas of cooperation, but there is a need to map these onto local realities. Events since the Arab Spring have seen opportunities and challenges for Arab regional institutions. There are also new trends in studies of regionalism, which, by breaking away from Eurocentric models, allow us to rethink the role of regions from new perspectives.

Introduction

How and why states cooperate, form alliances and institutions, and how such institutions contribute to regional and global order are issues that naturally exercise scholars of international relations. They are vital to the Middle East region—one which has been identified as a continuing source of insecurity and as posing a challenge to not only regional but also global order. Theories have been designed and refined to answer these questions, and applied to different regions. This intellectual effort is important in terms of explaining and predicting state behaviour, particularly in highlighting the ways in which states can cooperate for pacific and mutually productive purposes, promoting regional and international community. Building regional peace and security is a stepping stone to the construction of a more secure global order. As such, it has been singled out as a priority since the end of the Cold War, notably in United Nations reports such as *Agenda for Peace* (Boutros-Ghali 1992) and later in *The Responsibility to Protect* (R2P), which stated: 'Those states which can call upon strong regional alliances, internal peace and a strong and independent civil society seem best placed to benefit from globalization' (ICISS 2001: 7). The Middle East is a particularly important arena for discussion because of the high levels of insecurity that have prevailed; a fact highlighted in the UN-commissioned AHDR reports. Despite multiple attempts to promote regional order by Middle Eastern states, external powers, and international organizations the region remains deeply insecure and its security concerns poorly understood, as exemplified by the effects of the Arab Spring (Monier 2015).

Like IR scholars, scholars of the Middle East are also concerned with these themes, but their focus is local and empirical, rather than global and theoretical. Alliances, cooperation, and regional order are important because they guide and frame the debates over domestic politics and society, about peoples and governments. In this way, the state and society, the region and the world, are intertwined.

The **Introduction** and **Chapter 1** have noted some of the challenges involved in combining the diverse strands of Middle East studies and international relations scholarship; this chapter addresses the problem in terms of the processes of alliance and region-building. Although alliances, 'formal or informal arrangements for promoting security cooperation' (Walt 1987) are often treated separately in international relations literature, they are closely related to regional regimes and institutions—certainly, any discussion of regional order in the Middle East cannot avoid considering the intersections between alliances and institutions. In doing so, it seeks to explain why, in contrast to other parts of the world, interstate cooperation in the Middle East appears fragile and institutional development limited. The chapter looks first at some problems of relevant theory and its application to the Middle East; second, at the definitional issues that arise when speaking of 'regions' and 'regionalism'; third, at the historical record of alliance-making and cooperation across the region; and finally, it offers a contemporary balance sheet, including a review of events since the Arab uprisings, which have contributed both to shifts in alliances and the regional power balance while, arguably, afforded new importance to regional institutions.

A study of regionalism—the theory and practice of regional cooperation—and its potential is central to the study of the international politics of the Middle East, not only because of wider global trends in regionalism making it an increasingly important feature of international politics (Farrell et al. 2005), but also because of the high levels of regional tension and the nature of its security dilemma, which make the case for regional cooperation particularly pressing. As argued here, insecurity operates at three interconnected levels: the domestic, regional, and international—areas that regional institutions have the potential to address. Yet so far this insecurity has been only partially mitigated by the effects of cooperation between states. The short-term impact of the Arab uprisings saw attempts to strengthen regional institutions, evident in collective action and proposed reforms to the GCC and LAS, but given continuing regional instability, their long-term prospects remains uncertain (Rishmawi 2013; Al Tamamy 2015).

International relations theory and the case of the Middle East

Mainstream international relations theories depict alliance, or bloc building as self-interested, rational behaviour by states to enhance their security and power. When states cooperate, it is not because they seek to promote any greater regional or global good, but because their interests are ultimately served by so doing. Regional groups and regimes are seen as power and security maximizers. Strong states are often identified as key agents in this process, although weaker states also initiate cooperation to consolidate their strength or to balance opposing power (the GCC is a good example). States that lack security and influence on the international stage might be expected to construct alliances or regimes to bolster their power, or to look to stronger states for help in their construction and maintenance (Krasner 1985).

The most important of these theories, realism and neorealism, ascribe to states unitary properties, but while the former acknowledges certain human attributes or 'social texture' (Ruggie 1998: 7), the latter focuses narrowly on the structure and distribution of power in the international system (Waltz 1979). In giving prominence to security concerns and the state of anarchy in international relations, such theories have functioned well as all-purpose explanations of many patterns of state behaviour—relations between European states until the Second World War, for example, or the US and USSR during the Cold War (Mearsheimer 2001). In the Middle East, where cooperation between peoples across borders was far denser and which, until the Second World War, was still a state system in the making, they seem less appropriate. Nonetheless, realists view international cooperation as contingent upon the restless drive of states for security, evident in the alliance-making patterns of the Ottoman Empire in the nineteenth and early twentieth centuries, and in the short life of the modern Middle East: whether in the arrangements linking Arab and non-Arab states—the League of Arab States (LAS), the Baghdad Pact, or the Gulf Cooperation Council (GCC)—or the different bilateral alliances, including those of the United States with Israel and Iran (before 1979), the USSR with Egypt and Syria during the Cold War or Iran and Syria since Iran's revolution. In this account, states are engaged in securing or consolidating their own positions and power, or balancing against the power and threats of others (Walt 1987). Indeed, every major regional alignment—from the positions adopted in the Cold War and the Arab–Israeli conflict, to the current post-Arab Spring divisions—has been thus explained.

Dominant states or regional powers—sometimes referred to as 'hegemons' for their willingness to lead and provide public goods—are often facilitators of such projects, for they possess the requisite power to shape outcomes in the international system (Nabers 2010).

Yet while the history of Europe, the Americas, and parts of Asia offer examples of the uses of hegemonic power, and the ability of strong states to positively exercise their influence in the regional and international system, this pattern is less evident in the modern Middle East (Lustick 1997; Fuertig 2014; Fawcett 2015a), although events since the Iraq War and the Arab Spring have seen the emergence of more powerful regional players such as Turkey, Saudi Arabia, and Iran. States historically have held such aspirations: Egypt has been seen as the natural leader of the Arab world and has at times displayed the characteristics of hegemony, particularly under the charismatic presidency of Nasser, and also in the immediate aftermath of the Arab uprisings, but this position has not been sustained. Saudi Arabia has displayed similar qualities in terms of claims to religious legitimacy or the power conferred by oil wealth; both Iraq and Syria have made different bids for regional dominance, using military and nationalist tools. However, if power is about the ability to influence outcomes and to demonstrate institutional leadership, it is clear that most Middle Eastern states have so far failed to acquire it (Nye 2003: 67).

One outlier is Israel, an obvious regional great power (at least in military terms), buttressed by US support, yet one that has not, so far, contributed to a viable and successful regional order, for reasons that relate to its regional isolation, external dependence, and domestic structure alike. Most Arab states are reluctant openly to ally or cooperate with Israel. Another is Iran, a powerful regional player, whose position was strengthened after the 2003 Iraq War following the weakening of Sunni-dominated Iraq. Like Israel, however, Iran's domestic structure and international posture—notwithstanding its 'Southern' appeal as an anti-Western state—have not been easy to reconcile with a wider regional or international constituency. Iran's relatively strengthened position since the Arab uprisings, both as a comparatively stable regional state and following a successful nuclear agreement with the P-5, could see it playing a more important regional role (Fawcett 2015b).

Looking to regional great powers and power-balancing to explain and predict the behaviour of Middle Eastern states in war and peace has thus provided only a partial picture. Middle Eastern states overall have been poor balancers and weak hegemons. This may be explained by a number of factors including persistent rivalries; the absence of obvious and durable hierarchies between states; the presence of powerful identities that overlap and even conflict with the existing state system, and the often contrary influence of external influences. Outside powers have attempted to impose their security agendas on the Middle East, whether France and Britain before the Second World War, the US and USSR during the Cold War, and the US since, all with mixed results. The Middle Eastern system may be deeply 'penetrated', but it has also proved resistant to external pressures for change (Brown 1984: 3). System-level analysis alone is therefore inadequate, because the behaviour of the Middle East also demonstrates the power of ideas—both shared and conflicting identities—and their constant interaction with regimes and peoples. The international relations of the Middle East are shaped, and reshaped, by criss-crossing local, regional, international, and transnational pressures.

The limits of realism in analysing the behaviour of regional states are only partly resolved, however, by a consideration of competing approaches. Admittedly, these are diverse and cannot be done full justice here. Within the tradition of liberal theories, liberal institutionalists—like realists—employ rationalist arguments to explain cooperative behaviour. Such arguments depart from traditional liberal or idealist claims regarding growing interdependence, declining state salience, the emergence of supranational government, cooperative norms or the possibilities of a democratic peace, focusing instead on the possibilities and rewards of cooperation amid anarchy, through the positive role of regimes and institutions (Keohane 1984). Institutions, critically, allow states to overcome problems of collective action and enforcement, incomplete information, high transaction costs, and other barriers to efficiency and welfare (Barnett and Finnemore 1999).

Applying the latter type of theory to the Middle East has proved problematic. International regimes and institutions in the Middle East have been flimsy: states agree on certain principles and norms to govern behaviour, but cannot trust others to keep or enforce them; hence the rate of defection is high and the (relative) security of bilateralism, or 'minilateralism', often preferred. Bilateral alliances have proved robust and easier to maintain than regional cooperation. Formal institutions are still undeveloped and decision-making processes cumbersome. The weakness of institutions is related to the relatively weak interdependencies between states, at least of the tangible economic and political kind that would make states prone to cooperate, and here both regime type and the nature of the regional economy—notably, low levels of interregional trade—are important. Functional cooperation, as identified at the core of Europe, increasingly has taken place between Arab—particularly Gulf—states, but still remains limited in comparison with other regions. Oil policies, despite evidence of common strategy and design within the Arab states of the Organization of the Petroleum Exporting Countries (OPEC)—notably, in the embargo of 1973—demonstrates the limits of economic cooperation, while diversity of regime type and interests, together with sustained external influence, has in turn constrained political cooperation. Taken together, both liberal theories of interdependence, and new institutionalism, have not greatly helped in explaining regional cooperation, though the GCC may prove to be the exception given the expansion of functional cooperation. This may still hold true for many regions outside Europe or the North Atlantic area, but the Middle East remains a relative outlier in comparative terms. In this respect also, the use of the European Union as a model for regional cooperation in the Middle East is arguably limited. Indeed, attempts to export the European model have often posed obstacles to cooperation (Telo et al. 2015).

A partial exception to the above is historical institutionalism (HI), which invites us to 'go back and look': to scrutinize the conditions under which institutions are founded, and how they change over time (Thelen and Steinmo 1992: 2, 27). This looking back is important. As Pierson writes, 'achieving greater clarity about how history imparts its effects on the present will open up real possibilities for a more constructive intellectual dialogue' (Pierson 2004: 7–8).

Other theoretical arguments explaining the international system through a core–periphery perspective in describing post-imperial orders help in explaining the position the Middle East (Hinnebusch 2003: 14–53) and a range of developing countries in the international system. They provide clues as to alliance-making and institutional patterns by showing how states' choices are limited: they are coerced to join groups sponsored by stronger powers or may attempt to balance against them. Because they also focus on the unequal distribution of power and resources—economic, political, and social—they suffer from some of the weaknesses of realism in their failure to examine the diverse capabilities of states. Colonialism, for example, is very important in understanding the origins and persistence of external influence in the region, even after formal colonialism ended, but states both experienced and responded to the colonial legacy in different ways (Hinnebusch and Cummings 2011). But not all regional states can simply be classed as belonging to the periphery. In some cases, like Saudi Arabia, Iran, or Turkey, these once peripheral states are becoming part of the core. They are joining a group of 'rising powers', which are challenging and reshaping the contours of power in the international system (Nolte 2010). As such they are likely to play increasingly important roles in any potential regional organization.

Other approaches that critique traditional understandings of the international system add value in forcing us to rethink the appropriateness of existing paradigms (Bilgin 2010). This rethinking is particularly important when it comes to making judgements about parts of the 'non Western' world. Constructivism, with its attention to shared reality, historical experience and norms as opposed to the purely material attributes of states, appears useful in a region where conflicting identities predominate (Barnett 1996). States and peoples have been drawn to Arab and Islamic causes that may contradict narrow national interests. Still, a focus on identity cannot be taken too far, as Sami Zubaida (1989) has demonstrated for the case of Islam in the Middle East. Rejecting 'essentialist' or 'orientalist' theses that demand a different starting point for a study of Middle Eastern politics, he shows how Islam in its modern form has grown and developed alongside the state system. Despite the emergence of radical groups that contest state boundaries, this is true today when multiple versions of Islam compete in the political marketplace and sectarian interests are used instrumentally by states to enhance their power (see **Chapter 11**). Shared identity matters, but diversity is a feature in Arab and Islamic contexts, leaving states as the supreme organizational players (Esposito 1995: 202). Despite predictions of the demise of the regional states system amid a plethora of challenges from non-state actors, this is unlikely to change.

Of these theories, realist and structural approaches, historical institutionalism and elements of constructivism, are useful, justifying an approach to the Middle East that is analytically eclectic (Sil and Katzenstein 2010). The region has a long history of external interference and dependence explaining the attractiveness of realism and structuralism, but the short lives and artificial nature of many states, together with the common, often transnational, bonds of history, language, and religion—among the Arab states at least—highlight aspects of constructivism. Domestic-level explanations, which question the state system as the determinant of regional behaviour, also have a role to play in explaining the state of regional cooperation. Regime security and a range of considerations including state–society relations, as well as regional and systemic constraints, are crucial to understanding how they will position themselves in the international arena. Such factors help to explain the expansion of the GCC both before and after the Arab Spring.

Understanding the behaviour of Middle Eastern states in the international system therefore demands a flexible and inclusive theoretical framework—one that incorporates the politics of power and influence, but also the role of diverging ideas, norms, and domestic considerations. It also requires us to study the region carefully, emphasizing the point that we need good area studies to understand the region's international relations. No single theory or level of analysis offers a way of exploring satisfactorily the shifting dynamic of interregional politics, or the international politics of the region, or of explaining why high levels of cooperation sometimes coexist alongside high levels of competition and conflict. One reason for this lies in the relationship between state and identity in the Middle East (see **Chapter 7**), which explains the relative weakness and insecurity of states. State weakness, in turn, accounts for the low levels of institutionalism. Another reason is the high and continuing level of external interference.

This reiterates the difficulties that the Middle East presents for international relations scholars. The region defies attempts at generalization and resists explanations derived from Western experience. The unanticipated events of the Arab Spring, which refute popular arguments of exceptionalism, are a case in point. There is validity in the critique that theories of international relations have failed to take the developing world seriously and therefore cannot be relied upon to provide a guide to understanding its past or present (Ayoob 1995; Korany 1999a). This problem extends to the very language and terms used in the study of regionalism—often drawing directly on Europe's different history and experience of integration—questioning the appropriateness of IR theory in non-Western contexts.

Regions, regionalism, and understanding cooperation

Speaking of 'regionalism' and its properties invites a discussion of which regional unit or level of cooperation is optimal. The **Introduction** and **Chapter 1** noted the wide definition of the region now known as the Middle East—but, in talking about regional cooperation, is the 'Middle East' best understood as a single coherent unit, or as a set of distinct, if related, parts? If subdivision is necessary, which regional units are most useful? These are key questions, not only for the Middle East, but also for regions generally, as the process and practice of regionalism takes on greater significance in the international system.

The term 'region' has been analysed and explained in many different ways: from a geographical reality—a continent, a cluster of states or territories sharing a common space on the globe—to a more imagined community held together by common experience, identity, and custom. A common view describes a region as a group of states linked together by a geographical relationship and a degree of mutual interdependence (Nye 1968: vii). Alternative approaches focus on regional patterns or 'complexes' of security and conflict (Buzan and Waever 2003). Regions, however, can also be perceived differently by insiders and outsiders and this is part of the problem when thinking of the Middle East, as critical scholars have noted (Bilgin 2004).

If we think of the Middle East as a region, we can see how elements of such definitions are useful: geography, history, and a range of common security concerns do indeed 'unite' the region, at least in one sense. Certainly, any durable peace settlement of the Palestine–Israel or more recently the Iraqi and Syrian crises will necessitate broad regional engagement. But security and other interdependences do not imply cooperation. There are deep divisions reflected in the absence of 'pan-regional' (as opposed to pan-Arab or pan-Islamic) institutions, despite recent efforts by both Europe and the US to promote them in 'Greater Middle East' and 'Mediterranean' initiatives. Indeed part of the problem is that these initiatives, like definitions of the region, have come from the outside rather than the inside. Cooperation, when it occurs, particularly when prompted by outside actors, is often fragmentary and transient. Although some robust alliances have been constructed, the overall impression is one of a conflictual terrain where deep, institutionalized cooperation has been slow to develop.

If, at one level, the idea of the broader Middle East as a region or as a system has been a useful analytical and policymaking tool (Gause 1999; Hinnebusch 2002), at another it may be too general and artificial. Subdivision is needed to highlight patterns of affinity, activity, and cooperation. The Arab states, for example, once formed an obvious system (Sela 1998)—a tightly knit community revealing dense patterns of conflict and cooperation. For Paul Noble, 'the Arab world is arguably the only meaningful international political system among the various continental or macro-regional grouping of states in the Third World' (Noble 1991: 72–3). This claim, however, makes puzzling its relative lack of durable institutional cohesion, the LAS notwithstanding. It also looks weaker today, as the Arab world appears more divided after the fall-out of the Arab Spring and rise of inter-Arab sectarianism. Other patterns and insights emerge when we consider subregional domains, in which groups of states—Arab and non-Arab—come together for different purposes in a variety of settings. Some of these smaller settings—the Gulf, the Northern Tier, and the Mahgreb (North African) regions are examples—provide useful points of departure in studies of co-operation. One difficulty in defining regions—a difficulty that is especially pertinent to the Middle East—is that such definitions have often been provided by outsiders. This was true of the Northern Tier concept, which gave rise to the failed Baghdad Pact, and, more recently, the different European and US efforts to promote regional cooperation (see **Chapter 17**). If there is not a good match between outsider and insider definitions of a region and its purposes, it is unlikely that regions will yield successful regionalisms.

Defining regions and their membership is important when we turn to a discussion of regional institutions. Different configurations have yielded different regionalisms. There is no single or ideal model. Europe is often cited as one, but in reality there are many different European experiences, and not all are transferable elsewhere. In discussing regionalism and the related processes of regionalization, it is therefore important not merely to borrow frameworks from European-style institutions and structures, but also to consider the wider experiences of global regionalisms and the lessons that they offer.

Regionalism is a policy-driven process in which states (and other actors) pursue common goals and policies in any given region. At its softer end, it may involve little more than the promotion of regional awareness or consensus—moves towards the creation of a regional 'society of states' (Bull 1977; Buzan and Gonzalez-Pelanez 2009). At its harder end, it is represented by more complex and formalized arrangements and organization. Although studies of regionalism have typically focused on states, recent scholarship highlights the roles played by non-state actors: forces operating above and below the level of the state—whether transnational, non-governmental, private-sector, or civil-society—which also play important roles in promoting dialogue and cooperation. In formal arrangements—certainly in the case of the Middle East—the state continues to play the predominant role and the bulk of the literature on regionalism focuses on the more measurable institutional forms of interstate cooperation.

'Regionalization' is a related term that refers broadly to processes (as opposed to policies) encompassing an increase in regionally based interaction and activity. Like globalization, although narrower in scope, it may arise as the result of spontaneous forces and can precede or flow from institutional arrangements. Concentrations of economic, social, or security activity may be the precursor to the emergence of formal organization. The regionalization of security, identified as a feature of the post-Cold-War environment, describes the way in which regional states and other actors have engaged with local security dilemmas by becoming providers of security replacing or complementing the role of great powers or the United Nations (Pugh and Sidhu 2003).

These twin processes of regionalism and regionalization have received much attention since the end of the Cold War. A new wave of regionalism has been identified, with important consequences for regional order (Fawcett and Hurrell 1995). Regionalization has been identified as an important process both in relation to regionalism, but also globalization and international order. This discussion is relevant to the Middle East not because the region is replete with examples of successful action, but rather to highlight the hitherto low levels of regionalism (Aarts 1999; Harders and Legrenzi 2008; Zank 2009). Despite areas of actual or potential regional cohesion and integration—whether in labour markets, migration, resource use, private-sector networks, or the disbursement of aid and development funds—their still-limited nature or relative absence in other key spheres is notable (Cammett, Diwan, Richards, and Waterbury 2015). Where the processes of regionalization have long existed, they have been slow to generate common strategies or agreements and are overridden by external initiatives.

The regionalization of conflict, for example, is real enough, but has failed to produce unified responses. In the important area of non-UN peace support operations for example, Middle Eastern actors hardly feature (Centre on International Cooperation 2010). In a world where regional agencies have increasingly come to play a role in determining the parameters of peacekeeping and other activity within their respective areas, or where there are real signs of regionalization—as cases in Europe, the Americas, South-East Asia, and Africa demonstrate—giving rise to new elements of economic and security community, the Middle East remains on the periphery. This was true at least until the Arab Spring, which arguably represented a new dawn for regional organizations, as seen in their engagement with international institutions like the UN and NATO, and their embarking on independent initiatives.

Middle East regionalism: a review

This section reviews the history and experience of Middle Eastern cooperation and regionalism from a comparative and historical perspective, looking at the Cold War and post-Cold-War periods respectively. As such it endorses the importance of an historical institutionalism perspective. This temporal division may be somewhat artificial from the Middle Eastern viewpoint. There, unlike some other regions, the end of the Cold War had limited effects in terms of region-building and conflict management, but from an international relations perspective, the Cold War and post-Cold War provide rather different frameworks in which to analyse the experience of alliances and cooperation (Laidi 1994).

A long view

Viewed from a historical and comparative perspective, Middle Eastern regionalism has quite a respectable pedigree. During the Ottoman period, a regional order—an informal regime by all accounts—was clearly recognizable. The sense of community and belonging, born of Islamic authority and custom, was strong. Cohesion was assisted by a degree of pluralism in the sense of religious and minority toleration. The collapse of the Empire, the abolition of the Islamic Caliphate, and the parallel emergence of a new state system had deleterious effects, although the notion of Islamic community persisted alongside the more recently discovered notion of Arabism.

In the period between the two World Wars, as the new states moved towards independence, the absence of the formal institutions of cooperation was unremarkable. States were concerned with the building of domestic structures, and no other regions in the world outside the Americas and Europe had well-developed institutions. Still, Middle Eastern states became acclimatized to the new culture of international organization through membership of the League of Nations. Persia (later Iran), although not an original member, was invited to join the League in 1919; by 1935, Iraq and Turkey (and Afghanistan) were members, and by 1938 Egypt (Zimmern 1945: 526–7).

Meanwhile, regionalism, in theory and practice, met with mixed responses from the founders of the League of Nations and the United Nations (UN), for whom universalism lay at the base of a successful international order. In the case of the UN, however, the demands of American, Arab, and Commonwealth states influenced the final wording of the Charter, highlighting—in Chapter VIII—the role and responsibility of regional agency (Claude 1968: 5–6). And membership of the UN and its related institutions—most Middle Eastern states, with the exception of the Gulf and North Africa, joined in 1945 (Roberts and Kingsbury 1993: 530–6)—became an important vehicle for representation and legitimacy.

As regards the LAS, it was the 'UN's historical twin'—founded in 1945 and part of a growing family of international organizations (Moussa 2012: 107). If Arab 'unity' was the theme that underpinned discussions over its shape and form, the organization was built around statist principles, its charter emphasizing respect for independence and sovereignty. State sovereignty and pan-Arabism were incongruous partners, but fear of hegemony and the competing agendas of different regimes prevented any deeper union: 'the loose form of association provided for in the Pact represented the most that Arabs could agree on in the circumstances' (Gomaa 1977: 26).

The Arabs, however, were not alone in achieving limited interstate cooperation. Unity and solidarity were also the goals of the Organization of African Unity (OAU), but the scope of its activities was likewise modest. Sovereignty was a prize to be nurtured, not one to be sacrificed on the altar of a 'pan-' movement, or one extolling the virtues of integration. This was particularly the case among states whose regimes were insecure. Other agencies and alliances emerging in this period had a heavily statist, and often specifically Cold War, agenda. Selective security pacts such as the North Atlantic Treaty Organization (NATO), the Warsaw, Rio, and Baghdad Pacts, and the South-East Asian Treaty Organization (SEATO) developed as products of the East–West divide, designed in part to serve the interests of the superpowers. Outside NATO and the Warsaw Pact (until the end of the Cold War), superpower dominance and the absence of a regional rationale limited their acceptability and influence. The Baghdad Pact—later the Central Treaty Organization (CENTO)—was seen as a Western instrument of Cold-War containment, superseding failed US attempts to build a Middle East Defence Organization. It excited the hostility of non-members, while failing to command the support of its own (see **Box 9.1**). Its regional justification dissipated after Iraq's exit in 1959. Subsequent US initiatives to construct an effective regional alliance system met with equally mixed results.

The LAS and Cold War alliances were not the only options. The West European experience of integration seemed to offer a different model and became a source of emulation elsewhere. It is true that the early European institutions had a strong realist rationale—that of securing Europe in an anti-Soviet alliance—but they went much further. The early successes

---

Box 9.1 Regional groups/unity schemes in the Middle East 1945–90

League of Arab States (LAS)	1945–	Algeria, Bahrain, Comoros, Djibouti, Egypt, Iraq, Jordan, Kuwait, Lebanon, Libya, Mauritania, Morocco, Oman, Palestine, Qatar, Saudi Arabia, Somalia, Sudan, Syria, Tunisia, UAE, Yemen
Baghdad Pact/Central Treaty Organization (CENTO)	1955–79	(Great Britain) Iran, Iraq (left in 1959), Pakistan, Turkey
United Arab Republic (UAR)	1958–61	Egypt and Syria
United Arab Emirates (UAE)	1971–	Abu Dhabi, Ajman, Dubai, Fujairah, Sharjah Ras Al-Khaimah, Umm Aal Qaiwain
Federation of Arab Republics	1971–73	Egypt, Libya, Syria
Organization of the Islamic Conference (OIC)	1971–	LAS states, Iran, Turkey
Gulf Cooperation Council (GCC)	1981–	Bahrain, Kuwait, Oman, Qatar, Saudi Arabia, UAE
Economic Conference Organization (ECO)	1985–	Afghanistan, Iran, Pakistan, Turkey (plus Central Asian Republics)
Arab Mahgreb Union (AMU)	1989–	Algeria, Libya, Mauritania, Morocco, Tunisia
Arab Cooperation Council (ACC)	1989–90	Egypt, Iraq, Jordan, North Yemen
Unification of Yemen	1990	Creation of Republic of Yemen, uniting the former People's Democratic Republic of Yemen (PDRY) and the Yemen Arab Republic (YAR)

---

of the original six European Community members presented a new regional opportunity, which, although rooted in the particular experience of Europe, was seen as a starting point for other such experiments. Attempts to create common markets and free trade associations in Asia, Africa, the Pacific, and the Americas proliferated.

In the Middle East, Arab attempts between 1957 and 1967 to create a common market were too ambitious. The European example and the consequences of the Suez crisis of 1956, encouraged the drive towards economic cooperation and common resource management, leading to the signature in 1964 (through the League's Economic Council), of a treaty to establish an Arab Common Market, scheduled for 1974. But lack of consensus over common tariffs and trade policies meant that the scheme, like similar schemes elsewhere, failed (Owen 1999). The relevance of the European experience to what were mostly poor and insecure states with only the rudiments of a regional market, along with the assumption that such states would benefit from a customs union or similar, was rightly brought into question. By the late 1960s, the different experiments in regional integration had faltered. Even in Europe, their proponents questioned the relevance of regional integration theory.

External penetration, inter-Arab tensions, domestic politics, and the nature of the regional economy help to explain the fitful progress of cooperative efforts at the regional level. Despite the potential benefits of functional cooperation, evident in areas such as resource management or regional labour movements which grew significantly in this period, few durable achievements resulted. Regimes found that their economic and military interests were better supplied in either ad hoc or bilateral alignments; through oil sales to the developed world, or through the receipt of military assistance and material from one of the superpowers. This did not mean that schemes for greater Arab unity were irrelevant—they still served important rhetorical and even unifying purposes—but failed to provide a framework to overcome the security and development dilemmas that different regimes faced.

The limitations of an institution such as the LAS should, however, be placed in comparative perspective (Salamé 1988a; Pinfari 2009). If the idea of the League as a vehicle for collective security was largely unrealized, this was true of other similar ventures outside Western Europe. In a number of the different conflicts in which the League Council was involved— the Lebanon–United Arab Republic (UAR) conflict of 1958, the Kuwait–Iraq conflict of 1961; the Yemen civil war, 1962–67—the League played a significant negotiating role (Nye 1971: 161–5; Pinfari 2009: 12).

In the case of the Kuwait–Iraq dispute, LAS forces were deployed to thwart possible Iraqi aggression. Further, the League achieved unity of purpose in its stance against Israel— notably, in the Arab boycott of Israeli goods. Like the League of Nations, however, the LAS has been criticized for its failures and judged more for its 'high politics' record in conflict prevention than for its achievements in other areas, of which development support through the Arab Fund is one example (Cammett, Diwan, Richards, and Waterbury 2015).

Other attempts at union and cooperation, with mixed results, included the United Arab Republic (UAR), the Federation of Arab Republics, the United Arab Emirates (UAE), the Gulf Cooperation Council (GCC), and the Economic Conference Organization (ECO). In a different category—and not strictly speaking a Middle Eastern organization—was the Organization of the Islamic Conference (OIC) (**Box 9.1**). While the UAR and the Federation offered the prospect of greater Arab unity, both were short-lived. The UAR revealed the many tensions inherent in any pan-Arab project (Kerr 1971). Behind the rhetoric of unity and cooperation lay the reality of state and regime interest. While those of Syria and Egypt briefly coincided, the UAR survived; when seen as a vehicle for Egyptian hegemony, it collapsed.

The UAE and GCC, however, provide examples of how shared regime-type (monarchy) and security concerns can help to sustain groupings whose members believe their interests and freedom of action to be upheld by so doing (Tripp 1995). Britain's withdrawal from the Gulf in 1971 helped to bring the Emirates together as a federation—an arrangement reflecting 'political necessity', as well as 'economic and social convenience' (Heard-Bey 1999: 136). As regards the GCC, it was the continuing insecurity of the region in the face of common threats—the Soviet invasion of Afghanistan (1979), the Iranian Revolution (1978–79) and the Iran–Iraq War (1980–88)—that motivated Gulf states to create a formal organization. Security certainly appeared to be the major motivation behind the GCC—despite early talk of economic integration—and remained a central preoccupation during its first ten years of existence, which saw not only the continuation of the Iran–Iraq War, but also the Gulf War of 1990–91. External dependence and rivalry among its members prevented the emergence of a 'security community' (Deutsch 1957) despite the creation of a Peninsula Shield Force in 1984 (Deutsch 1957)—a force largely inactive until the Arab Spring. In this regard, the GCC did less well than a number of parallel subregional security organizations, such as the Association of Southeast Asian Nations (ASEAN), or the Economic Community of West African States (ECOWAS), although probably better than the South Asian Association for Regional

Cooperation (SAARC) (Barnett and Gause 1998). Despite its limitations, however, the GCC has proved over the years to be one of the region's more successful organizations, expanding its functional cooperation in a number of areas, even though the Gulf Wars and subsequent developments further tested its unity and independence of action, while exposing its limited capacity to act against powerful external threats.

There were other moments of collaboration for Arab states in this period. A high point of solidarity between 1967 and 1974 was followed by fragmentation until the outbreak of the Gulf War in 1990 (Sayigh 1991). During those years, a consensus emerged over the desired regional order—as evidenced in regular Arab summits, the 1973 October War, and the oil embargo—which briefly saw a coordinated set of Arab responses to the US–Israel position. However, the consequences of the war, the Camp David accords (1978) which saw Egypt and Israel sign a peace treaty, the lost economic opportunities, and the threatening regional environment caused introspection—a decline in support for core issues and a shift away from Arabism to state nationalism. The structures of cooperation were too fragile to endure: regional states proved as willing to break the consensus as they were to lead it.

Outside the region, there were other opportunities for Middle Eastern states to participate in diverse multilateral forums, in which bloc politics based on a looser 'southern' identity engaged different groups of developing countries. The Non-Aligned Movement (NAM) provided an important venue for Arab countries, while other developing states enjoyed the fruits of the short-lived Arab successes of the 1970s. Concerted action among Arab states in OPEC in raising oil prices was inspirational in terms of the broader Third World or 'Southern' movement, particularly in articulating demands by the G77 countries for a 'New International Economic Order'. These achievements proved ephemeral, but deserve mention in the context of broader regionalisms, seen as expressions of post-colonial resistance to the existing international order.

By the end of the Cold War, the collective achievements of Middle Eastern states were few. The system was in deep crisis, reverberating from the consequences of the Iranian Revolution, the Iran–Iraq War, and the Camp David accords, which exacerbated Arab divisions and resulted in Egypt's temporary expulsion from the LAS. Inter-Arab cooperation paled alongside the record of US and Soviet alliance building in the region. Neither superpower was fully satisfied with its efforts: the USSR, with the exception of Syria, failed to secure a reliable regional partner; and the US, despite a succession of initiatives, never achieved a viable containment strategy. Taken overall, however, the relationships forged between the US and Arab/non-Arab states—Israel, Iran (until 1979), and Turkey (a member of NATO since 1952)—and the USSR with Syria and (temporarily) Egypt, Iraq, and South Yemen provide a more robust memory of the international politics of the region than the sporadic efforts of the LAS or the GCC. Inter-Arab alignments, whether bilateral or multilateral, had proved transitory and fragile.

Beyond the Cold War

What changed with the end of the Cold War? From an international relations perspective, this was a period of major global change, with the perceived delivery of a substantial peace dividend and the expansion of the processes of globalization and regionalization. Globalization, with its revolution in communications, trade, and technology, assisted in the flow and fusion of ideas about politics and economics, and societies; regionalization, because of the greatly increased levels of regional activity, suppressed during the Cold War, and guided by the powerful example of Europe, experienced a revival from the mid-1980s. The growth of regional purpose and empowerment—'new regionalism'—affected different parts of the world in unequal ways. For some states, the old world of international relations—of inter-state war, alliances, balances of power, and threats—became less relevant; for others, the change was outwardly dramatic, but ultimately less profound.

In the Middle East, the response to the Cold War's end was mixed, for the new era was characterized by both continuity and change (Sayigh 2000; Miller 2003). As **Chapter 4** demonstrates, the region's most important rivalries and tensions were not of the Cold War type: the Arab–Israel conflict, the Iranian Revolution, and the Iran–Iraq War were all influenced by the Cold War and its ending, but their causes lay elsewhere. More generally, there was a rethinking of external alliances and commitments, particularly where the USSR and Eastern bloc were concerned (important for Syria), and, to some extent, the US—although, for the latter, Cold War or not, regional security and oil remained top priorities and continued to condition regional alignments. Still, the fear of globalization and possible marginalization, common to many developing countries, was also felt by states of the region, prompting new cooperative ventures. Early responses to these trends came in the form of two schemes: the Arab Mahgreb Union (AMU) and the Arab Cooperation Council (ACC), formed in 1989. The revival of the Yemeni unification movement that year was also related to the changed post-Cold-War environment and the drying up of Soviet support for the South Yemen regime (Halliday 2002: 272). In 1992, following an Iranian initiative to bolster indigenous security initiatives on a different axis, the ECO was expanded to include the six Muslim Central Asian states and Afghanistan. These developments were matched by a proliferation of new groups elsewhere, including the Common Market of the South (MERCOSUR) in South America, and the Asia Pacific Economic Conference (APEC) to name but two.

With regard to the Middle East case, a few points should be noted. The AMU was no new idea, and flowed logically from the renewal of diplomatic relations between Algeria and Morocco in 1988; it was also a response to, and borrowed from, the European experience. In its early commitment to a common market—commitments repeated in new regional experiments in South America and South-East Asia—the impact of Europe is clear. However, interregional trade was slow to take off and political quarrels kept AMU leaders away from the summit table. In contrast, relations between individual Maghrebi states and the European Union were consolidated as part of the Euro–Mediterranean Partnership, Neighbourhood Policy, and Union for the Mediterranean, respectively (see **Chapter 17**).

In relation to the short-lived experiment that was the ACC, it appears that the European challenge was also a factor; so was the chronic state of regional instability in the wake of the Iran–Iraq War and the eruption of the Palestinian intifada. Many speculated that the ACC aimed at containment of Iraq's power; as such, it was a failure. Iraq's invasion of Kuwait in 1990 demonstrated the fragility of previous attempts to build regional order and revealed that the end of the Cold War, for the Middle East at least, had not diminished its security dilemma, or even—unlike other parts of the world—the spectre of interstate war (Human Security Centre 2005).

The emergence of these new regional alignments within the space of a few years highlighted the impact of regional and global change. Two related developments—both to some extent products of the new era—were of particular importance and interacted with the ongoing debate about post-Cold-War regional cooperation: the Gulf War; and the start of the

Arab–Israeli peace process in 1991. The former had enormous knock-on consequences for the institutions and axes of cooperation, killing off the ACC, dividing the LAS, and loosening Arab alignments. The war was a salutary reminder of the limits of regionalism. Ultimately, Arab states lacked the power and the will to match Iraqi might, and this task fell to a US-led coalition—a tactical alliance par excellence.

Declared preferences for *Arab* solutions demonstrated the continuing power of identity politics, but their failure to deliver results merely reinforced the futility of such ideas unless accompanied by the appropriate level of commitment, whether of the military or the diplomatic kind. Again, this was mainly supplied by outside actors. In other parts of the world, by contrast, regional actors and their institutions started to take on larger roles in the management of regional security—whether in South-East Asia, where ASEAN became involved in regional consensus-building; in Africa, where regional institutions have taken on security and development tasks previously within the UN's remit; or in Latin America, where the Central American peace processes and democracy-building have been fashioned at least in part by regional actors.

The Gulf War had a profound long-term impact on regional order. In the short term, the League's Secretary General resigned as the organization divided over the invasion: this was perhaps the most serious crisis that it had faced. Its survival, however, also demonstrated the resilience of institutions to overcome internal strife. The GCC also weathered the storm, although the 1991 Damascus Declaration, with its talk of a 'six plus two' arrangement, which would have brought Egypt and Syria into the regional security frame, did not materialize. The GCC, however, continued to expand its functional cooperation and plans to develop a regional market and customs union. If levels of interregional trade remained relatively low, the organization facilitated regional contacts and networks in services and trade (Legrenzi 2008). On the critical question of security, however, the organization's weakness in respect of its powerful neighbours, both Iran and Iraq (at least until 2003), and continuing dependence on the US remained an insurmountable obstacle to strategic independence. Nevertheless, the GCC has embarked on a further stage of institution-building and taken on new security roles.

In regard to the Arab–Israeli peace process initiated in Madrid in 1991, the consequences of the Gulf War and the end of the Cold War were important facilitators, prompting external and internal actors to frame new responses to the conflict. While these efforts are dealt with in **Chapters 12** and **13**, a few observations are relevant here. In the early post-Oslo days, there was widespread talk of a new regional order: part of the 'New World Order' of President George W. H. Bush, and the 'New Middle East' concept of former Israeli Prime Minister Shimon Peres (Peres and Noar 1993).

The new order under discussion was inclusive and ambitious. Underpinning it was the belief that a peace settlement, and reduction of military expenditure, would free up resources for economic and social development, and promote wider economic integration on the European model. Reality soon tested such assumptions and, by the turn of the century, the hoped-for dividends of the Oslo accords, and the multilateral economic conferences that followed, failed to materialize. Still, many would agree that the initiatives of the decade, including the Euro–Mediterranean Partnership, remain an important point of reference and heralded the possibility of future change.

A snapshot of the region at the start of the twenty-first century, however, was hardly encouraging. The Palestine–Israel conflict had reached an impasse. Neither the intermediary efforts of foreign powers, including the European and US commitment to a Palestinian state, nor those of Arab states—such as the Saudi initiative in 2002—had succeeded in brokering a durable settlement.

The region's difficulties were compounded by the unilateral turn in US foreign policy since 9/11, characterized by the interventions in Afghanistan and Iraq which added to regional fragmentation and realignment, igniting discussions about new regional orders. Sympathy for the attacks on the US of 11 September 2001 became more muted, with the elaboration of an 'axis of evil' and its remedy—a war on terror and weapons of mass destruction—both with particular focus on the Middle East. Regional ambivalence over the Afghan intervention turned to hostility over the Iraq War. Most Arab states publicly pronounced against US intervention, signalling that acquiescence or cooperation, of the sort that some had offered in the previous Gulf War or Afghan invasion, would not be forthcoming.

For their part, the hopes of Western powers that a new Iraqi regime would contribute to regional stability and cooperation were soon disappointed. Different initiatives to promote security regionalism along European or NATO lines, or through a bilateral US–Gulf defence pact (Legrenzi 2011), failed. Other projects (still on the table) included the 'Road Map', a peace proposal envisaging the staged development of a Palestinian state, devised by the 'Quartet' (the US, Russia, the European Union, and the UN), the 'Greater Middle East Initiative', stemming from the G8 Summit in 2004, and the different European measures to promote regional integration and confidence-building (see **Box 9.2**). While some progress has been made, this has been overtaken by recent events in the Arab world and hampered by an overreliance on external agency, and the neglect of regional priorities and actors.

In hindsight, rather than opening up new vistas of unity and cooperation, the post-Cold War Middle East revealed forces of fragmentation and division—exacerbated by the destructive events of 2001 and 2003—which key regional actors struggled to check. Identity politics—the broad Arab consensus, which in the past had seemed to offer a way forward— were challenged by the blows of recurrent wars, ongoing crises, and the dismantling of the Iraqi regime, which in turn strengthened alternative regional alliances—that of Iran and Syria, for example. The allegiances that had characterized the region assumed new colours, with Islamism competing with Arabism and states for popular support. Particular challenges were posed by the calls to violence from radical Islamic groups, which threatened regime (and regional) stability and invited external responses to the threat to states. Again, in contrast to other regions where 9/11 and subsequent events reinforced cooperation, Arab states (at least until the Arab Spring) made little progress on core security issues. This was true of the oldest regional organization, the LAS, despite some success at mediation in the 2005–08 Lebanese crisis (Dakhlallah 2012) and attempts to revive, in its 2007 summit, an earlier Arab–Israel peace plan. Similarly, while Islamic states in the Organization of the Islamic Conference (see **Chapter 8**) have laid some groundwork for cooperative strategies, so far these have had a limited, and often symbolic, impact (Esposito 1995: 202; Akbarzadeh and Connor 2005). And here contrasts can be drawn with the growth and expansion of Africa's regional institutions since the 1990s (Fawcett and Gandois 2010).

Until the start of the Arab Spring, regional developments on one level seemed to validate a realist paradigm of regional anarchy with the US, the external hegemon, holding, albeit with increasing difficulty, a regional balance of power between Israel and diverse Arab interests, on the one hand, and regional pretenders such as Iran, on the other. However, the regional, but also the global, environment has become more complex, with the US showing greater

Box 9.2 Post-Cold-War regional initiatives		
Arab Mahgreb Union (AMU)	1989–	Algeria, Libya, Mauritania, Morocco, Tunisia
Arab Cooperation Council (ACC)	1989–90	Egypt, Iraq, Jordan, North Yemen
Unification of Yemen	1990	Creation of Republic of Yemen (ROY), uniting the former People's Democratic Republic of Yemen (PDRY) and the Yemen Arab Republic (YAR)
Damascus Declaration	1991	Egypt, Syria, the GCC
Madrid Peace Conference	1991	Multilateral conference to discuss peace between Israel and Arab neighbours
Euro–Mediterranean Partnership Programme	1995–	EU member states, Algeria, Cyprus, Egypt, Israel, Jordan, Lebanon, Malta, Morocco, Palestinian Authority, Syria, Tunisia, Turkey
Greater Arab Free Trade Area (GAFTA)	1997–	LAS proposal implemented in 2005
Gulf Cooperation Council (GCC) Customs Union	2001–	Proposal to remove trade barriers
Greater Middle East Initiative	2004–	US proposal including Middle Eastern and non-Middle Eastern states
Mediterranean Free Trade Area (Agadir Agreement)	2004–	Egypt, Jordan, Morocco, Tunisia
European Neighbourhood Policy	2004–	EU members, plus neighbours: Algeria, Egypt,
Arab Parliament	2004–	Israel, Jordan, Lebanon, Libya, Morocco, Palestinian Territory, Syria, Tunisia, Turkey
		Proposal for a permanent Arab Parliament
Union for the Mediterranean	2008–	EU, Israel, North African, Balkan, and Arab states
GCC/LAS support for UN Resolution 1973	2011	Arab support for Libyan intervention
GCC Union	2012	Saudi proposal for deeper GCC cooperation

restraint and newer players entering the scene. Russia, China, and the Central Asian states all condition the regional balance of power on a different axis, through their relations with Iran, Turkey, and Arab states such as Syria. While Turkey's stance is both to the East and the West, with EU and NATO links a priority, the country has recently assumed more important regional roles, particularly in conflict mediation. Iran offers a different model: a beneficiary of the new regional balance of power following the Iraq War, it has developed strategies to make the most of its immediate environment, from building regional and extra-regional links, attempting to consolidate an anti-Western front and developing its own nuclear programme. Europe's potential to mediate—and to offer new roads to regionalism by policy and example—remains real, but still under-utilized (Peters 2012).

The limitations of external agency in addressing regional issues were brought sharply into focus by the unanticipated events of the Arab Spring, which accelerated changes in the regional balance of power and revealed the extent to which Western policies had failed in their stated goals. Above all, however, it shifted attention away from external domain and to the realm of domestic politics (see **Chapter 15**) revealing how in understanding the region and its alignments the domestic domain deserves our close attention.

Beyond the Arab uprisings: new regionalism?

The rapid unfolding of events since the Arab uprisings, which commenced late in 2010, has affected the prospects for regionalism in a number of ways, although it is premature to assess their impact. Overall, there has been contradictory evidence of the Middle East embracing more fully the agenda of new regionalism.

Initial reactions to the uprisings saw action by Arab institutions, previously dubbed moribund, in response to regional events—in particular, in support of international initiatives to protect civilians against regime violence (Libya, Syria) and to promote peaceful regime change (Yemen, Syria). Regime change, and with it the possibility of wider reforms, may, in the longer term, encourage a regional environment more conducive to regional cooperation.

In respect of action by Arab institutions, a great deal of significance has been attached, particularly by Western powers, to their involvement and support for international initiatives in Libya such as the endorsement of UN resolution 1973, calling for a 'no-fly zone' and measures to protect the civilian population. Indeed, support from the GCC, LAS (and the OIC) was crucial in providing legitimacy to international action, and suggested also a move towards greater regional collaboration with multilateral institutions such as NATO and the UN. Such support also represented a break from these organizations' stance of strict respect for sovereignty and non-intervention, underwritten in their charters (Bellamy and Williams 2011) and as such a tentative move toward the acceptance of R2P (Elgindy 2012).

The LAS also supported talks to end the political crisis in Yemen, backing a GCC-brokered initiative under which President Salih handed power to his deputy early in 2012. Similarly, it called upon Syria's President Asad to step down, supporting two UN envoy's peace missions to Syria. In summer 2012, OIC members followed LAS in calling for Syria's expulsion from the organization. This regional activism, together with progress in areas like human rights, has prompted discussion of a new era for regional organization (Rishmawi 2010). Despite such positive signs, viewing the regional terrain in 2015, particularly given the continuing crises in Iraq, Syria, and Yemen, rather than new regionalism, what is striking is the incapacity to act decisively, making any celebration of the LAS's new roles premature.

The GCC presents a somewhat different picture with a more sustained effort at unity amid multiple dangers. Indeed, it was partly in response to the events of the Arab Spring and the challenges posed to incumbent regimes, that King Abdullah of Saudi Arabia first called, in December 2011, for the deeper integration of the GCC. This was followed in 2014 for a call for inclusion of Morocco and Jordan to strengthen the axis of monarchies in the region (Al Tamamy 2015).

The significance of such developments should not be understated, but do not necessarily herald a sea change in the capacity for regional organization. The GCC's call for unity can be understood as a bid to enhance regime security against external threats. Such threats include not only the contagion effects of the tumbling of fellow Arab regimes, once dubbed 'presidents for life' (Owen 2012), but also the dangers attached to a resurgence of Sunni–Shia tensions, already aggravated by the Iraq War, but even more acute following the effects of the Arab Spring and the rise of ISIS. The Sunni monarchs of the Gulf fear the implications of a strengthening Shia axis with Iran at its centre. It was in the light of such threats that the GCC announced an increase in its aid package to Bahrain and Oman, and used the Peninsula Shield force in Bahrain alongside Saudi troops and UAE police in spring 2011 to help to suppress Shia-led protests in the capital. However, GCC members, notably Saudi Arabia and Qatar, were openly divided over how to respond to the coup against the Muslim Brotherhood regime in Egypt in 2013.

It remains to be seen whether and how much the GCC states will move towards closer union; however a few observations about the nature of regional developments since the Arab Spring can be made. First, the activism of the GCC—notably, key states such as Saudi Arabia and Qatar—suggests the deepening of a trend towards regional realignment evident after the Iraq invasion. The old Arab core—the republican axis, which once dominated the regional land-scape—has loosened, producing fragmentation, and the rise of new regional players and alliances as discussed in **Chapter 10**. This new regional dynamic, and the alliances it has fostered, is crucial to understanding order and forthcoming directions in regionalism. It is those Gulf states with close US links that currently exercise dominance in regional forums; their position, based on economic performance and other indicators, is likely to remain strong. Second, in relation to regime change and the future of regional organization in the wider region, it is possible that, with a set of more accountable regimes in power, a new consensus on regional issues such as the Palestine–Israel question, which has eluded the LAS in the past, could emerge in the long term.

Conclusion

This chapter has emphasized the limitations of regional cooperation in the Middle East, particularly when contrasted with other regions. Until the events of the Arab Spring, the region was regarded as a backwater of regionalism, with cooperation and alliance-building seen as superficial and transitory acts accommodated within realist state-centred analysis—the cornerstone of traditional international relations theory. Institutional cooperation identified by liberal scholars has been hard to identify. There is a poor match between the externally defined Middle Eastern 'region' and existing institutions; there is no effective network of institutional arrangements (as in Europe for example), limited free trade, no security community, and no longer even a core community of shared ideals. Despite some of the advances since the 1990s, highlighted here and in other chapters of this book, the different regional groups and initiatives remain limited, revealing weak impulses to economic, political, and security cooperation. Events since 2011 initially gave some grounds for optimism—newer players are calling for regional reorganization—but while the political picture remains so uncertain, caution is called for. The most dynamic regional organization, particularly given the absence of leadership in LAS is the GCC. However, the GCC has also faced new challenges and the LAS will still remain important as a source of region-wide initiatives on larger security questions—the Arab Parliament is one example (Rishmawi 2013: 59).

It has been shown that institutional progress has been retarded by the influences of external powers and the contested shape of the regional order. Yet it is also evident that regime security and state type are important in determining the positioning and capabilities of Middle Eastern states in respect of cooperation. The state remains the essential ingredient in determining what makes for successful regionalism and cooperation in the long term. What initiates regional activity—external shocks or internal forces, for example—may not sustain it, so the role of states and domestic actors is central. Here, capacity and regime type are crucial: where regionalism and cooperation are to succeed, states, regimes, and interest groups have major roles to play in promoting and maintaining the processes that drive them. And when we look at state capacity and governance, in the Middle East, and a range of developing countries, the state is often weak, except in a coercive sense. It lacks legitimacy, being unaccountable to its own peoples—to say nothing of peoples and states belonging to any broader regional entity (Tripp 1995).

Middle Eastern states and regimes have often lacked both the capacity and the will to make cooperation and regional institutions work, except in a narrow and self-regarding sense; hence the need for short-term alliances or the propensity to turn outside to resolve their security dilemmas. In this formulation, regionalism and anything more than functional cooperation are merely a symbol: a valuable, but disposable, source of legitimacy for regimes whose own legitimacy quotient is low (Hudson 1977). The events of the Arab Spring have exacerbated these trends to weakening state capacity in key states and giving rise to contestation of borders and territories, making any united response difficult if not impossible. The rise of new alliances to protect regime interests is illustrative of this.

Democratization may be an important, if not sufficient, element in this process. It is true that successful, if still quite limited, cooperation at the regional level has occurred among soft authoritarian states in South-East Asia and this pattern may now be replicated among the monarchies of the Gulf. But it is also noteworthy that, in regions such as South America and parts of the wider Europe, the return or consolidation of democracy and more accountable government has helped to cement the processes of cooperation. In the Middle East, we may be witnessing a political transformation rather than a 'transition to democracy', with the prospects for enhanced regional engagement and cooperation lying beyond this transformationist phase. The prospects remain uncertain.

Tellingly, the UN-commissioned *Arab Human Development Reports* (UNDP 2003–12)—important documents cited elsewhere in this volume—highlight governance, modelled on universal democratic principles, as the key to change. While the reports are concerned with economic, or 'human', development, they stress repeatedly the necessity for fundamental political reform if the Middle East is to catch up with the rest of the world. And this relates as much to its international relations as to its economic and social development. The message here may be that only long-term regime change can finally give real purchase to the marriage of identity and interest, to viable forces and institutions of cooperation; hence the real interest in the possible implications of the Arab uprisings for processes of regional cooperation.

In the years following the Iraq War it was tempting to see the Middle East through the lens of US policy: part of a world of regions embedded in 'America's imperium' (Katzenstein 2005). This lens seems less appropriate however as the US downsizes its commitment, reduces its dependence on Middle East oil, and other states, like China and Russia become more involved not only in regional trade but also in politics. Nevertheless, Middle Eastern states have had few opportunities to develop collaboration and engagement at the regional level, and effectively to project power onto the international stage. For many, then, it remains a case of immature regionalism. But this is too simple a stereotype and is already changing. Regional progress has been encumbered by external influence, the product of its imperial past, strategic vulnerability, and resource capacity. External powers have contributed to the democracy deficit by keeping the authoritarian state alive. However, external agency is both part of the problem and part of a possible solution in enabling the region to move forward. Alone, of course, it will not suffice, for progress depends critically on the successful and meaningful engagement of its own members. And here, as suggested, we need to look harder at the fabric of Middle Eastern states and societies to appreciate their current situation. There are multiple opportunities for regional-level action—engaging not only states, but also a range of non-state or civil society actors—to enable the region to connect with the broader processes of regionalization and globalization. These are precisely the kinds of connections that regional scholars have called for.

While identity remains a factor in explaining regional alignments, there has been a shift away from Arabism towards Islamism, on the one hand, and towards regional fragmentation, on the other. While Islamism in multiple forms is set to condition political outcomes in the region, we do not yet know whether it will be Islamism based on a more moderate Turkish (or Tunisian) model or on the diverging and conservative Saudi and Iranian models. What we have seen in the Middle East, as in other parts of the world, is the rise of emerging powers or centres of power—one example of which is Turkey; another, the GCC—with alternative visions of regional order in which identity forms a part, but not the most important one.

The hypothesis that multiple identities and linkages bind and divide the Middle East, and that these will invariably affect regional outcomes and choices, remains valid. But identity is not enough: if states feel threatened by Israel or Iran, or by a drop in oil prices, the politics of identity will not save them; there must also be compelling material reasons to act. The success of the European Union project depended in the first instance on US power, and shared security and economic concerns; identity construction came later. Similar material considerations explain the initial success of regional arrangements elsewhere—ASEAN or MERCOSUR, for example. Together, in different combinations, the quest for power and security, the agency of strong states, levels of interdependence, institutional frameworks, and shared values all play a role in promoting community and cooperation at the regional level. Ultimately, however, we must focus upon the domestic level of analysis to explain what makes such arrangements work. In the Middle East, domestic arrangements have inhibited, rather than promoted, meaningful collective action. Region-building has suffered from the same legitimacy deficits as nation-building: both have been tarnished by the effects of authoritarianism and the often contrary influence of the West. This is why the Arab Spring—and Western responses to it—is so important.

The limitations of international relations theory, and the need for a flexible and multilevel approach to understanding the region, has been a constant theme of this and other chapters. IR offers some clues to understanding regional patterns of behaviour, but ultimately models designed to fit elsewhere have worked poorly. The need for an eclectic approach which draws selectively and builds upon existing theory while paying close attention to the region is key and is well illustrated by Paul Noble (1991: 49): 'Foreign policies are shaped by national situations, values and perceptions of policy makers and global and regional environments. Systemic conditions provide opportunities or constraints to action and generate pressure that push or pull states in different directions.' The history of alliances and regionalism in the Middle East amply bears this out.

Further reading

Barnett, M. N. (1998) *Dialogues in Arab Politics: Negotiations in Regional Order* (New York: Colombia University Press)
A constructivist approach to understanding inter-Arab relations.

Buzan, B. and Waever, O. (2003) *Regions and Powers: The Structure of International Security* (Cambridge: Cambridge University Press)
Examines regional security patterns from a comparative perspective.

Cammett, M., Diwan, I., Richards, A., and Waterbury, J. (2015) *A Political Economy of the Middle East*, 4th edn (Boulder, CO: Westview Press)
Comprehensive analysis of the region's political economy.

Harders, C. and Legrenzi, M. (2008) *Beyond Regionalism? Regional Cooperation, Regionalism and Regionalization in the Middle East* (Aldershot: Ashgate)
Case studies and analytical chapters explore the limits and opportunities of regionalism.

Hinnebusch, R. and Ehteshami, A. (2014) *The Foreign Policies of Middle Eastern States* (Boulder, CO: Lynne Reinner)
Analysis of the foreign policies of regional states, providing useful insights into their regional and their international relations.

Hudson, M. (1999b) *Middle East Dilemma: The Politics and Economics of Arab Integration* (London: I. B. Tauris)
A comprehensive volume describing the different experiments in regional integration and cooperation across the region.

Luciani, G. and Salamé, G. (eds) (1988) *The Politics of Arab Integration* (New York: Croom Helm)
A volume usefully read in conjunction with Hudson (1999b).

Questions

1. Why has the Middle East seen so few successful regional organizations?
2. Are theories of regionalism a poor fit for explaining Middle East regionalism?
3. Which have been the principal successes of the Arab League?
4. Have the Arab uprisings helped or hindered the prospects of improved regional integration?
5. Is the GCC an example of 'new regionalism'?

Middle East Security: Conflict and Securitization of Identities

MARINA CALCULLI WITH MATTEO LEGRENZI

Overview

This chapter explores the mechanisms and ways in which state and non-state actors seek to shape the regional balance of power in the Middle East, especially after the 2011 uprisings. It sheds light on the 'securitization of identities' and the production of security discourses through which rival regimes deliberately instigate hostility and conflicts, which are often accompanied by high levels of transnational social and political mobilization, a proxy to direct military confrontation. The chapter proposes a fresh understanding of the construction of 'identities' and their role in international politics, moving beyond essential understandings of sectarianism. Instead, it treats the manipulation of sectarianism and other ideological tools of mobilization as sophisticated ways of balancing and/or expanding power. Three main trends are taken into account: the long-standing rivalry between monarchies and republics; the opposition between Sunnis and Shia; and the rift between proponents and opponents of the Muslim Brotherhood. In considering the impact of both state and non-state actors on Middle East security, the chapter reveals how the distinction between these two types of actors is often blurred, especially when they cooperate or compete in the traditionally *domaine réservé* of states.

Introduction

This chapter analyses security in the Middle East with a focus on the consequences of the Arab uprisings of 2010–11 on alliances and alignments in the region. Interstate dynamics remain crucial to understand the shifts in the distribution of power, as well as how and why Middle East states have engaged in conflicts, remained neutral or made peace (Walt 1987; Barnett 1998; Korany 2011b). Yet, there is a need to encompass more transnational and intrastate actors in the analysis of security threats, with regards to their unconventional nature and directionality (David 1991a; Salloukh and Brynen 2004; Ryan 2009) issuing new challenges to prevailing security understandings.

The political consequences of the Arab uprisings have led to a reassessment of the assumptions framing Middle East security and the role of regional and international alliances. Moreover, the proliferation of violent non-state actors and especially their unprecedented ability to compete and/or cooperate with state-actors demands a reassessment of the question of Middle East security in all its multi-layered dimensions.

Building on existing literature the chapter argues that, in the wake of the popular uprisings that erupted across the region, the collapse of key long-standing regimes led to a reconstruction of the security *status quo*. However, at the interstate level there has not been a radical shift and redefinition of traditional alignments. On the contrary, old latent rivalries have increased, whilst traditional alliances have strengthened. For instance, whilst old tensions between Syria and the Gulf States have erupted, the axis of Arab monarchies has been further empowered. The only outlier in this trend is the Syria–Turkish relation, which has drastically deteriorated after 2011. Nonetheless, interstate wars do not characterize the contemporary Middle East, whereas intrastate/transnational conflicts and asymmetric warfare are now the markers of insecurity. Yet, in the aftermath of the Arab uprisings both interstate dynamics and asymmetric conflicts are compounded by confessional/ethnic discourses that drive the creation of coalitions or rivalries in the region.

Against this backdrop, it will be argued that the *securitization* of sectarian identities—that is, the elaboration of a security discourse by state and non-state actors—is the main tool through which certain key regional players have either attempted to capitalize on domestic instability, resulting from popular upheavals, or to elaborate new defensive strategies and coalitions in the aftermath of the Arab uprisings. Indeed, state actors remain central to the understanding of Middle East security, whilst cooperation and competition between state and non-state actors—some of them increasingly autonomous—is a recent development (Calculli 2015).

I identify three main trends that define patterns of conflict in the Middle East today. The first of these trends is a notable resurgence in the long-standing rivalry between monarchies and republics (Kerr 1967; Derichs and Demmelhuber 2014), although the legacy of this friction has assumed a new paradigm in the aftermath of the Arab uprisings. The second is the Sunni–Shia confrontation, mainly reflecting a geopolitical rift opposing the Sunni monarchy of Saudi Arabia and the Shia republic of Iran. The third is a rising antagonism against the Muslim Brothers in the region, mainly orchestrated by Saudi Arabia, which has led to violent ostracism towards Brotherhood-affiliated political actors.

Taken together, these three trends entail contradictory alignments: for instance, Saudi Arabia and Qatar are allied within the monarchical axis, but rivals in the support of/ opposition to the Muslim Brothers. Yet, the strategic salience of Gulf Arab monarchies—in spite of inner disputes over power and prestige—has consolidated the strategic alliance of the Gulf Cooperation Council (GCC).

This chapter is divided into three parts. The first part assesses the concepts and practices of security in the Middle East, as approached in the existing literature, and as for what the 'securitization of identities' implies; the second part is devoted to understanding interstate interaction with respect to the antagonism between republics and monarchies in a histori- cal perspective. Finally, it discusses the securitization of the Sunni–Shia rift and the rise of the Muslim Brotherhood as a political force after 2011, which involves states and non-state actors alike.

Security in the Middle East: concepts and practices

There is a burgeoning literature that addresses manifold aspects of security in the Middle East, especially its regional and international dimensions. For decades, the link between scholarship in Middle East security and Western interests in the region has been apparent (Bilgin 2005: 2–3). This is entrenched in the very fact that Western powers, and especially the United States, have exerted—and still exert—an unparalleled influence in the region. A more critical stream of scholarship has instead put forward new overarching approaches, shifting the attention onto regional 'agency' rather than external orchestration. Even as the United States has sought to limit its overall involvement, the security situation in the region is not conducive to such a move. At the same time, the US has failed to recalibrate its strategy toward the Middle East (Gerges 2012). Moreover, the unprecedented prominence of 'peo- ple's power' (Volpi and Stein 2015) in 2011 (see **Chapter 15**), as well as the consequence of popular movements on regional security, show that the US has by and large lost its capability to impose a security order on the Middle East (Amar and Prashad 2013; Heydemann 2014).

Two main approaches can be distinguished in the existing literature. One more traditional strand of the literature analyses primarily the role of states and how they respond to secu- rity threats by either creating alliances or waging war. A second and more recent approach focuses on the role and impact of non-state actors, particularly violent armed groups, and unconventional threats to domestic and regional security as well as some instances of co- operation and competition between state and non-state actors. These two approaches com- bined reflect various stages in the evolution of the Middle East system from the beginning of the post-colonial era to the aftermath of the Arab uprisings of 2010–11. Indeed, whilst newly created states became central players and gave rise to the emergence of an interstate system following the Second World War, an array of non-state actors emerged and gained centrality, particularly from the 1970s onwards. Some of them, such as the Lebanese Hezbollah and the Palestinian Hamas, have become powerful actors that play a complementary role to states in regional security (El Husseini 2010; Saad-Ghorayeb 2012). The emergence of groups like Al- Qaeda only added to the academic literature on the role of non-state actors in Middle East security, especially with regards to their motivations, goals, and functioning (Moghadam 2009; Gerges 2011). The emergence of a plethora of violent groups in the aftermath of the

US invasion of Iraq in 2003 and the popular uprisings of 2010–11 identifies the Middle East as a region that remains a good case for exploring the issue of how violent non-state actors affect regional and international security.

Realist and neorealist hypotheses have enriched the literature on Middle East security, especially the persistence of high levels of interstate mistrust and conflict, and the deep external penetration of the region (Walt 1987; Brown 1984; Korany 1999b: 35–59; Salloukh and Brynen 2004; Halliday 2005: 75–130). Constructivist and, more broadly normative analyses that emphasize the role of norms and ideas in international politics, also enjoy an important place in the literature on Middle East security; this scholarship has specifically focused on the role of Arab or Islamic identity in explaining regional conflicts and perception of threats, also emphasizing the systemic functionality of an 'Arab interstate system' as distinguished from a Middle East system (Mufti 1996; Barnett 1998; Noble 2008; Bilgin 2010).

Attempts to include different types of threats into an overarching analysis have focused on the 'permeability' of Middle Eastern states (Salloukh and Brynen 2004), and concentrated on the transnational dimension or the multiple directionality of challenges to national security— that is, from outside and from within the state (Halliday 2005: 229–60; Ryan 2009; Korany et al. 1993). These studies, more or less explicitly, owe much to Steven David's concept of *omni-balancing* that captures—from a neorealist angle—the difference between the threats posed to state leadership rather than to the state as such, especially in countries of the global South (David 1991a). Also, during the 1990s, an effort was made to distinguish between the dynamics of *national security* and those of *regime security*, although early debates over the relative merits of these two analytical concepts have now largely died out (Ayoob 1995).

Yet, this conceptual differentiation helps highlight a further systemic contradiction and it is particularly relevant to capture some of the security issues that mark the aftermath of the Arab uprisings. I argue that, since *regime interest* is essentially the interest of political elites to preserve their own domestic power, these elites do not—and cannot—share the same security concerns that are relevant to other segments of society. The triumph of *regime interest* is what defines the polity as a 'fierce state' (Ayubi 1995: 449–50), that is a system lacking a social pact, thus domestic legitimacy, and that entails resorting to models of internal coercion and external patronage and security provision in order to keep the status quo (Migdal 2001; Brownlee 2002). What does this domestic configuration of the polity imply for international security? On the one hand, given that the making of security and foreign policy is the work of political elites that are oblivious to the concept of the 'mandate' through which individuals confer legitimacy to state authority, the state itself ends up overshadowed by the regime, whilst apparently playing a role as a unitary actor in the international arena. On the other hand, societal groups can achieve strength and military autonomy to the point of challenging state authorities from within, and de facto overturning the formal distinction between legitimate and illegitimate use of force. Indeed, the most striking element of novelty in Middle East security today is the increased autonomy of non-state actors and traditional proxies, which is producing patterns of hybridity in 'agency' and warfare. The self-proclaimed 'Islamic State' is the most striking example of this dynamic, as it illustrates the process of transformation from a sovereignty-*challenger* into a sovereignty-*claimer*. Whilst renegotiating sovereignty is quite common in 'immature anarchies' and post-colonial interstate systems (Krasner 1999, 2001), state fragmentation, contestation of sovereignty, or claims of sovereignty—as in the case of Syria, Iraq, Yemen, or Libya—challenge not only the security, but also the territorial integrity of the Middle East. Protracted conflicts between states and new claimers of sovereignty deeply endanger the unity of traditional polities, and may eventually cause further fragmentation.

Securitization of identities

The focus on *regime security* helps reveal the historical legacy of the domestic divide between power elites and societies that has come to the fore during the Arab uprisings. Yet, in order to link the domestic to the international dimensions of Middle East security (see also **Chapter 3**), we need to delve into the practices and mechanisms that have produced such hybrid alliances between states and non-states. I distinguish three distinct fault lines of conflict. The first line of antagonism pits monarchies against republics, and represents a long-standing marker of Middle East (in)security, in an interstate dimension. The second and the third lines are associated with new intra-state and transnational confrontations, grounded in competing doctrinal versions of political Islam—most notably the struggle between Sunni and Shia, but also between the Muslim Brothers and other versions of Sunni Islam.

The 'Cold War' climate helps us to understand why these lines of antagonism have plunged some countries into a violent civil war, with external actors sponsoring one side or another partly on the basis of a sectarian discourse (Salloukh 2013; Gause 2014). However, classical realist and neorealist approaches, which see the balance of power in terms of material capabilities, fail to capture how and why transnational alliances based on identities and encompassing both state and non-state actors can push toward the militarization of societies. Identities shape representations of societal differences and cleavages, which are in turn instrumentally reproduced and reiterated by elite discourses. Against this backdrop, I intend to highlight the function that the *securitization* of sectarian identities has played in defining the present insecurity. The concept of securitization was coined to illustrate a 'speech act' that justifies emergency security measures against what is narrated as an 'existential threat' (Buzan et al. 1998: 6). Securitization theory is mainly grounded in the assumption that it is only 'by labelling something as a security issue, that it becomes one' (Wæver 2004: 13). In this sense, the illocutionary act of defining something as a threat in and of itself defines power relations, in Foucault's terms. By framing sectarian identities as conflicting sides of a zero-sum game, regional powers can mobilize fighters, militarize societies and create fragmentation inside neighbouring states in order to undermine the power of the foe. I consider such identities as opportunistically manipulated by sectarian political elites. It is in this sense that I propose to analyse the historical opposition between Arabism and Islam, the production of the Sunni–Shia conflict and the intra-Sunni rivalry. Indeed, the creation of an official and persuasive truth sold to or imposed on societies is an instrument of power that 'decides, transmits and itself extends upon the effects of power' (Foucault 1980: 94).

Therefore, even the (mis)representations of the 'foe' and/or the deliberate exaggeration of a threat coming from a given societal group or a state actor can produce fragmentation within a rival state, in order to undermine the power of the target regime (Corm 2012a; Calculli 2015); and a re-composition of allegiances and alliances on a transnational basis. Based on these assumptions, I consider the securitization of identities as an instrument of power and a function of regime security and not a driver of alliance-making or conflict. Indeed, the politicization of identity discourses accompanies a massive transfer of financial and military means to allies and sectarian proxies. However, identity discourses remain the driving force in attracting individuals to join a conflict, whilst material incentives only help to catalyse such a move. Herein lies the fracture between the elitist dimension of regime security and the wider dimension of regional (in)security. The securitization of identities provides a comprehensive view of the interdependence between elite and non-elite groups and their role in shaping Middle East security overall. It also helps explain the malleability of identities and their intimate link with the production and exercise of power. Finally, it sheds light on why some violent non-state actors gradually assume a more pragmatic and opportunistic stance than others. Indeed, the practice of power and expansion in size and control by specific violent groups transform the function of identities from simply societal markers into instruments of power. This is why some non-state actors compete with states, whilst others remain simple proxies.

Monarchies vs republics: the traditional structure of security in the Arab Middle East

The first occurrence of a region-based rivalry between monarchies and republics is what Michael Kerr has depicted as the 'Arab Cold War' and which took place between 1958 and 1970, mainly opposing the then Arab socialist Egypt, led by Gamal Abdel Nasser, and Saudi Arabia, a traditional monarchy grounding its legitimacy in Pan-Islamic credentials (Kerr 1967). The drivers of the conflict, involving domestic and regional/transnational dimensions alike, were actually engraved in the divide between secular Arab nationalism and Islam that were at once sources for legitimating domestic authority in various countries and projecting power in the region. While many Arab kings mainly relied and still rely on the Islamic tradition to inform the legitimacy of the *mamlāka* ('kingdom') and of their political authority, by depicting themselves as the defenders of that tradition, the original format of the *jumhūriya al-'arabiyya* ('Arab republic') was mainly secular and marked by a discourse of modernization.

The Arab Cold War never entailed an open military confrontation between regular armies but a number of 'proxies' in different countries, in the form of politicized oppositions or violent militant groups, that were sponsored, financed, and often armed by rival state-actors, especially Egypt and Saudi Arabia.

Along with conventional (military and economic-political) threats, ideational threats became particularly destabilizing, for the diffusion of ideas and ideologies was liable to dramatically erode the domestic bottom-up legitimacy of already fragile power authorities.

Yet, I analyse how identities and ideologies have been instrumentalized and exploited by rival powers in order to penetrate other states' societies and power structures, thus circumventing direct military threats. In fact, Gulf monarchies—especially after the creation of the Gulf Cooperation Council (GCC) in 1981—have created an alliance of convenience, more than ideological alliance, although the model of the 'Sunni traditional kingdom' is the unvarying identity of the six member states. Yet, the Gulf Cooperation Council is not a fully articulated *security community* (Legrenzi 2011: 73–85). The very adhesive holding the GCC alliance together is a common perception of threat and a focus on stability.

This strategic partnership is aimed at protecting the energy resources (oil and gas) of member states, which constitute the primary source of GCC members' wealth and economic activity, thereby allowing the monarchies to finance their foreign policy allies as well as to forestall demands for political rights by means of generous welfare policies. Furthermore, extra-Gulf monarchies over time have occasionally sided with Arab republics, as in the case of the Jordanian support for Iraq in the initial phase of the 1990–91 Gulf War.

Similarly, republics—although united in principle by a number of shared statements and the avowed commitment to an Arab security agenda—have balanced monarchies and republics alike. In contrast to the mainstream constructivist argument that Arab identity has shaped perceptions of threats in Arab regimes, I highlight the instrumental use of identity narratives. In fact, in their power projection, republics have by and large used the pan-Arab concept of *ummā 'arabiyya*, by generating pressure on other regimes to create a unified Arab nation, encompassing all Arab societies and overcoming the colonial interstate territorial and political order. Yet, the fact that the very notion of *ummā 'arabiyya* is de facto incompatible with a state system divided into sovereign, territorial units, its shadow made hegemonic ambition conceivable only in terms of 'empire'. Gamal Abdel Nasser emerged as the strongest Arab leader, especially in the 1960s, thus representing a direct threat to the very survival of other power elites in the Middle East, especially Arab monarchs. It is remarkable that even Saddam Hussein in 1990 invaded Kuwait, by making a claim against the illegitimacy of the British-imposed borders onto the 'pan-Arab land' in the document of *al-wihda al-intimajiyya*, the unification of Iraq and Kuwait (Tibi 1998: 166). Nevertheless, by colliding with the interests of other national authorities in different states of the region, the notion of the *ummā 'arabiyya* has hindered the emergence of any potential hegemon in the region.[1] Herein lies the structural illegitimacy of the interstate system, which has posed a doubly destabilizing threat to Arabist regimes: if the authority of the political-military elites has been legitimized by the coups d'état that brought them into power—thus representing no more than a transitional step towards the consolidation of the *ummā*—then, in the constitutive period of the new post-revolutionary states, an ad hoc political formula was required to legitimize the elites' subsequent refusal to relinquish their recently acquired sovereignty. In the contemporary Middle East—in radical republics such as Baathist Syria and Iraq as much as in republics that relinquished the original Arab nationalist identity, like Egypt—that formula has translated into a mantra of a 'revolutionary legality'. Transitory by nature, 'revolutionary legality' serves to consolidate the new order and is oriented towards the preservation of internal security, thus ultimately eschewing legal-rational legitimization. The continuation of several decades of emergency laws and other security measures that severely restrict freedom of association and speech—one of the main targets of the 2010–11 protests—is the result of perpetuating such temporary status. Herein lies the intimate link between populist-demagogic foreign policies on the one hand, and regime security and domestic societal control on the other.

Moreover, given this element of interstate insecurity, republican regimes have been induced to consider cooperation to be potentially destabilizing to their power. This also leads to heightened isolationism within the interstate system, while making stable alliances with mainly non-Arab actors—in contradiction with the Arabist principle of 'Arab brotherhood'—such as the case of the Egypt–US alliance, or the Syria–Iran alliance. The targeting of Saddam Hussein's regime after 1991 can be considered a case par excellence in which extra-regional action has been vital in order to preserve the regional status quo. By imposing a forced retreat and then overturning the one republic that harboured the strongest aspiration to hegemony, United States military intervention served the interests of the other Arab states (monarchies as well as republics), whose perception of Iraqi military superiority was that it posed a threat to their continued sovereignty.

The 2003 American invasion of Iraq highlighted the system's need for external guarantors to preserve interstate arrangements and 'balance of weakness' (Korany 2011b: 37), given the Arab states' collective incapacity to maintain the regional status quo. The lack of durable coalitions among regional powers generated a vacuum that allowed the US to deepen its political and military presence in the region, particularly after the attacks of 11 September 2001.

We can then distinguish two patterns of power projection, related to regime type, that exemplify the most crucial difference between them: no regional actor, whether monarchy or republic, managed to become a dominant player, in a position of primacy over the region but within the monarchical subsystem, Saudi Arabia became the leader amongst the Gulf Cooperation Council (GCC) countries (Gause 2011b: 173–5), and has succeeded in further extending its leadership over the two extra-Gulf monarchies, Morocco and Jordan as well as expanding its role in the aftermath of the popular uprisings of 2010–11.

Arab monarchies and republics after the uprisings

The Arab uprisings have deepened the divide between republics and monarchies, although this ideational-based rivalry is no longer structuring the balance of power in the region. On the one hand, the failure of Arab nationalism and Pan-Arabism, and the exhaustion of its remaining bastions, such as the Baath party in Iraq (after the US invasion in 2003) and in Syria (in the wake of the popular uprisings of 2011), has downsized the ideological threat that Arabism once posed to Islamic traditional monarchies. On the other hand, although popular protests have targeted monarchs and presidents alike, regime change has occurred only within republics, whereas kings have proven more resilient to popular contestation of their rule.

However, as a reaction to the societal upheaval across the region, there is a newly emerged monarchical common strategy, which has catalysed an inter-monarchical alliance, driven by kings' common interest in mutually preserving and boosting their popular legitimacy.

Domestically, this goal has been pursued through reproducing traditional (ethnic, religious, and civic) narratives in supporting the legitimacy of the regime in charge. For instance, the sovereign in Morocco is officially the *amīr al-mū'minīn* ('the prince of the believers'); in a similar vein, the Saudi kingdom has opened eight new state TV channels after the uprisings, each devoted to celebrate specific components of the history of the kingdom. Attempts to reinvigorate domestic narratives of power legitimacy in the Arab monarchies have been accompanied by extraordinary welfare measures, especially top-down distributions of resources, in order to dampen or contain socio-economic grievances.

Regionally, shared concerns with 'domestic threats' within monarchies have fuelled a common defensive strategy, even entailing military interventions in support of other regimes and other new foreign policy initiatives geared to reinforce the stability of Arab kingdoms. For instance, an ad hoc GCC armed coalition, the *Peninsula Shield Force*, intervened in Bahrain in March, 2011 to back the Bahraini army loyal to Emir al-Khalifa in repressing social protests that erupted at the Pearl roundabout in Manama. At the same time, Saudi 'foreign aid policy' witnessed an unprecedented acceleration and functioned as a shield to preserve monarchical stability. By providing additional aid to other Gulf monarchies and extra-Gulf monarchies (Jordan and Morocco), Saudi Arabia forestalled an extreme deficit and even bankruptcy that could exacerbate socio-economic discontent in other kingdoms. In a similar vein, the six Gulf monarchies have extended invitations to Jordan and Morocco to join the GCC in 2011 and in 2014, in order to promote the creation of a pan-monarchical military alliance (Ryan 2014). Although unlikely to result in full membership, the invitation has formalized a strategic alliance grounded in common security concerns, and been further reinvigorated by the proactive participation of Jordan and Morocco to the 'Pan-Arab army', launched in 2015 under the auspices of an Egyptian-Saudi initiative.

Foreign aid policy has become a crucial component of the regional strategy of the Gulf (especially the Saudi kingdom), and it is geared toward preserving monarchical stability across the region as well as to appease potential challengers and undermine resilient foes. The resources needed for financing such a revisionist foreign policy have been made possible by the oil boom of the 2000s; from this perspective, the regional role of the Gulf can be compared to the one played in the region during the 1970s. Especially after the October War of 1973, the increase in oil prices allowed Gulf monarchies to redraw the balance of power in the region, through an intense foreign aid policy mainly directed toward radical republics and former foes, such as Syria and Egypt. It is important to note that, by emerging as the main provider of military and development aid in intra-Arab relations, the Gulf monarchies have tremendously expanded their regional role at different points in time.

The fact that the GCC monarchies are a key player in all three axes of conflicts that define the security structure in the Middle East today testifies to their ability to affect and manoeuvre the regional balance of power. Yet, intra-monarchical relations have also witnessed unprecedented rifts following the Arab uprisings, with Saudi Arabia and Qatar becoming competitors for regional leadership. The contestation of a regional hierarchy also highlights the strategic, more than identity-grounded, nature of the alliance.

Strategic competition and the Sunni–Shia rift

The politicization of the Sunni–Shia rivalry in the contemporary Middle East is grounded in the legacy of the Iranian revolution of 1978–79, which led to the establishment of a Shia Islamic republic in the Persian Gulf. The destabilizing effects of the Iranian revolution in the Arab world resulted in the emergence of a new theocratic model to compete with the one that was already present, the Sunni *mamlāka*. At the same time, new political ties between the emergent Islamic Republic of Iran and Shia communities in the Arab world were established. These ties assumed strategic significance during the 1980s. Two major events mark this process: first, Syria's alignment with Iran in the Iran–Iraq war (1980–88); second, the creation of Hezbollah in Lebanon. Whilst confessional solidarity played a role in both events, it is, however, important to highlight the strategic rationale underpinning them.

With regards to the Iran–Syria alliance, whereas the elite ranks of the Alawi (Shia) community in Syria may have represented an important component of the power structure in Syria,
Damascus' alignment with Iran mainly functioned to counterbalance the rising influence of
Iraq, especially after the Egypt–Israel Camp David peace accords that cut Egypt out of the
regional game, leaving room for new hegemonic ambitions to develop. Furthermore, Syria
preserved and strengthened its identity as an Arab republic, with the Baath party fulfilling
the role of the last stronghold of Arab socialism even while the obstinately secular nature of
the Syrian regime was far from resembling—or wanting to resemble—an Iranian theocracy.
To highlight the instrumental use of confessional sectarianism, it is important to note that
the Alawites, to which the Asad family and some key political, military, and *mukhābarāt*
figures belonged, were recognized as part of the Shia community only in the 1970s by the
Lebanese Imam Musa al-Sadr, after a longstanding history of being labelled as heretics. The
operation clearly aimed to reinforce the identity of the family in power and its strategic alliance with both Iran and Harakat 'Amal, the Lebanese Shia party and militia, from which a
group of militants split in 1985, and gave birth to Hezbollah (Kramer 1990: 275).

However, it was mainly the longstanding competition between the Syrian and the Iraqi
Baathist republics that determined Syria's move towards an extra-Arab alignment with Iran,
whilst the relation between Hezbollah and Iran is deeply grounded in the Shia identity and
loyalty to the *wilāyat al-faqīh*. Yet, a notable strand of literature on Hezbollah has also highlighted the strategic development and posture of the triangulation between Iran, Hezbollah,
and Syria from the 1980s to the consequences of the Arab uprisings (Ranstorp 1998; Harb
and Leenders 2005; Norton 2007a; Daher 2014).

Nonetheless, it is after 2003 that this alliance produced a new redefinition of the regional
balance of power, also triggering a securitization of the confessional divide between the
Sunni and the Shia.

The narrative of the 'Shia crescent' and its impact from 2003 to the aftermath of the 2011 uprisings

As an Iranian diplomat put it, '[h]ad the United States not removed the Taliban regime in
2001 and Saddam Hussein's regime in 2003, Iran would now concentrate all its military and
strategic efforts in policing and controlling the borders it shares with Afghanistan and with
Iraq'.[2]

The forced regime change in Iraq in the wake of the US 'war on terror', and the first legislative elections of the post-Saddam era, brought to power a coalition of Shia parties—the
'United Iraqi Alliance' (*al-I'tilāf al-'Irāqī al-Muwaḥḥad*)—that welcomed a new era of Iraq–
Iran relations. In fact, the US invasion removed from the security equation of the Middle
East the latest strategic foe and main challenger of Teheran's power projection. The major
fact through which the US altered the structure of Middle East security was the dismantling
of the Baath party and the strong Iraqi army, considered the strongest remaining army in
the Arab World, after the Camp David agreement that downscaled the strategic role of the
Egyptian military (al-Marashi and Salama 2008). In this perspective, the year 2003 can also
be considered as inaugural of a new regional security order, marked by increased American
and Iranian influence in the Middle East.

As a consequence, Sunni monarchies sought to coordinate their efforts in the aftermath of the invasion of Iraq, in order to balance the newly strengthened axis of alliances, including Iran, key Iraqi political actors, Syria, and Hezbollah: the so-called 'Shia crescent'—a term coined by king Abdullah of Jordan and originating from a 'strategic narrative' of the actual growing influence of Iran over the Middle East, grounded in its confessional identity more than in its strategic nature, and paving the way for an interstate rivalry to penetrate and mobilize societies on the basis of the politicization of religious identities.

The politicization of the Sunni–Shia sectarian rift produced the internal fragmentation of post-2003 Iraq and post-2011 Syria, also shifting the dimension of regional rivalries from the interstate to the transnational and societal dimension (Hazbun 2010: 252). Domestically, the newly emerged Iraqi political leadership led by Nuri al-Maliki exploited the demographic advantage of the Shia population in the country to implement a sectarian policy of retribution, widely marked by corruption and abuse to the detriment of the Iraqi Sunni community (Ali 2014). Regionally, Gulf interests in preventing Iraq from becoming a new regional challenger dominated by a predominantly Shia political establishment, led a number of Gulf clerics, private intermediaries, and members of various Gulf elites, to unofficially sponsor and support Sunni jihadi groups, especially the *tanzim qaidat al-jihad fi bilād al-rafidaīn*, also known as Al-Qaeda in Iraq (or AQI) and led by Abu Mus'ab al-Zarqawi. On the other hand, Shia brigades emerged in the country, such as the *jaish al-Mahdi*, founded by Muqtada al-Sadr, and the Badr Brigades, respectively supported by Iran. Violence between Sunni and Shia in Iraq reached a peak during the 2006–07 civil war, and after a period of relative quiescence, has been revived after 2011, especially with the rise and consolidation of another violent jihadi actor, which emerged in Iraq as an evolution of Al-Qaeda in Iraq and later expanded into Syria to fight against the regime of Bashar al-Asad: the so-called Islamic State in Iraq and the Levant, which later became known as simply the 'Islamic State' (IS) or ISIS.

How did this plethora of violent non-state actors become part of the Saudi–Iran rivalry in the region? First, this was a result of the de-militarization of the Iraqi state, which brought about a militarization of society. In fact, violent non-state actors emerged as a de facto delegitimization of state institutions, and especially security institutions. After invading Iraq, the US decided to dismantle the Iraqi army and the Baath party—two decisions that have been seen as irresponsible and indicative of a lack of a post-invasion plan (Tripp 2004: 553). Indeed, the US tried to rebuild a new Iraqi army, without however succeeding in overcoming the sectarian struggle that was instead exacerbated by the first post-Saddam legislative elections. The new Iraqi army became at once instrument and victim of the sectarian rift, with Sunni and Shia officers incapable of cooperating among the ranks, thus also favouring the emergence and the consolidation of informal militias to fill the security vacuum in the country. Second, both Saudi Arabia and Iran tried to capitalize on the sectarian divide, by granting local militias external support, the two regional powers de facto transformed them into proxies. If material incentives were crucial to exacerbate the conflict, the securitization of identities played a fundamental role in mobilizing different societal groups.

Whilst containment policies succeeded in mitigating the intensity of the violence in Iraq after 2007, it was in the wake of the Syrian crisis that a new wave of societal militarization swamped Iraq. The pattern of societal militarization in Syria occurred similarly to the Iraqi one. In fact, the sectarian rift was not central at the beginning of the Syrian crisis but came as a result of the transformation of the Syrian *thāwra* ('revolution') into a regional war. The first wave of societal militarization was indeed national and grounded in a political anti-regime platform: the *jaish al-suri al-ḥurr* (the 'Free Syrian Army') was created in the immediate aftermath of the brutal repression by the regime of unarmed protesters, and mainly formed by defectors from the Syrian armed forces and Syrian citizens.

It was only after a shift in the regional alignments that the structure of the armed rebellion against the regime of Bashar al-Asad changed, and the narrative of Syria's internal fragmentation morphed accordingly. Turkey and the Gulf States were the main orchestrators of the regionalization of the domestic opposition to the Asad regime. Turkey was the first regional power to break the alliance with Syria and sponsored the creation of *al-majlis al-watani as-suri* (the Syrian National Council) in Istanbul on 1 October 2011, to claim the legitimization as the Syria authority. Subsequently, in an attempt to match the Turkish bid to control and drive a potential transition in Syria (Ennis and Momani 2013), many Arab States also broke ties with Syria and suspended it from the League of the Arab States in November 2011. Regional re-alignments produced the gradual radicalization of the armed opposition in Syria, and the appearance of Islamists among the rank and file of the Free Syrian Army and other fighting groups alike. Many of the salafi-jihadi cells, like the Jabhat al-Nusra, have infiltrated Syria from Iraq since August 2011 (Cafarella 2014: 46), while the Turkish border also became the transit path for world jihadists to penetrate the Syrian battleground. Turkey and the Gulf States, especially Saudi Arabia, the UAE, and Qatar, informally engaged in sponsoring defections from the Syrian army and the political establishment, but also in supporting the expansion of jihadi groups that have become increasingly prominent in the struggle against Asad.

Yet, the securitization of identities transformed the conflict. The radicalization of the Syrian war by external forces came with a new narrative, propagated primarily by Sunni clerics in the region, calling for jihad in Syria against the Shia and the 'Nusayris'—a belittling depreciative term for the Alawites, to which the Asad family belongs.[3] Relying on three fatwas by the Syrian scholar Taqi al-Din b. Taimiyya, a group of clerics, among which Yusuf al-Qaradawi, singled out the 'Alawite-Nusayri' as 'apostates' (*murtadd*) of the Islamic religion, guilty of disbelief (*kufr*) and 'more unbelieving (*akfar*) than Christians and Jewish'.[4] These discourses have largely eclipsed the original claims of the Syrian revolution, and encouraged the creation of a non-Syrian jihadi opposition which has penetrated the conflict in Syria, and largely contributed to its fragmentation.

The changing nature of the Syrian opposition has fostered the strengthening of two transnational alignments that confronted each other in Syria: one made of Sunni monarchies, Turkey, and their jihadi militias and proxies, directly or indirectly benefiting from their material support; the other made of the Syrian army, Hezbollah, and other Iran-sponsored informal groups that have joined the Syrian Army's ranks.[5] Indeed, whilst the radicalization and external penetration of the opposition against the Asad regime has marginalized the original endogenous armed and unarmed anti-regime movements, the Syrian regime has adjusted its discourse and strategy to the framework of ideological guerrilla warfare.

First, the Lebanese Shia party and militia Hezbollah has become one prominent actor of the Syrian war, backing the Syrian army in most military operations. Shia fighters from Iran and Afghanistan have also formally and informally joined the ranks of the Army or Hezbollah to confront Islamist militias. The Shia identity is a catalyser of cohesion, also pointing out the hybridization of state and non-state actors on a transnational basis. Indeed, the spreading of an identity-based narrative has also served the purpose and goals of the Syrian regime: by calling for the protection of 'religious pluralism' against the annihilation of the (Sunni) *takfir* attempt to clean out the Levant (*Sham*) from Christian, Shia, and other alleged 'apostates'—the Syrian regime has posed as the security provider of minority groups, fostering a sectarian alliance, but also justifying brutal military operations against Syrian villages mainly inhabited by civilians. In a similar vein, Asad himself has facilitated the radicalization of the opposition by releasing from the Saidnaya prison many radical Islamists, who have later joined al-Nusra, the so-called Islamic State, and other Islamist militias, whilst keeping non-violent political activists imprisoned. This move has served to substantiate the narrative of the opposition as a 'terrorist movement', in an attempt to expose and de-legitimize it in the eyes of the international community and public opinion.

Syrian Kurdish militias have also played a peculiar role in the post-2011 war. Traditionally allied with the Syrian regime, but forming a longstanding enclave grounded in the nationalist aspiration to the Kurdish nation, Kurdish militants have aligned with the Damascus–Teheran–Hezbollah axis, in order to gain leverage for the eventual achievement of an independent and sovereign or semi-sovereign Kurdish nation state (Gunter 2013; Charountaki 2015).

As Gregory Gause III has pointed out, war in Syria and Iraq can be understood in the terms of a 'new Middle East Cold War', where Iran, on the one hand, and a coalition of Sunni monarchies (under the leadership of Saudi Arabia), on the other, have formed two opposing transnational axes to secure their influence over the Levant and expand their regional role (Gause 2014). These two axes have been framed through securitizing instrumentally the Sunni–Shia divide. Both axes have used existing non-state actors and created new proxies. For instance Hezbollah, as an Iran-sponsored militia, has redefined its role, from the champion of the anti-Israel resistance (*muqawama*) to the defender of the Shia communities against Sunni radical jihadists. In a similar vein, Iraq-based Sunni militias have been strengthened by Gulf private donors—including members of the regimes in power—to penetrate Syria and fight against al-Asad. This is, for instance, the case of the former Al-Qaeda in Iraq, which later became 'Islamic State' (IS).

The war in the Levant has further transformed these actors, for IS has eventually developed from a challenger of the political *status quo* into a claimer of sovereignty. Against this background, IS can no longer be considered a 'proxy', for its agenda was only dictated by external patrons at the beginning; afterwards it became increasingly autonomous. Other actors, like the Jabhat al-Nusra or Harakat Ahrar al-Sham al-Islamiyya, sponsored by Turkey or the Gulf states, or the Shia militias in Iraq, sponsored by Iran, are newly-created proxies, and depend more on external powers.

It is noteworthy that, whereas in the beginning IS was part of the Sunni military bloc against the Shia counterpart, the practice of power and security has transformed the group from an identity-based militia into an opportunistic producer of new identity discourses, also differentiating it from other violent groups. Whilst evolving and performing state-like functions, IS has pragmatically used the securitization of identities, by labelling as a threat and a military target not only the Shia, but also other Sunni regimes and actors.

The securitization of the Sunni–Shia rift has informed a 'zero-sum game', as both confessional groups are constructed as an existential threat for the other. These dynamics have not only fostered the militarization of Levantine societies, but also attracted spur-of-the-moment fighters from all over the world to join one side or the other in the name of confessional identity. The de-nationalization of political struggles also has a potential for further expansion of this transnational conflict. The war in Yemen, started in 2015 when a Saudi-led coalition of Sunni Arab military forces attacked the Houthi, a Zaydi Shia militia group, financially and militarily supported by Iran, after it took over Sanaa and forced the president to resign, is indeed the latest hotspot of this Middle East Cold War.

A new rivalry: proponents and opponents of the Muslim Brotherhood

The third dynamic that has affected Middle East security after the Arab uprisings stems from the attempt of Qatar and Turkey to strengthen their positions in the regional hierarchy, through sponsoring the Muslim Brothers as a political actor in several Arab countries and establish external influence over them. This section explores how the ambitions of these two countries have affected the traditional alignments in the Middle East, and challenged the Saudi attempt to lead the establishment of a new regional status quo. It is in this context that we can understand the Saudi bid to cast the Brotherhood as a security threat to regional stability.

In the wake of the 2011 revolts that brought down several Arab regimes, Qatar and Turkey converged toward similar twin strategies, even though they did not coordinate their positions. On the one hand, they officially supported the popular revolts in several countries, thus seeking to project and bolster their respective *brands* regionally and globally at a point at which general enthusiasm for the Arab uprisings ran high;[6] on the other hand, they sought to help the Muslim Brothers (*al-Ikhwan al-Muslimun*) to seize power in key Arab countries, especially Egypt and Tunisia.

In offering financial support and electoral training to the newly-formed 'Freedom and Justice Party' in Egypt, *al-Nahda* in Tunisia or the 'Justice and Construction Party' in Libya, Qatar and Turkey have attempted to give shape to the political transition in these countries. However, they differed in their objectives and approach. Whilst Qatar pursued a very ambitious policy in order to establish a role as a newcomer in the region, Turkey mainly tried to restore the great influence it once exercised over the Middle East. Accordingly, the outcomes differed too. Qatar succeeded in carving out a role as the main reference point for the Muslim Brothers in the Middle East, including the *Ikhwan*-linked Palestinian movement Hamas, which moved its political headquarter from Damascus to Doha, after the outbreak of the Syrian revolution; whereas the Turkish policy has yielded appeal and influence, and in several case backfired, mainly as a result of resentment toward the alleged 'neo-ottomanism' of Turkey (Ayata 2015; Monier 2015).

However, Turkey has significantly interfered in the Syrian war, by sponsoring the outside opposition and supporting the inside armed rebellion against Asad, including the non-Syrian jihadi wing. Indeed, Turkey's border with Syria has been the main access channel for foreign jihadi fighters to access the conflict. By turning a blind eye on this development, Ankara has attempted to secure a major role in a potential post-Asad Syria.

Facing multidirectional challenges to the regional *status quo*, Saudi Arabia has tried to subvert the revisionist attitude of Qatar and Turkey. This has resulted in a broader intra-Sunni competition, including within the ranks of the GCC. Indeed, Qatar's ambition to climb up the regional hierarchy after 2011 has indirectly challenged Saudi hegemony over the GCC.

Against this backdrop, Saudi Arabia has, first and foremost, sponsored the ascent of Salafi political parties in several countries in order to balance the Brotherhood-affiliated parties, supported by Qatar and Turkey (Lacroix 2012); second, it has tried to ostracize and delegitimize the Muslim Brothers in the region, especially in the wake of the anti-Brotherhood popular protests that started in Egypt during June 2013 and ended with the overthrowing of Mohamed Mursi on 3 July 2013.

Indeed, whereas the Saudi-backed Salafi organizations and parties have gained momentum in different Arab countries, they were never able to surpass the *Ikhwan* or to capitalize on their electoral success. As a result, the balance of power in the region tilted towards Qatar, especially in the immediate aftermath of the uprisings. It was only after 2013 that the Saudi kingdom was able to reverse such a trend and to contain the expanding role of its Gulf neighbour in the region. The turning point was regime change in Egypt in July 2013.

To situate this process, after the Brotherhood gained 47 per cent of the seats in the *majlis al-Sha'b* and Mohammed Mursi became the first democratically elected president of the Muslim Brotherhood in Egypt in June 2012, Qatar had become the main influential power in Egypt, and the main investor and provider of financial aid for the country. Initially, the Saudis took a wait-and-see stance. However, when in June 2013 the *Tamarrud* movement demanded the resignation of the president and early presidential elections, Saudi Arabia explicitly sponsored the forced ousting of Mohammed Mursi from power, the establishment of a military-led interim government, and eventually the election of General Abdel Fattah al-Sisi as the new president of Egypt in May 2014. The coordinated political support by Saudi Arabia and UAE for the Egyptian army was followed by a package of $20 billion that eased the military-led transition and replaced the existing financial support by Qatar and Turkey, which had been key between 2011 and 2012 (Amin 2014: 403–4). In the process of transition, the first and most important measure taken by the interim government was the blacklisting of the Muslim Brothers as a 'terrorist group', which went in tandem with a de facto impunity of the security forces responsible for the killing of 638 supporters of the deposed President Mursi in al-Raba' al-Adawiyya Square on 14 August 2013. It was further followed by the decision of an Egyptian court that branded Palestinian Hamas as a terrorist organization in February 2015. These measures spread regionally with Saudi Arabia and the UAE labelling the Muslim Brothers a terrorist group. In a similar vein, Saudi Arabia, Bahrain, and the UAE jointly withdrew their ambassadors from Doha, claiming that Qatar had violated the pact of non-interference in other GCC members' internal affairs.

The intra-Sunni rift is also shaping the domestic transition in Libya, where two different governments have formed and claimed international legitimacy: the Ṭubruq government mainly supported and financed by Saudi Arabia, UAE, and Egypt; and the Tripoli government—led by the Brotherhood-affiliated 'Justice and Construction Party'—strongly backed by Qatar and Turkey.

These developments have resulted in the ostracism of the Brotherhood and relative isolation of Qatar in the GCC and the wider Middle East. This forced Qatar to recalibrate its foreign policy, with Doha falling back into the GCC ranks, and brought about a consequent normalization of intra-GCC relations as a result.

In a similar vein, whereas Turkey's ambitions had never openly confronted Saudi interests, and despite Ankara's aspiration to lead an international movement of the Muslim Brothers—by opening the country to exiled Muslim Brothers and continuing to sponsor them after the toppling of Mursi—its early foreign policy dreams withered away in the wake of the manifold failures of the political transitions in which the Turkish establishment sought to play a role.

The competition among rival Sunni regimes in the aftermath of the 2011 uprisings has been ideologically shaped in terms of support for/opposition to the Muslim Brotherhood. Yet, Turkey's and Qatar's support for the *Ikhwan*, as well as Saudi and Emirati measures to ostracize them, can be understood as sophisticated attempts to expand their regional influence and redraw the balance of power in Middle East. Whereas the immediate aftermath of the uprisings—when the Brotherhood emerged as a dominant political player—was a favourable juncture for both Turkey and Qatar in their respective bids for regional leadership, Saudi Arabia has later succeeded in reversing such a development and rolling back the rise of the *Ikhwan*. In so doing, the Saudi king has mainly resorted to its economic power and foreign aid policy, rather than its ideological appeal and capacity to spread Wahhabism throughout the region and has relied on a network of non-ideological—and rather strategic—alliances, especially the one with the al-Sisi regime in Egypt. Against this backdrop, it seems that after 2011, interest-oriented alignments, power competition, and material power resources are the ultimate drivers of the swift rise and decline of Qatar and Turkey as regional players.

Conclusion

Security in the contemporary Middle East is tied to a wide range of conflicts and rivalries, whilst the new waves of insecurity that have been discussed in this chapter increasingly blur the analytical boundaries between foreign and domestic affairs. State and non-state actors have been able to affect regional security in similar ways, which is an unprecedented development.

In summary, (i) a new strategic alliance among the monarchies; (ii) a political instrumentalization of the long-standing rivalry between Sunni and Shia; and (iii) increasing tensions among proponents and opponents of the Muslim Brotherhood, lead to one analytical and one theoretical conclusion.

First, at the crossroad of the three axes, the pivotal role of monarchies such as Saudi Arabia, Qatar, and the UAE, sanction the geopolitical triumph of the Gulf and the GCC's ability to play a leading role in the political transitions of neighbouring countries. However, a crucial dilemma rests on whether this shift in the centre of gravity in the direction of the Gulf will survive as a result of the weakness of these neighbouring countries or, conversely, whether such weakness will become an uncontainable factor of insecurity for the stable monarchies of the Gulf.

Second, offering new insights into the role of sectarianism and identities in international politics, the chapter argued that conflicts that seemingly embody sectarian antagonism could be better explained as a function of strategic competition involving instrumental use of religious discourses, symbolisms, and identities. This subtle strategy seeks to achieve objectives that would otherwise require direct military confrontation. This point is in line with the work of Georges Corm and his call for a 'profane'—rather than religious—reading of conflicts (Corm 2012b). Against this background, the 'securitization of identities'—the production of discourses about identity threats—can be seen as a sophisticated way to instantiate and manipulate the regional balance of power.

Acknowledgements:

I would like to thank Gjovalin Macaj and Louise Fawcett as well as Leila Kabalan and Karim Makdisi for their very useful comments and suggestions.

Further reading

Buzan, B. (1991) *People, States, and Fear: An Agenda for International Security Studies in the Post-Cold War Era* (Boulder, CO: Lynne Rienner)
  A classic redefinition of security studies in the wake of the Cold War. Required background reading for any student of strategy and international security.

International Institute of Strategic Studies (IISS) (2012) *The Military Balance 2012* (London: IISS)
  Annual publication summarizing the military balance around the world and in the Middle East. It is the basis of all calculations of the balance of power.

Kamrava, M. (ed.) (2012) *The Nuclear Question in the Middle East* (London: Curzon)
  An essential collection tackling the energy, as well as the security, aspects of nuclear programmes in the Middle East.

Korany, B., Noble, P., and Brynen, R. (eds) (1993) *The Many Faces of National Security in the Arab World* (London: Macmillan)
  A holistic overview of security challenges in the Arab world, highlighting the socio-economic imbalances that generate much of the insecurity for Middle East states.

Legrenzi, M. (2011) *The GCC and the International Relations of the Gulf: Diplomacy, Security and Economic Coordination in a Changing Middle East* (London: I. B. Tauris)
  A comprehensive look at the Gulf Cooperation Council, and the new role of the Gulf in the security and international relations of the Middle East, including the confrontation with Iran.

Monier, E. (ed.) (2015) *Regional Insecurity after the Uprisings: Narratives of Security and Threat* (London: Palgrave Macmillan)
  A collection of essays on security developments in the Middle East after the 2011 uprisings, through the lens of 'threat perception'.

Peterson, J. E. (1986) *Defending Arabia* (London: Palgrave Macmillan)
  Classic account of the difficulties in defending the territorial integrity of the states of the Arabian peninsula. The questions that it asks remain relevant today.

Potter, L. G. and Sick, G. G.(eds) (2002) *Security in the Persian Gulf* (New York: Palgrave)
  A collection of essays dealing with mutual threat perceptions in this key Middle East subsystem.

Sayigh, Y. (2000) *Armed Struggle and the Search for State: The Palestinian National Movement, 1949-1993* (Oxford: Oxford University Press)
  An extraordinarily in-depth and exhaustive history of Palestinian resistance. It illuminates the security implications and difficulties of conducting an armed struggle without a fixed territorial basis.

Walt, S. (1987) *The Origins of Alliances* (Ithaca, NY: Cornell University Press)
   Classic treatise on alliance theory, with the Middle East as a case study. While realist and parsimonious, it emphasizes perception of threat as opposed to balance of power as a key variable, thus paving the way for constructivist accounts of Middle East security.

Questions

1. To what extent can 'identity politics' help explain conflict in Middle East?

2. In what ways does cooperation and competition between state and non-state actors affect (in)security in the Middle East? What are the differences and commonalties between these two types of actors?

3. What are the strategic and political factors underpinning the divide between Arab monarchies and republics before and after the 2011 uprisings?

4. Which factors have caused the resurgence of a Sunni–Shia rift in the twentieth and twenty-first centuries, and what are their implications for regional security?

5. How has the Muslim Brotherhood affected traditional alignments in the Middle East after the 2011 uprisings?

Notes

1. One good illustration for this is the project of administrative union between Egypt and Syria in 1958—the *jumhūriya al-ʿarabiyya al-muttaḥida* ('United Arab Republic'—UAR)—a political step towards creating the *ummā*. However, the UAR was dissolved after three years in existence. The dissolution came as a result of the unequal weight of Egypt's and Syria's political and military establishments, which eventually lead Syrian officers to reject Nasser's overflowing interference in Syria's affairs. This was of course not the only case in which pan-Arabism had been instrumentalized in order to pursue hegemonic projects.

2. Author's interview with an Iranian diplomat (Beirut, 23 January 2015).

3. Yusuf al-Qaraḍāwī, 'Khuṭṭbat al-Jumaʿa liʾl-Duktūr al-Qaraḍāwī', *YouTube*, 31 May 2013, http://www.youtube.com/watch?v=QLHXSWCar78 (Retrieved: 23 February 2014).

4. On the three fatwas by Ibn Taymiyya, see Jon Hoover, 'Ibn Taymiyya', in *Oxford Bibliograpies Online*, 2012, http://www.oxfordbibliographies.com/view/document/obo9780195390155/obo-9780195390155-0150.xml?rskey=HPX03i&result=104&q (Retrieved: 14 March 2014).

5. In April 2015, around 4,000 Afghan, Iraqi, and Lebanese Shia fighters were incorporated into the ranks of the Syrian army. See, among others, Kozak (2015: 17).

6. Mehran Kamrava highlighted the capacity of small states like Qatar to use their unique 'brand' to acquire visibility and power in the international affairs (Kamrava 2012).

Part 3

Key Issues and Actors

Foreign Policymaking in the Middle East: Complex Realism

RAYMOND HINNEBUSCH AND ANOUSHIRAVAN
EHTESHAMI

Overview

This chapter lays out a framework of the factors that shape the foreign policies of
Middle East states, including their external environments and policy processes. It
then examines decision-making by four leading states—Saudi Arabia, Iran, Turkey,
and Egypt—towards key events of the early twenty-first century: the 2003 Iraq War;
the 2006 Hezbollah War; and the post-2014 War with the Islamic State of Iraq and
Syria (ISIS). Finally, it summarizes the relative weight of the various foreign policy determinants in these cases. As realists expect, states' foreign policies chiefly respond to
threats and opportunities, as determined by their relative power positions. However,
other factors largely discounted by realists were also important—notably, the level of
dependency on the United States, the extent of democratization, and the agency of
individual leaders.

Introduction: complex realism

Our approach to understanding politics in the Middle East and North Africa (MENA)
might be called 'complex realism'. It starts with realist basics, since Middle Eastern policymakers are quintessentially realists, preoccupied with the threats that are so pervasive
in MENA. They seek to counter threats, first of all, to ensure regime survival, although we
do not exclude that this could overlap with state/national interests, since policymakers also
value sovereignty and territorial integrity, and some have ambitions for regional leadership,
international acceptance, and economic development. However, the MENA environment in
which policymakers have to operate is more complex than that depicted by realists. In the
following framework of analysis, we adumbrate this complexity.

Framework of analysis

The MENA environment

The environment determines the challenges that policymakers face and in MENA it is constituted of several distinct levels, as follows.

1. The *global environment* for MENA is a hierarchy (not an anarchy), in that the region is highly penetrated by core states that lay down the rules (Brown 1984) and is hence chiefly a source of constraint on regional states' autonomy. It is, however, also a source of the resources that regimes need to confront regional and domestic threats. Some regimes sacrifice their autonomy, becoming clients, dependent for economic benefits or protection on a core patron state and must in return give political support to their patrons (Alnasrawi 1991); a few states are rebels against the global system, which for them is a source of threat (Nahas 1985). All regional states seek either to evade core constraints or to manipulate the core–periphery system, in what Ayoob (1998) called 'subaltern realism'. Their ability to do so was much higher under bipolarity (Gerges 1994), when the 'core' was split, than it is under the post-Cold-War relative unipolarity.

2. The *regional environment* in MENA has a unique dual character: a states system, embedded in supra-state (pan-Arab, Islamic) communities and cross-cut by trans-state and sub-state identities (Noble 1991). Hence the regional environment is both a source of *conventional military threats from other states*, but also threats to the legitimacy of regimes from *trans-state movements*, or *interrelated threats* (Harknett and VanDenBerg 1997), when the latter are manipulated by states, as when Nasser's Egypt mobilized pan-Arabism against rival regimes in the 1950s. But the trans-state arena is also a source of domestic legitimacy (when states are seen to champion or defend supra-state norms based in identity) and an arena for playing out leadership ambitions based on supra-state identity (pan-Arabism, Islam). The impact of trans-state identity, whether it constrains or is manipulated by the makers of foreign policies, has varied over time and place, partly according to levels of state formation.

State formation and foreign policy tangents

If the external environment of a regime determines the kind of challenge that it faces, state formation—specifically, variations in the level of 'stateness', the social composition of ruling coalitions, and a state's power position—is the major determinant of its response to these challenges.

The *level* of state formation determines the main threats that foreign policy is used to manage. When the consolidation of states in the regional system is low, the main threats are *within* and foreign policy is used to counter domestic opposition (for example, by getting resources from a patron or generating legitimacy from nationalist rhetoric); when state formation is sufficiently high that internal threats are manageable, the domestic environment becomes a source of support/resources, and if military capabilities also advance, the main threat is from neighbours, and foreign policy deals with external threats and ambitions (Mufti 1996; Salloukh 2000). High levels of state formation depend on institution-building and the inclusion of social forces in these institutions, and also on enough coincidence of identity and state boundaries to legitimize regimes. Unfortunately, few Middle East states enjoy these conditions; however, state formation level—hence the location of the main threats that policymakers address—is an empirical question and a matter of degree that has varied over time and among states. As regards time, in the early period of state formation (1945–55), weak regimes low in institutionalization and inclusion followed rhetorical foreign policies meant to protect precarious domestic legitimacy. In the next period of relative regime consolidation (1974–86), corresponding to the oil boom, regimes built institutions and included constituencies that reduced domestic instability and enhanced leaders' autonomy to pursue realist-like policies of power balancing against external threats. In the period 1986–2010, regimes became more vulnerable to domestic instability (from economic crises) and were more likely to bandwagon with a core patron to get protection. Finally, since 2011, the main threat to policymakers in many Arab states has been domestic rebellion. State formation also varies by state: thus the non-Arab states, such as Turkey and Israel, enjoy more legitimacy from relative nation-state congruence, while at the other extreme fragmented Arab states (Iraq, Lebanon) lack such congruence.

The *social basis* of state formation determines the initial orientation, or direction, of foreign policies. This is largely shaped by whether the social forces incorporated into the regime are privileged or plebeian and the extent to which identity is satisfied or frustrated by state boundaries. The original formation of regimes tended to set states on different tangents— either status quo (notably the Western aligned monarchies) or revisionist (among the initially revolutionary republics), the main historical distinction between the Arab regimes— but this tended to be altered over time by pressures on the regime from the environment (to become more pragmatic) or by changes in its social composition (as when radical elites were 'embourgeoised').

As regards *state power position*, states with greater resources and power capabilities (wealth, population, size, social coherence) are more likely to have activist foreign policies, including ambitions for regional hegemony, while weak states are more likely to concentrate on maintaining their sovereignty. The non-Arab states have generally enjoyed more such assets, notably Turkey and Iran, deriving from their size and historic coherence, and Israel from its special external connections; among the Arab states, Egypt, by virtue of its population, centrality and cohesion, has always been the potential hegemon.

The intra-state level: the 'black box' of policymaking

While the environment and state formation may determine regimes' challenges and bias their responses, much variance remains unaccounted for, since, in any given situation, there are always multiple possible interests or values and choices. This is especially so in the Middle East, where pressures from the environment often pull in contradictory directions, and to get some of one value often requires giving up some of another: thus security sought through foreign protection may sacrifice foreign policy autonomy; legitimacy from anti-imperialism clashes with economic dependency on the core powers (wealth). Governments must mediate, Janus-faced, between internal and external demands, with moves rational in playing the game at one level often impolitic on another. To understand choices, we must open the 'black box' of policymaking in which policies are drafted and decisions made and implemented. Here, the main tradition, *foreign policy analysis*, is mostly concerned with agency, and specifically how the features of the policy process enhance or detract from the ability of states to cope with their environments. How regimes prioritize and make trade-offs in any given situation will be affected by three components of the decision-making process: foreign policy role; the balance of power among interests in the foreign policy process; and leadership.

Foreign policy role

A state's foreign policy role (or ideology) implies an identity and defines orientations toward neighbours (friend or enemy), toward great powers (threat or patron), and toward the state system (revisionist or status quo). Roles are constructed by elites in interaction with other states and with their publics (likely reflecting the interests of dominant social forces in the regime). This role also includes a modus operandi that incorporates the experience (learning, accumulated memory) of state elites in balancing among economic needs, geopolitical imperatives, domestic opinion, and state capabilities (Korany and Dessouki 1991: 17–18).

Geopolitical position has a major impact on the conception of foreign policy roles. Thus Egypt's centrality and weight in the system has led its decision-makers to seek influence in the Arab East, North Africa, and the Nile Valley. But its view of it role has altered: Egypt's redefinition of its role from defender of the Arab revolution in the 1960s to status quo power (mediator between Israel and the Arabs, and then bulwark against Islamic extremism) in the 1980s and 1990s arguably paralleled the consolidation of a new bourgeois ruling class. On the other hand, the frustration of identity may also produce enduring roles: artificial or truncated states, such as Syria and Iraq, have sought protection and fulfilment in a wider Arab role. Israel's role conception as a besieged refuge for world Jewry imparts both insecurity and an irredentist need for more territory and water.

Although manipulated by elites, once a role is constructed, it sets standards of legitimacy and performance that, to a degree, constrain elites; it also shapes the socialization of the next generation of policymakers. It may therefore impart a certain consistency to foreign policy despite changes in leadership and environment. Roles do not, however, provide ready-made solutions to particular challenges, since they have to be applied in different and unique situations, allowing for differences over how the role is interpreted—a matter decided in the foreign policy process in which interested actors try to influence the choices of the top leader(s).

Power concentration and decision-making

When elites conflict, the power distribution among them and vis-à-vis society, which is defined by the state's governing institutions, decides outcomes. This distribution may affect the rationality of decisions, such as whether regimes overreact or underreact to threats. A balance between regime autonomy of, and accountability to, society and a balance among elites in the policy process arguably makes for more effective foreign policies: excessive leadership autonomy risks the pursuit of idiosyncratic policies that may be irrational, while excessive fragmentation among branches of the bureaucracy over decision-making may produce policy incoherence.

In the authoritarian republics, the leader-dominant model prevailed (Dawisha 1976). Foreign policy was constitutionally the reserved sphere of the chief executive, who was also the commander-in-chief of the armed forces, and enjoyed wide discretion and autonomy in foreign policy, although in reality presidential power depended on how secure the president's position was. Consolidated presidencies had great power to act and could make bold or risky decisions, such as Nasser's nationalization of the Suez Canal, Sadat's separate peace with Israel, and Saddam's invasion of Kuwait. In Arab monarchies, extended ruling families constitute informal groups with which the monarch is expected to consult and decision-making tends to be based on consensus (the lowest common denominator), and hence to be cautious and status quo. Monarchies may however, take bolder policies where the monarch has exceptional stature, such as King Faisal's oil embargo and Hassan of Morocco's invasion of Western Sahara. In pluralistic states, such as Israel, the prime minister must keep senior cabinet colleagues satisfied; in Turkey, the President assembles the cabinet and military chiefs under a National Security Council. Where such more collegiate leadership prevails, more information and input should allow for better policies unless it is vulnerable to 'group-think', hence fails to consider new options. Fragmented leaderships, as in Iran, tend to zigzag depending on which faction is in power; if none is in charge, effective foreign policymaking may be frustrated if, for example, the foreign ministry's effort to improve relations with the West is frustrated by the contrary policies of the revolutionary guards or the intelligence ministry.

Difference in leadership recruitment may also make a difference: where, as in early phases of authoritarian republics, leaders had to climb to power in a struggle, more competitive and power-hungry personalities tended to emerge than where a king inherited his crown. Leadership recruitment through competitive elections is supposed to make for more accountable, hence constrained, leaders, but in the Middle East, democratically elected leaders are not less bellicose: in Turkey, it was elected politicians (Menderes, Ozal) who occasionally departed from the cautious policies of the career bureaucracy, while in Israel, where electoral success usually requires being seen as tough on the Arabs, it is peace diplomacy, not war-making, that is most constrained. However, periodic competitive elections do allow for alternation between more and less hawkish governing teams—something apparent in both Israel and Iran.

The idiosyncratic variable: how much does the leader count?

In regimes in which power is personalized and concentrated, and especially in times of fluidity or crisis, the leader's personal style, values, perceptions, and misperceptions can make an enormous difference. Whether this is a liability depends in part on the experience and character of the leader. Thus, while Syria and Iraq were long ruled by branches of the same Baath party and had similar leader–army–party regimes, big differences between the styles of Asad (the cautious and calculating general) and Saddam (a risk-taking ex-street-fighter) seemed part of the explanation for key differences in their foreign policies (interacting with the geopolitical differences, such as the greater resources available to oil-rich Iraq and the formidable Israeli neighbour faced by Asad). Leadership miscalculations have had enormous consequences for the region, including Nasser's brinkmanship on the eve of the 1967 war and Saddam's failure to anticipate the reaction to his invasion of Kuwait. Because leaders and their bureaucracies tend to be too invested in existing policies, change in failing policy is most likely when an external shock is accompanied or followed by leadership change, with the new leader more willing to reinterpret the situation; with the change from Nasser to Sadat, and from Khomeini to Rafsanjani, successors, although building on alterations already initiated, ended up turning their predecessors' policies upside-down. The diplomatic skills and bargaining strategies of leaders, including intangibles such as 'credibility' and 'will', can also make a decisive difference. Thus Telhami (1990) argues that Sadat's failure to play his hand effectively in the Camp David negotiations produced a suboptimal outcome.

Intra-elite bureaucratic politics

In the Middle East, normally the leader decides, but other interested actors do try to influence him, such as presidential advisers, senior military and intelligence officers, key cabinet members, party apparatchiki, and foreign ministry officials. As the 'bureaucratic politics' model argues, each of these may propose different policies shaped by their special roles and material interests. Characteristic of the Middle East has been the dominating role of the military and intelligence services at the expense of the diplomats. The salient role of the former, even in pluralistic Turkey and Israel, and the relative weakness and limited professionalism of most foreign ministries, may bias policy toward coercive options and prioritize 'national security' issues over others. Important, however, is the change in the role of the military in the Arab republics, from vanguard of reform and nationalism, to pillars of the (conservative) status quo preoccupied with the Islamist threat from within. Economic and business elites have, until recently, had only limited access to decision-makers. Yet economic imperatives require state elites to remain cognizant of business needs: where a 'national bourgeoisie' is ascendant, its demands for protection from foreign competition may reinforce a nationalist foreign policy; satisfying *infitah* internationalist bourgeoisies, by contrast, is likely to require a pro-Western policy designed to entice foreign investment.

   Input into foreign policymaking from outside the governing establishment has typically been limited and indirect in the Middle East. Public opinion is likely to play a greater role in regimes having electoral accountability mechanisms, such as Turkey and Israel. In personalized authoritarian regimes, it may have an indirect impact on foreign policy if leaders must defend legitimacy under attack by rivals or if the mass public is aroused by crisis, such as conflict with the West or Israel. In normal times, when the public is divided, for example, by class or ethnicity, elites enjoy more autonomy to act as they please. Democratization resulting from the Arab uprising seemed likely to magnify the impact of public opinion in foreign policymaking; yet post-uprising states' options remain constrained by external factors, such as the balance of power with neighbours or dependency on the West, which can dilute the effect of popular demands in the policy process.

Explaining foreign policy outcomes

Given the typically contrary demands and constraints on their complex environment, decision-makers seek to balance between them: since *regime security* is normally the first priority, the location and intensity of the main security threat will be the main determinant of policy. The main threat may be internal or external, and regimes may either 'omni-balance' with (appease) or balance against threats. If the main security threat is *internal*, regimes may either bandwagon with an external power to get the support/resources to balance against it (even at the expense of autonomy), or they might use radical nationalist rhetoric to mobilize internal support—that is, to appease internal opposition. If the threat is an *external* power, the regime may either rely on a global protector or seek a power balance by means of self-help, through nationalist mobilization of domestic support, military build-up, and alliance-making. If the precarious economic health of a state threatens internal security, acquiring economic resources may move to the top of the foreign policy agenda. The choice of response to threat will depend on the dominant social forces in the regime, foreign policy role, and possibly leadership idiosyncrasies. State power position will also matter: if states are too weak to balance threatening stronger states, they may appease them or seek a patron-protector; in larger states (if internal threats are manageable), regional leadership (power) is more likely to be prioritized.

Comparative foreign policy in the 2000s: explaining foreign policy variation

The framework identifies the factors that matter in foreign policymaking, but not their relative weight. While this is contested by rival theories, with, for example, realists stressing the dominance of the states system, and liberals and foreign policy analysis arguing for the importance of internal politics, in fact these factors vary by country and over time, and their explanatory power is thus a matter of empirical research. In the sections that follow, we explain the foreign policies of four major powers—Saudi Arabia, Iran, Turkey, and Egypt—towards key events of the last decade: the 2003 Iraq War; the 2006 Lebanon War; and the post-2014 war with the Islamic State of Iraq and Syria (ISIS). In the conclusion, we summarize the relative weight of the various policymaking determinants in the 2000s.

The 2003 Iraq War

None of the regional states welcomed the US war on Iraq, since none saw Saddam's debilitated Iraq as a threat and all believed that the US-led invasion was likely to spread instability—but Saudi Arabia and Egypt acquiesced, while Turkey and Iran opposed or were ambivalent.

Egypt

Egypt's Mubarak, who had used the 1990 war on Iraq to prove his value to the US and to win massive debt relief, famously warned in 2003 that a new war would 'open the gates of hell' and spawn a hundred bin Ladens. Egypt did not join the 'coalition of the willing' that invaded Iraq, but it blamed Saddam Hussein for not fully complying with UN resolutions and, aside from verbal condemnation, did not really oppose the war. Mubarak ignored the resolution of the League of Arab States (LAS) summit against the war and Syria's urging that, under the Arab Collective Security Treaty, all Arab states were obliged to combine against a threat to another Arab state; rather, he allowed US forces to use bases in Egypt and to transit the Suez Canal to carry out the war. After the war, Egypt acknowledged and supported the US occupation of Iraq.

Mubarak had to defy Egyptian public opinion, which was inflamed against the war: massive demonstrations, fuelled by television coverage on the Al-Jazeera network, protested the war, burning the US flag and shouting anti-Mubarak slogans. The regime had to deploy an exceptional security presence as anger still mounted and, to appease the public, even sponsored anti-war demonstrations.

Egypt was too economically dependent on its US patron to say no. Not only did the economy depend on US aid, but the main pillar of the regime, the army, depended on US arms and financing. The contrast with Syria is instructive: the only Arab state to oppose the invasion, it was also the only one lacking clientage ties to Washington. Moreover, Mubarak was fearful of provoking the Bush administration, which professed to believe that the cause of the attacks on the US of 11 September 2001 ('9/11') was the lack of democracy in the Middle East. As US pressures on his regime for political liberalization mounted, Egypt tried to disarm its US critics by pursuing closer economic relations with Israel, selling it natural gas and opening investment to in its economic zones. This also reflected the rising lobbying power of American-connected businessmen associated with Gamal Mubarak's wing of the ruling party. In summary, the regime was omni-balancing with the US to contain the domestic opposition. But the cost was a growing erosion of domestic legitimacy: the anti-war demonstrations that had taken over Tahrir Square began a tradition of increasing street protest that would eventually culminate in Mubarak's fall.

Turkey

Turkey had also bandwagoned with the US in the 1990 war, similarly in order to demonstrate its strategic importance to Washington with the decline of the Soviet threat, but also driven by economic interests, such as access to the American market, investment, aid, and loans. What had changed in 2003 when Turkey declined to bandwagon? There had been no dramatic change in the degree of Turkey's dependency on the US; however, the Western 'core' was split, since key European powers opposed the 2003 war. Turkey's policy also reflected a changed perception of the utility of the US alliance, especially for countering its most pressing national security threat—that of Kurdish separatism and particularly the insurgency of the Kurdistan Workers' Party (PKK). In the 1990–91 war, Turkey had suffered severe economic losses and had seen US policy empower the Iraqi Kurds at the expense of the Baghdad government; a further war on Iraq risked a break-up of the country to the advantage of the Kurds and the encouragement of Kurdish separatism in Turkey. Still, on the eve of the war, Turkish–US negotiations had seemingly arrived at a agreement, backed by the ruling *Adaletve Kalkinma Partisi* (AKP) government, which would serve Turkish interests: not only would Turkey be given a significant economic package (US$4 billion in grants and US$20 billion in loans) needed to recover from a severe economic crisis (although less than it was asking for), but also Turkish forces would enter Iraq with the Americans and be in a position to counter threats from the PKK or the fragmentation of Iraq. That this deal fell apart in the end, failing to win parliamentary approval by a handful of votes, resulted from domestic politics—namely, widespread public opposition to the impending invasion, which seeped up into the ruling party and governing elite. Eighty-three per cent of the public opposed

even allowing the US to use Turkish air bases to support the war, and civil society organizations mobilized large-scale anti-war demonstrations. The main opposition Republican Peoples' Party, reflective of Kemalist nationalist opinion, argued against participation in a war
of aggression. The governing AKP was sharply split, with Parliament Speaker Bulent Arinc
insisting that a war lacked legitimacy without an endorsing UN Security Council Resolution
and the construction minister opposing the bombing of Muslims. With the prime minister
forced to allow a free vote, ninety-nine AKP parliamentarians, reflecting the views of their
constituents, joined the opposition in voting against the war. At the same time, the secular
President Ahmet Necdet Sezer, presiding over the National Security Council on which the
military chiefs were represented, argued that the war lacked international legitimacy and
prevented the Council from endorsing it, while the generals, themselves ambivalent, refrained from pushing for it, in spite of their intimate relations with the US military and
dependence on US military aid.

As a result of Turkey's decision, the strategic partnership between Turkey and the US
suffered a major setback. If Turkey had economic and strategic interests at least as weighty
as those of Egypt in pleasing its US patron, what seems to have made the difference for its
opposite choice was public opinion, registered through the democratic process, and also arguably an alteration in its conception of its role away from that of 'reliable US ally'. Not only
its emerging Muslim identity, but also Turkey's view of itself as conforming to international
legitimacy were seemingly important, the latter heavily influenced by its bid for EU membership (Winrow 2003).

Iran

Despite the chatter of war in the Persian Gulf, the war itself came as a total surprise to Iran,
for in its calculations the US had neither the resources nor the international backing for such
an audacious act. But, given the ideological context of US-led military action—to promote
democracy through regime change—and President Bush's 2002 State of the Union 'axis of evil'
speech, in which Iran was placed alongside Iraq and other 'pariah' states, any war that would
bring US forces to Iran's western borders (having already taken up residence in the countries
to the east) was an unwelcome development. After 2003, Tehran felt surrounded and vulnerable, and even made a covert effort to enter into a dialogue with Washington. Yet the US had
also done Iran a strategic favour by disposing of its greatest regional rival. This was the best
Persian New Year present for which Iran could have wished, it was whispered in Tehran, and
just two countries (Iran and Kuwait) welcomed the fall of the Saddam Hussein-led Baath state.

Iran's declared policy was one of 'active neutrality' in the 2003 Iraq War, meaning that it
would sidestep the war itself but be ready to deal with the fallout from it. There was a view
in Tehran at the time—as indeed in Damascus, Riyadh, and even Cairo—that, after Saddam,
Iran would likely be the next target on the US 'democratization' hit list. It would make sense,
therefore, for Tehran to regard Iraq as its first line of defence and thus to find ways of ensuring that the US did not find the time or the opportunity to secure decisive control of Iraq.
One effective course of action proved to be Iran's flexing of its muscles through Iraq's large
Shi'i constituency. But this would be a risky strategy for Tehran to adopt, for the liberation
of the Iraqi Shia was slowly exposing the deep policy and doctrinal tensions in Iran's own
Islamic political system. In a country where influence and political power are derived from

both religion and the religious hierarchy, where Tehran and Qom stand united only through the maintenance of the *vilayat-ifaqih* system, a new and powerful source of religious authority beyond Tehran's control can act as a new beacon of Shia Islam, seriously testing the doctrinal basis of a regime founded on a unique (and fairly narrow) interpretation of Shi'i thought. Najaf's rise, were it to happen, would not only challenge Qom, but also give Arab Shia a bigger say in Shi'i affairs across the region. The fall of Saddam thus had an impact on the factional rivalries in Iran and indeed encouraged some forces there to try to extend their power by infiltrating Iraq.

These calculations are somewhat separate from Tehran's more immediate concerns about Washington's intentions toward the Islamic Republic. The place of the US in Iran's agenda with respect to the Persian Gulf and Iraq is defined more by ideology than by immediate threat. Tehran still clearly separated its bilateral concerns with the US from those in the US–Iraq basket. This separation proved to be favourable for the US Iraq strategy, but the struggle against the US played a critical part in Iran's domestic power struggle and as long as that remained the case, no party in Iran could endorse any US action in the Persian Gulf. So, although ultimately it was the US that finally delivered on the most important of Iran's war aims in the Iran–Iraq War, because of the tensions between Washington and Tehran, the removal of Saddam Hussein's regime by overwhelming US force proved to be a new poisoned chalice with which Tehran had to contend.

Saudi Arabia

The Saudis were equally unsettled by the US action, seeing in the violent overthrow of the Baath regime regional chaos and more violence. While Riyadh had, since 1990, been as opposed to the Iraqi regime as was Iran, the Saudis were nevertheless unwelcoming of large-scale US troop deployments in their sphere of influence, because of the domestic political damage that such deployment would inflict on all the Gulf states. They therefore pressed for UN Security Council approval for any military action in Iraq, as a way of providing cover for any contribution that they would inevitably be asked to make by Washington. Having already seen the political and security consequences of the war on terror in the Afghani context and the destruction of the Taliban regime, which had, until October 2001, enjoyed diplomatic recognition by Riyadh, another war next door and so soon was threatening— particularly as, in their assessment, the Iraqi regime had been so weakened by international sanctions that it no longer posed a security threat to the countries of the Gulf Cooperation Council (GCC). More broadly, Saudi Arabia's confidence had been so shaken by the fallout from 9/11 and direct US criticism of it that it saw US-inspired conspiracies against it everywhere. An unnecessary assault on the only Arab country that had waged a sustained war to contain the contagion of Iran's (Shia) revolution must surely be a conspiracy against Saudi Arabia and its regional partners. Thus, when asked in 2002 if the kingdom would support any military action against Iraq (and Iran), the then Crown Prince declared Riyadh's position thus: 'I do not believe that the war on terrorism applies to Iran and Iraq. If you have a situation [of Iranian or Iraqi terrorism], it is the result of small fringe groups, and not government policy' (*Time*, 26 February 2002). Moreover, because the kingdom in 2002 was so squarely focused on the delivery of the Riyadh-sponsored Arab Peace Plan, unveiled in the March meeting of the LAS heads of state, it saw the impending war as a deliberate distraction from the kingdom's efforts finally to bring peace to Palestine. Thus, from the second half of 2002, it publicly opposed military action against Iraq. Indeed, the fourteenth Arab Summit's communiqué, orchestrated by the Saudis, made clear that the Arab world as a whole opposed any military action against Iraq. From the Saudi perspective, this was the wrong war to fight and at the wrong time: destabilizing Iraq would destabilize the Persian Gulf to the detriment of the US and the neighbouring Arab countries. The demise of Iraq as a regional power and the emergence of a pro-Iranian power elite there also strengthened Saudi Arabia's resolve to chart thereafter a more independent and proactive line in its foreign relations.

In calling for a regional solution to the Iraq crisis, Iran and Saudi Arabia had found a common cause in opposing US military action in Iraq, but the outcome of the conflict did much to change the regional balance of power (in favour of Iran) and also to worsen relations between the two Persian Gulf giants. Bush's war, ironically, had considerably strengthened the regional position of Iran and the hand of its own neo-conservative president, Mahmoud Ahmadinejad, whose bid for a greater regional role was to see Tehran extend its influence into Iraq and build a strong coalition of the 'resistance movement' in the Levant. This coalition's mettle was tested in 2006 and Hezbollah's thirty-four-day war with Israel.

The 2006 Lebanon War

What was remarkable about the 2006 Lebanon War was that the two main Arab powers, Egypt and Saudi Arabia, were complicit in an Israeli attack on an Arab country, while the two main non-Arab powers, Turkey and Iran, opposed it. For the first time in the history of Arab–Israeli military confrontations, Arab countries criticized the Arab party, Hezbollah, for undertaking 'uncalculated adventures that threaten Arab national security', referring to the cross-border raid and abduction of Israeli soldiers that sparked the crisis.

Egypt

Egypt's policy was based on its perception of rising domestic security threats from Islamism. First, the success of the Muslim Brotherhood in Egypt's 2005 parliamentary elections—allowed to appease US pressures for democratization—coincided with the electoral victory of its Palestine affiliate, Hamas (January 2006) in the Palestine territories, fuelling alarm in the Egyptian regime over the rise of Islamism in regional politics. Gaza, where Hamas dominated, was also seen as a security threat, reflected in the 2004–05 terrorist bombings in Sinai resorts perpetuated jointly by Egyptian and Palestinian militants. In parallel, Egypt saw itself as part of a 'moderate' Sunni Arab bloc engaged in a new Arab Cold War with a radical Iranian-led 'Shia crescent', empowered by the rise of the Shia in Iraq, and including Hezbollah in Lebanon and also Syria since its opposition to the war on Iraq. Seeing Hezbollah's actions as an effort to expose Egypt's impotence to defend the Arab cause and to delegitimize its ties with the US and Israel, Mubarak welcomed the possibility that Israel would cut Hezbollah down to size. Facing regional and domestic threats, the regime needed, all the more, to appease the US and to deflect its pressures for political reform by showing itself to be a bulwark against Islamic radicalism, and a bridge between Israel and the Arab world. In fact, the rise of Hamas and Hezbollah alarmed the US, and relieved the Mubarak regime of pressures for political reform.

Egypt's position in the 2006 war, however, only exposed the growing and dangerous gap between the ruling elite and public opinion. The prominence of security officials in Mubarak's inner circle fostered a preoccupation with a supposed subversive threat from Iran and Hezbollah. Among the public, however, Israel's excessive violence against Lebanon plus Hezbollah's effective resistance to it made Hassan Nasrallah a hero, with his portraits appearing alongside those of Nasser—a pointed reproach to an impotent Mubarak (Sedgwick 2010). Public anger against Israel melded with discontent against the government, again manifest in calls for the fall of Mubarak, who was viewed as a US puppet. The regime bent under public criticism, and started calling for a ceasefire and condemning the Israeli bombing, but activists, frustrated at the government's failure to reflect public views, were 'linking the lack of democracy in Egypt and what was happening to the Palestinians' (*New York Times*, 6 August 2006). The Muslim Brotherhood—which had, before the war, been moderating its stances, notably on the peace treaty with Israel, in parallel with its solicitation of US pressure on the regime for further democratization and its acquired stake in protecting its significant presence in parliament—now radicalized its discourse, supporting Hezbollah (against regime efforts to stir the Sunni–Shia cleavage), denouncing Israel, and linking the US and the Mubarak regime to its violence against Muslims.

Mubarak's policy was a relatively undiluted form of omni-balancing, seeking to strengthen support from its US patron in order to balance against domestic subversion perceived to be orchestrated by regional rivals, yet it was actually self-defeating: in so ignoring public opinion, it further increased domestic opposition. The regime's stance set it on a dangerous tangent that continued after the war, when, deepening its appeasement of the US and Israel, and its invocation of the Islamist threat, it collaborated in Israel's efforts to blockade the Gaza strip after Hamas's seizure of power there, further delegitimitizing it in public opinion and preparing the way for the 2011 uprising.

Turkey

The 2006 war had the opposite effect on Turkey, driving it toward the radical camp. Since the 1990s, Turkey, under the leadership of the military establishment, had developed significant security and economic ties with Israel, including intelligence cooperation and free trade agreements, initiated to appease the US, to balance against threats from Syria and Iran, who were supporting the PKK, and to acquire Israeli military technology. However, after Syria's 1998 ending of support for the PKK, and especially after the Iraq war led to rapprochement with Syria and Iran, Turkey's need for Israel had declined, especially because Israel was covertly supporting the Iraqi Kurds. The leader of the AKP government, Recep Tayyip Erdogan, was developing a new 'zero problems' relationship with Turkey's Arab neighbours, seeing the former Ottoman Islamic space as a natural sphere of influence and an outlet for Turkey's booming export capitalists, the Anatolian tigers.

During the war, some mainstream media joined Islamist and ultra-nationalist organs in demonizing Israel. Numerous non-governmental organizations condemned Israel and many anti-Israeli demonstrations were held in various cities, with 100,000 gathered at one rally in Istanbul. Reflecting the views of his constituents and encouraged by the positive acclaim in the Arab world, Turkey's Prime Minister Erdogan condemned Israel for the atrocities committed in Lebanon and for waging what he called an 'unjust war' that fuelled hatred.

He did not, however, terminate Turkey's links with Israel, and indeed, in 2008, was using Turkey's old ties to Israel and his new ones to Syria to broker peace negotiations between the two. When Israeli Prime Minister Olmert chose to sacrifice the negotiations by launching the 2008 attack on Gaza, Erdogan was infuriated and publically denounced Israel, again to acclaim in the Arab world; Turkey's engagement with and bid for leadership in the Middle East, a trend begun by the Iraq war, was thereby consolidated, as was the deterioration of relations with Israel.

Turkey's policy was reflective of the shift in its perception of regional threats and also of how to deal with them—away from the hard power and US–Israeli alliances to balance against the Arab Middle East, and toward the use of soft power and interdependencies to engage with it. This reflected the consolidation of the AKP as a majority party with wide public and Anatolian business support, and the consequent decline of the political power of the military establishment. It also reflected a parallel shift in Turkey's identity in a neo-Ottoman, moderate Islamic direction, reflective of a deepening of democratization—and hence of the role of mainstream public opinion in foreign policy.

Iran

For Iran, the war was a strategic blessing, for not only did Hezbollah perform well on the battlefield, but its favourable outcome also provided an emphatic endorsement of the Iran/ Syria-led 'resistance front'. The Hezbollah leader's regional elevation helped Iran to promote itself as the champion of Arab causes, and to make the case that it was thanks to Iran's leadership and the strength of its alliances that Israel was now suffering military, political, and moral defeats. The war in Lebanon illustrated an altogether new dimension to Iran's regional role in these rather tense circumstances. The perception of an Iranian-backed small, but dedicated, militia 'winning' the first Arab war against Israel in the Jewish state's sixty-year history persisted long after the war itself. Although the true costs of the war to the Arab side—Israel's unwillingness to give up any Palestinian or Syrian territory in an environment of insecurity, death, and destruction visited on Lebanon, and the deepening of factional and sectarian differences in the country—were indeed great, the feeling in the region was that Hezbollah and its 15,000 militants had managed to dent Israel's aura of invisibility. The fact that Hezbollah had apparently singlehandedly fought the Arabs' longest war with Israel to the bitter end—firing some 246 rockets into Israel on the last day of the war, superseding the previous record of 231 fired on 2 August—and had forced Israel to agree to an internationally negotiated ceasefire with it were sufficient reasons for it to feel victorious, and for Iran to feel proud of its own role.

Furthermore, if this campaign was ultimately a proxy war between Tehran and Washington, then the fact that mighty Israel, the US 'champion', had not managed to defeat Iran's much smaller Arab protégé made pro-American states feel vulnerable and blunted Israel's deterrence stance against hostile neighbours, and particularly against an emboldened Iran. But even more seriously, the fact that, in the eyes of the Arab masses, Israel (and by extension the US) in fact lost the war had a much bigger strategic implication: Tehran's neo-conservatives began to position themselves as the only force able and willing not only to challenge the US-dominated status quo, but also to change the regional balance of power in favour of 'the forces of Islam'.

Saudi Arabia

Riyadh had opposed the war as an unworthy adventure from the start; once the extent of the devastation of Lebanon became clear, it was able to point the finger of blame at Tehran and Hezbollah. This was an unnecessary war caused by an irresponsible movement, beholden to a non-Arab regional power. The war drew the Saudis closer to both Egypt and Jordan, who had been warning of the menace of a powerful 'Shia crescent' held together by Iran. But the Saudis could not help but feel vulnerable at the same time to the new revolutionary winds blowing from the direction of Iran; Iran was now playing an active part in Arab causes and its allies were able to expose the weaknesses of the neighbouring Arab regimes through their bold action—and military successes. Hassan Nasrallah's rocketing popularity in the 'Arab street', as the vanguard of a resurgent Arabism, threatened the 'moderate' Arab regimes and Israel's inability to destroy Hezbollah in anticipation of what the then Secretary of State had referred to as 'the birth pangs of a new Middle East' showed the limits of the power of their US patron. The Iranian government's open and unreserved support for Hezbollah stood in sharp contrast to the Saudi position, which rather swiftly changed from condemnation of Hezbollah's action as 'reckless' in the early days of the war to one of muted expression of support for the 'Lebanese resistance' halfway through the war. It was clear to all that this Arab adjustment was in small measure in response to a groundswell of support on the Arab street for what was portrayed by the Arab media as Hezbollah's heroism in the face of an unjust onslaught. Saudi Arabia's strategic position in the region was weakened for appearing to be supportive of Israeli aggression and for being on the wrong side of the fence.

Saudi Arabia's position was determined by its support for the Sunni communities of Lebanon and the al-Saud's close ties with the Hariri family in Lebanon (whose head had allegedly been assassinated by Hezbollah), and of course the geopolitical and ideological rivalry with Iran. This was articulated by a prominent Saudi columnist (Muhammad bin Ali Al-Mahmoud):

> Iran wants to control the region, not by spreading its ideology … but by maintaining armed organizations [in Arab countries] … it violates their loyalty to their homelands, replacing it with loyalty to Iran, … a country that [promotes] a culture of one-sided hegemony … to impose a kind of occupation.
>
> (*al-Riyad*, 29 May 2008)

But in order not to lose influence completely, Saudi Arabia led the international campaign to rebuild war-torn Lebanon, and it and two of its GCC allies (Kuwait and Qatar) committed some US$1.1 billion to reconstruction, with the Saudis taking the lead with a pledge of US$500 million and a further US$1 billion in supported loans to the Lebanon's central bank.

The ISIS war

Turkey

Turkey's policy toward ISIS was shaped by the frustration of the ruling AKP's ambition to make Turkey a regional leader through diplomatic and economic openings to its Arab neighbours and the soft power of its democratic Islamic model. Although Syria was the showcase of this 'zero-problems' policy, when Asad snubbed Turkish Prime Minister Erdogan's advice to respond to Syrian protesters with political reforms, he abandoned good relations with Damascus. Now resting its bid for hegemony on democracy promotion, Turkey aimed to oust Asad and bring the Syrian Muslim Brotherhood to power in Damascus.

As the AKP became increasingly frustrated by the tenacity of the Asad regime and the reluctance of the West to move against him, and as the AKP's Sunni identity became, amidst the region's sectarian identity wars, more salient, it started supporting jihadists as the most effective fighters against Asad and also to use against the PKK-linked PDY that had taken over the Syrian Kurdish areas on the Turkish border. But in the process, Ankara helped create ISIS. It gave its fighters weapons and training, allowed their free movement across its borders, permitted recruitment in Turkey (some 5,000 Turks joined ISIS, 7–10 per cent of its militants), and allowed ISIS to sell Syrian crude oil via Turkey, with an estimated $100 million hidden in Turkish banks. The AKP seemed to regard ISIS as protecting Sunni interests in Syria and Iraq against anti-Sunni regimes. After ISIS seized Mosul, this (and Turkey's stand on the ISIS siege of the Kurdish town of Kobane) became a major point of contention between Turkey and its Western allies. Under pressure from Washington, Turkey shut down the ISIS-controlled border crossings but continued to back other jihadists such as Al-Qaeda avatar, Jabhat al-Nusra. But alarmed that the Washington-led anti-ISIS coalition would tilt the balance of power in favour of its regional rivals (Iran, the Iraqi government, and, the Asad regime-whose policies Erdogan claimed had generated jihadists like ISIS), Turkey tried to make its participation in the coalition contingent on the Syrian regime being made a principal target. Since the global and regional priority was confronting ISIS, this isolated Turkey; fostering ISIS also precipitated opposition at home among Kurds and secularists and risked 'blowback' (Hinnebusch 2015a).

Iran

The arrival of ISIS in Iraq posed a major challenge to Iran, which until then had been able to demonstrate to the rest of the region its near total political and economic domination of Iraq. Indeed, in defence of the Asad regime, Tehran had recruited Iraqis to fight for the Syrian regime and had utilized Iraqi territory for the transfer of vital supplies to Syria. So, the takeover of Iraq's second largest city, Mosul, by ISIS fighters and usurpation of large tracts of Iraqi territory for the establishment of the new Islamic State or 'Caliphate', was a most unwelcome development and another sign of weakening state structures of its Arab allies. Beyond this, ISIS' military and political successes in Iraq (and Syria) put Iran in an impossible position: on the one hand, it had little choice but to bolster the position of its (mainly Shia) allies in Iraq, but on the other, it found itself frozen out of the international coalition against ISIS, headed by the United States and including a group of Arab allies (Egypt, Jordan, Saudi Arabia, the UAE) highly critical of Iran's regional policies. While Iran was the first country to commit military assets to the fight against ISIS, it was nevertheless also exposed to domestic and regional pressures for its policies. The neighbouring Arab states (and also Turkey) saw in Iran's policies a drive to strengthen the Shia belt now stretching from the Levant to the heart of the Yemeni capital. At home, the question was asked, why Iran was fighting other peoples' wars for them, and if it has to take a stance then why was it doing so in isolation? Tehran of course did not see things in these terms. First, the defence of the Shia-led government of Iraq was an essential part of its strategy of maintaining Iraq and

Syria under its influence and for ensuring access to its other allies in the Levant (Hezbollah, Hamas, and to a lesser extent Islamic Jihad). Second, from Tehran's perspective, ISIS was being aided by Sunni Arab states in order to weaken Iran's alliance structures and ultimately weaken Iran itself. Given Tehran's interpretation of events, ISIS' anti-Shia message was not only a clear warning to Tehran but also a call to arms for its Shia (and Kurdish) allies in Iraq. Tehran was both a prisoner of the new security crisis in Iraq and at the same time one of the critical actors able to change the dynamics of the theatre in favour of the Iraqi government (and its American backers).

Saudi Arabia

For Saudi Arabia, ISIS advances were a direct threat to its national security, and also to its Islamic worldview and status as the religious authority of the Sunni world. In terms of security, ISIS had now reached the frontiers of the Arabian Peninsula, encouraging Khaliji recruitment, and also threatening the security of the neighbouring monarchies. Furthermore, the establishment of the Caliphate on the soil of former great Islamic empires gave it a legitimizing edge not experienced since the middle ages in the Muslim world. In founding the Caliphate, ISIS presented the first 'state-type' Salafi-oriented political alternative with mass appeal in the region, notably for many Wahhabis and Salafis that Saudi Arabia had traditionally groomed as champions. ISIS' launch of *qadimun* ('we are coming' to take over the country) was a further direct threat to the al-Sauds. But, the ISIS war also presented an opportunity for Riyadh to try and further isolate Iran. Like Turkey, it encouraged the US to link the anti-ISIS campaign to the fight against the Syrian regime. Riyadh also used the ISIS threat to engage with the new government in Baghdad. In joining the forty-member coalition, Riyadh restored its strained ties with the US and managed to carve for itself a central place in the fight against ISIS, even hosting the coalition's first meeting in Jeddah in September 2014. In the words of the foreign minister (Prince Saud al-Faisal): 'The contribution of the Kingdom has not been confined to participation in military operations against the group, but also has extended to include humanitarian assistance to the brotherly Iraqi people and coordination with the international community to dry up the financing sources of terrorist groups and expose the criminal nature of these groups, which are contrary to the tolerant teachings of Islam' (Royal Embassy of Saudi Arabia, Washington, DC, 3 December 2014). Saudi Arabia also agreed with the US to host training bases for Syrian opposition forces. While it sought to depict itself as defender of the Sunni regional order against what it labelled as 'Kharijite' heretics, its own direct contribution to the military campaign remained small partly due to sensitivities at home about Saudi forces being seen as American allies involved in killing Arabs and Sunni Muslims.

Egypt

Egypt's weak regimes are *omni-balancers*, seeking external support against strong internal opposition, but changes in the ruling coalition—the overthrows of Mubarak and Mursi—changed both the opposition and Egypt's external alignments. President Mursi, in his brief tenure, used support from Turkey and Qatar against opposition from the military/deep state over which he never had full control. He reached out to Hamas amidst enmity from Israel and Saudi Arabia, but was forced to acquiesce in the military's blockade of Gaza to the benefit of Israel and at US urging. The killing of Egyptian soldiers by Islamist militants in the Sinai, blamed by the military on Hamas, and Mursi's call for a jihad against Syria's Asad, were factors in his overthrow (Morsy 2013).

The anti-Mursi coup and the near restoration of the old regime, marked by a draconian repression of the Muslim Brotherhood, provoked a widened Islamist insurgency centred on the Sinai. One faction, Ansar Bayt al-Maqdis, pledged allegiance to ISIS, renaming itself Wiliyat Sinai. President al-Sisi legitimized his regime in the name of a war on Islamic terrorism. In a parallel campaign against Hamas, which the military blamed for the Sinai insurgency, the Sisi regime closed Gaza's lifeline of underground tunnels and established a *cordon sanitaire* between it and the Sinai. During Israel's July 2014 war on Gaza, the regime coordinated its diplomacy with Israel to discredit Hamas, prolonging the Israeli assault on the Palestinians (Brown and Dunne 2014). While these moves sparked enmity with pro-Brotherhood Turkey and Qatar, they were supported by the United States, Israel, Saudi Arabia, and the UAE. This, plus Egypt's growing economic dependency on Saudi and Emirati funding, drove a close alignment with the latter. Egypt also aligned with Syria's Asad against the shared jihadist threat, particularly ISIS; it supported the anti-ISIS intervention in Syria, but opposed any US targeting of the Syrian military (Wagner and Cafiero 2013). In Libya, Egypt sided with Khalifa Hafter's anti-Islamist military faction, crowned by air strikes against the Libyan franchise of ISIS in February 2015. In Washington, the Israeli lobby defended Egypt from cuts in aid after the al-Sisi coup; later, with the US needing allies against ISIS and Cairo flirting with China and Russia, Washington moved closer to al-Sisi's regime. Egypt came under further pressure to act following the ISIS-claimed downing of the Russian plane over the Sinai peninsula in October in 2015. Thus, ISIS became an opportunity to reinvigorate Cairo's omni-balancing.

Conclusion

Our case studies enable us to draw some conclusions regarding the main determinants of foreign policy in the 2000s.

The 2003 War

All regional actors publicly opposed the war on Iraq as a threat to regional stability. Turkey and Iran also perceived threats to their immediate security interests, and began coordinating with Syria—notably, against the Kurdish threat exacerbated by US policy; Iran, fearing the US forces on its border, took advantage of the empowerment of the Iraqi Shia to extend its sphere of influence in order to contain the US threat. While Turkey and Iran pursued independent policies to minimize damage from the war, Egypt and Saudi Arabia covertly, if unwillingly, facilitated the war. Egypt's response was a function of US dependency and an authoritarian regime's ability to defy public opinion. As for the Saudis, caught between public opinion, including the powerful ulema, and the need to appease their US patron, they denied the Americans use of Saudi bases from which to attack Iraq, but allowed the US use of Saudi-based command-and-control facilities necessary to the war. Turkey's refusal to facilitate the war in spite of some US dependency was a function of democratic processes that channelled public opinion as a counterbalancing force.

The 2006 War

In 2006, Egypt and Saudi Arabia tacitly applauded an Israeli attack on an Arab country, while the two main non-Arab powers, Turkey and Iran, opposed it. Egypt saw the war as an answer to the domestic security threat from trans-state Islamist subversion that the regime believed was orchestrated by Iran, and also as an opportunity to demonstrate its utility to its US patron and hence ward off pressures for democratization—but it was still forced to alter its stance in the face of trans-state public rage. Saudi Arabia saw the war in similar terms, as an Iranian attempt to delegitimize the regime, but was similarly forced to change its public stance in the face of regional opinion. Thus, even non-democratic states were vulnerable to public opinion in times of crises that aroused the people. Turkey's leaders saw the war as an opportunity to mobilize Turkish public opinion and to decrease the influence of the military, with its intimate links to Israel, and also—driven by a shift in identity and its role in foreign policy, and by business interests—to build bridges with the Arab Middle East. Iran also took the war as an opportunity to assert its regional leadership and the neo-conservative president took it as an opportunity to consolidate his power.

The ISIS War

The war on ISIS is taking place against a backdrop of state destabilization from the Arab uprisings and the sectarian identity wars they inflamed; with regimes more vulnerable to penetration of their territory by trans-state movements and discourse, they naturally saw ISIS as a threat but also sought to turn it to their advantage against rivals. Although the war on ISIS was mounted by a US-led coalition, that fact that its most effective member was a US opponent, Iran, and its least enthusiastic participant was a US ally, Turkey, is indicative of the growing dominance of regional struggles over global level factors in shaping state policies. Turkey's ambition for regional hegemony had increasingly exceeded its capabilities, and was contested by Iran, Iraq, and Syria. As the AKP's Sunni Islamist identity come to the fore, it sought to use (even fostered) ISIS as a tool, particularly against Syria's Asad; hence, the AKP feared the anti-ISIS campaign would strengthen its rivals and sought to make its participation conditional on turning the campaign against Asad. For Iran, the need to strike a blow at the threat of Sunni jihadism, which threatened its main Arab allies in Baghdad and Damascus, and to contain Turkey's ambitions and Saudi influence, over-determined its policy against ISIS. Despite the affinities between ISIS ideology and Saudi Wahhabism, the al-Saud recognized the threat to its family rule from ISIS 'Kharijitism' although it also hoped the campaign could be turned against Asad and that it could be used to put Riyadh at the head of the 'anti-terrorism' coalition and thereby contain Iran's role. For Egypt's, the weakest of the four states, omni-balancing against Islamism at home and in the region was also a way for al-Sisi to demonstrate Egypt's value to the West's 'war on terrorism' and to sustain Gulf financial backing.

Summary of the balance of factors

As realists might have expected, MENA states' foreign policies chiefly responded to environmental threats and opportunities, in ways determined, in the first instance, by their relative power positions. All four of the states studied have had pretensions to regional leadership, but it was the stronger states, Turkey and Iran, that saw opportunities while vulnerable Egypt and Saudi Arabia mostly perceived threats. Turkish fears of Kurdish separatism in 2003 were eclipsed by opportunities in 2006 to project regional leadership. In the anti-ISIS war, however, Turkey saw its opportunities to weaken its rivals (Asad, Iran) enervated and tried to turn the campaign against Asad. Iranian fears of the US military threat on its borders in 2003 gave way to perceived leadership opportunities in 2006, and while Iran had been put on the defensive by the 2011 popular revolt against its Syrian ally, the war on ISIS enabled it to recover its stature. For Egypt, 2006 had begun as an opportunity to see its 'resistance axis' rivals damaged, but these rivals were ultimately strengthened; while in 2014, ISIS-like Islamism was an internal threat to be omni-balanced against while seeking to bandwagon with the anti-ISIS coalition.

However, the main threat to states was seldom military, but rather from legitimacy wars waged by sub- or trans-state identity movements, as constructivists (Barnett 1998) have argued, or from their manipulation by rival regimes. All four states—but especially Egypt, ruled by the most vulnerable regime—saw the three crises as inflaming regional instability, which could spill over domestically; 2003 and 2006 were threats to the Egyptian and Saudi regimes in delegitimizing their US alliances, although they also saw in these certain opportunities to show their value to, and hence ward off criticism from, their US patron. ISIS posed an ideological threat to all regimes, although Turkey sought to use it against enemies and all tried to use its threat to enhance their regional roles and alliances.

Responses to these threats and opportunities took quite different forms, and the policy process mattered in differentiating them. Responses in 2003 and 2006 were shaped by the relative balance between the power of core demands on client states and public resistance to these demands—a dimension that realists would not anticipate—although neo-classical realists would. Regimes ruled by client elites had no choice but to appease the US in 2003 against their own best interests, as structuralists might expect, while those not dependent (Iran) or democratically responsive to public opinion (Turkey) opposed the war. In 2006, regime self-interest in Egypt and Saudi Arabia (fear of Iranian-inspired subversion) coincided with the requirements of US dependency, although both were still forced to alter their discourses to minimize legitimacy losses in the court of public opinion. Iran and Turkey, which were less dependent or not dependent at all on the US, were better positioned to use 2006 to enhance their regional leadership positions by championing publicly popular opposition to Israel. In 2014, the unaccountable Saudi and Egyptian regimes could easily have ignored domestic Islamist opinion and joined the US coalition against ISIS.

The policy process had certain other effects on responses to systemic challenges. In Turkey, the ruling AKP leadership used the crises to push a foreign policy congruent with a new identity and foreign policy role that also weakened the military, its historic rival; increasingly, too, in the struggle over Syria, it mobilized Sunni Islamist opinion, while disquieting secularists. In Iran, hardliners—notably, Ahmadinejad and the Revolutionary Guard—used 2003 and 2006 to strengthen their position against reformist rivals; any convergence with the US precipitated by the ISIS war would strengthen pragmatists, although the anti ISIS campaign increased the role of the revolutionary guards in the regional power struggle. In Egypt, the pivotal role of the military and security chiefs, obsessed with Islamist/Iranian threats, dictated first omni-balancing with the US and later with similar anti-Islamist regimes in

Saudi Arabia and the UAE against threats to regime stability. In Saudi Arabia, the ulema may have been a certain constraint in 2003 on the default position—deferring to the US—of a royal family intimately connected to US elites; the Saudi–US link survived strains over policy toward the Arab uprisings and was reinvigorated by the Saudi's accession to the anti-ISIS coalition, with the ulama brought to sanction a war on a kindred fundamentalist entity.

In conclusion, foreign policy in each state was driven by a combination of threats, albeit mostly of domestic instability, and geopolitical rivalries, as realists might expect. Omni-balancing was most in evidence in the weaker regimes, especially Egypt. But responses varied according to factors that neo-realists largely discount, such as the level of dependency on the US and the extent of democratization.

Further reading

Ehteshami, A. (2007) *Globalization and Geopolitics in the Middle East: Old Games, New Rules* (New York: Routledge)

Hinnebusch, R. and Ehteshami, A. (2014) *The Foreign Policies of Middle East States* (Boulder, CO: Lynne Rienner)
  The only foreign policy text with a framework and case studies including the non-Arab states.

Korany, B. and Dessouki, A. E. H. (2008) *The Foreign Policies of Arab States: The Challenge of Globalization* (Cairo: American University in Cairo Press)
  Combines overviews of theory and the region, and country cases.

Telhami, S. (1990) *Power and Leadership in International Bargaining: The Path to the Camp David Accords* (New York: Columbia University Press)
  A classic that combines realism and the leadership variable.

Telhami, S. and Barnett, M. (2002) *Identity and Foreign Policy in the Middle East* (Ithaca, NY: Cornell University Press)
  Debates and case studies on the impact of identity.

Questions

1. Can realism explain the different response of regional states to the 2003 US invasion of Iraq?

2. How far do differences in the foreign policy role conceptions of the four states explain their contrasting reactions to the 2006 war?

3. How much difference has leadership made for the Iraq, Hezbollah, and ISIS wars?

4. What drives the responses of regional states to ISIS?

5. What explains the quite different responses of regional states to the ostensibly similar militant non-state Islamist movements, Hezbollah and ISIS?

The Arab–Israeli Conflict

CHARLES SMITH

Overview

The term 'Arab–Israeli conflict' refers to a condition of belligerency between the Arab states and Israel. The first Arab–Israeli War began immediately after the proclamation of the State of Israel on 14 May 1948, with assaults by Egypt, Jordan, Syria, and elements from the Iraqi and Lebanese armies. Subsequent wars in this conflict included the 1956 Suez crisis, in which Israel, Britain, and France attacked Egypt, the 1967 and 1973 wars, and the Israeli invasion of Lebanon in 1982. In addition, border tensions and armed clashes between Israel and Arab neighbours were frequent in the early 1950s and in the mid-1960s, the latter contributing to the 1967 war. Two Arab states, Egypt (1979) and Jordan (1994), have signed peace treaties with Israel, but tensions remain high because of the Palestinian question and Israeli settlement expansion in the occupied territories in the midst of uncertainty resulting from the Arab Spring—notably the ongoing turmoil in Syria and Iraq. As for the United States, some in the George W. Bush administration saw Saddam Hussein's overthrow in 2003 as a step towards enabling Israel to evade any peace agreement with the Palestinians and to consolidate its regional hegemony over its Arab neighbours. The efforts of the Obama administration to reverse that approach, and to oversee a Palestinian–Israeli and Arab–Israeli peace, failed as of summer 2015, with Israeli Prime Minister Netanyahu focusing the narrative instead on Iran's nuclear development and the Palestinian Authority (PA) turning to the United Nations rather than the US for support.

Introduction

The Arab–Israeli conflict is a direct outgrowth of the Palestinian question, which resulted from the inclusion of the Balfour Declaration (1917) in the mandate for Palestine. This obliged Britain to support Zionist aspirations to create a Jewish state against the wishes of the Palestinian Arab inhabitants. These two conflicts, Arab–Israeli and Palestinian–Israeli, have frequently intersected, with the Palestinian question often serving as a major factor in Arab state rivalries, as well as Arab–Israeli tensions.

Arab–Israeli hostility did not create alignments that paralleled the Cold War rivalry between the United States and the Soviet Union. The major dividing lines were among Arab states, which either sided with the US or Britain during the 1950s and 1960s, or pursued a policy of non-alignment. Non-alignment permitted its adherents to deal with the West and the Soviet bloc, but often resulted in major arms deals with the Soviets and their East European satellites. This split frequently coincided with one between states such as Egypt and Syria, which were governed by young, more radical military officers or politicians, and more conservative monarchies with close Western ties, such as Saudi Arabia, Jordan, and Iraq until the 1958 Revolution.

Cold War allegiances saw Jordan and Israel identified with Western powers, whereas Egypt and Syria were often linked to the Soviet Union. With respect to the Arab–Israeli conflict, Jordan, Egypt, and Syria, whatever their mutual animosities, were considered to be aligned against Israel.

A key element in examining the Arab–Israeli conflict is asking what conditions are required to resolve it. Realist theory has assumed a certain uniformity in states' calculations of their own interests based on their judgements of power relative to their rivals. For realists, 'internal, domestic factors, including identity, are relatively marginal in determining state interests' (Telhami and Barnett 2002: 2; Peleg 2004: 101).

This chapter considers the question of identity politics as key to the definition of nationality and whether such a definition corresponds to the basis of the state. Can conflicting visions of what constitutes the identity of the state and its security, based on religion, ethnicity, or language, block efforts for peaceful resolution of differences? To what extent can state actions and evaluations of what constitutes state security or insecurity represent the input of ideological actors whose views may endanger the state, not protect it? Here, constructivism serves as a useful tool of analysis for explaining state actions within a realist framework; state interests are defined according to the ideology of the group or party that rules. Examples of developments addressing the approaches of realism, identity politics, and constructivism include the following, placed under different headings.

Realism

Many proponents of realism assume a common view of state interests by policymakers within that state, including what constitutes the security of the state. Judgements of security reflect the evaluation of power relationships between neighbouring or rival states. The following examples challenge that assumption.

Israel

Major differences emerged in the early 1950s as to what was required for the security of the state. There were two options. First was an 'activist', aggressive policy that assumed that Arabs would seek peace only once they had been crushed militarily, known as the 'iron wall' doctrine. Originally espoused by revisionists, the Labour Zionist leadership centred in the first Prime Minister, David Ben-Gurion, also adopted it. Second was the 'Weizmannist' policy, which did not eschew force, but sought to resolve disputes initially by diplomacy and the mediation of outside agencies if necessary, such as the United Nations. This approach was linked to Moshe Sharett, the first Israeli foreign minister, who succeeded Ben-Gurion briefly as Prime Minister in 1954–55.

Officials loyal to Ben-Gurion activated a spy ring in Egypt in 1954 without informing then Prime Minister Moshe Sharett. Egyptian discovery of the spy ring played a role in Israeli reprisal actions in early 1955 and contributed to the 1956 Suez crisis. In 1982, Ariel Sharon lied to the Israeli cabinet, and possibly to his prime minister, Menachem Begin. He assured them that the planned invasion of Lebanon was a limited one, when he intended to proceed to Beirut, to destroy the Palestine Liberation Organization (PLO) infrastructure there, and to instigate a war with Syrian forces to oust them from Lebanon.

One of the major arguments for retaining the West Bank is security-based: the territory would form a buffer against any assault from the east. But ideology also plays a role here. The West Bank forms part of ancient Israel, known as Judaea and Samaria. Abandoning this region would violate the Likud party's platform, which insists on its retention. Ideology linked to national identity means that keeping the West Bank is preferable to negotiating peace agreements acceptable to Arab states or to the Palestinians (Podeh 2014).

Egypt

Accounts suggest that Gamal Abd al-Nasser did not control the Egyptian military during the 1967 war. Chief of Staff Abd al-Hakim Amr and Minister of Defence Shams al-Din Badran pursued a more aggressive military posture than Nasser may have intended, creating the opportunity and justification for an Israeli attack. There was no agreement on policy at the outset of the crisis, thereby threatening state security.

United States

During the 1967 Arab–Israeli War, the Lyndon B. Johnson administration made no policy decisions, but pursued suggestions offered by persons close to Israel. In doing so, it abandoned a commitment to the region's territorial integrity made prior to hostilities. Secretary of State Dean Rusk was never informed of decisions or of the White House's expectation that war was imminent (Smith 2012: 165–92).

During the Nixon administration, major differences emerged over the conduct of Middle Eastern policy between Secretary of State William Rogers, and National Defence Secretary Henry Kissinger and President Richard Nixon. Rogers backed UN efforts to induce a cease-fire between Egypt and Israel in 1969–70 as a prelude to peace talks; Israel, encouraged by Kissinger and Nixon, opposed Rogers's efforts. They objected to UN involvement in the peace process; rather, the US should control the process and exclude its Cold War rival, the Soviet Union. 'Beating' the Soviets counted more than seeking resolution of regional disputes through international cooperation. Rogers and Kissinger ordered their staffs not to talk to their counterparts.

In the build-up to the US attack on Iraq in March 2003, the Pentagon and Vice-President Richard Cheney's office bypassed the State Department and National Security Adviser Condoleezza Rice in order to present false intelligence to President Bush. This intelligence served as a basis for war despite being repeatedly challenged by CIA analysts. This intelligence was produced in the Office of Special Plans in the Pentagon, headed by Under-Secretary for Defence Douglas Feith, himself of a revisionist Zionist background.

Identity politics: nationalism, religion, and the state

Arab nationalism, State identity, and Islam

The Arab national idea in the twentieth century, defined on the basis of language and culture, sought to unite Arab peoples from Morocco to the Arabian Peninsula in one state. It failed, owing to rivalry for leadership of the movement, especially between Egypt and Syria, which ultimately became a major factor inciting the 1967 war.

The aftermaths of the American invasion of Iraq (2003) and the Arab Spring (2010–12) have witnessed the weakening or fragmentation of states such as Iraq, Syria, and Libya. Major Sunni–Shia divisions in Iraq have spread to Syria where Sunnis seek the overthrow of the Asad regime. The hostilities have drawn in or affected as refugee centres most central Middle East states such as Turkey, Iran, Lebanon, and Arab Gulf countries. Moreover, all are now confronted by the seemingly Wahhabist-inspired violently puritanical 'Islamic State' (IS) Sunni movement based in northern Iraq and Syria. Although a potentially unstable coalition of groups, the IS ideology challenges the bases of Sunni Muslim identity in the midst of the Sunni–Shia rivalry, while appearing to undermine loyalty to either Arab or existing state identities.

At the same time, Saudi Arabia's recent actions suggest that it will opt for dictatorship rather than democratically-elected Muslim governments. The Saudis opposed the ouster of Egypt's Husni Mubarak and the election of Muslim Brotherhood Muhammad al-Mursi as Egypt's president. They then backed Mursi's overthrow by General Abdel Fattah al-Sisi with financial aid. And whereas Mursi sought to reconcile Hamas and Fatah, al-Sisi has joined Israel in blockading Gaza and has declared Hamas a terrorist organization.

Israel: ideology and identity

Factions have always differed on what lands were essential to constitute the State of Israel. Menachem Begin's Herut Party consistently advocated, during the 1950s, an immediate Israeli takeover of the East, as well as the West, banks of Jordan, to fulfil revisionist Zionist expansionist principles. Today, revisionists insist that Israel retain all of the West Bank, as the Likud party platform declares, whereas a majority of Israelis appear to accept, with some territorial adjustments, a return to the pre-1967 war boundaries, granting the Palestinians a state of their own. These conflicting approaches to the identity of Israel directly affect the peace process and also call attention to the question of state security.

Would Israel be more secure with the absorption of the West Bank and its Palestinian Arab population, thus weakening the nature and identity of a Jewish state? Israeli census statistics for 2011 suggest that the Palestinian Arab populations of the West Bank and Gaza, together with the Israeli Arab population, equal the Jewish population of Israel, including Jews in expanded East Jerusalem and the West Bank (Bassock 2011). Or would Israel be more secure within boundaries resembling those of 1967, thus preserving its character as a Jewish state? In both cases, competing considerations of security are bound up with conflicting visions of what borders are required to constitute Israeli identity.

Finally, revisionist Zionist ideology assumes that Israel, as a Jewish state, can never achieve security because of anti-Semitism and Arab hostility unrelated to any actions that Israel might undertake. Identity and insecurity become a 'mutually constitutive process', requiring constant reassurance through affirmation of military might (Weldes et al. 1999: 11; Peleg 2004: 111). By this logic, Arab hostility will be ongoing with or without a peace agreement, meaning that no peace is possible: 'a culture of insecurity feeds on itself as a self-fulfilling prophecy' (Peleg 2004: 106).

A complicating factor is that right-wing Israeli ambitions, whether religious or secular in origin, acquire great support from the worldwide Christian evangelical movement, and especially Christian fundamentalists in the US. These Christian Zionists openly back Israeli retention of the West Bank, fund settlements, and view the ousting of the Palestinians as fulfilling Old Testament prophecy. They are a major factor in current US Middle Eastern policy, with strong representation in Congress, especially among Republicans, and close ties to the American Israel Public Affairs Committee (AIPAC) lobby. In short, definitions of what constitutes the legitimate identity of Israel go beyond the views of its citizens to include those of ardent believers of a different religion in another country.

Hamas/Islamic Jihad

Whereas official Palestinian policy recognizes Israel and supports a two-state solution, the major Islamic groups call for the eradication of Israel and the return of all former Palestine to Palestinian rule, preferably under an Islamic government. This definition of a Palestinian state, based on an Islamic identity, clearly conflicts with that offered by the Palestinian Authority. As with Likud in Israel, it establishes competing visions of the ideal state based on differing calculations of identity. The Hamas platform calls for full Muslim-Palestinian control from the Mediterranean to the Jordan River—the mirror image of Likud's platform for Jewish control of the same land.

Clashes of identity at Camp David, 2000: The Temple Mount and the Nakba

Two key issues obstructing Israeli–Palestinian agreement at Camp David were sovereignty/control over the Temple Mount/al-Haram al-Sharif, and the Palestinian right of return to lands from which most had been expelled in 1948. The former issue considers an area deemed sacred to both Jews and Muslims, with each side arguing for inclusion in its territory as basic to its identity. The right of return addresses events crucial to the national narratives of both Israelis and Palestinians. Israeli achievement of independence in 1948 is to them a triumph to be considered in itself, apart from its impact on others. For Palestinians, Israel's independence was, and is, their catastrophe (*nakba*).

Palestinians argue, and many Israeli analysts agree, that the Palestinians do not demand a literal right of return for all refugees who so wish, but simply Israeli acknowledgement of the principle of such a Palestinian right. This would entail Israeli recognition that Israel's actions in gaining its state created the Palestinian refugee problem—which is doubtful at the present time.

The United States

Key members of the George W. Bush administration had links with the Israeli Likud party and, in 1996, advised newly elected Israeli Prime Minister Binyamin Netanyahu to abandon the Oslo peace process in order to secure Israel's control of the West Bank.

They also argued for the overthrow of Iraq's Saddam Hussein as the first step in ensuring Israel's regional hegemony. Douglas Feith co-authored one paper, *Clean Break*, in June 1996 with Richard Perle (1996), and David Wurmser a second, *Coping with Crumbling States: A Western and Israeli Balance of Power Strategy for the Levant* (Wurmser 1996). Feith, as noted, was later given the number three post in the Defense Department and Wurmser became Middle Eastern adviser to Vice President Richard Cheney, stepping down in December 2007. In short, Likud sympathizers held sway over much of Bush's Middle Eastern, and especially Israeli–Palestinian, initiatives to the extent that, for one analyst, Bush 'subcontracted' Palestinian policy to Prime Minister Ariel Sharon during Bush's first term in office (Quandt 2005: 408).

From the creation of Israel to the 1967 war

Britain handed over responsibility for Palestine to the United Nations in February 1947, setting the stage for the General Assembly's partition decision of November. Fighting quickly erupted between Zionist forces and Palestinians. Zionist military superiority enabled Jewish forces to gain control of the territory awarded to them in the 1947 partition plan, resulting in the declaration of Israeli independence on 14 May 1948.

The Arab state assaults on Israel following this declaration of independence failed, owing to Israeli military superiority and Arab disunity. Most backed the creation of a Palestinian state, to be led by the former mufti of Jerusalem, Hajj Amin al-Husseini, who then lived in Egypt. Transjordan, to become the Hashemite Kingdom of Jordan in 1948, opposed Palestinian self-determination and accepted the idea of partition, hoping to divide Palestine with the new State of Israel. Jordan's Arab Legion sought to retain already-occupied territory, to be known as the West Bank, and clashed with Israeli forces only when challenged for control of the city of Jerusalem, which was divided. Jordan's King Abdullah was assassinated in 1951 because of his negotiations with Zionists over the partition of Palestine.

Israel and the combatant Arab states signed armistice agreements between January and June 1949, but a state of war still existed. Arab states boycotted companies trading with Israel and Egypt forbade Israeli ships from transiting the Suez Canal, although it permitted passage of foreign ships destined for Israel. Between 1948 and 1956, border tensions were strong, with frequent clashes between Israel and its neighbours, Syria, Jordan, and Egypt—especially Jordan.

The Suez crisis of 1956: background

During 1955, the focus of Arab–Israeli animosity shifted from the Jordanian front to the Egyptian, influenced by Cold War rivalries between the Soviet Union and the West. Washington wanted Egypt to be the linchpin of a Middle Eastern alliance to form part of the West's containment policy towards the Soviet Union and world communism. However, Egypt's Gamal Abd al-Nasser, the young colonel who had taken over in a coup in July 1952, espoused the doctrine of neutrality or non-alignment between the Cold War rivals. When Britain arranged a security pact with Nuri al-Said of Iraq in February 1955 (the Baghdad Pact), this ignited severe inter-Arab rivalries and regional tensions.

At the same time, February 1955, Nasser suddenly found himself confronted by a military crisis with Israel. This stemmed from an agreement that he had reached with Britain during the summer of 1954 for British withdrawal of forces from their 200-square-mile military base in the Suez Canal Zone, to be completed by June 1956. News of this pact led Israeli officials to activate a spy ring in Egypt without the knowledge of Prime Minister Moshe Sharett. The reason given was to buttress Israel's future security by forcing Britain to remain in the Suez Canal Zone, thus blocking the possibility of Egyptian troop movements into the Sinai. This would be done by having the spies blow up installations frequented by Westerners, forcing Britain to conclude that it should remain to protect its citizens.

An amateur affair, the spies were soon captured and placed on trial. The hanging of two spies and the imprisonment of others gave the Israeli public the impression of Egyptian racism towards Israel, since Sharett, once aware of Israeli responsibility for the ring, could not openly admit it. Popular alarm at Israel's apparent inability to counter Egypt's actions led to calls for Ben-Gurion's return to government, rewarded when he took over as Minister of Defence in January 1955, officially under Sharett's control, but in reality independent.

In February 1955, Israel undertook a massive raid into Gaza that resulted in major Egyptian casualties. The raid was primarily intended to reassure Israeli citizens of their government's military superiority in the face of supposed Egyptian provocations in the aftermath of the spy trials. It proved to be a landmark in the Arab–Israeli conflict within the Cold War context. Concerned at Egyptian military weakness, Nasser signed an arms pact with the Soviet Union in September 1955, causing Israel to seek more arms from its supplier, France. Tensions mounted in July 1956 when the US and Britain refused to finance the building of the Aswan Dam. Nasser retaliated by nationalizing the Suez Canal the same month.

As a result, Britain, France, and Israel, for different reasons, collaborated to attack Egypt. Israel sought to destroy the Egyptian blockade of shipping through the Tiran Straits into the Gulf of Aqaba, and to force Nasser's overthrow—the latter goal, shared by France. Humiliated by France's forced withdrawal from Vietnam in 1954, French officials were determined to retain control of Algeria, which they had invaded in 1830 and colonized, making it a *département* of France. Convinced that Nasser sustained the Algerian Revolt that had erupted in 1955, France saw Nasser's ouster as ensuring its position in Algeria. The British government viewed the canal's nationalization as an intolerable affront by a former imperial possession and a threat to international order.

The Suez war and its legacy

The Suez war of late October/November 1956 ended in political failure for France and Britain, despite the military defeat suffered by the Egyptians. Nasser's defiance in the face of aggression by the Western imperial powers, Britain and France, allied with Israel, which Arabs considered to be the product of British imperialism, reinforced his reputation as a defender of Arab nationalism. The war brought Israel ten years of peace on its Egyptian frontier, with open passage for Israeli shipping into the Gulf of Aqaba. United Nations Emergency Forces (UNEF) were stationed in the Sinai to serve as buffers between Israel and Egypt; Israel warned that Egyptian re-imposition of the blockade of the Tiran Straits from the Sinai promontory of Sharm el-Sheikh would be a *casus belli*—that is, a legitimate cause for war.

    The Suez crisis was the last Middle Eastern war in which European powers strove to retain or reassert an imperial presence. Henceforth the Arab–Israeli conflict involved only regional forces, although the US and the Soviets, along with European countries, were heavily involved in supplying arms to Arab states and Israel.

The 1967 war, Arab nationalist rivalries, and the re-emergence of the Palestinian factor

In contrast to the Suez crisis, the preliminaries to the 1967 Arab–Israeli War directly involved Palestinian factions: Palestinians served competing Arab state interests, while seeking to define their own objectives. The war's aftermath introduced a new stage in the Arab–Israeli conflict, the territorial ramifications of which remain unresolved into the twenty-first century.

Arab rivalries

The 1967 war stemmed as much from Arab nationalist debates and rivalries as from direct Arab–Israeli hostilities.

    Following its secession from the United Arab Republic (1958–61), Syria impugned Nasser's Arab nationalist credentials by accusing him of evading further confrontations with Israel. These charges and counter-charges became a staple of Egyptian–Syrian–Iraqi invective, as did similar accusations hurled by Jordan's King Hussein; both leftist and conservative governments used the same propaganda. The symbols of Nasser's supposed fear of challenging Israel were the UNEF forces stationed in the Sinai since the Suez war of 1956. Syria especially accused Egypt of hiding behind the UNEF because of Syrian–Israeli confrontations in 1963 over Syrian development of a water diversion system that Israel had attacked and destroyed.

    Palestinians and a concern for the Palestinian question became embroiled in these inter-Arab disputes. At an LAS meeting in Cairo in January 1964 called to discuss Syrian–Israeli clashes, Egypt's Nasser agreed to back the formation of an official organization that represented the Palestinians, the PLO. Nasser intended to use the PLO to focus Palestinian attention on political concerns under Egyptian control. Egyptian sponsorship of PLO activities would counter Syrian charges of ignoring the Palestinians, while defusing Syrian calls for war with Israel.

Syria continued to incite tensions with Israel, if only to bolster its own Baathist image as the leader of Arab nationalism. With Egypt controlling the PLO, Syria turned to a small, revolutionary group, Fatah. Founded in 1959 in Kuwait by young Palestinians who included Yasser Arafat, Fatah rejected the PLO as a tool of Egypt. Dedicated to Israel's destruction, in 1965 Fatah began undertaking raids into Israel, sponsored by Syria but frequently launched from Jordan. These incursions and Israeli reprisals inflamed Arab–Israeli and inter-Arab tensions, especially once Syria became directly involved in skirmishes with Israel in early 1967.

The 1967 war

In May, Israel threatened Syria with possible retaliatory strikes, leading the Soviets to warn Nasser, falsely, that Israel had massed forces on the Syrian border. Eager to boost his anti-Israeli image, Nasser sent Egyptian troops into the Sinai Peninsula on 14 May 1967. They ousted UNEF forces from the Sinai, including Sharm el-Sheikh overlooking the Straits of Tiran, and, in response to taunts from Jordan and Syria, reimposed a blockade of those straits to Israeli shipping. Nasser thus recreated the circumstances that had been in place prior to the Suez war of 1956. Egypt's actions, motivated primarily to prove its nationalist credentials against Syrian claims, established the *casus belli* for Israel that it had proclaimed in 1957. Jordan then allied itself with Egypt along with Syria, Jordan's enemy.

Israel attacked Egypt on 5 June 1967 after being informed by the US that an Egyptian envoy would arrive in the US on 7 June to seek terms for resolving the crisis peacefully (Schwar 2004). With the entrance of Jordan and Syria into the war, Israel conquered and occupied the West Bank and the Golan Heights, in addition to the Gaza Strip and the Sinai Peninsula. Israel immediately annexed East Jerusalem, with its religious sites holy to Judaism, Islam, and Christianity, and declared that unified Jerusalem would remain forever the capital of the Israeli state. Hundreds of thousands of West Bank and Gaza Palestinians now fell under Israeli rule.

The 1967 war and its legacy: UN Security Council Resolution 242

The consequences of the 1967 war have defined the parameters of negotiations to resolve the Arab–Israeli conflict ever since. Israel declared that it would return territories in exchange for full peace agreements, the extent of the lands involved left undefined. Arab countries meeting at Khartoum, Sudan, in August 1967 issued a document that called for full Israeli withdrawal, but without entering negotiations with that country. Still, the Khartoum Declaration was seen as presenting diplomatic opportunities, especially since Egypt's Nasser sided with Jordan's King Hussein in seeking international intervention via the United Nations. Syrian refusal to consider negotiations was consistent with Syrian hostility towards Israel prior to the war, as was Palestinian rejection of talks. For the Palestinians, however, the situation was more complicated. If Arab states were to recognize Israel, Israel would have had to accept the refugee status for Palestinians as a result of the 1948 wars—a condition in which there was no Palestinian political entity.

Palestinians sought to regain all of pre-1967 Israel or former Palestine, a position proclaimed in the modified 1968 PLO Charter, which referred to the attainment of this goal by 'armed struggle'. Palestinian groups and the PLO, with Arafat as its head from 1969 onward, constantly opposed international efforts to resolve the results of the 1967 war unless the Palestinian political objective—self-determination—was considered. This explains their attempts to undermine, or later modify, the document considered the basis of negotiations to resolve the changes brought about by that war: UN Security Council Resolution 242.

Passed by the United Nations in November 1967, Resolution 242 called for Arab–Israeli settlement of the consequences of the war based on exchanges of occupied land in return for peace. Its deliberate ambiguity led to conflicting interpretations at the Arab–Israeli state level, but none at all for the Palestinians.

Declaring its intent to achieve 'a just and lasting peace' for the region, the Resolution condemned 'the acquisition of territory by war' and called for all states 'to live in peace in secure and recognized boundaries'. Resolution 242's key statement was its clause stating that Israel should withdraw 'from territories occupied in the recent conflict'. This expression deliberately omitted the article 'the' before the word 'territories', owing to Israel's insistence that it should not be required to withdraw from *all* of the territories that it had occupied. Israel argued that the Resolution's statement that all states should live 'within secure and recognized boundaries' required that it retain some territories acquired in the war in order to establish those secure boundaries that it had lacked prior to the war.

Resolution 242 referred to the Palestinians solely as refugees whose condition would be resolved through Arab–Israeli state negotiations. As they had feared, the Palestinians were not considered to be a people with legitimate political aspirations. The PLO, from this time onwards, strove to block any settlement that enshrined the refugee status of the Palestinians, while working to modify Resolution 242 to permit Palestinian access to negotiations as a people with acknowledged political rights.

From the 1967 war to the Egyptian–Israeli peace treaty

In the aftermath of the 1967 war, Arab states worked to recover lands taken by Israel in that conflict by both military and diplomatic means. Their strategies differed according to their perceptions of their interests.

The war of attrition

Egypt undertook a war of attrition from 1968 to 1970, combating Israel across the Suez Canal. Although Israel was the victor militarily, its triumph was marred by significant casualties and ultimate setback. Its military advantage, especially air superiority, led Israel to bomb targets inside Egypt and not only on the canal—raids designed to humiliate Nasser and to cause his downfall. Instead, these attacks brought the Soviet Union more directly into the Arab–Israeli conflict. Nearly 15,000 Soviet troops and pilots were shifted to Egypt to bolster its defences.

This massive Soviet presence altered the Cold War equation in the Arab–Israeli conflict, but the Nixon administration still pursued its contradictory policy. Secretary of State William Rogers backed UN efforts to institute a ceasefire between Israel and Egypt, achieved in August 1970—a regionalist approach. National Security Adviser Henry Kissinger, with Nixon's approval and Israel's knowledge, strove to undermine Rogers's efforts. Their miscalculations led to the greatly enhanced Soviet presence in Egypt, stalemating the conflict and resulting in the ceasefire.

The Jordanian civil war, September 1970

For their part, the Palestinians were alarmed by the August 1970 ceasefire, fearing that it might lead to negotiations in which they would be excluded. Arafat, now head of the PLO, could not dominate that organization, challenged by groups such as the Popular Front for the Liberation of Palestine (PFLP) headed by George Habash and the Popular Democratic Front for the Liberation of Palestine (PDFLP) led by Nayif Hawatmah. Both called for the overthrow of conservative Arab regimes as a precondition for an assault on Israel, whereas Arafat and Fatah focused on Israel and endeavoured to distance the PLO from Arab state politics. Following the August 1970 ceasefire, the PFLP and PDFLP attempted to overthrow Jordan's King Hussein as the first step in creating a more radical Arab front that would challenge Israel. This led to the Jordanian civil war of September 1970, in which King Hussein's Jordanian army crushed Palestinian forces, with a major Arab–Israeli crisis barely averted.

The Palestinian–Jordanian clashes of August–September 1970 altered Arab state involvement in the Arab–Israeli conflict. The Palestinian defeat and subsequent losses in later engagements with Jordanian forces forced the PLO to move its command structure in 1971 from Jordan to Lebanon. From that time onward, PLO actions against Israel engaged Lebanon more directly in the Arab–Israeli conflict and became a major factor in instigating a Lebanese civil war in the mid-1970s.

The Jordanian civil war had another casualty: Egypt's Nasser died shortly after negotiating a ceasefire. He was succeeded by Anwar Sadat, who, from 1971 to 1973, sought unsuccessfully to negotiate an Israeli withdrawal from the Sinai via UN mediators, but failed to gain US backing for his efforts.

Nixon and Kissinger rejected Egyptian overtures, refusing to act while Soviet forces remained in Egypt. Then, when Sadat expelled them in July 1972—a Cold War victory for Washington—the US did not respond because Kissinger was diverted by scandals pertaining to Nixon's 1972 re-election campaign. US inaction contributed to the 1973 war.

The 1973 war and its consequences

With no diplomatic initiatives forthcoming, Egypt and Syria decided to attack Israeli forces in the Golan Heights and Sinai Peninsula. Expectations of continued diplomatic stalemate had been furthered when Israel declared it would annex a large area of the Sinai in defiance of Resolution 242. Minister of Defence Moshe Dayan proposed this plan as a condition of his remaining part of the Labour Party (formed in 1968) in forthcoming elections scheduled for November.

Egypt and Syria attacked Israel on 6 October 1973. Israeli forces fell back in the Golan Heights, but ultimately stopped the Syrians. Egyptian troops crossed the Suez Canal and overwhelmed the Israeli defences, advancing into the Sinai before being checked. Initial Egyptian successes were thwarted by Israeli counter-attacks that led to Israeli forces crossing the Canal and occupying its West Bank. Technically, Israel had won the war against Egypt, but Egyptian troops held out in pockets in the Sinai against fierce Israeli efforts to oust them and to restore the *status quo ante*.

Whereas the 1967 war had completely overturned the political–military parameters of the Arab–Israeli conflict existing since 1948, the 1973 war created a modified territorial framework within which the changes wrought by 1967 might be resolved. Henry Kissinger, now Secretary of State as well as Nixon's National Security Advisor, intervened to gain an Egyptian–Israeli ceasefire that left Egyptian forces in the Sinai, creating a situation that required negotiations. Kissinger now argued that limited agreements between Israel, Syria, and Egypt, with minor Israeli withdrawals from lands that it occupied, could create a climate of confidence and trust within which full peace treaties might ensue. He negotiated Israeli pullback accords in the Sinai and the Golan Heights with Egypt and Syria during 1974, pursuant to Security Council Resolution 338, passed on 22 October 1973, the last day of the war; it called for full implementation of Resolution 242.

Eager to pursue talks and to recover the Sinai, Sadat agreed to a second limited agreement with Israel in September 1975. For Arab leaders, the accord signalled Egypt's willingness to seek a separate agreement with Israel—anathema to them, but attractive to Israeli politicians, including Yitzhak Rabin, who had succeeded Golda Meir as prime minister in the summer of 1974.

Rabin, like most Israeli leaders, was primarily concerned with retaining the Golan Heights and the West Bank for Israel regardless of Resolution 242. From this perspective, a separate peace with Egypt would remove Egypt from the military equation of the Arab–Israeli conflict, enabling Israel to concentrate its forces against Syria and Jordan in order to impose its terms and to retain land. Here, Rabin was reassured by Kissinger that the US would not push for any limited withdrawal agreements between Israel and Jordan over the West Bank.

The American-sponsored peace efforts of 1974–75 and Israeli disinterest in any agreement with Jordan over the West Bank had important repercussions for Palestinians and the PLO within the framework of the Arab–Israeli conflict.

Jordan and the Rabat Declaration

Jordan's King Hussein had been humiliated by his exclusion from the pullback agreements of 1974—the product of Israel's refusal to negotiate over the West Bank. His inclusion would have reaffirmed Jordanian claims to the area, and undercut PLO calls for Palestinian self-determination and claims to represent all Palestinians.

Further humiliation awaited Hussein. In October 1974, Arab heads of state met in Rabat, Morocco, where they recognized 'the right of the Palestinian people to establish an independent national authority under the command of the Palestinian Liberation Organization, the sole legitimate representative of the Palestinian people, in any Palestinian territory that is liberated' (Cobban 1984: 60). The Rabat Declaration remains a landmark in the history of Palestinian efforts for self-determination within the framework of the

Arab–Israeli conflict. It declared that Hussein and Jordan had no right to represent Palestinian interests in any international forum. Hussein appeared to accept this decision, which acquired international recognition when Arafat spoke at the UN General Assembly in November 1974, and the PLO was awarded observer status over the strong objections of Israel and the US.

Henceforth, advocates of a diplomatic resolution of the Arab–Israeli conflict were divided. Most countries, including America's European allies, called for inclusion of the PLO and discussion of Palestinian political rights in any negotiations based on Resolution 242. In contrast, the US and Israel rejected PLO inclusion in talks, calling it a terrorist organization.

The Camp David talks and the Egyptian–Israeli peace accord

The election of Jimmy Carter as US president in November 1976 initiated a new approach to the Arab–Israeli conflict. Carter abandoned Kissinger's scheme of limited agreements and decided to seek a comprehensive Arab–Israeli accord, to be negotiated at an international conference that would include not only the Soviet Union, but also the Palestinians if the PLO could accept Resolution 242. In the end, Carter failed to achieve his objectives. The Camp David agreement of September 1978 between Egypt and Israel was a last-gasp effort to salvage something out of his search for a comprehensive peace.

Carter had overreached in seeking an international conference. Arab states had no common policy agenda and most suspected Sadat of seeking a separate arrangement with Israel. The PLO would not openly accept Resolution 242 unless the Palestinians' right to a state was acknowledged beforehand—a condition that Carter could not meet. Israel objected to an international conference, preferring US oversight of limited talks. Finally, Israeli opposition to negotiations involving territory or the Palestinians was now intransigent. Menachem Begin had succeeded Rabin as prime minister of Israel in June 1977. Leader of the right-wing Likud party and a pillar of Revisionist Zionism, he had continually advocated since 1948 the need for Israel to invade and capture the West Bank (Judaea and Samaria) to fulfil the Zionist goal of governing ancient Israel; the Likud coalition official platform (1977) rejected the idea of a Palestinian state, and stated that Israel would rule eternally over the land between the Mediterranean and the Jordan River.

Carter's difficulties convinced Sadat to approach Israel on its terms: those of a separate peace—an arrangement that would hopefully bring Western, especially US, economic aid to Egypt. On 9 November 1977, Sadat announced to the Egyptian National Assembly that he would go to Jerusalem in search of peace if invited, leading to his visit to that city the same month. The search for an Egyptian–Israeli peace had been set in motion.

The most tangible result of the Camp David accord was the Egyptian–Israeli peace treaty of March 1979, the first between an Arab state and Israel. Although a milestone in the history of the Arab–Israeli conflict, the Egyptian–Israeli treaty did not suggest progress towards resolution of the broader conflict through further negotiation. The LAS expelled Egypt and moved its headquarters from Cairo to Tunis.

Arab censure of Sadat focused on the conflicting interpretations of what Camp David had promised with respect to the Palestinians. The agreement referred to the 'legitimate rights of the Palestinian people' and Palestinian 'autonomy'. Begin interpreted these references to mean their non-political rights under Israeli sovereignty, whereas Carter and Sadat believed it meant political rights under Arab rule, probably Jordanian. Disputes also arose over the supposed moratorium on Israeli settlement-building after Camp David: Israel undertook such activity after three months; Sadat and Carter thought that they had an oral agreement for five years. From Begin's perspective, 'the Sinai had been sacrificed but Eretz Israel had been won', meaning that removing Egypt as a hostile neighbour would enable Israel to retain the West Bank and prove to the million Palestinians living there that they had no hope of true self-determination. Israel had already begun a massive settlement programme in the West Bank under Ariel Sharon's direction (Quandt 2005: 228–40).

The legacy of Camp David went beyond the achievement of an Egyptian–Israeli peace. The document's clauses for the West Bank envisaged a transition period of five years during which gradually implemented electoral and administrative procedures, including Israel's withdrawal from many areas, would lead to final status negotiations. Never attempted as part of the Camp David accord, this scheme would become the basis for the Oslo process following the first Oslo accord in 1993.

From Camp David to Oslo

With Egypt removed from Arab–Israeli hostilities, the conflict assumed new dimensions, which included state sponsorship of proxies—notably in Lebanon, that led to the Israeli invasion of that country in 1982.

Lebanon: civil war and foreign intervention

Lebanon had served as an unwilling base for PLO attacks into Israel since the later 1960s; hijackings of El Al planes by Palestinian factions based in Lebanon resulted in an Israeli assault on the Beirut airport in 1968. The shift of the PLO command from Jordan to camps outside Beirut in 1971 further destabilized an already-fragile Lebanese political structure and inspired the formation of Maronite Catholic militias independent of government control, as was the PLO. The Maronites in particular resented Lebanon being drawn into the Arab–Israeli conflict, but this confrontation became embroiled in local political tensions. Lebanese Muslim and leftist anger at Maronite political dominance, already expressed in the 1957–58 civil war, erupted again in the mid-1970s.

The clashes this time were far more destructive and involved state sponsors, Israel and Syria. In addition to arming and training the Maronites, Israel facilitated Maronite infiltration into southern Lebanon via Israel to seek to block Palestinian attacks. The Syrians briefly supported the Palestinians before allowing them to be crushed by the Israeli-backed Maronites, fearing that Palestinian dominance in Lebanon might lead to a Syrian confrontation with Israel. A truce in the civil war in 1976 permitted PLO groups to attack Israel again from the south, leading to a major Israeli invasion into southern Lebanon in March 1978 in response to a terrorist attack into Tel Aviv.

In the wake of Camp David and the Egyptian–Israeli peace treaty, Prime Minister Menachem Begin and his chief adviser, Ariel Sharon, reconsidered their strategy regarding the PLO. The treaty with Egypt seemed to ensure Israeli domination of the West Bank, but most West Bank Palestinians remained loyal to the PLO. Destruction of the PLO command in

Lebanon would relieve Israel of border strife and crush West Bank Palestinian hopes that they could escape Israeli rule.

Israeli ambitions meshed with those of Bashir Gemayel, leader of the Phalange, the premier Maronite militia; Gemayel had wiped out his leading Maronite rivals. He, like Begin and Sharon, hoped to oust, if not destroy, the PLO in Lebanon, with the goal of installing himself in power with Israeli assistance; this would ensure Maronite dominance of Lebanon despite their minority status and give Israel an ally on its northern border.

These calculations resulted in the Israeli invasion of Lebanon in June 1982, when Ariel Sharon misled the Israeli cabinet, which had been briefed for a limited incursion similar to that of 1978. The Israeli army encircled Beirut, where repeated assaults caused many civilian casualties, but did not destroy the Palestinian community or command. International intervention resulted in the PLO agreeing to leave Lebanon for Tunisia in August, with guarantees that the Palestinians who remained would be protected. Once the PLO left Lebanon, US military contingents were withdrawn. Almost simultaneously, Bashir Gemayel was assassinated. As a result, the Israeli army permitted Maronite Phalangists to enter the Sabra and Shatila refugee camps, where over a thousand Palestinians were slaughtered.

These massacres brought the return of US forces, which became increasingly caught up in Lebanese factional disputes. In 1983, the Reagan administration called for naval bombardments of Druze positions, over the strong objections of the marine commander in Beirut. Opposition forces retaliated with the suicide bombing of the marine barracks in October, causing 241 deaths. After a further show of force, Reagan ordered the withdrawal of US troops in early 1984, leaving Lebanon to its regional competitors.

The 1982 Israeli invasion of Lebanon proved, in retrospect, to be an undertaking the short-term triumphs of which masked long-term liabilities—in particular, the incitement of Lebanese Shia hostility towards Israel. The Lebanese–Israeli frontier remained a zone of conflict—notably, an enclave in southern Lebanon where Israel retained control. There, the Iranian-backed Hezbollah, formed in response to the Israeli invasion, engaged Israeli troops and client forces in a war of attrition that ultimately ended with Israel voluntarily withdrawing from most of the enclave in May 2000.

Israel and the intifada

These difficulties did not deter Israeli Likud prime ministers of the 1980s, Menachem Begin and later Yitzhak Shamir, from pursuing the real goal of the Lebanese venture: consolidation of the Israeli position in the West Bank. The decade saw the vast expansion of Israeli settlements in the area. Arab–Israeli state tensions were muted, with Egypt sidelined, Iraq involved in a protracted and costly war with Iran (1980–88), and Syria monitoring its position in Lebanon. Jordan sought entry into negotiations with US support and that of Labour politicians in Israeli coalitions, continually stymied by Likud objections. No major change in the diplomacy of the Arab–Israeli conflict occurred until December 1988, when the US agreed to talk to the PLO, declaring that it had satisfactorily renounced terrorism and accepted Security Council Resolution 242.

Taken with more reluctance than enthusiasm, the US decision appeared to be a major stepping stone towards resolution of issues within the framework of the broader Arab-Israeli conflict. However, the impetus for recognition lay not in diplomacy, but in the actions of Palestinians in the West Bank and especially in the Gaza Strip, who had rebelled against Israeli occupation. The rebellion, known as the intifada, began in December 1987 and lasted into 1991. The intensity of Palestinian protests and the brutality of the Israeli response focused international attention on the nature of Israel's role as occupiers of these lands, and called into question the future of the territories. In addition, the intifada gave legitimacy, if only indirectly, to PLO claims to represent the Palestinians in the territories. Still, US agreement to discuss matters with Arafat did not mean a willingness to negotiate with him; the Jordanian solution remained the favoured option. Matters remained stalemated, with Likud, guided by Yitzhak Shamir, ever more determined to resist pressures to compromise, despite US pressures to do so.

The Gulf War, 1990–91

The catalyst for an apparent breakthrough toward resolution of Arab–Israeli matters was a factor indirectly related to the conflict: the decision of Saddam Hussein to invade Kuwait in August 1990 and the counter-decision of President George H. W. Bush to forge a military coalition that included Arab armies to drive Iraqi forces out of that country. These developments, coupled with the disintegration of the Soviet Union, removed the Cold War justification of US–Soviet rivalry for control of Arab–Israeli negotiations. Arab states such as Syria, long a recipient of Soviet aid, but a foe of Iraq, now had incentives to join an American-led force. These incentives were not limited to defeat of an Arab rival; they included US promises to seek to broaden Arab–Israeli negotiations at the conclusion of the war and to confront more directly the militancy of Yitzhak Shamir.

The Madrid Conference

Herein lay the basic irony of the Gulf War: the ultimate, although not immediate, beneficiary of the Gulf War was to be Arafat, and with him the PLO, despite the fact that he had sided with Saddam against the US-led coalition and had, as a result, lost his funding from Saudi Arabia and Kuwait, his principal sources of revenue.

With the end of the Gulf War, Washington pressured Israel in order to fulfil US promises made to Arab leaders to gain their inclusion in the coalition against Saddam Hussein. Secretary of State James Baker's efforts resulted in an international conference in Madrid, convened in October 1991 attended by Syria, Jordan, and Lebanon. In addition, the Palestinians, for the first time, participated in such a conference, although the PLO was excluded and the Palestinian contingent was officially part of the Jordanian delegation.

The Madrid talks included several rounds of negotiations, from October 1991 to the summer of 1993. Arab states and Israel negotiated directly for the first time, as did Israelis and Palestinians. No formal agreements resulted, although Israel and Jordan drafted a peace accord that would not be signed until October 1994, following the 1993 Oslo accord. Exchanges between other delegations led nowhere—especially those between Palestinian delegates, who demanded a Palestinian state, and their Israeli counterparts during a period of increasing violence in the territories and in Israel, undertaken by the Islamic groups, Hamas and Islamic Jihad. These attacks reflected anger at Israel's settlement expansion and at Arafat's failure to represent Palestinian interests. Although Arafat had benefited from the Gulf

War to the extent that Palestinians were invited to the Madrid talks, he remained isolated in Tunisia, trying to influence Palestinian resistance from afar, while Hamas and Islamic Jihad led armed resistance as the intifada lost momentum.

Yitzhak Rabin's election as Israeli prime minister in 1992 gave impetus to peace efforts. He and Foreign Minister Shimon Peres saw the Islamic-inspired violence as a greater threat to Israeli security than Arafat and the PLO. They decided to resurrect Arafat and instil a sense of hope among Palestinians to undermine the appeal of the Islamists, a decision that led to the historic Oslo accord of August–September 1993.

The Oslo peace process in retrospect

The two Oslo accords, of September 1993 and October 1995, treated more fully in **Chapter 13**, were hailed by many as signalling an ultimate resolution of a problem that had festered for nearly half a century. But the apparent successes in implementing the process concealed inherent problems concerned primarily with acceptance by key parties in the Palestinian and Israeli political spectrum.

Not only Hamas, but also many Palestinians identified with a peaceful resolution of the conflict condemned the first Oslo accord ('Oslo I') because Arafat recognized Israel's right to exist without acquiring Israeli recognition of Palestinian statehood in return. Delays in implementing specific clauses of Oslo I pertaining to the Israeli handover of responsibilities increased tensions, as did terrorist acts from both sides. Ironically, these tensions led Prime Minister Yitzhak Rabin, initially reluctant to enter the Oslo process, to resolve to establish firmer procedures that would lead to the final resolution of outstanding issues. The second Oslo accord ('Oslo II'), with its promise of greater Israeli handovers of land and increased Palestinian political and security responsibilities, seemed to presage a final accord with a Palestinian state on most of the West Bank: Israel would retain only heavily populated settlements close to the Green Line. Rightist Israeli condemnation was harsh and swift, especially since Rabin said that the settlers were a greater threat to Israel's security than the Palestinians. Likud rivals Ariel Sharon and Binyamin Netanyahu competed to condemn Oslo II and Rabin. Both participated in rallies during which posters portraying Rabin as a Nazi were prevalent. This vilification, accompanied by calls for Rabin's assassination from rabbis in Brooklyn, as well as the West Bank, led to his killing on 4 November 1995.

Rabin's death and the election of Netanyahu to succeed him in June 1996 promised Likud determination to block adherence to Oslo II's goals, frustrating Palestinian hopes. By the time Labour Party candidate Ehud Barak replaced Netanyahu in July 1999, Yasser Arafat's reputation among Palestinians had plummeted. He had bowed to US encouragement to proceed with the appearance of a process even as Israel took more Palestinian lands for settlements and bypass roads to be used exclusively by Israelis. And despite Barak's declared commitment to resurrect negotiations, the fragmentation of Israeli politics required him to include in his coalition parties opposed to peace; settlement growth initially proceeded at a faster pace under Barak than it had under Netanyahu.

In such circumstances of mistrust and political instability, all sides approached the Camp David 2000 talks unprepared, with rifts within every camp. But it was the US–Israeli version of Palestinian responsibility for the talks' failure that would resonate and influence opinion as the al-Aqsa intifada exploded at the end of September 2000. Triggered by Ariel Sharon's provocation in visiting the Temple Mount/al-Haram al-Sharif on 28 September, that uprising could also be seen as a condemnation of the Oslo process, which to Palestinians represented further loss of land and of the possibility of achieving statehood.

Palestine–Israel: 2000–15

Camp David 2000: talks and their repercussions–the George W. Bush administration

The dominant narrative explaining the failed Camp David 2000 talks and the eruption of the al-Aqsa intifada stressed Palestinian rejection of Ehud Barak's offers at Camp David and Palestinian incitement that required harsh Israeli retaliation. This narrative, initiated by President Bill Clinton, was adopted by his successor George W. Bush, and underwrote Bush's approach to Palestinian–Israeli matters, an approach that condoned further Israeli settlement expansion.

Yet testimonies given by participants from all three delegations, Israeli, American, and Palestinian, challenge this narrative (Pressman 2003; Swisher 2004; Bregman 2005). Indeed, in the case of chief US negotiator Dennis Ross, he admitted to a European audience that both Israel and the Palestinians were responsible for the failure of the Oslo peace process, and specifically noted the doubling of Israeli settlements between 1993 and 2000 as causing justified Palestinian mistrust of Israeli motives. But, for a US audience, Ross withheld any mention of Israeli settlement growth from 1993 onwards in his own memoir of the period (Ross 2004; cf. Malley and Agha 2001; Enderlin 2003: 360–1; Swisher 2004: 362).

Similarly, whereas most reports cited Palestinian incitement, official records indicated that Palestinians initially demonstrated with rocks and tyre burnings, as in the first intifada, while Israeli troops filed live ammunition from the outset and fired rubber bullets to make them more lethal. With the advent of Ariel Sharon's government in March 2001, Palestinian suicide bombings reappeared and penetrated into Israel itself. One at a Passover seder in April 2002 led to Sharon ordering the retaking of all lands granted to the Palestinians during the Oslo process; the headquarters of the Palestinian Authority were destroyed and Yasser Arafat isolated in its ruins, essentially under Israeli supervision. The Bush administration's refusal to deal with Arafat led to Mahmoud Abbas becoming de facto head of the Palestinian Authority; he succeeded Arafat as president on the latter's death in November 2004.

In the meantime, Sharon ordered the construction of a security barrier in the West Bank, often 20 feet high. Justified to halt suicide bombings, its political intent was to incorporate most large settlements under Israeli control. It also cut through Palestinian towns, such as Bethlehem, and blocked tens of thousands of Palestinians from their fields or places of work. Announced as a temporary measure, its cost has exceeded US$1 billion and it will likely remain in place as an obstacle to any Palestinian acceptance of a peace agreement. Then, in April 2004, Sharon gained US approval for a unilateral withdrawal from the eight Israeli settlements in Gaza. His goal was to block any further peace talks on the West Bank.[1] President Bush in return promised that any future peace agreement would have to take account of 'new realities'—that is, large Israeli centres of population well within the West Bank, not just adjacent to the 1967 border, would become Israeli in any Palestinian peace accord. A controversial agreement contradicted by Bush's further statement that any Palestinian state should have territorial contiguity, Bush's 'new realities' phrase remains a staple of Prime Minister Netanyahu's rhetoric (Smith 2016: 512–13).

Israel withdrew from Gaza in August 2005, but retained leverage over the area and its Palestinian residents by encircling the Gaza Strip with a 15-foot wall, imposing naval surveillance of the coast, and restricting goods entering the Gaza Strip. These measures contributed to Hamas' stunning electoral victory in the January 2006 Palestinian Authority elections, placing Hamas's Ismail Haniya as prime minister under Fatah's Mahmoud Abbas, who remained president of the PA. Although the US had insisted on Hamas's participation in the elections to demonstrate its commitment to democracy, the Bush administration condemned the results, and joined Israel in furthering the military and economic blockade of Gaza. When news emerged that the two countries were funding new Fatah battalions to enter Gaza and crush the Hamas military, Hamas pre-empted by taking over all government functions and defeating those Fatah military cadres that remained. This would lead to a devastating Israeli attack on Gaza in December 2008, as much a result of Israeli domestic politics, with an upcoming election, as of any presumed Hamas violation of ceasefires.

Obama, Netanyahu, and the Arab Spring: stalemate?

Barack Obama took office as US president in January 2009; Netanyahu regained the Israeli premiership in March. The Obama administration consistently sought to advance Israeli–Palestinian peace talks based, for negotiating purposes, on the 1967 borders. Netanyahu consistently rejected this idea and proposals that he halt West Bank settlement expansion. Secretary of State Hillary Clinton appeared to gain a partial success when Netanyahu agreed to freeze new settlement construction for ten months in the West Bank, but not East Jerusalem; nonetheless, 2,400 units were constructed in the West Bank. Her successor, John Kerry, was equally unsuccessful.

Netanyahu's stance against the Obama administration was encouraged by the US Congress. Former House Majority Whip Eric Canter (Republican) told Netanyahu in 2010 that the House of Representatives 'would serve as a check on the administrations', referring to peace efforts where settlements would be abandoned (Cooper 2011) and he received repeated standing ovations when he addressed Congress in April 2011. Congress gave him a similar though more controversial welcome in March 2015 when he openly opposed US policy on Iranian nuclear development as the guest of the Republican members of Congress who had not informed the president of the invitation beforehand, introducing a new level of partisanship regarding Israel and US foreign policy with major implications for future elections. Domestic politics forced Obama to side with Israel in September 2011, when PA President Mahmoud Abbas sought UN Security Council recognition of a Palestinian state. The US blocked the measure, which had the backing of all other members. Similarly, when the UN Human Rights Council voted to undertake an inquiry on Israeli settlements and their impact on Palestinians in March 2012, the US was the only state to vote 'no', although some members abstained. The American stance on negotiations has, in turn, forced the PA to reconsider its reliance on US sponsorship of peace talks particularly given that daily existence for most Palestinians, especially in Gaza, has worsened considerably.

Palestinian Options: the 2014 Gaza War and Israel's March 2015 elections

From the Palestinian perspective, continued reliance on American oversight of the peace process with Israel, despite the efforts of Secretaries of State Hilary Clinton and John Kerry, has resulted in a stalemate at the same time that Israeli settlement expansion has intensified. The only progress has been in increased cooperation between PA security forces, trained by US advisers, and the Israeli military, employed primarily to block Palestinian attacks on Israelis that often occur in protest of that settlement growth. Once the latest round of American-sponsored talks collapsed at the end of April 2014, a process began where Palestinian politics and clashes with Israel interacted.

In April 2014, the PA and Hamas reached another accord to form a unity government—several past efforts had failed. Israel immediately suspended peace talks with the PA, a week before the deadline for negotiations to end, demanding it nullify the agreement. Then two Palestinian teenagers were killed by Israeli police on 14 May during demonstrations against commemoration of Israeli independence day—Palestinians call it 'Nakba remembrance day'. Massive Palestinian demonstrations followed and, on 12 June, three Israeli teenagers were kidnapped in the West Bank. Netanyahu immediately condemned Hamas for the abductions and ordered the arrests of hundreds of West Bank Palestinians while PA security forces helped Israelis search for the youths. With the bodies found on 30 June, Netanyahu ordered airstrikes on Gaza the next day, setting in motion further strikes following rockets fired from Gaza into Israel along with Palestinian anger as three Israelis confessed to burning alive a Palestinian teenager as revenge for the deaths of the three young Israelis. These developments led to the Gaza war of Summer 2014, officially dated 8 July—26 August, that devastated much of the Gaza Strip and killed over 2,200 Palestinians, at least two-thirds of them civilians; there were 72 Israelis killed, 66 of them soldiers. Israel used four times the artillery shells fired in the 2008 war while Hamas fired at least 3,000 rockets, less than 10 per cent of which struck Israeli residential areas. Gaza's isolation intensified as Israeli strikes and incursions destroyed many tunnels used for smuggling goods and Egypt, under General Abdel Fattah al-Sisi, imposed a blockade on Gaza's eastern side similar to that applied by Israel. Little if any reconstruction has occurred in Gaza as of spring 2015.

This sequence of events weakened Hamas militarily but did not boost Mahmoud Abbas's popularity among West Bankers. Apparently losing faith in American sponsorship of peace talks, at the end of 2014 he made a failed attempt to have the United Nations Security Council pass a motion calling for a peace pact with Israel within one year and Israel's withdrawal to the 1967 borders within three years, steps that would have signalled UN backing for a Palestinian state. The Obama administration would have vetoed the motion if it had had sufficient support. The next day Abbas applied for Palestinian membership on the International Criminal Court, a move whose legal and political ramifications are unclear.

The PA's perception of the futility of further American-backed negotiations appeared justified by the results of Israel's March 2015 elections where Netanyahu and Likud gained the most seats in parliament and he was asked to form a coalition government. Netanyahu had declared at the end of his campaign that he opposed a Palestinian state and rejected the formula of a two-state solution. Although he and his aides later sought to depict these comments as electoral strategies, they matched the policies set down in the Likud Party platform and appeared to confirm the overall strategy of Netanyahu' tenure in office. Attention to the implications of these statements was short-lived as Israel and its American allies in and outside of Congress focused on blocking a Great Power agreement with Iran on its nuclear programme. However, Netanyahu's freedom of action was short-lived. Having withheld payment of tax revenues to the PA since January because of Abbas's application for Palestinian membership on the International Criminal Court, he was forced to back down and hand over the funds after warnings from the Israeli military of an imminent Palestinian uprising.

Palestinians in both Gaza and the West Bank face uncertain futures. Gaza residents still confront the destruction wrought by the summer 2014 war and the near total enclosure of the Gaza Strip enforced by Egypt as well as Israel; no serious reconstruction has been undertaken in the aftermath of the war. For West Bank Palestinians, Netanyahu's electoral remarks confirm fears that American oversight of the peace process has failed because of the realities of settler presence in the West Bank and American domestic politics. Many Israelis, on the other hand, appear to accept the idea that retention of the West Bank offers more security than a peace accord. Lacking political options, Palestinians are faced with ongoing Israeli dominance at a time when international attention is focused on regional strife. In such circumstances, violence for many may become the only option.

Conclusion

These developments occur at a time when the attention of the Great Powers as well as most Middle Eastern states is focused elsewhere, on the ongoing civil strife in Syria, Iraqi attempts to oust IS militias from major urban areas in the north, especially Mosul, and the potential collapse of the Yemeni state that has led the Arab League to form a military coalition of Sunni forces to defeat a Yemeni uprising by the former Shi'i rulers of the country. These events have created unforeseen alliances that mitigate against any great attention being paid to the Arab–Israeli conflict. Israel and Saudi Arabia have had a tacit accord to back radical Sunni opponents of the Asad regime in Syria, an anti-Iran ploy that has been at least temporarily stymied by the growth of IS which both countries oppose. At the same time, the United States, hitherto leader in imposing sanctions on Iran, tolerates Iran's role in Iraq's war against IS, to the dismay of Saudi Arabia, still in principle a major American ally but one whose vision of the Middle East for the moment differs sharply from that of Washington; the 2002 Saudi-sponsored peace proposal to Israel has been set aside.

The first two decades of the Arab–Israeli conflict, often marked by armed hostilities, were notable for Arab refusal to recognize Israel's existence. Since the 1967 war, Arab states, notably Syria and Saudi Arabia, have displayed willingness to recognize Israel, and two, Egypt and Jordan, have signed peace treaties; Yasser Arafat recognized Israel's right to exist in the 1993 Oslo agreement.

This recognition has been premised on a two-state solution to the Palestinian–Israeli question, with Israel ceding the Gaza Strip and most of the West Bank. Revisionist Zionism rejects that notion as both Ariel Sharon and Netanyahu have ignored Arab state peace initiatives and opposed proposals that would require abandoning most of the West Bank along with seeking to undermine any Palestinian unity government (Podeh 2014). These developments suggest that the resolution of the Arab–Israeli conflict is now affected more by Israeli state militancy than by Arab, as was formerly the case. Likud expansionism to achieve ful-filment of its identity as a true Jewish state, with the apparent tolerance of many American politicians embraces ideological perspectives requiring the subjugation of neighbours as well as inclusion of West Bank Palestinians whose presence would appear to contradict the very idea of a Jewish state (see **Chapter 16**).

In this regard, most Arab states have adopted a realist approach to the Arab–Israeli con-flict, seeking coexistence based in part on acceptance of Israel's military supremacy. In contrast, Israel appears to insist on security through regional domination, coupled with re-tention of the West Bank as Greater Israel. Here, one finds no homogeneity of state interests, as realist theory sometimes assumes, but rather an assertion of identity based both on power and on claims to historic territory, the West Bank.

As a result of the Arab Spring and its fallout, with Egypt labelling Hamas a terrorist or-ganization as does Israel and the US, the Palestinian question is for the moment no longer central to relations between Israel and many Sunni Arab states with whom it has no diplo-matic relations. Indeed, the Middle East as a region has seen state alignments develop along the lines of religious identity, Sunni vs Shia, allowing Israel to tacitly ally itself with Sunni states against Syria and Iran, abandoning the Arab–Israeli dichotomy of the past.

Given this fluid regional situation, the Arab–Israeli conflict, as a state to state interaction, has achieved stasis, leaving the field to non-state actors such as Hezbollah. Any challenges to Israel from within the region in the near future will likely be military, not diplomatic, and would likely come from non-state organizations, whether Shia Hezbollah or Sunni jihad-ist groups if the latter survive the combined efforts of Western and regional governments to destroy them. Regional dynamics have been nearly totally transformed since the Arab Spring, placing the Arab–Israeli conflict in limbo and creating the possibility that European states may abandon acceptance of American leadership to resolve the issue and unilaterally recognize a Palestinian state, leaving the US isolated with Israel.

Key events

1948	May	Declaration of State of Israel
	May–July	First Arab–Israeli War: Arab states attack Israel
1956	October	Suez crisis: Israel, France, and Britain attack Egypt
1964		Formation of Palestine Liberation Organization (PLO)
1967	June	Six-Day War: Israel defeats Egypt, Jordan, and Syria, and occupies Sinai Peninsula, Golan Heights, Gaza Strip, and West Bank
1973	October	October War: Egypt and Syria attack Israel in the Golan Heights and Sinai Peninsula
1978–79		Camp David talks establish basis for an Egyptian–Israeli peace treaty
1987	December	Outbreak of first Palestinian intifada
1991	February–March	Gulf War
	October	Madrid Conference

1993	September	First Oslo accord (Oslo I)
1994	October	Israel–Jordan peace treaty
1995	September	Second Oslo accord (Oslo II)
	November	Yitzhak Rabin assassinated
	December	Israeli forces withdraw from areas outlined in Oslo II
1996	January	Palestinian Self-Governing Authority (Council) elected
	May	Binyamin Netanyahu elected Israeli prime minister
1997	January	Hebron redeployment agreement
1998	October	Wye Memorandum between Israel and Palestinians
	December	Palestinian National Council removes clauses from Palestine National Charter calling for Israel's destruction
1999	February	Jordan's King Hussein dies; succeeded by his son, Abdullah II
	May	Ehud Barak elected prime minister
2000	January–March	Syrian–Israeli peace talks end in failure
	June	Syrian President Hafiz al-Asad dies; succeeded by son, Bashar
	July	Camp David Israeli–Palestinian summit (final status talks)
	September	Ariel Sharon visits Temple Mount/al-Haram al-Sharif; triggers second intifada
	November	George W. Bush elected US president
2000–01		Israeli–Palestinian talks, building on Camp David
2001	February	Likud candidate Ariel Sharon elected prime minister
	September	9/11: Al-Qaeda terrorist attacks on the US
	October	US initiates attacks on Afghanistan in response to 9/11
2002	February	Israel rejects Saudi Arabian peace initiative
2003	January	Ariel Sharon re-elected prime minister; construction of Israeli 'security fence'
	March	US invades Iraq; Yasser Arafat appoints Mahmoud Abbas prime minister of new Palestinian Authority
	April	'Road Map' issued
2004	April	President Bush supports Ariel Sharon's proposal for full disengagement from Gaza, and appears to approve Israel's retention of major settlement blocs within the West Bank
	November	Death of Yasser Arafat

2005	January	Mahmoud Abbas elected Palestinian Authority president
	March	Secretary of State Condoleezza Rice calls for 'free and fair' Palestinian elections; Sasson Report documents official Israeli backing for settlement expansion; Hamas declares that it will enter Palestinian Legislative Council (PLC) elections
	August	Israel withdraws from all Gaza settlements and four settlements in northern West Bank
2006	January	Sharon incapacitated; Ehud Olmert succeeds him as acting prime minister; Hamas wins PLC elections; Ismail Haniya becomes PA prime minister in Gaza, while Mahmoud Abbas remains PA president in the West Bank; Olmert declares no negotiation with Hamas until it disarms and accepts Israel's existence and existing Israeli–PLO accords
	February	US rejects Palestinian election outcome and boycotts Hamas government; Quartet follows suit
	April	Olmert elected Israeli prime minister
	July–August	Major Israel–Hezbollah clashes in Lebanon
	September–October	Hamas–Fatah clashes in Gaza and West Bank
2007	June	Hamas forces take over Gaza; Israel imposes blockade
	November	Annapolis (Maryland) Conference: Bush, Olmert, and Abbas issue 'Joint Understanding'
2008	June	Israel and Hamas agree to a tentative, renewable sixty-day truce, arranged via Egyptian mediation
	June–July	Israel enters peace talks with Syria, sponsored by Turkey
	December	Israeli assault on Gaza
2009	January	Barack Obama assumes US presidency
	March	Binyamin Netanyahu becomes prime minister of Israel
	June	Barack Obama's speech at Cairo University, calling for Arab–Israeli peace based on the 2002 LAS peace plan and a halt to Israeli settlement-building
2010	December	Uprisings in Tunisia mark start of Arab Spring
2011	April	Obama declares US support for Palestinian–Israeli peace based on the 1967 borders; Netanyahu rejects Obama's conditions
	September	Obama blocks vote on UN Security Council measure calling for UN recognition of a Palestinian state; Netanyahu describes Obama's speech as 'heroic'

2012–14		Ongoing unsuccessful efforts by the Obama administration to achieve Palestinian–Israeli peace talks leading to a final settlement.
2012	June	Muslim Brotherhood candidate Muhammad al-Mursi elected President of Egypt. Seeks Hamas–PA reconciliation.
	August	General Abdel Fattah al-Sisi appointed Egyptian Minister of Defence.
2013	July	Muhammad al-Mursi ousted as Egyptian president by army
	November	Israeli–Hamas strife in Gaza
2014	June	Al-Sisi elected Egyptian president. Declares Muslim Brotherhood and Hamas terrorist organizations.
	July–August	New Gaza war destroys much of Gaza Strip infrastructure
2015	January	US Speaker of the House of Representatives John Boehner collaborates with Israel's ambassador to Washington to invite Netanyahu to speak to Congress, opposing possible agreement on Iran's nuclear capabilities without informing the White House in advance.
	March	Netanyahu reelected prime minister of Israel after disavowing support for a Palestinian state.

Further reading

Judis, John (2014) *Genesis: Truman, American Jews, and the Origins of the Arab–Israeli Conflict* (New York: Farrar, Strauss, and Giroux)
The latest and best study of American Zionism and Truman administration policies leading to the creation of Israel.

Kurtzer, D. and Scott, B. L. (2008) *Negotiating Arab–Israel Peace: American Leadership in the Middle East* (Washington, DC: United States Institute of Peace Press)
A forceful critique of US policy to the Arab–Israeli conflict and its resolution. Kurtzer was a former ambassador to Egypt and Israel.

Raz, Avi (2012) *The Bride and the Dowry: Israel, Jordan and the Palestinians in the Aftermath of the 1967 War* (New Haven: Yale University Press)
A carefully researched analysis of Israeli–Jordanian interactions following the 1967 War where Israel manoeuvred to retain control of the West Bank.

Robinson, Shira (2013) *Citizen Strangers: Palestinians and the Birth of Israel's Liberal Settler State* (Stanford: Stanford University Press)
The best study of Israel's policies toward its Palestinian Arab citizens after Israeli independence in 1948.

Roy, Sara (2013) *Hamas and Civil Society in Gaza: Engaging the Islamist Social Sector* (Princeton, NJ: Princeton University Press).
Excellent analysis of the socio-political reality of life in Gaza and Hamas's role in that society by the foremost scholar of Gaza.

Sayigh, Y. (1997) *Armed Struggle and the Search for State: The Palestinian National Movement, 1949–1993* (Oxford: Oxford University Press)
An important and detailed study of Palestinian nationalism, its politics, and factional disputes, and the difficulties of gaining acceptance in the international community as a non-state actor.

Shafir, G. and Peled, Y. (2002) *Being Israeli: The Dynamics of Multiple Citizenship* (Cambridge: Cambridge University Press)
A sophisticated and informative examination of the Israeli polity.

Shlaim, A. (2015) *The Iron Wall: Israel and the Arab World* (New York: W.W. Norton)
Expanded and updated, this is the basic study of Israel's attitudes and policies toward the Arab world.

Smith, C. D. (2016) *Palestine and the Arab–Israeli Conflict* (9th edn, Boston, MA: Bedford/St Martin's Press)
A comprehensive history.

Questions

1. How would you distinguish between the Palestinian–Israeli and Arab–Israeli conflicts? Have they always been and are they now interrelated?

2. How do the Palestinian Authority and Hamas differ in their goals? How have each been viewed by Israel and the international community?

3. What are the goals of Revisionist Zionism?

4. What is Security Council Resolution 242 and how is it interpreted?

5. How would you explain current regional Middle East conflicts, including the role, if any, that the Arab–Israeli conflict plays in these other disputes?

Note

1. Ari Shavit, 'The Big Freeze, Interview with Dov Weisglas', *Haaretz*, 8 October 2004. Weisglas, Sharon's chief aide, said that the Gaza withdrawal would put the peace process in 'formaldehyde'.

The Rise and Fall of the Oslo Peace Process

AVI SHLAIM

Overview

One of the salient strands in the international relations of the Middle East in the aftermath of the 1991 Gulf War was the US-sponsored peace process between Israel and the Arabs. On the Arab side, the principal participants were Syria, Jordan, and the Palestinians. This chapter focuses on the two principal parties to the Arab–Israeli conflict: Israel and the Palestinians. It traces the emergence, the development, and the breakdown of the peace negotiations between Israel and the Palestine Liberation Organization (PLO) from 1991 to 2001. The main landmarks in this process are the conclusion of the Oslo accord, the implementation of the accord, Oslo II, the Camp David summit, and the return to violence. The main conclusion is that the Oslo accord was not doomed to failure from the start; it failed because Israel, under the leadership of the Likud, reneged on its side of the deal.

Introduction

The Middle East is the most penetrated subsystem of the international political system. Ever since Napoleon's expeditionary force landed in Egypt in 1798, it has been an object of rivalry among the great powers. The strategic value of the Middle East was considerable as the gateway between Europe and the Far East. The discovery of oil, in the early part of the twentieth century, enhanced the region's importance for the global economy. After the Second World War, the Middle East became one of the major theatres of the Cold War. It was constantly caught up in superpower rivalry for political influence, power, and prestige. External sources of conflict combined with internal ones to produce frequent crises, violence, and wars. One of the most destabilizing factors in the affairs of the region is the dispute between Israel and the Arabs.

The Arab–Israeli conflict is one of the most bitter, protracted, and intractable conflicts of modern times. It is also one of the dominant themes in the international relations of the Middle East. There are two principal levels to this conflict: the interstate level and the Israeli–Palestinian level. In origin and in essence, this is a clash between the Jewish and Palestinian national movements over the land of Palestine. The Palestine problem therefore remains the core of the conflict. But the search for a settlement is complicated by inter-Arab relations and by the involvement of outside powers. The purpose of this chapter is to examine the peace process that got under way in the aftermath of the Gulf War, and, more specifically, the quest for a settlement between Israel and the Palestinians.

The Oslo peace process

The United States took the lead in convening an international conference to address the Arab–Israeli dispute following the expulsion of Iraq from Kuwait. The conference was held in Madrid at the end of October 1991. At the conference, the US adopted an even-handed approach and pledged to promote a settlement that would provide security for Israel and justice for the Palestinians. Negotiations were to be based on United Nations Security Council Resolution 242 of November 1967 and the principle of land for peace that it incorporated.

All of the parties to the conflict were invited to Madrid, but the Palestine Liberation Organization (PLO) was excluded on account of its support for Iraq following Saddam Hussein's invasion of Kuwait on 2 August 1990. The Palestinian delegation was made up of residents of the West Bank and the Gaza Strip, who went to Madrid not as an independent delegation, but as part of a joint delegation with Jordan. Jordan thus provided an umbrella for Palestinian participation in the peace talks. Although the PLO leadership in Tunis was formally banned from attending this major international gathering, the Palestinian negotiators kept in close contact with their colleagues in Tunis.

The Israeli delegation to Madrid was headed by Prime Minister Yitzhak Shamir, the leader of the right-wing Likud party. Whereas Labour is a pragmatic party committed to territorial compromise, the Likud is an ideological party committed to maintaining the West Bank as part of the ancestral lands of Israel. At Madrid, Shamir struck a tough and uncompromising posture. By arguing that the basic problem was not territory, but the Arab denial of Israel's very right to exist, he came close to rejecting the principle of swapping land for peace.

Two tracks for negotiations were established in Madrid: an Israeli–Arab track and an Israeli–Palestinian track. Stage two of the peace process consisted of bilateral negotiations between Israel and individual Arab parties. These bilateral talks were held under US auspices in Washington, starting in January 1992. Several rounds of negotiations were held in the US capital, but as long as the Likud remained in power, little progress was made on either track. It was only after Labour's victory over the Likud in June 1992 that the Israeli position began to be modified, at least on the Arab track. On the Palestinian issue, the Israeli position displayed more continuity than change following the rise of the Labour government under the leadership of Yitzhak Rabin. Consequently, the official talks between the Israeli and Palestinian delegations in Washington made painfully slow progress.

The road to Oslo

Stalemate in the official talks led both Israel and the PLO to seek a back channel for communicating. The decision to hold direct talks with the PLO was a diplomatic revolution in Israel's foreign policy and paved the way for the Oslo accord of 13 September 1993. Three men were primarily responsible for this decision: Yitzhak Rabin, Foreign Minister Shimon Peres, and Yossi Beilin, the youthful deputy foreign minister. Rabin held out against direct talks with the PLO for as long as he could. Peres took the view that, without the PLO, there could be no settlement. Expecting the PLO to enable the local Palestinian leaders to reach an agreement with Israel, he said on one occasion, was like expecting the turkey to help in preparing the Thanksgiving dinner. As long as Yasser Arafat, chairman of the PLO, remained in Tunis, Peres argued, he represented the 'outsiders'—the Palestinian diaspora—and he would do his best to slow down the peace talks (Peres 1995: 323–4).

Yossi Beilin was even more categorical in his view that talking to the PLO was a necessary condition for an agreement with the Palestinians. Beilin had always belonged to the extreme dovish wing of the Labour Party. He was the real architect behind the Israeli recognition of the PLO. Peres backed him all the way, and the two of them succeeded in carrying their hesitant and suspicious senior colleague with them.

The secret talks in Oslo got under way in late January 1993 with the active encouragement of Yossi Beilin, who kept Shimon Peres fully informed. Altogether, fourteen sessions of talks were held over an eight-month period, all behind a thick veil of secrecy. Norwegian Foreign Affairs Minister Johan Jørgen Holst and social scientist Terge Rød Larsen acted as generous hosts and facilitators. The key players were two Israeli academics, Dr Yair Hirschfeld and Dr Ron Pundik, and PLO Treasurer Ahmad Qurei, better known as Abu Ala. Away from the glare of publicity and political pressures, these three men worked imaginatively and indefatigably to establish the conceptual framework of the Israel–PLO accord. Their discussions ran parallel to the bilateral talks in Washington, but they proceeded without the knowledge of the official Israeli and Palestinian negotiators.

The unofficial talks dealt initially with economic cooperation, but quickly broadened into a dialogue about a joint declaration of principles. In May, Peres took a highly significant decision: he ordered Uri Savir, the director-general of the foreign ministry, and Yoel Singer, a high-flying attorney who had spent twenty years in the Israeli Defence Forces (IDF) legal department, to join Hirschfeld and Pundik on the weekend trips to Oslo. At this point, Peres began to report to Rabin regularly on developments in the Norwegian back channel. At first, Rabin showed little interest in this channel—but neither did he raise any objection to continuing the explorations. Gradually, however, he became more involved in the details and assumed an active role in directing the talks, alongside Peres. Since Abu Ala reported directly to Arafat, an indirect line of communication had been established between Jerusalem and the PLO headquarters in Tunis.

Another landmark in the progress of the talks was the failure of the tenth round of the official Israeli–Palestinian negotiations in Washington. To tempt the Palestinians to move forward, Peres floated the idea of 'Gaza first'. He believed that Arafat was desperate for a concrete achievement to bolster his sagging political fortunes and that Gaza would provide him with his first toehold in the occupied territories. Peres also knew that an Israeli withdrawal from Gaza would be greeted with sighs of relief among the great majority of his countrymen. Arafat, however, did not swallow the bait, suspecting an Israeli plan to confine the dream of Palestinian independence to the narrow strip of territory stretching from Gaza City to Rafah. The idea was attractive to some Palestinians, especially the inhabitants of the Gaza Strip, but not to the politicians in Tunis. Rather than reject the Israeli offer out of hand, Yasser Arafat came up with a counter offer of his own: Gaza and Jericho first. His choice of the small and sleepy West Bank town seemed quirky at first sight, but it served as a symbol of his claim to the whole of the West Bank.

Rabin did not balk at the counter-offer. All along, he had supported handing over Jericho to Jordanian rule, while keeping the Jordan Valley in Israeli hands. But he had one condition: the Palestinian foothold on the West Bank would be an island inside Israeli-controlled territory, with the Allenby Bridge also remaining in Israeli hands. Jordan, too, preferred Israel to the Palestinians at the other end of the bridge. Arafat therefore had to settle for the Israeli version of the 'Gaza and Jericho first' plan.

Rabin's conversion to the idea of a deal with the PLO was clinched by four evaluations that reached him between the end of May and July. First was the advice of Itamar Rabinovich, the head of the Israeli delegation to the talks with Syria, that a settlement with Syria was attainable, but only at the cost of complete Israeli withdrawal from the Golan Heights. Second were the reports from various quarters that the local Palestinian leadership had been finally neutralized. Third was the assessment of the IDF director of military intelligence that Arafat's dire situation, and possibly imminent collapse, made him the most convenient interlocutor for Israel at that particular juncture. Fourth were the reports of the impressive progress achieved through the Oslo channel. Other reports that reached Rabin during this period pointed to an alarming growth in the popular following of Hamas and Islamic Jihad in the occupied territories. Both the army chiefs and the internal security chiefs repeatedly stressed to him the urgency of finding a political solution to the crisis in the relations between Israel and the inhabitants of the occupied territories. Rabin therefore gave the green light to the Israeli team, and the secret diplomacy in Oslo moved into higher gear.

Rabin and Peres also believed that progress towards a settlement with the Palestinians would lower the price of a settlement with Syria by reducing the latter's bargaining power. Peres reduced the link between the two sets of negotiations to what he called 'the bicycle principle': when one presses on one pedal, the other pedal moves by itself. His formula was directed not at reaching a separate agreement with the Palestinians, but at gradual movement towards a settlement with the Palestinians, the Syrians, and the Jordanians.

On 23 August, Rabin stated publicly for the first time that 'there would be no escape from recognizing the PLO'. In private, he elaborated on the price that Israel could extract in exchange for this recognition. In his estimate, the PLO was 'on the ropes', and it was therefore highly probable that the PLO would drop some of its sacred principles to secure Israeli recognition. Accordingly, while endorsing the joint declaration of principles on Palestinian self-government in Gaza and Jericho, and mutual recognition between Israel and the PLO, he insisted on changes to the Palestinian National Charter as part of the package deal.

Peres flew to California to explain the accord to US Secretary of State Warren Christopher. Christopher was surprised by the scope of the accord and by the unorthodox method by which it had been achieved. He naturally assumed that the US had a monopoly over the peace process; his aides in the State Department had come to be called 'the peace processors'. Now, their feathers were ruffled, because they had been so thoroughly upstaged by the

Norwegians. All of the participants in the Oslo back channel, on the other hand, had the satisfaction of knowing that they had reached the accord on their own without any help from the US State Department. Their success showed that the fate of the peace process lay in the hands of the protagonists, rather than in the hands of the intermediaries.

The Oslo accord

The Declaration of Principles on Interim Self-Government Arrangements was essentially an agenda for negotiations, governed by a tight timetable, rather than a full-blown agreement. The Declaration laid down that, within two months of the signing ceremony, agreement on Israel's military withdrawal from Gaza and Jericho should be reached; within four months, the withdrawal should be completed. A Palestinian police force, made up mostly of pro-Arafat Palestinian fighters, was to be imported to maintain internal security in Gaza and Jericho, with Israel retaining overall responsibility for external security and foreign affairs. At the same time, elsewhere in the West Bank, Israel undertook to transfer power to 'authorized Palestinians' in five spheres: education, health, social welfare, direct taxation, and tourism. Within nine months, the Palestinians in the West Bank and Gaza were to hold elections to a Palestinian Council, to take office and assume responsibility for most government functions except defence and foreign affairs. Within two years, Israel and the Palestinians agreed to commence negotiations on the final status of the territories, and at the end of five years the permanent settlement was to come into force (Medzini 1995: 319–28). In short, the Declaration of Principles promised to set in motion a process that would end Israeli rule over the 2 million Palestinians living in the West Bank and Gaza.

The shape of the permanent settlement was not specified in the Declaration of Principles, but was left to negotiations between the two parties during the second stage. The Declaration was completely silent on vital issues such as the right of return of the 1948 refugees, the borders of the Palestinian entity, the future of the Jewish settlements on the West Bank and Gaza, and the status of Jerusalem. The reason for this silence is not hard to understand: if these issues had been addressed, there would have been no accord. Both sides took a calculated risk, realizing that a great deal would depend on the way in which the experiment in Palestinian self-government worked out in practice. Rabin was strongly opposed to an independent Palestinian state, but he favoured an eventual Jordanian–Palestinian confederation. Arafat was strongly committed to an independent Palestinian state, with East Jerusalem as its capital, but he did not rule out the idea of a confederation with Jordan.

Despite all of its limitations and ambiguities, the Declaration of Principles for Palestinian self-government in Gaza and Jericho marked a major breakthrough in the century-old conflict between Arabs and Jews in Palestine. On 13 September 1993, the Declaration was signed on the South Lawn of the White House, and sealed with the historic handshake between Prime Minister Rabin and Chairman Arafat.

The Oslo accord consisted of two parts, both of which were the product of secret diplomacy in the Norwegian capital. The first part consisted of mutual recognition between Israel and the PLO. It took the form of two letters, on plain paper and without letterheads, signed by Chairman Arafat and Prime Minister Rabin, respectively, on 9 and 10 September. Nearly all of the publicity focused on the signing of the Declaration of Principles, but without the mutual recognition there could have been no meaningful agreement on Palestinian self-government.

In his letter to Rabin, Arafat observed that the signing of the Declaration of Principles marked a new era in the history of the Middle East. He then confirmed the PLO's commitment to recognize Israel's right to live in peace and security, to accept UN Security Council Resolutions 242 and 338, to renounce the use of terrorism and other acts of violence, and to change those parts of the Palestinian National Charter that were inconsistent with these commitments. In his terse, one-sentence reply to Arafat, Rabin confirmed that, in the light of these commitments, the Government of Israel decided to recognize the PLO as the representative of the Palestinian people and to commence negotiations with the PLO within the Middle Eastern peace process.

Taken together, the two parts of the Oslo accord seemed, at the time, to merit the overworked epithet 'historic', because they reconciled the two principal parties to the Arab–Israeli conflict. The clash between Jewish and Palestinian nationalism had always been the heart and core of the Arab–Israeli conflict. Both national movements, Jewish and Palestinian, denied the other the right to self-determination in Palestine. Their history was one of mutual denial and mutual rejection; now, mutual denial made way for mutual recognition. Israel not only recognized the Palestinians as a people with political rights, but also formally recognized the PLO as its representative. The handshake between Rabin and Arafat at the signing ceremony, despite the former's awkward body language, was a powerful symbol of the historic reconciliation between the two nations.

The historic reconciliation was based on a historic compromise: acceptance of the principle of the partition of Palestine. Both sides accepted territorial compromise as the basis for the settlement of their long and bitter conflict. By accepting the principle of partition, the two sides suspended the ideological dispute as to who is the rightful owner of Palestine, and turned to finding a practical solution to the problem of sharing the cramped living space between the Jordan River and the Mediterranean. Each side resigned itself to parting with territory that it had previously regarded not only as its patrimony, but also as a vital part of its national identity. Each side was driven to this historic compromise by the recognition that it lacked the power to impose its own vision on the other side. That the idea of partition was finally accepted by the two sides seemed to support Abba Eban's observation that men and nations often behave wisely once they have exhausted all of the other alternatives (Eban 1993).

The breakthrough at Oslo was achieved by separating the interim settlement from the final settlement. In the past, the Palestinians had always refused to consider any interim agreement unless the principles of the permanent settlement were agreed in advance. Israel, on the other hand, had insisted that a five-year transition period should begin without a prior agreement about the nature of the permanent settlement. At Oslo, the PLO accepted the Israeli formula. In contrast to the official Palestinian position in Washington, the PLO agreed to a five-year transition period without clear commitments by Israel as to the nature of the permanent settlement (Beilin 1997: 152).

Reactions to Oslo

The Israeli–PLO accord had far-reaching implications for the interstate dimension of the Arab–Israeli conflict. Originally, the Arab states got involved in the Palestine conflict out of a sense of solidarity with the Palestine Arabs against the Zionist intruders. Continuing commitment to the Palestinian cause had precluded the Arab states, with the notable exception of Egypt, from extending recognition to the Jewish state. One of the main functions of the League of Arab States (LAS), which was established in 1945, was to assist the Palestinians in the struggle for Palestine. After 1948, the League became a forum for coordinating military policy and for waging political, economic, and ideological warfare against the Jewish state. In 1974, the LAS recognized the PLO as the sole legitimate representative of the Palestinian people. Now that the PLO had formally recognized Israel, there was no longer any compelling reason for the Arab states to continue to reject her.

Clearly, an important taboo had been broken. PLO recognition of Israel was an important landmark along the road to Arab recognition of Israel and the normalizing of relations with it. Egypt, which had been the first to take the plunge back in the late 1970s, felt vindicated and elated by the breakthrough. When Rabin stopped in Rabat on his way home after attending the signing ceremony in Washington, he was received like any other visiting head of state by King Hassan II of Morocco. Jordan allowed Israeli television the first ever live report by one of its correspondents from Amman. A number of Arab states, such as Tunisia and Saudi Arabia, started to think seriously about the establishment of diplomatic relations with Israel. And the LAS began discussions on the lifting of the economic boycott that had been in force since Israel's creation. Nothing was quite the same in the Arab world as a result of the Israel–PLO accord: the rules of the game in the entire Middle East had changed radically.

The change was no less marked in Israel's approach to its Arab opponents than in their approach to Israel. Zionist policy, before and after 1948, proceeded on the assumption that agreement on the partition of Palestine would be easier to achieve with the rulers of the neighbouring Arab states than with the Palestine Arabs. Israel's courting of conservative Arab leaders, such as King Hussein of Jordan and President Anwar Sadat of Egypt, was an attempt to bypass the local Arabs and to avoid having to address the core issue of the conflict. Recognition by the Arab states, it was hoped, would help to alleviate the conflict without conceding the right of national self-determination to the Palestinians. Now, this strategy was reversed: PLO recognition of Israel was expected to pave the way for wider recognition by the Arab states, from North Africa to the Persian Gulf. Rabin expressed this hope when signing the letter to Arafat in which Israel recognized the PLO: 'I believe', he said, 'that there is a great opportunity of changing not only the relations between the Palestinians and Israel, but to expand it to the solution of the conflict between Israel and the Arab countries and other Arab peoples' (*International Herald Tribune*, 11–12 September 1993).

On both sides of the Israeli–Palestinian divide, the Rabin–Arafat deal provoked strong and vociferous opposition on the part of the hardliners. Both leaders were accused of a betrayal and a sell-out. Leaders of the Likud, and of the nationalistic parties further to the right, attacked Rabin for his abrupt departure from the bipartisan policy of refusing to negotiate with the PLO and charged him with abandoning the 120,000 settlers in the occupied territories to the tender mercy of terrorists. The Gaza–Jericho plan was denounced as a bridgehead to a Palestinian state and the beginning of the end of Greater Israel. A Gallup poll, however, indicated considerable popular support for the prime minister. Of the 1,000 Israelis polled, 65 per cent said that they approved of the peace accord, with only 13 per cent describing themselves as 'very much against' (*The Guardian*, 16 September 1993).

Within the Palestinian camp, the accord also encountered loud, but ineffective, opposition. The PLO itself was split, with the radical nationalists accusing Arafat of abandoning principles to grab power. These included the Popular Front for the Liberation of Palestine, led by George Habash, and the Damascus-based Democratic Front for the Liberation of Palestine, led by Nayef Hawatmeh. Arafat succeeded in mustering the necessary majority in favour of the deal on the PLO's eighteen-member executive committee, but only after a bruising battle and the resignation of four of his colleagues. Outside the PLO, the deal aroused the implacable wrath of the militant resistance movements, Hamas and Islamic Jihad, which regarded any compromise with the Jewish state as anathema.

Opposition to the deal from rejectionist quarters, whether secular or religious, was only to be expected. More disturbing was the opposition of mainstream figures such as Farouk Kaddoumi, the PLO 'foreign minister', and prominent intellectuals such as Professor Edward Said and the poet Mahmoud Darwish. Some of the criticisms related to Arafat's autocratic, idiosyncratic, and secretive style of management; others related to the substance of the deal. The most basic criticism was that the deal negotiated by Arafat did not carry the promise, let alone a guarantee, of an independent Palestinian state.

This criticism took various forms. Farouk Kaddoumi argued that the deal compromised the basic national rights of the Palestinian people, as well as the individual rights of the 1948 refugees. Edward Said lambasted Arafat for unilaterally cancelling the intifada, for failing to coordinate his moves with the Arab states, and for introducing appalling disarray within the ranks of the PLO. 'The PLO', wrote Said, 'has transformed itself from a national liberation movement into a kind of small-town government, with the same handful of people still in command.' For the deal itself, Said had nothing but scorn. 'All secret deals between a very strong and a very weak partner necessarily involve concessions hidden in embarrassment by the latter', he wrote. 'The deal before us', he continued, 'smacks of the PLO leadership's exhaustion and isolation, and of Israel's shrewdness' (Said 1995: 2). 'Gaza and Jericho first ... and last' was Mahmoud Darwish's damning verdict on the deal.

Arab reactions to the Israeli–Palestinian accord were rather mixed. Arafat got a polite, but cool, reception from the nineteen foreign ministers of the LAS who met in Cairo a week after the signing ceremony in Washington. Some member states of the League, especially Jordan, Syria, and Lebanon, were dismayed by the PLO chairman's solo diplomacy, which violated Arab pledges to coordinate their negotiating strategy. Arafat defended his decision to sign the accord by presenting it as the first step towards a more comprehensive peace in the Middle East. The interim agreement, he said, was only the first step towards a final settlement of the Palestinian problem and of the Arab–Israeli conflict, which would involve Israeli withdrawal from all of the occupied territories, including 'Holy Jerusalem'. He justified his resort to a secret channel by arguing that the almost two years of public negotiations under US sponsorship had reached a dead end. Some of the Arab foreign ministers agreed with the PLO chairman that the accord was an important first step, even if they were not all agreed on the next step or the final destination.

Implementing the Declaration of Principles

Two committees were set up in early October 1993 to negotiate the implementation of the lofty-sounding Declaration signed in Washington. The first committee was chaired by Shimon Peres and Mahmoud Abbas, the leader who had signed the Declaration on behalf of the PLO. This ministerial-level committee was supposed to meet in Cairo every two or three weeks. The other committee, the nuts and bolts committee, consisted of experts who were supposed to meet for two or three days each week in the Egyptian resort of Taba on the Red Sea. The heads of the delegations to these talks were Nabil Sha'ath and Major-General Amnon Lipkin-Shahak, the number-two man in the IDF and head of its military intelligence. The two sides managed to hammer out an agenda and formed two groups of experts: one to deal with military affairs; the other, with the transfer of authority.

The IDF officers took a generally tough line in the negotiations. These officers had been excluded from the secret talks in the Norwegian capital and they felt bitter at not having been consulted about the security implications of the accord. Chief of Staff Ehud Barak believed that, in their haste to secure their place in history, the politicians had conceded too much to the PLO and that, when the time came to implement the agreement, it would be the responsibility of the army to tackle the security problems.

Underlying the labyrinthine negotiations at Taba was a basic conceptual divide. The Israeli representatives wanted a gradual and strictly limited transfer of powers, while maintaining overall responsibility for security in the occupied territories in their own hands. They wanted to repackage, rather than end, Israel's military occupation. The Palestinians wanted an early and extensive transfer of power to enable them to start laying the foundations for an independent state. They were anxious to get rid of the Israeli occupation and they struggled to gain every possible symbol of sovereignty. As a result of this basic conceptual divide, the Taba negotiations plunged repeatedly into crisis and took considerably longer to complete than the two months allowed for in the original timetable.

After four months of wrangling, an agreement was reached in the form of two documents: one on general principles, the other on border crossings. The two documents were initialled by Shimon Peres and Yasser Arafat in Cairo on 9 February 1994. Although the Cairo agreement was tactfully presented as a compromise solution, it was a compromise that tilted very heavily towards the Israeli position. The IDF had managed to impose its own conception of the interim period: specific steps to transfer limited powers to the Palestinians without giving up Israel's overall responsibility for security. The IDF undertook to redeploy, rather than to withdraw, its forces in the Gaza Strip and Jericho. The Cairo agreement gave the IDF full authority over Gaza's three settlement blocs, the four lateral roads joining them to the Green Line, and 'the relevant territory overlooking them'. The outstanding feature of the agreement was thus to allow the IDF to maintain a military presence in and around the area earmarked for Palestinian self-government, and to retain full responsibility for external security and control of the land crossings to Egypt and Jordan. Despite these serious limitations, the Cairo agreement formed a first step in regulating the withdrawal of the Israeli Civil Administration and secret services from Gaza and Jericho.

Another round of negotiations resulted in an agreement that was signed by Yitzhak Rabin and Yasser Arafat in Cairo on 4 May. The Cairo agreement wrapped up the Gaza–Jericho negotiations and set the terms for expanding Palestinian self-government to the rest of the West Bank. Expansion was to take place in three stages. First, responsibility for tourism, education and culture, health, social welfare, and direct taxation was to be transferred from Israel's Civil Administration to the Palestinian National Authority. Second, Israel was to redeploy its armed forces away from 'Palestinian population centres'. Third, elections were due to take place throughout the West Bank and the Gaza Strip for a new authority.

The Cairo document was billed by both sides as an agreement to divorce after twenty-seven years of unhappy coexistence in which the stronger partner forced the weaker to live under its yoke. This was true in the sense that Israel secured a separate legal system, and separate water, electricity, and roads for the Jewish settlements. It was not true in the sense that the document gave the stronger party firm control over the new relationship.

The Cairo document stressed repeatedly the need for cooperation, coordination, and harmonization in the new relationship. A large number of liaison committees, most of which were to have an equal number of representatives from the two sides, gave a superficial appearance of parity. But this parity was undermined in favour of the stronger partner by the fact that Israeli occupation laws and military orders were to remain in force unless amended or abrogated by mutual agreement. What this meant in practice was that any issue that could not be resolved by negotiation would be subject to the provisions of Israeli law rather than those of international law. This was a retreat from the Palestinian demand that international law, particularly the Fourth Geneva Convention, should be the source of legislation and jurisdiction during the transition period.

A week after the Cairo document was signed, a token force of thirty Palestinian policemen entered the Gaza Strip from Egypt to assume control for internal security from the retreating Israelis. This was the first tangible evidence that Israeli occupation was winding down. Until this point, all of the movement had been unilateral, as the Israeli army redeployed its forces so as to provide continuing protection for the tiny community of Jewish settlers in the strip. Now, a new Palestinian police force was to take charge of the nearby Palestinian population centres in accordance with a prearranged division of labour. The Israeli withdrawal was greeted with a sigh of relief at home, and great joy and jubilation among the Gazans. As the last Israeli soldiers pulled out of their military camps in Rafah and Nusairat to a final barrage of stones, the Israeli flag was replaced by the flag of Palestine. A twenty-seven-year-old experiment in imposing Israeli rule over 2 million recalcitrant Arabs was symbolically and visibly nearing the end of its life.

The Israeli government's policy of controlled withdrawal from Gaza and Jericho enjoyed broad popular support. Hard as they tried, the leaders of the opposition failed to arouse the nation against the decisions of the government. As far as the government was concerned, the real paradox was that it needed a strong PLO to implement the Gaza–Jericho settlement, but a strong PLO could only reinforce the determination of the Palestinians to fight for a state of their own.

The government maintained its commitment to peace with the Palestinians despite the protests from the right, and despite the terrorist attacks launched by Hamas and Islamic Jihad with the aim of derailing the peace talks. On 29 August 1994, the Agreement on Preparatory Transfer of Powers and Responsibilities was signed by Israel and the Palestinians. In accordance with the Oslo Accord, this agreement transferred powers to the Palestinian Authority in five specified spheres: education and culture; health; social welfare; direct taxation; and tourism.

Oslo II

Negotiations on the Syrian track proceeded in parallel to those on the Palestinian track. Rabin's strategy was to decouple the Syrian track from the Palestinian, Jordanian, and Lebanese tracks. He controlled the pace of the negotiations with Syria according to what was happening on the other tracks. The Americans offered their good offices in trying to broker a settlement with Syria. For Syria, the key issue was full Israeli withdrawal from the Golan Heights, by which it meant a return to the armistice lines of 4 June 1967. The Israelis preferred withdrawal to the 1923 international border, which was more favourable to them. In the second half of 1993, Rabin came close to accepting the Syrian condition if Syria would meet his demands—the 'four legs of the table', as he used to call them. Besides withdrawal, the other three legs comprised normalization, security arrangements, and a timetable for implementation. The Syrian response on these other points did not satisfy Rabin. Consequently, although considerable progress was achieved by the two sides in narrowing down their differences, it was not sufficient to secure a breakthrough on the Syrian track.

Jordan was more directly affected by the Israel–PLO accord than any other Arab country, because of its close association with the West Bank and because more than half of its population is of Palestinian origin. A day after the accord was presented to the world, in a much more modest ceremony in the US State Department, the representatives of Jordan and Israel signed a common agenda for negotiations aimed at a comprehensive peace treaty. Its main components were borders and territorial matters, Jerusalem, water, security, and refugees. The document bore the personal stamp of King Hussein, who had been deeply involved in the quest for peace in the Middle East for the preceding quarter of a century. A year of intensive negotiations culminated in the signing of a peace treaty in the Arava desert on 26 October 1994. This was the second peace treaty concluded between Israel and an Arab country in fifteen years, and the first to be signed in the region. The treaty between Israel and Egypt had been signed in 1979. But whereas Egypt had offered a cold peace, King Hussein offered Israel a warm peace.

On 28 September 1995, the Israeli–Palestinian Interim Agreement on the West Bank and the Gaza Strip was signed in Washington by Yitzhak Rabin and Yasser Arafat, in the presence of Bill Clinton, Hosni Mubarak, and King Hussein of Jordan. It became popularly known as 'Oslo II'. This agreement, which marked the conclusion of the first stage in the negotiations between Israel and the PLO, incorporated and superseded the Gaza–Jericho and the early empowerment agreements. The Interim Agreement was comprehensive in its scope and, with its various annexes, stretched to more than 300 pages. From the point of view of changes on the ground, it was highly significant. It provided for elections to a Palestinian Council, the transfer of legislative authority to this Council, the withdrawal of Israeli forces from the Palestinian centres of population, and the division of territories into three areas— A, B, and C. Area A was under exclusive Palestinian control; Area C under exclusive Israeli control; and in Area B, the Palestinians exercised civilian authority, while Israel continued to be in charge of security. Under the terms of this agreement, Israel yielded to the Palestinians control over nearly a third of the West Bank. Four per cent of the West Bank (including the towns of Jenin, Nablus, Kalkilya, Tulkarem, Ramallah, Bethlehem, and Hebron) were turned over to exclusive Palestinian control and another 25 per cent to administrative-civilian control. Oslo II marked the point of no return in the process of ending Israel's coercive control over the Palestinian people.

On 5 October, Yitzhak Rabin gave the Knesset a comprehensive survey of Oslo II and of the thinking behind it. His speech was repeatedly interrupted by catcalls from the benches of the opposition. Two Likud members of the Knesset (MKs) opened black umbrellas, the symbols of Neville Chamberlain's appeasement of Adolf Hitler at Munich. In the course of his speech, Rabin outlined his thinking for the permanent settlement: military presence, but no annexation of the Jordan Valley; retention of the large blocks of settlements near the 1967 border; preservation of a united Jerusalem with respect for the rights of the other religions; and a Palestinian entity that would be less than a state and whose territory would be demilitarized. The fact that Rabin sketched out the principles of the permanent settlement in a session devoted to the interim settlement suggested a strong interest in proceeding to the next stage.

The day on which the Knesset endorsed Oslo II by a majority of only one, thousands of demonstrators gathered in Zion Square in Jerusalem. Binyamin Netanyahu, the leader of the Likud, was on the grandstand, while the demonstrators displayed an effigy of Rabin in Nazi SS uniform. Netanyahu set the tone with an inflammatory speech. He called Oslo II a surrender agreement and accused Rabin of 'causing national humiliation by accepting the dictates of the terrorist Arafat'. A month later, on 4 November 1995, Rabin was assassinated by a religious-nationalist Jewish fanatic with the explicit aim of derailing the peace process. Rabin's demise, as the murderer expected, dealt a serious body blow to the entire peace process. Shimon Peres followed Rabin down the potholed road to peace with the Palestinians, but his efforts were cut short by his electoral defeat in May 1996.

Declaration of war on the peace process

The return to power of the Likud under the leadership of Binyamin Netanyahu dealt another body blow to the Oslo peace process. From the very beginning, the Likud had been bitterly opposed to the Labour government's 'land for peace' deal with the PLO. Netanyahu himself repeatedly denounced the accord as a violation of the historic right of the Jewish people to the State of Israel and as a mortal danger to their security. The foreign-policy guidelines of his government expressed firm opposition to a Palestinian state, to the Palestinian right of return, and to the dismantling of Jewish settlements. They also asserted Israel's sovereignty over the whole of Jerusalem and ruled out withdrawal from the Golan Heights. In the Arab world, this programme was widely seen as a declaration of war on the peace process.

Netanyahu spent 1996–99 in a relentless attempt to arrest, freeze, and subvert the Oslo accords. He kept preaching reciprocity, while acting unilaterally in demolishing Arab houses, imposing curfews, confiscating Arab land, building new Jewish settlements, and opening an archaeological tunnel near the Muslim holy places in the Old City of Jerusalem. Whereas the Oslo accord left Jerusalem to the final stage of the negotiations, Netanyahu made it the centrepiece of his programme in order to block progress on any other issue. His government waged an economic and political war of attrition against the Palestinians in order to lower their expectations.

Intense US pressure compelled Netanyahu to concede territory to the Palestinian Authority on two occasions. The Hebron Protocol was signed on 15 January 1997, dividing the city into a Palestinian zone and a Jewish zone. This was a milestone in the Middle Eastern peace process: the first agreement signed by the Likud government and the Palestinians. The second agreement was brokered by then President Bill Clinton at Wye Plantation in Maryland on 23 October 1998. By signing the Wye River Memorandum, Netanyahu undertook to withdraw from a further 13 per cent of the West Bank in three stages over a period of three months. But a revolt of his ultra-nationalist and religious partners brought down the government after only one pullback. The fall of the government was inevitable, because of the basic contradiction between its declared policy of striving for peace with the Arab world and its ideological makeup, which militated against trading land for peace.

Under the leadership of Ehud Barak, the Labour Party won a landslide victory in May 1999. Labour's return to power was widely expected to revive the moribund peace process. During the election campaign, Barak presented himself as Rabin's disciple—as a soldier who turned from fighting the Arabs to peacemaking. He was given a clear mandate to resume the quest for peace with all Israel's neighbours. Within a short time, however, Barak dashed the hopes that had been pinned on him. He lacked the vision, the political courage, and the personal qualities that were necessary to follow through on the peace partnership with the Palestinians. During his army days, Barak used to be called 'Little Napoleon'; in politics, too, his style was arrogant and authoritarian, and he approached diplomacy as the extension of war by other means.

The greatest barrier on the road to peace with the Palestinians raised by Barak was the expansion of Jewish settlements on the West Bank. Settlement activity is not contrary to the letter of the Oslo accord, but it is contrary to its spirit. True, settlement activity had gone on under all previous prime ministers, Labour as well as Likud. But under Barak, settlement activity gathered pace: more houses were constructed; more Arab land was confiscated; and more access roads were built to isolated Jewish settlements. For the Palestinian population, these settlements are not only a symbol of the hated occupation, but also a source of daily friction and a constant reminder of the danger to the territorial contiguity of their future state.

Another reason for the slowdown on the Palestinian track was the clear preference articulated by Barak for a deal with Syria first, on the grounds that Syria was a serious military power, whereas the Palestinians were not. During his first six months in power, Barak concentrated almost exclusively on the Syrian track, leaving the Palestinians to twist in the wind. When the late Syrian President Hafiz al-Asad rejected his final offer, Barak turned, belatedly and reluctantly, to the Palestinian track. His reservations about the Oslo accord were well known. He argued that the step-by-step approach of trading land for peace does not serve Israel's interests, because the Palestinians will always come back for more. This made him wary of further interim agreements and prompted him to insist that the Palestinian Authority commit itself to an absolutely final end to the conflict.

Camp David

One more interim agreement was necessary, however, before taking the plunge to the final settlement. It took ten months to break the deadlock created by the Likud government's failure to implement the Wye River Memorandum. Once again, Barak proved to be a tough negotiator, applying intense pressure on the Palestinians. His method was described as 'peace by ultimatum'. The accord that he and Yasser Arafat signed at Sharm el-Sheikh, on 4 September 1999, reflected the underlying balance of power between the two parties. It put in place a new timetable for the final status talks, aiming at a 'framework agreement' by February and a fully-fledged peace treaty by 13 September 2000.

The February deadline fell by the wayside, fuelling frustration on the Palestinian side and prompting Arafat to threaten to issue a unilateral declaration of independence if no agreement could be reached. To forestall this eventuality, Barak persuaded President Clinton to convene a trilateral summit in the US. With the announcement of the summit, Barak's chaotic coalition fell apart. Three parties quit the government, robbing him of his parliamentary majority on the eve of his departure for the summit. In a defiant speech, Barak told the Knesset that, although he no longer commanded a majority, as the directly elected prime minister he still had a mandate to make peace. But Barak's domestic political weakness inevitably reduced the diplomatic room for manoeuvre that he enjoyed. Once again, as so often in the past, the peace process was held hostage to the vagaries of the Israeli political system.

Negotiations at Camp David started on 11 July 2000 and lasted fourteen days. Barak approached the summit meeting in the manner of a soldier rather than as a diplomat. He dismissed Arafat's plea for more time to prepare the groundwork, believing that, with the help of the US 'peace processors', he would be able to impose his terms for the final settlement on the opponent. In fairness to Barak, it must be said that he crossed his own 'red lines' and put on the table a package that addressed all of the issues at the heart of the conflict: land, settlements, refugee rights, and Jerusalem.

Basically, Barak envisaged an independent Palestinian state over the whole of the Gaza Strip and most of the West Bank, but with the large settlement blocs next to the 1967 border being annexed to Israel. The Jordan Valley, long cherished as Israel's security border, would eventually be turned over to exclusive Palestinian sovereignty. Altogether, 20.5 per cent of the West Bank was to remain in Israel's hands: 10.5 per cent to be annexed outright and 10 per cent to be under Israeli military occupation for twenty years. Barak agreed to the return of Palestinian refugees, but only in the context of family reunification involving 500 people a year. On Jerusalem, he went further than any previous Israeli prime minister— and indeed broke a taboo by agreeing to the partition of the city. But his offer fell well short of the Palestinian demand for exclusive sovereignty over all of the city's Arab suburbs and over al-Haram al-Sharif (that is, Temple Mount) (Enderlin 2003: 213, 270, 324). The problem with this package was that it was presented pretty much on a 'take it or leave it' basis. Moreover, Barak insisted that an agreement would mark the final end of the conflict, with the Palestinians formally renouncing any further claim against the State of Israel.

The Palestinian delegation was divided in its response to the package. Some saw in it a historic opportunity for putting the conflict behind them; others felt that it would compromise their basic national rights, and in particular the right of return of the 1948 refugees. In addition, the Palestinian delegation came under pressure from Egypt and Saudi Arabia not to compromise Muslim rights over the Muslim holy places in the Old City of Jerusalem. At this critical juncture in his people's history, Yasser Arafat displayed neither courage nor statesmanship. His greatest mistake lay in rejecting many of the proposals put to him without putting forward any counter-proposals of his own. Consequently, when the summit ended in failure, Barak and Clinton were able to put all of the blame on Arafat. Arafat returned home to a hero's welcome, but he returned empty-handed.

The question of responsibility for the failure of the summit became the subject of heated controversy, not surprisingly given the serious consequences of failure. Both sides of the argument were forcefully presented over the pages of the *New York Review of Books* in articles and letters to the editor. Robert Malley and Hussein Agha launched the debate with a long revisionist article based on first-hand knowledge (Malley and Agha 2001). They believed that Bill Clinton consistently sided with Ehud Barak, leading Yasser Arafat to suspect that there was a conspiracy against him and leading him to dig in his heels. Ehud Barak repeatedly asserted that, at Camp David, he made a most generous offer, and that Arafat made a deliberate choice to abort the negotiations and to resort to violence in order to extract further concessions from Israel (Morris 2002; Morris and Barak 2002). Dennis Ross, Clinton's special envoy to the Middle East, also laid all of the blame at Arafat's door, arguing that at no point during Camp David or in the six months after it did the chairman demonstrate any capability to conclude a permanent status deal (Ross 2001a). Jeremy Pressman, an academic with no axe to grind, examined in depth both the Israeli and the Palestinian versions of the Camp David summit, and concluded that the latter is significantly more accurate than the former (Pressman 2003).

The al-Aqsa intifada

With the collapse of the Camp David summit, the countdown to the outbreak of the next round of violence began. On the Palestinian side, there was mounting frustration and deepening doubt that Israel would ever voluntarily accept a settlement that involved even a modicum of justice. Israel's apparent intransigence fed the belief that it understands only the language of force. On the Israeli side, there was growing disenchantment with the Palestinians and disillusion with the results of the Oslo accord. Ehud Barak succeeded in persuading virtually all of his compatriots that there was no Palestinian peace partner.

It was against this background that Ariel Sharon, the leader of the Likud, chose to stage his much-publicized visit to al-Haram al-Sharif (meaning 'Noble Sanctuary'), which the Jews call Temple Mount. On 28 September 2000, flanked by a thousand security men and in deliberate disregard for the sensitivity of the Muslim worshippers, Sharon walked into the sanctuary. By embarking on this deliberately provocative walkabout, Sharon in effect put a match to the barrel of gunpowder. His visit sparked off riots on the al-Haram al-Sharif that spread to other Arab areas of East Jerusalem and to other cities. Within a very short time, the riots snowballed into a full-scale uprising—the al-Aqsa intifada.

Although the uprising happened spontaneously, the Palestinian security services became involved and played their part in the escalation of violence. The move from rocks to rifles on the Palestinian side, and the resort to rockets, tanks, and attack helicopters by the Israelis, drove the death toll inexorably upwards. As so often in the past, the sound of gunfire drowned the dialogue of the diplomats. Violence is, of course, no stranger to the region. Even after the signing of the Oslo accord, diplomacy was sometimes interspersed with bursts of violence. Now, fierce fighting was interspersed with small doses of ineffectual diplomacy. Positions hardened on both sides and the tit-for-tat gathered its own momentum.

Neither side wanted to be seen as willing to back down. Yasser Arafat saw no contradiction between the intifada and negotiations. On the contrary, he hoped that the intifada would give him more leverage in dealing with the Israelis. Ehud Barak insisted that the incitement and the violence had to end before he would return to the negotiating table. His announcement of 'time out' signalled the abandonment of the political track until further notice. In the absence of talks, the security situation steadily deteriorated, clashes became more frequent and lethal, and the death toll increased at an alarming rate. Trust between the two sides broke down completely. The two societies became locked in a dance of death. The Oslo accords were in tatters.

Conclusion

Why did the Oslo peace process break down? One possible answer is that the Oslo accord was doomed to failure from the start because of its inherent shortcomings, and in particular because it did not address any of the core issues in the conflict between Israel and the Palestinians. This chapter's account of the rise and fall of the Oslo accord, however, suggests a different answer. It suggests that the basic reason for the failure of Oslo to resolve the conflict is that Israel, under the leadership of the Likud, reneged on its side of the deal. By resorting to violence, the Palestinians contributed to the breakdown of trust, without which no political progress is possible. But the more fundamental cause behind the loss of trust and the loss of momentum was the Israeli policy of expanding settlements on the West Bank, which carried on under Labour as well as Likud. This policy precluded the emergence of a viable Palestinian state, without which there can be no end to the conflict.

The breakdown of the Oslo peace process suggests one general conclusion about the international relations of the Middle East—namely, the importance of external intervention for the resolution of regional conflicts. According to an undoubtedly apocryphal story, Pope John Paul II believed that there would be two possible solutions to the Arab–Israeli conflict: the realistic and the miraculous. The realistic would involve divine intervention; the miraculous, a voluntary agreement between the parties. For the reasons explained in this chapter, the PLO and Israel were able to negotiate the Oslo accord without the help of a third party— but the imbalance in power between them made it exceedingly difficult to carry this agreement to a successful conclusion. The role of the US as the manager of the peace process was therefore essential to the success of the whole enterprise. In the final analysis, only the US could push Israel into a settlement. And, in the event, its failure to exert sufficient pressure on Israel to withdraw from the occupied territories was one of the factors that contributed to the breakdown of the Oslo peace process.

Key events

1990	2 August	Iraq invades Kuwait
1991	16 January–28 February	Gulf War
	30 September–1 October	Middle East peace conference convenes in Madrid

	10 December	Bilateral Arab–Israeli peace talks begin in Washington
1992	23 June	Labour defeats Likud in Israeli elections
1993	19 January	Knesset repeals ban on contacts with the PLO
	10 September	Israel and PLO exchange letters formally recognizing each other
	13 September	Israel–PLO Declaration of Principles on Palestinian Self-Government is signed at the White House
1994	4 May	Israel and PLO reach agreement in Cairo on application of the Declaration of Principles
	25 July	Washington Declaration ends state of war between Israel and Jordan
	26 October	Israel and Jordan sign peace treaty
1995	28 September	Israeli–Palestinian Interim Agreement on the West Bank and the Gaza Strip (Oslo II) is signed
	4 November	Yitzhak Rabin assassinated; Shimon Peres succeeds as prime minister
1996	21 January	First Palestinian elections
	24 April	Palestinian National Council amends Palestinian National Charter
	29 May	Binyamin Netanyahu defeats Shimon Peres in Israeli elections
1997	15 January	Hebron Protocol signed
1998	23 October	Binyamin Netanyahu and Yasser Arafat sign Wye River Memorandum
1999	17 May	Ehud Barak defeats Binyamin Netanyahu in Israeli elections
	4 September	Ehud Barak and Yasser Arafat sign Sharm el-Sheikh accord
2000	11–25 July	Camp David summit
	28 September	Ariel Sharon visits Temple Mount; outbreak of al-Aqsa intifada
	23 December	President Clinton presents his 'parameters'
2001	18–28 January	Israeli–Palestinian negotiations at Taba in Egypt
	6 February	Ariel Sharon defeats Ehud Barak in Israeli elections

Acknowledgement

The author would like to thank the US Institute of Peace for supporting his research on the Middle Eastern peace process.

Further reading

Eisenberg, L. Z. and Caplan, N. (1998) *Negotiating Arab–Israeli Peace: Patterns, Problems, Possibilities* (Bloomington, IN: Indiana University Press)
A useful comparative survey of peace negotiations between Israel and its neighbours.

Enderlin, C. (2003) *Shattered Dreams: The Failure of the Peace Process in the Middle East, 1995–2002* (New York: Other Press)
A detailed, but readable, account of the breakdown of the peace process, based on extensive research and interviews, and on minutes of conversations taken by the participants themselves.

Guyatt, N. (1998) *The Absence of Peace: Understanding the Israeli–Palestinian Conflict* (London: Zed Books)
A highly critical analysis of the nature of the Oslo accord, and of its political and economic consequences for the Palestinians.

Makovsky, D. (1996) *Making Peace with the PLO: The Rabin Government's Road to the Oslo Accord* (Boulder, CO: Westview Press)
A detailed account of the politics and diplomacy of the Rabin government by a well-informed Israeli journalist.

Meital, Y. (2006) *Peace in Tatters: Israel, Palestine, and the Middle East* (Boulder, CO: Lynne Reinner)
A concise and critical analysis of the Oslo accord, and the reasons for its failure.

Rabinovich, I. (1999) *Waging Peace: Israel and the Arabs at the End of the Century* (New York: Farrar, Straus and Giroux)
An overview of Israel's relationship with the Arab world by an academic who headed the Israeli delegation to the talks with Syria.

Ross, D. (2004) *The Missing Peace: The Inside Story of the Fight for Middle East Peace* (New York: Farrar, Straus and Giroux)
An extremely detailed, but one-sided, account of the Arab–Israeli peace negotiations, from Madrid to Camp David, by a senior US participant.

Said, E. W. (1995) *Peace and its Discontents: Gaza–Jericho, 1993–1995* (London: Vintage Books)
A collection of essays by a prominent Palestinian academic, with severe strictures on the PLO leadership and the peace that it made with Israel.

Said, E. W. (2000) *The End of the Peace Process: Oslo and After* (London: Granta Books)
A collection of articles dealing with the peace process and other aspects of Palestinian life.

Shlaim, A. (1995) *War and Peace in the Middle East: A Concise History* (London: Penguin Books)
A brief and basic introduction to the international politics of the Middle East since the First World War.

Shlaim, A. (2015) *The Iron Wall: Israel and the Arab World* (New York: W. W. Norton)
A detailed and highly critical study of Israel's policy in the conflict with the Arabs during the first fifty years of statehood.

Questions

1. Why were regional circumstances in the early 1990s favourable for the Oslo Peace Process?
2. How important were external states in fostering the Peace Process?
3. To which individual or individuals can most credit be given for success in the Oslo negotiations?
4. Why did Oslo II fail?
5. Why have subsequent peace efforts failed to build upon Oslo's achievements?

14

The International Politics of the Gulf

MATTEO LEGRENZI AND F. GREGORY GAUSE III

Overview

The international politics of the Gulf region are defined by the interplay of the local states and outside powers—primarily, in recent decades, the United States. The local states do not simply deal with each other on the basis of balance-of-power concerns, although those concerns are certainly present. With Arab nationalist, Islamic, and ethnic identities transcending Gulf borders, domestic security and stability concerns are as important in the foreign policies of the region's states towards each other and outside powers. The Gulf's strategic role as the source of 60 per cent of the world's known petroleum reserves has given it enduring importance in global US strategy. Since the Iranian revolution in 1979, Washington took an increasingly direct military and political role there, culminating with the US invasion and occupation of Iraq in 2003. However, the failure of the US to create a stable Iraqi regime and the still uncertain impact of the Arab uprisings highlight the local obstacles to outside power hegemony in the region, even if the would-be hegemon were the most powerful country in the world. The agreement reached between Iran and the major world powers in July 2015 after years of negotiation has the potential of ushering a new, less confrontational phase in the international politics of the Gulf in addition to instituting significant checks on Iranian nuclear activities. However, the hostility displayed towards the deal by veteran American allies Saudi Arabia and Israel highlights how the path to more cooperative relations between the two shores of the Gulf, let alone in the wider Middle East, is still bedevilled by a lack of mutual trust.

Introduction

Two almost contemporaneous events in the early 1970s created the international politics of the Persian/Arabian Gulf region (see **Figure 14.1**) as we know them today: the British withdrawal of its protectorate over the Arab states of the lower Gulf; and the dramatic increase in world oil prices. The Gulf had an important role in British imperial strategy from the outset of the nineteenth century, reinforced in the early twentieth century by the increasing importance of oil. The oil resources of the region made it important to both superpowers in the Cold War. The regional states all had 'open files' of contentious issues among them, including, but not limited to, border disputes. However, the early 1970s marks a dramatic change in the structure of power in the area.

Before that time, the states of the region were limited in their abilities to project their power and influence beyond their borders, and checked by what remained of British power in the area. After that time, the three major regional states—Iran, Iraq, and Saudi Arabia—all had vastly increased amounts of military and economic power. Their foreign policies became much more ambitious. At the same time, the restraint of great power presence in the area was removed, at least temporarily. Britain had left; the United States, mired in Vietnam and unwilling to take on new obligations, did not 'fill the vacuum'. The field was open for the regional states to take more forward and aggressive roles.

To some extent, these new ambitions on the part of the regional powers can be understood in classical realist, balance-of-power terms. However, classical realism and balance-of-power politics do not provide a perfect template for understanding the Gulf regional system; they are necessary, but not sufficient. The security agenda in the Gulf is complicated by the fact that the local states were, at the same time as they were competing with each other

Figure 14.1 The Gulf states

for power regionally, also confronting difficult domestic issues of state-building. The social dislocations brought on by great oil wealth brought down the Shah's regime in Iran. Centrifugal forces threatened the integrity of the Iraqi state at various times, up to the present. The Gulf monarchies were buffeted by challenges to their domestic stability. The importance of transnational identities in the Gulf states exacerbated the sense of threat that rulers faced. Baathist Iraq's Arab nationalism was deployed at various times to encourage opposition to rulers in Iran (in Khuzestan) and the Gulf monarchies. Revolutionary Shia Islam was an important threat to domestic stability in Iraq, Kuwait, Bahrain, and, to a lesser extent, Saudi Arabia. Iran's influence in post-Saddam Iraq is more the product of its close ties with Iraqi Shia groups than its military power. Kurdish identity cuts across the Iran–Iraq border, and was exploited by one regime to pressure another on various occasions.

So it is not simply the balancing of power, or the desire to extend one's power internationally, that has driven calculations of war and alliance in the Gulf. Threats are not simply military; they are also political. The Shah and the ayatollahs governed the same country, but the Arab states have viewed the nature of the threat emanating from different Iranian regimes in very different ways. Whether the Gulf states have viewed Iraq as a threat or a protector had more to do with their perceptions of Iraqi intentions towards their regimes than with estimates of Iraqi military power. Regime security—the ability of the ruling elites to stay in power domestically—was as important, if not more important, in determining foreign-policy choices than more traditional state security concerns, and the Arab uprisings have served to highlight this further.

The aim of this chapter is to demonstrate these points within a long time frame by considering two sets of issues: first, Iraqi war decisions, in 1980 and 1990, and also in 1975 (the Algiers agreement), when Iraq chose not to go to war, and in 1991, when Iraq chose not to withdraw from Kuwait in the face of superior power and almost certain defeat; and second, the different alliance choices made by Saudi Arabia at various times since 1971 in regional politics.

The regional security picture is not complete, however, without consideration of a third issue: the changes in US policy towards the region. US interest in the Gulf has been a constant, because of the strategic importance of oil, but the tactics that the US has pursued have changed significantly over time. These changes have brought the US into a much more direct role in the security picture of the Gulf from the late 1980s, constraining the freedom of action that the local states had enjoyed. However, the US's inability to create a stable post-Saddam regime increased Iran's relative power in the region and created a new arena of regional rivalry, with Iran, Saudi Arabia, Turkey, Syria, and other countries jockeying for influence in a weakened and fragmented Iraq. This rivalry, in turn, has been conditioned by the Arab uprisings that commenced at the end of 2010 and led to further fragmentation in Libya, Yemen, and Syria. The US military withdrawal from Iraq in 2011 opened a new chapter in Iraq's history, but given the heightened regional instability has hardly reduced the role of regional powers in its politics.

The above picture could definitely change if relations between Iran, the foremost regional power, and the United States, the over the horizon balancer, were to normalize in the wake of an agreement to regulate Iranian nuclear ambitions. A detailed preliminary agreement between the five permanent members of the UN Security Council and Germany, the so called P5+1, and Iran was reached in November 2013 and a formal declaration on the parameters of a formal agreement was signed in Lausanne on 2 April 2015 (Sick 2015.) These negotiations have been carefully presented as separate from the issue of US–Iran relations but a lifting of sanctions directed at the Iranian economy and a permanent deal over the Iranian nuclear programme would undoubtedly lead to a lessening of tensions between these two key actors and are fiercely resisted by the two stalwart American allies in the region: Israel and Saudi Arabia.

Regime security, political identity, and Iraqi War decisions

In both 1980 and 1990, the regime of Saddam Hussein launched wars against foes who were, or who seemed to be, considerably weaker than Iraq. It is tempting to conclude that the ambitious Iraqi president attacked a militarily weakened Iran and a practically defenceless Kuwait because he thought that he would win. Undoubtedly, the prospect for victory was an important element in Saddam's war calculations. However, the sequence of events and evidence from Iraqi sources indicate that these war decisions were driven as much, if not more, by fears about the prospects for regime security within Iraq itself—fears that were based on a belief that outside actors could manipulate Iraqi domestic politics against the Baathist regime. In each case, also, Iraqi calculations about the prospects of victory were inflated by the belief that the invasion would be met with at least some support both in the target state and in the larger region. Transnational connections inspired both the fears and hopes that lay behind the Iran–Iraq War of 1980–88 and the First Gulf War of 1990–91 (Gause 2002b).

The Iran–Iraq War 1980–1988

The Iranian revolution is the starting point for understanding the Iraqi war decision of 1980. The Shah's Iran and Baathist Iraq were never on particularly good terms. There were border crises between the countries in 1969 and 1975. The 1975 crisis led to the Algiers agreement, signed by then Vice-President Saddam Hussein and the Shah at an Organization of the Petroleum Exporting Countries (OPEC) meeting in the Algerian capital. Iraq agreed to accept the Iranian definition of their common border along the Shatt al-Arab river; in turn, Iran ceased supporting the Iraqi Kurdish rebellion that was raging in northern Iraq. While not close, relations between the two states after 1975 were not overtly hostile.

The weakening of Iran in conventional power terms, which began in late 1977 as the revolutionary movement gathered steam, did not immediately excite Iraqi ambitions. On the contrary, Baghdad expelled Ayatollah Khomeini from Iraq in October 1978 and engaged in security consultations with the Shah's government. When the monarchical regime fell in February 1979, Iraq's first reactions were mildly welcoming to the new regime. Relations soon deteriorated, however. In June 1979, Ayatollah Muhammad Baqir al-Sadr, a major Iraqi Shi'i religious leader, was arrested on the eve of a scheduled trip to Tehran. Violent demonstrations ensued in Iraqi Shi'i areas. Several prominent Iranian ayatollahs, including Khomeini, condemned the Iraqi regime as 'despotic' and 'criminal', warning Iraq's rulers of 'the wrath of God and the anger of the Muslim people' (Menashri 1990: 101). Border clashes in the Kurdish areas ensued. In July 1979, Mas'ud and 'Idris Barazani, the sons of Iraqi Kurdish leader Mustafa Barazani, crossed the border into Iran and received support from the revolutionary government (Hiro 1991: 35).

In the midst of these events, Saddam Hussein became president of Iraq on 16 July 1979. An explanation that focused purely upon Saddam's ambitions would expect a militant change in Iraqi policy towards Iran from that time. That did not happen. On the contrary, the two governments sought in the short term to de-escalate tensions and border skirmishes subsided. This did not, however, lead to any lessening of political ferment among Iraq's Shia majority. In July 1979, while under house arrest, Ayatollah Muhammad Baqir al-Sadr called for violent opposition to the regime. Shortly thereafter, the major Iraqi Shi'i political groups announced the formation of the 'Islamic Liberation Movement', ready to 'resort to all means' to bring down the Baathist regime. In October 1979, the Organization of the Iraqi 'Ulama declared its support for the use of violence against the government. Al-Da'wa, the major Iraqi Shi'i party, formed a military wing by the end of the year (Wiley 1992: 54–5; Tripp 2000: 229). In May 1980, the Iraqi interior minister told an interviewer that, while there were fewer than 1,000 members of al-Da'wa, 'the number of misguided supporters and religious sympathizers is considerable' (Foreign Broadcast Information Service (FBIS)-MEA-80–097, 16 May 1980: E2).

Against this rising tide of Shia opposition in late 1979, Iranian politics took a militant turn. Prime Minister Mehdi Bazargan resigned in November 1979, in the wake of the takeover of the US embassy in Tehran. Statements about the need to export the Iranian revolutionary model around the region became more frequent, and by 1980 there were explicit calls by Iranian government officials for the Iraqi people to overthrow the Baath regime (Chubin and Tripp 1988: 34; Khadduri 1988: 82; Menashri 1990: 157–8). On 1 April 1980, a member of one of the Shia opposition groups attempted to kill Deputy Prime Minister Tariq Aziz. During the funeral procession for some of those killed in that attempt, according to the Iraqi media, a bomb was thrown from a window of an 'Iranian school' in Baghdad (FBIS-MEA-80–068, 7 April 1980: E5–7). In retaliation, the Iraqi government executed Ayatollah Muhammad Baqir al-Sadr and began to expel tens of thousands of Iraqi Shia of Iranian origin from the country.

These events were the final straw for Saddam Hussein. He began to threaten Iran in the most obvious way. By late July 1980, Saddam was all but promising a war: 'We are not the kind of people to bow to Khomeini. He wagered to bend us and we wagered to bend him. We will see who will bend the other' (FBIS-MEA-80–144, 24 July 1980: E4–5). When news of Ayatollah Baqir al-Sadr's execution reached Iran, in mid-April 1980, the Iranian reaction matched the hostility now being exhibited by Saddam. Ayatollah Khomeini reiterated his previous calls to the Iraqi people and the Iraqi army to overthrow the regime, accusing the Baath of launching a 'war against Islam' (Hiro 1991: 35). Border clashes resumed.

Sources that have reported on the timing of the Iraqi decision to go to war almost unanimously place the decision in the spring of 1980, after the events of April (Gause 2002b: 68). The gap between the war decision and the actual initiation of conflict in September 1980 is attributable to two factors: the first is planning and organization, which would take some months to achieve; the second is the effort by Iranian exiles in Iraq to organize a military coup to overthrow the Islamic regime in Tehran. That effort was fully supported by Iraq and planned on Iraqi territory. Begun on 9 July 1980, it was a spectacular and immediate failure (Gasiorowski 2002). The failure of the coup was confirmation of the durability of the Islamic revolutionary regime.

The Iraqi war decision of 1980 is best explained by the change in Saddam Hussein's framing of the issue of how to deal with Iran. With the changes in Iran after November 1979 and the more open calls for the export of the Islamic revolution, domestic unrest in Iraq came to be seen as orchestrated by Tehran. Saddam's regime could only look forward to further Iranian efforts to foment revolution against it, if nothing changed in Tehran. Facing that prospect, Saddam chose the risky path of war. He certainly thought that he and Iraq would gain by victory, but the elements that made victory likely had been in place for some time. What had changed was his belief that a continuation of the status quo would only bring him more domestic problems.

Iraq's attack on Iran was spectacularly unsuccessful, both in destabilizing the revolutionary regime in Tehran and in securing Iraqi control of south-western Iran. By the summer of 1982, Iranian counter-attacks had driven Iraqi forces out of Iranian territory. The Khomeini regime was then faced with a decision: declare victory over Iraq and accept a ceasefire, or continue the war in Iraqi territory. Ayatollah Khomeini decided the issue with a call to continue the war until the downfall of the Baathist regime in Baghdad. Tehran hoped that an effort to spread the Islamic revolution would be met with support among the Iraqi Shia. That support was not forthcoming in any substantial way. The war dragged on for six more years. During most of that time, Iran was on the offensive and made occasional, limited gains, but was unable to break the Iraqi forces. Iraq turned the tide in 1988, recapturing lost territory in southern Iraq and demoralizing Iran with missile attacks on Tehran. From 1987, the US navy became directly involved in the war, protecting oil tankers from Kuwait and Saudi Arabia against Iranian attack. After a US naval vessel had shot down an Iranian civilian airliner in July 1988, Iran accepted UN Security Council Resolution 598, calling for a ceasefire. Khomeini likened this decision to 'drinking poison', but even he had become convinced that Iran could not win the war. Eight years of bloody war, with hundreds of thousands of casualties on each side, ended with the two sides basically in the same position as they had been when the war had begun.

The Gulf War 1990–1991

Establishing with certainty when Saddam Hussein decided to attack Kuwait is a difficult task. There are indications from Iraqi sources that the decision was made only a few months before the actual invasion (Gause 2002b: 53–4). No source that refers specifically to the timing of the decision places it earlier than the spring of 1990. The haste with which the decision was made was reflected indirectly in some of the (very mild) self-criticism exercised by Iraqi leaders after the invasion. At a meeting of the Iraqi Revolutionary Command Council and Baath party leadership on 24 January 1991, Taha Yasin Ramadan told his colleagues:

> I am not saying that August 2, 1990 [the date of the attack] was the best day for the mother of battles. We had not studied the situation for a year, or even for months, preparing for the mother of battles. But it was the will of God that decided the date.
>
> (al-Bazzaz 1996: 200)

There is every indication that the decision to invade Kuwait was made relatively shortly before the invasion, under feelings of time pressure. What had happened to trigger it?

Saddam Hussein's regime made it clear, before and after the invasion, that it saw an international conspiracy against it, meant to weaken Iraq internationally and to destabilize it domestically. Its economic problems were blamed on lower oil prices, which were in turn blamed on 'overproduction' by Kuwait and the United Arab Emirates (UAE), clients of the US. Small shifts in US policy (such as limits on US credits for Iraqi purchases of US rice exports and Congressional resolutions condemning Iraq for human rights violations) and damaging revelations (such as Iraq's use of the Atlanta branch of an Italian bank to launder arms purchase money) after the end of the Iran–Iraq War were read as evidence that the US had adopted a hostile attitude towards Iraq. Media attention to the Iraqi nuclear programme, and subsequent British and US efforts to block the export of dual-use technology to Iraq, were seen as part of a concerted effort to weaken Iraq.

Lurking behind many of these efforts, in the Iraqi view, was Israel, seen to be preparing for a strike on the Iraqi nuclear establishment similar to the one it had conducted in 1981 (Baram 1993; Freedman and Karsh 1993: chs 2–3; Heikal 1993: 158–231). Wafiq al-Samara'i, then deputy director of Iraqi military intelligence, says that, at the beginning of 1990, his office began receiving warnings from Saddam about Israeli plans to strike at Iraqi nuclear, chemical, and biological weapons facilities (al-Samara'i 1997: 365). Sa'ad al-Bazzaz, editor at the time of a major Baghdad daily newspaper, reports that the Iraqi leadership fully expected an Israeli military attack at some time in August 1990 (al-Bazzaz 1993: 345).

Saddam himself bluntly described this 'conspiracy' in March 1990:

> America is coordinating with Saudi Arabia and the UAE and Kuwait in a conspiracy against us. They are trying to reduce the price of oil to affect our military industries and our scientific research, to force us to reduce the size of our armed forces. ... You must expect from another direction an Israeli military airstrike, or more than one, to destroy some of our important targets as part of this conspiracy.
>
> (al-Samara'i 1997: 222–3)

There was also an internal aspect to the Iraqi regime's fears. In either late 1988 or early 1989, scores of officers were arrested and executed on the charge of conspiring to bring down the government. Hundreds of high-ranking officers indirectly connected to the accused were forced to retire (Baram 1993: 8; al-Bazzaz 1996: 36–7, 89–90; al-Samara'i 1997: 184–5; Tripp 2000: 249–50). Iraqi ruling circles came to believe during 1989 that a number of foreign powers, including Iran, Saudi Arabia, and the US, were attempting to infiltrate Iraqi society to collect intelligence and to pressure the government (al-Bazzaz 1993: 159–60, 210–13). Other sources report a failed coup attempt in September 1989 and the exposure of a coup attempt, coupled with a plan to assassinate Saddam, in January 1990 (Freedman and Karsh 1993: 29–30; al-Samara'i 1997: 185; Baram 1997: 5–6).

While Saddam Hussein increasingly saw his domestic political and economic situation in 1989 deteriorate, events in the larger world reinforced his growing sense of crisis. The fall of the Soviet client states in Eastern Europe increased his fears about the future of his own regime (al-Bazzaz 1993: 392). Saddam's sense that international and regional forces were conspiring with his domestic opponents against him had reached the point that, in October 1989, Tariq Aziz raised this issue in a meeting with Secretary of State Baker in Washington (Baker 1995: 265).

By early 1990, Saddam Hussein was convinced that his regime was being targeted. This belief was reflected in the changes in his rhetoric and the tone of Iraqi foreign policy. In February 1990, Saddam launched an attack on the US military presence in the Gulf at the founding summit of the Arab Cooperation Council and devoted much of the speech to criticism of Israel (Bengio 1992: 37–49). This was followed by Saddam's threat in April 1990 to 'burn half of Israel' if the Israelis attacked Iraq. The rhetorical temperature escalated from there. At the same time, Iraqi rhetoric towards Kuwait and the other Gulf states hardened, and in January 1990 Iraq first proposed that Kuwait 'loan' it US$10 billion, as well as write off Iraqi debts incurred during the war with Iran (Heikal 1993: 209). At the Arab summit of May 1990, Saddam likened overproduction of OPEC quotas to an act of war against Iraq (Freedman and Karsh 1993: 46–8).

This shift in Iraqi foreign policy came when Saddam concluded that there were international efforts afoot to destabilize him domestically (al-Bazzaz 1996: 198–9, 227–8). It culminated with the Iraqi occupation of Kuwait in August 1990. Saddam's unwillingness to accept a negotiated solution to the Kuwait crisis—which would have required him to withdraw from Kuwait, but would have spared his country and military the devastating attack by US and coalition forces—provides further evidence for the hypothesis that it was fear of domestic destabilization that was the most important factor prompting his decision to invade.

The Iraqi leadership did not believe that withdrawal from Kuwait would end what it saw as the international conspiracy against it. On the eve of the ground war, after enduring a month of air attacks, Saddam told Soviet envoy Yevgeny Primakov: 'If America decided on war it will go to war whether I withdraw from Kuwait or not. They were conspiring against us. They are targeting the leadership for assassination. What have the Iraqis lost? They might yet gain!' (al-Bazzaz 1993: 399). After the war, Tariq Aziz was asked on the PBS documentary *The Gulf War* why Iraq did not withdraw when defeat seemed inevitable. He replied: 'Iraq was designated by George Bush for destruction, with or without Kuwait. Inside Kuwait or outside Kuwait. Before the 2nd of August or after the 2nd of August.'[1]

The contrast with Iraqi acceptance of the Algiers agreement in 1975 is instructive. Then, Saddam Hussein believed that retreat internationally would strengthen the regime's domestic position; Saddam's belief that withdrawal from Kuwait in 1991 would not end the pressures on his domestic position emanating from abroad explains the different outcome in 1991. The Gulf War ended with Iraq's defeat on the battlefield, its humiliating withdrawal from Kuwait, and US dominance of the Gulf. However, for over a decade Saddam Hussein claimed victory in what Iraq termed the 'mother of battles' because his regime remained in power after the war.

Regime security, regional balancing, and Saudi Arabian alliance decisions

The importance of domestic regime security concerns in the foreign policies of Gulf states is highlighted by the alliance choices of Saudi Arabia during (and after) the different Gulf wars. Saudi manoeuvring between Iraq and Iran during the 1980s was dictated more by the ideological threat posed by the Iranian revolution than by balance-of-power concerns. The different Saudi reactions during the first and second Gulf Wars reflects the level of threat—both military and ideological—posed by Saddam Hussein's regime to the Saudi leadership and by the different public opinion reactions in Saudi Arabia to US military moves against Iraq. While the Saudis acted in both cases within the broad confines of their long-standing security relationship with the US, in the first they cooperated enthusiastically and publicly with the US military; in the second, their cooperation was much less extensive and largely hidden from their population.

Saudi Arabia and the Iran–Iraq War

The Iranian revolution changed the strategic picture dramatically for the Saudis. The new Islamic Republican government presented an open challenge to the legitimacy and stability of the Saudi regime, both as an example of Islamic revolution, and as a promoter of discontent within Saudi Arabia and the other monarchical states of the Gulf. A wave of unrest, concentrated mostly in Shi'i communities, swept Kuwait, Bahrain, and Saudi Arabia from 1978 through 1980 (Ramazani 1986: 39–40; Kostiner 1987: 179). The revolutionaries in Tehran continued to challenge the al-Saud's Islamic credentials through the 1980s. Central to this challenge was Iranian behaviour during the annual pilgrimage to Mecca. Iranian pilgrims held political demonstrations, forbidden by the Saudi authorities, during the 1982 and 1983 pilgrimages. In 1987, Saudi security forces clashed with Iranian pilgrims, resulting in more than 400 deaths. In contrast, during the 1980s Saddam Hussein's Iraq assiduously courted the Saudis, emphasizing their common interest in checking the Iranian threat.

The beginning of the Iran–Iraq War presented the Saudis with a serious dilemma. They were concerned about the ultimate intentions of Saddam Hussein. However, forced to choose between the two combatants, Saudi Arabia aligned with Iraq. When the war started, Saudi Arabia permitted Iraqi planes to use Saudi bases and Saudi ports were opened for the trans-shipment of goods to Iraq (Safran 1986: 369). Contemporary sources report substantial Saudi financial aid to Iraq in 1980 and 1981 (Nonneman 1986: 96–7). Once Iranian forces had entered Iraqi territory in 1982, Saudi support became more substantial. Billions of dollars of Saudi financial support helped Iraq to fund the war. That support, as detailed by King Fahd, included direct aid, loans, military equipment, and the sale of oil from the Saudi–Kuwaiti neutral zone, with profits going to Iraq, theoretically as a 'loan'. (al-Sharq al-Awsat, 17 January 1991: 4.) After Syria had cut the Iraqi oil pipeline to the Mediterranean in 1982, the Saudis permitted Iraq to build a pipeline into the kingdom, connecting to an existing Saudi line from the Gulf to the Red Sea. Saudi Arabia also publicly supported Iraq in various diplomatic forums.

The Saudis exploited the opportunities that the Iran–Iraq War presented. With Iran and Iraq consumed by their war, and the smaller states exposed to the myriad threats that war presented, the Saudis were able to organize under the Gulf Cooperation Council (GCC) in 1981. The Council brought together the smaller monarchies (Bahrain, Kuwait, Oman, Qatar, and the United Arab Emirates) under Saudi leadership and has proved to be one of the region's most successful regional groupings.

Saudi Arabia and the Gulf War

With the Iraqi invasion of Kuwait, the Saudi threat perception changed dramatically. Iraq was now an immediate military threat, moving troops up to the border of the oil-rich Eastern Province of Saudi Arabia. It was also an ideological/domestic threat to the Saudi regime: Iraq had overthrown a fellow monarchy. Iraq called openly, on both Islamic and Arab nationalist bases, for citizens in Saudi Arabia to revolt against their government. One Iraqi source reported that Saddam was confident that this propaganda barrage would destabilize the Saudi domestic scene so thoroughly that Riyadh would have no choice but to accept the new realities (al-Bazzaz 1996: 112).

The dire threat posed by Iraq, on both balance-of-power and regime security levels, led the Saudis to overcome their hesitations about an open military alliance with the US. Riyadh had preferred to keep the US military 'over the horizon', worried that too public an embrace of the US could lead to a domestic and regional public opinion backlash. The Saudis now chose to run the risk of alienating their own public and welcomed hundreds of thousands of US soldiers into the kingdom.

With the success of the US campaign to eject Iraqi forces from Kuwait, a new period in US–Saudi relations began. Riyadh was much more willing to cooperate openly with the US military, allowing it to use Saudi bases throughout the 1990s and into the 2000s to patrol the 'no-fly' zone in southern Iraq. This seemingly permanent US military presence excited domestic political opposition. It was one of the prime complaints levelled by Osama bin Laden against the Saudi rulers. American facilities were attacked in Saudi Arabia in November 1995 in Riyadh and in June 1996 in the Eastern Province. The former attack killed five Americans; the latter killed nineteen and wounded hundreds.

As the Saudis continued to see Saddam Hussein as a major threat after the first Gulf War, their relations with Iran slowly began to improve. This trend was facilitated by changes in Iran itself. The death of Ayatollah Khomeini in 1989 dissipated some of the fervour to 'export' the revolution, reducing at least one element of the threat that the Saudis perceived from Iran. The collapse of oil prices in the mid-1990s brought Riyadh and Tehran closer together, as they cooperated within OPEC and with major non-OPEC producers to push prices up. Riyadh still looked upon Tehran with suspicion, both as an ideological competitor in the Muslim world and as a major regional power. Tehran was equally mistrustful of Saudi–US relations, which it saw in the context of Washington's anti-Iranian policy. However, the hard edge of ideological hostility that characterized relations in the 1980s had been replaced by more normal and business-like ties in the 1990s.

Saudi Arabia and the Iraq War 2003

Riyadh was much less willing to cooperate with the US in its attack on Iraq in 2003 than it was in 1990–91. The Saudis officially opposed the US war. US ground troops and air forces were not permitted to use Saudi bases, with some exceptions that the Saudi government kept secret from its own population. The Saudi hesitancy to be publicly linked to this US attack on Iraq stemmed from two factors: first, Saddam Hussein was not nearly the threat to the Saudi rulers that he had been in 1990; and second, Saudi public opinion had taken a dramatic anti-American turn. However, the Saudi rulers also did not want to alienate their US allies, whom they continued to see as their long-term security guarantors. The Saudis therefore cooperated with Washington militarily when such cooperation could be kept removed from the glare of publicity.

Saudi public opinion, by the beginning of 2003, was extremely anti-American. The upsurge in Israeli–Palestinian violence in the second intifada, which began in the autumn of 2000, was one factor increasing the level of anti-Americanism in the kingdom. The US reaction to the attacks of 11 September 2001 ('9/11') was another. The debate in the US over Saudi complicity in the attack was seen by many in Saudi Arabia as an attack on their country and their religion. The Saudi response in the immediate aftermath, on both the governmental and popular levels, was defensive and hostile to the US. The US attack on the Taliban and Al-Qaeda in Afghanistan was depicted by many in Saudi Arabia as a superpower attack on a defenceless civilian population. A Gallup poll, conducted in late January–early February 2002, reported that 64 per cent of Saudi respondents viewed the US either very unfavourably or most unfavourably. Fewer than 10 per cent saw the US as either friendly or trustworthy (Burkholder 2002). A Zogby International poll conducted in February–March 2003 found that 95 per cent of the Saudis polled had either a very unfavourable or a somewhat unfavourable attitude towards the US (Zogby 2003).

In the face of this considerable public opinion rejection of US policy in the region and without the perception of an immediate threat from Saddam Hussein, the Saudi leadership made every effort to separate itself publicly from US policy towards Iraq. However, the importance of the Saudi–US security relationship was such that Riyadh sought to cooperate with Washington where that cooperation could be kept out of their public's eye. The Saudis increased oil production in the lead-up to the war, to try to prevent price spikes. They permitted the US to coordinate air attacks on Iraq from the command-and-control centre at Prince Sultan Airbase south of Riyadh. They allowed US special forces access to an isolated Saudi base in the northwest corner of the country, near the Iraqi border (Allen and Khalaf 2003; C. S. Smith 2003a).

The Saudis walked a tightrope in the second Gulf War, trying to do enough to keep Washington happy, but not so much as to alienate their own public. It was a tightrope that they had walked successfully before. The interesting point about their behaviour in this episode was not their cooperation with Washington, which could have been expected from both their long-standing ties with the US and their hostility to Saddam Hussein; rather, it was the way in which Saudi public opinion put serious limits on the extent of that cooperation. Saudi anti-Americanism in this episode was based, at least in part, on transnational Arab and Muslim ideological solidarity with Palestinians and Iraqis.

US policy in the Gulf

For the US, the strategic significance of the Gulf region has been a constant since the Second World War because of its oil resources. During the period between the end of the Second World War and 1971, the US developed close political, economic, and military relations with both Iran and Saudi Arabia, to safeguard its interests and to check the possibilities of Soviet moves in the area. Since the British withdrawal from the Gulf in 1971, US policy in the region has gone through a number of stages, reflecting changes in the US itself, in the Gulf, and in the world economic and strategic picture. Those stages have seen progressively greater US military involvement in the area, culminating in the second Gulf War of 2003.

The 1970s: oil revolution and the twin-pillar policy

The end of British military responsibilities in the smaller Gulf states in 1971 could have been an opening for the US to take on the British mantle directly, as it had in many other parts of the region since the Second World War. However, the British withdrawal occurred at the height of US involvement in Vietnam, and there was no public or Congressional support for new foreign military obligations. Washington sought to safeguard its interests in the Gulf by supporting the military build-up of its two local allies, Iran and Saudi Arabia (Gause 1985: 258–66). The Soviet Union responded by signing a treaty of friendship and cooperation with Iraq in 1972, providing a Cold War justification for continued US military support for the 'twin pillars' of Iran and Saudi Arabia.

The oil revolution of the early 1970s, culminating in the Saudi-led embargo by many Arab states of the sale of oil to the US in 1973–74 (in reaction to US support for Israel in the 1973 Arab–Israeli War), could have been seen as a direct challenge to the US 'twin pillar' policy in the Gulf. Saudi Arabia led the embargo against the US. Iran took advantage of the situation to push oil prices to their highest levels in history. By the time the dust had settled, oil prices had increased from around US$3 per barrel to more than US$12 per barrel, sending the US and much of the rest of the world into a recession that lasted through the decade. Paradoxically, the oil revolution strengthened the 'twin pillar' policy. The importance of the Gulf region for US foreign policy increased dramatically, but Washington was unable to take a direct military role there. With vast new oil revenues, Iran and Saudi Arabia were able drastically to increase their military spending, with most of their purchases coming from the US. The 1970s saw an intensification of military, economic, and political relations between the US and its Gulf partners (Safran 1986: ch. 12; Bill 1988: ch. 6).

The Iranian revolution and the Iran–Iraq War

The US 'twin pillar' policy in the Gulf came crashing down in 1979, as the Islamic revolution swept the Shah of Iran from power. The new Islamic Republic of Iran was intensely hostile towards the US—a hostility both signified and magnified by the Iranian hostage crisis. From November 1979 to January 1981, Iranian revolutionaries, with the support of Iran's leader, Ayatollah Ruhollah Khomeini, detained US diplomatic personnel in Iran. President Jimmy Carter attempted to free the hostages through a military raid in April 1980, which failed spectacularly, pointing to the weakness of the US military position in the area. Almost contemporaneously with the hostage crisis, in December 1979 the Soviet Union invaded Afghanistan in order to prop up a failing communist regime there. The Iranian revolution, the Soviet invasion of Afghanistan, and the subsequent Iraqi attack on Iran in September 1980 all further destabilized the world oil market, with oil prices increasing to over US$30 per barrel in 1980–81.

The US reaction to this set of strategic challenges was to reconfirm its commitment to its remaining Gulf ally, Saudi Arabia, and to commit more US military resources to the Gulf. President Carter declared that the US would use all of the military means at its disposal to confront any 'hostile power' trying to dominate the region. The Reagan administration, coming to power in January 1981, vastly increased the US military budget, fleshing out operationally the ambitious plans laid out at the end of the Carter administration for a 'Central Command' devoted to the Gulf region. Over intense Congressional objections, it sold airborne warning and control system (AWACS) aircraft to Saudi Arabia in 1981. The Reagan administration also continued efforts begun by Carter to negotiate basing rights in the region, most notably with Oman. Other Gulf states were more reluctant in the early 1980s to open their territory to the US military (Kupchan 1987: chs 4–6).

While the US increased its regional military capabilities in the early and mid-1980s, it did not find it necessary to use them, even though war raged between Iraq and Iran. Although the fortunes of war ebbed and flowed, neither side achieved a military breakthrough that might have drastically altered the regional power situation. Moreover, the price of oil, after spiking to more than US$40 per barrel at the beginning of the war, began to decline markedly from 1982. In 1986, prices briefly fell below US$10 per barrel, less in real terms than they had been before the 1973 oil price revolution. With the war generally stalemated and oil prices declining, the US saw no need for direct military intervention in the region.

From 1982, when Iraqi forces withdrew from Iran and the Iranians took the fight across the border into Iraq, Washington began to support Iraq directly. The US shared intelligence with Baghdad, encouraged (or did not discourage) allies from supplying Iraq with weapons, sold Iraq 'dual use' technologies such as helicopters, and extended economic credits for the Iraqi purchase of US agricultural goods (Jentleson 1994: ch 1). In 1985–86, the Reagan administration also conducted secret diplomacy with Iran in what became known as the 'Iran contra scandal'. The US arranged for Israeli arms to be sold to Iran, in an effort to secure the release of US hostages from Lebanon and channel funding to the US-supported Nicaraguan opposition forces, the 'contras'. Some in the administration hoped that this opening would lead to a renewal of a strategic partnership with Iran, but public revelation of these dealings led both sides to repudiate the initiative.

Seeking to pressure the Gulf monarchies to cut their support for Iraq, in 1986 Iran began to attack oil tankers shipping Kuwaiti, and occasionally Saudi, oil through the Gulf. (Iraq had been striking at Iranian tankers for some time.) Kuwait asked both the US and the Soviet Union to protect its ships. The combination of Washington's interest in balancing the Soviets and desire to restore its good faith with the Arab states after the revelation of the 'Iran contra scandal' in November 1986 brought the US navy into the Gulf in early 1987, where it engaged with Iranian forces on numerous occasions. In July 1988, a US ship shot down an Iranian civilian airliner over the Gulf, mistaking it for an Iranian air force jet. Days later, Iran accepted UN Security Council Resolution 598, calling for a ceasefire in the Iran–Iraq War.

The Gulf War and the 1990s

The US naval deployment at the end of the Iran–Iraq War represented a new level of military cooperation between the Gulf monarchies and the US. Kuwait opened up its ports to US naval vessels. Saudi Arabia, which had preferred that the US military be 'over the horizon', granted US forces new levels of access to Saudi facilities. This was the beginning of what would become an open security alliance with the US in the wake of the Iraqi attack on Kuwait in August 1990.

The end of the Cold War had removed the global strategic threat that had, in part, driven US policy towards the Gulf over the previous decades. However, the first Gulf War demonstrated to Washington that local actors could challenge US oil interests and US allies in the region as well. With Saddam Hussein still in power in Iraq after the war and the Islamic Republic of Iran still at odds with the US, Washington looked to the Gulf monarchies to provide bases for the US forces that took up a long-term station in the region. The monarchies, traumatized by the Iraqi invasion of Kuwait and wary of Iranian intentions, welcomed the security cover that US forces provided. US military bases were established in Kuwait and Qatar. The command of the US Gulf naval force, renamed the Fifth Fleet, moved onshore in Bahrain. Oman and the UAE provided regular access to their facilities for US forces. An American air wing operated out of Saudi airbases to patrol southern Iraq. There were some negative public reactions to this new level of US military presence—most notably, the June 1996 bombing of an apartment complex in eastern Saudi Arabia called Khobar Towers, housing US air force personnel. However, these events did not alter the course of US policy.

That policy was based on the containment of both Saddam's Iraq and Islamic Iran—what the Clinton administration called 'dual containment'. Containment of Iraq was legitimated by UN Security Council resolutions that maintained severe economic and military sanctions on the country. While the sanctions were altered at times during the 1990s to try to alleviate the sufferings imposed on the Iraqi population, their cumulative effect was to impoverish the country, while not destabilizing Saddam's regime (Graham-Brown 1999). US containment of Iran was unilateral, and largely ignored by the rest of the world.

9/11 and the Iraq War

The attacks of 9/11 by Al-Qaeda on New York and Washington marked an important turning point in US policy in the Gulf. Before 9/11, the US did not particularly like either the Iraqi or the Iranian regimes, but was willing to live with them. After the attacks of that day, the Bush administration was set on changing the Gulf status quo.

The most important change was towards Iraq. The new US 'war on terrorism' was not limited to Al-Qaeda and its direct state supporter, the Taliban regime in Afghanistan. President Bush defined the terrorist threat to include unfriendly states seeking to develop weapons of mass destruction (WMDs), because they could pass those weapons on to terrorist groups seeking to use them against the US. Iraq was named by the president as the centre of this new 'axis of evil' threatening US security. The administration succeeded in garnering US public and Congressional approval for war, but failed to receive the kind of UN mandate that had legitimated the first Gulf War. With limited international support, the US launched a war against Iraq in March 2003. In a matter of weeks, Saddam's regime had crumbled and US forces had occupied the country.

The contention that Iraq had large stockpiles of WMDs—the centrepiece of the Bush administration's public case for war—proved to be unfounded. However, the WMD issue was not the only factor in the US war decision. The belief that a US-reconstructed Iraqi polity could be a beacon of moderation and pro-Western democracy in the region, exerting pressure for reform on neighbouring states, which would then reduce the chances of terrorist groups developing in those states, was strongly held by some in the administration. The strategic benefits of increased US power in the centre of world oil production, and in an area directly connected to Arab–Israeli issues, were also part of the decision calculus. The failure of the US to build a stable successor regime in Iraq, however, turned what the Bush administration had hoped would be a strategic asset into a liability. The US became stuck in an expensive and debilitating counter-insurgency war in Iraq that drained its resources and prestige, and increased the power of Iran in the region.

The events of 9/11 also brought to an end the tentative steps, at the end of the Clinton administration, to re-engage with the Islamic Republic of Iran. Paradoxically, the 'war on terrorism' pitted the US against two Iranian adversaries: the Taliban regime in Afghanistan and Saddam Hussein in Iraq. Iran remained neutral in both wars, a stance that helped the US. There were even discussions between US and Iranian representatives on Afghan and Iraqi issues. However, Iran fell into the category of states targeted in the expansive definition of the 'war on terrorism', in that it was suspected of developing nuclear weapons and had links to groups identified by the US as terrorist. It was named by President Bush as one of the members of the 'axis of evil'. The Bush administration blamed Iran for supporting insurgent groups in Iraq, and sought to build a regional front of Arab states and Israel to contain Iranian influence. It also tried to mobilize international support for sanctions aimed at curbing Iran's nuclear programme. Confrontation, not cooperation, continued to dominate the US–Iranian relationship.

Surprisingly, the 9/11 attacks had the least effect on US relations with the Gulf country most directly involved in those attacks: Saudi Arabia. The mastermind of the attacks, Osama bin Laden, and fifteen of the nineteen perpetrators were from Saudi Arabia. Many in the US saw Saudi Arabia as, at best, an ambivalent ally in the 'war on terrorism' and, at worst, through its funding of Islamic groups and causes around the world, a supporter of terrorism. Anti-Americanism in Saudi Arabia, growing in the 1990s for reasons discussed under 'Saudi Arabia and the Iraq War', increased even further in reaction to what was seen by many Saudis as a US effort to blame them specifically, and Islam in general, for the attacks (Gause 2002a). It seemed that the relationship was at a crisis point. At the end of the second Gulf War, the US combat personnel who had been stationed in Saudi Arabia since 1991 were withdrawn. The Bush administration gave indications, particularly in 2004 and 2005, that it expected the Saudi leadership to undertake democratic reforms. For its part, Riyadh expressed its misgivings about US policy in Iraq. However, as the US Iraq adventure turned sour, and Iran took advantage of the regional changes to extend its power in Iraq and the broader region, Washington reverted to its traditional position of close relations with the Saudi regime. The dramatic increase in the price of oil after 2003, escalating toward US$100 per barrel in 2007, reminded the Bush administration of the importance of Saudi Arabia to US interests.

The Gulf after the US withdrawal from Iraq

At the end of 2008, the Bush administration negotiated a status of forces agreement with the Iraqi government of Prime Minister Nouri al-Maliki that called for the withdrawal of all US combat forces from Iraq by the end of 2011. The US military departure from Iraq did not signal a general withdrawal from the Gulf: the US maintains military facilities in all of the smaller Gulf states and a substantial naval presence in the area. But the withdrawal from Iraq in 2011 symbolized an end to the US effort to establish a hegemonic position in the region. It also signalled that the local states, particularly Iran and Saudi Arabia, would play a much larger role in driving the international politics of the region. The Saudi–Iranian rivalry is played out for the most part in the domestic politics of weak and divided Arab neighbours—not only Iraq, but also Lebanon, Palestine, and Yemen—with both states supporting local allies. The rivalry grew in intensity as the US presence in Iraq declined, both playing on and exacerbating sectarian tensions between Sunni and Shia throughout the Middle East. The domestic upheavals in the Arab world that began in Tunisia in late 2010 opened up new fronts in the rivalry, with Saudi Arabia (and the GCC) sending troops to Bahrain to support the ruling family against the demonstrations of its Shi'i majority population and supporting the revolts against Bashar al-Asad, Iran's closest Arab ally, in Syria. Tehran, while verbally supporting protests against pro-American rulers in Egypt and Bahrain, steadfastly stood by its Syrian ally.

Leaving aside the fall-out from the Arab Spring uprisings, the major international focus in the Gulf region after the US withdrawal from Iraq has been the Iranian nuclear issue. While Tehran steadfastly maintains that it is not developing a nuclear weapons capability and there is no evidence to date that it has done so, it took a number of steps that, in the eyes of many, increased the chances that it would be able to do so in the future. The Obama administration, joined by the European Union, progressively increased economic pressures on Iran, while Israel threatened military strikes unless Iran abandoned its nuclear programme. These efforts finally bore fruits and Iran, as a result of increasing external pressure and changes in its domestic politics came to the negotiating table in order to find a solution that would give relief to its economy, hit by sanctions and a steadfast drop in oil prices. As was noted at the beginning of the chapter, the Obama administration and the other major world powers initiated serious negotiations that culminated in a formal declaration on the parameters of a final agreement. The negotiations were successful and in July 2015 Iran and the P5+1 agreed on the Joint Comprehensive Plan of Action. The agreement was widely welcomed around the world as a diplomatic triumph. However, it encountered much resistance within American and, to a lesser extent, Iranian domestic political arenas. This was a symptom of the still significant distrust that permeates not only elected bodies but large swathes of the public in both countries.

The significance of the P5+1 negotiations with Iran and the Saudi–Iran war by proxy

The negotiations between the global powers and Iran have been strenuously resisted also by the two foremost American allies in the region: Saudi Arabia and Israel. This hostility towards a deal points to the fact that in addition to concerns about the Iranian nuclear programme, both Israel and Saudi Arabia are wary of an expanded Iranian role in the region following the lifting of economic sanctions. After the descent of Syria into civil war and the increased instability in Iraq, that necessitated the return of a significant number of American military personnel as 'trainers and advisors' after the withdrawal of combat troops, Saudi Arabia and Iran are engaged in a war by proxy throughout the region. The Saudi government, significantly more assertive after the ascent to the throne of King Salman, feels that it has to take matters into its own hands as it sees its interests in the regions as somewhat diverging from the ones of the United States. Whilst this distance will definitely not lead to a breakup of the Saudi–American axis it results in a much more assertive Saudi stance in areas where it perceives its interests to be threatened by Iran. In the first few months of his rule, King Salman initiated a war in Yemen to counter the Houthi rebellion that he sees as being inspired by Iran and stepped up Saudi involvement in the Syrian civil war.

The Saudi–Iran rivalry, which has waxed and waned since the 1960s, is shaping up to be crucial not only for the international politics of the Gulf but for the balance of power in the entire region. The fact that it is presented by both parties in increasingly sectarian terms does not bode well as it strikes a chord with public opinion on both sides of the Gulf and threatens to turn the conflict into an identity based one. This tension is further exacerbated by the vagaries of the global oil market. Lower oil prices brought about by hydraulic fracturing, so called 'fracking', can be withstood far more easily by Saudi Arabia than by Iran, Russia, or Venezuela and add a further element of tension to the rivalry.

Conclusion

During the 1970s and the 1980s, up to the first Gulf War, the driving force behind international political events in the Gulf was the regional states themselves: the oil embargo of 1973–74; the Iranian revolution; the Iraqi war decisions of 1980 and 1990. The US played an important, but largely reactive, role in that period. It was constrained by its own domestic politics from playing a more direct military role in the Gulf and by the superpower competition of the Cold War, in which US actions could be met by Soviet reactions. The first sections of this chapter thus dealt with the motivations behind regional state behaviour—Iraqi war decisions and Saudi alliance decisions—because it was the regional states that set the agenda. That agenda was greatly influenced by the importance of transnational Arab, Muslim, and ethnic (Kurdish) identities in the region. Regime security concerns, the desire to stay in power and to thwart domestic opponents, drove regional states' foreign policy behaviour as much as, if not more than, classic balance-of-power considerations.

The initiative in Gulf international politics passed from the regional states to the US during the Gulf War of 1990–91. The constraints of domestic public opinion and Cold War competition on US freedom of action were removed, and the Gulf monarchies were willing to associate themselves with the US military in an unprecedented way. The attacks of 9/11 marked a further escalation of US regional involvement, as the 'war on terrorism' became both the motive and the justification for the US to shed the last international constraint on its behaviour in the Gulf: the need for international legitimation provided by the United Nations. The invasion of Iraq was the first step in an ambitious effort to change not only the regional balance of power, but also the domestic politics of the Gulf states. Those hegemonic ambitions foundered on the realities of Iraqi domestic politics, with the Bush administration unable to consolidate a pro-American, democratic Iraqi regime that would be both a model of, and a base for pressing for, political change in Iran and Saudi Arabia. It had been a domestic political event—the Iranian revolution—that had scuttled an earlier US security policy in the Gulf. The complexities of Iraqi domestic politics seem to have put paid to Washington's more recent dreams of recreating the Persian Gulf in its own image. Now, after the withdrawal of combat troops from Iraq, local powers are once again take centre stage as the drivers of Gulf international politics. In particular, Saudi Arabia and Iran have become involved in a war by proxy throughout the entire region: not exclusively in the Gulf. This rivalry is unlikely to escalate into an armed conflict but it is nevertheless fierce. The fact that it is increasingly portrayed as identity based adds to the difficulty and contributes to the challenge of finding an accommodation that would lower the tension in the Gulf and throughout the region.

Key events

1968	Britain announces withdrawal from its remaining Gulf protectorates in 1971
	Military coup in Iraq brings Baath Party to power
1971	Independence of Bahrain, Oman, Qatar, and United Arab Emirates
1973	Arab oil embargo against the US during 1973 Arab–Israeli War
	Quadrupling of oil prices by early 1974
1975	Algiers accord between Iran and Iraq
1977	Beginning of unrest in Iran
1979	Fall of Shah's regime
	Establishment of Islamic Republic of Iran
	Second oil crisis, with oil prices doubling
	Saddam Hussein becomes president of Iraq
	Takeover of US embassy in Tehran
	Soviet Union invades Afghanistan
1980	Failed US military raid in Iran aimed at freeing embassy hostages
	Beginning of Iran–Iraq War
1981	Negotiated end of Iranian–US hostage crisis
1982	Iraqi troops retreat from Iranian territory
	Iranian troops carry war into Iraqi territory
1986	Oil prices collapse, briefly falling below US$10 per barrel
1987	US naval deployment in Persian Gulf to protect Kuwaiti and Saudi shipping 1988
	US navy shoots down civilian Iranian airliner over Persian Gulf
1988	Iran accepts ceasefire in Iran–Iraq War
1990	Iraq invades Kuwait
1991	US-led international coalition defeats Iraq and restores Kuwait government
	Large-scale uprisings in southern and north-eastern Iraq
	Baghdad restores control over the south
	Kurdish areas in north-east gain de facto independence from Baghdad under US protection

1996	Iraq accepts 'Oil for Food' Programme under UN auspices
	Explosion at US air force housing facility in Dhahran, Saudi Arabia, kills nineteen, and wounds hundreds
	Osama bin Laden declares war on US
1998	Three days of US air and missile strikes on Iraq in 'Operation Desert Fox'
2001	9/11 Al-Qaeda attacks on New York and Washington
2003	US invasion of Iraq
2004	Simultaneous uprisings in Sunni Arab and Shia Arab areas of Iraq against US forces
2005	Mahmoud Ahmadinejad elected president of Iran
2006	Phase of intense sectarian violence in Iraq
	UN Security Council calls on Iran to end uranium enrichment
2008	US 'surge' strategy of additional troops to Iraq
	Surge in world oil prices to US$140 per barrel, then collapse to below US$50 per barrel in world financial crisis
2009	World oil prices recover in 2009
2011	Withdrawal of US combat forces from Iraq
2012	World oil prices over US$100 per barrel
2013	Hassan Rouhani elected Iranian president
2013	Preliminary agreement between P5+1 and Iran
2015	Joint Comprehensive Plan of Action on Iran's nuclear programme

Further reading

Al-Rasheed, M. (2002) *A History of Saudi Arabia* (Cambridge: Cambridge University Press)
   A reinterpretation of the country's history that emphasizes power and domination.

Bill, J. (1988) *The Eagle and the Lion: The Tragedy of American–Iranian Relations* (New Haven, CT: Yale University Press)
   The essential background to understanding the fraught US–Iranian relationship.

Gause, F. G., III (2010) *The International Relations of the Persian Gulf* (Cambridge: Cambridge University Press)
   A comprehensive account of the events discussed in this chapter.

Keddie, N. R. (2003) *Modern Iran: Roots and Results of Revolution* (New Haven, CT: Yale University Press)
   The best single-volume history of modern Iran.

Marr, P. (2011) *The Modern History of Iraq* (3rd edn, Boulder, CO: Westview Press)
   A comprehensive and readable one-volume history.

Packer, G. (2005) *The Assassins' Gate: America in Iraq* (New York: Farrar, Straus and Giroux)
   One reporter's account of the political manoeuvrings leading up to the Iraq War and it consequences in both Iraq and the US.

Ricks, T. E. (2006) *Fiasco: The American Military Adventure in Iraq* (New York: Penguin)

    A searing journalistic exposé of US political and military blunders in Iraq.

Takeyh, R. (2009) *Guardians of the Revolution: Iran and the World in the Age of the Ayatollahs* (New York: Oxford University Press)

    The best recent account of Iranian foreign policy.

Vitalis, R. (2007) *America's Kingdom: Mythmaking on the Saudi Oil Frontier* (Stanford, CA: Stanford University Press)

    An outstanding revisionist history of the development of the Saudi–US relationship, the Saudi oil industry, and Saudi politics from the 1940s through the 1960s.

Questions

1. What changed in the international politics of the Gulf after the British withdrew from East of Suez in the 1970s?

2. Is the concept of a balance of power adequate in understanding the international politics of the region?

3. What are the main drivers of American policy in the Gulf and how have they evolved in the last four decades?

4. What is the nature of the Saudi–Iranian rivalry?

5. How have Iran–US relations evolved since the 1970s? Are these two countries destined to be adversaries?

Note

1. See http://www.pbs.org

The Arab Spring: The 'People' in International Relations

LARBI SADIKI

Overview

This chapter presents a timely and critical account of the Arab uprisings from an international relations (IR) perspective. It does so via a revisionist interpretation that stresses the importance of the interactions of civic (peaceful/ruly) and non-civic (violent/unruly), top-down and bottom-up, state and non-state, local and global manifestations of political behaviour. Conventional wisdom reduces the Arab Spring to a local phenomenon of 'street politics' unconnected with global trends. Challenging the conventional wisdom, the chapter throws the Arab 'revolution' into sharper relief, first, by tracing its origin and, second, by analysing its 'itinerary' through the region on a global train.

The whole matrix of oppositions—internal–external, state–society, democratic–non-demo cratic, peaceful–violent, and secular–religious—is underscored to upend conventional thinking about forces of mass democratic resistance (trade unions, secular and Islamist parties, NGOs) and unruly Islamism (Al-Qaeda, ISIS, militias in Libya and Yemen), local (Arab Spring states and regimes, armies, social movements, and sectarian identities), regional/global actors (ranging from Iran, Saudi Arabia, and the UAE to the US), and revolutionary and counter-revolutionary trends, by accounting for their local and global moorings and triggers.

A minimalist definition of the Arab Spring is offered here: a bottom-up ground swell of activism accompanied by cultural, political, and social transformation; or in the absence of transformation, a novel revolutionary or rebellious impulse, taking peaceful and violent forms, to exert pressure for change bottom-up.

Introduction: 'travel' of the Arab Spring

The Arab Spring defies essentialist-Orientalist narratives about the Arab Middle East (as shall be discussed). It reminds observers that the Arab Middle East is plugged into the global society like any other region. Arabs do not live detached from the world around them and all it offers through the 'travel' of ideas, goods, and peoples. They affect the world and are in turn affected by international happenings, ideas, norms, products and encounters with the cultures, agents, and structures of globalization. Young leaders and protesters from Agadir along Morocco's Atlantic shores to Aden on the Red Sea are socialized into the global ethos. But the Arab Middle East is also plugged into globalization. Economic management panders to policy preferences invented in the chancelleries of Europe and North America, in the core countries of the globalized North. These range from macro-economic management strategies devised to lessen the impact of creeping economic globalization to the lowering of food subsidies as often counselled by the International Monetary Fund (IMF). Arab classrooms have introduced curricula that coach learners into the Internet, computer literacy, and even Chinese. Linguists are seeking to equip Arabic with the means to keep up with rapid changes in IT and sweeping cultural homogenization in consumption patterns and greater interaction between global and local goods, ideas, and values deriving from globalization. The Arab region has not escaped globalization's perils (imbalances due to a dominant North; opening up of weak economies; the powerful economic interests of core countries from the North setting political, economic, and geostrategic agendas; the marginalization of poor areas and social classes; and privatization) and opportunities (regional integration; travel of goods; people, ideas, and investments; WTO membership; satellite TV such as Al-Jazeera redressing the New World Information and Communication Order; and greater awareness of democracy and human rights).

The Arab cities whose public squares have seen sustained protests, and all kinds of contests of authoritarian forms of power, are today joined to the 'indignant', the 'marginals' everywhere. Arab protesters (*thuwwar*) are part of the 'Global Village'—the shrinkage of time and space has not spared them. Like protesters elsewhere, the young protesters that spearheaded the Arab Spring relied on social media, such as Facebook, Google, and Twitter to disseminate their message. The deftness with which they deployed social media and other gadgets of globalization to challenge the postcolonial authoritarian order showed how they have mastered the technology of protest. Ideas of human rights, good governance, social awareness, and democratization travelled further afield from their origin in the West to the Arab heartland. These issues form a kind of thread that tie the marginalized masses across the globe regardless of nationality, gender, religious creed, or ethnic background.

Two interrelated ideas are in order. Partly, the emerging activism is driven by the desire to transform Arab Spring states; the aim is to put an end to intolerable disparities in political power and economic wealth between individuals and regions within countries such as Egypt and Tunisia. And, in so doing, the new types of activism have helped foment new fearless and leaderless democratic identities. The result is a movement of activists, in which marginal individuals coalesce with workers, students, opposition forces, women's groups, Islamists, leftists, and liberals, forming the nucleus of a multitude-based democracy, at least during the moment of public square mobilization and organization (Hardt and Negri 2005). The Arab Spring is stamped with the birthmarks of marginalization: inclusion-exclusion, self-other, centre/periphery, and inside–outside. However, the Arab Spring has also emerged from the womb of popular aspiration for greater freedom and dignity (*hurriyyah*, *karamah*) the common slogans of Arab protesters everywhere.

When these ideas were combined with the Muslim tradition of speaking truth to power at the risk of one's life, they created a powerful catalyst to overthrow the yoke of authoritarian tyranny. Abysmal levels of poverty and joblessness in some countries further minimized for many the opportunity cost of dying in anti-authoritarian protests. Co-optation, coercion, institutional design, and constitutional manipulation and distribution typically relied upon by tyrants were finally rendered impotent by the tsunami of mass protest—though not in all cases. Civic activism and moral protest in the name of 'freedom' (*hurriyyah*) and 'dignity' (*karamah*) put to rest any notions of Middle East 'exceptionalism'. Military might and seemingly uncontested hegemony collapsed when confronted with the tidal wave of relentless demonstrations by Arab youth. The authoritarian regimes that were ousted could no longer reproduce themselves by way of the 'social adhesive' (Kirby 2000) or 'deference' (Hudson 1977: 167) deployed to keep the masses at bay—on the margins of political power. Thus, since Egypt's Tahrir Square uprising in 2011, some of the world's longest-surviving dictators have fallen from power. Libyan strongman, Mu'ammar Gaddafi was brutally murdered in the same year and Yemen's Ali Abdullah Salih was forced to abdicate under a GCC-orchestrated deal by peaceful protesters. These were men who once seemed poised to stay in power till their death in their gilded beds and palaces. The Arab Spring that spread from Tunisia to Egypt continues to gun for Syria's Bashar al-Asad.

Global precedents

Global parallels are legion: the 1979 Khomenei Revolution in Iran that put an end to the tyranny of the Shah, the 1986 People's Power revolution that ousted Ferdinand Marcos in Philippines, or the 1989 'November-December' or 'Velvet' Revolution in Czechoslovakia which led to the demise of the Soviet-backed regime, the 2004 Orange Revolution against the erstwhile dictator Kuchma in Ukraine, and the 2005 Tulip Revolution which resulted in the overthrow of Askar Akayev in the Kyrgyz Republic are just a few examples. These were no different from the popular uprisings that led to the ousting of Zine Elabidine Bin Ali in Tunisia (14 January 2011) and Hosni Mubarak in Egypt (25 January 2011 Revolution). Although the so-called Arab *thuwwar* (revolutionaries) come in many political colours: secular, liberal, Islamist, and feminist, they stand on a shared space of 'peoplehood'. They form a new civic stratum. They hail from backgrounds as diverse as the Islamist Muslim Brotherhood, the liberal April 6 Movement (Egypt) as well as non-ideological or specific issue interest groups such as the General Union of Tunisian Workers (UGTT), *femmes Democrats* (democratic women), 'EKBES' ('Firmness') protesters in Al-Kasba Square (Tunisia), and workers, tribal leaders, women, students, and civil society activists (Bahrain, Yemen).

To an extent, the post-Cold War moment matters. The stress here is on 'peoplehood' as an important explanatory concept through which I undertake a reading of the Arab Spring complementing an international relations (IR) approach. It speaks to the dynamic of the post-Cold War moment. Peoplehood is in this context both prescriptive and analytical. In its prescriptive guise, it is a cosmopolitan ideal, a product of globalization transcending polarizations such as communist–capitalist, East–West, Orient–Occident, and even more recently North–South. The travel of discourses (understood as both ideas and social practices) via technology and the Internet has created various forms of subjectivities (individual and collective) which conform to or rebel against authority. Further, in the context of this chapter the focus will be on collective subjectivities and attendant social practices. As an analytical concept, 'peoplehood' (i) refers to a bottom-up mobilizational capacity in physical spaces seeking to subvert and transform the hegemony of the state; (ii) has a demotic and democratic dynamic, is people-driven and embodies the ideal 'for the people'; and (iii) is local and global in its reach and manifestation, in which solidarities are formed internally and transnationally.

What links the indignant voices of the Arab street and the 2011 angry protests of *Occupy Wall Street* in the US and the 2011–12 anti-austerity *acampadas* (encampments of protesters in public squares) in Spain? Evidence of commonality abounds in the global squares of protest and in the triggers of discontent. All of these protest groups seem to embrace, at least rhetorically, an emancipatory mantra of freedom and dignity. Again, the Arab Spring's protesters and groups do not differ much from those made popular by the movement of the *indignados*/M-15,[1] ATTAC,[2] *Democracia Real Ya* (genuine democracy), and *juventud sin future* (future-less youth) in Spain. They are driven by demands for inclusive citizenship shared by like-minded activists who took to the streets throughout 2014 in Thailand, Greece, Portugal, Venezuela, and Ukraine. The cries of 'indignation' at unchecked power, police brutality, corruption, cronyism, discrimination, and obscene levels of inequality hail, in varying degrees, from some of the richest (e.g. United States) to some of the poorest nations on earth (e.g. Yemen). It is moral outrage at the structural injustice inherent in the prevailing socio-economic and political order. While specific grievances vary from country to country, protests in diverse locales were bound together by displays of moral indignation at ill-governance (political and economic exclusion, cronyism, and corruption), familiarity with the gadgetry of globalization (Internet, Facebook, etc.), and usage of the 'technology' of resistance (moral protest, transnational solidarities, language of human rights).

Thus diverse backgrounds, levels of income, nationality and temporal and spatial distance are dissolved in the cauldron of shared moral outrage and revolt against the tyranny of existing political and socio-economic order. We witness the paradox of polyphony/plurality (of languages and cultures) and harmony/uniformity (of messages and activisms). The Arab Spring thus serves as a connector between Arab and non-Arab societies. As a historic moment of change, embodying anti-systemic protest, it has proven its worth. In many parts of the world, people seem to share the glee of despots fleeing, one of the most recent being Yanukovych in Ukraine in February 2014. They seem to act in unison: the banners of 'occupy' 'degage', or leave (*irhal*), and 'game over' have a kind of revolutionary and poetic synthesis: as if all of a sudden the world's rebellious youths, students, and other types of marginalized groups dissolved into a singular, cohesive, and solidaristic complex.

On the ground, the Arab Spring seemed unstoppable. Indeed, many argue that the Arab Spring, or at least the consequences of the uprisings, are still ongoing. In this sense, it continues to 'travel' steadily, eerily popping up in diverse socio-political terrains shaking apparently stable regimes, with host polities and societies deploying it in their locale according to their own needs. The initial spark was ignited by the Tunisian youth. The Egyptian and the Libyan youth intensified the flame of protest. Tunis was the trigger; Cairo built the momentum; Tripoli and Benghazi signalled a kind of 'domino effect'. From then on, the 'travel' of the Arab Spring took a life of its own. From this perspective, the Arab Spring is just another manifestation of the human desire for freedom, dignity and justice. From an IR perspective, we take three ideas from the foregoing. First, there is a dynamic of 'deterritorialization' of activism whereby new political imaginaries, solidarities, language and protest strategies render nationalist borders meaningless. Second, the resulting trans-border newly reconstituted identities, moral protests, and networks hint at the idea of social 'movement spillover' (Meyer and Whittier 1994), captured in this chapter by the notion of *al-harak* or 'peoplehood'. Third, for the first since the emergence of the modern Middle East, societies have led the drive to change, or forced it, in a fashion akin to a bottom-up redistribution of power, even if ephemerally taking advantage of disarray or powerlessness of power-holders. This speaks both to the Marxist idea of radical change from below (changing history, as it were, not describing it). Similarly, it accentuates the liberal standpoint of IR which exalts the dynamic of politically, ideationally, and socially differentiated power in which non-state actors contribute to the crafting of power relations, domestically as well as internationally.

A caveat is in order here. Popular revolutions are seldom smooth. Tribal solidarity, religiosity, sectarianism, democracy, social justice, and equal citizenship all seem to be part of the normative vision that animates these new activisms. The road to freedom and justice is bumpy. Thus, protracted protests when brutally suppressed can morph into militant campaigns and weaken states to the point of near collapse such as in Libya and Syria, or when states seem to melt away from specific regions, leaving the ground to be occupied by terrorists (as Al-Qaida in the Arabian Peninsula—AQAP—in South Yemen) or to be overrun by centrifugal forces (such as the Houthi campaign in Yemen).

Regional differences

It may be stated that parts of the Arab Middle East, such as the Gulf States, are islands of 'stability' and 'prosperity' amidst a sea of turmoil, and are immune from the contagion of the Arab Spring. However, this is a misreading of the situation on the ground. Although the spill-over and 'demonstration effects' of the Arab Spring have not been even across the vast Arab geography and demography, and—regardless of how the message of emancipation integral to the Arab Spring 'travels', that is, manifests itself, or mutates socially and politically—it resonates with wide publics within and without the region. The Arab Spring has inspired masses at the same time that it has struck fear among autocrats across the region. Protests have been spearheaded by both individuals and groups in these countries. The periodic protests of increasing frequency by Saudi women drivers are symptomatic of such protests, as are the individual voices of bloggers and poets. And that spooks up the state's security apparatuses. Thus, the reality lurking behind the appearance of stability is not pleasant.[3]

Perhaps an abundance of natural resources combined with a supernormal surplus of workers extracted from a seemingly infinite supply of cheap labour from South and South-East Asia has enabled the oil monarchies to set up a system of economic privilege and buy the acquiescence of their nationals. The unusual amount of wealth enjoyed by the oil exporting Gulf States has propelled the ruling elite into adopting a two-fold strategy to deal with the prospect of revolutionary contagion. On the one hand, it has led to the adoption of irrational or draconian measures—for example, the Qatari government gave a life sentence to Mohammad ibn al-Dheeb al-Ajami, a poet whose 2012 poem, 'Tunisian Jasmine,' supported the uprisings in the Arab world. 'We are all Tunisia in the face of repressive elites!' wrote al-Ajami. The sentencing of the Saudi blogger, Raif Badawi, to 1,000 lashes and 10 years in prison is another glaring example of the brutal silencing of protest. The combined Saudi and UAE intervention (14 March 2011) in Bahrain and the July 2013 Saudi–UAE-backed military takeover of power in Egypt, combined with massive aid packages, were complementary measures designed to contain people-driven system reforms. No process of dialogue between the Sunni ruling elite and the Shia majority in Bahrain was facilitated by neighbouring states, that is, a process that redistributes power and welfare in a way that produces a win–win outcome (positive-sum game) for the power holders and civil society. On the other hand, the oil-rich Gulf regimes are unique in their ability to effectively bribe entire national populations into silence. In the wake of the Arab Spring, the Gulf States, like Saudi Arabia, enhanced subsidies and other welfare payments for nationals.[4] Moreover, the measures put in place to appease the national population were not only financial. For instance, women were granted the right to vote and run in the 2015 municipal elections, without the permission of their male guardians. The Arab Spring's absence, thus far, in countries such as Saudi Arabia, may be thought to suggest a shadowy presence.

The Arab Spring and globalization

Equally important in understanding the expansion of the Arab Spring is the fact that the 'explosion' of protest and socio-political revolutions—as an ideational and moral dynamic—is on display as a consequence of the shrinking of time-space in the wake of globalization. This is often attributed to high-tech revolutions. With the shrinkage of time and space, disillusion with the prevailing socio-economic order appeared to be increasingly shared across the globe. The 'rebellious' citizens and denizens (in the global 'North') are the kind of individuals that today populate polities marked by disillusionment and contest of power. In this time-space collapse, there is an emerging tendency towards reclamation of citizenship rights. Issues of freedom and dignity and the desire to foment empowered identities resonate through all these societies. However, the question of timing must not be underestimated in the facilitation of 'movement spillover', from Egypt and Tunisia to other Arab countries. Through enactment of moral protest the people come together to challenge existing political organization, be it democratic or not. The bid to reconfigure power relations –in order to normalize state–society relations—has strong resonance in the Arab Spring. This it shares with protest movements that preceded it (e.g. in Eastern Europe) or followed it (across many an Arab state, as illustrated in **Figure 15.1**): there is dissolution of political thought practices that coached citizens to delegate (in democracies) or surrender and defer the management of their futures (in autocracies).

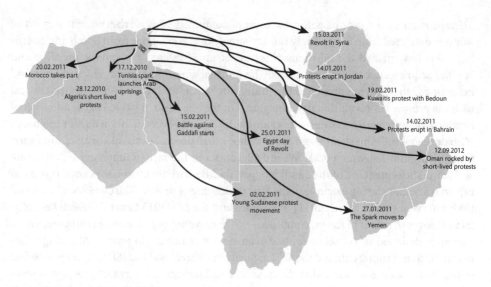

Figure 15.1 Travel of the Arab Spring

What has proved infectious in all of these instances of protest is the impulse towards self-organization, speaking back, writing back, and striking back at all symbols of power. The hitherto silent majorities in the West that had for so long been lulled to check out of political participation are inspired by the moral symbolism as well as the victories recorded against autocrats in the Middle East (West 2011). Social movements are playing a proactive role through moral protest and disruptive power, forcing either change in the political landscape (as with Greece's Syriza) or drawing wide support in favour of reforms (e.g. Spain).[5] Specifically, in the Arab Middle East, similar reference can be made to those who have until early 2011 opted out of political participation in delegitimized polities that took various forms from traditional autocracies to privatized polities such as the 'republican' dynasties (Libya, Tunisia, Egypt, Yemen; Sadiki 2009). They were the first to buckle under the juggernaut of anti-despotic popular defiance and resistance in 2011.

As far as moral symbolism goes, the death knell of the 'passive' Arab thrown into oblivion in the Orientalist discourse has been sounded. The revolutionary and visible Arab would not be 'voided' by Al-Jazeera, the Internet, Facebook, and the like. These have been perhaps 'over-romanticized' as drivers of change. Undoubtedly, the information and high-tech revolution has lent a helping hand to Arab uprisings. But, it is the free will and capacity of fearless and leaderless individuals to assume agency—more than the structural dynamic—that features prominently in the Arab uprisings. Agency matters when accounting for the Arab Spring as it did in the case of the Iranian Revolution of 1979. Because agency is primary in these revolutions (Sharp 2012), the techniques and technologies of protest, resistance, and communication would have been invented if they had not existed. At the time of the 1979 Islamic Revolution in Iran, Xerox and cassettes were the technologies of the time. They were no match to Facebook or Twitter today. Nonetheless, defiance led them to be used to optimum effect in the bid to reach a wider audience. Agency is what has turned people into a mobilizable 'monument', a critical mass that was able to assert itself against unjust rulers.

The position of international actors vis-à-vis these movements and the Arab Spring will be discussed in the chapter's last section.

Hopelessness in the face of systemic forces is what led Mohamed Bouazizi to take his own life in protest in December 2010. Bouazizi's individual act of desperation was just a dramatic manifestation of the feelings of marginalization shared by the youth across most of the natural resource poor Arab Middle East. Arab countries seemed to be susceptible to influence by the protests led by youths across a vast geography irrespective of local realities. This is where the Arab Spring impresses: the Arab region remains a cohesive cultural sub-system. It has continuously shared the quest for decolonization and modernization. This very quest is what the Arab region shares with other parts of the world (such as Africa) where merging solidarities as modes of collective against marginalization and joblessness have been present. These solidarities and protests are shaking established power and elites and range from civic and peaceful movements (e.g. Y'en a Marre movement in Senegal, April 6 in Egypt, Femmes Démocrates in Tunisia) to unruly and violent manifestations (such as Boko Haram in Nigeria, Ansar Dine in Mali, al Shabaab in Somalia, and ISIS in Iraq and Syria). While some champion the cause of re-Islamization (the quest for greater representation of Islam in polity, society, and economy), as in the cases of Ansare Dine and ISIS, others are leading struggles for social justice and socio-economic rights (e.g. in the Mozambique riots of 2010–12). Artistic expression as a mode of protest has entered the fray too. Rap music has emerged throughout the Arab World: for example, 'El General' led this wave in Tunisia with many songs against the dictatorial regime ousted in 2011.[6]

To sum up, that the Arab masses are connected with the rest of the world is evidenced by their proclivity to respond to and learn from other protest movements and revolts, such as those in Europe and Asia. There appears to be a new dynamic in the Arab Middle East: while there may be temporary setbacks and differential pace of protests, there is no winding back of the clock to pre-2011 state–society relations. The margin carved out by Arabs to speak back, write back, and engage in dissidence cannot be reclaimed by relics of the old regime, even in the states where vigilance against all dissidence has been heightened. That is the prosaic fact of life in the post-Arab Spring world.

Orientalism challenged

Orientalism as an attitude or a mode of speaking and writing about the Middle East (Said 1978; Mitchell 1988) persists. Orientalist narratives have historically relegated the Arab Middle East to a sphere of irrelevance, ahistoricity, and exile from the realm of civility and modernity—however understood. Theses of authoritarian 'resilience' have dogged the Middle East for the greater part of postcolonial history (Anderson 1991b).

The Arab Spring and the myth of exceptionalism

The Arab Spring poses a huge problem for conventional wisdom on the Middle East (or 'Orient') as a discursive formation produced by some Orientalists. Specifically, it warrants serious interrogation of the Arab Middle East 'exceptionalism' which manifests itself in the following two forms:

a) as an exilic and exclusionary device that situates the Arab Middle East outside the 'box' of modernity, democracy, legal-rationality, civility, etc., before the Arab Spring; and

b) as an attitude that elevates the Arab World (especially Arab Spring states) to a kind of beacon of light for the rest of the developing world suffering under the yoke of tyranny and oppression as they join the wave of protests in the wake of the Arab Spring.

The display of people power in the public squares of Cairo, Hama, Homs, Manama, Sanaa, Tripoli, and Tunis challenges Orientalist stereotypes of Arabs as passive, invisible, and resistant to the values of 'freedom'. The irony was not lost on keen observers as it was freedom that was one of the key demands of the *thuwwar* of the Arab Spring. Writing in the Ahram Centre's Arabic journal *Majallat Al-Dimuqratiyyah* (*Journal of Democracy*) in reference to the '25th of January Revolution', Hala Mustafa (2011: 6–14) observed that the Arab Spring represented 'a return of spirit and consciousness' for the eighty million-strong Egyptian nation. She notes that at the core of this revolution was the urge to create a 'democratic system', based on justice, dignity, and freedom (Hala Mustafa 2011: 7–8). This sums up the ethos of the Arab Spring from Tunisia to Yemen. A similar notion is encapsulated in the phrase 'the Tunisian people's charisma' (Qawi 2011: 143). This characterization draws attention to the empowering effect of the Tunisian people's success in ousting their dictator, thus setting in motion a revolutionary demonstration effect across the Arab Middle East. 'This charisma derives its moral flame from the long tradition of struggle all over the Arab Maghreb. This region led a fierce resistance against French colonialism, and [in Tunisia] led to the organization of labour unions of which the Federated Union of Tunisia Workers (UGTT) was a key force [during the 2011 revolution]' (Qawi 2011: 142).

These positive properties attributed to the enabling power of the Arab Spring are overlooked in some Orientalist discourses of the Oriental 'other'. The notions of 'spiritedness', 'consciousness', and 'charisma' stand in stark contrast to the invisibility and passivity attributed to Arabs, especially as agents of democratic change. Note how these terms of reference compare with those used by Steven Cook (Senior Fellow at the US-based Council on Foreign Relations) in his *Foreign Policy* article (Cook 2011): he talks about 'the Frankenstein of Tahrir Square' at the height of the 2011 protests. The phrase smacks of the old blinkered Orientalism. Doom and gloom is written all over his take on the protests : 'Egypt is spinning out of control. But it is not only the fault of the ruling military junta, but the protesters in the street deserve plenty of blame, too' (Cook 2011). Obsession with 'order' and 'stability' has created in the minds of international 'touristic' news-makers of Tahrir Square unrealistic expectations of 'orderly' protest. Revolutions are nothing short of messy historical moments.

The Arab Spring brought tremendous fervour. It galvanized Arab public squares into waves of sustained protest intermittently in Tahrir Square and the Kasba or Bardo squares in Tunisia, and escalated into armed conflict in places like Syria, Libya, and Yemen. It enthused the masses to dismantle the authoritarian structures of power (Egypt, Tunisia, Libya) similar to the democratizing energies of the Philippine, Indonesian, Czech, or Georgian peoples. Yet the emergence of this movement with its implications for civic reconstruction has not escaped the denigration typical of Orientalist depiction of the region. Early in 2011, Tahrir Square drew worldwide attention and admiration for the creative display of peacefully sustained protest, nine days before Mubarak was ousted. That admiration was not universal. There were concerns, some of them legitimate. American billionaire, Mortimer Zuckerman, warned that a takeover by the Muslim Brotherhood would be a disaster for US interests. What the Egyptians dared to think did not matter, it seems. Partly, this brand of thinking is a feature of a typically patronizing rhetoric (Zuckerman 2011).

The standard precautionary proviso, about 'Islamic militants' lurking to take over power after the departure of autocrats, is all-pervasive. The Israelis and their intellectual support-ers in the West, led by Bernard-Henry Levy, launched an organized campaign to unseat Mursi.[7] Thus the *Telegraph* (UK) quipped on 27 January 2011 that what Egyptians needed was 'reform not revolution' (Grant and Petersen 2011). 'Revolution' as the emblematic zeal of the Arab Spring tends to be represented as suspect. For Ziya Meral, a Turkish legal expert, the protests are a moment of 'evolution' not 'revolution'. He championed evolution, viewing it to be in 2011 pushing Egypt towards an Israeli model of political transformation. In that model, he intimates, the army would be the only force with the capacity to reign in fissiparous Islamists and secularists (Meral 2011). Maybe that is what Field Marshal Abdel Fattah al-Sisi attempted when he overthrew the elected Mursi government on 3 July 2013. His actions to date leave no doubt that democracy was the last thing on his mind. The role of external pow-ers as antagonists or backers of the Arab Spring will be touched upon in the final section of this chapter.

The use of the term 'awakening' is denounced by many Arab observers as a misnomer in reference to the Arab Spring. It is taken to be tainted by its usage in reference to the resur-gence of the 1980s during the height of antagonism between secular regimes and Islamists, on the one hand, and Islamists and the West, on the other. The usage is considered pejora-tive. Its connotations—intended or un-intended—signify contempt and communicate mis-understanding of the Arab Spring. One scholar writing in *Al-Jazeera English* criticizes the use of the term 'awakening' for ignoring Arab and Middle Eastern history of uprisings. The term is similarly questioned for assuming passivity (as opposed to participatory culture) to be the norm. 'Those who call what has unfolded since the last year in the Arab World as an Arab "awakening" are not only ignorant of the history of the last century, but also deploy Orientalist arguments in their depiction of Arabs as a quiescent people who put up with dictatorship for decades and are finally waking up from their torpor' (Massad 2011). For Massad, the advent of the Arab Spring has not stopped Orientalism.

Doubt over the 'Arab Spring' is widespread. It has elicited global debate. This is positive, since the discourse of the phenomenon is dispersed and plural. Yet this debate tends to be mired in a great deal of negativity about the actual or possible outcomes of the Arab Spring. Specifically, democratic outcomes are questioned. Some observers could see only a 'winter'. Indeed, the notion of the Arab Spring morphing into a winter is one of the most com-mon metaphors used in this respect. Writing in the well-known Israeli newspaper, *Haaretz*, Oudeh Basharat sounds off alarm bells about the rise of *fanatics*, a totalizing neat label in reference to Islamists (Basharat 2011). In an Op-Ed in the *Huffington Post*, New York University IR scholar, Alon Ben-Meir, also places 'the dark forces' of Islamism, including the emerging Salafist forces, as the harbingers of this winter (Ben-Meir 2011). He adds the following to the mix of factors conspiring against the Arab Spring: tribes, lack of 'tradi-tional liberalism', 'ethnic minorities' hold on power', the army, and 'the religious divide and extremism' (Ben-Meir 2011).

There is no denying that these dynamics exist. But they are not monoliths immune to any kind of shift. They are historically evolving. Furthermore, the voices and forces of democratic renewal do not come from a single or fixed bloc of 'liberals'. Use of common generalizations about Islamism, the Arab Middle East's lack of a liberal tradition, and the West's democratic repertoire are superficially assumed to be the main factors leading the Arab Spring to degenerate into a 'winter'. Paradoxically, many so-called liberals were cheerleading the military takeover of the democratically elected regime in order to stem the tide of Islamism in Egypt. Democratic values, practices, or struggles are not abstractions stored in an age-long repository, awaiting reification or reincarnation in a concrete form. They are instead constructed in the tensions, arguments, and disputations between these seemingly irreconcilable and inhospitable forces. The emerging sites of democratic struggle across boundaries of ideology, religion, sect, and even class that these forces share constitute the real terrain on which democratic compromises and learning take place.

Salman Masalha of *Haaretz* quips that the 'Recent revolutions are neither Arab nor spring' (Masalha 2011). He views the 'Arab Spring' as no more than a new phase in the nationalist crisis that has gripped the Arab Middle East for decades, making assertions that it is part of a bigger scheme to support Sunni Islam to stem the tide of Shia Islam. He concludes that the Arab Spring rather than a conscious spirited popular movement, 'is just another golem [an artificially created human being] that is liable to turn on its maker' (Masalha 2011). The Arab Spring warrants a questioning of persistent Orientalism. It allows observers and scholars to marshal evidence from the field with which to refute stereotypes of passivity and servility. The nature of postcolonial politics in the Arab Middle East cannot be explained by anything in Islam or Arab culture *per se*. Rather, one must look to the oppressive tactics of singular elites who ruled with an iron hand without any system of checks and balances. They did so, in fact, in a manner strikingly similar to elites in a number of predominantly Catholic (and non-communist) societies—Franco in Spain, Marcos in the Philippines, and junta-led regimes in Latin American countries such as Argentina, Brazil, Chile, and Nicaragua in the 1970s and 1980s. This Third Wave of Democratization was termed a Catholic wave even by Huntington (1991). However, all they see in the Arab uprising is a tendency for it to degenerate into a winter.

The main recipient of blame for this degeneration is the rise of Islamists. Yet, through Arab eyes,[8] the Arab Middle East is on the cusp of a democratic metamorphosis. Some Islamists (Nahda in Tunisia) are waging battles with the ballot, others with the bullet (ISIS). The October 2011 Constituent Assembly elections in Tunisia and the parliamentary elections in Egypt that took place in three phases between November 2011 and January 2012—the first two parliamentary elections of the Arab Spring—and the 2015 peaceful transfer of power from 'Islamists' to 'liberals' challenge the stereotypical constructions of the Arab Middle East. Fanaticism is not perennially cemented to Islamists; and an absence of civil society cannot be attributed to Islam. Resistance to authoritarianism, assumption of popular agency, and the new activism of plural political forces across the region are today defying Orientalist stereotypes. The people have in the wake of the Arab Spring emerged as agents of change, once the exclusive prerogative of states and political elites.

It is common ground to reject (neo)orientalism. However, more serious scholarship must be distinguished from extreme and unrepresentative voices. Nuanced and sophisticated representation of the Arab Spring, and the Middle East more generally, can be found in the views of more established Orientalists. Robert Irwin, a well-known British historian, offers a vigorous rebuttal of what he views as Said's mischaracterization of Orientalism and

Orientalists as tools of colonial powers. He gives a Pre-Saidian account of Orientalism as a serious undertaking to study Islam, Arab literature, language, culture, and history begun in the seventeenth century, untarnished by links to modern-day Western geopolitics or imperialism (Irwin 2006). Irwin's teacher, Princeton University historian Bernard Lewis expresses 'delight' at the advent of the Arab Spring. He stresses and lauds Islam's attention to the institution of justice (*adl*) and opposition to tyrannical rule (Weiss 2011). Moreover, he rejects any imposition of Western democracy on Arab Spring states. He champions a route of political renewal that, in his view, must be guided by local history and tradition. 'I don't think we can assume that the Anglo-American system of democracy is a sort of world rule, a world ideal … Muslims should be allowed—and indeed helped and encouraged—to develop their own ways of doing things' (Weiss 2011). In the same vein, Foud Ajami, senior fellow at Stanford University's Hoover Institution, promotes agency of the Arabs as being the main drivers of change in their region during the 2011 uprisings. This is a far cry from Orientalist generalizations about Arabs/Muslims as passive subjects, out of step with history. Ajami rejects suggestions that President Obama's June 2009 Cairo speech inspired the Arab Spring. As he puts it 'America should not write itself into every story: There are forces in distant nations that we can neither ride nor extinguish' (Ajami 2012). Moreover, he deprecates American officialdom's loss of credibility in the lead-up to the Arab Spring. Ajami specifies Obama's 'ease with the status quo'—driving home the message that his administration must not be credited with making the Arab Spring, which was the invention of Arab youth and protestors such as in Tahrir Square (Ajami 2012).

People-driven international relations

The study of IR within a Middle Eastern setting poses new challenges in the wake of the 'Arab Spring'. As noted already, the Arab Spring is loosely used here in reference to the people-driven actions. This includes protest, dissent, civic political organization, and unruly/violent political manifestations that have acted as catalysts for and against change. As briefly outlined in the section which follows, these challenges call for reflection on the dominant perspectives:

(a) **Bringing religion back in IR:** IR has been imported, in whole or in part, as part of wide-ranging Eurocentric disciplines and paradigms for interpreting and explaining a whole range of phenomena from state- and war-making to colonial and post-colonial encounters with Western powers in the region. As yet no uniquely Arab or Muslim analogues to IR's diverse theoretical approaches have emerged locally. Religion's lasting power—in an ideational or behavioural sense—suggests it continues to be a potent force common to Jews, Muslims, and Christians in this region (Armstrong 1994). The Middle Eastern perspective should be informed by the central place that religion has in it. This is not unique to this region. *Liberation theology* (Brown 1990) as a radical movement in the context of South America was deployed to bring about social change and justice to the working class. Demands for re-Islamization on behalf of democratic/civic and unruly/violent movements in the Middle East illustrate the point about the relevance of the religious perspective. Yet religion is seldom incorporated in studies of the IR of the Middle East with the possible exception of the Gramscian and the Constructivist models (Wendt 1992; Lawson 2006). Distinguished anthropologist Talal Asad's *Genealogies of Religion* (1993) interrogates the reigning wisdom that tends to construct religion and secularity as mutually exclusive categories. His study marshals empirical and textual evidence to argue that secularity alone is unable to explain social and political historical happenings. Juxtaposed with this is his view that liberal theory's stress on secularity renders it devoid of the tools to understand realities in non-Western societies. He questions liberal theory's categories and their ability to read 'different political futures in which other traditions can thrive' (1993: 306). He poses this question: 'Must our critical ethnographies of other traditions in modern nation-states adopt the categories offered by liberal theory?'

(b) **Counting realist narratives:** There still exists a conspicuous realist bent in the analytics of international events. However, it is appropriate in the wake of the Arab Spring to make use of the full range of alternative IR perspectives. This raises the level of sophistication and critical thinking when interpreting the complex dynamics of change in power relations, both within and without nations. IR theories are perennially subject to contestation and so are the interpretations of the events associated with the Arab Spring. Protest and dissent on behalf of 'freedom and dignity' were echoed in many an Arab public square. This fact points to the potency of ideas in explaining discontinuous change—deserving of special attention by the dominant schools of IR.

By the same token, violent and non-violent 'resistance' against authoritarianism (Hafez 2003) may intensify interest in alternative perspectives hitherto underrepresented in analytical discourses on global politics—along the lines of Gramscian and other critical theories, and 'revolution' as a driver and explanatory tool of change (see, for instance, Halliday 1990). It may be argued that religion fits into the Gramscian sense of 'hegemonic discourse'. At least, in so far as religion is used by the ruling regimes as a 'soft' mechanism to generate consent of civil society without recourse to brute force, it remains an important part of hegemonic discourse in Arab Gulf states. It is no less true of counter-hegemonic discourse across the Arab Middle East. In the same vein, constructivists may equally find plenty of food for thought in the 'explosion' of identity discourse (Hatina 2007). Identity narratives (e.g. Shia vs Sunni) are deployed to re-map out power relations. This may be within nations (e.g. Iraq, Bahrain, Syria, and Yemen) as well as between them (for example, Iran-backed Shia Houthis in Yemen pitted against a Saudi-led ten-Sunni majority states coalition in operation 'Firmness Storm' launched on 28 March 2015).

(c) **Marxists and revolution:** The idea of revolution as a driver of history is sketched out by many Marxist scholars. Revolution has been a major driving force in IR theory and in the regional life of the Arab Middle East. Examples abound of revolutions which targeted the state apparatus and old bureaucracy of monarchical realms from Iraq in 1920 to Egypt in 1952. Young officers who executed coups in many an Arab country (e.g. Libya, Syria, Yemen) adopted an anti-statist posture, viewing monarchies and their alliance with the landed class and acquiescence to colonial rule to be stifling progress and emancipation of polity and society. However, the military officers who came to power after smashing monarchical systems sought singular possession of the state—a kind of a 'booty' for the victorious officer class and their clients (workers, peasants, soldiers, Muslim clergy, and a parasitic state-dependent bourgeoisie).

Revolution is a regional dynamic in the Middle East. States are made and unmade in the process of unfolding revolutions. Although the persistence of authoritarian regimes has to a large degree obscured the presence of change, specifically radical political change, political actors within and across national boundaries in the Middle East have challenged incumbent regimes and threatened to introduce—and in a few cases have succeeded in introducing—a new political order. Thus revolutions have played a major role in speeding up the formation of state-building (1952 Egypt; 1979 Iran) and also shoring up counter-revolutionary regimes which have shored up their institutions of the state to stem the flow of revolution to their territories.

The late Fred Halliday's article (1990) is very sharp piece on the state of IR and the study of revolution. Grand moments ushering political change are products of a combination of national and international factors. The nation state and all that transpires within are not immune to the vicissitudes of the global theatre. Revolution can be counted among the various phenomena which bind the national to the international in a complex network of actors and institutions. In international relations, as Halliday aptly observed, revolution has been neglected in the theorizing of the international system. The presence of revolutions or other interruptions to the harmony of the state system are not exceptional, nor are they exclusively internal developments. Halliday cites Martin Wight's findings that revolution was dominant for 'over *half* the history of the international system' (Halliday 1990: 212). Decisive transformations such as the Bolshevik revolution have defined the very systemic nature of international politics, particularly in the twentieth century, in both war and post-war periods (Halliday 1990: 213). Interactions among states have been equally shaped by revolution as much as war. And moreover, wars have been preceded by revolutions. Revolutionary internationalism is contrasted with counter-revolutionary internationalism whereby conflicts ensue in a tendency to homogeneity seeking to export revolution or contain and overthrow revolutions (Halliday 1990: 215). The definition of revolution provided by Halliday is largely derived from Theda Skocpol's social revolution consisting of a combination of 'two coincidences' bringing together societal structural change with class upheaval on the one hand and political and social transformation on the other hand (Halliday 1990: 210). Popular mobilization against a weakened state, rendered so by international factors, produce revolutions with an emphasis on the latter (Halliday 1990: 213–14). The force of revolution gathers momentum through the deterioration of the state's coercive capacity to maintain order (or rather repression). The Arab Spring points to deleterious effects of international structural adjustment policies on societies linked to authoritarian policies. Bottom-up dynamics were produced by and in turn responded to the continuing political and economic marginalization of individuals and social groups (Sadiki 2000). Ostensibly durable authoritarian regimes in the Middle East were subject to challenges to their ability to repress against the backdrop of erosion of the post-colonial distributive arrangements (quasi 'republics of bread' that provided subsidies in return for political acquiescence and loyalty) due to international economic pressures. However, the reassertion of authoritarianism in some Arab countries (Libya, Egypt, and Syria) can be understood to be a region-wide counter-revolutionary trend seeking to privilege the most dominant actor in the region: the military.

(d) **Introducing a pluralist perspective:** While state-centric explanations remain important, a pluralist approach that incorporates alternative perspectives is necessary in grasping the full meaning of regional politics. To illustrate, 'Firmness Storm' can be read in multiple ways. On the one hand, it exemplifies the Saudi-led Gulf states' quest for regional leadership and their security, and, as such, it is a classic exercise of realpolitik à la realism. On the other hand, the operation can be assessed through a constructivist prism in so far as identity narratives (Shia vs Sunnis) underpin the conflict.

What the Arab Spring presents IR with is an opening for critically assessing the deep-rooted state-centric approaches to regional politics. Not so long ago, the region's 'game changers', as it were, belonged to a different IR imaginary. Such an imaginary was uniquely straddled by regional powers (e.g. Egypt, Israel, Iran, Iraq, Kingdom of Saudi Arabia, Syria, Turkey, and of late Qatar and UAE) and iconic statesmen, both local and global. That phalanx included a mix of figures such as Arafat, Asad, Begin, Gaddafi, Khomeini, Mubarak, Nasrallah, Nasser, Rabin, Reza Shah, Saddam, Henry Kissinger and his 'shuttle diplomacy' in the 1973 war, James Baker, Condoleezza Rice, Richard Pearl, Colin Powell, and Hilary Clinton, amongst others. The Arab Spring has changed all of that: for the first time since the 1979 Islamic Revolution that brought Shia clerics to power in Iran, peoples across a vast Arab geography have emerged as actual and potential 'game-changers', driving change from below (though interestingly still around an iconic leader in the Iranian case). This is one more reason why we must guard against mono-causal explanations of politics in the Arab Middle East. Non-state actors associated with the Arab Spring have challenged (Egypt), destabilized (Libya, Syria, Yemen), and radically reformed (Tunisia) the nation state.

Arab Spring: moment of 'peoplehood'

The Arabic term 'al-harak' (referring to 'peoplehood', and popular mobilization) captures the essence of the political, social, cultural, and religious people-driven ferment. It marks an important watershed in the life of the post-colonial Arab state. It partakes of both civil and uncivil manifestations of thought and practice across boundaries of rich diversity and complexity. Factors such as ethnicity, demography, history, geography, and varying degrees of political organization, good governance, and overall development make up such diversity.

This ferment is noted for its transformative impact on the region's politics. Actors, ideas, and events within one country seem to prove infectious or destabilizing in neighbouring countries. From the outset, the Arab Spring took on a life of its own: morphing from a national into a transnational phenomenon.

Four trends are integral to this people-based and driven ferment: migratory, transitory, participatory, and fragmentary. This four-fold process has impacted state–society relations within specific countries as well as state–state relations across the region. These trends have pushed a spectre of multi-faceted upheavals and transformations wide-open: power vacuum (Libya, Yemen), protracted contests and counter-contests over value allocation (Bahrain), reversals (Egypt), identity politics (Iraq, Yemen, Bahrain, Syria), power and resource distribution (Kuwait, Libya, Yemen), civil and unruly modes of engagement (Egypt, Yemen), patronage and client politics (Gulf states), and the consolidation of legitimate polities (Tunisia) (see **Table 15.1**).

Table 15.1 Emerging trends in the Arab Middle East

Transitory	Electoral processes	Democratic breakdown/reverse
	Constitution-framing	Counter-revolutionary reflexes
= motion and movement	Political party legalization	Political impasse
challenging *status quo*	Fledgling democratization	Civil war
		Insurgency / Terrorism
Participatory	Civil/Civic/Legal:	Uncivil/Unruly/Violent:
= agents of change made up	New political elites (Islamists,	Radicalized youth/forces
of individuals, old and new	Salafists, Leftists) + old elites	Militias (Iraq, Libya, Syria, Yemen)
groups, and solidarities	New social movements (youth	Warring tribes (Yemen, Libya)
	movements) + political parties	Warring sects (several countries including
	+ civic bodies	Lebanon)
	Emerging forms of citizenship	Warring ethnicities (Iraq, Syria, Libya)
	(protesters, dissidents, social	
	media agents)	
	Voters	
Fragmentary	Authoritarian power structures	Dissolution of political authority
	Post-colonial ruling houses	Regimes morphing into militias (Syria)
	Former ruling political parties and	Fragmentation of religious authority
	elites	(esp. in Sunni countries: Salafi vs. Muslim
	Old networks of patronage-	Brotherhood schools)
	clientelism	State dismembering scenarios
= break-up of collective	Mass mobilizational and populist	Regionalization (Libya, Syria, Yemen)
morality, laws, identity, and	ideologies (Iraq, Syria, Egypt,	Refuge in primordial templates of identity
conceptions of community	Tunisia, Yemen) and corporatist	Parochial solidarities (based on commonality
	forms of political organization	of region, sect, ethnicity, tribe, ideology, etc.)

Never before had such vociferous and diverse publics been at the heart of political contests. At the core of these contests lies the drive of peoplehood to reclaim and/or redefine power. That is, power in its multiple dimensions as governance, distribution of resources, morality, laws, belonging, citizenship, freedom, and dignity. The peoplehood moment represents a historical opening to strike back at the decaying post-colonial structures of authority and rule. To an extent, peoplehood is a novelty, with popular mobilizations being an integral part of the political landscape. Instructive examples range from mass-based resistance groups to cultural 'awakenings' (such as political and cultural salons) to autocratic regimes seeking to mobilize citizens for public shows of support in order to tame and channel their energies (sometimes nationalism and patriotism is invoked as we are currently seeing in al-Sisi's Egypt). From this perspective, peoplehood also marks a challenge to the whole discipline of IR. Even if marked by fluidity and susceptible to temporary setbacks, the Arab Spring seems to be irreversible in terms of enabling the region's peoples to transcend the threshold of fear. States no longer command all of the moral resources of defining change. Democratic participation and maturity (e.g. Tunisia) or violent resistance (e.g. Syria) call into question the ability of the Arab post-colonial order to reproduce itself intact.

The Arab Spring has been uneven in its impact. Nonetheless, peoples are empowered to contest, redefine and reclaim a space and a voice. Non-violent civic resistance and violent strategies are equally used. On the violent front, militias of all kinds have mushroomed—backed by internal and external constituencies. Their aim is to unseat authoritarian rulers (e.g. Asad in Syria) or have an input in the rebuilding of the nation state after overthrowing erstwhile leaders (e.g. Libya; Yemen). Peoplehood thus looms large on the IR and political horizon of the Middle East; the travel of positive ideas (freedom, moral protest) as well as of negative thought-practice (terrorism). Nonetheless, this new monumental force has been catapulted into political centre-stage after being relegated to the periphery for decades. It gives a flavour of the bottom-up dynamics to inform and transform polity, society, identity, information, and culture in the foreseeable future in this region. On the transitory front, democratization and constitution-making have begun a slow but sure induction into a few polities, with Tunisia being the most promising thus far. This is the biggest and most obvious trend shaping state–society relations in the wake of the Arab Spring. These processes are already impacting upon the state system itself, in the sense of changing the boundaries as well as the political arrangements, of that system. Fragile security is the hallmark of weakened states whose territories are today disputed, threatened, or divided among feuding militias (e.g. Iraq, Libya, Syria, and Yemen). A continuous youth bulge bereft of development goods (education, employment, and housing) remains vulnerable to heightened radicalization. Tunisia's paradox is a case in point. It is at once the Arab Spring's only democratizing polity and the country with one of the highest number of fighters (more than 3,000) in the ranks of terrorist groups such as ISIS. Politically, centralized authority is subject to fragmentation either along sectarian or ideological lines.

In one way, the Arab Spring-type revolts of 2011 and the events that attended upon them have set the stage for polarization of state–society power relations within and between states in the region. The fragmentary nature of this moment marks the new politics evident across the region's vast geography. The twin protest–contest dynamic and explosion of violence shall not wither away. The Arab Spring cannot be oversimplified by reducing it to manifestations of 'hungry mobs' or 'street politics' (Sadiki 2009). It is indirectly a public opinion barometer that speaks to important issues of distribution of power and wealth. For example, the Arab human development agenda is noted for glaring deficits in need of urgent attention. They include deficits in inclusiveness, freedom, equality, empowerment, and knowledge (UNDP 2003). The emerging trends that are driving the process of change—for and against stability—be they violent or non-violent, spontaneous or planned, top-down or bottom-up, and motivated by domestic or external agenda-setting, all point to a heightened state of polarity in state–society relations. The centre and margin seem to be locked into a kind of logic of rivalry.

In contradistinction to previous phases of postcolonial history, the political margin has rekindled the practice of speaking back (dissent and protest) or striking back (with physical force). The political margin has always challenged the centre, emerging every now and again when the state retreats or is complacent. Conventional wisdom in IR has ignored the stubborn persistence of the political margin or peoplehood in shaping politics, regional and global. Non-state actors have been potent, for example the Muslim Brotherhood spread from Egypt to Arab and non-Arab locales during the twentieth century. Externally, the Arab Spring has created openings for discourses and forces that have produced (ideologically and materially) transnational entanglements. The 'fallout' from these entanglements has complicated the region's politics. The proliferation of non-state actors, flowing from new national politics, has its imprint all over the chessboard that is the Middle East, seeking to transform the game with nonconventional gambits. The peoplehood (*al-Harak*), is today on full display, taking both civic and unruly permutations. Its drive to change the political landscape in the Arab Middle East such as on behalf of the forces of re-Islamization has from the outset accompanied the Arab Spring. It has manifested itself in various ways, such as by non-state actors, namely Islamists who have imprinted on the Arab Spring either as legal or illegal agents of indelible change. More or less, it seems to outweigh the impact of secularist forces and is checked only by forces of the so-called the 'deep state' (the armed forces) in countries such as Egypt and Syria. Peacefully and violently, Islamist non-state actors have contributed a great deal to the drive to reconfigure power in the Arab Middle East.

The renewed prominence of non-state actors during the Arab Spring has added new factors to regional and national political contexts. Key characteristics of non-state actors are identified in **Table 15.2** according to adoption or non-adoption of violence, sect, date of formation, and field of action, for example countries and elections. Political activity revolving around the poles of ruly and unruly forms have led to a state of affairs which includes longstanding regimes falling (such as those of Ben Ali, Gaddafi, and Mubarak), those stubbornly holding on to power (such as Asad and Bouteflika), and others co-opting opposition movements (King Mohamed VI). The use of violence and non-violent political methods by Hezbollah and Libya Dawn blurs these two categorizations, which is accounted for in the category of 'hybrid violent-non-violent movements'.

Three additional categories would further help to identify crucial aspects of the movements in this table. Ideology, activities (rather than field of action) and countries/country will enable the reader to make sense of a typology of movements in the Arab Spring period. Ideologies could be Salafism or Islamism. In the case of the latter, we have examples ranging from reformist/moderate (*Wasatiyyah*) to Khomeinist. Activities include elections, violence, armed resistance, etc. Some of the movements in the table are simultaneously national, regional, and global while others are merely located in one specific country.

Centre vs periphery: bottom-up change

The centre–periphery model is deployed here very loosely. This model views power relations in a quasi-concentric sense: the centre represents the powerful industrialized states. The periphery refers to the states which remain politically and economically dependent on these powerful states. Neo-Marxist scholars use it to explain disparity between the developed colonial and neo-colonial North and the developing and under-developed South in the world economy. In so doing, they underscore the underdevelopment and/or dependent development of the periphery as a structural feature of the world capitalist system. Wallerstein (1974), Amin (1974), and Frank (1978) take the centre–periphery cleavage to be integral to the development of capitalism. The core (colonial and neo-colonial developed North) has advantages over peripheral countries in terms of technology and capital-intensive production. At the centre of the core–periphery model there exists a reproducible structure of unequal power relations. What reproduces this structure of inequality is the near monopoly of technology and predominantly capital-intensive production of high value added products in the North, and specialization in labour-intensive low value added raw material and light industrial products in the South.

The post-colonial ruling houses and elites associated with the military bureaucratic and comprador capitalist groups are complicit in exploiting the working poor at both the centre and the periphery. They control financial, technical, and coercive resources.

Table 15.2 Islamist non-state actors and movements active in the Arab Spring

Violent movements			Movements of political Islam				
			Non-violent movements			Hybrid violent-non-violent movements	
Name & Muslim sect	Date of formation	Field of action	Name	Date of formation	Field of action	Date of formation	Field of action
Al-Qaeda Sunni	1996	Global	Freedom & Justice Party (political arm of Muslim Brotherhood)	2011	Egypt [Winner of 2012–13 elections]		
Islamic State of Iraq and Syria/Levant (ISIS/ISIL/Daesh) Sunni	2013	Iraq, Syria, and Libya	Hezbollah	1982		1982	Post-Arab Spring Lebanon & Syria conflicts
Nusra Front Sunni	2012	Syria	Al-Noor Party	2011	Egypt [2012–13 elections]		
Beit AL-Maqdis / Saini Emirate Sunni		Egypt/Sinai	Al-Wasat Party	Formed 1996/ legalized in 2011	Egypt [2012–13 elections]		
Houthis Shia	2008	Yemen	Justice and Development Party	1998	Morocco [winner of 2011 legislative elections; governing party since then]		
Ansar Al-Sharia/ Sunni	2012	Libya & Tunisia	Dawn Libya (alliance among Islamists and revolutionaries)	2014	Muslim Brotherhood came second to secularist front in 2012 National Congress elections	2013	Libya Civil war
Uqba Ibn Nafaa/ Sunni	2012	Tunisia	Nahda Party	1980/legalized in 2011	Tunisia [winner of 2011 Constituent Assembly elections; second in 2014 National Assembly elections]		
Al-Hashd al-Sha'bi/ Sha'bi/ Sha	2014	Iraq					
Peace Brigades (a new version of al-Mahdi Army-2003)/ Shia	2014	Iraq					

Parsimoniously, the centre–periphery model in which various globalized systems are entangled is used here as a metaphor to refer to the asymmetrical structural power relations within post-colonial Arab states. A variant of the centre–periphery metaphor depicts the territorial nation state in the Middle East. Charles Tripp connects the uneven power relations with the modelling of the post-colonial Arab state by colonial powers on the modern European Westphalian examples—though these are increasingly discredited. The post-colonial ruling elite that inherited power from the colonies engineered unequal state–society relations. The entire new statist foundation is built to control resources (e.g. politics, coercion, education, bureaucracy) and distribute goods (e.g. employment, status, power, etc. ...) (Tripp 2007: 13–15). This neutralized the traditional power-holders, pushing them to the periphery of polity and economy. In the same vein, Chalmer Johnson's outline of the anatomy of what he calls the 'developmental state' approximates this in terms of economic planning (Johnson 1982). It displays features of a strong state, acting autonomously of society, and having the means to control and determine the content and direction of economic development.

The neat characterization of the post-colonial Arab state as a 'strong' entity in control of a 'weak' society is problematized here (Ayubi 1990). The Arab Spring has not landed from the 'moon'. It has been incubated in a matrix of dynamics that has since the 1990s seen the profusion of protests, emergence of countervailing forces, and discourses from below. The post-colonial ruling elite relied on the classic divide-and-rule policy to sustain their political and socio-economic dominance over post-colonial societies. This fragmentation has come to haunt them. The very weakness of that fragmentary and weakened society became a site of resistance and even de-nationalization. The forces, voices, and discourses relegated by the centre to the margins of power refused to be sidelined and silenced. The periphery was refashioned into a site of visibility not invisibility, struggle not passivity, and resistance not acquiescence. Even the return to 'primordial' networks of solidarity facilitated the creation of civic spaces empowering society—at the expense of the state. From this angle, the Arab Spring has been in the offing since before 2011. The void of power (the peripheral sites abandoned by the state) was turned into a power of the void (the peripheral forces and voices that re-organized themselves) to strike back at the state (Sadiki et al. 2013).

Thus, the notion of 'peoplehood' is used here as a way of contextualizing the trend of rising sites of anti-systemic struggles in the Arab region. The periphery is the space from which society has launched its uprisings, revolts, and self-organization into a formidable adversary to the central core, the authoritarian state. This is what has given birth to a historical moment of 'peoplehood', literally a 'wave' of dynamically revolutionary change in the Arab Middle East. These bottom-up revolts happened in societies such as Egypt, Libya, Syria, and Yemen, where in the 1950s and 1960s army-led revolutions and coups unseated monarchical power-holders.

The tensions that have historically characterized the centre–periphery dyad are not necessarily flaws where the Arab Spring is concerned. Instead, they have set into motion processes that doomed excessively authoritarian structures of power to historical exit and signalled the return of the periphery to politics. These centrifugal processes are described below.

1. The 'over-stated Arab state' breathes its last: This type of Arab state (Ayubi 1996), which has historically invested itself with all the attributes of power (mostly coercive, but in varying degrees financial, legal, tribal, ideological, informational, social, etc.) has allocated little or no shared-space for normalizing state–society relations, and even less space for societal contests of state power. A great deal of the conflict to be generated over the next decade will be produced by the state's resistance to change. Since its emergence into territorial existence, the Arab post-colonial state's design of this brand of statecraft fulfils what might be called 'total politics' or 'total state'. That is, a state with a notable blind spot: the 'unoccupied sites of power' (such as in moral and distributive fields). This has resulted, especially after 2011, in a power vacuum, discussed in point 2.

2. There is a power vacuum: power is clearly up for grabs and the contests and counter-contests take many forms, ranging from civic (political, transparent, peaceful, legal) to unruly (secret, violent, illegal). Varying degrees of this power vacuum grip many an Arab polity and society. It is pronounced and unfolding in some (populist republics), and latent in others (monarchies).

3. People occupy vacant spaces: This trend is diverse and varies in substance, impact and sustainability across the Arab Middle East. Largely, it points to emerging, ongoing, hidden, or dormant attempts below the level of the state, by society to carve out a space for occupying vacuous sites of power (including in the realm of coercion: e.g. Al-Qaeda, Houthis, ISIS, and affiliates). However, this should not preclude civic struggles such as for good government and more equitable distribution. It is within these unoccupied sites that *power* seems to be susceptible to renegotiation, contest, protest, and anti-systemic challenges. By and large, these are the sites where society (civic and uncivil, legal and unruly) strikes back. This struggle manifests itself either as an urge (a) to invent the vocabulary of self-recognition and self-existence as well as the attendant thought-practice for speaking to and responding to the decaying authoritarian post-colonial state (newly emerging democratic discourses, forces and voices; Islamist and secular, liberal and illiberal); and (b) to cohabit or populate the unoccupied sites of power, as the new legitimate power holder and claimant (e.g. militias in Libya, Houthis in Yemen, ISIS in Syria and Iraq).

4. Society advances as the state retreats: In every retreat/absence by the state, there emerges the potential for advancement/presence by society. The Arab Spring's seismic political activity will be marked by contests at the boundaries of state authority/power and societal reclamation of some of that power. This explicates the attendant four trends: migratory, transitory, participatory, and fragmentary as shown in **Table 15.1**. These are trends that are integral to the shape of both domestic politics as well as IR to be witnessed by the Arab Middle East over the next decade, as has been noted in this chapter.

The Arab Spring: progenitor of democratization?

Two observations are in order. First, there is an aspect of 'contagion' that is useful to illuminate the nexus between indigenous agency or home-grown push to reform and the exogenous impact on democratization. The Arab Spring is one dimension of how to relate IR to democratization. It exemplifies the local energy summoned to democratize as well as the external dynamics that condition democratization or inhibit it (as argued in the final section of this chapter). The nexus between IR and democratization is under-studied. Order (security) not equality (freedom) has historically been the area singled out for scholarly investigation as a progenitor of stability, alliances, modernization-cum-development, oil-based economies (rentierism), and now terrorism. Comparative politics students concerned with questions of democratic transition in this region have tended to look at political culture, Islam and Islamism, and recently civil society. External dimensions are seldom analysed.

Second, preoccupation today by the US and the EU with democratization in the Arab Middle East is relatively new when compared with other regions. The US, for instance, has since the nineteenth century actively promoted democracy in Central and Latin America and the Caribbean, be it unevenly at times and through non-democratic means throughout the twentieth century. Such a commitment, not always motivated by principled ideals but by realpolitik and by pursuit of national interests, necessitated extreme measures such as intimidation (e.g. in Nicaragua) and invasion (e.g. in Panama, Haiti) (Whitehead 1996: 45–60). President Reagan's National Endowment for Democracy (NED) accorded priority for democracy promotion during the 1980s to Europe and Asia with little or no attention to the Arab Middle East.[8]

The indigenous inheritors of the post-colonial state fare no better than the ex-colons with regard to democratization. No sooner had the elites that were at the vanguard of the nationalist resistance against colonialism 'colonized' the newly founded states than they set out to erase all of the vestiges of foreign rule. They dismantled the emergent independent states' democratic façade, namely, political parties and parliaments. They made no effort to revamp, reform, or found on these institutions more representative and accountable government. The absence of an indigenous contagion effect, a democratic model, from within the Arab region has contributed to the routinization of autocracy.

Discussion of democratization in the context of the Arab Spring cannot ignore the notion of peoplehood. Peoplehood has not won out outright in its continuous quarrel with authoritarian structures of power. The notion of the 'deep state', often related to Turkey and Egypt, comes to mind as an example of the challenges facing bottom-up democratization and restructuring of the state and citizenship along legal, participatory, inclusive, and accountable means. Nonetheless, peoplehood can be introduced as a conceptual unit of analysis to put into sharp relief the role played by non-state actors in democratic transition, namely, in relation to the Arab Spring. This is an investigation at a very preliminary stage and lacks the long time-span and comparative attention that thus far allow only for tentative observations about the democratic potentialities, much less outcomes, in the context of the Arab Spring. Democratization here is not a reference to a bourgeois notion of democracy since what animates peoplehood, or *al-harak*, as noted earlier, are aspirations for an inclusive quasi-Rawlsian notion of justice and a form of redistribution of political and economic goods that serve as a harbinger for freedom or *hurriyyah*.

The crux of *al-harak* is public mobilization and organization through self-configuration and reconstructions of a brand of political organization, run by the people and driven by their quest for equality and dignity. Rebellion against authoritarianism does not necessarily have a democratizing effect in an institutional sense. Thus far, only a few years have elapsed since the uprisings and while the electoral gains may be significant in Tunisia (2011 October Constituent Assembly elections; 2014 parliamentary and presidential elections) they may hardly be indicative of democratic change in other countries where they were subject to reverses or total breakdowns of order and fledgling democratization (Egypt and Libya—both had elections in 2012). *Al-harak* is displayed simply as 'occupation in reverse' of spatial, temporal, and discursive fields, which have for so long been constructed, reproduced, and occupied by the post-colonial power-holders. In the quest for freedom and dignity (*hurriyyah*, *karamah*), *al-harak* is society's agential deployment against the 'occupiers' of the authoritarian state. Peoplehood facilitates practices whereby bottom-up notions of sovereign identities and participatory citizenship are engendered informally in the public squares of protest. Central to *al-harak* is the people's coming together to ephemerally substitute the authoritarian regimes' practice, thought, and language of controlling power. Peoplehood thus invents new conceptions of political practice (peaceful protest, civic organization, armed resistance, leaderless-ness), thought (a stress on social justice, radical change), and terminology (a mantra of freedom, dignity, public solidarity, revolution, and uprising's martyrs). Thus the regimes' routinized notions of stability, loyalty, and deference, for instance, are traded for spontaneously conceived practices, thought, and language. Stability cedes to fluidity, loyalty gives way to hostility and rebellion, and deference to resistance. To borrow a term from Paulo Freire's *Pedagogy of the Oppressed* 'critical consciousness' is thus forged and invented in the public squares of protest as a necessity to counter the hegemonic order with action, thought, and all kinds of signifiers of opposition and resistance (Freire 2006). While instantaneous and spontaneous, the critical consciousness summoned in the public squares of protest seems to generate (e.g. Egypt and Tunisia in 2011) the necessary democratic agency to unify the rebellious publics around a spirit beckoning a new beginning. The stand as a united public with unified practice, thought (perhaps dreams), and terminology constitute initial steps towards a reconstitution of democratic subjectivities, and rejection of subjection to authoritarian rule and rulers. The Arab Spring constitutes thus far, even if not a progenitor of democracy, an élan, an opening, and a space for popular empowerment. It will, for some time, be marked out by dialectics between a decaying old order and an emboldened peoplehood that has, across boundaries of geography and culture, tasted—directly or through neighbourly experiments—a sweet victory over challenged dictators and states.

The international relations of the Arab Spring

The Arab Spring has exposed the decay of the authoritarian Arab state system. Both in terms of politics and territory, the state continues in varying degrees to be rocked to its foundations. At least, this is the case of Arab Spring states—that is, states which have in some form or another experienced the travails brought about by the 'travel' of this phenomenon within their precincts of sovereignty: territory, polity, society, and culture. Therefore *the* 'conceptual, historical, and cultural' context within which Arab states (monarchical and republican) have emerged (Korany 1987) and reproduced their capacity to juggle nationalist, secularist, corporatist, rentier, traditional, and modernizing roles is tested by the new atmospherics. In the context of the Arab Spring atmospherics, in the case of the Arab state vs the people, the centre vs the periphery, and the internal vs the external, Arab polities look far more challenged than at any other moment since their establishment and consolidation in the course of their post-colonial careers. As Korany (1987: 47–74) rightly quipped, post-colonial Arab states looked 'alien and besieged' in the community of nation states, yet without doubtful prospects of survival: they were 'here to stay'. And stay they did through a combination of distribution of subsidized goods, status, a share of the 'booty' for client social groups (tribes, learned scholars, co-opted opponents, armies, and business interests), and coercive regulation of the political. However, the notion of permanence now looks tattered by time, practice, and the 2011 uprisings. For example, the Iraq that emerged following the 1958 revolution and eventually inherited by the Baathist power-holders ceased to exist in 2003. Bourguiba's Tunisia, the centre of which was 'occupied' by Ben Ali following the 1987 bloodless coup, was given its marching orders by the protesters who ousted the dictator and sacked an order which was until then thought to be sufficiently resilient and reproducible. Tunisians nowadays call the incipient democratic order that has unfolded through electoral and constitution-making process the 'Second Republic'. Scholars were more or less 'ambushed' by rapid historical events that led to post-Arab Spring conflict and weakened or failed states such as Libya, Syria, and Yemen. They are noted by the fragmentation of centralized authority, politically. Territorially, today none of these formerly assumed 'strong' states possess full control of their national geographies. Furthermore, violent non-state actors occupy huge tracts of land within these embattled states. All of a sudden, history's course is partly diverted in favour of the people. In the case of the Arab state vs 'peoplehood', the people (civic or unruly) are prevailing over the statist apparatuses and establishments affected by the Arab Spring. One thought to be gleaned from this is the notion that 'nation' and 'state' are now animated by competing sets of imaginaries for the onerous task of 'imagining' and 'reimagining' community, to paraphrase Benedict Anderson (2006).What complicates the unfurling order is that some of the forces competing with existing weakened centres (Yemen) or ruling houses (Asad in Syria) is that the new power configurations are not demanding the creation of new statist territorial realms. Rather, in the case of ISIS, their quest is for a Caliphate, a borderless realm based on faith, as opposed to territorial sovereignty, harking back to a re-envisioned model of a religio-political organization created by the Prophet Muhammad some 1,400 years ago. Thus if the national-secular politics of post-independence since the 1940s and 1950s have been deftly and surreptitiously used to conceal the fault lines of the newly created states, the unfurling post-Arab Spring order is revealing the potential of such fault lines in reconstructing states and reconstituting nationalist and legally protected and emancipated identities. To go back to Anderson's imagined communities, what seems to be at issue in the moment of the Arab Spring is that 'nationalization' and 'de-primordialization' of politics are being reversed (Yemen, Libya, and Syria). Narrow notions of self and other seem to animate the conflict over territory, polity, and culture. Religion, ethnicity, sect, ideology, regionalism, tribalism and wealth are all competing resources that fan the scramble for reconfiguration of power in recently destabilized countries. Little or no shared values are yet in sight in some of these countries: contestation (Tunisia) and/or state coercion (Egypt) may be seen as the 'midwife' to aspiring young Arabs struggling for better futures.

IR is never far from this narrative. The full potency of the realist armour with which external powers have in the course of post-coloniality sought to configure and reconfigure power to optimize their own and maximize the power ratios of their client regimes has more or less atrophied. Foreign powers had played a pivotal role in the creation of allied Arab states (e.g. Britain in the case of Jordan and France in the case of Lebanon), lending them continuous financial, political, and even military support.

That protective shield and overall tutelage have been seriously challenged, if not morally questioned, by the 2011 uprisings—not to mention public opinion, Arab and Western. The

US and the EU's foreign policy towards the Arab Spring display tensions and dilemmas but almost invariably these are resolved in favour of states or at least the governing entities at the apex of power, not the region's peoples.

The Arab Spring reveals two interrelated aspects of IR in the Middle East: first, to refer to Booth (1991: 317–19), the state-centric visions of realists rule the crafting of policy with exaggerated focus on security, power, and strategy as 'ethnocentrism writ large'. This vision leaves much to be desired in terms of moral standards given the self-interest motif that drives realist political agendas (Booth 2007: 35–6). Translated to the Middle East, this pessimistic assessment of IR seems to be validated by US and EU reactions to the Arab Spring. There is much trepidation even if somewhat favouring states over peoples. In the case of the US, there was from the outset a lack of coherence despite the odd declaratory rhetoric such as in 2011 when Obama championed the courage of young Tunisia before Congress after the ousting of Ben Ali on 14 January 2011. On the whole, however, caution won the day, with Obama and his foreign policymakers refraining from lucidly endorsing fast-moving events. It can be said that the pragmatic approach towards national interest prevailed over principles of democracy promotion and human rights (which constructivists would pinpoint as emblematic of US democratic identity). Obama perhaps erred on the side of caution, demonstrating contradiction between reality (geostrategic interests) and ideal (democracy). Of course, it is a moot point whether the US could actually influence the course of events by the time the Arab public squares swelled with the *al-harak* driven by peoples. In a nutshell, by indecision and calculated reaction (the US intervened in Libya in a secondary capacity to aid the anti-Gaddafi raids conducted by France and Britain), the US opened up room for dealing with the regimes that followed the fall of dictators such as in Egypt, Libya, and Tunisia.

Secondly, securing oil routes and markets, as well as good relations with Israel, remains paramount for the US, before and after the Arab Spring. These are more or less immutable interests that are at the heart of America's power calculus. This is an agenda driven by sustaining regional allies, preferences, and balances that promote these core interests. In principle, the US is committed to democracy promotion, although this did not apply when communism seemed to threaten ruling houses in possession of oil wells, especially where such houses tended to be risk-averse, and opposition to Israel tended to be mostly through rhetoric. This is perhaps one reason why the US led a coalition of the willing in the early 1990s to protect both Israel (a democracy) and the Kingdom of Saudi Arabia (an autocracy): security, oil, and alliance were all at stake. Just as the US deployed anti-communist containment in the 1980s and 1990s to stand by autocratic oil-rich states, today endorsing Abdel Fattah al-Sisi's regime in Egypt may be justified on grounds of preventing terrorist threats not only against the US and the Western world, but also allies in the Gulf region, the Middle East, and North Africa. In March 2015, Obama finally decided to fully endorse al-Sisi. In the same vein, the German Chancellor Angela Merkel received al-Sisi in Berlin in June 2015. In March, her Economic Minister had joined a huge business delegation to a Sharm el-Sheikh investment summit that resulted in a memorandum of understanding between Siemens, the engineering and blue chip company, and al-Sisi's regime, worth up to €10 billion to Germany (Salloum 2015).

Generally, it can be said that the EU was slow to react to the Arab Spring and often took cues on how to act following US initiatives or policies. The US treated each case on the basis of its merit and context. For example, Tunisia is less important strategically than Egypt. Even here the US was cautious and it was weeks before the Obama Administration endorsed the

Tunisian revolutionaries' right to self-determination. By contrast, the EU did not speak with uniformity, and each member state had its own historical, financial, and apolitical append-ages to the various Arab Spring states. France today supports al-Sisi unquestionably, siding with him against the Muslim Brotherhood and the regional fight against terrorism, espe-cially ISIS. On the other hand, France did not give up on Ben Ali and the reaction of Sarkozy's Foreign Minister at the time, Michelle Alliot-Marie, spoke of some EU powers' aversion to the Arab Spring. Alliot-Marie was in favour of a Special Forces dispatch and intervention to rescue Ben Ali's regime (Willsher 2011). Catherine Ashton, the EU's top diplomat, was not forthcoming with outright support of Tunisia's revolution and her rhetoric pointed to prudence. Only after Ben Ali's removal did she speak of peaceful democratization.

The above assessment still holds true today. The threat of terrorism has blunted enthu-siasm for the Arab Spring, and pragmatism overrides moralism. This has been rehearsed many times over in terms of real politik in the case of the Gulf oil-rich states, with the quali-fied exception of Qatar. Definitely KSA and the United Arab Emirates have invested billions in the counter-revolutionary movement in Egypt, including financial aid to al-Sisi's regime and military. The picture cannot be starker between the billions invested in ending an im-perfect experiment in democracy led by the Muslim Brotherhood in Egypt and the austerity of international development aid to Tunisia, the only democratizing Arab Spring state. Even a small percentage of the funds invested in counter-revolution (Hertog 2011) would provide a huge fillip for the cash-strapped Tunisian economy. This is a vignette that serves to drive one message: both Arab oil-rich states and Western powers are very circumspect in their approach to the Arab Spring. And security matters once again seem to have dictated that the fight against terrorism outweighs democracy promotion in terms of importance.

Conclusion

Regarding the aforementioned issue of Orientalism in IR, the introduction of contemporary history into the study of the Arab Spring can help to refute Orientalist claims about it as an 'exceptional' phenomenon. The latent and manifest dynamic of 'peoplehood' which privi-leges resistance, rebellion, and unruliness is not unlike other historical anti-authoritarian struggles past and present.

On another note, 'peoplehood' in the current juncture is a cosmopolitan ideal, arguably a product of globalization, transcending binaries like East–West and North–South. Peo-plehood or al-harak engenders a form of new politics from below. This development has changed the internal structures of the state as a result of broader global diffusions of ideas and practices. While in the West (for example, in the UK and US) politics from below has been primarily in opposition to increasing and unbearable austerity measures and the pro-nounced bias towards major corporations at the expense of ordinary people (e.g. the youth, disabled, and workers), in the Arab Middle East it has been directed at autocrats and the abuse of human rights. The former (in the West) has borrowed greatly from the latter (Arab Middle East) in mounting challenges to authorities in a variety of ways such as occupying physical spaces. In the same vein, the youth of the Arab Middle East deploy Western music and technology to mount challenges against the status quo.

Civilization in IR has recurred in studies as a unit of analysis in the post-Cold War milieu. 'Clashes' and rivalries, rather than cooperation, are the norm. This chapter has sought to challenge this idea and provide an alternative reading of the regional and global politics of the Arab Middle East, instead stressing the exchange of ideas and practices.

The Arab Spring has a charisma of its own—that is, a 'faceless charisma' or 'leaderless charisma'. Although post-revolutionary Iran has witnessed the institutionalization of charisma, that of Khomeini, it has experienced difficulty capitalizing on his legitimacy and this may expire. The Arab Spring seems to have democratized charisma and the likes of al-Sisi have encountered problems in generating charismatic authority. What keeps him in the seat of power, right now, are the tactical manoeuvres of the Western chancelleries of power. However, there is no guarantee of long-term survival in the age of the Arab Spring. The interim game is that states rule the region in consortium with Western powers. The endgame, however, will be what Arab youth will craft out of their dream to have dignity and freedom.

Key events

Year	Month	Day	Events	Details
2010	December	17	**Tunisia spark the flame**	In Sidi Bouzid Mohammed Bouazizi sets himself on fire in an act of protest against humiliation by local police for not having a permit to sell vegetables. The act is followed by mass young Tunisians protesting.
2011	January	14	**Fall Ben Ali**	Ben Ali bows to the protesters' pressure and announces his resignation. He flees to Saudi Arabia, opening a new page in Tunisia and the region: The Arab Spring begins.
		25	**Egypt: Day of Revolt**	Egyptians take to the streets in the first coordinated mass protest called 'day of rage', demand for Mubarak to step down after three decades in power.
		27	**The spark moves to Yemen**	Protests erupt in Yemen: call for Ali Abdullah Salih to stand down after three decades in power.

February	11	**New era in Egypt**	Vice-President Omar Suleiman appears on TV announcing Mubarak's resignation.
	14	**Protests erupt in Bahrain**	Thousands take to the streets across Bahrain demanding deep reforms.
	15	**Battle against Gaddafi starts**	Protesters take to the streets in Benghazi in East Libya followed by bloody Thursday on 17 February.
	20	**Morocco takes part**	Thousands of protesters take to the streets demanding a new government and reforms including reform of the constitution.
	15	**Revolt in Syria**	Protesters demonstrate against the country's hard-line and dictatorial Baath regime.
	20	**Gaddafi killed**	Gaddafi is captured and killed by rebels in the city of Sirte: first and only head of State killed during the Arab Spring.
	23	**Tunisia votes**	Tunisians vote in the first free election of the Arab Spring.
November	23	**Salih steps down**	The Yemeni President, Salih, is finally pressured to transfer power to his Vice-President, Abd Rabbu Mansour Al-Hadi, under an agreement brokered by the GCC states.
	28	**Egypt votes**	The first free parliamentary election in the post-Mubarak era takes place: second election of the Arab Spring.

	16	**Muslim Brotherhood in power**	Mohamed Mursi, the Muslim Brotherhood candidate, wins the second round of the presidential elections against Ahmed Shafiq.
	7	Libya's first elections	The National Transitional Council supervises democratic elections, the first in more than 40 years, for 200 members to form the General National assembly.
July	15	**A Syrian civil war declared**	The International Committee of the Red Cross issues an official declaration confirming the Syrian uprising to be a civil war.
July	3	**Army ousts Egypt's President**	Supreme Council of the Armed Forces (SCAF) member and Egypt's defence minister Field-Marshal Abdel Fattah al-Sisi removes the country's first democratically elected president, Mohamed Mursi. Al-Sisi suspends the constitution and installs an interim government. This is the Arab Spring's first military coup and first democratic breakdown.
August	14	**Rabaa massacre**	Thousands of Mursi's supporters killed by Egyptian police and Army. There is no precise figure of those killed in Nahda Square and Rabaa Al-Adawiya Square.

	21	**Syrian chemical attack**	Government forces carry out a chemical attack near Damascus which kills hundreds of Syrians.
September	23	**Egypt's Brotherhood banned**	An obscure Egyptian court outlaws the Muslim Brotherhood.
December	18	**Mursi charged with terrorism**	Mursi appears in court to face charges of terrorism.
January	14 and 15	**Egypt's third constitutional referendum**	The new ruling power, after the overthrow of the first elected president, holds a constitutional referendum and gets 98.1% yes votes. Anti-coup Alliance boycotts the vote.
February	14	**Libya's chaos starts**	A retired Major-General, Khalifa Haftar, appears on Al-arabia TV announcing suspension of the General National Assembly, the government and the constitutional Declaration: As in Egypt, Arab Spring setbacks for democratic transition are recorded in Libya
	26, 27 and 28	**Al-Sisi in power**	A presidential election in Egypt takes place between only two candidates in which General al-Sisi wins 96.1% of vote. Voter turnout: 38%, lower than the 52% voter turnout in the 2012 presidential election that brought Mursi to power. Thus al-Sisi, youngest SCAF member, becomes Egypt's 6th president since independence.

		23	**Tunisia holds presidential elections**	The leading candidates are: Beji Caid Essebsi (Nidaa Tounes), incumbent Moncef Marzouki, NCA Speaker, Mustafa bin Ja'afar, and former judge and anti-Ben Ali dissident Kalthoum Kannou, the only female to contest the presidential race.
2015	February	6		Houthis issue a constitutional declaration, dissolve the parliament and form a presidential council, as they enable the 'Revolutionary Committee' led by Mohammad Ali al-Huthi to lead the country on a temporary basis.
	March	26		A coalition led by Saudi Arabia hs launches air strikes against Shia Houthi rebels in Yemen, saying it is 'defending the legitimate government' of President Abdrabbuh Mansour Hadi.

Further reading

Buckner, El and Lina, K. (2014) 'The Martyrs' Revolutions: The Role of Martyrs in the Arab Spring', *British Journal of Middle Eastern Studies*, 41(4): 368–84
This is an insightful article, which evokes Qur'anic motifs of struggle against oppression.

Dabashi, H. (2012) *The Arab Spring: The End of Postcolonialism* (London: Zed Books)
This is a concise book, which stresses the idea of the end of postcolonialism, noting that the Arab uprisings result from a synergy of the national and the transnational.

Hatem, M. (2012) 'The Arab Spring Meets the Occupy Wall Street Movement: Examples of Changing Definitions of Citizenship in a Global World', *Journal of Civil Society*, 8(4): 401–15
This article provides an interesting argument, focusing on collective agency—the 'multitude' or 'global actor'—via the local experiences of the Arab Spring.

Howard, M. and Walters, M. (2014) 'Explaining the Unexpected: Political Science and the Surprises of 1989 and 2011', *Perspectives on Politics*, 12(2): 394–408
This article's approach goes beyond the formal façade of authoritarianism, by exploring popular mobilization.

Howard, P. N. and Hussain, M. (2013) *Democracy's Fourth Wave? Digital Media and the Arab Spring* (New York: Oxford University Press)
This is a good source for starting reflection on possible linkages between cyber activism and political change in the context of the Arab Spring.

Kassab, E. (2014) 'Critics and Rebels: Older Arab Intellectuals Reflect on the Uprisings', *British Journal of Middle Eastern Politics*, 41(1): 8–27.
This article provides a unique analysis of the intellectual dimensions of the Arab Spring, capturing Arab thinkers' readings of the uprisings.

Questions

1. How does the Arab Spring challenge current IR thinking in the context of the Middle East?

2. To what extent have peoples impacted on international relations of the Middle East?

3. How did local and external states react to the Arab Spring?

4. Has the Arab Spring precipitated a crisis within the Arab state system or has the crisis of the Arab state system precipitated the Arab spring?

5. What aspects of the Arab Spring caution against 'exceptionalism' when thinking about the Middle East?

Notes

1. M15 refers to 15 May the first day of the 2011–2013 Spanish protests.

2. ATTAC was originally a single-issue movement demanding the introduction of the so-called Tobin tax on currency speculation. ATTAC now devotes itself to a wide range of issues related to globalization.

3. The celebrated Lebanese-American author, Nassim Taleb, considers Saudi Arabia to be the most fragile country in the world (Taleb 2012).

4. Ulf Laessing, 'Saudi king back home, orders $37 billion handouts', *Reuters*, 23 February 2011.

5. The rise of grassroots organizations committed to the cause of social justice is not new. The Zapatista movement in Mexico and the Solidarity movement in Poland illustrate the point.

6. Rap music is a universal genre ranging from pop to conscious in various locales. It is a cultural expression for the youth, by the youth, exhibiting a no-nonsense attitude towards authority, at times anti-racist, also seeking liberation in culture and politics. It has 'travelled' across the world from its humble origins in the inner cities of America, mainly among black youth, reaching the refugee camps of Gaza and cities of Tunisia. Inclusion of culture in IR theorizing, hugely neglected, music, and art (graffiti) are part of the Arab Spring repertoire. See chapters on poetry, music, and graffiti as mediums of expression and protest in the Arab Spring in Sadiki (2015).

7. 'ISLAM WILL NEVER BE TOLERATED Bernard Henri Lévy / Tzipi Livni'. https://www.youtube.com/watch?v=DWnr27FvNhs (Retrieved: 12 March 2015).

8. However, it must be noted that some Arabs also feared the rise of Islamists in Egypt and Tunisia and elsewhere (such as in Libya and Syria), a backlash against them disguising a deeper disdain for democracy, mainly by so-called *azlam* and *fulool*, that is remnants of the ousted regime. Islamic law or *Shari'ah*-phobia in the Arab world is prevalent among these publics as well liberals and leftists, including women. See testimony by former NED President, Carl Gershman, in 'The National Endowment for Democracy in 1990: Hearing before the Subcommittee on International Operation of the Committee on Foreign Affairs', US House of Representatives, 28 September 1989, 31.

The United States in the Middle East

MICHAEL C. HUDSON

Overview

This chapter reviews and analyses US foreign policy in the Middle East. It begins with a historical sketch of US involvement in the area, discussing the traditional US interests. It then describes the structure of Middle Eastern policymaking and its domestic political context, as well as Washington's response to new regional tensions and upheavals since the late 1970s. Next, there is a survey of new regional developments, including socio-economic trends, the 'watershed' year of 1979, the rise of the Islamic Republic of Iran, and the emergence of a Shia regional coalition, the emergence of Al-Qaeda and the attacks of 11 September 2001 ('9/11') in the US, the US-led interventions in Afghanistan and Iraq, and the Palestinian–Israeli impasse. The next section traces the evolution of US policy since 2000 in the administrations of George W. Bush and Barack Obama. The chapter concludes with a discussion of an 'Obama doctrine' and 'American decline' in the Middle East and the world.

Introduction

Until recently, the United States exercised enormous influence throughout the Middle East. In a region historically penetrated by competing Western powers, there were no serious challengers to US hegemony following the collapse of the Soviet Union in 1990. Nevertheless, today, US policymakers see the Middle East as the source of unprecedented threats to national security. This is because they believe it to be a breeding ground for terrorist movements that are able to strike against the US homeland, as well as US interests overseas. They also see traditional US allies in the Arab world as threatened by Iran and its allies.

In this chapter, we seek to explain this puzzle. We will do so, first, by presenting an historical sketch of the US involvement in the area. This narrative focuses initially on the traditional trio of US interests: anti-communism, oil, and Israel. The second section describes the structure of Middle Eastern policymaking, emphasizing both the instruments of policy and the effects of domestic politics on policy. In the third part, we discuss how new regional tensions and upheavals since the late 1970s have challenged US interests, and how US policy has sought to cope with them. Finally, we will compare and contrast how the administrations of George W. Bush and Barack Obama have dealt with the growing volatility of the twenty-first-century Middle East.

The roots of US involvement

There was a time—very different from the present period—when the United States was popular and respected throughout the Middle East. That benign image began to dissipate around the period of the Second World War, when the US, as an emergent great power, became directly involved in a region that was itself undergoing great internal upheavals. Washington's concern about the Soviet Union, access to oil, and the project for a Jewish state in Palestine—concerns that clashed with the rising nationalism in the region—eroded the earlier positive image.

'The age of innocence'

The first US encounters with the Middle East and North Africa (MENA) date back to the founding of the republic (Bryson 1977). Relations revolved mainly around trade and missionary activity. In the late nineteenth and early twentieth centuries, as France, Britain, and Russia established an imperial presence in North Africa, Egypt, the Levant, Iran, and the periphery of the Arabian Peninsula, the US by contrast eschewed a colonial role in the Middle East. Indeed, in the aftermath of the First World War—that watershed event in which European countries replaced Ottoman Turkish administration in much of the Arab world—the Arabs indicated that if they could not have the independence that they most wanted, they would rather be governed by the US than by Britain or France. These were the findings of the King–Crane Commission, sent by President Wilson in 1919 to ascertain the wishes of 'the people' in the former Ottoman territories. Americans were seen to be good people, untainted by the selfishness and duplicity associated with the Europeans. As nationalist and religious movements reorganized to roll back European imperialism in the 1920s and 1930s, they spared the US from their anger.

Coming of age

The Second World War marked what US veteran 'Arabist' ambassador Raymond Hare called 'the great divide' in US relations with the Middle East, 'between our traditional national position of rejecting political responsibility in the Middle East and our postwar acceptance of responsibility on a global or great power basis' (Hare 1972). Three issues drove the US's new great power policies in the Middle East: communism, oil, and Israel.

Containing Soviet communism

In October 1947, as Hare (1993: 20) tells it, US and British officials met at the Pentagon to sketch out a geo-political blueprint for the Middle East in the light of the new threats of Soviet expansionism and communist ideology. Gone was the 'reverse Monroe doctrine' of the inter-war period in which the US left the Middle East to Britain (in contrast to President Monroe's insistence on keeping Britain out of Latin America in the nineteenth century). Already, President Truman had extended aid to Greece and Turkey to help those governments stave off communist or Soviet challenges. While still conceding to Britain 'primary responsibility' for the Middle East and the Mediterranean, Secretary of State Marshall was already contemplating an eventual leadership role for the US in the region.

A decade later, John C. Campbell from the Council on Foreign Relations published *Defense of the Middle East* (1958)—a revealing account of the concern with which the foreign-policy establishment viewed trends in the region. The fundamental problem was the threat to the security, even the survival, of the US in the face of the global Soviet challenge. As for the Middle East:

> The entrenchment of Soviet power in that strategic region would bring a decisive shift in the world balance, outflanking NATO. Soviet control of Middle Eastern oil could disrupt the economy of the free world. And the triumph of communism in the heart of the Islamic world could be the prelude to its triumph through Asia, Africa and Europe.
>
> (Campbell 1958: 4–5)

The study group asserted that the Arab–Israeli conflict:

> hangs like a poisonous cloud over the entire Middle East. … Time has not solved the problem of the Arab refugees. Something must be done about it. … The American commitment to Israel is to its continued independent existence, not to its existing boundaries or policies.
>
> (Campbell 1958: 351–2)

On the geo-strategic level, US policy sought to contain the Soviets in the Middle East through military alliances, as in Europe through the North Atlantic Treaty Organization (NATO). But this approach largely failed, as the examples of the Middle East Command proposal and the Middle East Defense Organization in 1951–52 indicate (Bryson 1977: 179–81). Even the Baghdad Pact (1955) generated more animosity than security in the Arab world (see **Chapter 9**). Nor were looser political–economic umbrella projects—such as the Eisenhower doctrine (1957), under which Washington promised financial aid and security assistance to Middle Eastern governments requesting US protection from 'international communism'— any more successful. Lebanon was the only Arab state to take up the offer—a decision that brought more instability than security to that small country. Indeed, under Stalin's less doctrinaire successors, the Soviet Union and its satellites succeeded in leaping over the Baghdad Pact into the Arab heartland through its arms deals with Syria and Egypt of 1954–56. To these governments, the real geo-strategic threat was Israel, not the Soviet Union—and therein lay a real problem for US diplomacy. The US–Soviet 'game' was not being played exclusively on the geo-strategic level; it was also being played on the volatile ideological terrain of Middle Eastern domestic politics.

The waning of European imperialism in the Middle East after the Second World War coincided with a powerful current of national assertiveness in Iran and the Arab countries, which were rapidly modernizing. Ascension to great power status and close wartime cooperation with colonialist European allies had not extinguished US liberal idealism. Accordingly, there was great curiosity and not a little sympathy with the emergence of independent states in what came to be called the 'Third World'. With these trends in mind, leading US government officials had correctly prophesied that support for a Zionist state in Palestine would set the US at odds with the emerging Arab nationalist currents. They were equally right in predicting that the Soviet Union would try to associate itself with this trend in order to advance its own interests throughout the region. Regimes friendly to Washington would be weakened. Developments during the 1950s and 1960s revealed the extent of the problem: nationalist coups or upheavals took place in Egypt, Iran, Iraq, Jordan, Lebanon, Libya, North Yemen, South Yemen, the Sudan; Syria suffered major instability. Ongoing eruptions (1956, 1967, 1969–70) in the unsolved Arab–Israeli conflict did not help matters.

If the US response to all of this was often improvised and contradictory, the results were not altogether negative. American diplomats tried to avoid a head-on confrontation with nationalist forces; US efforts to deal with Nasser are a fascinating case in point. Even US presidents occasionally made a supportive gesture: for example, Dwight Eisenhower in the 1956 war, and John F. Kennedy, who, as a senator, had spoken positively on Algeria, and, as president, initiated a dialogue with Nasser and supported the republican revolution in Yemen. On the other hand, the US worked to suppress Iranian nationalism by organizing the overthrow of Prime Minister Muhammad Mussadiq's government in 1953, and it opposed the nationalist upheavals in Syria and Iraq. While Kennedy had some temporary doubts about supporting a 'traditional' regime in Saudi Arabia, he did not hesitate to support the Saudis when they were challenged by Nasser in the 1960s.

US diplomacy in the field, and the presence of respected American educational and development organizations somewhat blunted the US confrontation with Arab nationalism, but it could hardly eliminate it. The Palestine problem lay at the heart of the pan-Arab cause and US support for Israel was too massive to allow for healthy relationships with most Arab states, let alone with Arab public opinion. The Soviet Union therefore had a clear field to plough. But the Soviets had their own problems and weaknesses: communism and Arab nationalism did not mix well together, and the Soviets were often clumsy in their military and aid relationships. Nationalist Arab regimes complained about the low level and poor quality of Soviet support. Nevertheless, Soviet patronage enabled the nationalist, anti-Israel camp to pose a serious challenge to US interests in the region.

The enfeeblement of the Soviet Union vis-à-vis the US was increasingly evident from the 1970s even to Arab governments heavily dependent on Moscow for arms and diplomatic support. Following Israel's smashing victory over the Arabs in the 1967 Six-Day War, an Arab 'rejectionist bloc' emerged that, with Moscow's support, had refused US and international plans for a negotiated settlement that would require recognition of Israel. But gradually this bloc began to disintegrate, and with it the influence in Arab public opinion of the pan-Arab nationalist movement. Egypt's President Anwar Sadat was the first Arab leader to recognize Moscow's decline, and he drew the logical realpolitik conclusion by throwing out his Soviet military advisers and dramatically turning towards Washington in search of a negotiated solution to the Arab–Israeli conflict. Later, Iraq and Syria would engage in their own, more cautious flirtations with the US. By the time of the Soviet Union's collapse in 1990, the US was able to enlist the one-time rejectionist governments in Egypt and Syria in the international coalition to remove Iraq as a threat to Kuwait and Saudi Arabia. The US–Soviet Cold War in the Middle East was over, and the Arab nationalist camp (what was left of it) no longer had a superpower patron to constrain the US and Israel.

Oil

US commercial interest in Middle East oil pre-dates Hare's 'great divide'. US companies got their foot in the door of the Middle Eastern oil cartel with the Red Line Agreement of 1928. Under the Red Line Agreement, the major international oil companies—including now a US group—pledged in a 'self-denying' clause to share proportionally the future oil discoveries in the former Ottoman Turkish territories, including the Arabian Peninsula (except for Kuwait), Iraq, the Levant (except for Sinai), Cyprus, and Anatolia. A decade later in Saudi Arabia, having outmanoeuvred their British rivals in Saudi Arabia, a subsidiary of Standard of California made a stupendous find at 'Dammam No. 7', which, over the next forty-five years, was to produce more than 32 million barrels of oil. But oil did not acquire a strategic security dimension until the Second World War. Just as the British at the beginning of the century had seen the military and economic value of Middle Eastern oil, so too did the Americans—not only for prosecuting the Second World War, but also as a cheap supplement to declining US reserves and the West's oil-driven post-war economic development. With the price of Middle Eastern oil a mere US$2 per barrel up until 1971, it is hardly surprising that Western Europe and even the US would become dependent on it.

While European and Japanese dependency was well over two-thirds of total consumption, Americans in the 1970s found that half their oil was imported and half of those imports were from the Middle East. Given, then, the importance of a secure supply of cheap Middle Eastern oil, US policymakers determined that their main tasks were to exclude Soviet influence from the region and to prevent any internal force from nationalizing Western companies, restricting production, and/or raising prices and overturning established regimes. Clandestine involvement by the US Central Intelligence Agency (CIA) and the British in a coup codenamed 'Operation Ajax', which returned the young shah to his throne in Iran in 1953, was an effective object lesson for would-be nationalist challengers (Bill 1988: 86–94). As for the US–Arab oil relationship, the Arabian-American Oil Company (ARAMCO), a consortium of US companies active in Saudi Arabia, had mounted a remarkably effective, indeed amicable, working relationship that has endured through to the first decade of the twenty-first century, weathering even the transfer to Saudi ownership.

In 1960, following an abrupt decision by the oil companies on a price cut, outraged governments of oil-producing states established the Organization of Petroleum Exporting Countries (OPEC). OPEC, inexperienced and weakened by internal rivalries, had little success in defending the price of oil during its first decade. But the situation was about to change. Growing world demand, the proliferation of small independent companies, and domestic nationalist pressures in several oil-producing countries set in motion the 'oil revolution' of the 1970s, which, by the end of the decade, had lifted the price to around US$35 per barrel. It also led to a shift in the balance of oil power from the companies to the producing countries, by breaking the cohesion of the producer cartel at a time when world oil demand was growing. Libya, following Colonel Muammar al-Gaddafi's nationalist revolution in 1969, led the charge, followed by Iran. Then, during the 1973 Arab–Israeli War, King Faisal of Saudi Arabia did what Americans had thought was unthinkable: he imposed a partial boycott on the US and on European consumers. Suddenly, the Arabs had 'the oil weapon' and, stung by US emergency war aid to Israel, they had used it.

The shock in the US and Europe was palpable, and it lent urgency to Secretary of State Kissinger's mediation of the war. In the long term, it also led to a comprehensive new energy policy designed to blunt the oil weapon in the future through the Strategic Petroleum Reserve, a vast underground oil storage facility, and conservation measures. Thus, by the time of the second major price hike in 1979, which resulted from the Iranian revolution of 1979–80 and the Iraq–Iran War of 1980–88, the global oil market was far more stable. Moreover, Saudi Arabia was both able and willing to cushion these shocks. With the collapse of world oil prices in 1986, OPEC and non-OPEC producers alike lost their collective effectiveness, and the Arab 'oil weapon' basically disappeared. For US policymakers, the main oil problem now was ensuring that the new Gulf Cooperation Council (GCC), formed in 1981, be 'protected' from regional (Iranian) or exogenous (Soviet) inroads. Fortunately for Washington, Iraqi President Saddam Hussein shared US concern over Ayatollah Ruhollah Khomeini's regional system-challenging proclivities. Iraq provided the military shield, the GCC states the money, and the US the intelligence data to beat back the Iranian Islamist challenge. Just over two decades later, however, as oil prices spiked to well over US$100 per barrel, Arab and other oil exporters were gaining new leverage in regional and global affairs.

This was not to last. From US$125 per barrel of Brent crude in 2008, the price plummeted to around US$50 per barrel by 2014, and industry experts were forecasting a long era of low prices. Even more profound was the reemergence of the US as a major producer and possibly, again, an exporter of oil and gas thanks to the new technique of hydraulic fracturing (or 'fracking') of shale. With America approaching energy independence, the importance of Middle East oil as a national security interest began to diminish.

Israel

So firm—indeed, fervent—has US support for Israel become since 1967 that it is easy to forget how bitter the policy debate in the US was over Palestine in the 1940s and how evenly matched the antagonists. On the one side were the pro-Zionists in the domestic political arena; on the other, the executive branch officials concerned with the global and regional implications of a US-supported Jewish state. In a well-known article published in the *Middle East Journal* in 1948, Kermit Roosevelt, an American intelligence expert on the Middle East, described (and criticized) the Zionist lobbying effort, observing that 'almost all Americans with diplomatic, educational, missionary, or business experience in the Middle East protest fervently that support of political Zionism is directly contrary to our national interests, as well as to common justice' (Roosevelt 1948: 1).

But President Harry Truman, influenced by Zionist friends and desirous of Zionist political support in the 1948 election campaign, decided that the US would support the establishment of a Jewish state in Palestine. Had he not taken that stand (and he himself wavered at one point), the Zionist enterprise in Palestine might have taken a weaker form and, indeed, might not have ultimately succeeded. It was not until 1967 that the executive branch diplomatic and defence establishment, impressed with Israel's military prowess and Arab weakness, was finally persuaded that Israel might be something more than a burden on the national interest. Since then, the deeply committed supporters of Israel have managed not only to mobilize most of the American Jewish community, but have also helped win US public opinion, in general, to support Israel and its policies in the region almost without reservation. Perhaps the best evidence for the political clout of Israel's supporters is the size of the annual US aid package: upwards of US$3 billion.

Israel in the first two decades of the twenty-first century is not only an established part of the Middle Eastern landscape, but has also become a regional superpower: its gross national product is more than twice that of the largest Arab state, Egypt, and it has a world-class military establishment. Yet the naysayers of the 1940s were not entirely wrong in their assessment. Indeed, they were right in forecasting that the US relationship with the Arab world would deteriorate, that repeated wars and immense suffering would result from the creation of a Jewish state, and that the Soviets would take advantage of this rancour and instability. US political leadership was prepared to accept these costs and to insist that the Arabs accept them too. For US leaders, the costs were bearable, because they included neither loss of access to Arab oil, nor the complete loss of the Middle East to the Soviet Union. For that, they may thank the Arabs, who failed to respond collectively to the challenges facing them, and the Soviets, who proved incapable of sustaining their empire.

As midwife at the birth of Israel in 1948, the US faced the task of helping to arrange a settlement that would see it through infancy and ensure it a prosperous life. To that end, the US has, over the years, supported a variety of diplomatic initiatives and projects to normalize the new state's relations with its neighbours. But owing to the manner in which Israel had been established—basically by force of arms, which led to the displacement of some 750,000 Palestinians into neighbouring countries—these efforts were largely unsuccessful until 1978. Only then, at Camp David, did the US government finally make a significant dent in the problem.

The Camp David accord is a milestone (see **Chapter 12**)—one of two pivotal events for US policy in securing the 'normalization' of Israel in the Middle East; the other is the Madrid/Oslo peace process that began in September 1991 (see **Chapter 13**). But the road from Camp David to Madrid was bumpy, to say the least. The presidency of Ronald Reagan (1980–88) proved sterile with respect to the Middle East. Reagan's officials maintained a quixotic and unrealistic fixation on 'strategic consensus', by which they meant agreement between Israel and its Arab neighbours to cooperate in rolling back what they saw as Soviet inroads in the Middle East. Reagan's first Secretary of State, Alexander Haig, is widely believed to have given 'an amber light' for Israel's invasion of Lebanon, a bloody adventure that only intensified Israeli–Palestinian hostility. The Reagan administration also sought to resuscitate the perennial 'Jordanian option' as a solution to the Palestine problem, even though Jordan's King Hussein was no longer in a position to represent Palestinian nationalism. So ill-equipped were the Reaganites to understand, let alone to deal with, the Middle East that they allowed valuable years to go by during which the Arab–Israeli situation only worsened. This paralysis of policymaking set the stage for the Palestinian intifada, a mass uprising of young, stone-throwing Palestinians in the occupied territories, which began in December 1987 and refocused world attention on Palestinian national grievances as the heart of the Arab–Israeli conflict. As we shall see, however, the ongoing diplomatic impasse, coupled with the rise of extremist trends both in Israel and among the Palestinians, would begin to fray the special relationship between the US and Israel.

Policymaking: structures and process

An examination of the internal workings of US Middle Eastern policy is essential for understanding why the US pursues policies that generally elicit hostility from people in the region and even exasperate traditional European allies. One key point emerges: Middle Eastern policy is decisively shaped by domestic US politics.

Unlike other major US foreign-policy issue areas, the Middle East is deeply embedded in US domestic politics. The process of Middle East policymaking involves interaction between the following key structures.

The White House

US presidents, as Quandt (1993) has observed, are by far the key actors in the shaping of Middle Eastern policy. They are driven by an awareness that what they do in the Middle East can have a significant positive or negative effect on their political future, because of the influence of the pro-Israel forces on the electoral process. They are also influenced by a panopoly of policy experts in the executive branch, and in the 'think tank' and academic communities, who shape their understanding of what is going on in the region and how this affects US security and economic interests.

The executive branch

The State Department is not the only organization in the vast executive branch of the US government that helps to shape Middle Eastern policy. It must compete with other bureaucracies, which often have divergent views. It must also contend with influential lobbies and elements in Congress, who see the State Department as 'anti-Israel'. The Defense Department has an important voice, especially present in the first decade of the twenty-first century, since the US military has a significant presence in almost every country in the region. The 'intelligence community' consists not only of the CIA, but also of several other similar organizations, such as the National Security Agency (NSA), which monitors electronic communications worldwide. Increasingly, the Federal Bureau of Investigation (FBI) plays an important role overseas, especially since the rise of transnational terrorist networks.

The legislative branch

Both houses of the US Congress—the Senate and the House of Representatives—play an important role in Middle Eastern policy formation. Each body has well-staffed committees on foreign relations, security issues, intelligence, and finance. These committees hold hearings on Middle Eastern policy issues, mobilizing the research arm of Congress, but also outside experts and lobbyists. Because the pro-Israel lobbies and the voting constituencies behind them exert such pervasive influence over members of Congress, who fear and respect the influence that they exert in elections, Congress regularly authorizes massive US financial aid to Israel (at the time of writing, over US$3 billion annually) and occasionally passes resolutions that even the White House finds excessively pro-Israel. Congressmen generally go along with the policy advice disseminated by pro-Israel think tanks on other Middle Eastern issues, such as arms sales to Arab governments or criticism of the Palestinian leadership. It should also be noted, however, that Congress does offer a limited opportunity for opponents of US policies in the Middle East to be heard.

The political parties

In general, Middle Eastern policy issues have been considered 'above partisan politics', at least by the politicians. Indeed, there is a bipartisan consensus that Israel's security and prosperity is a fundamental US priority. Similarly, the importance of access to oil and (until the demise of the Soviet Union) the need to contain communist influence in the region has been shared by both Democrats and Republicans. That said, until recently the Democratic Party has been regarded as more pro-Israel than the Republicans. But in recent election campaigns, especially in 2012, the increasingly influential neo-conservative elements in the Republican Party actively sought to present their party as more pro-Israel than the Democrats. Other Middle East issues also stimulated partisan conflict. In the 2004 and 2008 presidential campaigns, for example, Democratic candidate Barack Obama accused President Bush of needlessly invading Iraq and failing to advance in the 'war on terrorism'.

The 'opinion-makers'

Within the policy community, several think tanks attempt to influence the Middle Eastern policy debates. Those debates are still heavily shaped by organizations with a pro-Israel and neo-conservative agenda: the Washington Institute on Near Eastern Policy, a spin-off from one of the key pro-Israel lobbies; the Heritage Foundation; the American Enterprise Institute; and the Hudson Institute. But there are others, such as the New America Foundation, the Carnegie Endowment for International Peace, and the Middle East Institute, that eschew partisan positions. As for the news media, it is an exaggeration to assert, as some have done, that they are controlled by pro-Israel elements that dictate their coverage of the Middle East; if anything, news coverage in the US press has improved, in terms of reporting Arab as well as Israeli perspectives. On the editorial and opinion pages, however, anti-Arab and pro-Israeli commentary is abundant. On Middle Eastern issues not directly involving Israel, there is considerably greater diversity of opinion. Liberal and left-wing media outlets certainly exist, but their voices are relatively weak. It must be admitted that the American media in general have become weaker in their coverage of foreign news. On the positive side, however, the appearance of new media and information technologies in and on the Middle East—especially Al-Jazeera, and the reporting by PBS and NPR—has improved the coverage of Middle East issues in the US.

The lobbies

There is a consensus among observers of US politics (whatever their views on the Middle East) that the network of organizations that make up 'the Israel lobby' is one of the two or three most powerful lobbies in Washington (Tivnan 1987). The American–Israel Public Affairs Committee (AIPAC) is perhaps the most visible of these groups, and it has decades of experience in influencing both Congress and the White House, but it is only the tip of an iceberg of state and local organizations with a well-deserved reputation for being able to channel money and votes in election campaigns. The Israel lobby is thought to have more influence with the Democrats than with the Republicans, although it assiduously cultivates both. Democratic candidates typically win a large majority of 'the Jewish vote'. American Jews, who number around 5.3 million, make up around 2 per cent of the adult population, are concentrated in key states, and are politically active in terms of campaign contributions and voter turnout. It is also important to note that support for Israel is not at all confined to Jewish Americans. Large numbers of Christians, especially the increasingly influential evangelicals and fundamentalists, also enthusiastically support the hawkish elements that dominate Israeli politics. Pro-Israel organizations also benefit from generous funding from wealthy businessmen such as Sheldon Adelson, the Koch brothers, and Haim Saban. Criticism of the Israel lobby has been considered by many US politicians and analysts to be a taboo subject, because of fears of accusations of anti-Semitism—but, in 2007, two respected political scientists without Middle Eastern ties, Stephen M. Walt and John J. Mearsheimer, published a strong critique of the lobby as detrimental to US foreign-policy interests (Mearsheimer and Walt 2007), sparking a furious, but enlightening, debate. Nevertheless, the candidates for president in 2008 all appeared before AIPAC's annual meeting pledging one-sided support for Israel's positions in the ongoing conflict. But AIPAC's monopoly of the pro-Israel camp was challenged in 2008 with the appearance of a new Jewish organization—J-Street. J-Street offered a liberal-centrist alternative to its hawkish rival. Although lacking the organizational and financial clout of AIPAC, J-Street gained the attention and respect of the Obama administration and the foreign policy community with its more flexible and conciliatory stance toward the Palestinians.

The other major lobbying force—less focused than the Israel lobby, but still influential—is the oil and business lobby. Big oil companies, and construction and financial firms with major Middle Eastern interests, are concerned that the US should be able to do business in the region. The business lobby is generally closer to the Republicans than the Democrats. To a certain extent, this pits them against the 'Israel lobby', but not always. One reason why is that the American defence and high-tech industries find in Israel a very good customer. In the Republican administration of Ronald Reagan, Secretary of State George Shultz, an executive of Bechtel Corporation (a construction company with strong interests in the Arab world), turned out to be strongly pro-Israel. Many Arabs praised the election of George W. Bush in 2000, because they thought that the Arab oil and business connections of his family and key officials (such as Vice President Dick Cheney) would lead to greater 'understanding' by Washington of Arab points of view—but this did not happen.

Given the apparent structural complexity of the decision-making process on Middle Eastern policy, and the amount of information and expert opinion that is theoretically available to decision-makers, an academic observer is struck by the narrow, uninformed, and ad hoc nature of some policy outcomes. The decision-making on Palestine–Israel seems not to comprehend the dysfunctional side effects of US policy. In the decision to invade Iraq, the administration's contentions about the danger of weapons of mass destruction and Iraqi collaboration with Al-Qaeda terrorists were largely incorrect. And its post-invasion policy planning and implementation seem to have been utterly uninformed by any understanding of Iraq's history, culture, politics, or its place in the region. And as we shall see in the section entitled '**Obama's attempt to balance hard and soft power**', President Obama was hamstrung by domestic pressures in his fruitless effort to break the Palestinian–Israeli impasse.

A region in flux

While the US was growing in power and its interests in the Middle East were deepening, the region itself was and, as the 2011 Arab uprisings reveal, still is in the process of far-reaching social, economic, and political upheavals. It has been experiencing rapid population growth, and suffering from uneven and sluggish economic development. Oil wealth is mainly concentrated in only a few small, thinly populated countries; it has not been successfully deployed to promote region-wide sustainable development. Moreover, the collapse of oil prices in the mid-1980s and then again in the early-2000s continues to generate socio-economic strains on governments. Poor educational systems and a growing pool of unemployed young people pose a constant challenge to largely inefficient, authoritarian regimes. The annual series of *Arab Human Development Reports* prepared by Arab social scientists since 2002 (UNDP 2003–12) highlight these issues, which constitute important underlying factors behind several emerging political challenges to the role of the US in the region.

1979: the beginning of an era of change

These challenges were dramatically illustrated in 1979. That year was marked by five landmark events: first, the peace treaty between Egypt and Israel; second, the takeover of the Grand Mosque in Mecca, Saudi Arabia, by Islamist militants; third, the Islamist revolution in Iran; fourth, the Soviet invasion of Afghanistan; and finally, the emergence of Saddam Hussein as the sole ruler of Iraq.

On the surface, the Egypt–Israel treaty of 26 March 1979 represented a positive development, with the US playing the crucial role in bringing it about, thanks to the diplomacy of President Carter in the Camp David meetings the previous year. Momentous as it was, this breakthrough failed to address the heart of the Arab–Israeli problem: the conflict between Israel and the Palestinians. Indeed, because the 'Palestinian dimension' had not been successfully dealt with at Camp David, new pressures began to build up: Israel invaded Lebanon in 1982, trying to liquidate the Palestinian resistance. The Palestinians launched their first *intifada* in 1989; and Israel fought three wars in Gaza in 2008–09, 2012, and 2014. The US undertook two major new diplomatic initiatives: the Madrid conference under President George H. W. Bush in 1991 and the 'Oslo peace process' under President Bill Clinton in 1993. Unfortunately, both initiatives ultimately collapsed, and the ensuing brutal conflict between Israel and the Palestinians continues to erode US stature in the Arab and Islamic worlds.

But elsewhere in the region more ominous developments were occurring. On 20 November 1979, a well-organized group of Islamist radicals seized the Grand Mosque in Mecca—the holiest site in the Islamic world. It took three weeks for the Saudi authorities, reportedly with help from French commandos, to quell the rebellion. While the militants were executed immediately, the incident suggested that the Saudi regime—notwithstanding its conservative Islamic credentials—was vulnerable to Islamist opposition. Around the same time, there was an uprising by Shia militants, perhaps inspired by the Iranian revolution, in Saudi Arabia's heavily Shia Eastern Province. It was also quickly put down. But these events presaged the emergence of a much more serious threat from other religious dissidents in the 1990s (Fandy 1999: 47ff). Shia protest, mostly from Saudis abroad, reappeared. More significantly, a small number of radical salafi clerics, both inside and outside the kingdom, began to agitate for reforms of what they saw as a regime corrupted by Western—especially US—influences. Among these activists was a young man from one of Saudi Arabia's most successful business families: Osama bin Laden.

Farther to the east, in Iran, there was another major challenge. Iran's pro-American leader, Shah Muhammad Reza Pahlavi, was forced to leave Tehran in January 1979, and the Islamic revolution was fully under way a month later. The coming to power of Ayatollah Ruhollah Khomeini undermined a 'pillar' of US security interests in the region dating back to the early 1950s. It also signalled the resurgence of 'Islamist politics' throughout the region. Decades of Iranian popular resentment at US intervention erupted, symbolized by the seizure of the US embassy on 4 November 1979 and the holding of US hostages for over a year. The hostage crisis traumatized American public opinion and contributed to the defeat of President Carter in 1980. It also reignited negative perceptions of Islam among Americans and of the US among Muslims. During the first phase of the Islamic revolution, from 1979 until Khomeini's death in 1989, the Iranian regime waged an ideological campaign against the traditional (and pro-American) oil monarchies on the Arab side of the Gulf. So, when Iraq's leader, Saddam Hussein, decided to attack Iran in 1980, he was able to count on financial support from the Arab Gulf regimes and military intelligence support from the United States. But the Iranian challenge extended well beyond the Gulf: Tehran also cultivated a strategic alliance with the Baathist regime in Syria, and helped to develop and support the Islamist militant organization Hezbollah in Lebanon, elements of which were responsible for the murder and kidnapping of Americans and other Westerners, and for the disastrous bombings of the US embassy and US marine barracks in Beirut. The Islamist leadership also continued to develop Iran's nuclear capability (a project begun under the Shah); this would eventually precipitate a regional crisis, with the US, Israel, and Saudi Arabia (among others) vowing to utilize all necessary means to prevent Iran from attaining a military nuclear capability.

As if the 'fall' of Iran were not enough of a problem for Washington, the Soviet invasion of Afghanistan in December 1979 triggered fears among some American strategists that the Soviets would use Afghanistan as a springboard for extending their influence into the Persian Gulf area and perhaps beyond. Such fears revealed ignorance of geography and topography, as well as of Soviet capabilities. To prevent a new Russian march towards warmer waters, the Carter administration warned that Washington regarded the Gulf (on the Arab side at least) as vital to US interests, and it also undertook an energetic effort, with the support of Pakistan and Saudi Arabia, to roll back the Soviets in Afghanistan by mobilizing Islamist militants called mujahedin. Armed with US shoulder-launched Stinger missiles, the mujahedin were able to inflict severe damage on Soviet military helicopters and to entrap their ground forces in the rugged Afghan terrain. But the defeat of the Soviets, which led in part to the collapse of the Soviet Union itself, not only failed to bring security to Afghanistan and the Gulf area, but also left a chaotic 'failed state' of warring Islamist militias. Worse still, with the battle against the Soviets won, many thousands of these militants, who had come from Arab and other Muslim states, left Afghanistan in a mood to promote puritanical Islamic reform by force of arms (including terrorism) through organizations such as the Taliban and Al-Qaeda.

Finally, on 16 July 1979, Saddam Hussein consolidated his personal authority in Iraq upon the resignation of President Ahmad Hassan Al-Bakr, a decade after their Baath nationalist party had taken power in a military coup. At this juncture, Iraq was well placed to assume the leadership of the Arab world, especially since Egypt had been ostracized after President Anwar Sadat had signed the peace treaty with Israel without having achieved any gains for the Palestinians. Iraq's abundant oil revenues were actually used quite effectively to build the country's socio-economic infrastructure, as well as to support an ambitious military programme. Saddam Hussein's ambition and ignorance of political realities led him to go to war with Khomeini's Iran. In Washington, the Reagan administration (some of whose officials resurfaced in the administration of George W. Bush), attempting to play realpolitik, offered military intelligence assistance to Saddam in the hope of preventing an Iranian takeover of the vulnerable pro-Western Arab oil monarchies; it was also pleased that the war lasted a long time (from 1980 to 1988), giving Iraq a pyrrhic victory, and weakening both of these big and unfriendly Gulf countries. But Washington's satisfaction was short-lived, for in 1990 Iraq suddenly overran its small and oil-rich neighbour Kuwait. The administration of George H. W. Bush refused to countenance Saddam's takeover and US armed forces led an international coalition to expel the Iraqis from Kuwait. It was the first—but not the last— major US military action in the Arab world. Following Iraq's expulsion, for just over a decade Washington sought to maintain Gulf security through a strategy of 'dual containment' of both Iraq and Iran, with the emphasis on pervasive and debilitating sanctions against Iraq intended to diminish its military threat potential against its neighbours, and to eliminate its capabilities to produce or deploy weapons of mass destruction.

The emergence of Islamist transnational networks

The most important development toward the end of the twentieth century was militant political Islam, a force that challenged many of the states and the state system itself. With its hostility to America and the West in general and, in some cases, its readiness to utilize terrorist tactics, Washington came to see it as a national security threat. Its Islamic political discourse took two fairly distinct forms—Shi'ite and Sunni. The Shia-driven movement was inspired and supported by the revolutionary Iranian regime. It manifested itself most dramatically in Lebanon, which was in the throes of a civil war, in the form of the Amal movement and Hezbollah. Americans and other Westerners were taken hostage in Beirut, and some were killed. Groups affiliated with what would become Hezbollah twice bombed the US embassy and, in a suicide truck bombing, killed 241 US Marines on a peacekeeping mission in 1983. Other such incidents occurred outside Lebanon.

The other strand, marked by fundamentalist salafi and Wahhabi Sunni Islam, traced its lineage to the anti-colonial struggles between the two World Wars, but then was overshadowed by the relatively secular nationalist movements of the 1950s and 1960s. Inspired by radical offshoots from the Egyptian Muslim Brotherhood, it resurfaced in Egypt and Syria in the 1970s; it was responsible for the assassination of Egypt's President Anwar Sadat in

1980, and a bloody confrontation with the Syrian regime of President Hafiz al-Asad in the late 1970s and early 1980s. Islamist organizations also began to play a major role in Palestinian politics: the Islamist Hamas party carried the 2006 elections and subsequently took over control of the Gaza Strip. In the 1990s, Islamist movements successfully mobilized large numbers of followers in many Arab countries, leading in some cases, such as Algeria, Tunisia, and Egypt, to violent confrontations. The movement assumed a transnational aspect, in as much as its leading ideologues, such as the Sudanese activist Dr Hassan al-Turabi, sought to build a loose, broad-based front across the entire Arab world. All of these developments were deeply worrying to US officials, because of the anti-Israeli and anti-American tone of their discourse. By the early twenty-first century, groups such as Al-Qaeda, the Nusra Front, and the so-called Islamic State (ISIS) were implanting themselves in states throughout the region, and US policymakers were scrambling to contain or destroy them with advanced military technologies, notably drones.

The 1990s: Kuwait, the 'peace process', and militant Islamism

At the beginning of the 1990s, there were many reasons to suppose that the US had achieved much in the Middle East. Yet these successes were shadowed by negative after-effects. The Americans had played the leading role in defeating Soviet communism in Afghanistan. And then, of course, the Soviet Union itself had collapsed. But success in Afghanistan was achieved by utilizing the militant mujahedin Islamists. When many of these 'Arab Afghan' fighters returned home, they turned their attention to combating pro-American regimes.

In Iraq, Washington reacted quickly to Saddam Hussein's invasion of Kuwait. Immediately sensing a direct threat to its oil and security interests in the Gulf, the US determined that it had to go to war to evict the Iraqis. The war was quick, inexpensive, and relatively painless for the victors. President George H. W. Bush effectively mobilized an international coalition, including several Arab states, to liberate Kuwait, but he lacked an international mandate to occupy Iraq to bring down the Saddam Hussein regime. Instead, a decade-long sanctions regime was imposed, which wreaked devastating effects on the Iraqi civilian population without undermining the regime. Along with US support for Israel's occupation of the Palestinian territories, the US-led sanctions on Iraq contributed to the growing hostility towards the US in Arab and Muslim public opinion. The US policy of 'dual containment' of Iraq and Iran seemed at best a palliative, not a cure, for Gulf insecurity. A small, but influential, group of hawkish officials, former officials, and policy analysts—later to be known as 'neo-conservatives'—fervently believed that Iraq under Saddam Hussein was so dangerous to US (and Israeli) interests that merely 'containing' him was insufficient. With the election of George W. Bush as president in 2000, this group would be catapulted into power.

In the Arab–Israeli theatre, President Clinton, elected in 1992, inherited a promising new peace process from his defeated predecessor. The mechanisms laid down by former Secretary of State James Baker, which led to the Madrid Conference in 1991, had brought together the conflicting parties and created an elaborate multi-track structure of negotiations. By the time that Clinton took office early in 1993, the initial momentum of Madrid had flagged, and the subsequent bilateral talks in Washington between Israel and its neighbours had got bogged down. But then Clinton received an even better gift from Israel and the PLO themselves: the secret negotiations in Oslo led to the breakthrough 'Declaration of

Principles', signed in September 1993 on the White House lawn, and the beginning of the Oslo peace process, which initially appeared to be the best hope ever for Arab–Israeli peace (see **Chapter 13**). However, Washington's failure at the highest levels to prod the parties into keeping to the Oslo timetable and its failure to stop new Israeli settlement construction finally led to the collapse of the Oslo process—ironically, at Camp David—in August 2000. And so the vision of a 'new Middle East' articulated by Israel's Shimon Peres (Peres and Naor 1993) never materialized.

Meanwhile, networked Islamist terrorism—exemplified by fundamentalist Sunnis such as Osama bin Laden—was gaining ground. In the 1990s, there were several terrorist attacks on US targets, including one on New York's World Trade Center in 1993. In the late 1990s, American personnel in Saudi Arabia and embassies in Africa were also targeted. Although increasingly aware of this serious new threat, the Clinton administration responded in a relatively ad hoc manner (Gerges 1999). After the bombing of US embassies in Kenya and Tanzania in 1996, President Clinton ordered limited military strikes in Afghanistan and on what turned out to be a legitimate pharmaceutical factory in Khartoum. Following the bombing of US military facilities in Saudi Arabia in 1998, administration officials became even more alarmed, but were unable to fashion an effective counter-terrorism strategy. And President Clinton made no military response at all to the bomb attack on the USS *Cole* in Aden harbour in October 2000, just a few months before the end of his term. To its credit, Washington undertook efforts to reassure the Islamic world that the US was not anti-Islamic. For example, American Muslim leaders were invited to the White House for the *iftar* (the fast-breaking meal) in the month of Ramadan. But such gestures were mainly symbolic and the American attitude towards rising political Islam remained ambivalent at best, if not hostile.

The encouraging developments of the early 1990s—the removal of the Soviet threat from Afghanistan; the expulsion of Saddam Hussein from Kuwait; the Oslo peace process; President George H. W. Bush's talk of a 'new world order'—had turned to ashes by the end of the decade. Tensions in the Persian Gulf between Iran and its Arab neighbours remained high; Saddam's Iraq was still dangerous and unpredictable in spite of punishing international sanctions; Afghanistan was in turmoil and Al-Qaeda was on the rise; the Palestinian–Israeli conflict was about to erupt again in violence. And beneath the surface, the region's social and economic problems, and growing popular disaffection with corrupt and incompetent governance, were eroding the apparent stability of authoritarian regimes. Despite its uncontested military presence in the region, the US found itself unable to exercise sufficient 'soft power' to impose a Pax Americana on this turbulent region.

US responses to twenty-first-century challenges

US politics took a sharp rightward swing with the election of Republican George W. Bush in 2000 for two consecutive terms, the first of which especially was characterized by a muscular response to a threat emanating from the Middle East: the trauma of the 9/11 terrorist attacks on US soil. The election of Democrat Barack Obama in 2008 began with an effort to repair the rift with the Muslim and Arab worlds, but by the end of 2012, observers had begun to note significant continuities with the policies of his predecessor.

The George W. Bush era and the 'neo-conservative revolution'

The administration of President George W. Bush (2001–08) was marked by a dramatic escalation of tension and instability throughout the broader Middle East region. With the collapse of the Oslo peace process under President Clinton, the Palestinian–Israeli conflict erupted into violence once more; while Bush initially showed interest in restarting serious diplomacy, he in fact allowed the situation to fester. It was only in November 2007 that he and Secretary of State Condoleezza Rice belatedly tried to restart negotiations by calling an international conference in Annapolis, Maryland—but lack of preparation and the approaching end of his presidency were among the factors that prevented much progress from being made.

The US response to the attacks of 9/11 was encapsulated in the term 'global war on terror'. Eschewing a law-enforcement strategy, the administration advanced a military approach, focusing initially on regime change in Afghanistan, where the Taliban rulers had given sanctuary and protection to Osama bin Laden and Al-Qaeda. Washington deployed its intelligence agencies to hunt down radical Islamist terrorists around the world, and established special prisons in Guantanamo Bay, Cuba, and elsewhere to detain 'enemy combatants' indefinitely, without charges or legal recourse. Next, the administration turned its attention to a long-time objective of the neo-conservatives: overthrowing Saddam Hussein. It justified its invasion by citing intelligence reports about Iraqi weapons of mass destruction that later proved to be false. Equally incorrect were the allegations that Saddam had been harbouring terrorists. What had been expected to be a quick military and political operation turned out to be a swamp. One consequence of the US's misadventure in Iraq was the strengthening of Iran's influence throughout the region, even though the administration viewed 'Iranian-sponsored terrorism' (Shia, exemplified by its support of Hezbollah in Lebanon), along with Al-Qaeda and related terrorist groups (Sunni), as an existential threat to the US and its Middle Eastern allies—Israel, Egypt, Saudi Arabia, and Jordan, among others. As Bush's second term came to an end, even his supporters were conceding that the 'global war on terrorism' was far from over. And the manner in which Washington was prosecuting this 'war' was creating intense and widespread hostility toward the US throughout the Arab and Muslim world.

In less than two years after 9/11, the administration of George W. Bush had launched three wars: the war in Afghanistan, the larger 'war on (Islamist) terrorism', and the invasion and occupation of Iraq. The president believed that there was still another front in the new struggle: the terrorism practised by Palestinian Islamist organizations against Israel. To that end, he undertook to effect 'regime change' (as he had in Afghanistan and Iraq) among the Palestinians by trying to sideline President Yasser Arafat with a more 'moderate' Palestinian leadership but was thwarted when Hamas won the Palestinian election in 2006. While professing to be an 'honest broker' role in breaking the Palestinian–Israeli impasse with a diplomatic agenda called the 'Road Map', the president made it clear that the real problem was on the Palestinian side, not the Israeli.

With over 130,000 US troops occupying Iraq and the administration declaring 'a generational commitment to helping the people of the Middle East transform their region' (Rice 2003), it was obvious that the US had moved away from its traditional stance of upholding the regional status quo towards a proactive, interventionist policy. In what was widely hailed as a landmark speech, President Bush himself committed the US to the goal of actively promoting liberal democracy and free-market economic reforms, not only in Iraq, but also throughout the region (Bush 2003). The 'neo-conservative' network of hawkish policymakers who had fashioned the new approach justified the US's new boldness as 'manifest destiny', on the one hand, and the ineluctable workings of realism in international politics, on the other. As the neo-conservative commentator Robert Kagan (2003: 85–8), wrote, it was a policy driven by two imperatives: security in the post-9/11 era, and an ideological sense of moral mission, the origins of which can be traced to the very beginnings of the American republic.

Thus the greater Middle East became the testing ground for the new US project, and within it the Arab world was 'ground zero': the source of what the US administration insisted was the new danger—Islamist terrorists, irrational and therefore undeterrable, possessed of low-tech portable weapons of mass destruction and therefore uncontainable, who could strike at the US heartland unless they were pre-emptively liquidated. The Middle East, and indeed the vaster Islamic world, was, in this view, a breeding ground for this terrorism. Not only must terrorist organizations be rooted out, but the 'swamp' in which they breed must be drained. The new task of US foreign policy was not only to conduct regime change by force if necessary, but also—through vigorous democracy promotion—to reshape the domestic environment of states whose educational systems, religious organizations, incompetent governments, and stagnant economies nurtured anti-American terrorism. It proved to be an impossible project.

Obama's attempt to balance hard and soft power

With the election of Barack Obama in 2008, the 'neo-conservative revolution' that had shaped his predecessor's foreign policies seemed to be over. Obama, facing a hostile, turbulent Middle East when he took office in January 2009, set out to reshape US policy in two contentious areas after the abrasive approach of his predecessor: the Palestinian–Israeli conflict and the US attitude toward the Islamic world.

He tried to revive the moribund Palestinian–Israeli 'peace process' by appointing former Senator George Mitchell as his special envoy and by calling bluntly for a halt in the expansion of Israeli settlements in the occupied Palestinian West Bank. He also called for new negotiations based on the 1967 borders. This effort, however, did not bear fruit. Mitchell's shuttling between Israeli and Palestinian leaders produced no breakthroughs, because neither party took his mission seriously. Mitchell was undercut by some of Obama's own officials, the Israel lobby and its friends in Congress who opposed the President's attempt at balance as 'anti-Israeli'. Then in May 2011, in a joint press conference with Obama, Israeli Prime Minister Netanyahu rudely criticized the president for his lack of understanding of Middle East realities, prompting a senior White House official to say: 'I can think of no other time when a president has been lectured to in the Oval Office' (Wilson 2012). But Obama turned the other cheek, and as the 2012 election campaign began, he backed away from his initial determination to settle the Palestinian–Israeli issue.

On the second issue, in a dramatic speech at Cairo University, President Obama extended the hand of friendship to the Muslim world in an effort to win back hostile Muslim and Arab public opinion: 'We seek a new beginning based on mutual interest and mutual respect and based on the truth that America and Islam are not exclusive and need not be in competition', he said. But this gesture too proved ineffective. Two years after the speech, according to a poll in six Arab countries (Arab-American Institute 2012), more than 75 per cent of respondents in Morocco, Egypt, Lebanon, Jordan, and Saudi Arabia (and 41 per cent in the United Arab Emirates) stated that their expectations had not been met. Large majorities in each country indicated that 'US interference in the Arab world' and 'the continuing occupation of Palestinian lands' were the chief obstacles to peace and stability in the Middle East. Between 50 and 62 per cent of those polled stated that the killing of bin Laden made them less favourable toward the US. Only 10 per cent or fewer of those polled approved of Obama's policies—far lower than the approval ratings given to Sarkozy (France), Erdogan (Turkey), Ahmadinejad (Iran), or Abdullah bin Abdel Aziz (Saudi Arabia). And a Zogby poll in November 2014 found that almost eight out of ten respondents in Lebanon, Jordan, Egypt, Saudi Arabia, the United Arab Emirates, Iran, and Turkey disagreed with statement that the US 'contributes to peace and stability in the region'.

A wartime president

The president then turned his attention to extracting US forces from the wars in Iraq, which he had criticized as 'a war of choice'; and Afghanistan, which he called 'a war of necessity'. Having campaigned on a promise to pull US forces out of Iraq (which, at the height of the war, numbered more than 150,000), he withdrew the last combat troops in 2010 and completed the final withdrawal in December 2011. But the war had cost the lives of some 4,500 US soldiers and over US$1 trillion, and the 'new' Iraq was deeply divided, unstable, and subject to Iranian influence. In the US's other war—Afghanistan—Obama took a different tack, ordering a 'surge' of 30,000 in US troop strength, bringing the total to more than 100,000, promising to start withdrawing them in 2011, and completing the withdrawal by 2014. But well into Obama's second term (2012–16), the Taliban were gaining ground, the Afghan government continued to flounder, and a substantial number of US military 'advisors' remained in the country.

As for the war against Islamist extremism, Obama, who had been criticized by the Republicans for being 'soft' on national security, actually intensified military action against the Taliban, Al-Qaeda, and its offshoots in Afghanistan, Pakistan, and Yemen. On 2 May 2011, Obama authorized the US Special Forces attack that killed Osama bin Laden in his compound in Abbotabad, Pakistan—the crowning achievement for the US war on Al-Qaeda and one that would burnish the President's credentials as a strong leader. In the first three years of Obama's presidency, the US conducted at least 239 covert remotely piloted aircraft (better known as drone) strikes compared with the forty-four approved during George W. Bush's tenure. Despite public outcry over the targeting of American 'terrorist' citizens, the accidental killing in 2015 of an American hostage, and the 'collateral damage' inflicted on civilians, the Obama administration appeared determined to continue and even expand the use of drones. Some saw a certain irony in his having been awarded the Nobel Peace Prize in 2009.

Obama and Iran

As part of his plan to promote US 'engagement' with the Middle East Obama declared that he would reach out to Iran on the basis of mutual respect, despite the history of bitter relations dating back to 1979. But Iran's president Mahmoud Ahmadinejad rebuffed this overture.

Iran continued to provide support to Syria and the Lebanese Hezbollah organization, and to develop its nuclear programme, which it claimed was for peaceful purposes only. These activities were anathema to Israel especially, and they also resonated badly in the US and Saudi Arabia. However, when the Iranian regime crushed the 'green revolution' uprising surrounding the 2009 Iranian presidential election, the US administration basically stood aside. Instead, it resorted to a policy of increasingly severe economic sanctions and encouraged the European Union and other industrialized, oil-consuming countries to do the same. Unimpressed by Iran's commitment as a signatory to the Nuclear Non-Proliferation Treaty (which neighbouring nuclear-armed Israel, Pakistan, and India have refused to sign), Washington and its allies remained deeply concerned that Iran was secretly developing a military nuclear capability. As continuing negotiations were proving unproductive, the possibility of an Israeli attack on Iran's nuclear facilities increased and, along with it, the likelihood that the US would be drawn in. Administration officials were aware of the negative consequences of US military action in yet another Middle Eastern Muslim country, given the experiences in Iraq and Afghanistan. For a time the possibility of a new war in the Gulf, initiated by Israel with the likelihood of the US being drawn in, seemed real, but the election of Hassan Rouhani in 2013 cooled the situation, as the new President was far less bellicose than his predecessor. Negotiations over Iran's nuclear programme between Iran and the five permanent members of the UN Security Council plus Germany had begun in 2006 but gained momentum in 2014. In a distinct break with the past, high level American and Iranian diplomats negotiated face-to-face in a business-like manner leading to a framework agreement in 2015. Were the negotiations to succeed, leading to curbs on the Iranian nuclear programme in exchange for the lifting of sanctions, the tantalizing prospect arose of a major diplomatic realignment in the region and the possibility of reduced tensions. But America's traditional allies, Israel and Saudi Arabia, viewed the process with alarm.

The United States and the 'Arab Spring'

Nothing could better illustrate the strengths and weaknesses of US Middle East policies than the Obama administration's reaction to the 'Arab Spring'—the series of uprisings that began late in 2010 and continue to reverberate throughout the region. There is no denying the 'epidemic effect' of this phenomenon and the commonalities of mass protest that toppled dictators in Tunisia, Egypt, Libya, and Yemen, challenged regimes in Bahrain and Syria, and panicked rulers in neighbouring states, to co-opt or pre-empt upheavals in their own countries. But, four years on, it was clear that the affected countries have different trajectories. A challenge for the Obama administration was to fashion a broadly consistent position on the challenges to Arab authoritarianism, while taking into account the particularities of each case.

On the rhetorical level, President Obama and then-Secretary of State Hillary Clinton asserted the classical US *idealist* stance: in principle, Washington supports transitions to democracy. On the *realist* level, however, prudence was the watchword. Having initially hesitated to abandon authoritarian allies in Tunisia and Egypt, the administration calculated that qualified support for the oppositions was the intelligent position to take. In Libya, despite the 'brother leader' Muammar al-Gaddafi's earlier abandonment of his military nuclear ambitions, there was no love lost; the question was how much support to give an opposition movement that initially seemed destined to be liquidated by the dictator. Not wanting to plunge unilaterally into yet another military adventure, Obama elected to 'lead from behind' a NATO-led coalition, which used a Security Council Resolution calling for humanitarian protection of protesters to destroy the regime and its military forces. In chaotic Yemen, the administration was torn between the regime of President Ali Abdullah Salih, a willing and compliant ally in the war on Al-Qaeda terrorism, and a disaffected populace in which the opposition included elements considered neither democratic nor pro-American. Again, 'leading from behind' seemed the most prudent course—in this case, behind the multilateral efforts of the Arab GCC countries. But in Bahrain the Obama administration faced a dilemma. Nobody could doubt the massive popular antipathy to the regime of King Hamad bin Issa Al-Khalifa and the brutal reaction of his security forces to the protests. But here Obama punted. Under strong pressure from the rulers of Saudi Arabia, who chose to see the Bahrain uprising as a Shia–Iranian plot, the administration criticized the Bahrain rulers for their bad behaviour, but issued only pro forma protest against the Saudi intervention to try to crush the protests. Oil and strategic interests trumped democratic principles.

It was the Syrian uprising, however, that proved to be the biggest challenge. Initially, President Bashar al-Asad delusionally claimed that his regime would be immune from the Arab Spring because of its apparent fidelity to the Arab cause in Palestine. As it became obvious that popular discontent was widespread and deeply rooted, Bashar al-Asad's ill-advised response was to administer a 'shock and awe' dose of brutality in the hope of nipping the uprising in the bud—perhaps following the example of his father in the notorious crackdown in the city of Hama in 1982, in which at least 10,000 people were killed. Remarkably, however, the protests continued and deepened to the point at which the conflict became militarized. Syria was plunged into a civil war in which both the regime and the opposition attracted outside military assistance. As of 2015 over 200,000 Syrians had died and millions had become displaced in what was said to be the worst humanitarian catastrophe of the twenty-first century. For the Obama administration, Syria was seen both as a golden opportunity and a trap. Rarely were principle and interest more closely aligned. On the one hand, there was the prospect of bringing down a brutal dictatorship, giving democracy a chance, and delivering a body blow to Iran's regional influence, while strengthening the security of Israel, Saudi Arabia, and other friendly Sunni regimes. On the other hand, the Asad regime was politically cohesive at the elite level, and possessed of formidable military and security assets, while the opposition, initially at least, appeared poorly armed and deeply divided. Moreover, Washington was concerned about its potential Islamist character and the possibility of Al-Qaeda or other such groups taking power in a post-Asad period—which would hardly bode well for Israeli or US interests. Obama's advisers did not want to see the US drawn into problematic new military engagements in Syria and/or Iran, especially since there was little support for a multilateral approach along the lines of NATO's Libyan campaign. UN mediation was proving ineffectual. Moreover, Russia and China had blocked UN Security Council resolutions opening the way for military intervention. In 2012, President Obama—laying down a 'red line'—warned Syria that its use of chemical weapons would have serious consequences. In 2013 the Syrian regime unleashed a chemical weapons attack against an opposition stronghold in a Damascus neighbourhood, killing many civilians. But the Obama administration refused to state that the 'red line' had been crossed, and instead of ordering a military response the President accepted a Russian proposal that Syria destroy its chemical weapons stocks. With the US reluctant to support the opposition forces robustly, the Asad regime gained strength and the opposition found itself increasingly dominated by Islamist extremist groups. By 2015 one of those groups, the so-called Islamic State (or ISIS), which had originated in chaotic Iraq, had occupied substantial territory in Syria as well as Iraq. In 2014 Obama had spoken dismissively of ISIS, but a year later he sought Congressional authorization to use military force against it.

There were at least three points of view about Obama's handling of the Arab Spring. From the left, there were those who faulted the administration for not being consistently on 'the right side of history'. They pointed to the initial reluctance to abandon Ben Ali in Tunisia and Mubarak in Egypt, to foot-dragging in Yemen (because of Washington's close anti-terrorism cooperation with Ali Abdullah Saleh), to pusillanimity in Bahrain (where Saudi pressure and US military relations trumped supporting the protesters), and to timidity in Libya and, especially, Syria. From the right, there was anger at insufficient support for traditional allies in Tunisia, Egypt, and Bahrain, and alarm about the possible rise of anti-American Islamism in the guise of the Arab Spring. From the relatively non-partisan 'realist centre', there was approval of Obama's 'nimble' Middle East policies, citing his nuanced approach to the complexities of the Arab Spring and other regional issues (Gause and Lustick 2012).

Conclusion

In reviewing some 200 years of US involvements in the Middle East, we observe the interplay of idealism and realism. Missionaries and educators tried to bring what they felt were the benefits of Christianity and Western enlightenment in the nineteenth century. President Wilson sought to advance 'self-determination'. In the period after the Second World War, US governments gave foreign economic assistance and, lately, have sought to promote democracy. With the rise of the US as a global power after the First World War, interests took priority over ideals: hence the emphasis on 'protecting' oil interests and Israel, and promoting 'friendly' regimes by means both overt and covert. Following the collapse of the Soviet Union, some US commentators spoke of a Pax Americana over the Middle East, considering the US military's formidable presence throughout the region.

But a mere fifteen years later, America's influence seemed to have dramatically waned. If preserving regional stability was Washington's top priority, clearly its policies were not working. Four major Arab states—Iraq, Syria, Libya, and Yemen—were falling apart. Islamist militant movements, fundamentally hostile to the US, were in the ascendency not just in those countries but throughout the region. Iran and its Arab allies in Iraq, Syria, Lebanon, and Yemen were challenging the dominance of America's traditional Sunni allies—the Gulf states, Egypt, Jordan, and Lebanon. US-sponsored diplomacy in the Palestinian-Israeli conflict had stalled, fuelling public anger toward America throughout the Arab and Muslim worlds. Long-time US partners—Israel, Saudi Arabia, and Turkey—looked with dismay at what they saw as American irresoluteness.

An Obama doctrine?

President Obama clearly tried to rein in the foreign policy triumphalism of the previous administration. He did so mindful of the relative decline of the United States in the changing global balance of power. Having faced (and slowly overcome) the financial crisis of 2008, and having tried to deal with serious domestic problems such as budget deficits, inadequate health care, growing socio-economic inequality, and decaying infrastructure, the President was also aware of the robust rise of China in Asia. To that end, in 2011 Obama and his Secretary of State Hillary Clinton articulated what they called a 'rebalancing' (or 'pivot') of US attention toward Asia, with an eye to containing the expansion of Chinese power and influence. The reaction among America's Middle East allies was one of dismay. They feared that an America whose military assets were shrinking would have to contract its Middle East presence in order to bolster its presence in Asia. And in the Middle East itself they observed a reluctance on the part of Washington to involve itself. They remembered that Obama had come to power promising to extract the US military from Afghanistan and Iraq, and they puzzled at his 'leading from behind' in the Libyan uprising. Worse still, they faulted his failure to intervene actively on behalf of the opposition to the Bashar al-Asad regime. His meek acceptance of Israel's rejection of his call for an end to settlement expansion in the West Bank was seen as further evidence of American weakness. Most worrisome to them was the realization of a US (and other major powers) agreement with Iran over its nuclear programme, and the prospect that an Iran relieved of sanctions would seek to dominate the region.

President Obama, of course, rejected such criticism. In a lengthy interview with the *New York Times* in April 2015 (Thomas L. Friedman, 'Iran and the Obama Doctrine', *New York Times*, 5 April 2015) he said 'We will engage, but we preserve all our capabilities. ... at this point, the US's core interests in the region are not oil, are not territorial, our core interests are that everybody is living in peace, that it is orderly, that our allies are not being attacked, that children are not having barrel bombs dropped on them, that massive displacements aren't taking place.' If those were the objectives, they were far from being achieved as Obama neared the end of his presidency.

Key events

1919	King–Crane Commission, sent by President Wilson in 1919 to ascertain the wishes of former Ottoman peoples
1928	Red Line Agreement opens the Middle East to US oil companies
1947	Truman doctrine: promise of US aid to Greece and Turkey
1953	CIA coup to remove Iran's Prime Minister Mussadiq
1955	Baghdad Pact: pro-Western security alliance
1956	Suez crisis
1957	Eisenhower doctrine promises US support to Arab regimes
1967	Six-Day War
1973	Arab–Israeli War

1978	Camp David accord
1979	Egypt–Israel treaty
	Iranian Revolution and subsequent hostage crisis provoke a major rupture in US–Iran relations
1991	Gulf War: US and allies expel Iraq from Kuwait
	Madrid Conference initiates Arab–Israel peace talks
1993	'Declaration of Principles' on the White House lawn
2000	Oslo process collapses at Camp David summit
	Election of George W. Bush
2001	Terrorist attacks of 9/11 against US targets
	US initiates attacks against Taliban regime in Afghanistan
2002	President Bush delivers 'axis of evil' speech
2003	US invasion of Iraq begins
	Publication of 'Road Map for an Israeli–Palestinian Peace'
2007	Annapolis Conference (Maryland): attempts to restart peace talks
2009	Obama's speech at Cairo University
2011	Tunisia's Ben Ali flees; Egypt's Hosni Mubarak resigns; Libya's Gaddafi is overthrown
	Killing of Osama bin Laden in Pakistan by US Special Forces
2012	Yemen's Ali Abdullah Salih steps down
2013	Egypt's Muslim Brotherhood President Muhammad Mursi is ousted by the military
	The Raba'a Square massacre of Muslim Brotherhood supporters in Cairo
2014	Abu-Bakr Al-Baghdadi, leader of ISIS, declares a new caliphate
	ISIS captures Mosul, Iraq's second-largest city
	President Obama authorizes air strikes against ISIS in Iraq and Syria
2015	Re-election of Benjamin Netanyahu as Israel's prime minister
	Saudi Arabia carries out air attacks in Yemen against the Houthi movement
	Iran and the P5+1 reach a framework agreement on Iran's nuclear programme

Further reading

Al-Sumait, Fahed, Lenze Nele, and Hudson, Michael C. (eds) (2015) *The Arab Uprisings: Catalysts, Dynamics and Trajectories* (Lanham, MD: Rowman and Littlefield)
   A collection of scholarly analyses of the 'Arab spring'.

Bill, J. A., Jr (1988) *The Eagle and the Lion: The Tragedy of American-Iranian Relations* (New Haven, CT: Yale University Press)
   A well-researched study of US-Iran relations from the Second World War until the Revolution.

Clinton, Hillary (2011) 'America's Pacific Century,' *Foreign Policy*, 11 October
   The former Secretary of State articulates a US 'rebalancing' toward Asia.

Gerges, F. A. (2012) *Obama and the Middle East: The End of America's Moment?* (London: Palgrave Macmillan)
An evaluation of the decline of US hegemony.

Lesch, D. W. and Haas, Mark L. (eds) (2014) *The Middle East and the United States: History, Politics and Ideologies* (5th edn, updated, Boulder, CO: Westview Press)
Essay collection on different aspects of US policy from the nineteenth to the twenty-first century

Mann, J. (2004) *The Rise of the Vulcans: The History of Bush's War Cabinet* (New York: Viking)
A solid account of the neo-conservative network.

McClellan, S. (2008) *What Happened: Inside the Bush White House and Washington's Culture of Deception* (New York: Public Affairs)
A former White House spokesman reveals his dismay at how the administration misled the public on Iraq.

Mearsheimer, J. J. and Walt, S. M. (2007) *The Israel Lobby and US Foreign Policy* (New York: Farrar, Straus and Giroux)
A vigorously argued critique of the lobby's enormous influence on US Middle Eastern policy.

Nasr, Seyyed Vali Reza (2013) *The Dispensable Nation: American Foreign Policy in Retreat* (New York: Doubleday)
A well-informed discussion of American decline in world politics.

Quandt, William B. (2005) *Peace Process: American Diplomacy and the Arab-Israeli Conflict Since 1967* (revised edn, Berkeley: University of California Press)
The standard account of US policy toward the Palestine conflict.

Sanger, D. (2012) *Confront and Conceal: Obama's Secret Wars and Surprising Use of American Power* (New York: Crown)
An analysis of Obama's applications of 'hard power'.

Wright, L. (2006) *The Looming Tower: Al-Qaeda and the Road to 9/11* (New York: Alfred A. Knopf)
One of the best studies of Osama bin Laden and his movement.

Questions

1. What are America's core national interests in the Middle East today?
2. What challenges do the recent upheavals within the region pose for US policymakers?
3. What is the relation between US domestic politics and its Middle Eastern policies?
4. Is American influence declining in the Middle East and is this perhaps a good thing?
5. How would you account for the waning of American popularity in the Middle East?

Europe in the Middle East

ROSEMARY HOLLIS

Overview

In the early twentieth century, two European powers dominated the Middle East and North Africa (MENA), transforming 'the Arab world' into a system of separate states and facilitating the establishment of a Jewish homeland that became the state of Israel, before retreating in the face of independence movements. By the end of the century, the United States was unrivalled power-broker across the region, but the Europeans had turned old imperialist relationships into commercial ones. Bound to MENA by economic interdependence and migration flows, the European Union formulated a series of initiatives designed to address new transnational security concerns through the deployment of 'soft power', in conjunction with partial involvement in increased US military engagement in the region—with mixed results. By 2011 and the eruption of popular uprisings across the Arab world, the European Union was itself in the throes of an economic crisis that forced a rethink in European policies toward the region and a reassertion of bilateralism. This chapter traces this evolution in relations between the two contiguous regions, noting the interplay between changes in both; it outlines the role of the European Union in the quest to resolve the Arab–Israeli conflict; and summarizes European responses to the so-called 'Arab Spring', ensuing regional instability, and the related refugee crisis.

Introduction

There are four discernible phases to the story of Europe and the Middle East in the last hundred years. The first, spanning the First World War and collapse of the Ottoman Empire to the 1950s, is the era of European imperialism in the Middle East, out of which was born the contemporary state system in the region. (See **Box 17.1** for a chronology.)

Box 17.1 European imperialism and the emergence of the state system

1800s — Britain establishes a semi-colonial role (responsible for external relations) in Arab Gulf sheikhdoms (Kuwait, the last to join the British 'trucial system', is first to gain independence in 1961; others—United Arab Emirates, Qatar, Bahrain—gain independence in 1971)

Separate arrangements are made in Sultanate of Oman (replaced with treaty in 1971) and South Arabia (Yemen), with Aden a British colony (until evacuated in 1967)

1834–1962 — Algeria becomes a colony of France (independent in 1962)

1881 — Tunisia becomes a French protectorate (independent in 1956)

1882 — Britain takes control of Egypt (officially ends role in 1936, but retains presence until 1950s)

1899 — Sudan made an 'Anglo-Egyptian condominium'

1906 — Discovery of oil in Iran; foundation of the Anglo-Persian Oil Company

1911 — Italy takes Libya from the Ottomans (independent, with extended British involvement, in 1951)

1912 — Morocco, previously under French and Spanish areas of control, is made a French protectorate, with administration in north ceded to Spain (independent in 1956)

1919 — Attempted imposition of Anglo-Persian Agreement

1920–23 — France acquires the League of Nations mandate for Syria (independent in 1946), from which it separates Lebanon (officially independent in 1943, French left in 1946)

Britain gains the mandates for Palestine and Mesopotamia (Iraq); establishes Hashemite monarchies in Transjordan (separated from Mandatory remit) and Iraq (independent in 1932; monarchy overthrown in 1958); rules Palestine effectively as a colony, within which a 'Jewish homeland' takes shape on the basis of the Balfour Declaration of 1917, as stipulated under the mandate

1941 — Allied invasion of Iran: Britain in south; Soviets in north; abdication of Reza Shah, succession of Muhammad Reza Shah

1945–46 — British and Soviets withdraw from Iran

1948 — Britain withdraws from the Palestine mandate—establishment of the State of Israel; West Bank incorporated in Jordan; Gaza Strip under Egyptian administration until Israel captures both in 1967 war

1951–53 — Nationalization of Iranian oil; diplomatic relations with Britain severed; Britain assists CIA-instigated coup to overthrow Mussadiq/National Front government, reinstate Shah, and reverse oil nationalization

1956 — Suez crisis

The second coincides with the Cold War, during which Europe was part of the Western camp, but the United States unilaterally increased its power and influence in the Middle East as Britain and France retreated. While superpower rivalry was the dominant motif during the Cold War, with independent and in most cases militaristic regional states playing off one against the other, the subtext was rivalry between the Western powers for commercial gain.

The third, post-Cold War, period dates from the beginning of the 1990s to 2010, during which time the European Union came into being—briefly challenging US 'hard power' with its 'soft power' approach to regional developments. The EU member states set about devising a common foreign and security policy toward their neighbours in the Mediterranean, including a coordinated position on the Israeli–Palestinian conflict, but such efforts fell short of turning the EU into a unified actor with decisive influence across the Middle East writ large. Crucially, EU members differed in their reactions to the US invasion of Iraq in 2003. The ensuing conflict in Iraq, inclusive of sectarian violence, defied US and allied European efforts to restore enduring stability and in the case of the British at least, their military performance in Iraq was deemed a failure. The unravelling of Iraq, only partially contained sufficiently for US troops to withdraw in 2011, was a portent of more chaos to come, following the Arab uprisings.

The fourth phase in the story of European involvement in the Middle East dawned at the end of 2010, when the uprising in Tunisia presaged a wave of revolts across the region that took Europe and the US by surprise, and, in conjunction with the legacy of the intervention in Iraq, obliged both to re-examine their policies and assumptions. By 2015 the deepening war in Syria, the rise of the self-styled Islamic State (IS), and outflow of refugees had catapulted Europe into a crisis of major proportions.

The analysis offered here draws on a number of theoretical approaches. The literature on imperialism, neo-imperialism, and post-colonialism is instructive for understanding: first, early twentieth-century European predominance in the Middle East; second, subsequent US hegemony in the region; and third, the legacy of post-colonialism in contemporary European relations with the Arab and Muslim world.

Realism comes into its own during the Cold War period, not least in the cynical commentaries of Arab columnists as a predictor of not only superpower, but also US–European competition for clients, access to resources, and military sales, as well as the paramountcy of military force (Waltz 1979). However, the realist and neo-realist paradigms are limiting, in so far as they reinforce the perception that states are rational actors calculating and acting upon their interests in a global competition.

Issues of identity do not feature in the realist paradigm, yet they help to explain the resistance to and nature of anti-imperialism, anti-Westernism, and the Arab revolts. Critical theory (Doty 1996; Fierke 2007) is helpful in deconstructing Europe's depiction of the Middle East and its counter-terrorism policy, and related efforts to control migration (Basaran 2008). Recent examinations of narrative construction and multiculturalism, deploying discourse analysis, offer perhaps important insights on the contemporary phenomenon of radicalization in Europe, as well as the Middle East (Roy 2004; Croft 2012). Meanwhile, theories of regionalism in world politics are instructive in identifying how regions take shape, not only internally, but also in relation to one another.

The contention here is that while imperialism was done to the Middle East by Europe, the experience has shaped Europe as well as the regions colonized, and the process is dynamic. The contemporary identity of the EU has been, and continues to be, defined in relation to neighbouring regions, as well as in juxtaposition to the US. Its culture and politics are also informed by Europe's secular and Christian heritage, and the presence within of Muslim émigré communities alongside Jewish Europeans, with links including family ties to the Arab world and Israel, respectively.

By the same token, initiatives to develop regional institutions and consciousness in the Middle East, as discussed in **Chapter 9**, have met with limited results, despite a rare indication of assertiveness from the League of Arab States (LAS) in the context of the Libyan revolt, and Gulf Cooperation Council (GCC) mediation in the Yemeni crisis and Bahrain. Meanwhile, as of 2011, it is clear that the US, even with EU support, is incapable of imposing order on a region overtaken by competing transnational and sub-national actors and forces.

In economic terms, the MENA region is the periphery and Europe the core. In the 1990s, when globalization became the fashionable paradigm, theorists puzzled over whether the Middle East region as a whole and the Arab economies in particular had somehow been left behind in a global liberalization trend. European policy initiatives, especially in the Mediterranean, promoted liberal market capitalism, yet could find no alternative when parallel economic crises overtook the EU as well as MENA from 2009, and populist voices gathered momentum.

Social theory and constructivism are of use here in explaining how depictions of the problems can vary so profoundly from region to region, across and within societies (Wendt 1999: 157–90; Fierke 2007: 75–98). It helps to alert the scholar to the coexistence of contrasting world views and 'narratives', which serve a purpose for their proponents, but cannot be reconciled. By 2015 the Europeans were uncertain about the future of the EU itself, yet clung onto their traditional advocacy of human rights, civil society activism, and free speech, while seemingly powerless to stop a resurgence of dictatorship in the Middle East.

Phase I: the imperial era and its legacy

Early twentieth-century European imperialism in the Middle East was almost entirely a British and French endeavour, but the legacy of this period informs contemporary thinking about Europe's role in the region. Their period of dominance spawned a lasting resentment and/or suspicion of external interference. More importantly, these powers were responsible between them for devising the map of the Middle Eastern state system in the aftermath of the First World War which appeared durable until directly challenged by IS in 2014. (For a list of the milestone dates in the evolution of the state system, see **Box 17.1**.)

Imperial interests

British and French imperial policies were derivative of their global ambitions and interests. Britain initially sought access to coastal ports along the Persian Gulf, Indian Ocean, and Red Sea littorals, to protect the communication routes to its imperial possessions in India and beyond. The building of the Suez Canal, which opened a new sea route from the Mediterranean to the Red Sea, was a French, and later a British, business venture. It presaged progressive British interference in Egypt and protection of the canal was cited as a reason for British designs on Palestine in the early twentieth century.

Britain's decision to convert its navy from steam to oil was made at the beginning of the twentieth century, and prompted its quest to control access to the oil resources of Iran and the Ottoman-controlled province of Mosul (subsequently part of Iraq). Even before the collapse of the Ottoman Empire, therefore, the scene was set for a century of competition between the major oil companies, and thus the governments of Britain, France, and the US.

French ambitions in North Africa were more about extending the francophone empire than securing trade routes. French colonization of Algeria, begun in 1830, lasted until 1962—leaving the Algerians with an identity crisis post-independence. Morocco and Tunisia were made protectorates for several decades. The French interest in the Levant, meanwhile, had in part to do with proprietorial connections to the Christian (mainly Maronite) community in the Lebanon, as well as competition with the British.

The way in which the British and French manoeuvred and schemed to carve up Ottoman domains even before that empire had collapsed gave them a reputation for double-dealing. Three sets of documents bear witness to the machinations that took place,[1] and are important because they are cited by Arabs to this day as evidence of European interference and perfidy. First, the exchange of letters between Sir Henry McMahon, British High Commissioner in Egypt, and Sharif Hussein of Mecca, from July 1915 to January 1916 (the Hussein–McMahon correspondence), encouraged Hashemite leadership of an Arab revolt in return for British recognition and support for Arab independence, including in areas that eventually came under British and French mandatory rule from 1920.

Second, in January 1916, a secret agreement negotiated during the previous year between Sir Mark Sykes for the British and François Georges-Picot for the French (the Sykes–Picot Agreement) provided for British and French spheres of influence and control across whole swathes of the Ottoman Empire, including in those areas that subsequently became the League of Nations mandates of Syria/Lebanon, Iraq, and Palestine. In its specifics, this deal undercut the British understandings reached with Sharif Hussein.

Third, in a letter dated 2 November 1917 from the British Foreign Secretary Lord Balfour to Lord Rothschild, the British minister stated:

> His Majesty's Government views with favour the establishment in Palestine of a national home for the Jewish people, and will use their best endeavours to facilitate the achievement of this objective, it being clearly understood that nothing shall be done which may prejudice the civil and religious rights of existing non-Jewish communities in Palestine, or the rights and political status enjoyed by Jews in any other country.

The 'Balfour Declaration', and by extension the British, are still held responsible among Arabs for enabling the creation of the state of Israel at the expense of the Palestinians, and thus generating the Arab–Israeli conflict. The records suggest that the British did not foresee the difficulties that they would encounter in managing Jewish immigration to Palestine or the eventual outcome.

After 1920, Palestine and Iraq were established as separate entities, administered by the British as League of Nations mandates on the way to independent statehood. France took responsibility for what became the states of Syria and Lebanon. British acquiescence enabled the emergence of the Kingdom of Saudi Arabia, at the expense of the Hashemite emirate in the Hijaz. By way of partial recompense, the British installed Hashemite monarchs in what became Transjordan and Iraq.

These arrangements meant that the Arabs of the Levant and Mesopotamia transited from subjects of the Ottoman caliphate to citizens in the client states of the European victors of the First World War. The new borders cut across pre-existing age-old lines of communication, administration, kinship, and association. Iraq had previously been three Ottoman provinces, not one entity. In the Eastern Mediterranean, economic links had grown up that tied a string of port cities to the towns in the interior rather than to each other, but the mandate system separated coastal communities from those in the interior.

Thus it was that European imperialism came to take the blame for dividing up the Arab world, and for setting up a competitive state system that undercut Arab unity and produced militarist, undemocratic, and client regimes thereafter. In the popular Arab narrative, this was an imperial plot to divide and rule, which the Americans stand accused of perpetuating subsequently.

Phase II: imperial retreat and Cold War rivalries

Nationalist backlash

From their inception, in the Arab states the rallying cry became Arab nationalism and independence. Post-independence governments espoused anti-imperialist credentials to bolster their legitimacy. In Algeria, for example, the *Front de Libération Nationale* (FLN) based decades of political dominance on its leadership of the liberation from France. The republicans who murdered the Iraqi king in 1958 overthrew not only the monarchy, but also related British influence.

The British retreated from mandate Palestine in 1948 in the face of two nationalist movements, the aspirations of which they had failed to reconcile. They had repressed Arab opposition to Jewish immigration, but also fell foul of the Zionist movement by attempting to limit the inflow of Jewish migrants. The rise of Nazism and thence the Holocaust in Europe meant that British attempts to block the entry to Palestine of Jews fleeing systematic extermination was indefensible and widely criticized, not least in Washington. Various formulae were mooted for partitioning Palestine between Jews and Arabs, culminating in the United Nations partition plan of 1947 (UN General Assembly Resolution 181). This was accepted by the Jewish leadership, but rejected by the Arabs.

Lacking the will or the wherewithal, in the aftermath of the Second World War, to implement the UN plan by force, the British simply packed up and left. As they did so, the first Arab–Israeli war, resulting in the establishment of the State of Israel in 1948, decided the issue. For the Palestinians, the majority of whom became refugees, the legacy of the British mandate was a catastrophe. For the Israelis, there was no love for the British and a fierce sense that their very survival depended on self-reliance.

The ultimate humiliation for the British and French came in 1956, when they secretly colluded with the Israelis to seize control of the Suez Canal, nationalized by Egyptian President and hero of Arab nationalism, Gamal Abd al-Nasser, and to overthrow his government. Furious at their deception, the US administration ordered their immediate withdrawal. To press home the point, the US triggered a run on the pound sterling that was so serious that it forced the British to comply, leaving the French and Israelis with no choice but to follow suit.

France saw Nasser as the inspiration behind resistance to French rule in Algeria. The British encountered opposition to their colony in Aden from rebels assisted by Nasser. In both cases, the imperialists were ultimately driven out. In Britain's case, the subsequent departure from the Arab sheikhdoms of the lower Gulf was achieved relatively peacefully, by negotiation, in 1971. That finally was the last step in Europe's imperial retreat from the Middle East.

Oil wealth and commercial competition

The year 1971 was also the moment at which the oil-producing states of the region nationalized their oil industries, ending half a century of predominance of the Western oil companies in the energy sector and their control over price levels. The ensuing rise in oil prices, coupled with the Arab embargo on oil sales to Western countries supporting Israel in the 1973 Arab–Israeli War, delivered a profound shock to the developed economies. Meanwhile, the oil booms of the mid-1970s and early 1980s fuelled a spending spree in the oil-producing states, from which European contractors and suppliers of consumer goods and arms competed to benefit. The international banking system absorbed surplus Arab capital.

Cold War rivalry between the US and the Soviet Union encompassed both the Persian Gulf and the Arab–Israeli confrontation zone (Reich 1987). Even though the US came to Nasser's rescue during the Suez War, its reluctance to finance the Aswan High Dam project or to supply arms led Egypt to turn to the Soviet bloc. Thus began a period of superpower rivalry in the Arab–Israeli conflict, which saw the US take over from France as the principal arms supplier to Israel, and the Soviet Union siding with the Arab republics of Egypt, Syria, and Iraq.

The Shah of Iran, who owed his throne to British and US connivance in the coup of 1953 that ended both the republican government of Mohammad Mussadiq and nationalization of Iranian oil production, became the principal US ally and proxy policeman in the Gulf. After the British withdrew their forces from the Persian Gulf in 1971, Washington built up the Shah's Iran as a bulwark against Soviet expansion and sold him whatever arms he asked for. Saudi Arabia was the other pillar in US Gulf policy.

In the shadow of the US

Since the Israelis were effective in lobbying against the US sale of some high-tech weaponry sought by the Saudis, Britain had Washington's blessing to make up the difference. This arrangement was behind the British Al Yamamah defence sales contract with Saudi Arabia, which kept production lines of the British Tornado aircraft running pending the development of the Eurofighter. The British–Saudi deal was worth billions of pounds over several years and formed the bedrock of bilateral relations into the twenty-first century, when a follow-up deal for (Eurofighter) Typhoons was forged.

In fierce competition with the Americans and British, French arms manufacturers ranked third as suppliers to the Arab Gulf states, and alongside the Soviets they were the principal suppliers to Iraq in the 1980s. By this stage, Iraq was at war with Iran. The Iranian revolution that toppled the Shah in 1979 had brought to an end Iran's special relationship with the US and also presaged an upset in relations with Europe, especially with the British. Even though Iraq was the instigator of the Iran–Iraq War (1980–88) and a number of states instituted a ban on arms sales to both countries, the Iraqis continued to receive supplies, including covert help from both the Americans and the British.

Following the fall of the Shah and the Soviet invasion of Afghanistan in 1979, Washington moved away from a policy of securing its interests in the Gulf, including protection of the free flow of oil, by relying on proxies, and became directly involved in patrolling Gulf waters. Washington also gave its backing to the mujahedin and Arab volunteers fighting the Soviets in Afghanistan—the precursors of Al-Qaeda.

Meanwhile, in the Arab–Israeli sector, Washington became the principal architect of moves towards peace. The treaty between Egypt and Israel of 1979, presaged by the Camp David accords of 1978, was bankrolled and sustained by US aid to both parties. Relegated to the sidelines, the Europeans used the vehicle of the European Community to articulate a common stance on the conflict, deemed by both the US and Israel as unwelcome. Meanwhile, the identity of Europe was itself developing, with plans to move from an Economic Community to a Union of member states by 1992.

Phase III: the European Union and regional security

As the transition from the EC to EU drew nigh, Europe was overtaken by the momentous events surrounding the collapse of the Soviet Union, symbolized by the tearing down of the Berlin Wall. This meant a complete rethink of defence and security issues, as well as a preoccupation with forging new relationships with former Soviet bloc states to the east.

Concerns about 'failed states', refugee flows, gun-running, the drug trade, and all aspects of international crime supplanted the old preoccupations of the Cold War and the strategic nuclear threat. While the US, the sole remaining superpower, could boast the military capacity to police the new world order, the Europeans advocated, of necessity, the utility of 'soft power', international law, and institution-building as the means to contain conflict.

War, sanctions, and trade

The scene was set for a decade in which the US and the EU pursued distinct (and complementary) approaches to relations with the Middle East. When Iraq invaded Kuwait on 2 August 1990, the United Nations, Europe, and the US immediately imposed sanctions on Iraq, but it was the US that took the lead in marshalling a massive military force with European backing, UN endorsement, and significant Arab support. After Kuwait's liberation, the US-led coalition forces dispersed, but a US (and small British and French) military presence was retained in order to contain both Iraq and Iran (Gause 2010: 127–8).

For a time, the Europeans went along with the US-led containment of Iraq, including sanctions and weapons inspections. Britain and France joined the US in imposing 'no-fly zones' over both the Kurdish region of northern Iraq and in the south, ostensibly to protect the Shia population there, but arguably more to defend Kuwait. The French eventually ended their involvement. Only the British stayed the course and assisted the Americans in several bombing operations, purportedly to force Iraqi compliance with weapons inspections, although these were suspended following the Allied Operation Desert Fox in 1998.

With respect to the Arab Gulf states, the Europeans pursued independent and competitive commercial agendas, although the EU instituted a dialogue with the GCC—the alliance that links Saudi Arabia, Kuwait, Bahrain, Qatar, the United Arab Emirates, and Oman. Following the introduction of a GCC customs union, the EU–GCC dialogue was expected to deliver a free trade agreement between the two blocs, but disagreements over how this would apply to petroleum products stymied progress.

During the 1990s, the adoption of a common EU strategy toward Iran proved more productive. The European approach, which favoured dialogue over isolation, was initially dubbed 'critical dialogue' and, after the election of reformist President Mohammad Khatami in 1997, progressed to 'comprehensive engagement'. Having negotiated the restoration of full diplomatic relations with Tehran, Britain was a full participant in the coordinated EU approach. Khatami made official visits to a number of European capitals, although not London, cementing diplomatic, trade, and cultural links. At the end of 2002, negotiations began for an EU–Iran trade and cooperation agreement, and a dialogue on human rights was initiated. By this time, however, Washington was gearing up for the invasion of Iraq and subsequently, as discussed in the section entitled '**Phase IV: Europe, the Arab uprisings, and the refugee crisis**', EU relations with Iran became preoccupied with the issue of Iran's nuclear programme.

9/11 and the 'war on terror'

When terrorists attacked in New York and Washington on 11 September 2001 ('9/11'), the Europeans were in the forefront of pledges of support for the Americans. The US went on to a war footing and declared a 'war on terror', to which allies around the world committed support—at least in terms of security and intelligence cooperation.

Members of the North Atlantic Treaty Organization (NATO) offered to assist the anticipated US reprisals against Al-Qaeda in Afghanistan, although the Americans initially preferred to go it alone, with some British assistance. British Prime Minister Tony Blair capitalized on Britain's improved access in Iran to help to secure Tehran's cooperation in Afghanistan. Germany hosted an international gathering in Bonn, intended to lay the ground for a new democratic polity in Kabul following the fall of the Taliban.

In due course, most NATO members committed forces and aid to the reconstruction of Afghanistan, and eventually took overall command of military operations there while US forces concentrated on pursuing Al-Qaeda fighters, including Osama bin Laden, along the border with Pakistan. The US and the Europeans underestimated the challenges of reconfiguring the politics of Afghanistan in the name of democracy. Meanwhile, Washington switched its focus to Iraq; in January 2002, President Bush named Iran, Iraq, and North Korea as the 'axis of evil'.

As the possibility of a US invasion of Iraq gathered momentum, the Europeans split ranks. The British, along with the US State Department, did convince Bush to take his case to the United Nations in September 2002, and the Security Council agreed Resolution 1441, requiring Iraq to submit to new weapons inspections. However, these proved inconclusive, and France and Germany refused to support military action in the absence of UN authorization.

Britain sought UN cover for the intervention that Washington had prepared, but eventually opted to join US forces in the invasion of March 2003 without UN endorsement. European public opinion was largely opposed to the war, although Prime Ministers Berlusconi of Italy and Aznar of Spain sided with Bush and sent troops to Iraq following the invasion. The governments of the East European states—lined up to become new EU members, yet equally keen to support the US—also committed forces to the stabilization effort, but except for the Polish forces, their numbers were comparatively small.

Ultimately, the fallout for European unity and EU expansion was damaging, but not fatal. It did, however, contribute to subsequent timidity in Europe about criticizing Washington's policies in other parts of the Middle East.

Arab governments were generally fearful that a US success in Iraq could portend a more ambitious US agenda for regime change in the region, but when the occupation met increasing Iraqi opposition in early 2004, fears of a spill-over effect in the region loomed larger. Token European support for the rebuilding effort in Iraq also began to peel away as all foreign nationals there began to fear kidnap, and some were executed by the newly emergent Al-Qaeda in Iraq and other extremists. After mass attacks on Iraqi civilians triggered sectarian warfare in 2006, the US military was left virtually alone to try to restore security.

In the meantime, a terrorist bombing in Madrid in early 2004, apparently inspired by Al-Qaeda, turned public opinion there decisively against involvement in Iraq. Yet even though intelligence assessments indicated US policy in Iraq and support for Israel were contributing to the radicalization of Muslim opinion everywhere, the sense dawned in Europe that the problem was more deep-rooted and at least partly domestic.

In Britain, suicide bombings on the London transport system, in July 2005, and other incidents perpetrated by British nationals prompted the government to pass new counter-terrorism legislation and to re-examine its assumptions about 'British multiculturalism'. Social tensions in other parts of Europe erupted around areas of urban deprivation and across religious divides. The place of Muslims in Europe became the subject of heated debate and prejudice, with almost all governments introducing new measures to manage immigration, as well as to combat the possibility of terrorism within the EU.

The Mediterranean neighbourhood

The EU is the most important destination for exports from the MENA region, and the overall trade balance has long been in Europe's favour, although Europe as a whole is heavily dependent on energy supplies from North Africa and the Gulf, and more so than the US. Israel's primary market is Europe.

These economic ties, together with geographic proximity and inward migration from the Arab countries, Turkey and Iran, to Europe make for a relationship between the two regions that contrasts with relations between the Middle East and the more distant US. Reflecting these differences, European policies in the Middle East concentrated on socio-economic strategies toward their neighbours (Behrendt and Hanelt 2000).

Thus, in their dealings with each other, the Europeans and the Arabs manoeuvred around the imperatives of economic interdependence and attendant security issues in a way that suggests that both were as influenced by political considerations as by economic imperatives.

In the mid-1990s, the EU embarked on a new initiative for relations with its southern neighbours, which was conceived in parallel with its more ambitious arrangements for incorporating former Soviet satellite states into the EU. The central objective was the creation of a Euro-Mediterranean economic area, to come into effect by 2010. The intention was to dismantle tariff and non-tariff barriers to trade in manufactured products between the EU and neighbouring states on the southern and eastern shores of the Mediterranean. Taking into account traditional trade flows and existing agricultural policies, trade in agricultural produce was also to be progressively liberalized, as was provision of cross-border services and capital movements. (A list of successive EU initiatives for the Mediterranean, starting in the 1990s, is provided in **Box 17.2**.)

In the Barcelona Declaration of 1995,[2] the fifteen member states of the EU and Algeria, Cyprus, Egypt, Israel, Jordan, Lebanon, Malta, Morocco, the Palestinian Authority, Syria, Tunisia, and Turkey embraced a three-tier agenda for economic, political and cultural, and security cooperation in the Mediterranean. The EU allocated funds to promote new communication and trade links between the Maghreb and the Levant and by 2004 was spending about €1 billion a year on the programme.

It was counted a notable achievement of this Euro-Mediterranean Partnership (EMP) that Syria and Lebanon were involved as well as Israel, notwithstanding the unresolved conflict

---

Box 17.2 Europe and the Middle East since the Cold War

1991	Wide European support for sanctions and use of force against Iraq in the Gulf War
1995	The Barcelona Declaration
	EU member states, plus Algeria, Cyprus, Egypt, Israel, Jordan, Lebanon, Malta, Morocco, the Palestinian Authority, Syria, Tunisia, and Turkey, embrace a three-tier agenda for economic, political and cultural, and security cooperation intended to turn the Mediterranean into a more integrated region
	The arrangement becomes known as the Euro-Mediterranean Partnership (EMP)
1990s	Initiation of EU–GCC dialogue encompassing EU members and the Gulf states of Bahrain, Kuwait, Oman, Qatar, Saudi Arabia, and the United Arab Emirates envisages the creation of an EU–GCC free trade area
1990s	Development of an EU common strategy towards Iran known as 'critical dialogue', aims to promote political, economic, and cultural links
2001	Wide European support for the US following 9/11, including NATO support of action in Afghanistan
2002–03	EU participation in 'the Quartet' (the EU, US, UN, and Russia) to produce the 'Road Map' to promote a two-state solution to the Palestine–Israel conflict
2003	Limited European support for the Iraq invasion (initially supported by Britain, Italy, Spain, and East European states)
2004	Launch of the European Neighbourhood Policy (ENP) following EU enlargement from fifteen to twenty-five members, to complement EMP; ENP applies to the EU's immediate neighbours by land or sea, with bilaterally agreed action plans for partner states
	EU3: a diplomatic initiative involving Britain, France, and Germany to encourage Iran to curb its nuclear enrichment programme
2008	Mediterranean Union: a proposal by French President Sarkozy, builds on the EMP to create a new Union for the Mediterranean (UfM), including EU, North African, Balkan and Arab states, and Israel
2011	Limited EU support for NATO intervention in Libya

between them. In the mid-1990s, progress in Middle Eastern peace-making through the Oslo process had been expected to deliver an end to the conflict, and the Barcelona initiative was intended both to complement and capitalize on that process, but not directly interact with it. As it transpired, the EMP survived the demise of the Oslo process, but not without some stormy encounters at ministerial meetings of the participants and the collapse of early efforts at security cooperation across the Arab–Israeli divide.

By 2003, the broad parameters and shortcomings of the EMP were apparent. Instead of an integrated region around the Mediterranean, what had emerged was a hub-and-spokes arrangement, with the EU as the hub connected to each partner state by bilateral trade links, or spokes (Xenakis and Chryssochoou 2001). A series of bilateral association agreements were concluded between the EU and Algeria, Egypt, Israel, Jordan, Lebanon, Morocco, the Palestinian Authority, and Tunisia. Negotiations with Syria failed to produce a similar agreement, complicated in part by a new requirement for partner states to renounce weapons of mass destruction. Libya remained under sanctions until Gaddafi's decision to renounce weapons of mass destruction in 2003, and then only accepted observer status in the EMP.

The failure of the EMP to transform the Mediterranean into a cohesive new economic area of shared prosperity and security cooperation stemmed from the continuation of disputes between the partner states (not least the Arab–Israeli conflict), the reluctance of the Arab regimes to adopt the political reforms advocated by Europe, and the persistence of barriers to the free movement of labour around the region, kept in place by EU measures to control immigration. In addition, none of the Arab partner states had the capacity to match the European Commission in managing the bureaucratic complexities of the relationship. This enabled the EU to set the pace, at least in terms of trade relations, while the partner states feared exposure of their fragile domestic industries to European competition.

Realization of the limited achievements of the EMP led to a rethink and the launch of a new European Neighbourhood Policy (ENP) in 2004. This reflected a decision, in the wake of EU enlargement, to develop a comprehensive formula to embrace non-candidate countries around the periphery, the better to enhance their stability and prosperity, to mutual benefit. The new policy was also a response to a US initiative to promote economic and political reform in what Washington called 'the Wider Middle East' (including Pakistan and Afghanistan).

The core concept of the ENP was to complement the EMP with a differentiated approach to bilateral relations with each of Europe's neighbours, taking account of the size and relative level of development of partner economies.[3] The EU undertook to assist with indigenously generated reform programmes, and 'Action Plans' were agreed accordingly with Egypt, Israel, Jordan, Lebanon, Morocco, and Tunisia, as well as East European neighbours outside the EU.

By the end of 2007, however, the Europeans were professing disappointment that their efforts to help to combat corruption, to promote accountability and transparency, and to export European norms for human rights protection were still failing to meet their aspirations. For the Arab states, the ENP was even less attractive than the EMP, since it offered them only the distant promise of economic benefits as and when they achieved greater harmonization with internal EU standards. Disparities in wealth within the Arab states, as well as between the Arab economies and Europe, intensified.

Running for the French presidency in 2007, Nicolas Sarkozy floated a new initiative to complement the EMP that led to the launch of the Union for the Mediterranean (UfM) in Paris in 2008 (Bicci and Gillespie 2011). This proved little more than a repackaging of the concept of partnership, elevated to the intergovernmental level, with a joint presidency (initially France and Egypt) and a dedicated secretariat (in Barcelona). In substance, it prioritized various joint projects, most already mooted under the EMP, and looked to the private sector to deliver funding. In essence, the UfM represented a retreat from the aspirations for the creation of a new Mediterranean area of economic cooperation and development espoused in the 1990s.

Europe and the Middle East peace process

Individually and collectively, the Europeans have traditionally championed the view that the 'land for peace' formula that underpinned the Egypt–Israel peace treaty of 1979 offers the best formula for a comprehensive peace deal. The concept was adopted by the UN Security Council in the aftermath of the 1967 war in Resolution 242, and repeated in Resolution 338 after the 1973 war. All EC and EU statements on the Arab–Israeli conflict thereafter have sought implementation of all relevant UN resolutions, adherence to international law, and the exchange of land for peace.

As of 2002, the EU has formally embraced the goal of a 'two-state solution' to the Israeli–Palestinian conflict, but always with the caveat that this must be achieved by negotiation between the protagonists. In practice, also, the Europeans have generally proceeded on the assumption that only the US has the leverage necessary to bring the contending parties to agreement.

In 1980, the European Community demonstrated both unity and prescience when it issued the Venice Declaration,[4] calling for the Palestinian people to be able 'to exercise fully their right to self-determination' and stating that the Palestine Liberation Organization (PLO) would have to be involved in peace negotiations.

For several years, the Venice Declaration formed the basis of the European stance on the conflict, but the US was the peace broker. Following the Israeli invasion of Lebanon in 1982, the US adopted the lead in mediation efforts, including the evacuation of the PLO leadership from Beirut to Tunis. Europe called for Israel's unconditional withdrawal in accordance with UN Resolution 425 (of 1978). Israel did pull back its forces to southern Lebanon, but then remained there until 2000.

Meanwhile, when the Palestinian uprising, or intifada, erupted in Gaza and the West Bank in December 1987, European opinion was shocked by television coverage of Israel's military response to stone-throwing Palestinians. The European Parliament voted to deny finalization of three protocols on Israel's trade and financial relations with the EC. The Parliament also criticized conditions set by Israel for implementation of an EC provision for direct trade between Palestinians and Europe. The move achieved an alleviation of those conditions prior to passage of the protocols later in the year.[5]

The tactic of delaying approval of bureaucratic instruments affecting trade with Israel was to be used on subsequent occasions, as a way in which to convey European disapproval of Israeli policies in relation to the Palestinians. For example, ratification of Israel's partnership agreement with the EU, reached in 1995 under the EMP, was held up the following year to signal dissatisfaction with the policy of the Netanyahu government (which took office in 1996) with respect to the peace process. However, over the years such moves have not affected the trajectory of Israel's settlement expansion in the occupied West Bank and East Jerusalem and under the ENP Israel has attained ever closer economic relations with the EU. In effect, the EU has pursued a twin track approach of improving ties to Israel while also criticizing its policies on the Palestinians.

The Europeans were given only observer status at the November 1991 Madrid Conference that launched the peace process following the Gulf War. However, the conference gave birth to both bilateral and multilateral tracks, and the EC was made convener of the working group dealing with regional economic development. For the duration of the multilateral process—which eventually ceased because of problems on the bilateral tracks—the EU used this platform to take a number of initiatives, including commissioning a World Bank report that laid the basis for an economic aid and development plan for the West Bank and Gaza (World Bank 1993).

Under the Oslo process, initiated in 1993, the EU became the largest single donor to the Palestinian Authority. The US administration kept to itself management of actual peace negotiations, but acknowledged that the whole process was facilitated by the EU role. Nonetheless, neither the Americans nor the Europeans were able to save the peace process when the make-or-break summit at Camp David in July 2000 collapsed without agreement and the second intifada ensued. Under the premiership of Ariel Sharon, from February 2001, the conflict raged anew, with Palestinian suicide attacks in Israel reaching unprecedented levels and the Israelis reoccupying Palestinian autonomous areas in spring 2002.

The EU did not support the decision of the Bush administration to boycott and sideline PLO Chairman Yasser Arafat, and emergency aid from the EU kept the Palestinian Authority afloat when US assistance was suspended. Responding pragmatically to US President Bush's endorsement of a two-state solution to the conflict, in spring 2002, the EU worked through the mechanism of 'the Quartet' (the EU, the US, the UN, and Russia) to produce the 'Road Map', formally launched in 2003, spelling out steps to reach that goal.

Responding to Hamas

While the EU, along with other members of the Quartet, continued to cite the Road Map as the recipe for peace, Sharon preferred a unilateralist strategy, and evacuated Israeli settlements and troops from Gaza in 2005. The EU then took the initiative of organizing new Palestinian legislative elections, held in January 2006.

Contrary to expectations in Europe and Washington, the Palestinian Islamist movement Hamas won a clear victory. This presented a problem for the EU, since it had included Hamas in a list of terrorist organizations and EU law prevented Brussels from funding such groups. The Quartet called on Hamas to renounce violence, to accept agreements previously reached by the Palestinian leadership, and to recognize Israel. In the meantime, Brussels introduced a temporary mechanism to funnel aid to vital service personnel in the West Bank and Gaza.

In summer 2006, Israel launched an offensive on the Gaza Strip to counter Palestinian attacks into Israel, but the ensuing battle was soon overtaken by war on the Israeli–Lebanese front triggered by a raid across the Israeli border by Hezbollah. Most European governments pressed for an early ceasefire, while the US and Britain initially held out for the defeat of Hezbollah, which the Israeli armed forces proved unable to deliver.

Hezbollah won plaudits from around the Arab world for its readiness to take on the Israelis and survive. The links between Hezbollah, its patrons Syria and Iran, and Hamas were enhanced, and after Hamas won sole control of the Gaza Strip following a showdown with the rival Fatah organization in 2007, Hamas was able to survive the blockade imposed by Israel by means of aid from Iran, among others. The EU denounced the Israeli blockade on Gaza as 'collective punishment', but proved powerless to lift or circumvent it. At the end of 2008, Israel launched another offensive to curtail Hamas rocket attacks from Gaza, in which more than 1,300 Palestinians and thirteen Israelis died. This time, the Europeans were united in criticizing the Israeli use of force as 'disproportionate'.

In the meantime, the EU focused on helping a reconstituted Palestinian Authority in the West Bank to develop the infrastructure of a state, including new police and security forces. Washington took the lead on renewed peace negotiations, excluding Hamas. However, even when President Barack Obama took office in 2009 and reinvigorated US efforts to achieve a 'two-state' agreement, his strategy foundered over the issue of settlement expansion in the occupied territories.

In a statement issued by the EU Council of Ministers at the end of 2009, just before the European External Action Service (EEAS) came into being and Catherine Ashton was appointed the new EU foreign policy chief, the Europeans spelled out their position on the Israeli–Palestinian conflict in detail (Council of the European Union 2009). The statement was explicit on the illegality of the Israeli occupation and the need for it to end. Yet little was said thereafter by the EU to articulate ways in which Europe might hold Israel, or the Palestinians, to account for their actions and transgressions. Another round of war on the Israeli-Gaza front in November 2012 left 167 Palestinians and six Israelis dead.

A new attempt by the US to rejuvenate negotiations during Obama's second term, led by Secretary of State John Kerry, collapsed in April 2014. This time, the US was more inclined than ever before to hold Israel primarily responsible. The following summer the Israelis engaged Hamas in a more prolonged and devastating war in which over 2,000 Gazan Palestinians, sixty-six Israeli soldiers, and seven Israeli civilians were killed. Various donors, including the EU and Arab states, pledged support for the rebuilding of Gaza, but by early 2015 only a fraction of what was pledged had been spent. Meanwhile, the Palestinians took their cause to the UN but, having won recognition as a 'non-member observer state' in November 2012, their bid for recognition as an independent state was defeated by the UN Security Council in December 2014. The EU Parliament, as too the parliaments of several EU member states, did vote for such recognition of Palestinian statehood, but still held to the position that this should come about as the result of agreement with the Israelis.

Phase IV: Europe, the Arab uprisings, and the refugee crisis

EU relations with the Middle East entered a new phase in 2010, as a result of several factors. By then, Europe was in the grips of the financial crisis that has dominated the agenda of the EU and its member states ever since, relegating other issues, including relations with the Middle East, to the periphery. Deferring to Washington to lead on resolving the

Israeli–Palestinian conflict, the EU had no alternatives to offer when US efforts faltered. EU initiatives for the Mediterranean, from the EMP to the ENP and then the UfM did not deliver the reforms in the Arab states that they were intended to encourage. Part of the problem was that the Europeans had used the ENP action plans to oblige Arab governments to control migration in Europe's interests to the detriment of human rights (Basaran 2008).

Meanwhile, the Islamic Republic of Iran, under an increasingly hardline leadership, aligned with Syria, Hezbollah, and Hamas, and on friendly terms with a Shia-dominated government in Iraq, looked poised to become the new regional hegemon, in defiance of the US and its regional allies. Simultaneously, the Europeans had come round to the US position on the Iranian nuclear issue, fearing that Tehran was developing the capability to turn its civil nuclear programme into a military one. When the various incentives offered to Iran by Britain, Germany, and France—the so-called 'EU3'—failed to persuade Iran to suspend its nuclear enrichment programme, the US became more directly involved and the issue was taken to the UN Security Council.

UN-imposed sanctions on Iran were followed up with additional sanctions by both the US and the EU. Only when an embargo on Iranian oil exports was threatened in 2011 did the Iranians agree to new talks, but the possibility of war loomed, if diplomacy and pressure failed, fuelled by Israeli warnings that it might take unilateral action. However, the Obama administration was more inclined to pursue negotiations with Iran than the previous Bush administration, and when Hassan Rohani was elected President of Iran in 2013, the stage was set for more serious negotiations in which the US acted in concert with the EU (represented by Ashton), plus Russia and China.

In the meantime, the Arab world was overtaken by a series of popular uprisings that began in Tunisia in December 2010.

The Arab Spring

The Europeans were caught off guard by the Tunisian revolt not least because they thought the secular Western-aligned government of Ben Ali was the exemplar of economic and gradual political reform advocated by the EU. France initially contemplated bolstering Ben Ali, but when the Tunisian army refused to suppress mass demonstrations that combined all elements of the population, secular and Islamist, middle class and working class, France joined other Europeans in supporting the protesters. Within days of Ben Ali's flight into exile in Saudi Arabia, on 25 January 2011, a revolution erupted in Egypt.

Faced with the dilemma of whether to stand by Mubarak, its long-time ally, Washington wavered and the Europeans demurred, but when regime security forces turned violently on the demonstrators in Cairo's Tahrir Square, broadcast live around the world, the Americans and the Europeans abandoned Mubarak. In any case, Mubarak's fate was not in their hands. This was an Egyptian revolution and the army initially went along with the protesters, sacrificed Mubarak, and set up an interim administration pending new elections that delivered a victory for the Muslim Brotherhood's Mohammed Mursi. His administration antagonized many Egyptians, but crucially the army, and Mursi was ousted in 2013 amid a more brutal crackdown on the Brotherhood than even Mubarak had countenanced. EU initiatives to give Mursi cautious support in the name of democracy were rendered irrelevant.[6]

When the revolution spread to Libya in 2011, Gaddafi mobilized the armed forces to crush the rebels and both the UN and the LAS called for action. British Prime Minister David Cameron and French President Sarkozy grasped the moment to champion intervention. Germany initially opposed proposals for NATO to mount an air and naval operation, and only some NATO members participated in the campaign that led to the fall of Gaddafi. Washington chose to 'lead from behind'. Yet toppling the regime proved easier than building a new one, and by 2015 internal conflict had rendered Libya a no-go area for EU and US nationals.

The intervention in Libya did not set a precedent for action elsewhere in the region. The Europeans and Americans deferred to GCC mediation in Yemen (which represented only a temporary fix before the Saudis launched military action against Houthi forces in 2014), and, in the case of Bahrain, while criticizing the methods used by the rulers to suppress demonstrations, the Europeans stood aside. When opponents of the Asad regime in Syria faced increasingly harsh repression by government forces, the Europeans and Americans sought UN Security Council condemnation, but were thwarted by Russia and China. An LAS- and UN-initiated mediation effort subsequently foundered and civil war raged.

European and US efforts to galvanize the Syrian opposition into a coherent fighting force foundered and anti-Asad Islamist militia gained in strength. By 2014 a new configuration of such forces, the self-styled Islamic State in Syria and the Levant (IS) had captured vast swathes of eastern Syria and western Iraq. The US-trained and equipped Iraqi army crumbled, leaving only Kurdish and Iranian-backed Shia militia to push back. Appalled by the beheadings of kidnapped Westerners, broadcast by IS over the Internet, and IS recruitment of hundreds of Muslim volunteers from Europe, by 2015 several European states had sent forces to join in US-led bombing raids on IS. France's activities against IS were stepped up significantly following the Paris attacks of November 2015. By then, however, the US-backed Syrian opposition forces had begun to lose ground to the Asad regime backed by Russia, which entered the fray in September 2015.

Describing itself as a new caliphate, IS declared its intention to unravel the legacy of the British–French 'Sykes–Picot' agreement that presaged the shape of the Arab state system in the Middle East for a century. To counter IS and its ambitions, the Europeans have made common cause with a collection of Arab governments and Iran, none of which seek to uphold the values of human rights and democracy espoused by the Europeans since the demise of European imperialism. Meanwhile, as a direct consequence of war in Syria, large numbers of refugees have sought entry to the EU, creating a migrant crisis that has severely tested the limits of European cooperation.

Conclusion

Half a century on from the retreat of the European imperial powers from MENA, a brief interlude of US hegemony had also peaked and Europeans could only look on in consternation as the regional state system that they had devised in the 1920s looked set to unravel. The confidence with which the EU had sought to export its values and neoliberal economic model in the 1990s had given way to anxiety in the face of Islamist-inspired terrorism at the turn of the century, and greater preoccupation with controlling immigration and countering 'radicalization' within Europe.

Over the same period, the EU had become increasingly integrated into the economic fabric of the Middle East, both as aid donor and supplier of arms, infrastructure projects, and consumer goods. Europe remains the principal market for exports from the Middle East, and is dependent on energy supplies from North Africa and the Persian Gulf. Migration flows—of Jews from Europe into Israel, and of Arabs, Iranians, and Turks into Europe—bind the populations and politics of these two contiguous geographic regions. Yet this is not just a simple tale of harmonious interchange; there is ambivalence and friction with clear historical roots.

European efforts to promote Arab–Israeli peace are an expression of Europe's own security interests and ties on both sides of the divide, but there is little to show for EU engagement in the Israeli–Palestinian peace process, except the dependence of the Palestinian Authority on EU financial support. The EMP has been supplanted by the UfM and that has achieved little. The ENP and its action plans for Arab reform, intertwined with the deals done by the Europeans with Arab dictators to protect European security, did not address the problems that led to the Arab uprisings, while the forces of political Islam, which the Europeans had hoped to contain, are resurgent.

During the course of 2015 over 1 million refugees arrived in the EU, including Afghans, Iraqis, and Eritreans, as well as Syrians. Some came overland from Turkey; most (over 800,000) risked their lives trying to reach the shores of Greece in overcrowded boats organized by people-traffickers. When European coastguards and/or volunteers were not on hand to rescue them, they drowned. The Greek authorities, already struggling to cope with the impact of the debt crisis, were overwhelmed by the influx. When Chancellor Angela Merkel announced that Germany would take the lead in accepting migrants and proposed a quota system to spread the load, some other EU members refused to cooperate. Poland declared it impossible to implement the quotas for fear of the security risk. France, then Denmark, reintroduced border checks, signalling at least a temporary end to the Schengen system. Sweden accepted more refugees per capita than any other EU state but then closed its border; Hungary processed the most asylum applications per head of population before closing its border to new arrivals.

The twin crises of an increased terror threat posed by IS and its sympathizers inside Europe and the relentless flow of migrants toward Europe represented a challenge of unprecedented proportions to the cohesion of the EU and the values it espouses. The member states agreed that a resolution to the war in Syria and the defeat of IS were essential. Yet to achieve this would necessitate a level of cooperation between the MENA states, the US, and Russia hitherto absent.

Further reading

Al-Fattal, R. (2010) *European Union Foreign Policy in the Occupied Palestinian Territory* (Jerusalem: PASSIA)
An explication of how EU dealings with the Palestinians were framed by EU instruments for relations across the Mediterranean.

Basaran, T. (2008) 'Security, Law, Borders: Spaces of Exclusion', *International Security Review*, 2: 339–54
An examination of how laws passed in the EU and agreements forged with Arab governments were used to control migration and asylum seekers.

Bicci, F. and Gillespie, R. (eds) (2011) 'Special Issue: The Union for the Mediterranean—Continuity or Change in Euro-Mediterranean Relations?', *Mediterranean Politics*, 16(1)
A thorough examination of the genesis, parameters, and implications of EU initiatives for the Mediterranean.

Croft, S. (2012) *Securitizing Islam: Identity and the Search for Security* (Cambridge: Cambridge University Press)
An examination of British constructions of 'Britishness', security, and insecurity.

Doty, R. (1996) *Imperial Encounters* (Minneapolis: University of Minnesota Press)
A very readable introduction to the politics of representation in North-South discourse.

Fawcett, L. and Hurrell, A. (1995) *Regionalism and World Politics: Regional Organisation and International Order* (Oxford: Oxford University Press)
A discussion of regionalism in theoretical and historical perspective, and its application in different contexts, including Europe and the Middle East, thereby providing a context within which to understand relations between the two.

Fierke, K. M. (2007) *Critical Approaches to International Security* (Cambridge: Polity Press)
A very useful detailed overview of critical theory approaches to specific issues in international relations.

Gause, G. (2010) *The International Relations of the Persian Gulf* (Cambridge: Cambridge University Press)
In this work, Gause—a specialist on the politics of the Arab Gulf states—explores the idea of the Gulf as a 'regional system'.

Owen, R. (2004) *State, Power and Politics in the Making of the Modern Middle East*, revd edn (London: Routledge)
Points to how the European colonial legacy in the Middle East affected state-building and politics in the region.

Radwan, S. and Reiffers, J.-L. (2005) *The Euro-Mediterranean Partnership, 10 Years after Barcelona: Achievements and Perspectives* (Paris: Institut de la Méditerranée)
A report focusing on the economic aspects of the partnership, with input from Arab and European experts.

Roy, O. (2004) *Globalised Islam: The Search for a New Ummah* (London: Hurst)
A revealing analysis of the causes and implications of radicalization among young European Muslims, and relations between the West and the Muslim world.

Teti, A. (2012) 'The EU's First Response to the "Arab Spring": a Critical Discourse Analysis of the Partnership for Democracy and Shared Prosperity', *Mediterranean Politics*, 17(3): 266–84.
This article provides a critical analysis of the initiative taken by the EU to re-work the ENP to support democratization in the wake of the Arab uprisings.

Wendt, A. (1999) *Social Theory of International Politics* (Cambridge: Cambridge University Press)
An exposition of social theory from which to derive applications to the Middle East; useful specifically for understanding competing narratives about identity, states, regions, and society in this context.

Youngs, R. (ed.) (2006) *Survey of European Democracy Promotion Policies 2000–2006* (Madrid: FRIDE)
A useful survey of individual and collective EU approaches to political (and economic) reform in the Middle East and other parts of the world.

Questions

1. Describe and analyse the legacy of European imperialism in the Middle East after 1971.

2. In what ways did the EU model the use of 'soft power' in its dealings with the Middle East after 1992?

3. Analyse the role of the EU in the 'Middle East Peace Process'.

4. Compare and contrast the usefulness of the EMP and the ENP in pursuing EU goals for the Mediterranean neighbourhood.

5. What do European responses to the Arab uprisings reveal about Europe as a regional actor?

Notes

1. For the texts of these documents, see Laqueur and Rubin (1995).

2. Barcelona Declaration, 28 November 1995, available online at http://ec.europa.eu/research/iscp/pdf/barcelona_declaration.pdf

3. See European Commission (2004).

4. Venice Declaration 1980, *Bulletin of the EC*, 6–1980: 10–11, point 1.1.6.

5. For sources, see Hollis (1997).

6. See Teti (2012).

Bibliography

Aarts, P. (1999) 'The Middle East: A Region without Regionalism or the End of Exceptionalism?', *Third World Quarterly*, 20 (5): 911–25.

Aarts, P. and Nonnemann, G. (eds) (2005) *Saudi Arabia in the Balance: Politics, Economics and International Relations between 9/11, the Iraq Crisis and the Future* (London: Hurst).

Abd al-Raziq, A. (1925) *Al-islam wa usul al-hukm* (Cairo: Misr Press).

Abdulla, A. K. (1999) 'The Gulf Cooperation Council: Nature, Origin and Process', in M. Hudson (ed.) *Middle East Dilemma: The Politics and Economics of Arab Integration* (London: I. B. Tauris) pp. 150–70.

Abrahamian, E. (1982) *Iran between Two Revolutions* (Princeton, NJ: Princeton University Press).

Abu Khalil, A. (1992) 'A New Arab Ideology? The Rejuvenation of Arab Nationalism', *Middle East Journal*, 46 (1): 22–36.

Abu Khalil A. (2012) 'Opposition to the Syrian Opposition: Against the Syrian National Council', Jadaliyya, 8 March, available online at http://www.jadaliyya.com/pages/index/4593/opposition-to-the-syrian-opposition_against-the-s

Abu Sulayman, A. (1993) *Towards an Islamic Theory of International Relations: New Directions for Methodology and Thought* (Herndon, VA: International Institute of Islamic Thought).

Abu-Lughod, J. (1989) *Before European Hegemony: The World System, AD 1250–1350* (New York: Oxford University Press).

Acharya, A. and Buzan, B. (2010) *Non-Western International Relations Theory* (London: Routledge).

Action Against Iraq. Web. http://www.cctv.com/lm/942/19/14.html

Adib-Moghaddam, A. (2006) *The International Politics of the Persian Gulf: A Cultural Genealogy* (London: Routledge).

Adler, E. (1997) 'Seizing the Middle Ground: Constructivism in World Politics', *European Journal of International Relations*, 3 (3): 319–63.

Aghrout, A. and Sutton, K. (1990) 'Regional Economic Union in the Maghreb', *Journal of Modern African Studies*, 28 (1): 115–39.

Ajami, F. (1977–78) 'Stress in the Arab Triangle', *Foreign Policy*, 29: 90–108.

Ajami, F. (1992) *The Arab Predicament: Arab Political Thought and Practice since 1967* (updated edn, Cambridge: Cambridge University Press).

Ajami, F. (2012) 'Five Myths about the Arab Spring', in the *Washington Post*: http://www.washingtonpost.com/opinions/five-myths-about-the-arab-spring/2011/12/21/gIQA32TVuP_story.html (Retrieved: 18 April 2015).

Akbarzadeh, S. and Connor, K. (2005) 'The Organization of the Islamic Conference: Sharing an Illusion', *Middle East Policy*, 12 (2): 79–92.

Akun, M., Percinoglu, G., and Gundogar, S. S. (2009) *The Perception of Turkey in the Middle East* (Istanbul: Economy and Social Studies Foundation).

Al Tamamy, S. (2015), 'GCC membership expansion: possibilities and Obstacles', Al Jazeera Center for Studies Dossier (15 March).

Al-Ali, Zaid (2014) *The Struggle for Iraq's Future: How Corruption, Incompetence and Sectarianism Have Undermined Democracy* (New Haven: Yale University Press).

al-Bazzaz, S. (1993) *harb tulid'ukhra [One War Gives Birth to Another]* (Amman, Jordan: alàhliyya lil-nashr wa al-tawzi').

al-Bazzaz, S. (1996) *al-janaralat àkhr man ya'lam [The Generals are the Last to Know]* (Amman, Jordan: alàhliyya lil-nashr wa al-tawzi').

Albright, M. K. (2003) 'Bridges, Bombs or Bluster?', *New York Times*, 19 August, available online at http://www.nytimes.com/cfr/international/20030901FAESSAY82501_albright.html?pagewanted=print&position=&_r=0

Al-Fattal, R. (2010) *European Union Foreign Policy in the Occupied Palestinian Territory* (Jerusalem: PASSIA).

al-Ghamdi, A. A. S. (1996) 'The Saudi-Yemeni Boundary: Towards a Peaceful Resolution', Unpublished PhD thesis, Durham University.

al-Hariri, J. U. (2011) 'Israeli Penetration of Central Asian Nations and Repercussions for Relations with the Arab World', *Contemporary Arab Affairs*, 4 (3): 322–40.

Alianak, S. (2007) *Middle Eastern Leaders and Islam: A Precarious Equilibrium* (New York: Peter Lang).

al-Khalil, S. (1989) *The Republic of Fear: The Politics of Modern Iraq* (Berkeley, CA: University of California Press).

Allawi, A. A. (2007) *The Occupation of Iraq* (New Haven, CT: Yale University Press).

Allen, R. and Khalaf, R. (2003) 'Saudis Allow Use of Key Facilities to US', *Financial Times*, 9 March.

Allin, D. H. (2007) 'American Power and Allied Restraint: Lessons of Iraq', *Survival*, 49 (1): 123–40.

Allin, D. H. and Simon, S. (2003) 'The Moral Psychology of US Support for Israel', *Survival*, 45 (3): 123–44.

Al-Marashi, I. and Salama, S. (2008) *Iraq's Armed Forces: An Analytical History* (London: Routledge).

Alnasrawi, A. (1991) *Arab Nationalism, Oil* and the Political Economy of Dependency (New York and London: Greenwood Press).

Al-Rasheed, M. (2002) *A History of Saudi Arabia* (Cambridge: Cambridge University Press).

al-Samara'i, W. (1997) *hatam al-bawaba al-sharqiyya [The Destruction of the Eastern Gate]* (Kuwait: dar al-qabas).

al-Sayyid, M. K. (1991) 'Slow Thaw in the Arab World', *World Policy Journal*, 8 (4): 711–38.

al-Sayyid, M. K. (1999) 'The Rise and Fall of the United Arab Republic', in M. Hudson (ed.) *Middle East Dilemma: The Politics and Economics of Arab Integration* (London: I. B. Tauris) pp. 109–27.

Al-Sumait, F., Lenze, N., and Hudson, M. C. (eds) (2015) *The Arab Uprisings: Catalysts, Dynamics and Trajectories* (Lanham, MD and New York: Rowman and Littlefield)

Alvandi, R. (2014) 'Guest Editor's Introduction: Iran and the Cold War', *Iranian Studies*, 47 (3): 373–8.

Amar, P. and Prashad, V. (2013) *Dispatches from the Arab Spring: Understanding the New Middle East* (London: University of Minnesota Press).

Amin, S. (1974) *Accumulation on a World Scale* (New York: Monthly Review Press).

Amin, S. (1978) *The Arab Nation: Nationalism and Class Struggles* (London: Zed Press).

Amin, K. (2014) 'International Assistance to Egypt after the 2011 and 2013 Uprisings: More Politics and Less Development', *Mediterranean Politics*, 19 (3): 392–412.

Anderson, I. H. (1981) *Aramco, The United States, and Saudi Arabia: A Study in the Dynamics of Foreign Oil Policy, 1933-1950* (Princeton, NJ: Princeton University Press).

Anderson, B. (1991a) *Imagined Communities: Reflections on the Origin and Spread of Nationalism* (revd edn, London: Verso).

Anderson, B. (2006) *Imagined Communities* (London: Verso).

Anderson, L. (1986) *The State and Social Transformation in Tunisia and Libya, 1830-1980* (Princeton, NJ: Princeton University Press).

Anderson L. (1987) 'The State in the Middle East and North Africa', *Comparative Politics*, 20: 1–18.

Anderson, L. (1991b) 'Absolutism and the Resilience of Monarchy in the Middle East', *Political Science Quarterly*, 106 (1): 1–15.

Anderson, L. (1991c) 'Legitimacy, Identity and the Writing of History in Libya', in E. Davis and N.

Gavrielides (eds) *Statecraft in the Middle East* (Miami, FL: PN Florida International University Press).

Anscombe, F. (1997) *The Ottoman Gulf: The Creation of Kuwait, Saudi Arabia and Qatar* (New York: Columbia University Press).

Appadurai, A. (1996) *Modernity at Large: Cultural Dimensions of Globalization* (Minneapolis, MN: University of Minnesota Press).

Arab-American Institute (2012) *Arab Attitudes 2011* (Washington, DC: Arab-American Institute).

Aras, B. and Polat, R. K. (2008), 'From Conflict to Cooperation: The Securitization of Turkey's Relations with Syria and Iran', *Security Dialogue*, 39 (5): 495–515.

Armstrong, J. (1982) *Nations before Nationalism* (Durham, NC: University of North Carolina Press).

Armstrong, K. (1994) *A History of God: The 4000-year Quest of Judaism, Christianity and Islam* (New York: Ballantine Books)

Asad, T. (1993) *Genealogies of Religion: Discipline and Reasons of Power in Christianity and Islam* (Baltimore: Johns Hopkins University Press).

Ashley, R. K. (1988) 'Untying the Sovereign State: A Double Reading of the Anarchy Problematique', *Millennium*, 17: 227–62.

Ashraf, A. (1988) 'Bazaar-Mosque Alliance: The Social Bases of Revolts and Revolutions', *Politics, Culture and Society*, 1 (4): 558–67.

Ashraf, A. (1990) 'Theocracy and Charisma: New Men of Power in Iran', *International Journal of Politics, Culture and Society*, 4 (1): 113–52.

Ashton, N. J. (2007) *The Cold War in the Middle East: Regional Conflict and the Superpowers, 1967–1973* (London: Routledge).

Ayalon, A. (ed.) (1991) *Middle East Contemporary Survey, Vol. XV* (Boulder, CO: Westview Press), pp. 141–52.

Ayalon, A. (1993) *Middle East Contemporary Survey, Vol. XVII* (Boulder, CO: Westview Press).

Ayata, B. (2015) 'Turkish Foreign Policy in a Changing Arab World: Rise and Fall of a Regional Actor?' *Journal of European Integration*, 37 (1): 95–112.

Ayoob, M. (1995) *The Third World Security Predicament: State Making, Regional Conflict and the International System* (Boulder, CO: Lynne Rienner).

Ayoob, M. (1998) 'Subaltern Realism: International Relations Theory Meets the Third World', in S. Neuman (ed.) *International Relations Theory and the Third World* (Basingstoke: Macmillan), pp. 31–54.

Ayubi, N. (1990) 'Arab Bureaucracies: Expanding Size, Changing Roles', in G. Luciani (ed.) *The Arab State* (Berkeley-Los Angeles: University of California Press), pp. 129–50.

Ayubi, N. (1995) *Overstating the Arab State: Politics and Society in the Middle East* (London: I. B. Tauris).

Ayubi, N. (1996) *Over-stating the Arab State: Politics and Society in the Middle East* (London: I. B. Tauris).

Azar, E. E. (1972) 'Conflict Escalation and Conflict Reduction in an International Crisis: Suez, 1956', *Journal of Conflict Resolution*, 16 (2): 183–201.

Bahadur, J. (2011) *Deadly Waters* (London: Profile Books).

Baker, J. A., III (1995) *The Politics of Diplomacy* (New York: G. P. Putnam's).

Baker, R. W. (2004) *Islam without Fear: The New Islamists* (Cambridge, MA: Harvard University Press).

Balzacq, T. (2011) *Securitization Theory* (London: Routledge).

Baram, A. (1993) 'The Iraqi Invasion of Kuwait: Decision-Making in Baghdad', in A. Baram and B. Rubin (eds) *Iraq's Road to War* (New York: St Martin's), pp. 5–36.

Baram, A. (1997) 'Neo-Tribalism in Iraq: Saddam Hussein's Tribal Policies, 1991–1996', *International Journal of Middle East Studies*, 29 (1): 1–31.

Barkawi, T. (2004) 'On the Pedagogy of "Small Wars" ', *International Affairs*, 80 (1): 19–38.

Barnett, M. N. (1996) 'Identity and Alliances in the Middle East', in P. J. Katzenstein (ed.) *The Culture of National Security: Norms and Identity in World Politics* (New York: Colombia University Press), pp. 400–40.

Barnett, M. N. (1998) *Dialogues in Arab Politics: Negotiations in Regional Order* (New York: Columbia University Press).

Barnett, M. N. and Finnemore, M. (1999) 'The Politics, Power and Pathologies of International Organizations', *International Organization*, 53 (4): 699–732.

Barnett, M. N. and Gause, F. G., III (1998) 'Caravans in Opposite Directions: Society, State and the Development of a Community in the Gulf Cooperation Council', in E. Adler and M. Barnett (eds) *Security Communities* (Cambridge: Cambridge University Press), pp. 161–97.

Basaran, T. (2008) 'Security, Law, Borders: Spaces of Exclusion', *International Security Review*, 2: 339–54.

Basharat, O. (2011) 'The Arab Spring Turned into Arab Winter', *Haaretz*, 19 December, http://www.haaretz.com/print-edition/opinion/the-arab-spring-turned-into-arab-winter-1.402208 (Accessed: 26 December 2011).

Bassel F. S. and Bryner, R. (eds) (2004) *Persistent Permeability? Regionalism, Localism, and Globalization in the Middle East* (Aldershot: Ashgate).

Bassock, M. (2011) 'Israel's Population Stands at 7.8 Million with 2012 around the Bend', *Haaretz*, 29 December.

Batatu, H. (1978) *The Old Social Classes and the Revolutionary Movements of Iraq: A Study of Iraq's Old Landed and Commercial Classes and of its Communists,*

Ba'thists and Free Officers (Princeton, NJ: Princeton University Press).

Bayat, A. (2007) *Making Islam Democratic: Social Movements and the Post-Islamist Turn* (Stanford, CA: Stanford University Press).

Bayat, A. (2010) *Life as Politics: How Ordinary People Change the Middle East* (Stanford, CA: Stanford University Press).

Beblawi, H. (1987) 'The Rentier State in the Arab World', in H. Beblawi and G. Luciani (eds) *The Rentier State* (London and New York: Croom Helm), pp. 85–98.

Beblawi, H. and Luciani, G. (eds) (1987) *The Rentier State* (London and New York: Croom Helm).

Beeston, R. (2006) 'Six Arab States Join Rush to go Nuclear', *The Times*, 4 November.

Behrendt, S. and Hanelt, C. (eds) (2000) *Bound to Cooperate: Europe and the Middle East* (Gütersloh: Bertelsmann Foundation Publishers).

Beilin, Y. (1997) *Touching Peace* (in Hebrew) (Tel Aviv: Yediot Aharonot).

Beinin, J. (2003) 'Pro-Israeli Hawks and the Second Gulf War', *Middle East Report*, 6 April.

Beinin, J. (2010) *The Struggle for Worker Rights in Egypt: A Report by the Solidarity Center*, February, available online at http://www.solidaritycenter.org/files/pubs_egypt_wr.pdf

Bellamy, A. and Williams, P. (2011) 'The New Politics of Protection', *International Affairs*, 87 (4): 825–50.

Bellin, E. (2002) *Stalled Democracy: Capital, Labor, and the Paradox of State-Sponsored Development* (Ithaca, NY: Cornell University Press).

Bellin, E. (2004) 'The Robustness of Authoritarianism in the Middle East: Exceptionalism in Comparative Perspective', *Comparative Politics*, 36 (2): 139–57.

Ben Dor, G. (1999) *Minorities and the State in the Arab World* (Boulder, CO: Lynne Rienner).

Bengio, O. (ed.) (1992) *Saddam Speaks on the Gulf Crisis: A Collection of Documents* (Tel Aviv: Dayan Center for Middle Eastern and African Studies).

Benli-Altunisik, M. (2011) 'Challenges to Turkey's Soft Power in the Middle East', in Turkish Economy and Social Studies Foundation, *Turkey and the Middle East* (Istanbul: TESEV), pp. 14–17.

Ben-Meir, A. (2011) 'Arab Spring Could Turn into a Cruel Winter', *The Huffington Post*, 14 December, in http://www.huffingtonpost.com/alon-benmeir/the-arab-spring-could-tur_b_1143442.html (Accessed: 27 December 2011).

Benoit Challand, B. (2011) 'Counter-Power of Civil Society and the Emergence of a New Political Imaginary in the Arab World', *Constellations*, 18 (3): 271–83.

Berdal, M. and Zaum, D. (eds) (2013) *Political Economy of Statebuilding* (NewYork: Routledge).

Berman, S. (1997) 'Civil Society and the Rise of the Weimar Republic', *World Politics*, 49 (3): 401–29.

Berman, S. (2003) 'Islamism, Revolution, Civil Society', *Perspectives on Politics*, 1 (2): 257–72.

Bicci, F. and Gillespie, R. (eds) (2011) 'Special Issue: The Union for the Mediterranean—Continuity or Change in Euro-Mediterranean Relations?', *Mediterranean Politics* 16 (1).

Bienen, J. (2010). 'Egyptian Workers Demand a Living Wage', *Foreign Policy*. http://foreignpolicy.com/2010/05/12/egyptian-workers-demand-a-living-wage/

Bigo, D. (2011) 'Pierre Bourdieu and International Relations: Power of Practices, Practices of Power', *International Political Sociology*, 5 (3): 225–58.

Bilgin, P. (2004), 'Whose Middle East? Geopolitical inventions and practices of security', *International Relations*, 18 (1): 25–41.

Bilgin, P. (2005) *Regional Security in the Middle East: A Critical Perspective* (London: Routledge Curzon).

Bilgin, P. (2008) 'Thinking Past Western IR', *Third World Quarterly*, 29 (1): 5–23.

Bilgin, P. (2010) *Regional Security in the Middle East: A Critical Perspective* (London and New York: Routledge).

Bilgin, P. (2011) 'The Politics of Studying Securitization? The Copenhagen School in Turkey', *Security Dialogue*, 42 (4–5): 399–412.

Bill, J. A. (1988) *The Eagle and the Lion: The Tragedy of American-Iranian Relations* (New Haven, CT: Yale University Press).

Bill, J. (1996) 'The Study of Middle East Politics 1946–1996: A Stocktaking', *Middle East Journal*, 50 (4): 501–12.

Binder, L. (1958) 'The Middle East as a Subordinate International System', *World Politics*, 10 (3): 408–29.

Binder, L. (1999a) 'The International Dimensions of Ethnic Conflict in the Middle East', in L. Binder (ed.) *Ethnic Conflict and International Politics in the Middle East* (Gainesville, FL: University of Florida Press), pp. 1–40.

Binder, L. (ed.) (1999b) *Ethnic Conflict and International Politics in the Middle East* (Gainesville, FL: University of Florida Press).

Blainey, G. (1973) *The Causes of War* (New York: Free Press).

Blechman, B. M. (1972) 'The Impact of Israel's Reprisals on Behavior of the Bordering Arab Nations Directed at Israel', *Journal of Conflict Resolution*, 16 (June): 155–81.

Bleiker, R. (2001) 'The Aesthetic Turn in International Political Theory', *Millennium*, 30: 509–33.

Booth, K. (1991) 'Security and Emancipation', *Review of International Studies*, 17 (4): 313–26.

Booth, K. (2007) *Theory of World Security* (Cambridge: Cambridge University Press).

Booth, K. and Wheeler, N. J. (2008) *The Security Dilemma* (London: Palgrave Macmillan).

Botman, S. (1998) 'The Liberal Age, 1923–1952', in M. W. Daly (ed.) *The Cambridge History of Egypt*, vol. 2 (Cambridge: Cambridge University Press).

Boutros-Ghali, B. (1992) *Agenda for Peace* (New York: United Nations).

Boyd, D. (2014) *It's Complicated, the Social Lives of Networked Teens* (New Haven: Yale University Press).

BP (2007) BP Statistical Review of World Energy, available online at http://www.bp.com

BP (2011) BP Statistical Review of World Energy, available online at http://www.bp.com

BP (2012) BP Statistical Review of World Energy, available online at http://www.bp.com

Brand, L. A. (1994) *Jordan's Inter-Arab Relations: The Political Economy of Alliance Making* (New York: Columbia University Press).

Brecher, M. (1972) *The Foreign Policy System of Israel: Setting, Images, Process* (Oxford: Oxford University Press).

Bregman, A. (2005) *Elusive Peace: How the Holy Land Defeated America* (New York: Penguin Books).

Bronson, R. (2006) *Thicker than Oil: America's Uneasy Partnership with Saudi Arabia* (Oxford; New York: Oxford University Press).

Brown, C. (1994) '"Turtles All the Way Down": Anti-Foundationalism, Critical Theory and International Relations', *Millennium*, 23 (3): 213–36.

Brown, C. (2012) 'The "Practice Turn": Phronesis and Classical Realism—Towards a Phronetic International Relations Theory?', *Millennium*, 40 (3): 439–56.

Brown, L. C. (1984) *International Politics and the Middle East: Old Rules, Dangerous Game* (Princeton, NJ: Princeton University Press).

Brown, L. C. (2000) *Religion and State: The Muslim Approach to Politics* (New York: Columbia University Press).

Brown, L. C. (ed.) (2001) *Diplomacy in the Middle East: The International Relations of Regional and Outside Powers* (London: I. B. Tauris)

Brown, L. C. (ed.) (2004) *Diplomacy in the Middle East: The International Relations of Regional and Outside Powers* (revd edn, London: I. B. Tauris)

Brown, N. (2011) *Post-Revolutionary Al-Azhar* (Washington, DC: Carnegie Endowment).

Brown, N. and Dunne, M. (2014) 'How Egypt Prolonged the Gaza War', *Foreign Policy*, 18 August. http://foreignpolicy.com/2014/08/18/how-egypt-prolonged-the-gaza-war/

Brown, R. M. (1990) *Gustavo Gutiérrez: An Introduction to Liberation Theology* (New York: Orbis).

Brownlee, J. (2002) 'And Yet They Persist: Explaining Survival and Transition in Neopatrimonial Regimes', *Studies in Comparative International Development*, 37: 35–63.

Brynen, R. and Noble, P. (1991) 'The Gulf Conflict and the Arab State System: A New Regional Order?', *Arab Studies Quarterly*, 13 (1): 117–40.

Brynen, R., Korany, B., and Noble, P. (eds) (1993) *The Many Faces of National Security in the Arab World* (London: Macmillan).

Brynen, R., Korany, B., and Noble, P. (eds) (1995) *Political Liberalization and Democratization in the Arab World: Theoretical Perspectives* (Boulder, CO: Lynne Rienner).

Bryson, T. A. (1977) *American Diplomatic Relations with the Middle East, 1784–1975: A Survey* (Metuchen, NJ: Scarecrow Press).

Brzezinski, Z. K. (2004) *The Choice: Global Domination or Global Leadership* (New York: Basic Books).

Brzezinski, Z. K. (2007) *Second Chance: Three Presidents and the Crisis of American Superpower* (New York: Basic Books).

Budeiri, M. (1997) 'Palestinians' Nationalist Religious Identities', in J. Jankowski and I. Gershoni (eds) *Rethinking Nationalism in the Arab Middle East* (New York: Columbia University Press).

Bull, H. (1977) *The Anarchical Society* (London: Macmillan).

Bull, H. (1984) 'The Emergence of a Universal International Society', in H. Bull and A. Watson (eds) *The Expansion of International Society* (Oxford: Oxford University Press), pp. 117–26.

Bull, H. and Watson, A. (eds) (1984) *The Expansion of International Society* (Oxford: Oxford University Press).

Burchill, S., Linklater, A., Devetak, R., Donnelly, J., Nardin, T., Paterson, M., Reus-Smit, C., and True, J. (2010) *Theories of International Relations* (4th edn, London: Palgrave Macmillan).

Burkholder, R. (2002) 'The US and the West—through Saudi Eyes', *Gallup Tuesday Briefing*, 6 August, available online at http://www.gallup.com

Burrowes, R. and Muzzio, D. (1972) 'The Road to the Six Day War: Towards an Enumerative History of Four Arab States and Israel, 1965–67', *Journal of Conflict Resolution*, 16 (2): 211–26.

Bush, G. W. (2003) 'President Bush Discusses Freedom in Iraq and the Middle East', Remarks by the President at the 20th Anniversary of the National Endowment for Democracy, US Chamber of Commerce, 6 November, available online at http://www.whitehouse.gov

Buzan, B. (1991) *People, States, and Fear: An Agenda for International Security Studies in the Post-Cold War Era* (Boulder, CO: Lynne Rienner).

Buzan, B. (2004) *From International to World Society?* (Cambridge: Cambridge University Press).

Buzan, B. and Gonzalez-Pelaez, A. (eds) (2009) *International Society and the Middle East* (London: Palgrave Macmillan).

Buzan, B. and Waever, O. (2003) *Regions and Powers: The Structure of International Security* (Cambridge: Cambridge University Press).

Buzan, B., Wæver, O., and de Wilde, J. (1998) *Security: A New Framework for Analysis* (Boulder, CO: London: Lynne Rienner).

Cafarella, L. (2014) *Jabhat al-Nusra in Syria: An Islamic Emirate for Al-Qaeda*. Middle East Security Report 25. Institute for the Study of War (Retrieved: 23 March 2015).

Calculli, M. (2015) 'Sub-regions and Security in the Arab Middle East: Managing Isolationism and Interdependence', in Elizabeth Monier (ed.) *Regional Insecurity After the Uprisings. Narratives of Security and Threat* (London: Palgrave Macmillan), pp. 58–81.

Cammett, M. (1999) 'Defensive Integration and Late Developers: The Gulf Cooperation Council and the Arab Maghreb Union', *Global Governance*, 5 (3): 379–402.

Cammett, M., Diwan, I., Richards, A., and Waterbury, J. (2015) *A Political Economy of the Middle East* (4th edn, Boulder, CO: Westview Press).

Campbell, D. (2010) 'Poststructuralism', in T. Dunne, M. Kurki, and S. Smith (eds) *International Relations Theories: Discipline and Diversity* (2nd edn, Oxford: Oxford University Press).

Campbell, J. C. (1958) *Defense of the Middle East: Problems of American Policy* (New York: Council on Foreign Relations).

Carlsnaes, W., Risse, T., and Simmons, B. A. (eds) (2002) *Handbook of International Relations* (London: Sage).

Carr, E. H. (1961) *What is History?* (London: Macmillan).

Carrère d'Encausse, H. (1975) *La Politique soviétique au Moyen Orient, 1955–1975* (Paris: Presses de la Fondation Nationale des Sciences Politiques).

Center of Arab Unity Studies, Beirut (January 2000), *El-mustaqbal Al Arabi*

Central Intelligence Agency (CIA) (2011) 'Saudi Arabia', available online at https://www.cia.gov/library/publications/the-world-factbook/geos/sa.html

Centre on International Cooperation (2007) *Annual Review of Global Peace Operations* (Boulder, CO: Lynne Reinner).

Centre on International Cooperation (2010) *Annual Review of Global Peace Operations* (Boulder, CO: Lynne Reinner).

Chagnollaud, J. and Souiah, S. (2004) *Les Frontières au Moyen-Orient* (Paris: L'Harmattan).

Challand, C. (2011) 'Counter-Power of Civil Society and the Emergence of a New Political Imaginary in the Arab World', *Constellations*, 18 (3): 271–83.

Chaqueiri, C. (1995) *The Soviet Socialist Republic of Iran, 1920-1921: Birth of the Trauma* (Pittsburgh, PA: Pittsburgh University Press).

Charountaki, M. (2015) 'Kurdish Policies in Syria under the Arab Uprisings: A Revisiting of IR in the New Middle Eastern Order', *Third World Quarterly*, 36(2): 337–56.

Chernoff, F. (2004) 'The Study of Democratic Peace and Progress in International Relations', *International Studies Review*, 6 (1): 49–77.

China Central Television (CCTV) (undated) 'War's impact on world economy', *Action against Iraq*, available online at http://www.cctv.com/lm/942/19/14.html

Choucri, N. and North, R. (1975) *Nations in Conflict* (San Francisco, CA: Freeman).

Choueiri, Y. (2000) *Arab Nationalism: A History* (Oxford: Blackwell).

Chubin, S. and Tripp, C. (1988) *Iran and Iraq at War* (Boulder, CO: Westview Press).

Chubin, S. and Tripp, C. (1993) 'Domestic Politics and Territorial Disputes in the Persian Gulf and the Arabian Peninsula', *Survival*, 35 (4): 3–27.

Clapham, C. (1996) *Africa and the International System: The Politics of State Survival* (Cambridge: Cambridge University Press).

Clarke, V. (2011) *Dancing on the Snakes* (New Haven, CT: Yale University Press).

Claude, I. (1968) 'The OAS, the UN and the United States', in J. Nye (ed.) *International Regionalism* (Boston, MA: Little, Brown & Co.) pp. 3–21.

Clinton, H. (2011) 'America's Pacific Century', *Foreign Policy*, 11 October.

Cobban, H. (1984) *The Palestine Liberation Organization: People, Power, and Politics* (Cambridge: Cambridge University Press).

Coldwell, D. (2003) 'Egypt's Autumn of Fury: The Construction of Opposition to the Egyptian-Israeli Peace Process', Unpublished MA thesis, St Antony's College, University of Oxford.

Colgan, J. D. (2010) 'Oil and Revolutionary Governments: Fuel for International Conflict', *International Organization*, 64 (4): 661–94.

Colgan, J. D. (2013) 'Domestic Revolutionary Leaders and International Conflict', *World Politics*, 65 (4): 656–90.

Colgan, J. D. and Weeks, J. L. P. (2015) 'Revolution, Personalist Dictatorships and International Conflict', *International Organization*, 69 (1): 163–94.

Collier, P. and Hoeffler, A. (2004) 'Greed and Grievance in Civil War', *Oxford Economic Papers*, 56 (4): 563–95.

Constantinou, C. (1994) 'Diplomatic Representations—or Who Framed the Ambassadors?', *Millennium*, 23 (1): 1–23.

Cook, S. (2011) 'The Frankenstein of Tahrir Square', *Foreign Policy*, in http://foreignpolicy.com/2011/12/19/the-frankenstein-of-tahrir-square/ (retrieved: 28 May 2015).

Cooley, J. K. (1991) *Payback: America's Long War in the Middle East* (Washington, DC: Brassey's (US)).

Cooley, J. K. (2002) *Unholy Wars: Afghanistan, America and International Terrorism* (2nd edn, London: Pluto Press).

Cooper, S. (2003–04) 'State-Centric Balance-of-Threat Theory: Explaining the Misunderstood Gulf Cooperation Council', *Security Studies*, 13 (2): 306–49.

Cooper, H. (2011) 'Invitation to Israeli Leader Puts Obama on the Spot', *Washington Post*, 21 April, available online at http://www.washingtonpost.com

Copeland, D. C. (2000) *The Origins of Major War* (Ithaca, NY: Cornell University Press).

Copeland, D. C. (2003) 'A Realist Critique of the English School', *Review of International Studies*, 29 (3): 427–41.

Cordesman, A. (2001) *Economic, Demographic, and Security Trends in the Middle East* (Washington, DC: Centre for Strategic and International Studies).

Cordesman, A., Burke, A. A., and Nerguizian, A. (2010) *The Gulf Military Balance in 2010: An Overview* (Washington, DC: Center for Strategic and International Studies), available online at http://csis.org/files/publication/100422_GulfMilBal.pdf

Cordsman, A. (2001) *Economic, Demographic, and Security Trends in the Middle East* (Washington, DC: Centre for Strategic and International Studies).

Corm, G. (2012a) *Le Proche-Orient Éclaté. 1956–2012* (Paris: La Découverte).

Corm, G. (2012b) *Pour une lecture profane des conflits. Sur le « retour du religieux » dans les conflits contemporains du Moyen-Orient* (Paris: La Découverte).

Council of the European Union (2009) 'Council Conclusions on the Middle East Peace Process', 2985th Foreign Affairs Council Meeting, Brussels, 8 December, available online at http://www.consilium.europa.eu/uedocs/cms_Data/docs/pressdata/EN/foraff/111829.pdf

Council on Foreign Relations (1999) *Task Force Report: Strengthening Palestinian Public Institutions*, available online at http://www.cfr.org/middle-east/strengthening-palestinian-public-institutions/p3185

Cox, M. (2007) 'Is the United States in Decline—Again? An Essay', *International Affairs*, 83 (4): 643–53.

Cox, R. (1996) 'Social Forces, State and World Orders', in R. Cox and T. Sinclair (eds) *Approaches to World Order* (Cambridge: Cambridge University Press).

Croce, B. (1941) *History as the Story of Liberty* (New York: W. W. Norton).

Croft, S. (2012) *Securitizing Islam: Identity and the Search for Security* (Cambridge: Cambridge University Press).

Cummings, S. and Hinnebusch, R. (2014) 'Empire and After', *Journal of Historical Sociology*, 27 (1): 103–31.

Daher, A. (2014) *Le Hezbollah* (Paris: Presse Universitaire de France).

Dakhlallah, F. (2012) 'The Arab League in Lebanon 2005–2008', *Cambridge Review of International Affairs*, 25: 53–74.

Dann, U. (1984) *Studies in the History of Transjordan, 1920–1949: The Making of a State* (Boulder, CO: Westview Press).

David, S. (1991a) 'Explaining Third World Alignment', *World Politics*, 43 (2): 233–56.

David, S. R. (1991b) *Choosing Sides: Alignment and Realignment in the Third World* (Baltimore; London: Johns Hopkins University Press).

Dawisha, A. (1976) *Egypt in the Arab World: The Elements of Foreign Policy* (New York: Wiley).

Dawisha, A. (ed.) (1983) *Islam in Foreign Policy* (Cambridge: Cambridge University Press).

Dawisha, A. (1999) 'The Assembled State: Communal Conflicts and Governmental Control in Iraq', in L. Binder (ed.) *Ethnic Conflict and International Politics in the Middle East* (Gainesville, FL: University of Florida Press), pp. 61–76.

Dawisha, A. (2005), *Arab Nationalism in the Twentieth Century: From Triumph to Despair* (Princeton: Princeton University Press).

Dawisha, A. (2008) 'The Unravelling of Iraq: Ethnosectarian Preferences and State Performance in Historical Perspective', *Middle East Journal*, 62 (2): 219–31.

Derichs, C. and Demmelhuber, T. (2014) 'Monarchies and Republics, State and Regime, Durability and Fragility in View of the Arab Spring', *Journal of Arabian Studies*, 4 (2): 180–94.

Dessouki, A. E. H. (1983) 'The Crisis of Inter-Arab Politics', in A. E. H. Dessouki (ed.) *International Relations in the Arab World 1973–1982* (Tokyo: Institute of Developing Economies)

Dessouki, A. E. D. H. (2015) 'The Arab Regional System: A Question of Survival', *Contemporary Arab Affairs*, 8 (1): 96–108.

Deutsch, K. (1953) *Nationalism and Social Communication* (Cambridge, MA: MIT Press).

Deutsch, K. (1957) *Political Community and the North Atlantic Area* (Princeton, NJ: Princeton University Press).

Deutsch, K. and Singer, J. D. (1964) 'Multipolar Power Systems and International Stability', *World Politics*, 16 (April): 390–406.

Devenny, P. (2006) 'Hezbollah's [sic] Strategic Threat to Israel', *Middle East Quarterly*, 13 (1): 31–8.

Devlen, B., James, P., and Ozdamar, O. (2005) 'The English School: International Relations and Progress', *International Studies Review*, 7 (2): 171–97.

Dhillon, N. and Yousef, T. (eds) (2009) *Middle East Youth Initiative, Generation in Waiting: The Unfulfilled Promise of Young People in the Middle East* (Washington, DC: Wolfensohn Center for Development, Brookings Foundation)

DiCicco, J. M. and Levy, J. S. (1999) 'Power Shifts and Problem Shifts: The Evolution of the Power Transition Research Program', *Journal of Conflict Resolution*, 43 (6): 675–704.

Diehl, P. F. and Goertz, G. (2000) *War and Peace in International Rivalry* (Ann Arbor, MI: University of Michigan Press).

Diskin, A. and Mishal, S. (1984) 'Coalition Formation in the Arab World: An Analytical Perspective', *International Interactions*, 11 (1): 43–59.

Dodge, T. (2007) 'The Causes of US Failure in Iraq', *Survival*, 49 (1): 85–106.

Dodge, T. (2012) 'The Resistible Rise of Nuri al-Maliki', *Open Democracy*, 22 March, available online at http://www.opendemocracy.net/toby-dodge/resistible-rise-of-nuri-al-maliki

Dor, B. G. (1999) *Minorities and the State in the Arab World* (Boulder, CO: Lynne Rienner).

Doran, C. F. (1980) 'Leading Indicators of the June War: A Micro Analysis of the Conflict Cycle', *International Journal of Middle East Studies*, 11 (1): 23–58.

Doran, C. F. (1991) *Systems in Crisis* (Cambridge: Cambridge University Press).

Doty, R. L. (1996) *Imperial Encounters* (Minneapolis, MN: University of Minnesota Press).

Dunne, T., Kurki, M., and Smith, S. (eds) (2010) *International Relations Theories: Discipline and Diversity* (2nd edn Oxford: Oxford University Press).

Dyer, P. D. (2008) 'Demography in the Middle East: Implications and Risks', in A. Pandya and E. Laipson (eds) *Transnational Trends: Middle Eastern and Asian Views* (Washington, DC: The Stimson Center) pp. 62–90.

Eban, A. (1993) 'Building Bridges, Not Walls', *The Guardian*, 10 September.

Economist, The (2012) 'Unfinished Business: Revolutions Have Hurt the Wallets of Bosses and Workers Alike',

4 February, available online at http://www.economist.com/node/21546018

Edkins, J. (1999) *Poststructuralism and International Relations* (Boulder, CO: Lynne Rienner).

Ehteshami, A. and Murphy, E. (2011) *The International Politics of the Red Sea* (London and New York: Routledge).

Eickelman, D. F. and Anderson, J. W. (eds) (2003) *New Media in the Muslim World: The Emerging Public Sphere* (Bloomington, IN: Indiana University Press).

Eickelman, D. F. and Piscatori, J. (1996) *Muslim Politics* (Princeton, NJ: Princeton University Press).

Eilstrup-Sangiovanni, M. (2009) 'The End of Balance-of-Power Theory? A Comment', *European Journal of International Relations*, 15 (2): 347–80.

Eisenberg, L. Z. and Caplan, N. (1998) *Negotiating Arab-Israeli Peace: Patterns, Problems, Possibilities* (Bloomington, IN: Indiana University Press).

El Badawi, I. and Makdisi, S. (eds) (2011) *Democracy in the Arab World: Explaining the Deficit* (London and New York: Routledge).

El Badri, H., El Magdoub, T., and El-Din Zhody, M. D. (1978) *The Ramadan War* (Dunn Loring, VA: T. N. Dupuy Associates).

El Husseini, R. (2010) 'Hezbollah and the Axis of Refusal: Hamas, Iran and Syria', *Third World Quarterly*, 31 (5): 803–15.

Elgindy, K. (2012) *A New and Improved Arab League* (New York: Brookings).

El-Saadani, N. (1997) 'Conferences of Middle East Cooperation', *El-Siasa El-Dawliyya*, 38 (1): 246–54.

El-Saadani, N. (1998) 'The Doha Economic Conference', *El-Siasa El-Dawliyya*, 42 (1): 299–301.

El-Shazly, N. and Hinnebusch, R. (2002) 'The Challenge of Security in the Post-Gulf War Middle East System', in R. Hinnebusch and A. Ehteshami (eds) *The Foreign Policies of Middle East States* (Boulder, CO: Lynne Rienner), pp. 79–90.

El-Sherif, A. (2011) 'Will Islamists Accept Political Pluralism?', *Current History*, 110 (740): 358–63.

Enderlin, C. (2003) *Shattered Dreams: The Failure of the Peace Process in the Middle East, 1995–2002* (New York: Other Press).

Ennis, C. A. and Momani, B. (2013) 'Shaping the Middle East in the Midst of the Arab Uprisings: Turkish and Saudi Foreign Policy Strategies', *Third World Quarterly*, 34 (6).

Esposito, J. L. (ed.) (1990) *The Iranian Revolution: Its Global Impact* (Gainesville, FL: University Press of Florida).

Esposito, J. L. (1995) *The Islamic Threat: Myth or Reality* (Oxford: Oxford University Press).

European Commission (2004) *Interim Report on an EU Strategic Partnership with the Mediterranean and the Middle East* Euromed Report 73, 23 March, available online at http://www.euromedi.org/inglese/home/partenariato/report/report/euromed_report73_en.pdf

Evron, Y. (1987) *War and Intervention in Lebanon* (Baltimore, MD: Johns Hopkins University Press).

Evron, Y. (1994) 'Gulf Crisis and War: Regional Rules of the Game and Policy and Theoretical Implications', *Security Studies*, 4 (1): 115–54.

Faksh, M. (1993) 'Withered Arab Nationalism?', *Orbis*, 37 (3): 425–38.

Fandy, M. (1999) *Saudi Arabia and the Politics of Dissent* (New York: St Martin's).

Farah, T. E. and Al-Salem, F. (1980) 'Group Affiliations of Children in the Arab Middle East (Kuwait)', *Journal of Social Psychology*, 111 (1): 141–2.

Farman Farmaian, S. and Munker, D. (1992) *Daughter of Persia: A Woman's Journey from her Father's Harem through the Islamic Revolution* (New York: Crown).

Farouk-Sluglett, M. (1982) 'Socialist' Iraq 1963–1978: Towards a Reappraisal', *Orient*, 23 (2): 206–19.

Farouk-Sluglett, M. (1994) 'Power and Responsibility: US Hegemony and the Arab States in the Post-Gulf War Middle East', in J. O'Loughlin, T. Mayer, and E. S. Greenberg (eds) *War and its Consequences: Lessons from the Persian Gulf Conflict* (New York: HarperCollins College Publishers) pp. 105–24.

Farouk-Sluglett, M. and Sluglett, P. (1983) 'Labor and National Liberation: The Trade Union Movement in Iraq, 1920–1958', *Arab Studies Quarterly*, 5 (2): 139–54.

Farouk-Sluglett, M. and Sluglett, P. (2001) *Iraq since 1958: From Revolution to Dictatorship* (3rd edn, London: I. B. Tauris).

Farrell, M., Hettne, B. and van Langenhove, L. (eds) (2005) *Global Politics of Regionalism: Theory and Practice* (London: Pluto Press).

Fawcett, L. (1992) *Iran and the Cold War: The Azerbaijan Crisis of 1946* (Cambridge: Cambridge University Press).

Fawcett, L. (2009) 'Alliances, Cooperation and Regionalism', in L. Fawcett (ed.) *The International Relations of the Middle East* (2nd edn Oxford: Oxford University Press), pp. 188–207.

Fawcett, L. (2011a) 'Regional Order in the Middle East', in A. Acharya and H. Katsumata (eds) *Beyond Iraq: The Future of World Order* (Singapore and London: World Scientific Publishers) pp. 35–64.

Fawcett, L. (2011b) 'Regional Leadership? Understanding Power and Transformation in the Middle East', in N. Godehardt and D. Nabers (eds) *Regional Powers and Regional Orders* (London and New York: Routledge), pp. 155–72.

Fawcett, L. (2013) 'The Iraq War ten years on: assessing the fallout', *International Affairs*, 89 (2): 325–43.

Fawcett, L. (2014a) 'Revisiting the Iranian Crisis of 1946: How Much More Do We Know?' *Iranian Studies*, 47 (3): pp. 379–99.

Fawcett, L. (2014b) 'The Arab League', in J. Sperling (ed.) *Handbook of Governance and Security* (Cheltenham: Edward Elgar).

Fawcett, L. (2015a) 'Rising Powers and Regional Organization in the Middle East' in J. Gaskarth (ed.) *Rising Powers, Global Governance and Global Ethics* (London: Routledge), pp. 133–51.

Fawcett, L. (2015b), 'Iran and the Regionalization of (in) Security', *International Politics*, 52: 646–56.

Fawcett, L. and Gandois, H. (2010) 'Regionalism in Africa and the Middle East: Implications for EU Studies', *Journal of European Integration*, 32 (6): 617–36.

Fawcett, L. and Hurrell, A. (eds) (1995) *Regionalism and World Politics: Regional Organization and International Order* (Oxford: Oxford University Press).

Fearon, J. D. (2003) 'Ethnic Structure and Cultural Diversity around the World', *Journal of Economic Growth*, 8 (2): 195–222.

Fierke, K. M. (2007) *Critical Approaches to International Security* (Cambridge: Polity Press).

Filiu, J.-Pi. (2011) *The Arab Revolution: Ten Lessons from Democratic Uprising* (translated from the French, New York: Hurst & Co.).

Findley, C. V. (1989) *Ottoman Civil Officialdom: A Social History* (Princeton, NJ: Princeton University Press).

Finlay, A. (2011) *Governing Ethnic Conflict: Consociation, Identity and the Price of Peace* (London: Routledge).

Flemes, D. (ed.) (2010) *Regional Leadership in the Global System* (Aldershot: Ashgate).

Foucault, M. (1980) 'Two Lectures', in C. Gordon (ed.) *Power/knowledge: Selected Interviews and Other Writings by Michel Foucault, 1972–1977* (New York: Pantheon Books), pp. 78–108.

Frank, A. G. (1978) *Dependent Accumulation and Underdevelopment* (New York: Monthly Review Press).

Frankel, J. (1988) *International Relations in a Changing World* (4th edn, Oxford: Oxford University Press).

Franzén, J. (2011) *Red Star over Iraq: Iraqi Communism before Saddam* (London: Hurst).

Freedman, L. and Karsh, E. (1993) *The Gulf Conflict, 1990-1991* (Princeton, NJ: Princeton University Press).

Freire, P. (2006) *Pedagogy of the Oppressed* (New York: Bloomsbury).

Fritz, P. and Sweeney, K. (2004) 'The (de)Limitations of Balance of Power Theory', *International Interactions*, 30 (4): 285–308.

Fromkin, D. (2000) *A Peace to End All Peace: Creating the Modern Middle East, 1914-22* (Harmondsworth: Penguin).

Fukuyama, F. (1992) *The End of History and the Last Man* (London: Penguin/New York: St Martin's Press).

Fuertig, H. (2007) 'Conflict and Cooperation in the Persian Gulf: The Interregional Order and US Policy', *Middle East Journal*, 61 (4): 627–40.

Fuertig, H. (2014) *Regional Powers in the Middle East: New Constellations after the Arab Revolts* (New York: Palgrave).

Furia, P. and Lucas, R. (2006) 'Determinants of Arab Public Opinion on Foreign Relations', *International Studies Quarterly*, 50 (3): 585–605.

Gaddis, J. L. (2005) *Strategies of Containment* (Oxford: Oxford University Press).

Garnham, D. (1976) 'Dyadic International War 1816–1965: The Role of Power Parity and Geographical Proximity', *Western Political Quarterly*, 29 (2): 231–42.

Gartzke, E. and Simon, M. W. (1999) 'Hot Hand: A Critical Analysis of Enduring Rivalries', *Journal of Politics*, 61 (3): 777–98.

Gary, M. (2011) *A Theory of 'Late Rentierism' in the Arab States of the Gulf* (Qatar: Center for International and Regional Studies, Georgetown University School of Foreign Service in Qatar), available online at http://www12.georgetown.edu/sfs/qatar/cirs/MatthewGrayOccasionalPaper.pdf

Gasiorowski, M. J. (2002) 'The Nuzhih Plot and Iranian Politics', *International Journal of Middle East Studies*, 34 (4): 645–66.

Gause, F. G., III (1985) 'British and American Policies in the Persian Gulf, 1968–1973', *Review of International Studies*, 11 (4): 247–73.

Gause, F. G., III (1992) 'Sovereignty, Statecraft and Stability in the Middle East', *Journal of International Affairs*, 45 (2): 441–67.

Gause, F. G., III (1999) 'Systemic Approaches to the International Relations of the Middle East', *International Studies Review*, 1 (1): 11–31.

Gause, F. G., III (2002a) 'Be Careful What You Wish for: The Future of US-Saudi Relations', *World Policy Journal*, 49 (1): 37–50.

Gause, F. G., III (2002b) 'Iraq's Decisions to Go to War, 1980 and 1990', *Middle East Journal*, 56 (1): 47–70.

Gause, F. G., III (2003) 'Balancing What? Threat Perception and Alliance Choice in the Gulf', *Security Studies*, 13 (2): 273–305.

Gause, F. G., III (2004) 'Theory and System in Understanding Middle East International Politics: Rereading Paul Noble's "The Arab System: Pressures, Constraints and Opportunities"', in B. F. Salloukh and

R. Brynen (eds) *Persistent Permeability?* (Aldershot: Ashgate), pp. 15–28.

Gause, F. G., III (2007) 'Saudi Arabia: Iraq, Iran, the Regional Power Balance, and the Sectarian Question', *Strategic Insights*, 4 (2), available online at http://www.isn.ethz.ch/isn/Digital-Library/Publications/Detail/?ots591=0c54e3b3-1e9c-be1e-2c24-a6a8c7060233&lng=en&id=30995

Gause, F. G., III (2010) *The International Relations of the Persian Gulf* (Cambridge: Cambridge University Press).

Gause, F. G., III (2011a) 'Why Middle East Studies Missed the Arab Spring: The Myth of Authoritarian Stability', *Foreign Affairs*, July/August, available at: http://www.foreignaffairs.com/print/67865

Gause, F. G., III (2011b) 'Saudi Arabia's Regional Security Strategy', in Mehran Kamrava (ed.), *International Politics of the Persian Gulf* (Syracuse, NY: Syracuse University Press) pp. 169–83.

Gause, G. (2014) 'Beyond Sectarianism: The New Middle East Cold War'. *Brookings Doha Centre Analysis Paper Number 11*, July, available at: http://www.brookings.edu/research/papers/2014/07/22-beyond-sectarianism-cold-war-gause

Gause, F. G., III, and Lustick, I. S. (2012) 'America and the Regional Powers in a Transforming Middle East', *Middle East Policy*, 19 (2), available online at http://mepc.org/journal/middle-east-policy-archives/america-and-regional-powers-transforming-middle-east

Gellman, B. (1992) 'Pentagon Would Preclude a Rival Superpower', *Washington Post*, 11 March.

Gelvin, J. L. (1997) 'The Other Arab Nationalism: Syrian/Arab Populism in its Historical and International Contexts', in J. Jankowski and I. Gershoni (eds) *Rethinking Nationalism in the Arab Middle East* (New York: Columbia University Press), pp. 23–48.

Gelvin, J. L. (1998) *Divided Loyalties: Nationalism and Mass Politics in Syria at the Close of Empire* (Berkeley, CA: University of California Press).

Gerges, F. (1991) 'The Study of Middle East International Relations: A Critique', *British Journal of Middle Eastern Studies*, 18 (2): 208–20.

Gerges, F. (1994) *The Superpowers and the Middle East: Regional and International Politics, 1955–1967* (Boulder, CO: Westview Press).

Gerges, F. (1999) *America and Political Islam: Clash of Cultures or Clash of Interests?* (Cambridge: Cambridge University Press).

Gerges, F. (2005) *The Far Enemy: Why Jihad Went Global* (Cambridge and New York: Cambridge University Press).

Gerges, F. A. (2011) *The Rise and Fall of Al-Qaeda* (Oxford; New York: Oxford University Press).

Gerges, F. (2012) *Obama and the Middle East: The End of America's Moment?* (London: Palgrave Macmillan).

Gerges, F. (2014) *The New Middle East: Protest and Revolution in the Arab World* (Cambridge, Cambridge University Press).

Gershoni, I. (1997) 'Rethinking the Formulation of Arab Nationalism', in J. Jankowski and I. Gershoni (eds) *Rethinking Nationalism in the Arab Middle East* (New York: Columbia University Press), pp. 3–25.

Ghoneim, W. (2012) *Revolution 2.0: The Power of the People is Greater than the People in Power—A Memoir* (Berkley, MA: Houghton Mifflin Harcourt).

Gills, B. K. (2002) 'World System Analysis, Historical Sociology and International Relations: The Difference a Hyphen Makes', in S. Hobden and J. M. Hobson (eds) *Historical Sociology of International Relations* (Cambridge: Cambridge University Press), pp. 141–61.

Ginor, I. (2007) *Foxbats over Dimona: The Soviets' Nuclear Gamble in the Six-Day War* (New Haven, CT: Yale University Press).

Glaser, C. L. (1997) 'The Security Dilemma Revisited', *World Politics*, 50 (1): 171–201.

GlobalSecurity.org (2011) 'Iran-Iraq War (1980–1988)', available online at http://globalsecurity.org/military/world/war/iran-iraq.htm

Göcek, F. (1987) *East Encounters West: France and the Ottoman Empire in the Eighteenth Century* (New York: Oxford University Press).

Gochman, C. S. and Maoz, Z. (1984) 'Militarized Interstate Disputes, 1816–1976: Procedures, Patterns and Insights', *Journal of Conflict Resolution*, 28 (4): 585–615.

Goertz, G. and Diehl, P. F. (1993) 'Enduring Rivalries: Theoretical Constructs and Empirical Patterns', *International Studies Quarterly*, 37 (2): 147–71.

Golan, G. (1992) *Moscow and the Middle East: New Thinking on Regional Conflict* (London: Royal Institute of International Affairs/Washington, DC Council on Foreign Relations Press).

Gomaa, A. (1977) *The Foundation of the League of Arab States* (London: Longman).

Graham-Brown, S. (1999) *Sanctioning Saddam: The Politics of Intervention in Iraq* (London: I. B. Tauris).

Grant, G. and Petersen, A. (2011) 'Egypt needs reform, not revolution', *The Telegraph*, 28 January, in http://www.telegraph.co.uk/news/worldnews/africaandindianocean/egypt/8289505/Egypt-needs-reform-not-revolution.html

Gray, J. (1998) *False Dawn: The Delusions of Global Capitalism* (New York: New Press).

Greenwald, G. (2015) 'Obama personally tells the Egyptian dictator that the US will again send weapons (and cash) to his regime'. https://firstlook.org/theintercept/2015/03/31/obama-lifts-freeze-weapons-transfer-egyptian-dictator/ (Retrieved: 12 May 2015).

Grieco, J. M. (1988) 'Anarchy and the Limits of Cooperation', *International Organization*, 42 (3): 485–507.

'Gulf War Fast Facts' CNN. Cable News Network, n., d. Web. http://edition.cnn.com/2013/09/15/world/meast/gulf-war-fast-facts/

Gunter, Michael M. (2013) 'The Kurdish Spring', *Third World Quarterly*, 34 (3): 441–57.

Guyatt, N. (1998) *The Absence of Peace: Understanding the Israeli-Palestinian Conflict* (London: Zed Books).

Guzzini, S. and Leander, A. (eds) (2006) *Constructivism and International Relations: Alexander Wendt and his Critics* (London: Routledge).

Haass, R. (2003) 'Toward Greater Democracy in the Muslim World', *Washington Quarterly*, 26 (3): 137–48.

Haass, R. (2008) 'What Follows American Dominion?', *Financial Times*, 16 April.

Hafez, M. (2003) *Why Muslims Rebel: Repression and Resistance in the Islamic World* (Boulder, CO: Lynne Rienner).

Halliday, F. (1990) 'The Sixth Great Power': On the Study of Revolution and International Relations', *Review of International Studies*, 16 (3): 207–21.

Halliday, F. (1997) 'The Middle East, the Great Powers and the Cold War', in Y. Sayigh and A. Shlaim (eds) *The Cold War and the Middle East* (Oxford: Oxford University Press), pp. 6–26.

Halliday, F. (2002) 'The Foreign Policy of Yemen', in R. Hinnebusch and A. Ehteshami (eds) *The Foreign Policies of Middle Eastern States* (Boulder, CO: Lynne Reinner), pp. 257–82.

Halliday, F. (2005) *The Middle East in International Relations: Power Politics and Ideology* (Cambridge: Cambridge University Press).

Hamati-Ataya, I. (2013) 'Reflectivity, Reflexivity, Reflexivism: IR's "Reflexive Turn" and Beyond', *European Journal of International Relations*, 19 (4): 669–94.

Hammoudi, A. (1997) *Master and Disciple: The Cultural Foundations of Moroccan Authoritarianism* (Chicago, IL: University of Chicago Press).

Hansen, B. (2000) *Unipolarity and the Middle East* (Richmond, VA: Curzon).

Harary, F. (1961) 'A Structural Analysis of the Situation in the Middle East in 1956', *Journal of Conflict Resolution*, 5 (2): 167–78.

Harb, M. and Leenders, R. (2005) 'Know Thy Enemy: Hizbullah, "terrorism" and the Politics of Perception', *Third World Quarterly*, 26 (1): 173–97.

Harders, C. (2008) 'Analyzing Regional Cooperation after September 11, 2011: The Emergence of a New Regional Order in the Arab World', in C. Harders and M. Legrenzi (eds) *Beyond Regionalism? Regional Cooperation, Regionalism and Regionalization in the Middle East* (Aldershot: Ashgate), pp. 33–50.

Harders, C. and Legrenzi, M. (eds) (2008) *Beyond Regionalism? Regional Cooperation, Regionalism and Regionalization in the Middle East* (Aldershot: Ashgate).

Hardt, M. and Negri, A. (2005) *Multitude: War And Democracy in the Age of Empire* (New York: Penguin).

Hare, P. J. (1993) *Diplomatic Chronicles of the Middle East: A Biography of Raymond Hare* (Washington, DC: Middle East Institute).

Hare, R. A. (1972) 'The Great Divide: World War II', *The ANNALS of the American Academy of Political and Social Science*, 401: 23–30.

Harik, I. (1987) 'The Origins of the Arab State System', in G. Salame (ed.) *The Foundations of the Arab State* (London: Croom-Helm), pp. 19–46.

Harik, I. (1990) 'The Origins of the Arab State System', in G. Luciani (ed.) *The Arab State* (Berkeley, CA: University of California Press), pp. 1–28.

Harik, I. (2006) 'Democracy, "Arab Exceptionalism", and Social Science', *Middle East Journal*, 60 (4): 664–84.

Harknett, R. J. and VanDenBerg, J. A. (1997) 'Alignment Theory and Interrelated Threats: Jordan and the Persian Gulf Crisis', *Security Studies*, 6 (3): 112–53.

Hasanli, J. (2006) *At the Dawn of the Cold War: The Soviet-American Crisis over Iranian Azerbaijan, 1941–1946* (Lanham, MD: Rowman & Littlefield).

Hashmi, S. (ed.) (2002) *Islamic Political Ethics: Civil Society, Pluralism, and Conflict* (Princeton, NJ: Princeton University Press).

Hashmi, S. (2009) 'Islam, the Middle East and the Pan-Islamic Movement', in B. Buzan and A. Gonzalez-Pelaez (eds) *International Society and the Middle East* (Basingstoke: Palgrave Macmillan).

Hatina, M. (2007) *Identity Politics in the Middle East: Liberal Thought and Islamic Challenge in Egypt* (London: I. B. Tauris).

Hazbun, W. (2010) 'US Policy and the Geopolitics of Insecurity in the Arab World', *Geopolitics*, 15 (2): 239–62.

Healy, B. and Stein, A. (1973) 'The Balance of Power in International History: Theory and Reality', *Journal of Conflict Resolution*, 17 (1): 33–61.

Heard-Bey, F. (1999) 'The United Arab Emirates: A Quarter Century of Federation', in M. Hudson (ed.) *Middle East Dilemma: The Politics and Economics of Arab Integration* (London: I. B. Tauris), pp. 128–49.

Hebron, L., James, P., and Rudy, M. (2007) 'Testing Dynamic Theories of Conflict: Power Cycles, Power Transitions, Foreign Policy Crises and Militarized Interstate Disputes', *International Interactions*, 33 (1): 1–29.

Hefner, R. H. (ed.) (2004) *Muslim Democrats: Prospects and Policies for a Modern Islamist Politics* (Princeton, NJ: Princeton University Press).

Hegghammer, T. (2006) 'Global Jihadism after the Iraq War', *Middle East Journal*, 60 (1): 11–32.

Heikal, M. (1993) *Illusions of Triumph: An Arab View of the Gulf War* (London: HarperCollins).

Helmreich, P. C. (1974) *From Paris to Sevres: The Partition of the Ottoman Empire at the Peace Conference of 1919–1920* (Columbus, OH: Ohio State University Press).

Henry, C. and Springborg, R. (2001) *Globalisation and the Politics of Development in the Middle East* (Cambridge: Cambridge University Press).

Henry, C. and Springborg, R. (2009) *Globalization and the Politics of Development in the Middle East* (2nd edn, Cambridge and New York: Cambridge University Press).

Hensel, P. R. (1996) 'Charting a Course to Conflict: Territorial Issues and Interstate Conflict, 1816–1992', *Conflict Management and Peace Science*, 15 (1): 43–73.

Hensel, P. R. (2000) 'Theory and Evidence on Geography and Conflict', in J. A. Vasquez (ed.) *What Do We Know about War?* (Lanham, MD: Rowman & Littlefield), pp. 57–84.

Heradstveit, D. and Bonham, G. M. (2007) 'What the Axis of Evil Metaphor Did to Iran', *Middle East Journal*, 61 (3): 421–40.

Herb, M. (1999) 'Subordinate Communities and the Utility of Ethnic ties to a Neighbouring Regime: Iran and the Shia of the Arab States of the Gulf', in L. Binder, (ed.) *Ethnic Conflict and International Politics in the Middle East* (Gainesville, FL: University of Florida Press), pp. 154–80.

Herb, M. (2005) 'No Representation without Taxation? Rents, Development, and Society', *Comparative Politics*, 37 (3): 297–316.

Hertog, S. (2011) *Foreign Policy* (31/05/2011) http://foreignpolicy.com/2011/05/31/the-costs-of-counter-revolution-in-the-gcc/ (Retrieved: 6 June 2015).

Herzig, E. (2004) 'Regionalism, Iran and Central Asia', *International Affairs*, 80 (3): 503–17.

Herzog, M. and Robins, P. (eds) (2014) *The Role, Position and Agency of Cusp States in International Relations* (Abingdon: Routledge).

Heydarian, R. (2014) *How Capitalism Failed The Arab World* (London: Zed.)

Heydemann, S. (1993) 'Taxation without Representation: Authoritarianism and Economic Liberalization in Syria', in E. Goldberg, R. Kesaba, and J. Migdal (eds) *Rules and Rights in the Middle East: Democracy, Law, and Society* (Seattle, WA: University of Washington Press)

Heydemann, S. (ed.) (2000) *War, Institutions and Social Change in the Middle East* (Berkeley, CA: University of California Press).

Heydemann, S. (ed.) (2004) *Networks of Privilege in the Middle East: The Politics of Economic Reform Revisited* (New York: Palgrave Macmillan).

Heydemann, S. (2007) *Upgrading Authoritarianism in the Arab World*, Saban Center Analysis Paper Series 13 (Washington, DC: Saban Center at The Brookings Institution), available online at http://www.brookings.edu/papers/2007/10arabworld.aspx

Heydemann, S. (2014) 'America's Response to the Arab Uprisings: US Foreign Assistance in an Era of Ambivalence', *Mediterranean Politics*, 19 (3): 299–317.

Heydemann, S. and Leenders, R. (2014) 'Authoritarian Learning and Counterrevolution', in M Lynch (ed.) *The Arab Uprisings Explained: New Contentious Politics in the Middle East* (New York: Columbia University Press), pp. 75–92.

Hilsum, L. (2012) *Sandstorm: Libya in the Time of Revolution* (New York: Penguin Press).

Hinnebusch, R. (1982) 'Children of the Elite: Political Attitudes of the Westernised Bourgeoisie in Contemporary Egypt', *Middle East Journal*, 36 (4): 535–61.

Hinnebusch, R. (2002) 'The Middle East Regional System', in R. Hinnebusch and A. Ehteshami (eds) *The Foreign Policies of Middle Eastern States* (Boulder, CO: Lynne Reinner), pp. 29–54.

Hinnebusch, R. (2003) *The International Politics of the Middle East* (Manchester: Manchester University Press).

Hinnebusch, R. (2007) 'The US Invasion of Iraq: Explanations and Implications', *Middle East Critique*, 16(3):209–28.

Hinnebusch, R. (2015a) 'Back to Enmity: Turkey-Syria Relations Since the Syrian Uprising', *Orient 1*: 14–22.

Hinnebusch, R. (2015b) *The International Politics of the Middle East* (Manchester: Manchester University Press).

Hinnebusch, R. and Cummings, S. (2011) *Sovereignty after Empire: Comparing the Middle East and Central Asia* (Edinburgh: Edinburgh University Press).

Hinnebusch, R. and Ehteshami, A. (eds) (2014) *The Foreign Policies of Middle Eastern States* (Boulder, CO: Lynne Reinner).

Hinnebusch, R. and Quilliam, N. (2006) 'Contrary Siblings: Syria, Jordan and the Iraq War', *Cambridge Review of International Affairs*, 1 (3): 513–28.

Hiro, D. (1991) *The Longest War: The Iran-Iraq Military Conflict* (New York: Routledge).

Hobson, J. (2000) *The State and International Relations* (Cambridge: Cambridge University Press).

Hobson, J. (2009) 'Provincializing Westphalia: The Eastern Origins of Sovereignty', *International Politics*, 46 (6): 671–90.

Hobson, J. (2012) *The Eurocentric Conception if World Politics* (Cambridge: Cambridge University Press)

Hoffmann, S. (1977) 'An American Social Science: International Relations', *Daedalus*, 106 (3): 41–59.

Hollis, R. (1997) 'Europe and the Middle East: Power by Stealth?', *International Affairs*, 73 (1): 15–29.

Hopf, E. (1998) 'The Promise of Constructivism in International Relations Theory', *International Security*, 23 (1): 171–200.

Hourani, A. (1961) *A Vision of History and Other Essays* (Beirut: Khayats).

Hourani, A. (1962) *Arabic Thought in the Liberal Age, 1789-1939* (Oxford: Oxford University Press).

Hourani, A. (1993) 'Introduction', in A. Hourani and M. Wilson (eds) *The Modern Middle East* (London: I. B. Tauris) pp. 1–20.

Hourani, A. (2002) *A History of the Arab Peoples* (London: Faber).

Howard, H. N. (1963) *The King-Crane Commission: An American Inquiry into the Middle East* (Beirut: Khayats).

Hudson, M. (1977) *Arab Politics: The Search for Legitimacy* (New Haven, CT: Yale University Press).

Hudson, M. (1992) 'Democracy and Foreign Policy in the Arab World', *The Beirut Review*, 4: 3–28.

Hudson, M. (1999) *Middle East Dilemma: The Politics and Economics of Arab Integration* (London: I. B. Tauris).

Human Security Centre (2005) *Human Security Report 2005: War and Peace in the Twenty-First Century* (Oxford: Oxford University Press).

Huntington, S. (1991) *The Third Wave: Democratization in the Late Twentieth Century* (Norman, OK: University of Oklahoma Press).

Huntington, S. (1996) *The Clash of Civilizations* (New York: Simon & Schuster).

Huntington, S. (1997) 'After Twenty Years: The Future of The Third Wave', *Journal of Democracy*, 8 (4): 1–12.

Hurewitz, J. C. (1975) *The Middle East and North Africa in World Politics: A Documentary Record, vol. 1, European Expansion, 1535-1914* (2nd edn, New Haven, CT: Yale University Press).

Hurewitz, J. C. (1976) *The Struggle for Palestine* (New York: Schocken Books).

Hurewitz, J. C. (1979) *The Middle East and North Africa in World Politics: A Documentary Record, vol. 2, British-French Supremacy, 1914-1945* (2nd edn, New Haven, CT: Yale University Press).

Hurrell, A. (1995) 'Explaining the Resurgence of Regionalism in World Politics', *Review of International Studies*, 21 (4): 331–58.

Huth, P. K. (1996) *Standing Your Ground: Territorial Disputes and International Conflict* (Ann Arbor, MI: University of Michigan Press).

Huth, P. K. (2000) 'Territory: Why Are Territorial Disputes between States a Central Cause of International Conflict?', in J. A. Vasquez (ed.) *What Do We Know about War?* (Lanham, MD: Rowman & Littlefield), pp. 85–110.

Ibrahim, S. E. (1995) 'Civil Society and the Prospects for Democratization in the Arab World', in A. R. Norton (ed.) *Civil Society in the Middle East, vol. I* (Leiden: E. J. Brill) pp. 27–54.

Ignatiev, M. (2003) 'The Burden', *New York Times Magazine*, 5 January.

Indyk, M. (2002) 'Back to the Bazaar', *Foreign Affairs*, 81 (1): 75–88.

International Commission on Intervention and State Sovereignty (ICISS) (2001) *The Responsibility to Protect* (Ottawa, ON: IDRC).

International Energy Agency (IEA) (2010) *World Energy Outlook* 2010 (Paris: IEA).

International Energy Agency (IEA) (2011) *World Energy Outlook* 2011 (Paris: IEA).

International Institute of Strategic Studies (IISS) (2006) 'Islamic Republic News Agency: Iran's Defense Spending "a Fraction of Persian Gulf Neighbours"', 31 May, available online at http://www.payvand.com/news/06/jun/1011.html

International Institute of Strategic Studies (IISS) (2012) *The Military Balance* 2012 (London: IISS).

International Institute of Strategic Studies (IISS) (2015) *The Military Balance* 2015 (London: IISS).

International Journal of Middle East Studies (2011) 'Round table discussion on the Cold War in the Middle East', 43: 313–25.

International Monetary Fund (IMF) (2007) *World Economic Outlook* 2007, available online at http://www.imf.org/external/pubs/ft/weo/2007/02/pdf/text.pdf

Internet World Statistics (2014) http://www.internetworldstats.com/ (accessed 7 January 2016).

Iraq Centre for Research and Strategy (IraqCRSS) (2006) *Public Opinion Survey in Iraq: Security and Political Situation*, November, available online at http://www.irqcrss.org/pdf/56.pdf

Irwin, R. (2006). *For Lust of Knowing: The Orientalists and their Enemies* (New York: Allen Lane).

Isaac, S. K. (2014) 'Explaining the Patterns of the Gulf Monarchies' Assistance after the Arab Uprisings', *Mediterranean Politics*, 19 (3): 413–30.

Ismael, T. Y. (1986) *International Relations of the Contemporary Middle East: A Study in World Politics* (Syracuse, NY: Syracuse University Press).

Ismael, T. Y. (2008) *The Rise and Fall of the Communist Party of Iraq* (Cambridge: Cambridge University Press).

Ismail, S. (2013) 'Urban Subalterns in the Arab Revolutions: Cairo and Damascus in Comparative Perspective', *Comparative Studies in Society and History*, 55 (4): 865–94.

Itzkowitz, N. and Mote, M. (1970) *Mubadele: An Ottoman-Russian Exchange of Ambassadors* (Chicago, IL: University of Chicago Press).

Jankowski, J. and Gershoni, I. (eds) (1997) *Rethinking Nationalism in the Arab Middle East* (New York: Columbia University Press).

Jarvis, A. (1989) 'Societies, States and Geopolitics: Challenges from Historical Sociology', *Review of International Studies*, 15 (July): 281–93.

Jentleson, B. W. (1994) *With Friends Like These: Reagan, Bush and Saddam, 1982–1990* (New York: W. W. Norton).

Jentleson, B. W. and Dassa Kaye, D. (1998) 'Security Status: Explaining Regional Security Cooperation and its Limits in the Middle East', *Security Studies*, 8 (Autumn): 204–38.

Jervis, R. (1978) 'Cooperation under the Security Dilemma', *World Politics*, 30 (2): 167–213.

Johnson, C. (1982) *MITI and the Japanese Miracle* (Stanford, CA: Stanford University Press).

Judis, J. (2014) *Genesis: Truman, American Jews, and the Origins of the Arab-Israeli Conflict* (New York: Farar, Strauss, and Giroux).

Kagan, R. (2003) *Of Paradise and Power: America and Europe in the New World Order* (New York: Knopf).

Kahler, M. and Lake, D. A. (2009) 'Economic Integration and Global Governance: Why So Little Supranationalism?' in W. Mattli and N. Woods (eds) *The Politics of Global Regulation* (Princeton, NJ: Princeton University Press), pp. 242–76.

Kaldor, M. (1999) *New and Old Wars: Violence in a Global Era* (Cambridge: Polity Press).

Kalyvas, S. (2006), *The Logic of Violence in Civil War* (Cambridge, Cambridge University Press).

Kamrava, M. (2000) 'Military Professionalization and Civil-Military Relations in the Middle East', *Political Science Quarterly*, 115 (1): 67–85.

Kamrava, M. (ed.) (2011) *International Politics of the Persian Gulf* (Syracuse, NY: Syracuse University Press).

Kamrava, M. (ed.) (2012) *The Nuclear Question in the Middle East* (London: Curzon).

Kandil, H. (2014) *Inside the Brotherhood* (Cambridge: Polity).

Kanovsky, E. (1968) 'Arab Economic Unity', in J. Nye (ed.) *International Regionalism* (Boston, MA: Little, Brown & Co.) pp. 370–6.

Karasipahi, S. (2009) 'Comparing Islamic Resurgence Movements in Turkey and Iran', *Middle East Journal*, 63 (1): 69–86.

Karawan, I. (1997) *Islamic Impasse*, Adelphi Paper 314 (London: IISS).

Karawan, I. (2002) 'Identity and Foreign Policy: The Case of Egypt', in S. Telhami and M. Barnett (eds) *Identity and Foreign Policy in the Middle East* (Ithaca, NY: Cornell University Press), pp. 155–68.

Karsh, E. (1990) 'Geopolitical Determinism: The Origins of the Iran—Iraq War', *Middle East Journal*, 44 (2): 256–68.

Kashani-Sabet, F. (1999) *Frontier Fictions: Shaping the Iranian Nation, 1804–1946* (Princeton, NJ: Princeton University Press).

Katib, L. (2011) *Islamic Revivalism in Syria: The Rise and Fall of Ba'thist Secularism* (New York: Routledge).

Katz, M. (2008) 'Russian-Iranian Relations in the Ahmadinejad Era', *Middle East Journal*, 62 (2): 202–16.

Katzenstein, P. (2005) *A World of Regions: Asia and Europe in the American Imperium* (Ithaca, NY: Cornell University Press).

Kaufman, A. (2001) 'Who Owns the Shebaa Farms? Chronicles of a Territorial Dispute', *Middle East Journal*, 56 (4): 576–96.

Kaufman, A. (2006) 'Between Palestine and Lebanon: Seven Shi'i Villages as a Case Study of Boundaries, Identities and Conflict', *Middle East Journal*, 60 (4): 686–706.

Kaufman, A. (2009) ' "Let Sleeping Dogs Lie": On Ghajar and other Anomalies in the Syria-Lebanon-Israel Tri-Border Region', *Middle East Journal*, 63 (4): 539–60.

Keck, M. and Sikkink, K. (eds) (1998) *Activists beyond Borders: Advocacy Networks in International Politics* (Ithaca, NY: Cornell University Press).

Keddie, N. R. (2003) *Modern Iran: Roots and Results of Revolution* (New Haven, CT: Yale University Press).

Kedourie, E. (1992) *Democracy and Arab Political Culture* (Washington, DC: Washington Institute for Near East Policy).

Keene, E. (2013) 'International Hierarchy and the Origins of the Modern Practice of Intervention', *Review of International Studies*, 39 (5): 1077–90.

Kelsay, J. (1993) *Islam and War: A Study in Comparative Ethics* (Louisville, KY: Westminster/John Knox Press).

Keohane, R. O. (1984) *After Hegemony: Cooperation and Discord in the World Political Economy* (Princeton, NJ: Princeton University Press).

Keohane, R. O. and Martin, L. L. (1995) 'The Promise of Institutionalist Theory', *International Security*, 20 (1): 39–51.

Kerr, M. H. (1967) *The Arab Cold War, 1958–1967: A Study of Ideology in Politics* (Oxford: Oxford University Press).

Kerr, M. (1971) *The Arab Cold War: Gamal abd al-Nasir and his Rivals, 1958–70* (Oxford: Oxford University Press).

Kerr, M. and El Sayed, Y. (eds) (1982) *Rich and Poor Nations in the Middle East: Egypt and the New Arab Order* (Boulder, CO: Westview Press).

Khadduri, M. (1955) *War and Peace in the Law of Islam* (Baltimore, MD: Johns Hopkins Press).

Khadduri, M. (1988) *The Gulf War: The Origins and Implications of the Iraq-Iran Conflict* (New York: Oxford University Press).

Khalaf, A. and Luciani, G. (eds) (2006) *Constitutional Reform and Political Participation in the Gulf* (Dubai: Gulf Research Center).

Khaled, A. (2014) 'International Assistance to Egypt after the 2011 and 2013 Uprisings: More Politics and Less Development', *Mediterranean Politics* 19 (3): 392–412.

Khalidi, R. (1997) 'The Formation of Palestinian Identity 1917–23', in J. Jankowski and I. Gershoni (eds) *Rethinking Nationalism in the Arab Middle East* (New York: Columbia University Press), pp. 171–90.

Khalidi, R. (2009) *Sowing Crisis: The Cold War and American Dominance in the Middle East* (Boston, MA, Beacon Press).

Khalidi, R., Anderson, L., Muslih, M., and Simon, R. S. (eds) (1991) *The Origins of Arab Nationalism* (New York: Columbia University Press).

Khoury, N. (1982) 'The Pragmatic Trend in Inter-Arab Politics', *Middle East Journal*, 36 (3): 374–87.

Khoury, P. S. (1987) *Syria and the French Mandate: The Politics of Arab Nationalism, 1920–1945* (Princeton, NJ: Princeton University Press).

Khoury, P. S. and Kostiner, J. (1990) *Tribes and State Formation in the Middle East* (Berkeley, CA: University of California Press).

Kienle, E. (1990) *Ba'th vs Ba'th: The Conflict between Syria and Iraq* (London: I. B. Tauris).

Kienle, E. (1995) 'Arab Unity Schemes Revisited: Interest, Identity, and Policy in Syria and Egypt', *International Journal of Middle East Studies*, 27 (1): 53–71.

Kim, M. and Wolford, S. (2014) 'Choosing Anarchy: Institutional Alternatives and the Global Order', *International Theory*, 6 (1): 28–67.

Kim, T. (2011) 'Why Alliances Entangle but Seldom Entrap States', *Security Studies*, 20 (3): 350–77.

Kirby, O. (2000) 'Want a Democracy? Get a King', *Middle East Quarterly*, 7 (4): 3–12.

Kirpatrick, D. D. (2012) 'Islamist Victors in Egypt Seeking Shift by Hamas', *New York Times*, 24 March.

Knafo, S. (2010) 'Critical Approaches and the Legacy of the Agent/Structure Debate in International Relations', *Cambridge Review of International Affairs*, 23 (3): 493–516.

Kocs, S. A. (1995) 'Territorial Disputes and Interstate War, 1945–1987', *Journal of Politics*, 57 (1): 159–75.

Korany, B. (1987) 'Alien and Besieged yet Here to Stay: The Contradictions of the Arab Territorial State', in G. Salamé (ed.) *The Foundations of the Arab State* (London: Croom Helm), pp. 47–74.

Korany, B. (1998) 'The Arab World and the New Balance of Power in the New Middle East' in Michael Hudson (ed.) *Middle East Dilemma: The Politics and Economics of Arab Integration*. London: IBTauris, pp.35–59.

Korany, B. (1999a) 'International Relations Theory: Contributions from Research in the Middle East', in M. Tessler, J. Nachtway, and A. Banda (eds) *Area Studies and Social Science: Strategies for Understanding Middle East Politics* (Bloomington, IN: Indiana University Press), pp. 148–58.

Korany, B. (1999b) 'The Arab World and the New Balance of Power in the New Middle East', in M. C. Hudson (ed.) *Middle East Dilemma* (New York: Columbia University Press).

Korany B. (2009) 'The Middle East since the Cold War: Still Insecure', in L. Fawcett (ed.) *The International Relations of the Middle East* (Oxford: Oxford University Press), pp. 61–78.

Korany, B. (ed.) (2010) *The Changing Middle East: A New Look at Regional Dynamics* (New York and Cairo: American University in Cairo Press).

Korany, B. (2011a) 'Middle East Regionalisms: Can an Institution Bridge Geo-Culture to Geo-Economics?', in T. M. Shaw, J. A. Grant, and S. Cornelissen (eds) *The Ashgate Research Companion to Regionalisms* (Aldershot: Ashgate), pp. 273–93.

Korany, B. (ed.) (2011b) *The Changing Middle East: A New Look at Regional Dynamics*. A Tahrir studies edition (Cairo, Egypt New York: American University in Cairo Press)

Korany, B. (2012) 'Egypt and Beyond: The Arab Spring, The New Pan-Arabism and the Challenge of Transition', in B. Korany and R. El-Mahdi (eds) *The Arab Spring in Egypt: Revolution and Beyond* (Cairo: American University in Cairo Press), pp. 271–94.

Korany, B. (ed.) (2014) *Arab Human Development in the 21st Century* (Cairo and New York: American University in Cairo Press).

Korany, B. and Dessouki, H. A. E. (eds) (1991) *The Foreign Policies of Arab States: The Challenge of Change* (Boulder, CO: Westview Press).

Korany, B. and Dessouki, H. A. E. (eds) (2008) *The Foreign Policies of Arab States: The Challenge of Globalization* (Boulder, CO: Westview Press).

Korany, B. and El-Mahdi, R. (eds) (2012) *Arab Spring in Egypt: Revolution and Beyond* (New York and Cairo: American University in Cairo Press).

Korany, B., Noble, P., and Brynen, R. (eds) (1993) *The Many Faces of National Security in the Arab World* (London: Macmillan/New York: St Martin's Press)

Korany, B., Brynen, R., and Noble, P. (eds) (1998) *Political Liberalization and Democratization in the Arab World: Comparative Experiences vol. 2* (Boulder, CO: Lynne Rienner).

Kostiner, J. (1987) 'Shi'i Unrest in the Gulf', in M. Kramer (ed.) *Shi'ism, Resistance and Revolution* (Boulder, CO: Westview Press), pp. 173–86.

Kostiner, J. (2010) 'Saudi Arabia and the Arab-Israeli Peace Process: The Fluctuation of Regional Coordination', in M. Legrenzi (ed.) *Security in the Gulf: Historical Legacies and Future Prospects* (London: Routledge).

Kozak, C. (2015) 'An Army in All Corners. Assad's Campaign Strategy in Syria'. *Middle East Security Report 26*. Institute for the Study of War. http://understandingwar.org/sites/default/files/An%20Army%20in%20All%20Corners%20by%20Chris%20Kozak%201.pdf (Retrieved: 20 May 2015).

Kramer, M. (1986) *Islam Assembled: The Advent of the Muslim Congresses* (Colombia, NY: Columbia University Press).

Kramer, M. (1990) 'Syria Alawis and Shi'ism', in M. Kramer (ed.) *Shi'ism: Resistance* (London: I. B. Tauris) pp. 237–54.

Kramer, M. (2001) *Ivory Towers on Sand: The Failure of Middle Eastern Studies in America*, Policy Papers 58 (Washington, DC: Washington Institute for Near East Policy).

Krasner, S. D. (1985) *Structural Conflict: The Third World against Global Liberalism* (Berkeley, CA: University of California Press).

Krasner, S. D. (1999) *Sovereignty: Organized Hypocrisy* (Princeton, NJ: Princeton University Press).

Krasner, S. D. (2001) *Problematic Sovereignty: Contested Rules and Political Possibilities* (New York; Chichester: Columbia University Press).

Kratochwil, F. (2000) 'Constructing a New Orthodoxy? Wendt's "Social Theory of International Politics" and the Constructivist Challenge"', *Millennium*, 29 (1): 73–101.

Krause, K. (2004) 'State-Making and Region-Building: The Interplay of Domestic and Regional Security in the Middle East', in Z. Maoz, E. B. Landau and T. Malz (eds) *Building Regional Security in the Middle East* (London: Cass), pp. 99–124.

Krauss, C. and Lipton, E. (2012) 'US Inches toward Goal of Energy Independence', *New York Times*, 22 March, available online at http://www.nytimes.com/2012/03/23/business/energy-environment/inching-toward-energy-independence-in-america.html?_r=1&partner=rss&emc=rss&pagewanted=all

Kuniholm, B. (1980) *The Origins of the Cold War in the Near East: Great Power Conflict and Diplomacy in Iran, Turkey and Greece* (Princeton, NJ: Princeton University Press).

Kunz, D. B. (2002) 'The Emergence of the United States as a Middle Eastern Power, 1956–1968', in W. R. Louis and R. Owen (eds) *A Revolutionary Year: The Middle East in 1958* (London: I. B. Tauris/Washington, DC: Woodrow Wilson Center Press) pp. 77–100.

Kupchan, C. A. (1987) *The Persian Gulf and the West: The Dilemmas of Security* (Boston, MA: Allen & Unwin).

Kurtzer, D. and Scott, B. L. (2008) *Negotiating Arab-Israel Peace: American Leadership in the Middle East* (Washington, DC: United States Institute of Peace Press).

Kydd, A. (1997) 'Sheep in Sheep's Clothing: Why Security Seekers Do Not Fight Each Other', *Security Studies*, 7 (1): 114–54.

Labs, E. J. (1992) 'Do Weak States Bandwagon?', *Security Studies*, 1 (3): 383–416.

Labs, E. J. (1997) 'Beyond Victory: Offensive Realism and the Expansion of War Aims', *Security Studies*, 6 (4): 1–49.

Lacroix, S. (2010) *Les Islamistes Saoudiens* (Paris: Presses Universitaires de France).

Lacroix, S. (2012) 'Sheikhs and Politicians: Inside the New Egyptian Salafism', *Brookings Doha Centre Analysis Paper Number 16*, June 2012, http://www.brookings.edu/research/papers/2012/06/07-egyptian-salafism-lacroix

Ladiki, L. (2009) *Rethinking Arab Democratization: Elections without Democracy* (Oxford: Oxford University Press).

Lahn, G. and Stevens, P. (2011) *Burning Oil to Keep Cool: The Hidden Energy Crisis in Saudi Arabia* (London: Chatham House).

Lai, D. (2001) 'Alignment, Structural Balance and International Conflict in the Middle East, 1948–1978', *Conflict Management and Peace Science*, 18 (February): 211–50.

Laidi, Z. (1994) *Power and Purpose after the Cold War* (Oxford: Berg Publishers).

Lake, D. A. (1997) 'Regional Security Complexes: A Systems Approach', in D. A. Lake and P. M. Morgan (eds) *Regional Orders* (University Park, PA: Pennsylvania State University Press), pp. 45–67.

Lake, D. A. (2009) *Hierarchy in International Relations* (Ithaca, NY: Cornell University Press).

Landau, J. (1990) *The Politics of Pan-Islam: Ideology and Organization* (New York: Oxford University Press).

Laqueur, W. and Rubin, B. (eds) (1985) *The Israel-Arab Reader: A Documentary History of the Middle East Conflict* (Harmondsworth: Penguin).

Laqueur, W. and Rubin, B. (eds) (1995) *The Arab-Israeli Reader: A Documentary History of the Middle East Conflict* (5th edn, New York: Penguin).

Laron, G. (2013) *Origins of the Suez Crisis: Postwar Development Diplomacy and the Struggle over Third World Industrialization, 1945–1956* (Washington, DC: Woodrow Wilson Center Press).

Lawson, F. H. (1985) 'Positive Sanctions and the Managing of International Conflict: Five Middle Eastern Cases', *International Journal*, 40 (Autumn): 628–54.

Lawson, F. H. (1999) 'Theories of Integration in a New Context: The Gulf Cooperation Council', in K. P. Thomas and M. A. Tetreault (eds) *Racing to Regionalize* (Boulder, CO: Lynne Rienner), pp. 7–32.

Lawson, F. H. (2006) *Constructing International Relations in the Arab World* (Stanford, CA: Stanford University Press).

Lawson, F. H. (2007a) 'Syria's Relations with Iran: Managing the Dilemmas of Alliance', *Middle East Journal*, 61 (1): 31–47.

Lawson, F. H. (2007b) 'New Twists, More Intricate Configurations: The Changing Israel-Palestinian Regional Security Complex', *Perspectives on Global Development and Technology*, 6: 345–62.

Lawson, F. H. (2008) 'Comparing Regionalist Projects in the Middle East and Elsewhere: One Step Back, Two Steps Forward', in C. Harders and M. Legrenzi (eds) *Beyond Regionalism? Regional Cooperation, Regionalism and Regionalization in the Middle East* (Aldershot: Ashgate), pp. 13–32.

Lawson, F. H. (2011) 'Security Dilemmas in the Contemporary Persian Gulf', in M. Kamrava (ed.) *International Politics of the Persian Gulf* (Syracuse, NY: Syracuse University Press), pp. 50–71.

Lebovic, J. H. (2004) 'Unity in Action: Explaining Alignment Behavior in the Middle East', *Journal of Peace Research*, 41 (1): 167–89.

Lebow, R. N. and Valentino, B. (2009) 'Lost in Transition: A Critical Analysis of Power Transition Theory', *International Relations*, 23 (3): 389–410.

Legrenzi, M. (2008) 'Did the GCC Make a Difference? Institutional Realities and (Un)intended Consequences', in C. Harders and M. Legrenzi (eds) *Beyond Regionalism? Regional Cooperation, Regionalism and Regionalization in the Middle East* (Aldershot: Ashgate), pp. 107–224.

Legrenzi, M. (2010) *Security in the Gulf: Historical Legacy and Future Prospects* (London: Routledge).

Legrenzi, M. (2011) *The GCC and the International Relations of the Gulf: Diplomacy, Security and Economic Coordination in a Changing Middle East* (London: I. B. Tauris).

Legrenzi, M. and Momani, B. (2011) *Shifting Geo-Economic Power of Gulf: Oil, Finance and Institutions* (New York: Ashgate).

Lemke, D. (1996) 'Small States and War', in J. Kugler and D. Lemke (eds) *Parity and War* (Ann Arbor, MI: University of Michigan Press), pp. 77–92.

Lemke, D. (2010) 'Dimensions of Hard Power: Regional Leadership and Material Capabilities', in D. Flemes (ed.) *Regional Leadership in the Global System* (Aldershot: Ashgate).

Lesch, D. W. (ed.) (1996) *The Middle East and the United States: A Historical and Political Reassessment* (Boulder, CO: Westview Press).

Lesch, D. W. (2007) *The Arab-Israeli Conflict: A History* (Oxford: Oxford University Press).

Lesch, D. W. and Haas, M. L. (2012) *The Middle East and the United States: History, Politics, Ideologies* (5th edn, Boulder, CO: Westview Press).

Levy, J. S. and Thompson, W. R. (2005) 'Hegemonic Threats and Great-Power Balancing in Europe, 1495–1999', *Security Studies*, 14 (1): 1–33.

Levy, J. S. and Thompson, W. R. (2010) *Causes of War* (Chichester: Wiley-Blackwell).

Lieberman, E. (1994) 'The Rational Deterrence Theory Debate: Is the Dependent Variable Elusive', *Security Studies*, 3 (3): 384–427.

Lieberman, E. (1995) 'What Makes Deterrence Work? Lessons from the Egyptian-Israeli Rivalry', *Security Studies*, 4 (4): 851–910.

Linklater, A. (2009) 'The English School', in S. Burchill, A. Linklater, R. Devetak, and J. Donnelly (eds) *Theories of International Relations* (4th edn, London: Palgrave Macmillan), pp. 86–110.

Linklater, A. and Suganami, H. (2006) *The English School of International Relations: A Contemporary Assessment* (Cambridge: Cambridge University Press).

Little, R. (2000) 'The English School's Contribution to the Study of International Relations', *European Journal of International Relations*, 6 (3): 395–422.

Llewellyn, T. (2008) 'Obituary', *The Guardian*, 14 February.

Long, D. and Koch, C. (eds) (1997) *Gulf Security in the Twenty-First Century* (London: British Academic Press for Emirates Centre for Strategic Studies and Research).

Louis, W. R. (1984) *The British Empire in the Middle East 1945–1951: Arab Nationalism, the United States and Postwar Imperialism* (Oxford: Oxford University Press).

Louis, W. R. (1986) 'British Imperialism and the End of the Palestine Mandate', in W. R. Louis and R. W. Stookey (eds) *The End of the Palestine Mandate* (Austin, TX: University of Texas Press), pp. 1–31.

Louis, W. R. (ed.) (1988) *Mussadiq, Nationalism and Oil* (Austin, TX: University of Texas Press).

Louis, W. R. and Owen, R. (2002) *A Revolutionary Year: The Middle East in* 1958 (London: I. B. Tauris/ Washington, DC: Woodrow Wilson Center Press).

Louis, W. R. and Shlaim, A. (eds) (2012) *The 1967 Arab-Israeli War: Origins and Consequences* (Cambridge: Cambridge University Press).

Luciani, G. (1987) 'Allocation vs. Production States: A Theoretical Framework', in H. Beblawi and G. Luciani (eds) *The Rentier State* (London and New York: Croom Helm).

Luciani, G. (1990) *The Arab State* (Berkeley, CA: University of California Press).

Luciani, G. (1994) 'The Oil Rent, the Fiscal Crisis of the State and Democratization', in G. Salamé (ed.) *Democracy without Democrats: The Renewal of Politics in the Muslim World* (London: I. B. Tauris) pp. 130–55.

Luciani, G. (2013) 'Businesses and the Revolution' in S. Hertog, G. Luciani, and M. Valeri (eds) *Business Politics in the Middle East* (London: Hurst).

Luciani, G. (2015) 'On the Economic Causes of the Arab Spring and its Possible Developments', in K. Selvik and B. O. Utvik (eds) *Oil States in the New Middle East*, Routledge Abingdon and New York

Luciani, G. and Salamé, S. (eds) (1988) *The Politics of Arab Integration* (New York: Croom Helm).

Lustick, I. (1993) *Unsettled States, Disputed Lands: Britain and Ireland, France and Algeria, Israel and the West Bank-Gaza* (Ithaca, NY: Cornell University Press).

Lustick, I. (1997) 'The Absence of Middle Eastern Great Powers: Political "Backwardness" in Historical Perspective', *International Organization*, 51 (4): 653–83.

Lynch, M. (2006) *Voices of the New Arab Public: Iraq, al-Jazeera, and Middle East Politics Today* (New York: Columbia University Press).

Lynch, M. (2012) *The Arab Uprisings: The Unfinished Revolutions of the New Middle East* (New York: Public Affairs).

Lynch, M. (ed) (2014) *The Arab Uprisings Explained: New Contentious Politics in the Middle East* (Columbia: Columbia University Press).

Lynn-Jones, S. M. (1995) 'Offense-Defense Theory and its Critics', *Security Studies*, 4 (4): 660–91.

McClellan, S. (2008) *What Happened: Inside the Bush White House and Washington's Culture of Deception* (New York: Public Affairs).

McDonald, P. J. (2007) 'The Purse Strings of Peace', *American Journal of Political Science*, 51 (3): 569–82.

Mahdavy, H. (1970) 'The Patterns and Problems of Economic Development in Rentier States: The Case of Iran', in M. Cook (ed.) *Studies in the Economic History of the Middle East* (Oxford: Oxford University Press), pp. 428–67.

Makiya, K. (1993) *Cruelty and Silence: War, Tyranny, Uprising and the Arab World* (London: Jonathan Cape).

Makiya, K. (1998) *Republic of Fear: The Politics of Modern Iraq* (3rd edn, Berkeley, CA: University of California Press).

Makovsky, D. (1996) *Making Peace with the PLO: The Rabin Government's Road to the Oslo Accord* (Boulder, CO: Westview Press).

Malley, R. and Agha, H. (2001) 'Camp David: The Tragedy of Errors', *New York Review of Books*, 9 August.

Mandaville, P. (2001) *Transnational Muslim Politics: Reimagining the* Umma (London: Routledge).

Mandaville, P. (2007) *Global Political Islam* (London: Routledge).

Mandaville, P. (2014) *Islam and Politics* (London: Routledge)

Mann, J. (2004) *The Rise of the Vulcans: The History of Bush's War Cabinet* (New York: Viking).

Mann, J. (2008) 'What Will the Pillars of His Foreign Policy Be?', *Washington Post*, 15 June.

Mansfield, E. D. and Snyder, J. (1995) 'Democratization and the Danger of War', *International Security*, 20 (1): 5–38.

Mansfield, E. D. and Solingen, E. (2010) 'Regionalism', *Annual Review of Political Science*, 13: 145–63.

Maoz, Z. (1998) 'Regional Security in the Middle East: Past Trends, Present Realities and Future Challenges', in Z. Maoz (ed.) *Regional Security in the Middle East* (London: Frank Cass), pp. 1–45.

Maoz, Z. (2009) *Defending the Holy Land* (Ann Arbor, MI: University of Michigan Press).

Maoz, Z. and Mor, B. (2002) *Bound by Struggle: The Strategic Evolution of Enduring International Rivalries* (Ann Arbor: University of Michigan Press).

Marr, P. (2011) *The Modern History of Iraq* (3rd edn, Boulder, CO: Westview Press).

Martin, L. L. (1992) 'Interests, Power and Multilateralism', *International Organization*, 46 (4): 765–92.

Martin, L. L. and Simmons, B. A. (1998) 'Theories and Empirical Studies of International Institutions', *International Organization*, 52 (4): 729–57.

Masalha, N. (2000) *Imperial Israel and the Palestinians: The Politics of Expansion* (London: Pluto Press).

Masalha, S. (2011) 'Recent Revolutions are neither Arab nor Spring', *Haaretz*, 5 December, in http://www.haaretz.com/print-edition/opinion/recent-revolutions-are-neither-arab-nor-spring-1.399552 (Accessed: 27 December 2011).

Massad, J. (2011) 'Arab Revolts, Past & Present', *Al-Jazeera English*, 18 November, http://aljazeerait.net/indepth/opinion/2011/11/2011111810259215940.html (Accessed: 29 December 2011).

Matar, G. and Dessouki, A. H. (1983) *al-Nizam al-Iqlimi al-'Arabi* (Beirut: Dar al-Mustaqbal al-'Arabi).

Mayer, J. and Rotte, R. (1999) 'Arms and Aggression in the Middle East,1948–1991', *Journal of Conflict Resolution*, 43 (1): 45–57.

Mearsheimer, J. J. (2001) *The Tragedy of Great Power Politics* (New York: Norton).

Mearsheimer, J. J. and Walt, S. M. (2007) *The Israel Lobby and US Foreign Policy* (New York: Farrar, Straus and Giroux).

Medzini, M. (ed.) (1995) *Israel's Foreign Relations: Selected Documents, 1992–1994*, vol. 13 (Jerusalem: Ministry of Foreign Affairs).

Meital, Y. (2006) *Peace in Tatters: Israel, Palestine, and the Middle East* (Boulder, CO: Lynne Reinner).

Melman, Y. (2007) 'Inside Intel/Not a Reactor—Something Far More Vicious', *Haaretz*, 22 November, available online at http://www.haaretz.com/print-edition/features/inside-intel-not-a-reactor-something-far-more-vicious-1.233789

Menashri, D. (1990) *Iran: A Decade of War and Revolution* (New York: Holmes and Meier).

Mendelsohn, B. (2012) 'God vs. Westphalia: Radical Islamist Movements and the Battle for Organising the World', *Review of International Studies*, 38 (3): 589–613.

Meral, Z. (2011) 'Israel: A model for the Future of Egypt', Channel 4 News, 3 February, http://www.channel4.com/news/israel-the-model-for-the-future-of-egypt (Accessed: 20 September 2011).

MERMI. http://www.memri.org/bin/articles.cgi?Page=archives&Area=ia&ID=IA26506

Meyer, D. and Whittier, N. (1994) 'Social Movement Spillover', in *Social Problems*, 41 (2): 277–98.

Migdal, J. S. (2001) *State in Society: Studying How States and Societies Transform and Constitute One Another*. Cambridge Studies in Comparative Politics (Cambridge: Cambridge University Press).

Miller, B. (1992) 'Explaining Great Power Cooperation in Conflict Management', *World Politics*, 45 (1): 1–46.

Miller, B. (2003) 'Conflict Management in the Middle East: Between the "Old" and the "New"', in P. F. Diehl and J. Lepgold (eds) *Regional Conflict Management* (Lanham, MD: Rowman & Littlefield), pp. 153–208.

Miller, B. (2004) 'The International System and Regional Balance in the Middle East', in T. V. Paul (ed.) *Balance of Power: Theory and Practice in the 21st Century* (Stanford, CA: Stanford University Press).

Miller, B. (2006) 'Balance of Power or the State-to-Nation Balance: Explaining Middle East War-Propensity', *Security Studies*, 15 (4): 658–705.

Milton Edwards, B. (2011) *Contemporary Politics in the Middle East* (revd edn, Cambridge: Polity Press).

Mitchell, T. (1988) *Colonising Egypt* (New York: Cambridge University Press).

Mitzen, J. (2005) 'Reading Habermas in Anarchy: Multilateral Diplomacy and Global Public Spheres', *American Political Science Review*, 99 (3): 401–17.

Mockli, D. and Mauer, V. (eds) (2011) *European-American Relations and the Middle East* (London and New York: Routledge).

Moghadam, A. (2009) 'Motives for Martyrdom: Al-Qaida, Salafi Jihad, and the Spread of Suicide Attacks', *International Security*, 33 (3): 46–78.

Mojtahed-Zadeh, P. (1994) 'A Geopolitical Triangle in the Persian Gulf: Actions and Reactions among Iran, Bahrain and Saudi Arabia', *Iranian Journal of International Affairs*, 6 (1–2): 47–59.

Monier, E. (2014) 'The Arabness of Middle East regionalism: the Arab Spring and competition for discursive hegemony between Egypt, Iran and Turkey'. *Contemporary Politics*, 20 (4): 421–34.

Monier, E. (ed.) (2015) *Regional Insecurity After the Arab Uprisings. Narratives of Security and Threat* (Basingstoke: Palgrave).

Moore, C. H. (1980) *Images of Development: Egyptian Engineers in Search of Industry* (Cambridge, MA: MIT Press).

Mor, B. D. (2003) 'The Onset of Enduring Rivalries: A Progress Report', *International Politics*, 40 (1): 29–57.

Morris, B. (2002) 'Camp David and After: An Interview with Ehud Barak', *New York Review of Books*, 13 June.

Morris, B. and Barak, E. (2002) 'Camp David and After: Continued', *New York Review of Books*, 27 June.

Morsy, A. (2013) 'Morsi's Unrevolutionary Foreign Policy', Middle East Institute, April 4, http://www.mideasti.org/content/morsi%E2%80%99s-un-revolutionary-foreign-policy

Mosely, P. E. (1969) 'Soviet Search for Security', in J. C. Hurewitz (ed.) *Soviet-American Rivalry in the Middle East* (New York: Praeger, for the Academy of Political Science Columbia University), pp. 216–27.

Moul, W. B. (1985) 'Balances of Power and European Great Power War 1815–1939: A Suggestion and Some Evidence', *Canadian Journal of Political Science*, 18 (3): 481–528.

Moul, W. B. (1993) 'Polarization, Polynomials and War', *Journal of Conflict Resolution*, 37 (4): 735–48.

Moul, W. B. (2003) 'Power Parity, Preponderance and War between Great Powers, 1816–1989', *Journal of Conflict Resolution*, 47 (4): 468–89.

Moul, W. B. (2005) 'Counting the Seven Weeks War: Dyads, Disputes and Balances of Power', *Canadian Journal of Political Science*, 38 (March): 153–74.

Moussa, A. (2012) 'The UN and the League of Arab States', in P. Lombaerde, F. Baert, and T. Felicio (eds) *The United Nations and the Regions* (Dordrecht: Springer).

Mowle, T. (2007) *Unipolar World* (London: Palgrave Macmillan).

Mufti, M. (1996) *Sovereign Creations: Pan-Arabism and Political Order in Syria and Iraq* (Ithaca, NY: Cornell University Press).

Murden, S. (2002) *Islam, the Middle East, and the New Global Hegemony* (Boulder, CO: Lynne Rienner).

Muslih, M. (1991) 'The Rise of Local Nationalism in the Arab East' in R. Khalidi, L. Anderson, M. Muslih, and R. Simon (eds) *The Origins of Arab Nationalism* (New York: Columbia University Press), pp. 167–85.

Mustafa, H. (2011) 'Al-Thawrah al-Masriyyah: 'Awdat al-Ruh wa al-Wa'y' [The Egyptian Revolution: The Return of Consciousness and Spiritedness to Egypt], *Majallat Al-Dimuqratiyyah*, 42: 6–14.

Mutawi, S. (1987) *Jordan in the 1967 War* (Cambridge: Cambridge University Press).

Nabers, D. (2010) 'Power, Leadership and Hegemony in International Politics', in D. Flemes (ed.) *Regional Leadership in the Global System* (Aldershot: Ashgate), pp. 51–70.

Nabli, M. (2007) 'Talking points: MENA 2007 Economic Developments and Prospects Press Conference' Saturday, 14 April. http://siteresources.worldbank.org/INTMENA/Resources/TalkingpointsMustapha.pdf

Naff, T. (1984) 'The Ottoman Empire and the European States System', in H. Bull and A. Watson (eds) *The Expansion of International Society* (Oxford: Clarendon Press), pp. 143–70.

Nahas, M. (1985) 'State Systems and Revolutionary Challenge: Nasser, Khomeini and the Middle East', *International Journal of Middle East Studies*, 17 (4): 507–27.

Narang, V. and Nelson, R. M. (2009) 'Who Are These Belligerent Democratizers? Reassessing the Impact of Democratization on War', *International Organization*, 63 (2): 357–79.

Nasr, V. (2005) 'The Rise of 'Muslim Democracy', *Journal of Democracy*, 16 (2): 13–27.

Nasr, V. (2006) *The Shia Revival: How Conflicts within Islam Will Shape the Future* (New York: W. W. Norton).

Nasr, S. V. R. (2013) *The Dispensable Nation: American Foreign Policy in Retreat* (New York: Doubleday).

Neumann, S. (ed.) (1998) *International Relations Theory and the Third World* (New York: St Martin's Press)

Nevakivi, J. (1969) *Britain, France and the Arab Middle East, 1914–1920* (London: Athlone Press).

Niblock, T. (1990) 'The Need for a New Arab Order', *Middle East International*, 385: 17–8.

Noble, P. (1991) 'The Arab System: Pressures, Constraints, and Opportunities', in B. Korany and H. A. E Dessouki (eds) *The Foreign Policies of Arab States: The Challenge of Change* (Boulder, CO: Westview Press), pp. 41–78.

Noble, P. (2008) 'From Arab System to Middle Eastern System? Regional Pressures and Constraints', in B. Korany and A. E. Dessouki (eds) *The Foreign Policies of the Arab States* (New York and Cairo: American University of Cairo Press), pp. 67–166.

Nolte, D. (2010) 'How to compare regional powers: analytical concepts and research topics', *Review of International Studies*, 36 (4): 881–901.

Nonneman, G. (1986) *Iraq, the Gulf States and the War* (London: Ithaca Press).

Nonneman, G. (1996) 'The (Geo)Political Economy of Iraqi-Kuwaiti Relations', *Geopolitics and International Boundaries*, 1 (2): 178–223.

Nonneman, G. (2001) 'Rentiers and Autocrats, Monarchs and Democrats, State and Society: The Middle East between Globalization, Human Agency and Europe', *International Affairs*, 77 (1): 141–62.

Norton, A. R. (1995) 'The Challenge of Inclusion in the Middle East', *Current History*, 97: 1–6.

Norton, A. R. (2003) 'The New Media, Civic Pluralism and the Struggle for Political Reform', in D. F. Eickelman and J. W. Anderson (eds) *New Media in the Muslim World: The Emerging Public Sphere* (Bloomington, IN: Indiana University Press), pp. 19–32.

Norton, A. R. (ed.) (2005) *Civil Society in the Middle East* (2 vols, Leiden: E. J. Brill)

Norton, A. R. (2007a) *Hezbollah: A Short History* (Princeton, NJ: Princeton University Press).

Norton, A. R. (2007b) 'The Role of Hezbollah in Lebanese Domestic Politics', *The International Spectator*, 42 (4): 475–91.

Nye, J. (ed.) (1968) *International Regionalism* (Boston, MA: Little, Brown & Co.)

Nye, J. (1971) *Peace in Parts* (Boston, MA: Little Brown & Co.).

Nye, J. (1997) *Understanding International Conflicts* (New York: Longman).

Nye, J. (2003) 'US Power and Strategy after Iraq', *Foreign Affairs*, 82 (4): 60–73.

Nye, J. (2004) *Soft Power: The Means to Success in World Politics* (New York: Public Affairs Press).

O'Hanlon, M. E. and Livingston, I. (2011) *Iraq Index: Tracking Variables of Reconstructions and Security in Post-Saddam Iraq*, available online at http://www.brookings.edu/~/MEDIA/CENTERS/SABAN/IRAQ%20INDEX/INDEX20120131.PDF

Okruhlik, G. and Conge, P. J. (1999) 'The Politics of Border Disputes on the Arabian Peninsula', *International Journal*, 54 (2): 230–48.

Oneal, J. R. and Russett, B. (1999) 'The Kantian Peace: The Pacific Benefits of Democracy, Interdependence and International Organizations, 1885–1992', *World Politics*, 52 (1): 1–37.

OPEC Annual Report (2015) http://www.opec.org/opec_web/en/publications/337.htm

OPEC World Oil Outlook (2015) http://www.opec.org/opec_web/en/publications/340.htm

Oren, I. (1990) 'The War Proneness of Alliances', *Journal of Conflict Resolution*, 34 (2): 208–33.

Organization of the Petroleum Exporting Countries (OPEC) (1991) *OPEC Annual Statistical Bulletin* 1990vn (Vienna: OPEC).

Organization of the Petroleum Exporting Countries (OPEC) (2005) *OPEC Annual Statistical Bulletin* 2004 (Vienna: OPEC).

Organization of the Petroleum Exporting Countries (OPEC) (2008) *OPEC Annual Report* 2007, available online at http://www.opec.org/opec_web/static_files_project/media/downloads/publications/AR2007.pdf

Organski, A. F. K. and Kugler, J. (1980) *The War Ledger* (Chicago, IL: University of Chicago Press).

Osiander, A. (2001) 'Sovereignty, International Relations and the Westphalian Myth', *International Organization*, 55 (2): 251–87.

Osman, T. (2011) *Egypt on the Brink* (New Haven, CT: Yale University Press).

Osterhammel, J. (1997) *Colonialism: A Theoretical Overview*, trans. S. L. Frisch (Princeton, NJ: Markus Wiener).

Ottaway, M. and Muasher, M. (2011) *Arab Monarchies: Chance for Reform, Yet Unmet*, Carnegie Paper, available online at http://carnegieendowment.org/2011/12/16/arab-monarchies-chance-for-reform-yet-unmet/8e7t

Owen, R. (1981) *The Middle East in the World Economy, 1800–1914* (London: Methuen).

Owen, R. (1999) 'Inter-Arab Economic Relations during the Twentieth Century: World Market versus Regional Market?', in M. Hudson (ed.) *Middle East Dilemma: The Politics and Economics of Arab Integration* (London: I. B. Tauris) pp. 217–32.

Owen, R. (2004) *State Power and Politics in the Making of the Modern Middle East* (revd edn, London: Routledge).

Owen, R. (2012) *The Rise and Fall of Arab Presidents for Life* (Cambridge, MA: Harvard University Press).

Oye, K. (1985) 'Explaining Cooperation under Anarchy', *World Politics*, 38 (1): 1–24.

Packer, G. (2005) *The Assassins' Gate: America in Iraq* (New York: Farrar, Straus and Giroux).

Parasiliti, A. (2003) 'The Causes and Timing of Iraq's Wars: A Power Cycle Assessment', *International Political Science Review*, 24 (1): 151–65.

Parasiliti, A. (2012) 'Leaving Iraq', *Survival*, 54 (1): 127–33.

Paris, T. J. (2003) *Britain, the Hashemites and Arab Rule, 1920–1925: The Sherifian Solution* (London: Frank Cass).

Parker, R. (1993) *The Politics of Miscalculation in the Middle East* (Bloomington, IN: Indiana University Press).

Parker, R. (ed.) (1996) *The Six Day War: A Retrospective* (Gainesville, FL: University of Florida Press).

Parsi, V. E. (1998) *Interesse Nazionale e Globalizzazione* (Milan: Yacabook).

Parsi, T. (2005) 'Israel-Iranian Relations Assessed: Strategic Competition from the Power Cycle Perspective', *Iranian Studies*, 38 (2): 247–69.

Parsi, V. E. (2009) 'L'entropia dell'ordine mediorientale e l'ascesa dell'Iran', in E. Brighi and F. Petito (eds) *Il Mediterraneo nelle Relazioni Internazionali* (Milan: Vita & Pensiero, Milan) pp. 78–91.

Patten, C. (2003) 'Democracy Doesn't Flow from the Barrel of a Gun', *Foreign Policy*, 138 (September–October): 40–4.

Peceny, M. and Beer, C. C. (2002) 'A Dictatorial Peace?' *American Political Science Review*, 96 (March): 18–26.

Peceny, M. and Beer, C. C. (2003) 'Peaceful Parties and Puzzling Personalists', *American Political Science Review*, 97 (2): 339–42.

Peceny, M. and Butler, C. K. (2004) 'The Conflict Behavior of Authoritarian Regimes', *International Politics*, 41 (4): 565–81.

Peleg, I. (2004) 'Israeli Foreign Policy under Right-Wing Governments: A Constructivist Interpretation', *Israel Studies Forum*, 19 (3): 1–14.

Pennell, C. R. (2000) *Morocco since 1830* (London: C. Hurst & Co.).

Penrose, E. T. (1967) *The Large International Firm in Developing Countries: The International Petroleum Industry* (Cambridge, MA: MIT Press).

Peres, S. (1995) *Battling for Peace: Memoirs* (London: Weidenfeld & Nicolson).

Peres, S. and Noar, A. (1993) *The New Middle East* (New York: Henry Holt and Co.).

Perle, R. (1996) *Clean Break: A New Strategy for Security the Realm*, IASPS Research Papers in Strategy (Jerusalem: Institute for Advanced Strategic and Political Studies).

Peters, J. (ed.) (2012) *The European Union and the Arab Spring: Promoting Democracy and Human Rights in the Middle East* (Lanham, MD: Lexington).

Peterson, J. E. (1986) *Defending Arabia* (London: Palgrave Macmillan).

Peterson, J. E. (2011) 'Sovereignty and Boundaries in the Gulf States', in M. Kamrava (ed.) *International Politics of the Persian Gulf* (Syracuse, NY: Syracuse University Press), pp. 21–49.

Phillips, C. (2011) 'Arabism after the Arab Spring', 31 July, available online at http://cjophillips.wordpress.com/2011/07/31/arabism-after-the-arab-spring/

Pierson, P. (2004) *Politics in Time, History, Institutions and Social Analysis* (Princeton: Princeton University Press).

Pinfari, M. (2009) *Nothing but Failure? The Arab League and the Gulf Cooperation Council as Mediators in Middle Eastern Conflict*, Crisis States Working Paper 45 (London: Crisis States Research Centre, LSE), available online at http://www2.lse.ac.uk/internationalDevelopment/research/crisisStates/download/wp/wpSeries2/WP452.pdf

Piscatori, J. (1986) *Islam in a World of Nation-States* (Cambridge: Cambridge University Press).

Podeh, E. (1993) 'The Struggle over Arab Hegemony after the Suez Crisis', *Middle Eastern Studies*, 29 (1): 91–110.

Podeh, E. (1999) *The Decline of Arab Unity: The Rise and Fall of the United Arab Republic* (Brighton: Sussex Academic Press).

Podeh, E. (2003) 'To Unite or Not to Unite—That is Not the Question: The 1963 Tripartite Unity Talks Reassessed', *Middle Eastern Studies*, 39 (1): 150–85.

Podeh, E. (2014) 'Israel and the Arab Peace Initiative, 2002–2014', *The Middle East Journal*, 68 (4): 584–603.

Pope, H. and Harling, P. (2011) 'Are There "Zero Problems" for Turkey?', *Daily Star* (Beirut), 29 November.

Posen, B. (1993) 'The Security Dilemma and Ethnic Conflict', *Survival*, 35 (1): 27–47.

Posusney, M. P. and Angrist, M. P. (eds) (2005) *Authoritarianism in the Middle East: Regimes and Resistance* (Boulder, CO: Lynne Rienner).

Potter, L. G. and Sick, G. G. (eds) (2002) *Security in the Persian Gulf* (New York: Palgrave).

Powell, R. (1991) 'Absolute and Relative Gains in International Relations Theory', *American Political Science Review*, 85 (4): 1303–20.

Pressman, J. (2003) 'Visions in Collision: What Happened at Camp David and Taba?', *International Security*, 28 (2): 5–43.

Priess, D. (1996) 'Balance of Threat Theory and the Genesis of the Gulf Cooperation Council', *Security Studies*, 5 (4): 143–71.

Primakov, Y. (2009) *Russia and the Arabs: Behind the Scenes in the Middle East from the Cold War to the Present* (New York: Basic Books).

Project for the New American Century (1997) 'Statement of Principles', 3 June, available online at http://www.newamericancentury.org/statementofprinciples.htm

Project for the New American Century (1998) 'Letter to President Clinton', 26 January, available online at http://www.newamericancentury.org/iraqclintonletter.htm

Pugh, M. and Sidhu, W. P. S. (2003) *The United Nations and Regional Security. Europe and Beyond* (Boulder, CO: Lynne Reinner).

Qawi, B. (2011) 'Karisma al-Shariʿ al-Tunisi wa Quwwat al-Taghyeer al-Siyasi' [The Tunisian People's Charisma and the Capacity for Political Transformation], *Majallat Al-Dimuqratiyyah*, 42: 141–52.

Quandt, W. B. (1993) *Peace Process: American Diplomacy and the Arab-Israeli Conflict Since 1967* (Washington, DC: Brookings Institution/Berkeley, CA: University of California Press).

Quandt, W. B. (2005) *Peace Process: American Diplomacy and the Arab-Israeli Conflict Since 1967* (3rd edn, Washington, DC: Brookings Institution/Berkeley, CA: University of California Press).

Rabinovich, I. (1999) *Waging Peace: Israel and the Arabs at the End of the Century* (New York: Farrar, Straus and Giroux).

Rabinovich, I. (2004) *Waging Peace: Israel and the Arabs 1948–2003* (Princeton, NJ: Princeton University Press).

Radwan, S. and Reiffers, J.-L. (2005) *The Euro-Mediterranean Partnership, 10 Years after Barcelona: Achievements and Perspectives* (Paris: Institut de la Méditerranée).

Rahim, A. H. (2011) 'Wither Political Islam and the Arab Spring', *Hedgehog Review*, 13 (3): 8–22.

Rahman, H. (1997) *The Making of the Gulf War: Origins of Kuwait's Long-Standing Territorial Dispute with Iraq* (Reading: Ithaca Press).

Ramazani, R. K. (1986) *Revolutionary Iran: Challenge and Response in the Middle East* (Baltimore, MD: Johns Hopkins University Press).

Ramsbottom, O. (2005) 'The Analysis of Protracted Social Conflict: A Tribute to Edward Azar', *Review of International Studies*, 31 (1): 101–26.

Ranstorp, M. (1998) 'The Strategy and Tactics of Hizballah's Current "Lebanonization Process"', *Mediterranean Politics*, 3 (1): 103–34.

Raphaeli, N. (2006) 'Unemployment in the Middle East: Causes and Consequences', 11 February, available online at http://www.imra.org.il/story.php3?id=28479

Rasler, K., Thompson, W. R., and Ganguly, S. (2013), *How Rivalries End* (Philadephia: University of Pennsylvania Press).

Rattinger, H. (1976) 'From War to War: Arms Races in the Middle East', *Journal of Conflict Resolution*, 20 (4): 501–31.

Ray, J. L. (1995) *Democracy and International Politics: An Evaluation of the Democratic Peace Proposition* (Columbia, SC: University of South Carolina Press).

Raz, A. (2012) *The Bride and the Dowery: Israel, Jordan and the Palestinians in the Aftermath of the 1967 War* (New Haven: Yale University Press).

Record, J. (2007) 'The Use and Abuse of History: Munich, Vietnam and Iraq', *Survival*, 49 (1): 163–80.

Redaelli, R. (2009) *L'Iran Contemporaneo* (Rome: Carocci).

Reich, B. (ed.) (1987) *The Powers in the Middle East: The Ultimate Strategic Arena* (New York: Praeger).

Reich, B. (ed.) (1998) *Handbook of Political Science Research on the Middle East and North Africa* (Westport, CT: Greenwood Press).

Reiser, S. (1984) 'Islam, Pan-Arabism and Palestine: An Attitude Survey', *Journal of Arab Affairs*, 3 (2): 189–204.

Rice, C. (2003) 'Remarks Delivered at the National Association of Black Journalists Convention', *Washington Post*, 7 August.

Ricks, T. E. (2006) *Fiasco: The American Military Adventure in Iraq* (New York: Penguin).

Rida, R. (1923) *Al-khilafa aw al-imama al-'uzma* (Cairo: Matba'at al-Manar).

Rishmawi, M. (2010) 'The Arab Charter on Human Rights and the League of Arab States: an update', *Human Rights Law Review*, 10: 169–78.

Rishmawi, M. (2012) 'The League of Arab States in the Light of the Arab Spring', at: http://www.cihrs.org/wp-content/uploads/2013/09/Arab-Leage.pdf

Rishmawi, M. (2013) 'The League of Arab States in the Wake of the Arab Spring', Cairo Institute for Human Rights Studies. http://www.cihrs.org/wp-content/uploads/2013/09/Arab-Leage.pdf

Ritchie, N. (2008) *From the Swamp to Terra Firma: The Regional Role in the Stabilization of Iraq* (London: Oxford Research Group), available online at http://www.oxfordresearchgroup.org.uk:sites:default:files:fromtheswamp.pdf

Roberson, B. (1998) *The Middle East and Europe: The Power Deficit* (London: Routledge).

Roberts, A. (2008) 'International Relations after the Cold War', *International Affairs*, 84 (2): 335–50.

Roberts, A. and Kingsbury, B. (1993) *United Nations Divided World* (2nd edn, Oxford: Oxford University Press).

Robins, P. (2002) "The Foreign Policy of Turkey", in R. Hinnebusch and A. Ehteshami (eds) *The Foreign Policies of Middle Eastern States* (Boulder, CO: Lynne Reinner), pp. 311–34.

Robins, P. (2014) 'Introduction: "Cusp States" in International Relations', in Marc Herzog and Philip

Robins (eds) *The Role, Position and Agency of Cusp States in International Relations* (Abingdon: Routledge).

Robinson, S. (2013) *Citizen Strangers: Palestinians and the Birth of Israel's Liberal Settler State* (Stanford, CA: Stanford University Press).

Rogan, E. (1998) 'Instant Communication: The Impact of the Telegraph in Ottoman Syria', in T. Philipp and B. Schaebler (eds) *The Syrian Land: Processes of Integration and Fragmentation in Bilad al-Sham from the 18th to the 20th Century* (Stuttgart: Franz Steiner Verlag) pp. 113–28.

Rogan, E. (1999) *Frontiers of the State in the Late Ottoman Empire: Transjordan, 1850–1921* (Cambridge: Cambridge University Press).

Rogan, E. (2009) *The Arabs: A History* (New York: Basic Books/Harmondsworth: Penguin).

Rogan, E. (2015). *The Fall of the Ottomans: The Great War in the Middle East* (London: Allen Lane).

Rogan, E. and Shlaim, A. (eds) (2007) *The War for Palestine: Rewriting the History of 1948* (2nd edn, Cambridge: Cambridge University Press).

Roosevelt, K. (1948) 'The Partition of Palestine: A Lesson in Pressure Politics', *Middle East Journal*, 2 (1): 1–20.

Rosenberg, D. (2011) 'Unrest Divides Mideast Economies into Winners, Losers', *The Jerusalem Post*, 11 April, available online at http://www.jpost.com/MiddleEast/Article.aspx?id=216142&R=R3

Rosenberg, D. (2012) 'Web Grows in the Mideast, But So Does Censorship', *The Jerusalem Post*, 14 March, available online at http://www.jpost.com/Features/InThespotlight/Article.aspx?id=261847

Ross, D. (2001a) 'Camp David: An Exchange', *New York Review of Books*, 20 September.

Ross, D. (2004) *The Missing Peace: The Inside Story of the Fight for Middle East Peace* (New York: Farrar, Straus and Giroux).

Ross, M. (2001b) 'Does Oil Hinder Democracy?' *World Politics*, 53 (3): 325–61.

Ross, M. (2012) *The Oil Curse* (Princeton, NJ: Princeton University Press).

Rothkopf, D. (2012) 'Iran is the Great Distraction', *Foreign Policy*, 5 March, available online at http://www.foreignpolicy.com/articles/2012/03/05/iran_is_the_great_distraction

Roy, O. (2004) *Globalised Islam: The Search for a New Ummah* (London: Hurst).

Roy, S. (2013) *Hamas and Civil Society in Gaza: Engaging the Islamist Social Sector* (Princeton, NJ: Princeton University Press).

Rubin, B. (1981) *Paved With Good Intentions: the American Experience and Iran* (Harmondsworth: Penguin).

Ruggie, J. G. (1998) *Constructing the World Policy: Essays on International Institutionalization* (London: Routledge).

Rustow, D. (1970) 'Transitions to Democracy', *Comparative Politics*, 2 (3): 337–63.

Ryan, C. R. (2009) *Inter-Arab Alliances: Regime Security and Jordanian Foreign Policy* (Gainesville, FL: University Press of Florida).

Ryan, C. R. (2014) 'Jordan, Morocco and an expanded GCC', *Middle East Research and Information Project* (MERIP), 15 April, http://www.merip.org/jordan-morocco-expanded-gcc?ip_login_no_cache=717df6c6a c153649fd48872c6627efa9 (Retrieved: 3 April 2015).

Saad-Ghorayeb, A. (2012) *The Iran Connection: Understanding the Alliance with Syria, Hizbullah and Hamas* (London: I. B. Tauris).

Sadiki, L. (2000) 'Popular Uprisings and Arab Democratization', *International Journal of Middle Eastern Studies*, 32: 71–95.

Sadiki, L. (2009) *Rethinking Arab Democratization: Elections without Democracy* (Oxford: Oxford University Press).

Sadiki, L. (ed.) (2015) *The Routledge Handbook of the Arab Spring* (London: Routledge).

Sadiki, L., Wimmen, H., and Al-Zubaidi, L. (2013) *Democratic Transition in the Middle East: Unmaking Power* (Abingdon: Routledge).

Safran, N. (1986) *Saudi Arabia: The Ceaseless Quest for Security* (Cambridge, MA: Harvard University Press).

Said, E. (1978) *Orientalism* (New York: Random House).

Said, E. (1994) *Culture and Imperialism* (New York: A. A. Knopf).

Said, E. (1995) *Peace and its Discontents: Gaza-Jericho, 1993–1995* (London: Vintage Books).

Said, E. (2000) 'Travelling Theory', in M. Bayoumi and A. Rubin (eds) *The Edward Said Reader* (London: Granta), pp. 195–217.

Salamé, G. (1988a) 'Integration in the Arab World: The Institutional Framework', in G. Luciani and S. Salamé (eds) *The Politics of Arab Integration* (New York: Croom Helm), pp. 256–79.

Salamé, G. (1988b) 'Inter-Arab Politics: The Return of Geography', in W. Quandt (ed.) *The Middle East: Ten Years after Camp David* (Washington, DC: Brookings Institution), pp. 319–56.

Salamé, G. (ed.) (1994) *Democracy without Democrats: The Renewal of Politics in the Muslim World* (London: I. B. Tauris).

Salibi, K. (1977) *The Modern History of Lebanon* (New York: Caravan Books).

Salibi, K. (1998) *The Modern History of Jordan* (London and New York: I. B. Tauris).

Salloukh, B. (2000) 'Organizing Politics in the Arab World: State-Society Relations and Foreign Policy Choices in Jordan and Syria', Unpublished PhD thesis, McGill University.

Salloukh, B. F. (2013) 'The Arab Uprisings and the Geopolitics of the Middle East', *The International Spectator*, 48 (2): 32–46.

Salloukh, B. F. and Brynen, R. (2004) *Persistent Permeability? Regionalism, Localism, and Globalization in the Middle East* (Aldershot: Ashgate Pub. Company).

Salloum, R. (2015) 'Selling out: Berlin send wrong message by welcoming Sisi', Spiegel International Online, 3 June, http://www.spiegel.de/international/world/editorial-on-egyptian-president-sisi-and-his-visit-to-germany-a-1036876.html (Retrieved: 6 June 2015).

Samii, A. B. (2008) 'A Stable Structure on Shifting Sands: Assessing the Hizbullah-Iran-Syria Relationship', *Middle East Journal*, 62 (1): 35–53.

Sanger, D. (2012) *Confront and Conceal: Obama's Secret Wars and Surprising Use of American Power* (New York: Crown).

Sassoon, J. (2012), *Saddam Hussein's Ba'th Party: Inside an Authoritarian Regime* (Cambridge: Cambridge University Press).

Sassoon, J. (2014), 'The East German Ministry of State security and Iraq 1968–1989', *Journal of Cold War Studies*, 16 (1): pp. 3–31.

Sayigh, Y. (1991) 'The Gulf Crisis: Why the Arab Regional Order Failed', *International Affairs*, 67 (3): 487–507.

Sayigh, Y. (1997) *Armed Struggle and the Search for State: The Palestinian National Movement, 1949–1993* (Oxford: Oxford University Press).

Sayigh, Y. (2000) 'Globalization Manqué: Regional Fragmentation and Authoritarian-Liberalism in the Middle East', in L. Fawcett and Y. Sayigh (eds) *Third World beyond the Cold War* (Oxford: Oxford University Press), pp. 200–33.

Sayigh, Y. and Shlaim, A. (eds) (1997) *The Cold War and the Middle East* (Oxford: Oxford University Press).

Schlumberger, O. (2007) *Debating Arab Authoritarianism: Dynamics and Durability in Non-Democratic Regimes* (Stanford, CA: Stanford University Press).

Schofield, R. (2011) 'The Crystallisation of a Complex Territorial Dispute: Britain and the Saudi-Abu Dhabi Borderland, 1966–71', *Journal of Arabian Studies*, 1 (1): 27–51.

Schölch, A. (1981) *Egypt for the Egyptians! The Socio-Political Crisis in Egypt 1878–82* (London: Ithaca Press).

Schroeder, P. W. (1994) 'Historical Reality vs Neo-Realist Theory', *International Security*, 19 (1): 108–48.

Schulze, R. (1990) *Islamischer Internationalismus im 20. Jahrhundert* (Leiden: E. J. Brill).

Schwar, H. D. (ed.) (2004) *Foreign Relations of the United States 1964–1968, vol. xix: Arab-Israeli Crisis and War, 1967* (Washington, DC: US Government Printing Office).

Schwedler, J. (2006) *Faith in Moderation: Islamist Parties in Jordan and Yemen* (Cambridge: Cambridge University Press).

Schwedler, J. and Clark, J. (2007) 'Islamist-Leftist Cooperation in the Arab World', *ISIM Review*, 18: 10–1.

Schweller, R. L. (1994) 'Bandwagoning for Profit', *International Security*, 19 (1): 72–107.

Schweller, R. L. (1996) 'Neorealism's Status Quo Bias: What Security Dilemma?', *Security Studies*, 5 (3): 90–121.

Seale, P. (1965) *The Struggle for Syria: A Study of Post-War Arab Politics, 1945–1957* (Oxford: Oxford University Press).

Sedgwick, M. (2010) 'Measuring Egyptian Regime Legitimacy', *Middle East Critique*, 19 (3): 251–67.

Segev, T. (2000) *One Palestine, Complete: Jews and Arabs under the British Mandate* (London: Abacus Books).

Sela, A. (1998) *The End of the Arab-Israeli Conflict: Middle East Politics and the Quest for Regional Order* (Albany, NY: State University of New York Press).

Senese, P. D. and Vasquez, J. A. (2008) *The Steps to War* (Princeton, NJ: Princeton University Press).

Seth, S. (2009) 'Historical Sociology and Postcolonial Theory: Two Strategies for Challenging Eurocentrism', *International Political Sociology*, 3 (3): 334–8.

Seth, S. (2013) *Postcolonial Theory and International Relations: A Critical Introduction* (Abingdon: Routledge).

Sfeir, A. (ed.) (2009) *Dictionnaire Géopolitique de l'Islamisme* (Paris: Montrouge Bayard).

Shafir, G. and Peled, Y. (2002) *Being Israeli: The Dynamics of Multiple Citizenship* (Cambridge: Cambridge University Press).

Shain, Y. and Barth, A. (2003) 'Diasporas and International Relations Theory', *International Organization*, 57 (3): 449–79.

Shambayati, H. (1994) 'The Rentier State, Interest Groups, and the Paradox of Autonomy: State and Business in Turkey and Iran', *Comparative Politics*, 26 (3): 307–31.

Shapland, G. (1997) *Rivers of Discord: International Water Disputes in the Middle East* (New York: St Martin's Press).

Sharm el-Sheikh Fact-Finding Committee (2001) *Report of the Sharm el-Sheikh Fact-Finding Committee (The Mitchell Report)*, 30 April, available online at http://unispal.un.org/UNISPAL.NSF/0/6E61D52EAACB860285256D2800734E9A

Sharman, J. C. (2013) 'International Hierarchies and Contemporary Imperial Governance', *European Journal of International Relations*, 19 (2): 189–207.

Sharp, G. (2012) *From Dictatorship to Democracy* (New York: Serpent's Tail).

Shaw, S. and Shaw, E. K. (1978) *History of the Ottoman Empire and Modern Turkey, vol. II: Reform, Revolution and Republic* (Cambridge: Cambridge University Press).

Shazli, S. (1980) *The Crossing of the Suez* (San Francisco, CA: American Mideast Research).

Shlaim, A. (1988) *Collusion across the Jordan: King Abdullah, the Zionist Movement, and the Partition of Palestine* (New York: Columbia University Press).

Shlaim, A. (1995) *War and Peace in the Middle East: A Concise History* (London: Penguin Books).

Shlaim, A. (2000) *The Iron Wall: Israel and the Arab World* (New York: W. W. Norton).

Shlaim, A. (2015) *The Iron Wall: Israel and the Arab World* (New York: W. W. Norton).

Sick, Gary (2015) Saudi Arabia's Widening War, *Politico*, June.

Sifry, M. and Cerf, C. (eds) (2003) *The Iraq War Reader* (New York: Simon & Schuster).

Sil, R. and Katzenstein, P. (2010), 'Analytic Eclecticism in the Study of World Politics', *Perspectives on Politics*, 8 (2): 411–31.

Singer, J. D., Bremer, S. A., and Stuckey, J. (1972) 'Capability Distribution, Uncertainty and Major Power War, 1820–1965', in B. Russett (ed.) *War, Peace and Numbers* (Beverly Hills, CA: Sage), pp. 19–48.

Singerman, D. (1995) *Avenues of Participation: Family, Politics, and Networks in Urban Quarters of Cairo* (Princeton, NJ: Princeton University Press).

Sirriyeh, H. (2000) 'A New Version of Pan-Arabism? ', *International Relations*, 15 (3): 53–66.

Siverson, R. M. and Sullivan, M. P. (1983) 'The Distribution of Power and the Onset of War', *Journal of Conflict Resolution*, 27 (3): 473–94.

Skovgaard-Petersen, J. (2004) 'The Global Mufti', in B. Schaebler and L. Stenberg (eds) *Globalization and the Muslim World: Culture, Religion, and Modernity* (Syracuse, NY: Syracuse University Press).

Slaughter, A.-M. (2003) 'Everyday Global Governance', *Daedalus*, 132 (1): 83–90.

Sluglett, P. (1986) 'The Kurds', in Committee against Repression and for Democratic Rights in Iraq (CARDRI) (ed.) *Saddam's Iraq: Revolution or Reaction?* (London: Zed Press), pp. 177–202.

Sluglett, P. (2002) 'The Pan-Arab Movement and the Influence of Cairo and Moscow', in W. R. Louis and R. Owen (eds) *A Revolutionary Year: The Middle East in 1958* (London: I. B. Tauris/Washington, DC: Woodrow Wilson Center Press)

Sluglett, P. (2014) 'The Waning of Empires: The British, the Ottomans and the Russians in the Caucasus and North Iran, 1917–1920', *Middle East Critique*, 23 (2): 189–208.

Smith, A. (1981) 'States and Homelands: The Social and Geopolitical Implications of National Territory', *Millennium*, 10 (3): 187–202.

Smith, A. (1995) *Nations and Nationalism in a Global Era* (Cambridge: Polity Press).

Smith, C. D. (2012) 'The United States and the 1967 War', in W. R. Louis and A. Shlaim (eds) *The 1967 Arab-Israeli War: Origins and Consequences* (Cambridge: Cambridge University Press), pp. 165–92.

Smith, C. D. (2016) *Palestine and the Arab-Israeli Conflict* (9th edn, Boston, MA: Bedford/St Martin's Press).

Smith, C. S. (2003a) 'Reluctant Saudi Arabia Prepares Its Quiet Role in the U.S.-Led War on Iraq', *New York Times*, 20 March.

Smith, N. (2003b) *American Empire: Roosevelt's Geographer and the Prelude to Globalization* (Berkeley, CA: University of California Press).

Smith, S., Booth, K., and Zalewski, M. (eds) (1996) *International Theory: Positivism and Beyond* (Cambridge: Cambridge University Press).

Snidal, D. (1991) 'Relative Gains and the Pattern of International Cooperation', *American Political Science Review*, 85 (3): 701–26.

Snyder, G. H. (1997) *Alliance Politics* (Princeton, NJ: Princeton University Press).

Soffar, M. (2008) 'Foreign Policy under Occupation: Does Iraq Need a Foreign Policy?', in B. Korany and A. E. Dessouki (eds) *The Foreign Policies of the Arab States* (New York: American University of Cairo Press), pp. 195–252.

Solingen, E. (2003) 'Toward a Democratic Peace in the Middle East', in A. Saikal and A. Schnabel (eds) *Democratization in the Middle East* (Tokyo: United Nations University Press), pp. 42–62.

Solingen, E. (2007) 'Pax Asiatica versus Bella Levantina: The Foundations of War and Peace in East Asia and the Middle East', *American Political Science Review*, 101 (4): 757–80.

Solingen, E. (2008) 'The Genesis, Design and Effects of Regional Institutions: Lessons from East Asia and the Middle East', *International Studies Quarterly*, 52 (1): 261–94.

Somel, S. A. (2001) *The Modernization of Public Education in the Ottoman Empire, 1839-1908* (Leiden: Brill).

Sorli, M. E., Gleditsch, N. P., and Strand, H. (2005) 'Why Is There So Much Conflict in the Middle East?', *Journal of Conflict Resolution*, 41 (1): 141–65.

Spiezio, K. E. (1993) 'Power Cycle Theory and State Involvement in Militarized Interstate Disputes', *Conflict Management and Peace Science*, 13 (1): 87–100.

Spiro, D. J. (1994) 'The Insignificance of the Liberal Peace', *International Security*, 19 (2): 50–86.

Springborg, R. (2011) 'Wither the Arab Spring? 1989 or 1948?', *The International Spectator*, 46 (3): 5–12.

Sreberny-Mohammadi, A. and Mohammadi, A. (1994) *Small Media, Big Revolution: Communication, Culture, and the Iranian Revolution* (Minneapolis, MN: Minnesota University Press).

Starrett, G. (1998) *Putting Islam to Work: Education, Politics, and Religious Transformation in Egypt* (Berkeley, CA: University of California Press).

Stein, E. (2012) 'Beyond Arabism vs. Sovereignty: Relocating Ideas in the International Relations of the Middle East', *Review of International Studies*, 38 (4): 881–905.

Stein, J. G. (1985) 'Calculation, Miscalculation, and Conventional Deterrence I: The View from Cairo', in R. Jervis, R. N. Lebow, and J. G. Stein (eds) *Psychology and Deterrence* (Baltimore, MD: Johns Hopkins University Press).

Stein, J. G. (1993) 'The Security Dilemma in the Middle East: The Prognosis for the Decade Ahead', in B. Korany, P. Noble, and R. Brynen (eds) *The Many Faces of National Security in the Middle East* (London: Macmillan), pp. 56–75.

Stein, J. G. (1996) 'Deterrence and Learning in an Enduring Rivalry: Egypt and Israel, 1948–73', *Security Studies*, 6 (1): 104–52.

Stern, S. N. (ed.) (2011) *Saudi Arabia and the Global Islamic Terrorist Network: America and the West's Fatal Embrace* (New York: Palgrave Macmillan).

Stockholm International Peace Research Institute (SIPRI) (2008a) 'The 15 Major Spender Countries in 2007', available online at http://www.sipri.org

Stockholm International Peace Research Institute (SIPRI) (2008b) *SIPRI Yearbook 2008: Armaments, Disarmament and International Security* (Stockholm: Stockholm International Peace Research Institute).

Stockholm International Peace Research Institute (SIPRI) (2011) *SIPRI Yearbook 2011: Armaments, Disarmament and International Security* (Stockholm: Stockholm International Peace Research Institute).

Stockholm International Peace Research Institute (SIPRI) (2014) *SIPRI Yearbook 2014: Armaments, Disarmament and International Security* (Stockholm: Stockholm International Peace Research Institute).

Stocking, G. W. (1970) *Middle East Oil* (Knoxville, TN: Vanderbilt University Press).

Stork, J. (1975) *Middle East Oil and the Energy Crisis* (New York: Monthly Review Press).

Struever, G. and Wegenast, T. (2011) Ex Oleo Bellare? *The Impact of Oil on the Outbreak of Militarized Interstate Disputes*. GIGA Working Paper 162 (Hamburg: German Institute of Global and Area Studies).

Sunayama, S. (2007) *Syria and Saudi Arabia: Collaboration and Conflict in the Oil Era* (London: I. B. Tauris).

Swearingen, W. D. (1988) 'Geopolitical Origins of the Iran-Iraq War', *Geographical Review*, 78 (4): 405–16.

Swisher, C. (2004) *The Truth about Camp David* (New York: Nation Books).

Takeyh, R. (2008) 'Iran's New Iraq', *Middle East Journal*, 62 (1): 13–30.

Takeyh, R. (2009) *Guardians of the Revolution: Iran and the World in the Age of the Ayatollahs* (New York: Oxford University Press).

Taleb, N. (2012) *Anti-fragile: How to Live in a World We Don't Understand* (London: Penguin).

Taliaferro, J. W. (2000–01) 'Security Seeking under Anarchy: Defensive Realism Revisited', *International Security*, 25 (4): 128–61.

Taylor, A. R. (1982) *The Arab Balance of Power* (Syracuse, NY: Syracuse University Press).

Telhami, S. (1990) *Power and Leadership in International Bargaining* (New York: Columbia University Press).

Telhami, S. (1999) 'Power, Legitimacy and Peace-Making in Arab Coalitions: The New Arabism', in L. Binder (ed.) *Ethnic Conflict and International Politics in the Middle East* (Gainesville, FL: University of Florida Press), pp. 43–60.

Telhami, S. (2006) *Annual Arab Opinion Survey* (College Park, MD: University of Maryland/Washington, DC: Zogby International).

Telhami, S. (2007a) 'America in Arab Eyes', *Survival*, 49 (1): 107–22.

Telhami, S. (2007b) *Annual Arab Opinion Survey* (College Park, MD: University of Maryland/Washington, DC: Zogby International).

Telhami, S. (2011) *Annual Arab Opinion Survey* (College Park, MD: University of Maryland/Washington, DC: Zogby International).

Telhami, S. and Barnett, M. (eds) (2002) *Identity and Foreign Policy in the Middle East* (Ithaca, NY: Cornell University Press).

Telhamy, Y. (2009) 'The Syrian Muslim Brothers and the Syrian-Iranian Relationships', *Middle East Journal*, 63 (4): 561–80.

Telo, M., Fawcett, L., and Ponjaert, F. (2015) *Interregionalism and the European Union* (Ashgate: Farnham Surrey).

Tessler, M., Nachtway, J., and Banda, A. (eds) (1999) *Area Studies and Social Science: Strategies for Understanding Middle East Politics* (Bloomington, IN: Indiana University Press).

Teti, A. (2004) 'A Role in Search of a Hero: Construction and the Evolution of Egyptian Foreign Policy, 1952–67', *Journal of Mediterranean Studies*, 14 (1–2): 77–105.

Teti, A. (2007) 'Bridging the Gap: IR, Middle East Studies and the Disciplinary Politics of the Area Studies Controversy', *European Journal of International Relations*, 13 (1): 117–45.

Teti, A. (2012) 'The EU's First Response to the "Arab Spring: a Critical Discourse Analysis of the Partnership for Democracy and Shared Prosperity"', *Mediterranean Politics*, 17 (3): 266–84.

Thelen, S. and Steinmo, S. (2008) 'Historical institutionalism in comparative politics', in S. Steinmo, K. Thelen, and F. Longstreth (eds) *Structuring Politics: Historical Institutionalism in Comparative Analysis* (Cambridge: Cambridge University Press), pp. 1–32.

Thomas, S. M. (2000) 'Taking Religious and Cultural Pluralism Seriously: The Global Resurgence of Religion and the Transformation of International Society', *Millennium*, 29 (3): 815–41.

Thomas, S. M. (2001) 'Faith, History and Martin Wight: The Role of Religion in the Historical Sociology of the English School of International Relations', *International Affairs*, 77 (4): 905–29.

Tibi, B. (1998) *Conflict and War in the Middle East: From Interstate War to New Security* (2nd edn, New York: St Martin's Press/Basingstoke: Macmillan).

Tickner, A. (2003) 'Seeing IR Differently: Notes from the Third World', *Millennium*, 32 (2): 295–324.

Tivnan, E. (1987) *The Lobby: Jewish Political Power and American Foreign Policy* (New York: Simon & Schuster).

Tripp, C. (1995) 'Regional Organizations in the Arab Middle East', in L. Fawcett and A. Hurrell (eds) *Regionalism and World Politics: Regional Organization and International Order* (Oxford: Oxford University Press).

Tripp, C. (2000) *A History of Iraq* (Cambridge: Cambridge University Press).

Tripp, C. (2002) 'The Foreign Policy of Iraq', in R. Hinnebusch and A. Ehteshami (eds) *The Foreign Policies of Middle Eastern States* (Boulder, CO: Lynne Reinner), pp. 167–92.

Tripp, C. (2004) 'The United States and State-Building in Iraq', *Review of International Studies* 30 (4): 545–58.

Tripp, C. (2007) *A History of Iraq* (New York: Cambridge University Press).

Tyler, P. E. (1992) 'Pentagon Drops Goal of Blocking New Superpowers', *New York Times*, 23 May.

Ulrichsen, K. C. (2010) *The GCC States and the Shifting Balance of Global Power*, CIRS Occasional Paper 6 (Qatar: Center for International and Regional Studies, Georgetown University School of Foreign Service in Qatar).

Ulrichsen, K. C. (2011) *Insecure Gulf* (New York: Hurst).

Ulrichsen, K. C. (2014) *The First World War in the Middle East* (London: Hurst).

United Nations (1992) *Agenda for Peace* (New York: United Nations Publications).

United Nations, Economic and Social Commission for West Asia (UNESCWA) (2002) *Annual Review of Developments in Globalization and Regional Integration in the Countries of the ESCWA Region: Summary* (New York: United Nations).

United Nations Development Programme (UNDP) (2003) *Arab Human Development Report 2002: Creating Opportunities for Future Generations* (New York: United Nations Publications).

United Nations Development Programme (UNDP) (2004) *Arab Human Development Report 2003: Building a Knowledge Society* (New York: United Nations Publications).

United Nations Development Programme (UNDP) (2005) *Arab Human Development Report 2004: Towards Freedom in the Arab World* (New York: United Nations Publications).

United Nations Development Programme (UNDP) (2006) *Arab Human Development Report 2005: Towards the Rise of Women in the Arab World* (New York: United Nations Publications).

United Nations Development Programme (UNDP) (2008) *Arab Human Development Report 2007* (New York: United Nations Publications).

United Nations Development Programme UNDP (2009) *Arab Human Development Report, 2008: Human Security in the Arab World* (New York: United Nations Publications).

United Nations Development Programme (UNDP) (2010) *Arab Human Development Report 2009: Challenges to Human Security in Arab Countries* (New York: United Nations Publications).

United Nations Development Programme (UNDP) (2012) *Arab Human Development Report 2011: The People Want Empowerment* (New York: United Nations Publications).

US Congress Senate Committee on Foreign Relations (1975) *A Select Chronology and Background Documents Relating to the Middle East*, 94th Congress, First Session (Washington, DC: US Government Printing Office).

US Energy Information Administration (US EIA) (2011) 'US Imports by Country of Origin', in *US EIA Database*, available online at http://www.eia.gov/dnav/pet/pet_move_impcus_a2_nus_ep00_im0_mbbl_m.htm

US Energy Information Administration (US EIA) (2012) '[Table 3.1:] Petroleum Overview', *Monthly Energy Review*, August, available online at http://www.eia.gov/totalenergy/data/monthly/pdf/sec3_3.pdf

US Government (2004) 'G8: Greater Middle East Partnership', Working Paper circulated for G8 Summit, June, published in *al-Hayat*, 13 February.

Valbjorn, M. (2004a) 'Culture Blind and Culture Blinded: Images of Middle Eastern Conflicts in International Relations', in D. Jung (ed.) *The Middle East and Palestine* (New York: Palgrave).

Valbjorn, M. (2004b) 'Towards a "Mesopotamian Turn": Disciplinarity and the Study of the International Relations of the Middle East', *Mediterranean Studies*, 14 (1–2): 47–75.

Valbjorn, M. (2008) 'Before, during and after the Cultural Turn: A "Baedeker" to IR's Cultural Journey', *International Review of Sociology*, 18 (1): 55–82.

Valbjorn, M. (2009) 'Arab Nationalism(s) in Transformation: From Arab Interstate Societies to an Arab-Islamic World Society', in B. Buzan and A. Gonzalez-Pelaez (eds) *International Society and the Middle East* (Basingstoke: Palgrave Macmillan), pp. 140–69.

Valbjorn, M. and Bank, A. (2007) 'Signs of a New Arab Cold War: The 2006 Lebanon War and the Sunni-Shi'i Divide', *Middle East Report*, 242 (Spring): 6–11.

Valbjorn, M. and Bank, A. (2012) 'The New Arab Cold War: Rediscovering the Arab Dimension of Middle East Regional Politics', *Review of International Studies*, 38 (1): 3–25.

Van Evera, S. (1999) *Causes of War* (Ithaca, NY: Cornell University Press).

Vasquez, J. A. (2004) 'The Probability of War, 1816–1992', *International Studies Quarterly*, 48 (1): 1–27.

Vasquez, J. A. (2009) *The War Puzzle Revisited* (Cambridge: Cambridge University Press).

Vitalis, R. (2007) *America's Kingdom: Mythmaking on the Saudi Oil Frontier* (Stanford, CA: Stanford University Press).

Volpi, F. and Ewan S. (2015) 'Islamism and the State after the Arab Uprisings: Between People Power and State Power', *Democratization*, 22 (2): 276–93.

Wæver, O. (2004) 'Aberystwyth, Paris, Copenhagen: New Schools in Security Theory and the Origins between Core and Periphery'. Montreal: ISA Conference, March.

Wagner, D. and Cafiero, G. (2013) 'Syria's New Friend in Cairo', *Huffington Post*, 18 September, http://www.huffingtonpost.com/daniel-wagner/syrias-new-friend-in-cair_b_3950421.html

Walker, R. B. J. (1984) *Culture, Ideology, World Order* (Boulder, CO: Westview Press).

Wall Street Journal (2011) 'Interview with Syrian President Bashar al-Assad', 31 January, available online at http://online.wsj.com/article/SB10001424052748703833204576114712441122894.html?KEYWORDS=bashar+interview+Syria

Wallerstein, I. (1974) *The Modern World-System* (New York: Academic Press).

Walt, S. M. (1987) *The Origins of Alliances* (Ithaca, NY: Cornell University Press).

Walt, S. M. (1996), *Revolution and War* (Ithaca, NY: Cornell University Press).

Waltz, K. N. (1964) 'The Stability of a Bipolar World', *Daedalus*, 93 (3): 881–909.

Waltz, K. N. (1979) *Theory of International Politics* (New York: McGraw-Hill).

Ward, S. R. (2005) 'The Continuing Evolution of Iran's Military Doctrine', *Middle East Journal*, 59 (4): 559–76.

Warde, I. (2007) *The Price of Fear: Al-Qaeda and the Truth behind the Financial War on Terror* (London: I. B. Tauris).

Watson, A. (1984) 'European International Society and its Expansion', in H. Bull and A. Watson (eds) *The Expansion of International Society* (Oxford: Oxford University Press), pp. 13–32.

Watson, A. (1992) *The Evolution of International Society* (London: Routledge).

Wayman, F. W. (1984) 'Bipolarity and War', *Journal of Peace Research*, 21 (1): 61–78.

Weber, C. (1995) *Simulating Sovereignty* (Cambridge: Cambridge University Press).

Weber, C. (1999) 'IR: The Resurrection or New Frontiers of Incorporation', *European Journal of International Relations*, 5 (4): 435–50.

Weede, E. (1976) 'Overwhelming Preponderance as a Pacifying Condition among Contiguous Asian Dyads, 1950–1969', *Journal of Conflict Resolution*, 20 (3): 395–411.

Weeks, J. L. (2012), 'Strongmen and Straw Men: Authoritarian Regimes and the Initiation of International Conflict', *American Political Science Review*, 106 (2): 326–47.

Weiss, B. (2011) 'The Tyrannies are Doomed', http://www.wsj.com/articles/SB100014240527487037125045762346 01480205330 (Retrieved: 20 April 2015).

Weitzman, E. (2007) *Hollow Land: Israel's Architecture of Occupation* (London: Verso Press).

Weldes, J., Laffey, M., Gusterson, H., and Duvall, R. (eds) (1999) *Cultures of Insecurity: Communities and the Production of Danger* (Minneapolis, MN: University of Minnesota Press).

Wendt, A. (1992) 'Anarchy is What States Make of it: The Social Construction of Power Politics', *International Organization*, 46 (2): 391–425.

Wendt, A. (1999) *Social Theory of International Politics* (Cambridge: Cambridge University Press).

West, C. (2011) Cornel West links 'revolution' in the USA, what he describes as 'US autumn', to the Arab Spring in the following article, 29 November: http://www.democracynow.org/blog/2011/9/29/cornel_west_on_occupy_wall_street_its_the_makings_of_a_us_autumn_responding_to_the_arab_spring (Retrieved: 21 March 2015)

Westad, O. A. (2005) *The Global Cold War: Third World Interventions and the Making of our Times* (Cambridge: Cambridge University Press).

Weulersse, J. (1946) *Paysans de Syrie et du Proche-Orient* (Paris: Gallimard).

White, J. B. (2002) *Islamist Mobilization in Turkey: A Study of Vernacular Politics* (Seattle, WA: University of Washington Press).

White, J. B. (2014) *Muslim Nationalism and the New Turks* (Princeton, NJ: Princeton University Press).

Whitehead, L. (1996) 'The Imposition of Democracy: The Caribbean' in L. Whitehead (ed.) *The International Dimensions of Democratization: Europe and the Americas* (Oxford: Oxford University Press).

Whiteneck, D. J. (2001) 'Long-Term Bandwagoning and Short-Term Balancing: The Lessons of Coalition Behaviour from 1792 to 1815', *Review of International Studies*, 27 (2): 151–68.

Wiegand, K. E. (2011) *Enduring Territorial Disputes* (Athens, GA: University of Georgia Press).

Wiley, J. R. (1992) *The Islamic Movement of Iraqi Shias* (Boulder, CO: Lynne Rienner).

Wilkenfeld, J., Lussier, V. L., and Tahtinen, D. (1972) 'Conflict Interactions in the Middle East, 1949–1967', *Journal of Conflict Resolution*, 16 (June): 135–54.

Wilkinson, J. C. (1991) *Arabia's Frontiers* (London: I. B. Tauris).

Willsher, K. (2011) 'French minister defends offer of security forces to Tunisia', *The Guardian*, 18 January, http://www.theguardian.com/world/2011/jan/18/french-minister-tunisia-offer (Retrieved: 27 April 2015).

Wilson, M. C. (1987) *King Abdullah, Britain and the Making of Jordan* (Cambridge: Cambridge University Press).

Wilson, S. (2012) 'Where Obama Failed on the Middle East', *Washington Post*, 15 July, p. A15.

Winrow, G. (2003) 'Turkey: Recalcitrant Ally', in R. Fawn and R. Hinnebusch (eds) *The Iraq War: Causes and Consequences* (Boulder, CO: Lynne Rienner), pp. 197–208.

Wohlforth, W. C., Little, R., Kaufman, S. J., Kang, D., Jones, C. A., Tin-Bor Hui, V., Eckstein, A., Deudney, D., and Brenner, W. J. (2007) 'Testing Balance-of-Power Theory in World History', *European Journal of International Relations*, 13 (2): 155–85.

World Bank (1993) *Developing the Occupied Territories: An Investment in Peace* (Washington, DC: World Bank).

World Bank (1997) *World Development Report 1997: The State in a Changing World* (Washington, DC: World Bank).

World Bank (2000) *Basic Development Report* (Washington, DC: World Bank).

World Bank (2003) *MENA Development Report: Trade, Investment, and Development in the Middle East and North Africa: Engaging with the World* (Washington, DC: World Bank).

World Bank (2006) *World Bank Development Report* (Washington, DC: World Bank).

World Bank (2008) *The World Bank annual report 2008: year in review* (Washington, DC: World Bank).

World Bank (2011) 'Overview: Water Sector Brief', available online at http://web.worldbank.org/WBSITE/EXTERNAL/COUNTRIES/MENAEXT/EXTMNAREGTOPWATRES/0,contentMDK:20536156~menuPK:497170~pagePK:34004173~piPK:34003707~theSitePK:497164,00.html

World Bank Group (2015) *Global Economic Prospects: The Global Economy in Transition* (Washington, DC: IBRD/World Bank) at: http://www.worldbank.org/content/dam/Worldbank/GEP/GEP2015b/Global-Economic-Prospects-June-2015-Global-economy-in-transition.pdf

Wright, L. (2006) *The Looming Tower: Al-Qaeda and the Road to 9/11* (New York: Alfred A. Knopf).

Wright, S. (2011) 'Foreign Policy in the GCC States', in M. Kamrava (ed.) *International Politics of the Persian Gulf* (Syracuse, NY: Syracuse University Press), pp. 72–93.

Wurmser, D. (1996) *Coping with Crumbling States: A Western and Israeli Balance of Power Strategy for the Levant*, IASPS Research Papers in Strategy (Jerusalem: Institute for Advanced Strategic and Political Studies), available online at http://www.iasps.org/strat2.htm

Xenakis, D. and Chryssochoou, D. (2001) *The Emerging Euro-Mediterranean System* (Manchester: Manchester University Press).

Yaniv, A. (1986) 'Syria and Israel: The Politics of Escalation', in M. Ma'oz and Avner Yaniv (eds) *Syria under Assad* (London: Croom Helm), pp. 157–78.

Yaniv, A. (1987) *Dilemmas of Security: Politics, Strategy and the Israeli Experience in Lebanon* (New York: Oxford University Press).

Yapp, M. E. (1987) *The Making of the Modern Near East, 1792–1923* (London: Longman).

Yapp, M. E. (1991) *The Near East since the First World War* (London: Longman).

Yergin, D. (1991) *The Prize: The Epic Quest for Oil, Money and Power* (New York: Simon & Schuster).

Yilmaz, B. (2012) 'Turkey and the Arab Spring', in S. Calleya and M. Wohlfeld (eds) *Change and Opportunities in the Emerging Mediterranean* (Msida: University of Malta Press), pp. 46–69.

Youngs, R. (ed.) (2006) *Survey of European Democracy Promotion Policies 2000–2006* (Madrid: FRIDE).

Zank, W. (2009) *Clash or Cooperation of Civilisations? Overlapping Integration and Identities* (Farnham: Ashgate).

Zartman, I. W. (1999) 'The Ups and Downs of Maghrebi Unity', in M. Hudson (ed.) *Middle East Dilemma: The Politics and Economics of Arab Integration* (London: I. B. Tauris)

Zehfuss, M. (2002) *Constructivism in International Relations* (Cambridge: Cambridge University Press).

Zertal, I. and Eldar, A. (2007) *Lords of the Land: The War over Israel's Settlements in the Occupied Territories, 1967–2007*, trans. V. Eden (New York: Nation Books).

Zimmern, A. (1945) *The League of Nations and the Rule of Law* (London: Macmillan).

Zogby, J. (2002) *The Ten Nation Impressions of America Poll* (Washington, DC: Zogby International).

Zogby, J. (2003) 'Saudis Reject Bin Laden and Terrorism', available online at http://www.mediamonitors.net/zogby99.html

Zogby Research Services (2014) 'Today's Middle East: Pressures and Challenges', November, at b.3cdn.net/aai/a6466ad6476c08d752_bum6b4j61.pdf

Zorob, A. (2008) 'Intraregional Economic Integration: The Cases of GAFTA and MAFTA', in C. Harders and M. Legrenzi (eds) *Beyond Regionalism?* (Aldershot: Ashgate), pp. 169–84.

Zubaida, S. (1989) *Islam, the People and the State: Political Ideas and Movements in the Middle East* (London: I. B. Tauris).

Zuckerman, M. (2011) Speaking to Jeremy Paxman on 'Hard Talk', British Broadcasting Corporation, 1 February.

Index

The prefix 'al', when referring to personal names, is ignored for sorting purposes.